MEDIATION

Mediation
Skills and Techniques

SECOND EDITION

Laurence J. Boulle, B.A., LL.B., LL.M., Ph.D.

BELL WIESE PROFESSOR OF LAW
UNIVERSITY OF NEWCASTLE, AUSTRALIA
ADJUNCT PROFESSOR, BOND UNIVERSITY, AUSTRALIA
ACCREDITED MEDIATOR, AUSTRALIA
DIRECTOR, INDEPENDENT MEDIATION SERVICES LTD

Michael T. Colatrella Jr., J.D., LL.M.

PROFESSOR OF LAW
MCGEORGE SCHOOL OF LAW, UNIVERSITY OF THE PACIFIC
FORMER DIRECTOR OF THE CENTER FOR DISPUTE RESOLUTION,
SCHOOL OF EDUCATION AND HUMAN DEVELOPMENT,
SOUTHERN METHODIST UNIVERSITY

Anthony P. Picchioni, Ph.D.

EDUCATIONAL CONSULTANT, BAYLOR UNIVERSITY MEDICAL CENTER
FORMER CHAIR OF THE DEPARTMENT OF
DISPUTE RESOLUTION AND COUNSELING,
SIMMONS SCHOOL OF EDUCATION AND HUMAN DEVELOPMENT,
SOUTHERN METHODIST UNIVERSITY

CAROLINA ACADEMIC PRESS
Durham, North Carolina

LIBRARY OF CONGRESS CATALOGING-IN-PUBLICATION DATA

Names: Boulle, Laurence, 1949- author. | Colatrella, Michael T., Jr., author. |
 Picchioni, Anthony P., author.
Title: Mediation : skills and techniques / by Laurence Boulle, Michael Colatrella,
 Anthony Picchioni.
Description: Second edition. | Durham, North Carolina : Carolina Academic Press, 2023. |
 Includes index.
Identifiers: LCCN 2022059508 (print) | LCCN 2022059509 (ebook) |
 ISBN 9781531026134 (paperback) | ISBN 9781531026141 (ebook)
Subjects: LCSH: Mediation--United States. | Dispute resolution (Law)--United States. |
 Conflict management--United States.
Classification: LCC KF9084 .B68 2023 (print) | LCC KF9084 (ebook) |
 DDC 347.94/09--dc23/eng/20230206
LC record available at https://lccn.loc.gov/2022059508
LC ebook record available at https://lccn.loc.gov/2022059509

Carolina Academic Press
700 Kent Street
Durham, North Carolina 27701
(919) 489-7486
www.cap-press.com

Printed in the United States of America

Summary of Contents

ONE · Introduction to Learning Mediation Skills
and Techniques   3

TWO · Establishing the Foundation: Introductions,
Intake, Screening, and Preparation   29

THREE · Maintaining a Favorable Climate   55

FOUR · Managing the Mediation Process   71

FIVE · Assisting the Communication Process   137

SIX · Managing Conflict from Crisis to Opportunity   167

SEVEN · Facilitating the Negotiations   207

EIGHT · Encouraging Settlement   269

NINE · Managing Power in Mediation   287

TEN · Variations in the Mediation Process   305

ELEVEN · Virtual Mediation   325

TWELVE · Use of Evaluation in Mediation   339

THIRTEEN · Special Issues in Mediation   353

FOURTEEN · Avoiding Mediator Traps   377

FIFTEEN · Becoming a Mediator, Careers in Mediation, and
Establishing a Private Mediation Practice   395

Contents

About the Authors   xxvii

Acknowledgments   xxix

One · Introduction to Learning Mediation Skills and Techniques   3
  I. Mediation's Role and Benefits   3
    A. Mediation Defined   3
    B. Benefits of Mediation   5
      1. Greater Participant Control Over the Proceedings
        and Outcome   6
      2. Greater Likelihood of Preserving and Enhancing the
        Relationship of the Participants   7
      3. Greater Access to Creative and Adaptable Solutions   7
      4. Quicker Resolutions for Participants   8
      5. Less Expensive Proceedings for Participants   8
      6. Conservation of Court Resources   8
    C. Uses and Applications of Mediation   9
      1. Labor Disputes   9
      2. Civil Cases   10
      3. Community Disputes   10
      4. Family Matters   10
      5. Business Disputes   11
      6. Special Education Disputes   11
      7. Public Policy Disputes   12
        a. A Note on International Commercial Mediation   12
    D. Limitations of Mediation   14
  II. Scope and Organization of This Book   14
 III. Mediation Is a Skill, Not a Talent   15
 IV. The Mediator's Skills and Techniques Toolbox   17
  V. Mediation Models   18
    A. The Models Defined   18
      1. Facilitative Mediation   18
      2. Transformative Mediation   19
      3. Evaluative Mediation   19

B. The Eclectic Use of the Models 20
VI. Functions of the Mediator 20
A. Creating Favorable Conditions for the Parties 21
B. Assisting the Parties to Communicate 21
C. Facilitating the Parties' Negotiations 21
D. Encouraging Settlement 22
E. Identifying and Managing Cultural Differences 22
1. Culture and Mediation 23
VII. Evaluating Your Effectiveness 24
VIII. Overview of a Real Mediation 25
IX. Exercises 28

Two · Establishing the Foundation: Introductions, Intake, Screening, and Preparation 29
I. Overview 29
II. Entering the Dispute 30
A. Joint Introductions and Communications 30
B. Preliminary Conferences 31
C. The "One-Party" Approach 32
III. Gathering Information 33
A. Identifying the Participants 34
B. Identifying the Issues 35
C. Status of the Litigation 35
D. Reviewing Documents 36
E. Written Party Statements 37
F. Scheduling 37
IV. Assessment 38
A. Conflicts of Interest 38
B. Mediator Competence 39
C. Appropriateness for Mediation 39
D. Authority of Participants 41
V. Educating the Parties About the Mediation Process 42
A. The Mediation Process 43
B. Mediator's Particular Approach to Mediation 44
C. Mediator's Background and Experience 45
D. The Agreement to Mediate, Fees, and Charges 46
VI. Practical Preparation for the Mediation Meeting 47
A. Timing 47
B. Duration 48
C. Facilities 49
D. Amenities 49
E. Arrivals, Waiting Facilities, and Departures 50
F. Seating 50

G. Visuals 52
H. Security 52
VII. Special Circumstances and Techniques 52
A. Team Negotiations 52
B. Pre-Mediation Conferences with the Parties Separately 53
VIII. Exercises 54

Three · Maintaining a Favorable Climate 55
I. The Role of the Mediator in "Climate Control" 55
II. Reasons for a Poor Climate 56
A. Reasons Pertaining to Pre-Mediation Developments 56
B. Reasons Pertaining to the Individual Parties 57
C. Power Imbalances and Fear of Losing 58
D. Reasons Pertaining to the Mediation Process 59
III. Strategies for Improving the Climate 59
A. The Trust Factor 59
1. Why Trust Is Important 59
2. Generating Trust in the Mediator 60
3. Generating Trust in the Mediation Process 60
4. Helping the Parties Develop Faith in Their Own
Negotiating Abilities 61
B. Managing Expectations 61
C. Other Ways to Improve Climate 62
1. Promoting Optimism, a Positive Tone, and a
Mood of Confidence 62
2. Productive Communication, Structure, and Security 62
3. Acknowledging Concerns 63
4. Normalizing 63
5. Getting Out of the Past and Into the Future 63
6. Mutualizing the Unhappiness 64
7. Reducing the Pressure to Settle 64
8. Relieving Tension Through Humor 64
9. More Ritual for Mediation 65
IV. Dealing with Intense Emotions 65
A. Overview 65
V. Discourage the Expression of Intense Emotion 66
A. Ignore the Emotion and Proceed with the Mediation 67
B. Acknowledge the Emotion, and Then Continue 67
C. Encourage Some Venting of the Emotion 68
D. Identify and Deal with the Underlying Problem Therapeutically 68
E. Selecting a Strategy 69
F. Overcoming Clients' Fundamental Fears 69
VI. Exercises 70

Four · Managing the Mediation Process   71
  I. The Power of Process   71
 II. Stages in the Process   72
     A. Mediator's Opening Statement   72
        1. Purpose   72
        2. Principles   73
           a. Clear   73
           b. Concise   74
           c. Conversational   74
           d. Confident   74
           e. Constructive   74
        3. Elements   74
           a. Preliminaries   75
           b. Explaining the Nature of Mediation   76
           c. Explaining the Mediation Process   77
           d. Explaining the Guidelines   78
           e. One Person Speaks at a Time   78
           f. No Personal Attacks   78
           g. Anyone Can Take a Break at Any Time for Any Reason.   79
              i. No Binding Agreement Until Reduced to Writing and
                 Signed by the Parties.   79
             ii. Confidentiality Obligations.   79
            iii. Commitment to Comply.   80
           h. Commitment to Begin the Mediation   80
        4. Confidentiality in Mediation   80
           a. Mediator's Duty to Keep Mediation Communications
              Confidential   81
           b. Mediator's Duty to Keep Information Shared by One
              Party Confidential from Other Parties   82
           c. Mediation Participants May Also Be Bound
              by Confidentiality   82
           d. Exclusion of Using Mediation Communications as
              Evidence in Subsequent Legal Proceedings   83
           e. Exclusion of Calling Mediators as Witnesses or of
              Subpoenaing Mediator Notes   84
           f. Exceptions to Mediation Confidentiality   84
           g. Mediator's Duty to Explain Confidentiality to Participants   85
        5. Example of a Mediator's Opening Statement   86
        6. Other Matters   90
           a. Omitting an Important Element of the Opening Statement   90
           b. Mediator's Opening Statement Where There Are
              Two or More Mediators   90

B. The Parties' Initial Statements 90
   1. The Parties' Statements 90
      a. Purpose 90
      b. Scope 91
      c. Focus 91
      d. Who Makes the Party Statements? 92
      e. Party Speaking Order 93
      f. Deciding Who Speaks First 94
         i. Private Rationales for Who Speaks First. 94
         ii. Public Explanations for Who Speaks First. 94
         iii. Allowing the Parties to Choose Who Speaks First. 95
      g. Preventing a Defensive Response from the Second Speaker 95
      h. The Party Statements Should Be Addressed to the Mediator 95
      i. The Mediator's Role During the Parties' Initial Statements 96
      j. Note-Taking by the Mediator 97
      k. Requests for a "Right of Reply" 98
   2. Mediator Summaries of the Parties' Statements 99
      a. Purpose 99
      b. Process 99
      c. Types of Summaries 99
         i. Actual Summary. 99
         ii. Reframed Summary. 99
         iii. Cross-Summaries. 100
C. Defining the Problem 100
   1. Purpose 100
   2. Process 101
   3. Using Pre-Mediation Conferences 101
   4. Uncovering Interests 102
      a. Positions and Interests 102
      b. Types of Interests 102
      c. Uncovering Interests 102
   5. Identify Areas of Agreement 104
   6. Developing An Issue Agenda 105
      a. Crafting the Issues 105
      b. Different Levels of Defining the Issues 107
      c. Form for the List of Issues 107
      d. Avoid Framing the Problem as a Single Issue 108
      e. Addressing "One-Party" Issues 109
      f. Presenting the List of Issues Visually 109
      g. Prioritizing the Issues 110
      h. Standard Issue Lists 111
      i. Using the List of Issues 111

D. Problem Solving and Negotiation 112
   1. Purpose 112
   2. Style 112
   3. Storytelling 113
     a. Benefits of Permitting Storytelling 113
     b. Limitations of Storytelling 114
     c. Guidelines to Manage Storytelling 115
   4. Procedure 117
     a. Packaging Issues 117
     b. Problem-Solving Processes 118
       i. Open Discussion. 118
       ii. Interest-Based Negotiation. 118
       iii. Positional Negotiation. 120
E. Final Decision and Closure 120
   1. Purpose 120
   2. The Agreement 120
     a. Level of Commitment 120
       i. Oral Agreements. 121
       ii. Non-Binding Written Agreements. 121
       iii. Binding Written Agreements. 122
     b. Drafting the Agreement 122
     c. Content of the Agreement 123
   3. Closing Statement and Termination 124
   4. Evaluations 126
   5. Post-Mediation Activities 126
III. The Separate Meetings 126
 A. Definition 126
 B. Purpose 127
 C. Confidentiality in Separate Meetings 128
 D. When Separate Meetings Should Be Called 129
 E. Separate Meetings and Physical Space 130
 F. How Dynamics Change in Separate Meetings 131
 G. When to End Separate Meetings 131
   1. Duration of Separate Meetings 131
   2. Calling and Managing Separate Meetings 132
   3. Balancing the Duration of Separate Meetings 132
 H. The Separate Meeting Transitions 133
   1. Breaking Into Separate Meetings Transition 133
   2. Commencing a Separate Meeting Transition 133
   3. Ending a Separate Meeting Transition 133
   4. Resuming the Joint Session Transition 134
 I. Potential Dangers with Separate Meetings and Ways of
   Handling Them 134
IV. Exercises 135

Five · Assisting the Communication Process   **137**

   I. Introduction   137

  II. Communication and Culture   138

 III. Basic Issues in Communication   140

    A. Encoding and Decoding Messages   140

    B. Professional Terminology   141

    C. Experiences, Behavior, and Affect   141

  IV. Communication Style and Terminology   142

   V. Non-Verbal Communication in Mediation   143

    A. Body Language and Visuals   143

    B. Vocals   145

    C. The Mediator's Role in Relation to Visuals and Vocals   146

    D. The Mediator's Own Non-Verbal Communication   146

  VI. Effective Listening   147

    A. Causes of Ineffective Listening   148

    B. Listening Effectively   148

 VII. Elements of Active Listening   148

    A. Detracting from Effective Listening   149

VIII. Communication in Telephone Mediations   150

  IX. Reframing   152

    A. Reframing Defined   152

      1. A Note on the Similarity Between Reframing and
the Design of Jokes   153

    B. Functions and Examples of Reframing   154

    C. Potential Problems with Reframing   155

   X. Appropriate Questioning   156

    A. Introduction   156

    B. The Types of Questions   157

      1. Open Questions   157

      2. Focused Questions   157

      3. Closed Questions   157

      4. Clarifying Questions   157

      5. Reflective Questions   158

      6. Probing Questions   158

      7. Leading Questions   158

      8. Cross-Examining Questions   158

      9. Hypothetical Questions   159

     10. Disarming/Distracting Questions   159

     11. Rhetorical Questions   159

     12. Suggestive Questions   159

    C. Choosing the Appropriate Question   159

      1. Use Questions Judiciously   159

      2. The Hypothetical Question   160

      3. Empathic Versus Probing Questioning   160

XI.	Mediators' Tools to Promote Effective Communication	161
	A. Reiterating	161
	B. Paraphrasing	162
	C. Summarizing	162
	D. Note-Taking	164
XII.	Exercises	164

Six · Managing Conflict from Crisis to Opportunity — **167**

I.	Benefits of Conflict	167
II.	Productive vs. Unproductive Conflict	170
	A. Identifying and Encouraging Productive Conflict	171
	1. Flexible	171
	2. Recognition of Others' Needs and Interests	172
	B. Identifying and Discouraging Unproductive Conflict	172
	1. Personal Attacks	172
	a. Criticizing	173
	b. Stonewalling	173
	c. Contempt	175
	d. Defensiveness	176
	2. Over-Competitiveness	177
	3. Issue Proliferation	178
III.	Conflict Style	179
	A. Introduction	179
	B. The Styles	180
	1. Competing—"My Way or the Highway."	180
	a. Common Tactics	180
	b. Working with This Style	181
	2. Avoiding—"I'll Think About it Tomorrow."	182
	a. Common Tactics	182
	b. Working with This Style	183
	3. Compromising—"Half a Loaf Is Better Than None."	183
	a. Common Tactics	183
	b. Working with This Style	184
	4. Accommodating—"I Am Happy to Oblige."	185
	a. Common Tactics	185
	b. Working with This Style	185
	5. Collaborating—"Two Heads Are Better Than One."	186
	a. Common Tactics	187
	b. Working with This Style	187
IV.	The Path of the Storm	188
	A. Introduction	188
	B. The Escalation Stages	189

1. Inciting Incident 189
2. Progressive Complication 190
3. Crisis 190
4. Climax 191
5. Resolution 192
C. Complications that Occur During Conflict Escalation 192
1. Light Tactics Give Way to Heavy Tactics 193
2. Issue Proliferation 194
3. Sweeping Generalizations 195
4. Increased Commitment 195
5. Proliferation of Parties 196
D. Other Factors Contributing to Conflict Escalation 196
1. Attribution Distortions 196
2. Face-Saving 198
E. Factors Contributing to Conflict De-Escalation 200
1. Encouraging Contact and Communication 201
2. Initiating De-Escalatory Cycles 202
3. Generating Optimism 202
4. Diagnosing the Dispute 203
F. Who Are the Parties to the Conflict? 203
G. Why Are the Parties in Conflict? 204
1. Relationship Conflicts 204
2. Data Conflicts 205
3. Interest Conflicts 205
4. Structural Conflicts 205
5. Value Conflicts 205
V. Exercises 206

Seven · Facilitating the Negotiations 207
I. The Mediator's Role in Negotiations 207
A. The Negotiation Expert 207
B. Common Negotiating Mistakes 208
C. Many People Are Ineffective Negotiators 208
D. The Negotiator's Dilemma: Creating and Claiming Value 209
II. Assisting in Preparing for Negotiation 211
A. Nature and Importance of Preparation in Negotiation 211
B. Setting the Stage—Gathering Information 212
C. The Parties' Interests 213
1. The Power of Uncovering Interests 213
2. The Process of Understanding Each Other's Interests 215
a. Change the Parties' Point of View 215
b. Role Reversal 215

3. Sorting and Prioritizing Interests 216
  a. Identifying Common Ground 216
  b. Identifying Divergent Interests 217
    i. Different Valuations. 218
    ii. Different Expectations. 218
    iii. Different Risk Attitudes. 218
    iv. Different Time Preferences. 218
    v. Different Capabilities. 219
D. Trading on Divergent Interests 219
E. The Parties' Alternatives 219
  1. BATNA—Negotiating With the Lights On 219
  2. Mediator's Role in Assessing BATNA 220
  3. Relationship Between BATNA and Reservation Point 221
  4. The Other Party's BATNA 222
  5. BATNA in Litigated Matters 222
    a. The Decision to Go to Trial 222
    b. Calculating Expected Value 223
    c. Bias in Calculating Expected Value 226
    d. Other Factors that Affect Expected Value 227
      i. Time Value of Money. 227
      ii. Other Costs. 228
      iii. Benefits of Trial. 229
    e. Conclusion 229
F. Identifying Objective Standards 229
G. Generating Options 231
III. Assisting the Negotiation Process 232
A. Orientation and Positioning 232
  1. Orientation 232
  2. Positioning 233
    a. Overview 233
    b. Assisting the Parties in Formulating Opening Offers 234
      i. High/Soft or Low/Soft Offers. 234
      ii. Reasonable/Firm Offers. 235
      iii. High/Low Firm Offers. 235
      iv. Integrative Offers. 236
    c. Understanding the Other Side's Initial Offer 236
B. Argumentation 237
  1. Overview 237
  2. Managing the Rule of Reciprocity 237
    a. Social Foundations of the Rule 238
    b. How the Rule Works 239
    c. How Mediators Can Manage the Rule 240
  3. Managing the Pattern of Concessions 242
    a. Planning the Concessions 242

	i.	Opening Point.		243
	ii.	Reservation Point.		244
	iii.	Target Point.		247
	b.	Reciprocity of Concessions		247
	c.	Concessions Are Communication		249
		i.	Magnitude of Concessions.	249
		ii.	Timing of Concessions.	250
	d.	Record of Concessions		250
4.	Responding to and Packaging Offers			251
	a.	Provide a Rationale for the Offer Before Making the Offer		251
	b.	Emphasize Areas of Agreement by Communicating Them First		251
	c.	Acknowledge Agreement at the Level of Principle		252
5.	Dealing With the Tactics of Positional Bargaining			252
	a.	The Tactics		252
		i.	Intimidation and Threats.	252
		ii.	Stonewalling.	252
		iii.	Phantom Trades.	252
		iv.	Good Cop/Bad Cop.	253
		v.	Claiming Lack of Authority.	253
	b.	Possible Interventions		253
		i.	Educate.	253
		ii.	Anticipate.	253
		iii.	Identify.	254
		iv.	Enforce.	254
6.	Mediator's Role in Promoting Interest-Based Bargaining			254
	a.	Shifting Focus from Positions to Interests		254
	b.	Considering Creative Settlement Options		255
	c.	Brainstorming		256
	d.	Eliciting Participants' Solutions		257
7.	Special Techniques in Negotiation			257
	a.	Reframing to Enhance Negotiability		258
	b.	Shifting Between Principle and Detail		258
	c.	Making More than One Offer Simultaneously		259
	d.	Linked Bargaining		259
	e.	Accommodating Future Contingencies		260
C. Emergence and Crisis				261
1.	Crossing the Last Gap			261
2.	Dealing With Impasses			264
	a.	Possible Interventions for Substantive Impasses		265
	b.	Potential Interventions for Procedural Impasses		265
	c.	Potential Interventions for Emotional Impasses		266
D. Agreement or Final Breakdown				266
IV. Exercises				267

Eight · Encouraging Settlement   **269**
   I. Introduction   269
  II. Sources of Mediator Power and Influence   269
 III. Categories of Encouragement to Settle   270
     A. Providing Information   271
     B. Expressing an Opinion   272
     C. Advising   272
     D. Being Critical or Judgmental   274
     E. Acting as the Agent of Reality   275
        1. Weaknesses   276
        2. Quality of Agreement   277
  IV. Methods of Encouraging Settlement   277
     A. Modes of Encouraging Settlement   277
        1. Verbal   278
        2. Non-Verbal   278
        3. Procedural and Structural   278
        4. Environmental   278
        5. Visual   278
     B. Styles of Encouraging Settlement   279
     C. Using Power to Encourage Settlement: Some Illustrations   280
   V. Dangers in Encouraging Settlement   282
     A. Dangers Relating to the Parties and Their Agreement   282
     B. Dangers Relating to the Mediator   283
     C. Dangers Relating to the System of Mediation   283
  VI. Creating the Balance   283
 VII. Exercises   285

Nine · Managing Power in Mediation   **287**
   I. Introduction   287
  II. What Is Negotiation Power and Why Does It Matter?   288
     A. Negotiation Power Defined   288
     B. Why Does Being Attentive to Negotiating Power Matter?   289
     C. Types of Negotiation Power   290
        1. Substantive Power   290
          a. Positive Leverage   291
          b. Normative Leverage   291
          c. Negative Leverage   291
          d. Best Alternative to a Negotiated Agreement (BATNA) 292
          e. Asymmetry of Information   292
        2. Personal Power   293
        3. Relationship Power   293
 III. Mediator Interventions to Manage Power   293

A. Introduction   293
B. General Interventions   294
   1. Mediator Presence   294
   2. Educating the Parties About Mediation   295
   3. Modeling Appropriate Communication and Behavior   295
C. Balancing Substantive Power   295
   1. Encourage Parties to Share Information   295
   2. Help Parties Objectively Explore Their BATNA   296
   3. Assist Parties in Understanding Their Interests and the
      Interests of Other Parties   297
   4. Recommend the Use of Experts, Like Lawyers, Accountants,
      Financial Advisors, or Other Expert Sources of Information   297
   5. Provide Legal Information to Parties   298
   6. Provide an Evaluation   299
D. Managing Personal Power   300
   1. Ensure That Each Party Has Their Say   300
   2. Paraphrase and Summarize Frequently   300
   3. Encourage Persistence and Patience   300
E. Managing Relationship Power   301
   1. Assure Party Safety   301
   2. Tailor Mediation and Communication Guidelines to Manage
      Undue Power Imbalances   302
   3. Use Separate Meetings and Breaks Liberally   302
F. Dangers in Managing Power Imbalances   303
IV. Exercises   303

Ten · Variations in the Mediation Process   305
  I. Introduction   305
  II. Multiple Meetings   305
 III. Shuttle Mediation   306
   A. Shuttle Mediation Defined   306
   B. Differences in Shuttle Mediation   307
   C. When to Use Shuttle Mediation   307
   D. Practical Considerations   308
   E. Some Potential Drawbacks and Dangers in Shuttle Mediation 309
   F. Ways of Improving Shuttle Mediation   311
 IV. Using More than One Mediator   311
   A. When to Adopt Co-Mediation   311
   B. Creating a Favorable Environment in Co-Mediation   312
      1. Planning and Organization   312
      2. Conduct of the Process   313
      3. Using Each Mediator's Expertise   314

        4. Avoiding Bias and Partiality   314
        5. Staying Together   314
        6. Improving the Communications in Co-Mediation   315
        7. Facilitating the Negotiations in Co-Mediation   315
    C. Avoiding Traps in Co-Mediation   316
        1. Good Cop-Bad Cop Routine   316
        2. Modeling Inequality or Lack of Teamwork   316
        3. Appointing Incompatible Personalities   316
    D. Preparation for Co-Mediation   317
    E. Debriefing by Co-Mediators   317
  V. Telephone Mediation   318
 VI. Med-Arb   320
VII. Other Variations in the Mediation Process   321
    A. Alternating Venues   321
    B. Variations in Separate Meetings   321
    C. Involving Support Persons   322
    D. Consultation with Outside Parties Before Ratifying Agreement   323
VIII. Exercises   323

Eleven · Virtual Mediation   325
  I. Introduction to Online Dispute Resolution   325
 II. Virtual Mediation   326
III. The Advantages of Using Virtual Mediation   326
    A. Decreased Demands on Time and Money   326
    B. Ease of Attendance and Enhanced Participation   327
    C. Heightened Ability to Manage Negotiation Power Among Parties   327
    D. High Efficacy   328
 IV. The Disadvantages of Using Virtual Mediation   329
    A. Diminished Non-Verbal Communication   330
    B. Increased Difficulty in Building Trust and Rapport   330
    C. Risk of Technical and Practical Problems   331
    D. Videoconferencing Fatigue   331
    E. Confidentiality and Privacy Concerns   332
    F. Perceptions of Diminished Procedural Justice   332
  V. Best Practices in Conducting Virtual Mediation   334
    A. General Considerations   334
    B. Use of Videoconferencing Platform Features   335
    C. Protect Confidentiality   336
 VI. Exercises   337

Twelve · Use of Evaluation in Mediation   339
  I. Introduction   339
 II. Benefits of Evaluative Mediation   340

A. Provides Parties With a Better Understanding of the Issue(s)   341
B. Provides Objective Insight   341
C. Especially Beneficial for Unrepresented Parties   341
D. May Provide a More Cathartic Experience   342
III. Dangers of Evaluative Mediation   342
A. Risk of the Mediator Being Perceived as Having Lost Neutrality 343
B. May Discourage Interest-Based Problem Solving   343
C. Threatens Party Self-Determination   343
D. Evaluations Can Be Flawed   344
IV. Recommendations for Using Evaluative Mediation   346
A. Familiarize Yourself with Jurisdictional Variations   346
B. Use Best Practices in Evaluative Mediation   347
1. Choose to Evaluate Judiciously   347
2. Have Relevant Expertise   348
3. Ask Permission to Evaluate   348
4. Emphasize That It Is Only Your Opinion   349
5. Evaluate as Narrowly as Practicable   349
6. Delay an Evaluation as Long as Possible   350
7. Provide Evaluations to Parties Privately   350
V. Conclusion   350
VI. Exercises   351

Thirteen · Special Issues in Mediation   353
I. Introduction   353
II. Dealing with Violence   353
A. Policy Issues   354
B. Screening for Violence   354
C. Mediator Interventions in Relation to Violence Issues   355
III. Using Interpreters in Mediation   357
IV. Dealing with Proposed Settlements "Outside the Range"   358
V. Dealing with Absent Parties   361
VI. Involving Children in Mediation   362
VII. Dealing with Experts in Mediation   364
VIII. Dealing with Lawyers and Other Professional Advisers   366
A. Issues for Professional Advisers   366
B. Degrees of Involvement by Advisers   368
C. Seating of Advisers   369
D. Documentation   369
E. Parties' Initial Statements   370
F. Accommodating the Need to Be Involved   370
G. Taking Instructions   370
H. Assisting Advisers in Modifying Their Advice   371
I. Using the Advisers as Quasi-Mediators   372

IX. Dealing with Complex Multi-Party Disputes   372
X. Dealing with the Walk-Out   374
XI. Exercises   374

Fourteen · Avoiding Mediator Traps   377
I. Introduction   377
II. Unrealistic Expectations   378
   A. The Trap   378
   B. Avoidance Strategies   379
III. Losing Impartiality   379
   A. The Trap   379
   B. Avoidance Strategies   381
IV. Dominating the Process   382
   A. The Trap   382
   B. Avoidance Strategies   382
   C. Avoiding Technical Language   383
V. Losing Control of the Process   383
   A. The Trap   383
   B. Avoidance Strategies   384
   C. The Trap of Allowing Professional Advisers to
      Dominate the Process   385
VI. Ignoring Emotions   386
   A. The Trap   386
   B. Avoidance Strategies   386
VII. Moving to Solutions Too Quickly   387
   A. The Trap   387
   B. Avoidance Strategies   387
VIII. Pushing the Parties   388
   A. The Trap   388
   B. Avoidance Strategies   389
   C. Distorting the Parties' Views During Shuttle Mediation   390
IX. Assuming a Differing Professional Role   390
   A. The Trap   390
   B. Avoidance Strategies   391
X. Being Unprepared   391
   A. The Trap   391
   B. Avoidance Strategies   392
XI. Allowing the Agreement to Be Left Undocumented   392
   A. The Trap   392
   B. Avoidance Strategies   392
XII. Ignoring External Parties   393
   A. The Trap   393
   B. Avoidance Strategies   393
XIII. Exercises   394

Fifteen · Becoming a Mediator, Careers in Mediation, and
      Establishing a Private Mediation Practice   395
  I. Introduction   395
 II. Developing Mediator Credentials   396
    A. Training and Qualifications   396
       1. Where Training Is Available   396
          a. Community Mediation Centers   396
          b. Professional Mediation and Dispute-Resolution Organizations   396
          c. Private Mediators   397
          d. Colleges and Universities   397
       2. Basic Mediation Training   397
       3. Advanced Training   398
       4. Making the Decision   399
    B. Licensure, Certification, and Accreditation   400
    C. Gaining Experience as a Mediator   403
       1. Formal Avenues for Developing Experience   403
       2. Experience Through Co-Mediation   403
       3. Reflective Practice   403
       4. Informal Methods for Developing Mediation Experience   404
 III. Employment Opportunities   404
    A. Opportunities for Salaried Positions   404
       1. Court-Connected Programs   404
       2. State and Federal Agencies   405
       3. Community Mediation Centers   405
       4. Colleges and Universities   405
       5. Corporate   406
       6. Private Dispute-Resolution Companies   406
    B. Private Practice   407
    C. Mediation-Related Employment   407
       1. Teaching   407
       2. Associations and Organizations   407
       3. Consulting   408
    D. Developing Frontiers   408
       1. Victim-Offender Mediation   408
       2. Private International Mediation   409
       3. Online Mediation   409
 IV. Marketing Your Private Mediation Practice   410
    A. Introduction   410
    B. Mediation Is a Service Industry   412
       1. Characteristics of Successful Mediators   412
          a. People   412
          b. Passion   412
          c. Excellence   413
          d. Authenticity   413

2. Importance of Reputation   413
C. Determine Your Desired Level of Practice   414
    1. Volunteer Practice   414
    2. Part-Time Practice   415
    3. Full-Time Practice   415
    4. Premier Practice   416
D. Developing a Marketing Plan   416
    1. Identifying the Target Market   416
        a. Market Segmentation   416
        b. Market Niche   417
    2. Include Measurable Business Goals   417
    3. Strategies for Reaching the Target Market   418
        a. Professional Networks   418
            i. Internal Networks.   418
            ii. External Networks.   419
        b. Speaking Engagements   420
        c. Training and Teaching   421
        d. Publishing   421
        e. Website and Social Media   422
V. Practical Business Considerations   422
A. Meeting Facilities   422
B. Getting Paid   423
C. Business Entity   424
D. Professional Indemnity Insurance   424
E. Client Satisfaction Surveys   424
F. Conclusion   424
VI. Exercises   425

Appendix One · Standard Forms for Mediation Practice   427
Appendix Two · Forms Related to the Agreement to Mediate   433
Appendix Three · Mediated Agreements   439
Appendix Four · Reframing   447
Appendix Five · Guidelines for Lawyers Representing
    Clients in Mediation   449
Appendix Six · Evaluation   451
Appendix Seven · Mediator's Opening Statement Checklist   455
Appendix Eight · Pre-Mediation Conference Preparation Form 457
Appendix Nine A · Expected Value Calculation Form—Plaintiff 459
Appendix Nine B · Expected Value Calculation Form—Defendant 461
Appendix Ten · Ethical Standards   463

Index   471

About the Authors

Laurence J. Boulle, B.A., LL.B., LL.M., Ph.D., has worked at universities in Africa, Europe, North America, the Pacific, and Australasia. He was William J. Cook fellow at the University of Michigan Law School in Ann Arbor. He is currently Bell Wiese Professor of Legal Ethics, University of Newcastle, and Adjunct Professor in the School of Law, Bond University. He is nationally accredited as a Mediator and as a Family Dispute Resolution Practitioner and has practiced in family, franchising, leasing, workplace, native title, and organizational mediation. He is former chair of the Mediator Standards Board in Australia, and his books on mediation and dispute resolution have been published in seven countries.

Michael T. Colatrella Jr., J.D., LL.M., is a Professor of Law at University of the Pacific, McGeorge School of Law, and former Director of the Southern Methodist University's Center for Dispute Resolution and Conflict Management in Plano, Texas. He teaches and writes in the areas of Alternative Dispute Resolution, Mediation, Negotiation, Lawyering Skills, Legal Education, and Leadership. Professor Colatrella is a court-approved mediator in California, Texas, New Jersey, and Kansas, practicing in the areas of workplace, commercial, consumer fraud, and personal injury mediation. He has consulted for Fortune 500 companies and governments across the United States and abroad.

Anthony P. Picchioni, Ph.D., holds a Ph.D. from UNT in counseling. For the last 20 years he has been a professor at SMU in Dallas as well as an educational consultant for Baylor University Medical Center, the academic hospital in Dallas. Dr. Picchioni created two master's-level programs at SMU, one in dispute resolution and another in clinical counseling, and has served as chair of the Human Development Department for eighteen years. He has written and published extensively in the fields of counseling, mediation, conflict management, and health care. He has chaired the Texas licensing board for counseling and the ethics review board. He has also consulted internationally for Fortune 500 and Fortune 50 companies around the world. He and his wife (Debby) live in Plano, Texas.

Acknowledgments

Laurence Boulle would like to thank colleagues at the Dispute Resolution Centre, Bond University, in particular, John Wade, Pat Cavanagh, Libby Taylor, Jane Hobler, and Cheryl Hensel, for their support, as well as the many students and professionals whose observations, insights, and feedback have always made teaching mediation skills and techniques such a delight. Particular thanks go to his student research assistants on this project, Yvette Zegenhagen, Joshua Underhill, and Marian Pond. Finally, gratitude for assistance of both the mediational and non-mediational varieties goes to Nadja, Mark, Sarah, Philippa, and Jono.

Michael Colatrella and Anthony Picchioni would like to thank their colleagues at the Center for Dispute Resolution and Conflict Management, Southern Methodist University, in particular, Robert Barner, Ph.D.; Thomas Cinti, J.D., M.S.; Thomas Hartsell, J.D.; Joel Goldman, J.D.; Jeffrey Kreisberg Ph.D.; and John Wade, LL.B, LL.M. Particular thanks also go to Jacqueline Field and Kay Barclay for administrative support, to Ava Hall and Deborah Jean Schmidt for research assistance, and to Carlos Martín. Additional thanks go to students who volunteered their time to proofread various sections of this book: Enrique Arroyave, Brandi Colón, Kristyne Evanoski, Stacy M. Gibson, Ellen Lee, Robin T. Mathew, Allison Morrow, and Bridget A. Okpa. Finally, special thanks go to Jean Mary Shanley, J.D., for her support, advice, and editing suggestions that have greatly contributed to this book.

For the second edition, the authors wish to thank Kristina Lee and Heather Mills, McGeorge School of Law students, whose diligence in research and proofing contributed significantly to this edition.

The expectations of life depend upon diligence: the mechanic that would perfect his work must first sharpen his tools.

—CONFUCIUS (PHILOSOPHER)

MEDIATION

ONE

Introduction to Learning Mediation Skills and Techniques

I was ruined but twice. Once when I lost a lawsuit and once when I won.

—VOLTAIRE (WRITER)

I. Mediation's Role and Benefits

Mediation is a rapidly growing and developing field, recognized for its flexibility and application in many litigated and non-litigated conflicts. In response to this positive national trend, this book addresses the subject of mediation in a broad sense, since the skills and techniques that mediators use in their roles as helpers, facilitators, and supporters of decision-making are the same regardless of whether a formal dispute has been initiated. Indeed, there would likely be far fewer formal disputes ever docketed with the courts if mediation support was introduced earlier in the conflict-development phase to help the parties manage their emerging dispute.

A. Mediation Defined

Mediation is a process where the parties to a dispute are assisted by someone external to the dispute, the mediator, who aids their decision-making about the dispute in various ways. Mediation is unique because it is consensual and gives the parties the opportunity to make their own decision rather than have it imposed on them, as happens in many other forms of binding dispute resolution such as arbitration or adjudication. The mediator is there to guide and assist, not to render binding judgments and rulings.

This book includes all forms of assisted decision-making where the parties are supported by a mediator. The principal goal of the mediator is to employ skills and techniques to assist the parties in making practical decisions about their dispute. Reaching a definitive agreement is not the primary objective, although it is a secondary goal and usually the natural result of the involvement of an effective mediator.[1]

---

1. Some support the theory that merely "making decisions" is too vague and indeterminate, and they advocate a focus on "dispute resolution" as the goal of mediation. Although we do not subscribe to this limited view, we acknowledge the existence of contrary opinions.

3

For some, especially in the legal community, the goal of mediation is rather singular—to get the parties to reach an agreement. For proof of this mindset, one may look at the Uniform Mediation Act (hereinafter "UMA"), where mediation is more specifically defined as "a process in which a mediator facilitates communication and negotiation between parties to assist them in reaching a voluntary agreement regarding their dispute."[2] This view is too limited and, as we will address later, potentially problematic. Mediation sometimes resolves disputes, sometimes contains them, and sometimes defines them more clearly. Mediation may even serve as a gateway to self-awareness, empowerment, forgiveness, and reconciliation.[3] Always, however, mediation provides the opportunity for making better decisions, even if only the decision to submit the dispute to a court, a boss, an international tribunal, or some other authoritative decision-maker.

In the legal profession, mediation has enjoyed improved credibility and financial support, yet its application is still limited and its full benefits have not yet been realized. Mediation is often sought after the parties have initiated litigation, and very often well into the progress of the litigation matter or even just prior to trial. It is generally understood to be a means of encouraging settlement to save the additional costs of a trial. However, applying mediation to disputes in this way unfortunately does not avoid much of the costs of pre-suit and pre-trial litigation, which are often daunting. Well-known mediator Eric Green has explained that in the litigation context, "[o]ne of the keys to successful settlement practice is that 'attorneys and parties need to prepare just enough to make economic decisions in a minimal risk setting.'"

Mediation is sometimes also referred to as *conciliation, facilitation,* or *assisted decision-making.* Mediators may also be referred to as *conciliators, facilitators, intermediaries, go-betweens, peacemakers, brokers,* and the like, and may come from any

2. The Uniform Mediation Act (UMA) was approved in 2001 by the National Conference of Commissioners on Uniform State Laws (NCCUSL), a non-profit, state-sponsored organization that provides model legislation to bring clarity and uniformity to various areas of the law. The UMA was created with the participation of a variety of organizations interested in dispute resolution, including the ABA Section on Dispute Resolution and the Association of Conflict Resolution, as well as many others. The UMA has no independent force of law. Rather, it is prototype legislation for states to adopt, in whole or in part, to govern legal and policy issues regarding mediation. The NCCUSL is a highly regarded institution that has been responsible for a large number of now well-established and respected laws such as the Uniform Commercial Code, to name just one. As of this writing, states that have enacted the UMA, or some variation, as law are as follows: District of Columbia, Georgia, Hawaii, Idaho, Illinois, Iowa, Nebraska, New Jersey, Ohio, South Dakota, Utah, Vermont, and Washington.

3. Although we advocate a pragmatic model of mediation and believe that participants should not seek mediation principally for counseling, therapy, or personal transformation, we acknowledge that these may be secondary benefits flowing from participation in a competent process. Such expectations may be too high for many participants and disputes. High aspirations can also be an undue burden for the mediator in many situations, such as volunteer community mediations. The skills and techniques associated with these loftier objectives are beyond the scope of this text.

walk of life. No attempt is made to distinguish among these terms and labels. Even if valid distinctions could be made, the core mediation skills and techniques dealt with here are applicable to all of them and are the general subject matter of this book.

Those who are directly involved in mediation are referred to in this book as *participants* or *parties*, although *parties* does have a legalistic connotation. Sometimes they are referred to as mediation *clients*. The term *disputant* is not used because of its negative connotation. Where it is necessary to distinguish between the mediation participants, common usage is followed in referring to "Party A" and "Party B." For the sake of simplicity, we will generally presume that the mediation will consist of two parties, although multi-party mediations are common.

B. Benefits of Mediation

There are considerable benefits to both the parties and the court system by engaging in a future-oriented, problem-solving process rather than a past-oriented, adjudicatory process. Many of the benefits of mediation, although not all, flow from the nature of mediation as essentially a problem-solving process as opposed to an adjudicatory process. This problem-solving approach is more positive and naturally results in happier solutions, lower costs for the parties and the courts, and significant time savings. Also, as we will explore more fully in later chapters, mediation frequently results in more nuanced and better-tailored results that the parties could not have obtained in an adjudicatory process.

Unlike mediation, adjudicatory processes such as litigation and arbitration rely on a neutral decision-maker to decide the dispute and are "rights-based." This means that the decision-maker decides which of the participants is correct under some predetermined standard; in litigation, the standard is usually the law, but in arbitration, it can be common business practices or even the arbitrator's sense of fairness. The applicable standard is applied to the participants' past actions and behavior to arrive at a decision. Thus, the facts surrounding the dispute are of paramount importance in resolving it. A great deal of time, energy, and expense must be expended in discovering the relevant facts of the dispute and preparing for their presentation. Further complicating the process, the neutral decision-maker carries enormous power and responsibility when deciding who has the more valid claim. Accordingly, adjudicatory proceedings have extensive formal rules regarding the gathering of evidence, the presentation of evidence, and the conduct of the proceedings to ensure fairness to the parties at all times and unbiased treatment from the judge, jury, or arbitrator.

Mediation, on the other hand, is a problem-solving process. Emphasis is placed on the future lives of the parties rather than their past behavior. The energy of the parties is shifted toward creating an amicable agreement that will enable the parties to move past the dispute and move on with their lives. While this may involve some consideration and evaluation of the past by the parties, and possibly the mediator, this is not required and it is certainly not the primary focus of the process. Moreover, although some mediators make judgments about the merits of the participants' claims that require evaluation of their past interactions and behavior, the mediator's judgment does not finalize the dispute. This control remains with the parties. Thus, considerably less time, energy, and expense are usually required in gathering and presenting evidence.

Specifically, the benefits of mediation can be grouped as follows: (1) *greater participant control over the proceedings and outcome*, (2) *greater likelihood of preserving and enhancing the relationship of the participants*, (3) *greater access to creative and adaptable solutions*, (4) *quicker resolutions for participants*, (5) *less expensive proceedings for participants*, and (6) *conservation of court resources.*

1. GREATER PARTICIPANT CONTROL OVER THE PROCEEDINGS AND OUTCOME

Mediation provides participants greater control over both the process and the outcome in resolving their dispute. Mediation participants determine what facts are relevant to present and discuss, in contrast to an adjudication where the judge or arbitrator decides what matters may be presented. Mediation participants can engage in direct dialogue with the mediator, the other disputant, or the other disputant's counsel. In contrast, in adjudicatory proceedings, parties participate only as witnesses, through the prescribed rules of direct- and cross-examination. Mediation participants also have significant say in whether the mediation is conducted in joint sessions with all participants present or whether it is conducted in separate sessions that require the mediator to shuttle information and settlement offers back and forth between participants. While mediators do exercise control over the structure of the mediation, participants retain significant control over the process. With adjudication, on the other hand, pre-determined rules and the adjudicator direct the proceedings almost exclusively.

Mediation participants also have complete control over the outcome. In fact, the concept of disputant "party-self-determination" is central to the definition of mediation.[4] Mediators can influence outcomes, and can even recommend outcomes, but they cannot impose outcomes. Participants decide if they will agree to resolve the dispute and to what they will agree. This empowers participants instead of marginalizing them and increases the likelihood that they will comply with any agreement that is made. It also eliminates the risk of having a decision imposed on a participant that contains requirements that later cannot be fulfilled.

---

4. "A Mediator shall Recognize that Mediation is Based on the Principle of Self-Determination by the Parties." MODEL STANDARDS OF CONDUCT FOR MEDIATORS STD. I (2005).

2. GREATER LIKELIHOOD OF PRESERVING AND ENHANCING THE RELATIONSHIP OF THE PARTICIPANTS

Mediation is a problem-solving process more likely to preserve and enhance personal relationships than to destroy them. While some mediations may proceed in an adversarial manner, this is not by design of the process. Adjudications, on the other hand, are adversarial by design. They are structured as contests to distinguish true from false, right from wrong, and winners from losers. This promotes competitive behavior that increases personal animosity among participants (including the lawyers) and de-emphasizes areas of agreement, which can often be substantial.

By contrast, mediations are venues for collaboration, problem solving, and compromise. There is less fear, since the participants know they will not be "ruled against." When participants approach one another in this spirit, they are more likely to be forthright in sharing information, feelings, concerns, fears, and needs—what we call their "interests." They are more likely to be open to acknowledging the common ground that they share, instead of focusing on the battleground of what divides them. The atmosphere, whether spoken or unspoken, implies that cooperation is expected for success of the process. Success means the parties agree, not that someone wins and the other loses. The parties need each other for an agreement to happen. Thus, mediation requires a working relationship to be successful, even if the cooperation is through a mediator that shuttles communications back and forth. The upside is often a healthy interactive process that can lead to a better or restored relationship. This is especially important where it is in the participants' best interests to maintain an amicable relationship, as in the case of divorcing parents with minor children, profitable business partners, landlords and tenants, and organizations in long-term contracts.

3. GREATER ACCESS TO CREATIVE AND ADAPTABLE SOLUTIONS

The potential solutions available to participants involved in mediation are, with few exceptions, limitless and potentially better tailored to the participants' needs. Participants in mediation are free to resolve the dispute based on creative collaborative solutions or compromises that are potentially more responsive to their needs than deciding the dispute on the basis of who is right or who is wrong. In a contract dispute between an employer and employee concerning the terms of employee compensation, the participants in mediation are free to completely re-negotiate the employment contract. In doing so, they may reach a very different compensation arrangement than the original contract contemplated, one that both parties deem is fair, responsive to their concerns, and eliminates any confusion or mistakes that caused the original dispute. Both parties leave satisfied with the result and can continue a mutually beneficial arrangement. The solutions available in adjudication, conversely, are much more limited. Judges, juries, and usually arbitrators are confined to granting awards that are permitted under the prevailing law. This most often involves picking a winner and loser and awarding the winning party money damages. Thus, adjudication is a blunt instrument that at best provides a generic remedy that often is untailored to the dispute.

4. QUICKER RESOLUTIONS FOR PARTICIPANTS

Mediation can lead to quicker resolutions than adjudicatory proceedings and often can be conducted as soon as the dispute arises—before the participants engage in formal discovery or fact-finding that often can be time-consuming. Also, unlike adjudicatory processes, mediation does not usually entail formal presentations of evidence and does not employ a formal decision-maker to resolve the dispute. Consequently, on balance, mediations do not take as long as trials or arbitrations.

In the pre-litigation context, mediation is particularly beneficial in bringing about expedient resolutions for the parties because it emphasizes communication and cooperation. When parties address their dispute before their lawyers put on boxing gloves, the parties are much more likely to be willing to communicate openly and there is less risk of posturing. Once accusations begin to appear in writing and the dispute is launched in the court, there are more psychological barriers preventing the parties from coming together again and talking through a solution.

5. LESS EXPENSIVE PROCEEDINGS FOR PARTICIPANTS

Mediation is less expensive for the participants than adjudicatory proceedings because it often does not require the extensive discovery, fact-finding, preparation and exchange of formal pleadings, interviewing, and preparation of witnesses that are the hallmarks of adjudicatory processes.[5] This informality minimizes the time and cost to prepare, allowing most mediations to be completed in one day.

6. CONSERVATION OF COURT RESOURCES

There is strong evidence to suggest that mediation helps to relieve overcrowded court dockets.[6] At the trial court level, it eases pressure on court resources by reducing the time the dispute is in the legal system, not by appreciably increasing overall settlement rates. Most cases filed at the trial courts are never adjudicated but are

---

5. Jeanne M. Brett, Zoe I. Barsness & Stephen B. Goldberg, *The Effectiveness of Mediation: An Independent Analysis of Cases Handled by Four Major Service Providers*, 12 NEGOTIATION J. 259, 260–67 (1996) (The study looked at 449 cases mediated by four different service providers and found that "mediation participants are more satisfied with the process, the outcome, implementation… than arbitration participants." It also found it cost about a quarter of what arbitration costs.).

6. *See* FED. JUDICIAL CTR., REPORT TO THE JUDICIAL CONFERENCE COMMITTEE IN COURT ADMINISTRATION AND CASE MANAGEMENT: A STUDY OF FIVE DEMONSTRATION PROGRAMS ESTABLISHED UNDER THE CIVIL JUSTICE REFORM ACT OF 1990, at 7–10 (1997). In addition to the federal government's earlier experiments with the use of mediation and other dispute resolution methods in the federal court system, it passed the Alternative Dispute Resolution Act of 1998, which requires, among other things, that all federal courts establish alternative dispute resolution programs. 5 U.S.C.A. 575 (2007).

instead resolved through settlement. However, the longer a case stays in the legal system, the more likely it is that court administrative resources will need to be expended on it in the form of administrative notices, court conferences, and disposition of motions in resolving procedural, discovery, and substantive disputes that arise between the parties during the litigation. Well-organized, court-sponsored mediation programs require parties to enter settlement discussion relatively early in the litigation process and can achieve settlement rates of over 75%.[7]

C. Uses and Applications of Mediation

Mediation has grown exponentially in the United States over the last five decades in both the number and type of cases mediated. A comprehensive list of the types of disputes that are mediated would be difficult, if not impossible, to assemble because of the pervasiveness of mediation throughout all spheres of life. The following, however, are the more common categories of disputes in which mediation is used to resolve problems. Mediation is now widely used to settle: (1) *labor disputes*, (2) *civil cases*, (3) *community disputes*, (4) *family matters*, (5) *business disputes*, (6) *special educational disputes*, and (7) *public policy disputes*. There is even a growing trend to utilize mediation in criminal matters, a concept known as restorative justice.[8]

1. LABOR DISPUTES

Employee-employer relations was one of the first areas to use mediation. In 1913, the U.S. Department of Labor created the "commissioners of conciliation" to mediate disputes between organized labor and management. The commissioners evolved into the current Federal Mediation and Conciliation Service, the goal of which is to promote "sound and stable industrial peace" and "settle issues between employers and employees through the processes of conference and collective bargaining."[9] The mediation service was created to avert strikes, lockouts, and other industrial and economic maladies associated with the actions of organized labor. Based on the suc-

---

7. Jeanne M. Brett, Zoe I. Barsness & Stephen B. Goldberg, *The Effectiveness of Mediation: An Independent Analysis of Cases Handled by Four Major Service Providers*, 12 NEGOTIATION J. 259, 260–67 (1996) (The study looked at 449 cases mediated by four different service providers and found that 78 percent of the cases that were mediated were resolved.); Miguel A. Olivella, Jr., *Toro's Early Intervention Program After Six Years Has Saved $50 M*, 17 ALTERNATIVES TO THE HIGH COST OF LITIG. 65, at 81 (1999) (Toro Corp.'s in-house mediation program reported a 95 percent settlement rate and a $50 million costs savings in handling products liability, personal injury, and commercial claims against it and its subsidiaries.).

8. Thalia González, *The Legalization of Restorative Justice: A Fifty-State Empirical Analysis*, 2019 UTAH L. REV. 1027 (2019); Henry J. Shea, *Restorative Justice, Law, and Healing*, 17 U. ST. THOMAS L. REV. 1 (2020); Amy B. Cyphert, *The Devil Is in the Details: Exploring Restorative Justice as an Option for Campus Sexual Assault Responses Under Title IX*, 96 DENV. U. L. REV. 51, 51–52 (2018).

9. Labor-Management Relations Act of 1947, 29 U.S.C.A. 151 (2021) (also known as the Taft-Hartley Act).

cess of this model, many private and public companies, union and non-union, adopted mediation to resolve disputes among employees and between employees and management.

2. CIVIL CASES

Nearly every federal and state trial-level civil court system in the United States has a court-sponsored mediation program to resolve litigation. These programs, some voluntary and some mandatory, give parties the opportunity to mediate without forcing them to settle. Additionally, all federal appellate courts and many state appellate courts maintain enormously effective mediation programs. In Texas and Florida, most civil cases are mediated.[10]

3. COMMUNITY DISPUTES

Throughout the United States, community mediation centers provide a venue for people to resolve problems with the assistance of a mediator at little or no cost. These centers handle all types of disputes, many of which are ill-suited to the legal system or involve litigants that cannot afford legal counsel. Common disputes mediated by these centers are landlord-tenant matters, minor vandalism, truancy, and neighbor disputes involving barking dogs as well as other easily imaginable problems that can arise between people who share property lines or proximity. These centers were originally funded by the Federal Justice Department and were called Neighborhood Justice Centers. Today many of these centers now have become part of the state or municipal system in which they are located or are privately-funded, non-profit organizations.

4. FAMILY MATTERS

Perhaps no participants benefit more from mediation than parties to family disputes. Given the personal nature of these disputes and the sensitivity of the emotions involved, mediation is a highly effective process for family matters. Common issues mediated in these cases are division of assets between divorcing spouses, financial support for a spouse, child custody and visitation, child maintenance, child rearing issues, termination of parental rights, and disputes between the child and parent. These disputes can be factually complex, making it difficult, if not impossible, for a judge to determine who is "right" or "wrong." They are also highly emotional and can be very expensive to litigate, quickly using up the very assets being fought over. The confidential, problem-solving atmosphere of mediation is often more appropriate for such matters than the public, adversarial atmosphere of formal litigation proceedings.

---

10. Bennett G. Picker, *The Changing Landscape of Mediation: Personal Observations Over the Past 40 Years*, 36 ALTERNATIVES TO THE HIGH COST OF LITIG. 145 (2018).

5. BUSINESS DISPUTES

Increasingly, businesses, large and small, are turning to mediation to resolve their commercial disputes, such as conflicts regarding purchase or service agreements, with other businesses. Mediation is often part of a dispute-resolution clause in the business agreement that requires parties to the agreement to try to resolve the dispute through negotiation and mediation before they are permitted to pursue resolution through litigation or even arbitration.[11] On balance, both litigation and arbitration are more time-consuming and expensive than mediation. Moreover, because mediation is a potentially collaborative process, there is a greater chance of resolving the parties' differences quickly and amicably, thus preserving their mutually beneficial business relationship.

6. SPECIAL EDUCATION DISPUTES

For more than three decades, mediation has been used to resolve disputes among parents and representatives of schools and school districts regarding the special education needs of children. These disputes, for example, often involve the number of hours of extra tutoring or therapy. The Individuals with Disabilities Education Act ("IDEA"), a federal statute, in part states "that all children with disabilities have available to them a free appropriate public education that emphasizes special education and related services designed to meet their unique needs and prepare them for further education, employment, and independent living…"[12] For each qualifying child, the IDEA requires the school to develop a written "individualized education program ('IEP')."[13] The IEP must be developed with the input of teachers, administrators, and parents.[14] As one might suppose, disputes can arise among parents and school representatives regarding the appropriate educational plan for the child. Although IDEA provides for adjudicatory procedures to resolve these disputes, it also mandates that "[a]ny State educational agency or local educational agency that receives assistance under [IDEA]" provide parents the opportunity to mediate the dispute by a "qualified and impartial mediator who is trained in effective mediation techniques."[15] The IDEA further requires that the state maintain a list of qualified mediators for this purpose and pay for the mediation. Thousands of special education mediations are conducted across the country each year.[16]

---

11. Kathleen M. Scanlon & Harpreet K. Mann, *A Guide to Multistep Dispute Resolution Clauses*, 20 ALTERNATIVES TO THE HIGH COST OF LITIG. 1 (Sept. 2002).

12. 20 U.S.C. 1400(d)(1)(A) (2022).

13. 20 U.S.C 1400(d)(1)(B).

14. *Id.*

15. 20 U.S.C. 1415(e)

16. Carolyn Jones, *How California Plans to Deter Costly Special Education Disputes*, EDSOURCE (July 22, 2021), https://edsource.org/2021/how-california-plans-to-deter-costly-special-education-disputes/658226 (stating that in the 2020–21 academic year, California had 3,098 special education complaints, all but 87 of which were resolved through mediation).

7. PUBLIC POLICY DISPUTES

Mediation is also widely used to resolve disputes involving public policy. Public policy disputes are those that concern private citizens or businesses and a governmental entity, and they often concern environmental or social issues. Examples of public disputes commonly involve waste management, location of airports, sports stadiums, wetland protection, building of dams, natural resource management, greenhouse gas emissions, and location of halfway houses for the mentally ill. These issues are also usually complex and involve multiple "stakeholders" who have an interest in the resolution of the dispute, making any litigation extraordinarily lengthy and expensive. Many of these disputes spend decades in litigation as they bounce back and forth between trial and appellate courts with no appreciable progress or resolution.

Recognizing the appropriateness of applying a problem-solving approach to public issues, the U.S. Congress has authorized federal agencies empowered to create administrative rules to engage in negotiated regulation, commonly referred to as "reg-neg."[17] In this process, stakeholders are invited by the agency to participate in the rulemaking process that is managed by a neutral third party who facilitates the process. Thus, it is a mediated negotiation. The traditional way of passing administrative rules and actions was to have the agency draft the rule and then allow for a period of comment. However, because the agency had already committed to the rule's general structure and provisions, the rule often changed little as a consequence of stakeholder comments, leaving it extremely vulnerable to court challenge later. Moreover, if a commenter raised a valid issue that went to the very structure of the proposed regulation, often it was too late to "patch" the regulation, and the only thing that could be done was to scrap the entire proposed rule and start from the beginning, with the attendant expense and delay. But under reg-neg procedures, those with the greatest interest in an administrative rule are invited to participate in the process of creating it. The goal is to address the stakeholders' most important fears and concerns up-front, decreasing the likelihood that the rule will be challenged in court and creating more efficient governance. Federal agencies that have been particularly active in reg-neg are the Environmental Protection Agency, the Department of Health and Human Services, the Nuclear Regulatory Commission, and the Department of Education. Many states have also passed similar reg-neg legislation.

a. *A Note on International Commercial Mediation*

International commercial mediation involves business disputes between or among parties whose places of operation are in different countries. From World War II through the first decade of the twenty-first century, arbitration had been far and away the predominant form of dispute resolution for international commercial disputes. More recently, however, businesses increasingly choose to resolve their

---

17. Originally Congress passed the Negotiated Rulemaking Act of 1990, which was later more formally codified in 1996 in the Administrative Dispute Resolution Act, 5 U.S.C. 571–84 (2000).

international disputes through mediation.[18] This trend is due, in part, to the creeping formalism of international arbitration that has exponentially increased its complexity, duration, and costs.[19] Further fueling the recent increased use of commercial mediation in the international arena is the creation and adoption of the Singapore Convention on Mediation (the "Singapore Convention").[20] The Singapore Convention "is a multilateral treaty which offers a uniform and efficient framework for the enforcement and invocation of international settlement agreements resulting from mediation."[21] Adopted by the United Nations General Assembly in December 2018, there are 55 country signatories to the Singapore Convention as of the time of this writing, including the United States. Among the Singapore Convention's most important contributions is its streamlining of the enforcement of mediated agreements in signatory countries. Before the Singapore Convention, if a party defaulted on a mediated settlement, the non-defaulting party would need to litigate the matter as a breached contract, commencing a new lawsuit.[22] Under the Singapore Convention, a valid mediated settlement is treated like a final judgment that needs only to be enforced. The relevant enforceability language from the Singapore Convention is as follows:

> If a dispute arises concerning a matter that a party claims was already resolved by a settlement agreement, the party may invoke the settlement agreement in accordance with the rules of procedure of this State [country], and under the conditions laid down in this section, in order to prove that the matter has already been resolved.[23]

Since 1958, arbitration awards have been enforceable under The New York Convention, another multinational treaty that, among other things, streamlined the process of the enforcement of arbitration awards between businesses whose places of operation were in different countries.[24] With the advent of the Singapore Convention, mediated agreements are now on similar enforcement footing with arbitration awards, which will undoubtedly be a boon for international mediation.[25]

---

18. *See generally* S.I. Strong, *Realizing Rationality: An Empirical Assessment of International Commercial Mediation*, 73 Wash. & Lee L. Rev. 1973 (2016).

19. *Id.* at 1982.

20. Robert Butlien, Note, *The Singapore Convention on Mediation: A Brave New World for International Commercial Mediation*, 46 Brook. J. Int'l L. 183, 189 (2020). *See also* Hal Abramson, *The New Singapore Mediation Convention: The Process and Key Choices*, 20 Cardozo J. Conflict Resol. 1037 (2019).

21. *About the Convention*, Singapore Convention on Mediation, https://www.singaporeconvention.org/convention/about.

22. Butlien, *supra* note 20, at 198–99.

23. The Singapore Convention Art. 17(2).

24. Butlien, *supra* note 20, at 192–93. *See* New York Arbitration Convention, https://www.newyorkconvention.org/.

25. It is worth noting that the New York Convention also protects the forcibility of agreements to arbitration in additional to making arbitration awards easier to enforce in signatory

D. Limitations of Mediation

Although mediation offers a participant many potential benefits, mediation is not always the most appropriate dispute resolution procedure. Unlike litigation, mediation cannot provide a participant with a legal precedent, which is sometimes desirable to parties pursuing constitutional or civil rights violations, or even business rights violations. Because of the private and confidential nature of the mediation process, mediation may also not be desirable where public awareness of an issue is deemed important, as might be the case in some kinds of employment disputes. Finally, productive mediation requires some level of cooperation between the parties, so where at least one of the parties is overly aggressive or intransigent, mediation is not an advisable option. However, there is almost no category or type of dispute where mediation can be excluded out of hand. Any dispute that can be negotiated can be mediated. Mediation is simply assisted negotiation.

II. Scope and Organization of This Book

This text is designed to provide a fundamental background education to the beginning student of mediation and to serve as a reference or practice guide for the more seasoned mediator. We assumed little or no prior training or experience in mediation to make this text friendly to the brand-new student. Nonetheless, we designed the scope and content of the material to be sufficiently comprehensive and detailed to be useful to experienced mediators as well.

There are, of course, immense differences in *how* people learn new skills and techniques. Some learn best *cognitively*, that is, by absorbing information intellectually before applying it in concrete situations. Others learn best through *observation*, that is, through seeing others perform the particular skills and modeling their behavior on what they have seen. And others learn best through *doing*, that is, by practicing the skills clinically or in simulation and reflecting critically on their performance. This text addresses only the first form, or cognitive learning, by examining various scientific principles and theories underlying effective mediation skills and techniques. To be a successful mediator in practice, however, the student must take this knowledge and apply it in the real world by observing quality mediators at work and practicing their own skills in actual dispute settings. This text provides a basis for introducing mediation concepts to the new student, but it also serves as a tool for the reflective practitioner of mediation for evaluating his or her experiences in light of its suggestions.

---

countries. *Id.* at 194-95. In other words, if a party to a valid arbitration award files a court action in a signatory country, the New York Convention can be used to dismiss the court action in favor of arbitration. Not so of the Singapore Convention, as its provisions apply only to enforce valid mediated agreements and not to enforce valid agreements to mediate. *Id.* at 199.

This book is based on the reality that mediation is not always a linear process moving from A to Z and all stations in between. Problem solving, negotiation, and decision-making are often recursive processes which defy neat attempts to advance them through sequential stages. If the methodology of the natural sciences is sometimes serendipitous, accidentally stumbling on important discoveries while looking for something else, then so too must be the methodology of human sciences such as mediation.

There are some mediation topics that are beyond the scope of this book. This book does not deal comprehensively with some aspects of mediation skills, such as the impact of cultural factors and the role of children in mediation. In addition, other more theoretical and critical issues in mediation are not addressed, such as the desirability of mandatory mediation or the fairness and equity of mediation outcomes. This is a result of selective focus of the material and space constraints and not of the relative importance of these issues.

This book does not address all of the many different models of mediation, areas of mediation practice, and styles of mediator behavior. Generally, however, this book explores a more facilitative model of mediation, where the mediator's primary purpose is to assist their parties in communication and problem solving. Mediation can also be used for many other purposes: to settle disputes, define problems or disputes, manage conflict, prevent conflict, negotiate contracts, and formulate policy and standards. There are *universal* mediation skills and techniques relevant to the practice of mediation in most contexts, and *situational* skills and techniques relevant to specific situations, for example, family, commercial, or international diplomatic disputes. This book focuses predominantly on the universal, or core, skills and techniques of mediation, with occasional references to the situational.

III. Mediation Is a Skill, Not a Talent

Although some people seem to have certain personality traits, background experience, or natural talents that uniquely position them to serve as effective mediators without the benefit of any formal mediation training, this is the exception rather than the rule. It is true that certain notable figures in history, such as Gandhi, Nelson Mandela, and Benjamin Franklin, had undertaken no specific formal mediation training and received no accreditation as mediators but nevertheless made remarkable contributions by using their dispute resolution instincts and skills. Most successful mediators' skills and techniques, however, are not the result of "natural good instincts" but rather have been learned, developed, assessed, and improved through concerted study and practice over a period of time. It is of course also true that some people do appear to be naturally good at helping others resolve disputes. But just as those who are naturally good at caring for ill people require training and education to practice in health services, so too do those who are naturally good at dispute resolution.

Mastery of any skill comes with study, practice, and hard work. Michelangelo, the Italian Renaissance artist, once stated, "If people knew how hard I had to work to gain my mastery, it wouldn't seem wonderful at all." Recent advances in brain science and brain imaging supports what Michelangelo seems to have known long ago, that superior performance, even what we might call genius, has as much or more to do with how much effort we put into developing a particular skill as it does with the natural aptitudes with which we are born.[26]

There is also a misconception that simply gaining experience in conducting mediations is sufficient by itself to become a quality mediator. While performing a task repeatedly can lead to some increased aptitude initially, a much higher level of ability is attainable if the practitioner increases his or her knowledge of the underlying subject matter and critically evaluates his or her performance against science-based practices. For instance, most of us drive our car every day, but do we get much better at it simply because we have had more practice doing it? Certainly, experience improves driving skills in the first few months or perhaps even years of driving, but are we significantly better drivers after many hundreds or thousands of hours of driving experience? For most adults, our driving skill level is about the same this year as it was last year. Why? We drive as if we are on autopilot after we learn the rules of the road and with minimal skill to keep us reasonably safe. Without new knowledge about driving technique or feedback about our own driving ability, our skills will remain about the same. It is the same for any skill, such as golf, music, or mediation.

Modern brain science tells us that superior practitioners of a skill, like mediation for instance, "develop the capacity to break down t[heir] experience into multiple components and work on each of those separately."[27] They not only break down the general skill into sub-skills, but they also identify those sub-skills that need improving, and they work to improve them. We call this reflective learning. Reflective learning marries experience with critical evaluation of the quality of that experience.[28] This is the type of practice that leads to improved performance, and the kind that we recommend you apply in learning the skill of mediation.

This text breaks down the general skill of mediation into its component sub-skills, such as active listening, summarizing, reframing, reality testing, and many others. Some of these sub-skills will come easily to you, and some will be more challenging. You must identify those sub-skills you need to improve the most. It is through such reflective practice that you will become better at the general skill of mediation, just as the tennis player who hones a weak backhand elevates his or her entire game.

---

26. Philip Ross, *The Expert Mind,* SCIENTIFIC AMERICAN, Aug. 2006, at 64.
27. RICHARD RESTAK, M.D., THE NEW BRAIN 19 (2003).
28. *See* NADJA M. SPEGEL, BERNADETTE ROGERS & ROSS P. BUCKLEY, NEGOTIATION: THEORY AND TECHNIQUES 2–4 (1998).

If you wish to truly distinguish yourself as a mediator, reflective practice will be a life-long pursuit, not just limited to the classroom or the first weeks or months of study. The concert pianist F.B. Busoni wrote, "I never neglect the opportunity to improve no matter how perfect a previous interpretation may have seemed to me. In fact, I often go directly home from a concert and practice for hours upon the very pieces that I have been playing because during the concert certain new ideas came to me." While it may not be your goal, or a necessity, to become the Mozart of mediation, true mastery of the skill requires hard work and practice.

IV. The Mediator's Skills and Techniques Toolbox

Mediators use many skills and techniques and must be equipped to reach into their "toolbox" for the right skill or technique at the right time. We draw a distinction between the terms "skills" and "techniques," although in some circles these terms are used interchangeably. In this book, a "skill" is generally meant to be a particular proficiency or expertise that an individual has in a certain area. Examples of skills are common sense, organization skills, comfort in social situations, listening proficiency, interviewing skills, and verbal or written communication ability. A "technique" is meant to be a specific task, action, or systematic procedure or set of procedures employed by the mediator in a situation. Techniques are also sometimes referred to as "interventions." Examples of techniques include paraphrasing, reframing, and separating the parties. There is no bright-line distinction between a skill and a technique, and some overlap does exist, but distinguishing the terms is helpful in exploring the various things mediators do to assist people in conflict.

Although these skills and techniques we will examine are relevant for many different types of professions, it is their combination, organization, and interrelation in the process of mediation that makes the mediation profession unique. For example, many types of skilled professionals, such as managers, interviewers, arbitrators, judges, parents, and others, use these skills in their daily problem-solving processes. Viewed individually, none of the skills and techniques you will use as a mediator is strictly unique to mediation. However, the mediator must be able to pull it all together.

As you learn the skills and techniques that you will need to mediate disputes, you may find that some abilities you have already developed extensively as a result of your prior personal and professional experiences, while others may be more challenging for you. You will apply your own life experiences to your work as a mediator. You will then want to shift your attention to honing those skills and techniques that require further development. For example, you may have the skill to organize data systematically and ease awkward social situations, but you may not have much background experience in employing techniques to manage unrealistic expectations of the parties or to de-escalate conflict. You will need to identify your existing strengths and then focus on developing those areas which are more challenging for you.

For some prospective mediators, their prior training and experience may actually necessitate some "deskilling," in the sense of consciously unlearning existing skills and approaches and replacing them with those more appropriate for mediation. For example, some experienced lawyers have an ability to reduce a complex array of circumstances to a narrow set of facts relevant to legal advocacy. This tendency needs to be subordinated in mediation and replaced with a broader awareness of the relevance of all the factors, both legal and non-legal, which gave rise to the dispute. Likewise, some counselors may have developed a high level of skill in refraining from imposing any pressure on their clients, which might be an inappropriate technique in some mediations.

Another area for consideration is developing the ability to select and apply your "toolbox" skills and techniques in appropriate situations. Encompassed in this process is the ability to discriminate between using your own skills and techniques and assisting others in the use of their skills and techniques. There is a subtle but important difference between assisting others to communicate and negotiate well and being a good communicator or negotiator oneself. Likewise, there is sometimes only a subtle difference between assisting others to make decisions and making good decisions yourself. The key to choosing the right approach for the circumstances is to be clear and mindful about what you are trying to achieve.

V. Mediation Models

The particular skills and techniques that you choose to apply in a mediation will depend in part on which model of mediation you are providing to the parties. Mediation "models" refer to different styles of mediation. Some mediators may find that the mediation model they use is based on their personality and mediation philosophy, and accordingly does not change based on the circumstances of the mediation. Other mediators may find that they prefer to use a different style depending on the nature of the dispute being mediated. There are three common mediation models available to a mediator: (1) *facilitative*, (2) *transformative*, and (3) *evaluative*.

A. The Models Defined

1. FACILITATIVE MEDIATION

In facilitative mediation, which is the primary model espoused in this book, the mediator conducts the process along strict lines in order to define the problem comprehensively, focusing on the parties' needs and concerns and helping them to develop creative solutions that can be applied to the problem. The facilitative mediator views his or her role as facilitating communication and helping the parties avoid common pitfalls in problem solving.[29] They are "process" experts, not necessarily

---

29. See the classic treatment of mediator style, Leonard L. Riskin, *Mediator Orientations, Strategies and Techniques*, 12 ALTERNATIVES TO THE HIGH COST OF LITIG. 111 (1994). Professor

"content" experts. They do not provide opinions about the quality of settlement options, although they may, through questioning and other techniques, assist the parties in evaluating the quality of the settlement options for themselves.

2. TRANSFORMATIVE MEDIATION

In transformative mediation, the mediator assists parties in conflict to improve or transform their relationship as a basis for resolving the dispute. Transformative mediation theory posits that parties in conflict are in a "vicious circle of disempowerment, disconnection, and demonization."[30] A transformative mediator's primary focus is assisting the parties to have constructive interaction to improve the relationship, not settling the dispute at hand. By improving the quality of the relationship, the parties are better equipped to resolve not only the problem at hand but future conflicts as well.[31]

3. EVALUATIVE MEDIATION

In evaluative mediation, the mediator guides and advises the parties on the basis of his or her expertise with a view to reach a settlement that accords with their legal rights and obligations, industry norms, or other objective social standards. In doing so, the mediator will often provide opinions concerning an acceptable settlement range and likely outcome in court if the dispute is not settled. The primary focus of the evaluative mediator is to highlight the strengths and weakness of the parties' positions and arguments, as he or she sees them, in order to bring about a compromise.[32] An extreme form of evaluative mediation is sometimes referred to as "settlement mediation." As the name suggests, the only concern in this type of mediation is achieving settlement. The mediator encourages the parties to reach a point of compromise between their positional claims through various forms of persuasion, "reality testing," and pressure, without any significant emphasis on the process of decision-making. Although the primary focus of this book is on facilitative mediation, we include a chapter exploring evaluative mediation because of its ubiquity.

Riskin has updated and revised his thinking regarding mediator style, believing "elicitive" more accurately captures the qualities that he originally described as "facilitative," and "directive" more accurately describes the qualities that he originally described as "evaluative." Leonard L. Riskin, *Decision-making in Mediation: The New Old Grid and the New New Grid System*, 79 NOTRE DAME L. REV. 1, 30 (2003). Professor Riskin's original terms are used in this book because they are firmly established in the dispute resolution lexicon. For an exploration of the utility of Professor Riskin's grid as an educational tool for mediators, see Michael T. Colatrella Jr., *"True Enough," in* DISCUSSIONS IN DISPUTE RESOLUTION: THE FOUNDATIONAL ARTICLES (Art Hinshaw, Andrea Kupfer Schneider, & Sarah Rudolph Cole, eds. 2021).

30. ROBERT A. BARUCH BUSH & JOSEPH P. FOLGER, THE PROMISE OF MEDIATION 52 (2005).

31. *Id.* at 65–66. The United States Postal Service's REDRESS program uses the transformative mediation model exclusively. *Id.* at 52. *See* USPS, *Legal REDRESS*, https://about.usps.com/who/legal/redress/welcome.htm.

32. *See* Riskin, *Mediator Orientations*, *supra* note 29, at 111.

B. The Eclectic Use of the Models

The various terms of art used in the above descriptions are explained and illustrated in different parts of the book. It is important to note that few mediators can be neatly associated with a single form of mediation. Moreover, some mediations may begin in one mode, frequently facilitative, and be transformed later to another, for example, evaluative. As the model of mediation changes, so too will the role of the mediator. The skills and techniques examined in this book are potentially applicable in all the mediation models listed above, although how the skills are used and to what degree will be different for different models.

VI. Functions of the Mediator

Once you have assembled your mediator's "toolbox" of skills and techniques, you are ready to perform the functions of a mediator. As discussed previously, mediation is generally the process by which the mediator uses his or her various skills and selectively applies various techniques or interventions to assist the participants in practical decision-making about their dispute. Specifically, this process can be divided into the following five categories: (1) *creating favorable conditions for the parties*, (2) *assisting the parties to communicate*, (3) *facilitating the parties' negotiations*, (4) *encouraging settlement*, and (5) *identifying and managing cultural differences*.

In conducting this process, you will apply various skills and techniques as the circumstances require. You might use them separately or in combination with one another. While you will use some techniques, known as *general interventions*, in each mediation you perform, especially to provide structure and control, many techniques will be used only as the circumstances call for it. For instance, you may apply *contingent interventions* to shuttle messages between the participants or invite professional advisers to discuss particular issues. You will apply *primary interventions* when you introduce a concept to the participants or when you want to initiate a response from one or both participants. You will apply *reactive interventions* in response to situations or dilemmas that may arise during the course of the mediation. Throughout the mediation, the mediator is engaged in a constant process of initiating, reacting, adapting, and retreating—selectively choosing and applying the appropriate skills and techniques needed as matters evolve. If all this sounds exhausting, it is; however, it is also an immensely fulfilling pursuit.

To be successful in this role, an understanding of the fundamental nature of conflict is also important for the mediator. There is increasing knowledge about many aspects of conflict: its sources, the ways in which it escalates and de-escalates, strategies for dealing with it, and ways in which it can be managed and resolved. Knowledge in these areas not only assists mediators in terms of their choice of interventions but also enables them to inform and educate parties about normal patterns of conflict and ways of productively responding to it.

A. Creating Favorable Conditions for the Parties

Mediators can contribute to the resolution of a problem or dispute by creating favorable conditions for its treatment. As neutral observers with expertise in the nature of conflict and its management, they can do things that the participants and their advisers are unable to do on their own. There are at least three ways in which mediators can contribute toward a favorable climate for decision-making and dispute resolution:

- *Procedural framework.* The mediator is responsible for controlling the proceedings, establishing basic ground rules, establishing an effective problem-solving process, monitoring behavior, allowing equal air-time for all participants, allowing for necessary adjournments, setting parameters for the role of professional advisers, and otherwise providing a framework of control, impartiality, and security.

- *Physical environment.* The mediator should provide an appropriate physical environment for dispute resolution in terms of neutral venues, accessible buildings, adequate meeting rooms and amenities, and other physical facilities that provide convenience, security, confidentiality, and symbolically appropriate seating for decision-making and problem solving.

- *Emotional environment.* The mediator can contribute to an appropriate emotional environment for the participants in a dispute by providing a person and process in which they can trust; by ensuring an absence of threats, aggression, and intimidating behavior; by providing an atmosphere of neutrality and impartiality; by reducing defensiveness; and by otherwise providing a hospitable emotional climate for decision-making and problem solving.

B. Assisting the Parties to Communicate

Mediators can contribute to the communication process among the participants in a variety of ways. Parties in conflict tend not to communicate accurately, comprehensively, or constructively. Accordingly, mediators should aid communication by modeling good speaking and listening skills, ensuring clarity and accuracy in communication, being attentive to the non-verbal communication of the parties, engaging in appropriate questioning, making use of visual communications, reframing and summarizing what the parties say, and otherwise attending to communication factors which contribute to good decision-making and problem solving.

C. Facilitating the Parties' Negotiations

As experts in negotiation, mediators can contribute to the parties' negotiating endeavors so as to make them more constructive, interest-driven, efficient, and otherwise productive. Mediators accomplish this by ensuring that their clients prepare for their negotiating roles, focusing on the parties' needs and interests, preventing premature offers and rejections of offers, educating parties about good negotiation practice, coaching the parties in separate sessions on how to negotiate, assisting the parties with brainstorming and packaging an agreement, and otherwise facilitating a negotiation process which is positive and productive. A mediator may also further assist by limiting the options available to the participants to only those that are realistic and feasible and asking the parties to make practical decisions from that point.

D. Encouraging Settlement

Settlement may be encouraged through either the passive influence or the active participation of the mediator. For some participants, the mere presence of a mediator may be perceived as pressure to moderate their behavior and come to a settlement that they would not have reached without this presence. Thus, passive pressure to settle is a potential reality of all mediation situations. Among the active ways in which mediators can encourage settlement are by questioning the parties about their realistic options away from the mediation, acting as the "agent of reality," providing encouragement and rewards, imposing deadlines, and being assertive in separate meetings. The role of the mediator in encouraging settlement is controversial and there is much debate about the appropriateness and ethics of the ways in which these functions are performed.[33] This debate primarily centers on the question of whether "evaluative" mediator techniques are appropriate. Nonetheless, the mediator's role in encouraging settlement is a reality of mediation practice, regardless of whether the mediator adopts a facilitative or evaluative approach.

While the mediator's role will necessarily change from situation to situation, it is worth reiterating that the mediator's role is always to take the parties through a recognized and efficient process that assists them to make decisions but does not make decisions for them. With this approach, a mediator will not necessarily have done a good job merely because the parties reached a settlement. Conversely, the failure to reach a settlement will not necessarily mean that the mediator has not conducted the process satisfactorily and that the parties will not have derived some benefits from it. There is always an underlying assumption that it is better for the participants to make their own decisions through a systematic decision-making process than it is to have decisions made for them.

E. Identifying and Managing Cultural Differences

Good mediation is problem solving with an awareness of cultural differences. Here "cultural" is used in a broad sense to refer to differences based on class, gender, ethnicity, national origin, professional background, geography, and the like. The

---

33. Lela P. Love, *The Top 10 Reasons that Mediators Should Not Evaluate: Reflections on the Facilitative-Evaluation Debate*, 24 FLA. ST. U. L. REV. 937 (1997); MARJORIE CORMAN AARON, *Evaluation in Mediation, in* MEDIATING LEGAL DISPUTES: EFFECTIVE STRATEGIES FOR LAWYERS AND MEDIATORS 267 (Dwight Golann, ed. 1996).

core process of mediation certainly offers something of value for people with widely varying cultural attributes. However, the practical application of mediation skills and techniques is not culturally neutral. In particular, factors of ethnicity, class, and gender make difficult any broad generalizations about skills and techniques since many of them are culturally derived and circumscribed. Cultural differences may be a factor in the following issues relevant to the mediation process:

- Verbal or written communication (including tone, volume, etc.);
- Non-verbal communication (body language);
- Attitudes towards physical space and personal boundaries;
- Approaches to time;
- Approaches to problem solving and negotiation;
- Attitudes towards privacy and involvement of third parties;
- Acceptance of compromise and concession;
- Relationship values;
- Roles of lawyers and other professional advisers.

The skills and techniques used in this book are based on the predominant culture of the United States. Although this culture is shared in part by many other inhabitants of the globe, no assumptions can be made as to the universal applicability of any particular skill or technique.[34]

1. CULTURE AND MEDIATION

Bee Chen Goh, author of *Negotiating with the Chinese* (1996), writes as follows on the significance of culture in mediation:[35]

It needs to be noted that culture plays a significant role in determining and shaping one's perception of conflicts and their resolution. In the case of the Chinese, for instance, they are predominantly collectivists by nature. Collectivism favors group goals. Therefore, the Chinese are generally used to the ideals of harmony and compromise. Further, they subscribe to the anthropo-cosmic conception. What this means is that a conflict or a dispute is not just perceived by the Chinese as human, but it bears a cosmic dimension too. In the Chinese cosmological view, a conflict is seen as disrupting social harmony and disturbing the natural harmony. As such, a dispute is to be avoided lest it incurs the 'wrath of Heaven'. In ancient China, it was believed that a lack

---

34. For an excellent exploration of how cultural differences affect negotiation, see JEANNE M. BRETT, NEGOTIATING GLOBALLY (2001).

35. BEE CHEN GOH, NEGOTIATING WITH THE CHINESE 20 (1996). Reprinted with permission of the author.

of peace on earth and human conflicts resulted in natural disasters, the most common being severe floods.

Thus, in terms of disputes, the Chinese prefer the dissolution of disputes to a resolution of disputes. In the former case, when a problem is perceived, the people involved work around the problem and try to dissipate it. The Chinese tend to act in preventative ways so that the problem does not get out of proportion and escalate into a messy conflict. It is usually messy because a conflict, in the collectivistic Chinese sense, is communal and not personal. There is a popular Chinese saying: 'Let big problems become small, and let small problems disappear'. Their general intention lies in the preservation of social harmony. In this sense, collectivists are less interested in the pursuit of individual rights. Rather, their concern is the social good.

Quite naturally, litigation essentially runs counter to the observance of harmony and the Chinese discomfort at direct confrontation. Due to this, in the event of inevitable conflicts, the prime method for solving them is conciliation or mediation. Mediation also serves the objective of the Confucian Chinese in the adherence to *li*, i.e., correct behaviour and ritualistic propriety. Litigation is at odds with the Confucian spirit of self-criticism. A person who practises self-criticism is considered to be morally disposed, one who does not insist on rights but who prefers to settle a dispute through the means which enables both parties to save personal embarrassment and not to lose face. A lawsuit will certainly cause one to lose face.

Confucianism has further inculcated a hierarchical social structure which establishes stability and orderliness through its members observing the rules made appropriate to rank and status. If each one observes his or her place, there will be peace in society. Mediation is regarded as congruent with this process, as the disputants can be reminded of their own specific roles.

It can thus be seen that mediation as the primary method of conflict resolution is culturally ideal for the Chinese as it enables them to pursue their group goals of harmony and compromise, encourages face-saving behaviour, and supports the hierarchical nature of the Chinese society.

VII. Evaluating Your Effectiveness

Your effectiveness as a mediator should be assessed in broad terms, based on the totality of the experience for the participants. As discussed previously, whether or not the parties reached a settlement should not be the only criterion for your success. While this measure of effectiveness is obviously important, there is a wider range of indicators of competent mediation. By way of example, mediation could be assessed in terms of the following:

- *Process*: the extent to which the parties are satisfied with the mediator's conduct of the mediation and their experience of the process and its fairness;

- *Efficiency*: the extent to which the process is cost and time-effective and maximized the value of the outcome;

- *Empowerment*: the extent to which the mediation educates the parties about constructive problem solving and equips them to deal with disputes in the future;

- *Effectiveness*: the extent to which the mediation achieves a settlement outcome;

- *Durability*: the extent to which the mediation outcome endures over time; and

- *Relationship*: the extent to which the mediation process increases understanding and improves the relationship between the parties.

Further discussion of these and other indicators is beyond the scope of this text. However, they constitute some of the standards by which mediator competence can be assessed and demonstrate other avenues for critical evaluation of your performance besides whether settlement was achieved.

VIII. Overview of a Real Mediation

When cooking, it is helpful to use a recipe that contains good-quality color photographs of the completed dish. This is particularly helpful where the recipe goes under a foreign name and one has no idea what the final product should look like. Regrettably, a book on mediation is not to mediators what a recipe book is to cooks. This is because the human players in mediation do not have the objective and standardized qualities of cooking ingredients. And even if this work was like a mediation recipe book, it would be difficult to provide a picture of the final product.

Nevertheless, for those eager to enter the world of mediation, it is sometimes frustrating that they cannot see the finished product, particularly where the process and skills are divided into multiple chapters with many subheadings and numbered sections. Because of confidentiality arrangements, it is not easy to observe a mediation, nor is this form of dispute resolution well-represented in the media, drama, or entertainment. With this in mind, the following summary of a real mediation has been provided to present a "finished product." It is designed to give an overall feel of a mediation from start to finish without, of course, being able to provide all the detail or human drama. Here the story of a mediation is presented in plain English with an avoidance of the technical terms, acronyms, and other mediation jargon:

A small business (SB) in a rural area was in conflict with the publishers (DP) of a printed directory which was produced annually for a specific industry. The dispute originated from an ambiguous communication which led to the small business (SB) not receiving the advertising it had expected in the directory. It alleged that the omission of the directory publisher (DP) had caused loss of business and loss of income. DP rectified the problem in the next annual directory and waived all fees and charges which would otherwise have been owed by SB for another two years of the directory. SB sought damages directly from DP for their alleged losses, but there was a lengthy delay in dealing with their claim because of changes of personnel in DP.

Over time, SB became aware of other successful complainants who had experienced similar problems and decided to institute legal proceedings for breach of contract, claiming damages of $150,000 for additional advertising expenses, loss of business, and loss of goodwill. DP was offended by the size of the damages claim and refused to negotiate. SB made a formal offer of settlement for $75,000 and DP counteroffered with $6,000. The court made a compulsory referral to mediation. The parties, on the advice of their lawyers, agreed on the selection of the mediator.

The mediator sent the parties written information about mediation, the mediator's résumé, and an Agreement to Mediate. The mediator had telephonic discussions with the parties' lawyers, one of whom sent copies of the court papers and relevant reports. The mediator also had discussions with the clients themselves, explaining the nature of mediation, the role of the mediator, and the responsibilities of the clients. In these discussions, SB indicated an intention to "go along and see what happens" at the mediation, and DP indicated an intention to reach a commercial settlement because of the bad publicity they were facing. The mediator made arrangements with the lawyers about venue, timing, identity of participants, exchange of documents, and other housekeeping matters.

The mediation began at 11:00 a.m. at a neutral venue. SB was represented by the proprietor and a lawyer, and DP was represented by a middle manager from the head office, an in-house lawyer from another city, and a regional manager. Both sides indicated that they had authority to settle. The parties were formally seated at a boardroom table with the mediator at the head.

The mediation meeting began with the mediator explaining the nature of the mediation process, the mediator's role, the order of proceedings for the mediation, and the roles of the clients and their lawyers. The lawyer for DP raised a concern about the fact that the mediator knew the owner of SB, both having grown up in the area, but agreed to proceed when it was pointed out that this fact had been conveyed to the client when the mediator was appointed.

The parties then made short opening statements to the mediator, with some amplification of each by their lawyers. The DP representatives acknowledged their mistake right at the outset and expressed regret for its consequences for SB. The owner of SB accepted the apology. The mediator listed a number of points for discussion and all participants then talked about these one by one.

SB made use of an accountant's report in support of the monetary damages being claimed. DP criticized various aspects of the report. DP suggested possible ways of meeting SB's interests by providing new advertising products on favorable terms in the future; SB indicated some potential interest in these options but also asked for $75,000 by way of a monetary settlement.

The joint meeting then adjourned and the mediator spoke with each side separately on a confidential basis. The representatives of DP expressed criticism over SB's "patronizing attitude" and "gold-mining approach" and SB expressed concern over the "terrible delays" and "DP's lack of seriousness" in dealing with his claim. DP also indicated that they were eager to settle as it was the in-house lawyer's last day with the company. They also indicated that they could not remain at the mediation beyond 1:00 p.m. because of other commitments.

There followed a series of joint and separate meetings between the parties and the mediator during which the parties and their lawyers made the following offers and counteroffers:

$75,000 (again) from SB;

$15,000 ("inclusive of costs") from DP;

$60,000 from SB;

$25,000 from DP;

$45,000 from SB;

$32,000 ("absolute bottom line") from DP; and

$40,000 ("and not a cent less") from SB.

There was then an impasse over the gap of $8,000, and SB refused to consider the offer of new products until this was resolved. It was now 12:30 p.m., and DP's representatives indicated that they had to leave in 30 minutes. The mediator met with the parties separately to explore ways of crossing the gap. At 12:50 p.m., the parties came together, and SB offered to come down to $35,000, provided payment was within seven days. On these figures, the head office manager from DP shook hands with SB across the table. DP's in-house lawyer produced a prepared contract, filled in the agreed figures and period of payment, and all parties signed the settlement, which included a confidentiality clause. The parties agreed verbally that a sales representative from DP would make an appointment with SB to discuss new products. There were handshakes all around and the DP representatives left the meeting at 1:01 p.m. for their appointments.

In follow-up phone calls to the parties a few weeks later, the mediator established that there had been full compliance with the agreement and that they all regarded the matter as fully settled.

IX. Exercises

1. Interview a person you know who is good at dispute resolution. Ask them to identify the particular skills and techniques that they find helpful. Ask them to indicate which of these skills they regard as innate and which they developed through education and experience.

2. Select one or two of the skills identified above. Ask a person from a different cultural background how that skill would be regarded in their culture, and why. What are the implications of this answer for mediators?

3. Write out a list of some of the skills and techniques for which lawyers (or another occupational group) are renowned. Which of these do you think would be suitable for mediation, and which do you think would need to be adapted?

TWO

Establishing the Foundation

Introductions, Intake, Screening, and Preparation

A bad beginning makes a bad ending.

—EURIPIDES (ANCIENT GREEK PLAYWRIGHT)

I. Overview

Mediators have the responsibility to foster an environment for effective mediation from the moment they enter the dispute. From the mediator's first point of contact, his or her overarching goal should be to build trust with the participants and confidence in the mediation process. The more the parties trust you (and your staff), the more likely it will be that they will share useful information about the dispute with you and follow the mediation process, all of which increases the efficacy of the mediation. This earliest phase involving introductions, intake, screening, and preparation constitutes the participants' "first impression" of you and the process of mediation generally. As with all first impressions, the conduct of this phase will set the tone for the mediation to follow and create expectations, for better or worse, regarding your abilities and the mediation process. Thus, the importance of this early experience being neutral, forthright, personalized, organized, thorough, and professional cannot be overstated.

The mediator establishes this foundation of trust by generally promoting an environment of transparency about the mediation process where everyone knows what to expect. This sets the stage for calm, thoughtful decisions about how to best resolve the dispute. From the outset, the mediator's task is to learn about the dispute and the disputants, to promote the legitimacy of mediation generally and themselves as mediators, to make strategic judgments about the mediation process, and to schedule the timing, duration, and venue of the mediation. The mediator should act at all times in a non-partisan way and not become an advocate of either party, even in relation to the question of whether or not to mediate. Being a good listener, communicating clearly, and empathizing with the parties also creates trust and helps build rapport.

This chapter explores this early phase of the mediation process in the context of the following basic categories of actions by the mediator: (1) *entering the dispute*, (2) *gathering information about the dispute*, (3) *assessing the dispute*, (4) *educating the parties about the mediation process and your credentials*, and (5) *preparing for the mediation*. Mediators can enter the dispute in various ways, with different issues arising depending upon how this happens. Once the mediator is introduced into the dispute and to the parties, the next phase of the mediation process is called "intake and screening." The intake and screening phase is conducted with each party *separately* and occurs *before* the initial session where all parties are present. The intake aspect of this phase of the mediation involves mostly gathering information about the dispute. Screening refers to the other part of the process, involving an overall assessment of the suitability of the dispute for mediation. Both intake and screening involve educating the disputing parties about the mediation process. The preparation part of this phase involves practicalities, for example, the timing, duration, and facilities for the mediation. Finally, this chapter addresses some special considerations for mediations that involve "teams" and prior contacts with parties.

II. Entering the Dispute

A. Joint Introductions and Communications

The term "entering the dispute" refers to the early involvement of mediators in the parties' dispute. When mediators enter a dispute, there is usually a joint awareness by all parties that the option of mediation is being explored. Introductions and initial communications may be done, jointly or separately, in person, by telephone, or through e-mails, as long as the discussions are objective and everyone is on board.

A mediator can be introduced to a dispute in a variety of ways. First, participation in mediation is either mandatory or voluntary. Mandatory mediation is where the parties have been compelled to mediate by a governmental entity, such as a court or a state or federal agency. Voluntary mediation is where the parties elect to mediate. Regarding selection of the mediator, this is either by the choice of the parties (i.e., private mediation) or by appointment by a court, private referral service, or agency.

From the mediator's perspective, mandatory appointments often involve the least amount of initial communication with the parties. A mediator working with a court or agency or other institutional mediation service provider is usually given little or no information about the dispute apart from the names of the parties and the general nature of the dispute. Intake and screening are conducted by court or agency staff. To address this disadvantage, the mediator should take the initiative upon assignment of the matter to contact the parties and gather any additional information needed to mediate the dispute effectively.[1] Even where time or circumstances does not permit additional information to be gathered, a brief contact in the foyer

---

1. Some referring institutions may prohibit this contact in an effort to preserve neutrality. The mediator must confirm the rules of the referring organization.

or corridor before the mediation begins can often be enormously helpful. Such brief and informal contacts afford the mediator the opportunity to gain insight into the conflict and the parties and to create rapport.

To the extent that the mediator has an opportunity to communicate with the parties in advance, the mediator has the option of undertaking the task of intake and screening personally or relying upon trained employees or intake officers. In most cases of private mediation, the mediator elects to reach out to the participants directly so as to begin building rapport. Intake and screening are a specialized function, particularly where the circumstances require adequate screening of cases. In any case, this process is best not left to individuals unfamiliar with the mediation process or without good people skills. If the mediator is relying upon intake staff, the mediator should ensure the staff is adequately trained.

The method of communication throughout the intake and screening process is another matter for consideration. The mediator has the option of communicating in person, over the telephone, in writing by submission of forms, video conference, through on-line communication, or any combination of the above. Conducting in-person meetings makes it easier for the mediator or intake personnel to establish rapport with participants and communicate more effectively about the dispute and mediation process. Although it is almost always beneficial to conduct the intake and screening process in person, it is frequently impractical. Intake and screening are very often conducted over the telephone or video conference. Some mediators require the participants to submit an initial questionnaire, often available online at the mediator's website, which provides the mediator with the essential particulars of the dispute. Although this can be a helpful first step, it is by no means a substitute for interpersonal communication and information gathering that can be accomplished in person or by telephone.

B. Preliminary Conferences

In some situations, the mediator might consider holding a preliminary conference before the mediation meeting as an occasion for introductions and building the mediation foundations. Many of the intake and screening functions can be performed in a preliminary conference. They are particularly helpful where there are several parties to the mediation, the mediation is complex, or where the mediation will likely occur over multiple sessions. The preliminary conference is usually convened and chaired by the mediator and can be attended by all relevant parties. In some situations, only lawyers attend, and the parties have no direct involvement. Apart from the fact that this arrangement overlooks the reality that it is the parties' dispute, there are advantages in having the parties present. It gives them an opportunity to meet the mediator and become familiar with his or her style, and it allows the mediator to assess the parties' suitability for mediation and to predict their likely attitudes and behavior at the subsequent meetings.

In addition, a number of subtle developments can take place at preliminary conferences. Where large organizations are involved, such as local authorities or insurers, this may be the first occasion the mediating parties have to meet one another. It usually provides an opportunity for each party to meet the other's legal or other professional advisers for the first time, thereby preventing surprises or shocks at the mediation meeting. There is a general acclimatization between the parties and some tentative negotiations on matters of process. In some cases, settlement has been known to occur at the preliminary conference or shortly thereafter.

C. The "One-Party" Approach

Occasionally, mediation is not pursued jointly by the parties but rather by only one party to the dispute. This party might approach a mediator or mediation service directly requesting their assistance in contacting the second party to obtain their agreement to mediate.

This situation does raise some ethical concerns. Some mediators will decline this role to avoid the perception that they are agents of the first party or that they are not independent and impartial.[2] Rather, they prefer to redirect the party seeking mediation to communicate directly with the other party about the possibility of mediation. In situations where separate intake staff exists, this task may be appropriately delegated to the staff so as to avoid any contact with the mediator.

The predominant view, however, suggests that mediators may appropriately undertake the function of inviting and encouraging the second party to come to the mediation table as part of their overall service.

Some common-sense guidelines for the mediator's approach to the second party follow. First, the mediator should be diplomatic and tactful when approaching the second party, recognizing they did not ask for the mediator's involvement. Next, the mediator should immediately disclose the nature and extent of communications with the first party to promote an atmosphere of neutrality. It is best not to overstate the virtues of mediation, but simply inform and educate the second party about it. The mediator should speak on a general level about the nature of the dispute, being careful to avoid disclosing any specific knowledge of the substantive issues in breach of confidentiality obligations toward the first party. The mediator should not appear to be taking the side of the initiating party nor suggest a working alliance with them. The mediator may anticipate some resistance, uncertainty, or suspicion from the second party. Maintaining an attitude of neutrality and trustworthiness is the best way to counter this and promote the legitimacy of mediation. The mediator may

---

2. Some commentators with regard to family mediation, for example, argue that where a mediator joins one spouse in any way before establishing a working relationship with both parties, this compromises the mediator's usefulness to that couple. JOHN M. HAYNES & STEPHANIE CHARLESWORTH, THE FUNDAMENTALS OF FAMILY MEDIATION 37–38 (1996).

need to educate the second party about the mediation process so that they can make an informed commitment to it.

There are more ethical complexities in this approach. For example, where a mediator is approaching the second party, he or she will have to disclose some information about the dispute and can expect questions about the first party's motivations and goals. The same will apply when the mediator reverts to the first party. The mediator may find it challenging to maintain adherence to confidentiality requirements. The mediator must also resist any natural inclination to give more credence to the initiating party simply because their story was shared first. It may be advisable to limit the amount of information received from the initiating party in the first contact as much as possible. The mediator may advise both parties that the normal policy is to provide the same preliminary information to both parties during the entry stage.

If the second party says no to mediation, respect their choice. However, a desire not to show weakness or the need to take time out for advice may motivate the second party. As in other aspects of mediation, some probing and persistence may be necessary here. The classic problem-solving reaction to a negative response is to diagnose the reason for it. If you perceive that either ignorance, unfounded suspicion, or prejudice influenced the decision, consider other procedural options, including low-key contacts or approaches by respected outsiders such as colleagues. An Austin, Texas-based mediator suggests that the mediator aim for small behavioral steps in the face of stubbornness.[3] For example, ask whether the party would allow the mediator to send them informative mediation material, or possibly agree to speak again in a week's time, or even attend a short, informal meeting involving one or both parties.

There are some other procedural tactics to consider when the second party says no to you as the mediator. You might suggest to the first party that they make, or remake, the approach. If at the end of these strategies you still have a negative response, you should consider moving on to another client.

III. Gathering Information

It is extremely beneficial to the mediator and to the mediation process if the mediator has a general understanding of the nature of the dispute before he or she meets with the participants for the first time. This general knowledge helps the mediator to undertake any necessary preparation and planning to conduct the mediation effectively. These preparations might include researching relevant law, reading particularly relevant legal pleadings, or reviewing relevant documents concerning the dispute, such as contracts, expert reports, or correspondence. It also provides the mediator an opportunity to begin to formulate a mediation strategy based on his or her experi-

---

3. KARL SLAIKEU, WHEN PUSH COMES TO SHOVE 61 (1996).

ence with similar disputes he or she has mediated in the past. Finally, gathering information about the dispute is critical to properly planning the logistical needs of the mediation, such as setting the time, duration, and place, as well as arranging for any special needs the participants may have. Special needs might include arranging for security in particularly hostile disputes or a large enough room to accommodate several advisors who will join the participants in the mediation.

The following discussion outlines the areas in which information needs to be gathered during intake. These topics do not need to be discussed in any particular order as long as they are addressed at some point during the intake procedure. It is, however, advisable to use a checklist or form so that nothing is forgotten. It is also important to note that the person who calls to schedule the mediation may not know very much about the substance of the dispute. Although participants or attorneys often do make the initial contact with the mediator, in some types of disputes, administrative assistants or governmental personnel arrange for the mediation. These people often only have a passing understanding of the dispute, and can provide little more than the parties' names and potential mediation dates. In such situations, you need to decide whether to proceed with the mediation with only this minimal information or reach out to the participants or their representatives directly to gain a more complete understanding of the dispute.

A. Identifying the Participants

"Participants" include the parties to the dispute and anyone else they want to bring along for advice, contribution, or emotional support. Begin by getting a list of all the participants to the dispute (including attorneys) and contact information. Contact information should include address, work and cellular telephone numbers, and e-mail address. There may be scheduling changes, so the more information on hand, the easier it is to reach the parties on short notice, if necessary. Be certain to determine that a party with authority to settle the matter will be present. In cases of court-mandated mediations, this is a typical requirement, but it is a good practice to check that this requirement is met or make it a requirement if the mediation is voluntary.[4]

Finally, it is important to determine who else in addition to the parties and their representatives will be at the mediation. This is both a strategic and practical concern. The strategic concern is that as the number of participants grows, the dispute will become more complex and typically take longer. The practical concern is making sure that the facility in which the mediation will be held can accommodate the number of participants. For instance, do not presume that in a two-party litigated case there will only be four participants, one party from each side and their respective counsel. Sometimes a business will send several people to the mediation. In a contract dispute, a company might send its manager who was involved with negoti-

---

4. For further discussion of authority, see *supra* section IV D of this chapter.

ating the contract, the vice-president with authority to settle, in-house legal counsel, and its outside legal counsel. In a dispute involving divorcing spouses, one spouse might wish to bring a parent, a sister or a brother, or even a close friend. To plan appropriately, it is necessary to know how many people will attend the mediation.

B. Identifying the Issues

At minimum, it is helpful to know what the nature of the dispute is. It is also helpful to know whether the mediation is voluntary or compelled in order to gauge how cooperative the participants might be. If the intake is done with an administrative assistant, whether from an attorney's office or a referral program, the general nature of the dispute and whether it is voluntary is often all that can be learned. However, if you are performing the intake with the participant or their attorney, you can also uncover important details about the dispute. It is helpful to know some details about the main points of disagreement. In a landlord-tenant dispute, for example, is the tenant's failure to pay because he has no money, or is it because he alleges some problem with the leased space, such as no hot water or a leaky roof? In a commercial contract dispute, is the validity of the contract being questioned, or is there a dispute over the meaning of the contract? This also provides the mediator an opportunity to identify documents that might be helpful for him or her to review before the mediation, such as contracts, legal pleadings, letters, or expert reports. Identifying and understanding these issues before the mediation allows the mediator to prepare questions and strategies for appropriately addressing the dispute.

C. Status of the Litigation

Many disputes that are mediated are already being litigated, meaning that a legal action has commenced. When this is the situation, it is important to know where the dispute is in the litigation process. Most importantly, it should be determined if the matter has been set for trial. Obviously, the matter needs to be mediated before the trial date, but parties often come to mediation at the last minute, making scheduling sometimes problematic. In litigated matters, uncover how much discovery has been completed in the case and whether any discovery needs to be completed before the mediation can be held.[5]

Although mediation can be held at nearly any time during the discovery process, just as it might be negotiated to a settlement at any time, some matters require a more complete exchange of information before the parties are in a position to make informed decisions about settlement. For example, in personal injury cases it is very rare for a defendant to settle the dispute for anything more than "nuisance value"

---

5. Discovery consists of "[t]he pre-trial devices that can be used by one party to obtain facts and information about the case from the other party in order to assist the party's preparation for trial." BLACK'S LAW DICTIONARY (1979).

until an independent medical examination is completed by a physician of his or her choice. In divorce cases, a settlement is unlikely (and unwise) until the couple's assets and financial information have been assembled. Thus, mediation may need to be scheduled far enough in advance to complete these essential tasks. Another helpful area to explore is the extent to which the parties have had settlement discussions. If so, have any issues been resolved? What offers have been made? Have the settlement discussions been amicable or hostile? All of this information enables the mediator to better address the salient issues, to build on prior successes, or to prepare for more adversarial discussions.

D. Reviewing Documents

In many instances, there will be relevant documents connected to the conflict. These documents can include legal pleadings, contracts, financial information, correspondence, and much else. The extent to which a mediator will need to review relevant documents will be greatly influenced by his mediation style and philosophy. More evaluative mediators tend to like to review the key relevant documents, whereas more facilitative mediators tend to feel the need to review few, if any, documents.

Regardless of style or philosophy, however, there are a few guidelines that are valuable to follow concerning a mediator's review of documents. First, a mediator is not a judge or an arbitrator who will make a decision in the matter. Thus, a mediator should be selective about what documents to review so as not to give the parties the impression that mediation is just another form of adjudication. In making that selection, mediators should seek to review documents that will best aid him or her in gaining an understanding of the parties' concerns, previous negotiations, or the issues to be resolved. For example, in litigated matters it is often helpful to obtain a copy of the Complaint and Answer, as these legal pleadings can help to narrow the issues that will be discussed at the mediation. If the matter concerns a breach of contract, whether litigation has commenced or not, it is usually helpful to obtain a copy of the relevant agreement or correspondence that forms the basis for the agreement.

Second, we recommend that a mediator obtain documents desired for review before the mediation. This provides an opportunity to review them thoroughly if needed. More importantly, reviewing documents during the mediation is often impractical and disruptive to the process. To reduce the likelihood that a party will submit documents for review during the mediation, make a point during the intake process to ask the parties if there are any particular documents that they think might be helpful in understanding the matter.

Finally, mediators will need to exercise sensitivity when deciding to agree to a party's request to review documents. Parties sometimes view presenting documents to the mediator as part of their "story." Thus, in their decisions to review documents, mediators should weigh the advantages of having the parties feel "heard" against weighing down the process with "historical facts" that, as we will see, usually do not advance the process.

E. Written Party Statements

Some mediators ask the parties for, and oversee the exchange of, "party statements" or "issue statements." These documents are written specifically for the mediation and are intended to be short in length (not more than three or four pages) and to summarize the background, issues, and intended outcomes from each side's perspective. The intention is that, regardless of prior definitions of the problem and information exchanges between the parties, these statements will provide an up-to-date summary of the problem from each side's point of view for the benefit of the parties and the mediator. There are both benefits and drawbacks to this practice. Thus, while the statements may encourage the parties and lawyers to "get to the point" in a focused and disciplined way, they also tend to provide simplistic definitions of and solutions to the problem that the parties might regurgitate later. As one commentator, Karl Slaikeu, points out, the issue statement can lead to greater emotional investment in a party's position ("I told you in my issue statement I wanted a million dollars and now you don't seem to be taking that seriously…"), making the mediator's job more difficult later.[6] Instead, he suggests asking the parties to submit and exchange only materials that have already been generated beforehand. Some of the other potential benefits and drawbacks of position statements are portrayed in the following table:

Potential Benefits	Potential Drawbacks
Succinct statement of the problem	Over-simplification of the problem
Current version of issues and demands	Positional and adversarially worded style
Efficient way of informing mediator	Legalistic definition of the problem
Shortens time needed for mediation	Extra pre-mediation time and costs
Gets parties prepared for mediation	Reinforces parties in entrenched positions

One way of attempting to derive the benefits and minimize the drawbacks of issue statements is for mediators to give instructions to the parties on the desired format and style of the documents, and better still to provide them with copies of *model issue statements* to serve as guides for their endeavors.

F. Scheduling

The more common, but nevertheless important, task of intake is simply to schedule the mediation. Agreeing on a date and time for the mediation session can take several telephone, text, or e-mail exchanges, depending on the number of parties that are involved. It is imperative that the mediator confirm the final agreed-upon date and time in writing or by e-mail to all participants. There is nothing more frustrating to participants than assembling for a mediation, often paying lawyers

---

6. SLAIKEU, *supra* note 3, at 60.

considerable money to be present, only to have it rescheduled because an essential party is not there as a consequence of a lack of diligence in scheduling.

IV. Assessment

The assessment feature of the intake and screening phase can be very sophisticated depending on the mediator's preference and available time. There are, however, only four principal questions that a mediator needs to evaluate when taking on a new assignment: (1) are there any conflicts that prevent the mediator from meditating the dispute, (2) is the mediator competent to mediate the dispute, (3) is the dispute appropriate for mediation, and (4) will there be an individual present at the mediation who has the decision-making authority to settle the dispute?

A. Conflicts of Interest

Although a full discussion of mediation ethics is beyond the scope of this book, it is necessary to emphasize here that a mediator's ethical obligations commence the moment he or she enters the dispute. (See Model Standards of Conduct for Mediators included in Appendix 10.) Conflicts of interests concern relationships a mediator has with participants that raise questions about his or her ability to be neutral in conducting the mediation. Generally, if a mediator believes a past relationship with the participant will affect her ability to be neutral in managing the dispute, she must not agree to mediate the dispute. If, on the other hand, she feels that the relationship will in no way affect her ability to conduct the mediation fairly, then she may mediate the matter as long as the potential conflict is revealed to the participants.

The Model Standards of Conduct for Mediators ("Model Standards") set forth guidelines regarding conflicts of interest. They state in relevant part that "a mediator shall disclose . . . all actual and potential conflicts of interest reasonably known to the mediator."[7] The Model Standards go on to define a conflict of interest as a "dealing or relationship that might create an impression of possible bias."[8]

Some but not all conflicts of interest can be waived. The Model Standards state that "[i]f all the parties agree to mediate after being informed of conflicts, the mediator may proceed with the mediation." Although the Model Standards do not require it, we strongly recommend that any waiver of conflict be in writing.[9] However, the participants cannot waive all conflicts of interest. The Model Standards further state

---

7. MODEL STANDARDS OF CONDUCT OR MEDIATORS STD. III (2005). The Model Standards of Conduct for Mediators was prepared and adopted by the American Arbitration Association, American Bar Association, and the Association for Conflict Resolution, and is the premier Code of Conduct for mediators in the United States.

8. *Id.*

9. See Appendix 2D for a Prior Contact with Participant Waiver Form.

that if "'the conflict of interest casts serious doubt on the integrity of the process, the mediator shall decline to proceed."

Although what rises to the level of casting "serious doubt" on the integrity of the mediation process is not clear-cut, there are situations that will meet that standard in most reasonable people's minds. For example, regardless of whether a mediator believes that he or she could be neutral and fair, having a financial stake in the outcome would likely cast serious doubt on the integrity of the process, as would mediating a dispute in which one of the parties was a close family member. In such situations, most reasonable people would have serious doubts about whether the process could be fairly conducted, which would in turn cast doubt on the fairness of the agreement.

The purpose of this section is to make the mediator aware of the existence of conflicts in the world of mediation. If there is a suspicion of a conflict of interest in a dispute, one will need to seek further guidance on the matter. Conflicts is an important ethical issue, a full discussion of which is beyond the scope of a skills and techniques book.

B. Mediator Competence

Another ethical consideration in assessing a matter for mediation is whether a mediator possesses the competence to serve as mediator in a particular dispute. The Model Standards state that "a mediator shall mediate only when the mediator has the necessary qualifications to satisfy the reasonable expectations of the parties."[10] Fulfilling this obligation is different depending on the context of the mediation. When serving as a mediator in a court-connected case, a mediator should possess the state-mandated training and experience. In private mediations, i.e., those not connected with a governmental program, the obligation is typically filled by providing accurate information regarding "relevant training, education, and experience."[11] Even in private mediations, formal training is highly advisable, although not strictly required by most states.

C. Appropriateness for Mediation

Mediators have a responsibility to determine if the dispute is appropriate for mediation. As discussed previously, any dispute that can be negotiated can in theory be mediated. However, there are circumstances in which mediation may not be an appropriate dispute-resolution process because it is highly unlikely to produce a resolution or because it is highly likely to produce an unfair or invalid resolution. A private mediator can refuse to take a case if it is deemed inappropriate for any reason. The mediator can also help guide the parties to a more appropriate

---

10. MODEL STANDARDS OF CONDUCT FOR MEDIATORS STD. IV (2005).
11. *Id.* (comment).

dispute-resolution process. While some mediators may be reluctant to refuse a case regardless of how unsuitable it might be for mediation, this is a pitfall to be avoided. The desire for more referrals, more practical experience, or more revenue is not sufficient grounds for accepting an otherwise unacceptable matter. Sometimes being a good mediator means declining to mediate a dispute or referring it to a more appropriate dispute-resolution venue.

Whether a dispute is ill-suited for mediation is a highly subjective assessment driven by the particular facts of the dispute and the mediator's style and philosophical viewpoint concerning mediation. Declining to mediate the dispute can be advantageous if it prevents wasteful or destructive mediation sessions, forces postponement of mediation until conditions are more suitable, or motivates clients to rely more on their own resources. It also recognizes that in some disputes there might be no realistic solution at all, regardless of the dispute-resolution process used, just as for some illnesses there may be no cure, regardless of the medical treatment followed.

The following are some factors that suggest a dispute might be unsuitable for mediation because mediation will likely provide little benefit or make the situation worse. This is not, however, intended to be an exhaustive list of potential scenarios.

1. The parties' psychological or intellectual states are not conducive to successful mediation.

2. The parties will use mediation for ulterior purposes, for example, to indulge in destructive conflict or to fish for information.

3. A gross imbalance of power exists between the mediating parties, for example, where there is a history of domestic violence or where one party does not have the financial or personal resources for mediation.

4. At least one party desires revenge, has a "jackpot" syndrome,[12] or has an inappropriate mental or psychological state.

5. The mediator uncovers a history of child abuse in a matrimonial dispute, elder abuse in a family dispute, or a history of an unfair trade practice in a commercial dispute, and mediation may adversely affect external parties' interests.

6. Allegations of fraudulent or criminal behavior surface, such that the public court system is a better venue for the of dispute.

There is no consensus among mediators concerning what are the circumstances under which a dispute is not appropriate for mediation. For example, some mediators believe that the presence of domestic violence should not automatically

---

12. "Jackpot" syndrome is where a party believes that a "big" financial payoff is likely in the matter and is not receptive to compromising or problem solving.

disqualify a dispute from mediation.[13] This alternative philosophy holds that many of mediation's cost and time-saving benefits as well as the opportunity it provides to come up with creative and value-creating solutions should not be denied to parties in disputes where domestic violence is also an issue. Special precautions might need to be taken in such matters, such as hiring security, keeping the parties in separate rooms during the mediation, or conducting the entire mediation remotely.

Intake allows not only for the screening of disputes but also for streaming. Streaming refers to the reference of disputes to appropriate dispute-resolution options, such as arbitration, early neutral evaluation, mini-trial, summary jury trial, or litigation. This is not an exact science, but dispute-resolution advisers in various organizations and industry bodies perform this function in light of the information they have on hand. For present purposes, it is sufficient to note that the streaming aspect of intake might result in the referral of potential mediation clients to another venue.

D. Authority of Participants

It is always desirable that those present at the mediation table have authority to settle. The issue arises where the participating individuals are present in a representative capacity, for example, a professional adviser on behalf of a client, a director on behalf of a company, or a public official on behalf of a government department. All veteran mediators have experienced situations where the representative party has indicated toward the conclusion of mediation that they lack authority to settle. They then request an adjournment to contact and seek ratification of the proposed agreement from their client, the company board, or the director or administrator of the government department, as the case may be.

This can have fatal consequences for the mediation. To avoid this, the mediator should anticipate that claims of "no authority" may arise and attempt to secure the presence at the mediation table of a person or persons with the necessary authority. The mediator can easily address the issue by asking all participants at the earliest stage whether they will have authority to settle, and if not, what would be necessary to obtain it. Sometimes, the representative has genuinely overlooked the question of authority, although this is not a common occurrence. Thorough preparation by the mediator can prevent this from happening.

It may not always be possible to attain full settlement authority of all participants at the table. There are some situations in which the "no authority" problem might be unavoidable. The following is a discussion of three examples of such situations.

First, for practical or policy reasons, it may not be possible to obtain any authority at all. For example, some municipal governmental decisions require approval by

---

13. *See* Rene L. Rimelspach, *Mediating Family Disputes in a World with Domestic Violence: How to Devise a Safe and Effective Court Connected Mediation Program*, 17 Ohio St. J. on Disp. Resol. 95 (2001).

a formal vote of the governing body. In this situation, nothing can be done to secure authority, but the mediator can advise all parties in advance that any decision requires approval so that it does not come as a trust-threatening surprise later.

Second, the representative at the mediation may have authority but it is limited, and the proposed settlement agreement is in excess of that limit. This situation is a fact of life for many defendants who will have authority to settle up to their "bottom line." Here the mediator may have to create some doubt by asking whether the representative can obtain some additional discretion to take account of new information or disclosures from the other side or other unexpected developments.

Third, despite careful questioning of the parties in advance of the mediation to secure settlement authority, a representative at the mediation claims to have no authority as a tactic to buy time or to impose negotiation pressure on the other side. This is a most problematic situation, even where the mediator has strong grounds for believing that it is a power tactic. No amount of diligence will inevitably pre-empt the tactical ploy. Even when the mediator openly and timely raises the authority issue with all parties, a party can still insist that the "final" offer exceeds their limited authority.

Some experienced mediators probe in advance the limits of each representative's authority to settle. They may ask whether it includes up to the extent of offers previously made by that side, in which case it might be expedient to suggest that they obtain more authority. They may ask whether it extends to the full amount of the other party's claim, in which case it is likely to be sufficient. They may ask to see confidentially in advance a written statement of authority to ensure that any limited authority claim is genuine and not a devious tactic. None of these strategies will guarantee that the parties are open with the mediator, but they are, however, good risk-minimization strategies. Thus, canvass the question of authority as early into the dispute as possible and revisit it at later stages as well. The mediator may have to act as "reality agent" in pointing out the short-term and long-term disadvantages for the party who plays the "no authority" card. Unfortunately, here, as in other aspects of mediation, there are no guarantees.

V. Educating the Parties About the Mediation Process

Educating the parties about mediation occurs throughout the entire process, but it is of paramount importance in the initial contact with clients. When participants understand what to expect from the process and the mediator, it promotes a general atmosphere of trust and confidence. Information is the best way to minimize the potential for fear and anxiety during the mediation as a result of surprises along the way. While not all developments can be anticipated, there are certain basics of the mediation process that are predictable and should be disclosed in advance.

Educating the participants is usually easier in private mediations, where the mediator has more control over the process. The participants select and initiate contact with the mediator directly, establishing a line of communication. Consequently, the mediator has ample opportunity to explain the process from the outset, answer questions, establish ground rules, and allay fears.

By contrast, where the parties are referred to mediation through an administrative process, education of the participants may fall into the hands of intake staff. This is the case for many government and agency-based mediations. The skill of intake staff varies considerably. Many institutional mediation providers thoroughly and skillfully fulfill their educational responsibilities. Participants arrive at the mediation with a solid understanding of the mediation process and its potential benefits. In most situations, however, participants are inadequately educated about mediation. Inadequate resources, such as time, staff, or money, are usually the problem, rather than the institution's lack of appreciation or conscious disregard for the importance of providing this education. In these situations, the burden shifts to the mediator to set time aside, either in advance of or at the beginning of the mediation, to provide the participants with the necessary information to prepare them for the process. Managing the participants' expectations about the process is always time well spent.

Information about the mediation should be communicated both verbally and in writing or by e-mail. Verbal discussions, either in person or by telephone, allow the participants to ask questions and give the mediator an opportunity to clarify any ambiguities. Written information allows participants more time to absorb and reflect on the explanation of the process. Written documentation also protects the mediator from subsequent allegations by the participants that certain information was not disclosed or explained to them. Some examples of written material a mediator might provide to the participants include: a brochure explaining the mediation process, the mediator's professional biography, a standard form agreement to mediate, and the mediator's compensation arrangement.

Specifically, there are four general areas for education of the participants by the mediator: (1) *the mediation process generally*, (2) *the mediator's particular approach to mediation*, (3) *the mediator's background and experience*, and (4) *the Agreement to Mediate, fees, and charges*.

A. The Mediation Process

For many participants, mediation will be a new experience, and so they will appreciate general information explaining mediation, its potential benefits, and the roles and responsibilities of the mediator and participants.[14] First, it is important to

---

14. See Chapter 4—*Managing the Mediation Process*, section II A, which covers opening statements. See also Appendix 1B for a form describing the mediation process that should be sent to the participants before the mediation.

make certain the participants understand what mediation is and what it is not. You should explain your role in the process, which is to help them make decisions about the dispute and to facilitate discussions. Emphasize that you are not there to decide the dispute and they are free to agree to settle the matter or not. You should also explain to the disputants what their roles and responsibilities are in the mediation. Additionally, this is a good opportunity to raise their awareness about the many potential benefits of mediation, including providing them with evidence of settlement rates and the high participant satisfaction rate.

B. Mediator's Particular Approach to Mediation

Since mediators bring different personal styles, philosophies, processes, and techniques to the mediations they conduct, it is appropriate and helpful to explain your approach to mediation with participants at the earliest possible stage. For example, some mediators view their role as that of a facilitator of negotiations. Others see their role as providing honest evaluation of the strengths and weaknesses of the parties' positions based on some decision standard, such as law, the contract, or the mediator's own sense of fairness. Giving the participants an idea about what to expect from you promotes overall satisfaction in the process.

Specifically, sharing information about your planned style or philosophy for the mediation helps to create reasonable expectations about the mediation in the minds of the participants. A common reason for parties to become disappointed with a mediation process is simply because they expected something else from the experience, not necessarily because the experience was intrinsically problematic. Managing expectations in this way can minimize conflicts between the mediator and participants over the "best processes" to follow during the mediation. It also provides an opportunity for the participants to communicate with you about their preference in mediation styles.

Managing expectations may be particularly important for participants who have prior experience with mediation, such as lawyers or corporate executives. For example, a lawyer who is accustomed to a mediator providing unvarnished opinions about the merits of the competing positions in a case might believe that a mediator who sees their role more as a discussion facilitator is "weak" or "unskilled," or simply "not doing their job," even where the case was settled. Communication about this issue beforehand will either help the participants adjust their expectations to coincide with the intentions of the mediator, cause them to seek to discuss the possibility of changes in approach to mediation, or cause them to seek out a mediator whose philosophy is more compatible with their goals and expectations.

In an effort to educate the participants about a personal philosophical approach or style in mediation, an effective tool is to explain the process through metaphors. The following is a list of some metaphors that may be useful in explaining the mediator's role or style. Their suitability in a particular situation will also depend on the personal attributes of the clients.

1. The mediator's role is to direct the traffic; the parties will do all the driving.

2. Mediation is like a jigsaw puzzle. Lots of attempts to fit the pieces together, but it may take perseverance to achieve the final image.

3. Think of the mediator as a director and the parties as the actors in a play without a script.

4. The mediator's role can be similar to a sports umpire, controlling the game and providing a safe environment but leaving the action to the parties.

5. The mediator's role is to guide the parties down the path of decision-making, but how far they go depends on the individual.

C. Mediator's Background and Experience

The mediator should provide parties with his or her background and experience to help establish credibility and authority with the participants. This may be especially important and helpful where the parties have been compelled to mediation and have not selected the mediator. The more the participants view the mediator as competent, the more credible he or she will appear, and the greater control he or she will have over the mediation process. The more command the mediator has over the process, the more likely it will be that good decisions will be made about how to resolve the dispute. When good decisions are made, it is more likely the matter will be resolved in a productive way.

Appropriate information to provide to the participants includes training and degrees and work experience generally. The mediator should emphasize particularly relevant work or life experience.[15] In addition, some mediators also provide information about their past settlement record. Obviously, a new mediator will not have extensive experience in mediating disputes. This does not mean, however, that a credibility statement should not be given. For example, in a divorce mediation involving custody, a mediator might say, "Although I have just begun mediating divorce matters, I am familiar with these issues from my experience as a social worker where I have been involved with custody issues in various capacities for over 10 years." In this statement the mediator emphasizes her social work experience and not her mediation experience. In describing one's background and experience to a participant, whether in writing or orally, the mediator should always be truthful and accurate.[16]

Some mediators are reluctant to provide their background and experience directly to participants, believing that it might be perceived as boastful or arrogant, and thus make it more difficult for them to establish rapport, or worse, invite the

---

15. See Appendix 1C for a sample professional biography.

16. The Model Standards of Conduct for Mediators state that "[a]dvertising or other communication with the public concerning services offered or regarding the education, training, and expertise of the mediator shall be truthful." MODEL STANDARDS OF CONDUCT FOR MEDIATORS STD. VI (2005).

participants' contempt. Although this concern is not entirely without merit, the far greater risk is to conduct a mediation lacking credibility and authority with the participants. One way to minimize the legitimate concern of appearing boastful to the participants is to send a professional biography to them before the mediation by mail or e-mail as part of normal business practice along with the contract to mediate and other applicable forms. In this way, there is no need to speak directly to the participants about background, but the mediator is providing the helpful information in a business-like manner.

It may still be appropriate for a mediator to briefly mention background and experience highlights directly to participants. If this is done, it should be short and relevant to the mediation at hand. For example: "As you may know from the materials my office sent you, I am an attorney, although I am not serving in that capacity today. But as an attorney I have worked on many matters involving commercial leases similar to the one we're here to discuss today. And as a mediator for the last fifteen years, I have mediated many matters involving commercial lease disputes, so I am familiar with these types of issues." This short, general statement provides some basis for the participants to trust the mediator's judgment about how to proceed with the mediation.

D. The Agreement to Mediate, Fees, and Charges

Prior to any mediation, it is advisable to have a written agreement to mediate signed by the participants and the mediator. This agreement typically sets forth the roles and responsibilities of the participants and the mediator, as well as the fee structure. Discussing fees at the beginning of the process is good business practice. It helps to avoid confusion, surprise, and conflict at the end of the mediation service over the terms of compensation. The role of the mediator is typically described and the mediator's obligation regarding the confidentiality of the parties is explained. The contract should also set forth the participants' responsibilities, including the duty of full disclosure of all relevant facts and documents and the duty of good faith cooperation.

An Agreement to Mediate should be in plain English and as short and simple as possible so that it does not "over-legalize" an extra-legal dispute-resolution procedure. Its content should be explained to those parties who might have difficulty understanding it. Sometimes this is done before the mediation, sometimes at the preliminary conference, and sometimes as the first item in the mediation meeting. Most mediators and mediation services have form-agreements. In complex mediations, the mediator and the parties might negotiate an agreement that suits the specific needs of the situation. There is considerable variation among mediation agreements, in particular regarding their level of detail and legalistic orientation. Appendix 2 contains a sample Agreement to Mediate that contains a moderate level of detail and is written in a non-legalistic form.

Concerning the mediator's fee and charges, the Model Standards of Conduct state, "a mediator shall fully disclose and explain the basis of compensation, fees, and charges to the parties."[17] These Standards go on to explain that the mediator's fees must be reasonable, taking into consideration, among other things, "the mediation service, the type and complexity of the matter, the expertise of the mediator, the time required, and the rates customary in the community." We recommend, and the Model Standards of Conduct encourage, the fee agreement to be in writing.[18] In addition to the amount of the fee, you should also address how and when the fee is to be paid. Some mediators require payment at the beginning of the mediation and some bill their clients. Whichever practice you adopt, be sure to make your policy clear to participants before you agree to mediate the matter.[19]

VI. Practical Preparation for the Mediation Meeting

The mediator has primary responsibility for organizing the mediation. He or she is the host. Like any good host, the mediator must pay the utmost attention to all details of the meeting. The more convenient and comfortable the mediation experience is for the parties, the more energy they will have to focus their attention on the substantive issues of the discussion. Specific areas requiring planning and preparation are the timing and duration of the mediation, the facilities and amenities required by the parties, and other issues involving the conduct of the mediation such as arrivals, departures, waiting facilities, seating, visuals, and security.

A. Timing

A mediator must take into account several factors when determining the most appropriate timing for mediation. The mediation should not be scheduled too soon, so as to allow enough time for the participants to procure relevant information. However, since mediation is not driven predominantly by the facts, there does not have to be an exhaustive pursuit of information. The emotional state of the parties is also relevant to timing. Where one or more participants are experiencing emotional upset such as shock, denial, severe depression, or uncontrollable anger, it is not advisable to proceed with mediation. From a practical standpoint, the timing needs to be convenient for all parties and take into account any approaching trial or other litigation events that the mediation needs to precede.

---

17. MODEL STANDARDS OF CONDUCT FOR MEDIATORS STD. VIII (2005).

18. "The better practice in reaching an understanding about fees is to set down the arrangement in a written agreement." *Id.*

19. See Chapter 15—*Becoming A Mediator, Careers in Mediation, and Establishing a Private Mediation Practice*, section V.B, for a more detailed discussion of fees. See also Appendices 2A & B for a sample Agreement to Mediate and Fee Schedule.

B. Duration

The length of the mediation is another critical matter that is often decided during the intake procedure. Except where a court or governmental agency has set the duration of the mediation by order, the mediator should work with the parties to determine a reasonable duration of the mediation. Mediators should use their experience with disputes to help guide the parties in setting the proper duration of the mediation as they will typically be in a better position as result of their training and experience to know how much time it will take to conduct a productive mediation.

As a general rule, the more complex the dispute and the more participants that are involved, the longer the dispute will take to resolve. Most disputes can be mediated in one day. There are, however, disputes that can be handled in a half day and those that will require several days. Sometimes clients will advocate a block of time inappropriate for the dispute, usually shorter than necessary. For example, an employer might attempt to schedule a half-day mediation for an employment discrimination dispute the complexity of which clearly will require at least a full day of mediation. In such circumstances, you should explain your desire to extend the mediation time, providing your reasons for such a request. Good problem-solving and decision-making takes time.[20] Our experience is that most clients will follow advice regarding duration if it is supported with thoughtful explanation. In cases in which clients do not, it is then up to the mediator to decide whether to mediate a dispute that might have an increased chance of failing to be resolved because of insufficient time.

Set a specific duration for the mediation, 9:00 a.m. to 5:00 p.m., for example. This has two benefits. First, parties can plan their schedule accordingly and have advisors and constituents available by telephone or e-mail if necessary. Second, setting an ending time has strategic benefits. When faced with a deadline in negotiation, people have a tendency to become more flexible as that deadline approaches.[21] This potential benefit is greatly diminished when ending-times are open-ended.

Setting the duration in advance does not mean, however, that mediation cannot or should not be extended. If parties are making progress and/or the resolution of the matter appears promising with continued discussion, mediation can be continued past the planned ending-time or additional days can be scheduled in the future. These extensions should be discussed with parties and consented to by them. Moreover, there is usually a provision in the agreement to mediate regarding additional fees for extensions of the mediations, so parties have the option of continuing to try to work through the conflict. If there are any additional fees for extensions, parties should be reminded of them before an extension is agreed to.

---

20. LEIGH L. THOMPSON, THE MIND AND HEART OF THE NEGOTIATOR 67 (3d ed. 2005).
21. ROGER DAWSON, SECRETS OF POWER NEGOTIATING 173 (2d ed. 2001).

C. Facilities

The mediation facility ideally should be convenient, comfortable, and safe. In the case of private mediations, the mediator has the option of selecting the facilities and can ensure that these conditions are met. Very often, the mediator will hold the mediation at his or her own facilities so that he or she retains significant control over the environment. In mediations conducted at institutional facilities like courthouses or community mediation centers, however, mediators usually have little control over the facilities. Thus, the mediation facility may not always be ideal. Although issues pertaining to the mediation facility are more fully discussed in Chapter 12, the following are some guidelines to consider in preparation for the mediation.

1. It is prudent for the mediator to provide participants with written directions to the mediation facility. This helps to prevent parties from getting lost and arriving late and frustrated to the mediation, which is usually not a good start to the mediation.

2. The facility should be accessible to the clients, have convenient parking facilities, and have sufficient lighting if mediations will be held in the evening.

3. The facility should be neutral, to prevent the "home ground" syndrome that can provide tactical advantages for the "home team." Alternatively, the mediation can be held "on site," for example, at the place of employment in a workplace dispute. If convenience and travel are an issue for one or more participants, the venue might be rotated if multiple meetings are to be held, in order to promote fairness and convenience of the parties.

4. There should be at least two meeting rooms for joint and separate sessions.

5. The rooms should be relatively soundproof to promote privacy.

D. Amenities

Proper amenities might include communication facilities (e.g., telephones, and internet access), refreshments, tissues, and other creature comforts. While the refreshment issue may seem trite, it is not just about physical comfort for the participants. Having bottled water and empty glasses and even snacks on the table provides the opportunity for some ritual serving between the parties. Even where the mediator does the pouring, it symbolizes the equality of the participants and initiates a common activity for all. Where tea and coffee are available away from the mediation table, or in the room, there is a common activity of moving toward it and the movement provides an opportunity for informal discussion away from the table. From this standpoint, refreshments are a way to make the parties feel more comfortable and create a common experience that may create an atmosphere of sharing and cooperation that carries over into the negotiations.

E. Arrivals, Waiting Facilities, and Departures

Mediators must plan and supervise the arrival, waiting, and departure of all parties. It is sometimes a good practice, especially in highly contentious disputes, to arrange for the parties to arrive at the mediation venue at separate times. The mediator or a receptionist should greet them and allocate separate waiting rooms. Having the parties wait in separate rooms before the joint session begins prevents parties from becoming quarrelsome without the mediator's supervision. It also provides the mediator the opportunity to speak privately with each party before the joint session to answer questions or address any last-minute concerns. When one party arrives before the other, the mediator should not be seen in conversation with this party when the other arrives. If the mediation evokes strong emotions, especially between parties with a past history of violence, then the parties' departures also require careful attention. The normal practice is to allow the "victim" or threatened party to leave the building first and complete his or her departure before allowing the other party to leave.

F. Seating

Generally, seating should be as comfortable as possible. The basic approach is to provide what is socially appropriate for the circumstances of the participants. For example, formal tables work best for commercial disputes and easy chairs for community disputes. Again, the mediator should seek to promote the overall goal of comfort of the parties. Chief executives would not feel any more comfortable on couches than neighbors who are accustomed to chatting on the front lawn would feel sitting in very formal boardroom seating. In some cases, a mediator may actually consider choosing the mediation facility based on the type of seating and environment that is preferable for the particular dispute.

Regarding actual seating arrangements, there are many different variations, and the issue is a source of a surprising amount of debate in mediation circles. Figure 2–1, below, shows some seating possibilities. Most mediators sit at the head of the table, equidistant from the parties. The parties should have their own physical space, separate and equal. Mediators try to avoid the parties facing one another across the table in a "confrontational" mode, preferring round or oval settings, or seating at the corners of tables, in a less adversarial mode. Some mediation services have custom-designed "kitchen" layouts to symbolize the notion of "sorting this out around the kitchen table." However, to the extent that the facilities provide little choice in seating, mediators will have to make the best of whatever tables and chairs are available. At minimum, it is best for all parties' chairs to be of similar size and comfort (or discomfort), so as to prevent anyone from feeling inferior or subordinate.

Seating can change during the mediation. Initially, the parties' chairs may be facing the mediator, to whom they should speak in the beginning. During adjournments, the mediator might adjust the chairs so that the parties face each other as a basis for communicating directly across the table in later stages of the mediation. During the separate meetings, the mediator might move to a different chair and ask the relevant party to move as well, so that they are not physically associated with the stress and positional demands which occurred in the joint meeting. In all situations mediators make practical choices based on their informed judgment.

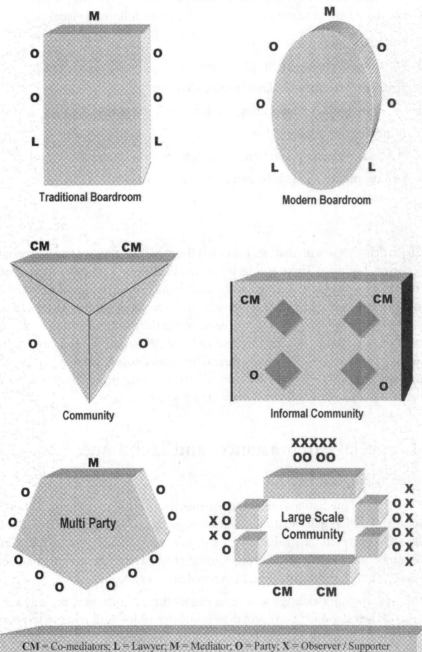

CM = Co-mediators; L = Lawyer; M = Mediator; O = Party; X = Observer / Supporter

G. Visuals

There is a saying in mediation that "the visual is vital." Mediators may find the use of visual aids helpful in certain situations, and recent advances in technology provide the mediator with more options than ever before. Many mediation clients benefit from seeing agendas, mathematical calculations, mud maps and sketches, points of agreement, and so on, in written or drawn form. For this purpose, mediators may find it helpful to organize one or more of the following visual aids:

1. Butcher's paper: promotes retention;
2. Whiteboard: enables writing to be erased;
3. Electronic whiteboard: allows printing/copies;
4. Overhead projector: educating and informing the parties;
5. Technology to display video;
6. PCs and computer projection: "high tech" versions of the above; and
7. Writing and drawing tools: avoid permanent markers.

H. Security

All participants in a mediation, including the mediator, require arrangements for their personal security. These arrangements can include supervised or separate waiting rooms for each party. The mediator will normally sit closest to the door to allow a quick exit and also to provide a "barrier" against the sudden exit of a party. In some service-provider agencies there is a panic button in the mediation room to alert outsiders if there is violence or the threat of violence. Where circumstances require it, the weaker or more vulnerable party should be allowed to leave first so that the dominant party cannot lie in wait for him or her. Holding the mediation via video conference is also an option when there are safety concerns.

VII. Special Circumstances and Techniques

A. Team Negotiations

Some types of mediations raise unique issues that require special preparation and arrangements. One such situation is a "team negotiation," which refers to a situation where each "party" in the mediation consists of a group of two or more individuals. For example, a voluntary association, a group of taxpayers, a trade union and even multiple plaintiffs may be involved in the mediation as a team.

The predominant challenge with team negotiations is managing the teams, both in terms of their size and in terms of their group dynamics. A number of techniques can be used to assist the mediator in controlling the situation. For example, nominating spokespersons and participants for each group is an important step in managing the size of large teams. It may also be necessary to establish methods for constituent groups to communicate with members of the principal team, which might involve modifications to the normal confidentiality arrangements. Additionally, making decisions regarding the division of labor within each group can help improve efficiency. The mediator might also consider whether it is desirable to appoint a process control group.

Perhaps the most challenging task of the mediator is to find a method for effective decision-making within each group. The following case illustration demonstrates the importance of the last-mentioned point. In a mediation involving a non-profit organization, the mediator undertook considerable preparatory work over a number of sessions involving extensive education on the nature of conflict and interest-based bargaining. The subsequent mediation commenced well, but it soon became apparent that it would be difficult to reach an agreement because of the presence of a destabilizing individual in one of the team groups. It was clear that this person would not commit to any agreement and her dominant role within the particular group precluded the group from being able to do the same. With hindsight, the mediation would have been more productive if the mediator, in the preparatory stages, had required the participating groups to commit to a decision-making process before any proposals were on the table. Had this been a system of majority vote, or two-thirds majority, it would have marginalized the sole dissenter and allowed the groups collectively to have come to a decision. It was difficult to impose a decision-making procedure on the groups once concrete proposals were on the table and individuals had taken up positions in respect of them. The lesson learned from this experience is that where the parties in mediation consist of several individuals it is worth insisting that each team stipulate and commit to a decision-making procedure in advance of the mediation. This should preferably not involve a unanimity requirement.

B. Pre-Mediation Conferences with the Parties Separately

Some mediators choose to conduct pre-mediation conferences, which are contacts with each party individually prior to the mediation that can be conducted in person or by telephone. They maintain that this contact is the most important factor in a successful mediation. It can be used to deal with many of the preliminary intake and screening matters referred to in this chapter and, in addition, allows the mediator to develop a productive working relationship with each party. This approach to mediation is sometimes referred to as the "prior contact system." It differs from preliminary conferences, which are addressed in this chapter above. In preliminary conferences, the mediator will meet with *all* parties together. In pre-mediation conferences, the mediator meets separately with each party. Pre-mediation conferences also go beyond basic housekeeping matters, such as mediation schedule and duration, and begin defining the problem and working on potential solutions. In particular mediators can help parties prepare for the mediation, so they are in the best possible position to make informed decisions about the conflict. (See Chapter 7 for a discussion on how to prepare parties for mediation.)

While most mediators recognize the potential benefits of this approach to mediation, there are conflicting views on the wisdom of the practice. Some argue that there should be no separate contact with the parties before the mediation as this might provide grounds for suspicion, unease, or loss of trust. As usual, much will depend on the circumstances, including the nature of the dispute and the clients. There is also a pragmatic consideration in that this system requires at least some additional resources in terms of time and money. We generally favor pre-mediation conferences and believe they can be a most valuable tool.

VIII. Exercises

1. Develop some additional metaphors which might be suitable for explaining mediation to a person involved in:

   • a building dispute;

   • a divorce dispute; and

   • an information technology dispute.

2. You are consulted by an agency that provides family mediation. They need a checklist of factors to consider in screening out cases in which domestic violence makes mediation inappropriate. Design an appropriate document for their use.

3. You are establishing a mediation center with a single mediation room which will accommodate the mediation of a wide variety of disputes. Your budget is limited. Design a set of furniture to cater for this situation.

THREE

Maintaining a Favorable Climate

You don't need a weatherman to know which way the wind blows.

—BOB DYLAN (SINGER/SONGWRITER)

I. The Role of the Mediator in "Climate Control"

Mediators have a role in creating and maintaining a favorable "climate" for the mediating parties as they communicate, negotiate, and make decisions. As with the development of the foundations referred to in the previous chapter, "climate control" is not something that occurs at only one stage of the mediation process; it has to be considered and attended to through the entire mediation. However, it tends to be a more important responsibility for mediators before and during the early stages of mediation when the parties are likely to be most apprehensive, confused, and defensive. In one sense, a mediator must be a type of counselor who helps to control the emotional climate to promote an atmosphere where effective problem solving can occur.

While counseling is distinguishable from mediation, counseling concepts are of significance for mediators, as they are for other skilled helpers. A difficulty for a book on mediation skills is that there are many different theories of psychology and counseling on matters such as motivation, behavior, and grief. It is not possible to canvass all relevant theories, nor is it wise to link mediation skills to a particular theory in one area. Therefore, the book, especially this chapter, works eclectically with counseling and psychological concepts and recommends reference to more specialized texts on these topics.[1] This chapter focuses on some of the reasons for the discomfort of mediation clients and on some of the ways in which mediators can deal with this factor.

---

1. As a starting point only, there is a very good chapter on the relevance of counseling concepts for mediators. See Chapter 4 of the classic mediation text JAY FOLBERG & ALISON TAYLOR, MEDIATION: A COMPREHENSIVE GUIDE TO RESOLVING CONFLICTS WITHOUT LITIGATION (1984).

II. Reasons for a Poor Climate

Conflict can be debilitating. To some people it appears confusing, even chaotic. It stirs the emotions and saps the energy, and it almost always feels difficult to manage and resolve. Mediators can expect that parties coming into the process will be in negative emotional and psychological states. They will feel that their cause is just and that the other side has acted unfairly, or worse. They may also have invested a great deal of energy in the "struggle" and be unwilling to negotiate toward a compromise on "matters of principle."

There may be several reasons for the negative state of mediation clients. These reasons will be explored throughout this section by reference to the following scenario.

Case Illustration: Sarah and Southern Gold Farms

Sarah was leaving the ABC Superstore when she stumbled over a concrete stair that was crumbling and in disrepair. She fell to the ground and severely injured her lower back. Since the accident she has not worked and has been restricted in her movements, affecting her usual activities. She has had no treatment other than taking pain management medication and some physical therapy, which she attended irregularly.

The medical reports suggest that Sarah suffered a "significant amount'" of pain and suffering but not as substantial as she claimed. They suggest that she will ultimately be capable of resuming suitable light work and the bulk of her household duties.

Sarah alleges that since the accident she has had difficulty socializing and sleeping, her sex life with her husband has been disrupted, and she has had to abandon plans for starting a family. She complains of constant throbbing in her back and occasional spasms and bruising. She has lost self-confidence and self-respect since the accident.

Proceedings were instituted in the District Court for negligence. The lawyers arranged a mediation, attended by Sarah, an ABC Superstore manager, and their respective attorneys.

A. Reasons Pertaining to Pre-Mediation Developments

Between the time of the accident and the mediation there could be a number of developments that contribute to a further deterioration in Sarah's original negative state. Seen from her perspective, these might include the following:

- Insulting settlement offers from the insurer that have "poisoned the well";
- The attitude and treatment of the defendant's doctors, who were abrupt, rough, disbelieving, and uncaring;

- The approach of the insurer in giving her the "run around" with gross delays in authorizing payment for medical treatment or in making a "decent" offer;

- Increasing concern that her injuries might get worse;

- Well-meaning advice from friends or relatives not to talk to the insurer, not to trust any lawyer, and not to settle the case;

- Her growing belief that the defendant treats all customers badly and must be taught a lesson;

- A slow realization that the whole system is "loaded against her" and her rights have been unreasonably disregarded, or the defendant will not be reasonable until the door of the court; and

- The very high expectations that her counsel's advice has raised in her mind, particularly in relation to the dollar amounts mentioned.

Comparable considerations could have put the insurer's representative in a negative frame of mind, in particular where Sarah is from a "certain socio-economic class," her lawyer has a notorious reputation among insurers, and there have been "grossly inflated" monetary claims for a "minimal injury." The effect of these factors is to escalate the conflict beyond its original scope, rendering mediation more problematic than it otherwise might have been.

B. Reasons Pertaining to the Individual Parties

Most parties in conflict, and hence in mediation, have experienced an actual loss or a perception of loss and are consequently undergoing a process of grieving.[2] The sense of loss could be over a matrimonial partnership, a promising business venture, the full use of limbs or other bodily parts, or security of employment. According to different writers on attachment theory, the grieving process could involve a number of elements, though not in any strict sequence or linear progression. Thus, Sarah could have experienced the following emotions in her grieving process:

- *Shock*: the state of numbness in which there is no ability to analyze, understand, or feel what has happened and what is going on;

- *Denial*: the inability to accept or come to terms with the loss, and the belief that her health, job, and family prospects, as the case may be, will be restored to what they were before;

- *Bargaining*: an attempt, usually futile, to recover whatever has been lost by "negotiating" with the employer, insurer, or even God, accompanied by firm commitments to reform in the future;

---

2. See the classic account in KUBLER ROSS, ON DEATH AND DYING (1969).

- *Anger*: characterized by extreme hostility toward the "cause" of the loss, such as Sarah's employer, her boss, or fate, or even the victim herself;

- *Despair and disorganization*: a loss of hope for the future and inability by the depressed person to plan, act, and make logical decisions in her best interests; and

- *Acceptance and reorganization*: in which Sarah comes to terms with the loss and decides that she "wants to get on with my life."

As the grieving elements do not occur in a strict linear progression, persons may move between them with some irregularity, and at times slip "backwards," for example, from partial acceptance to denial. It is also not unusual for persons who have been in a close relationship, such as marriage or business partners, to be in different stages of the grieving process from each other. For instance, one party might be at the stage of acceptance while the other party is still in denial. The latter party may be seen as unfeeling and the former as unable to manage, further exacerbating the dispute.

Some writers, such as Robert Emery, talk of a cyclical theory of grief, revolving around love, anger, and sadness, in which there is a constant cycling back and forth between these conflicting emotions.[3] While the intensity of these emotions lessens over time, they can involve a lengthy and confusing process with the possibility of the person becoming stuck on one of the emotions of grief. Furthermore, where there are two parties, one the "leaver" from a personal or business relationship and the other the "left," the guilt of the former, rejection of the latter, and the continued contact between them can perpetuate the cyclical process. As the leaver's emotions are usually less intense than those of the left party, the same misunderstanding and exacerbation can occur as described above.

Parties in all stages of grieving will be in a complicated emotional state. In some cases, for example, where there is prolonged shock or denial, it might be inappropriate to negotiate, and mediation should be deferred until these stages have passed. In other situations where one party is in the anger phase and the other is at acceptance, the mediator will have to be aware of their different emotional realities without resorting to amateur counseling.

C. Power Imbalances and Fear of Losing

Some parties come to mediation with a perception that they have grossly inferior bargaining power. This is likely to be the case for someone in Sarah's position. Even if the imbalance operates only at the level of perception, it is still a reality for the

---

3. ROBERT E. EMERY, RENEGOTIATING FAMILY RELATIONSHIPS: DIVORCE, CHILD CUSTODY, AND MEDIATION 26–29 (1994).

party concerned. In many situations both parties might feel at a disadvantage in terms of their bargaining power, causing anxiety and defensiveness all around. Specific ways of dealing with power imbalances are referred to in Chapter 13—*Special Issues in Mediation.*

Some parties come to mediation with a perception that they might lose altogether in the course of the mediation process. Even if this is, objectively speaking, an unlikely eventuality, it is not less real in the subjective world of the fearful party. Again, someone in Sarah's position may have this fear. Specific ways of dealing with this fear are also referred to below in this chapter

D. Reasons Pertaining to the Mediation Process

The mediation process itself can be a source of anxiety and concern. At least one of the parties in mediation has usually not experienced the system before, and "first-timers" such as Sarah are likely to have more anxieties than the "repeat users." The negative factors relating to the mediation process could include the following:

- Resentment at having been forced by a court, agency, or stronger contracting party to attend mediation against the relevant person's will;
- Ambivalence about being at mediation, even where they have chosen this option themselves;
- Unfamiliarity with and ignorance about the mediation process and the mediator;
- Uncertainty over the actual role and likely behavior of the mediator;
- Anxiety about their negotiating abilities; and
- Concern about having to compromise on "matters of principle."

Cumulatively these factors could have a deeply negative and distrustful effect on disputing parties as they come into mediation and as they begin participating in the process. The rest of this chapter deals with ways in which the mediator can change the climate to a more positive one.

III. Strategies for Improving the Climate

A. The Trust Factor

1. WHY TRUST IS IMPORTANT

Experience suggests a number of factors that can contribute to a stormy climate for many mediations. This is compounded by the fact that parties in dispute frequently distrust each other. Here the word "trust" refers to one person's *willingness to believe, to be open to, and to take risks with* another person. Another way to talk about trust is in terms of "risk assessment." The question then becomes, "How can the mediation process favorably modify a party's assessment of the risks involved in coming to the negotiations, disclosing interests and needs, and exploring settlement options with the other side?"

Levels of trust may improve, deteriorate, or stay the same during the course of the mediation, and a mediation is by no means a failure if the level of trust has not improved. It is too high an expectation of mediators that they turn embattled business partners or skeptical government officials into trusting comrades. However, high levels of distrust can make it difficult or impossible to come to a joint decision. In these circumstances, mediators can generate some degree of trust in themselves and the mediation process, as a basis for getting the parties to move toward reaching an agreement with each other. The central assumption here is that if the parties trust the mediator and the mediation process, then they are more likely to remain at the negotiating table and to make attempts at settlement than if this trust were absent. Needless to say, there are no guarantees.

2. GENERATING TRUST IN THE MEDIATOR

The objective is that the parties develop trust in the mediator so that they may be able to take risks with him or her that they would not take with each other. Mediators can use the following techniques to impress on the parties that they are individuals who can be trusted:

- Affirming their credentials as mediators and dispute resolvers;
- Showing respect and concern for the parties;
- Establishing a personal rapport with the parties;
- Using good active listening skills and acknowledging the parties' concerns; and
- Being impartial and even-handed in the conduct of the process.

3. GENERATING TRUST IN THE MEDIATION PROCESS

Here the objective is that the parties develop trust in the mediation process so that they are more likely to remain committed to it and to persist in their attempts to work through the problem. Mediators can use the following techniques to help the parties generate trust in the process in which they are participating:

- Explaining, normalizing, and validating the mediation process;
- Reassuring the parties, where possible, on their anxieties about the process;
- Providing for equality of speaking time for the parties;
- Applying the mediation guidelines appropriately and even-handedly; and
- Using separate meetings to keep the process moving.

4. HELPING THE PARTIES DEVELOP FAITH IN
THEIR OWN NEGOTIATING ABILITIES

As negotiation experts, mediators can identify relatively minor issues on which the parties can develop trust before moving on to more substantial matters. By initiating successful discussion and decision-making on a "process" issue, such as the venue for the mediation or the appropriate role for advisers or outsiders, the mediator can stimulate faith in the parties' ability to negotiate successfully together. The same can be achieved by the mediator targeting and gaining negotiated agreement on "easy" matters first, for example, on where the children will spend Mother's and Father's Day in a parenting dispute or on how interest will be calculated in a commercial dispute.

B. Managing Expectations

In our experience, managing expectations is one of the most important functions of mediators. It is the *M* and *E* in *Me*diation. This function is relevant in relation to the pre-mediation activities of the mediator, to developments within the mediation, and even to what occurs after the mediation.

Reference has already been made to the problems caused by parties who come to mediation in a negative frame of mind and the role of the mediator in dealing with this phenomenon. Conversely, some parties come to mediation with wildly optimistic expectations about the process, the role of the mediator, and likely mediation outcomes. These are some of the unrealistic expectations encountered in practice:

- That the mediation will vindicate the relevant party's version of the facts; that it will establish the "truth";
- That the mediator will find and hold the relevant party's case to be essentially just;
- That the parties are negotiating over a "fixed pie" that will not be diminished in mediation, litigation, or any other dispute-resolution process;
- That the mediation outcome will be in accordance with the party's most optimistic settlement prospects; and
- That if the mediation is not successful, the party will be vindicated by a judge in court and receive what they could not obtain in mediation.

These and other similar expectations are often quite unrealistic. One of the ways in which the mediator maintains a favorable climate during the mediation is by attempting throughout the process to manage expectations by bringing them down to reality. They administer the drug of realism. This is done through the strategies and interventions referred to in this chapter and throughout the book. This is a constant function of mediators, from the earliest stages of the mediation to its termination, and sometimes thereafter. What the mediator is doing is making the relevant party a good mediation client, as opposed to a client of litigation, lottery, or the fantasy of wishful thinking.

C. Other Ways to Improve Climate

The following are suggestions for ways in which mediators might improve the mediation climate. The appropriateness of each strategy will depend on the status and circumstances of each mediation.

1. PROMOTING OPTIMISM, A POSITIVE TONE, AND A MOOD OF CONFIDENCE

The mediator sets a positive tone from the outset with a quiet, confident approach and a mood of optimism. This is reinforced by emphasizing and upholding the fairness of the process, highlighting its problem-solving nature, and pointing out its ultimate goal, which is to make good decisions concerning the resolution of the conflict. Themes of mutuality and cooperativeness are emphasized from the beginning ("We are here to make decisions to suit both your needs and interests..."). Confidence and optimism are maintained throughout the process by emphasizing progress, particularly through the intervention of summarizing.

2. PRODUCTIVE COMMUNICATION, STRUCTURE, AND SECURITY

Mediation is not the forum to continue destructive fighting, and the mediator must neutralize the situation to some extent. The mediator provides a non-threatening productive atmosphere; controls the parties' accusations, criticisms, and defenses to accusations; emphasizes the confidentiality of the discussions; and otherwise creates a secure environment for dispute resolution. The causes for destructive behaviors and possible mediator interventions in response are discussed in Chapter 6—*Managing Conflict from Crisis to Opportunity*.

Another way in which mediators provide a favorable climate for decision-making is by providing a structure to the mediation procedure and by keeping it moving according to an appropriate plan. This function is referred to more fully in Chapter 4—*Managing the Mediation Process*. These stages are designed to ensure that the process is even-handed, that each side has sufficient "air-time," and that neither side is able to take control of the mediation or disadvantage the other through tactical maneuvers. Therefore, at least initially, mediators should be assertive in their control function.

The mediation guidelines listed in Chapter 4 are an important part of the mediation structure that promote productive communication and provide security for the parties. They provide a simple set of standards for behavior during the mediation and give the mediator some "objective" criteria against which to measure and control party behavior. However, where a party breaches the guidelines, the mediator has a range of possible responses, depending on the severity of the breach and other circumstances of the mediation. Thus, the mediator might, in ascending degrees of assertiveness:

- Ignore the breach if it is not significant or if it is very early in the mediation, and continue without any reference to it;
- Distract or disarm the party or parties with a deflective question;
- Neutrally restate the guidelines and ask both parties to recommit to them;
- Rebuke or reprimand the offending party or parties;
- Break into separate meetings in order to discuss the breach; and
- Terminate the mediation—a rare last resort.

In each case, the mediator will have to make a tactical judgment as to the appropriate intervention. The judgment is made with the overall objective of providing a good climate for decision-making through the appropriate amount and form of control. Sometimes the judgment will be correct, but sometimes it will not, and there is no exact formula that can be applied to all situations. Such is the ambiguity which mediation shares with life.

3. ACKNOWLEDGING CONCERNS

Here the mediator does what might not have been done by any other professional or helper with whom the client has been involved, namely, to acknowledge the nature and intensity of their concerns. This is achieved through the technique of active listening and is dealt with further in Chapter 5—*Assisting the Communication Process*.

4. NORMALIZING

Normalizing is the other side of the acknowledging coin. While mediation clients might be convinced that their problems are unique and unprecedented in their gravity, it is appropriate at certain times to normalize their situation. Thus, they might be informed that it is normal for people in business to make mistakes and normal to attribute malice where the other side errs. Likewise, the difficulties that the parties are encountering in their negotiations can be normalized. A mediator might explain that it is usual for negotiating parties to feel that they have conceded too much and have difficulty making the final concession.

One objective of normalizing is to open the parties to the notion that other persons have been in their situation, and so they might consider how those individuals resolved the same kinds of problem. This is intended to shift their perception that their situation is hopeless and without remedy to one in which there are precedents and possibilities that they could be thinking about.

5. GETTING OUT OF THE PAST AND INTO THE FUTURE

It is normal to feel more intense emotion, particularly anger, about the past than about the future. While a mediator might have to devote some time to dealing with prior events, mediation is not obsessed with the past and with historical facts, unlike other forms of dispute resolution such as adjudication. The mediator is able to redirect the parties' attention from a negative and destructive past to a future that can be different and more attractive.

6. MUTUALIZING THE UNHAPPINESS

Parties often assume that the unhappiness in the mediation room is theirs alone, and that the other side is in a state of bliss or mild euphoria. Where this is not the case, and it seldom is, the mediator can point out that the other side is in reality unhappy that they have had to move considerably off their bottom line or have had to make a concession on key issues. This technique has been referred to as "mutualizing the unhappiness."[4] This has the potential effect of reassuring each side on the acceptability of a proposed settlement—while it may not be what they wanted, it is certainly not what the other side wanted either. The disclosure of the mutual unhappiness might require the consent of the parties, however—one or both may not wish to reveal the extent of their dissatisfaction with the way the mediation is unfolding or with an imminent settlement.

7. REDUCING THE PRESSURE TO SETTLE

Where there is a great sense of pressure to settle in mediation, it can provoke resentment, resistance, and, ironically, a major obstacle to settlement. One way of reducing the feeling of pressure on the parties is by reassuring them that they are not obliged to settle in the mediation. This is to emphasize the self-determination principle, namely that it is up to the parties to make decisions on all matters, including on whether mediation is the right place for them to be. It is a defining feature of mediation that there will only be a settlement if both parties agree, and the "no deal unless you both accede" theme can be a reassurance for some parties. It could be taken further, with a light touch, for example, "It's OK not to agree—someone has to make up the three percent of cases that do not settle in mediation."

8. RELIEVING TENSION THROUGH HUMOR

Humor can be an appropriate way of relieving tension in many situations, from the classroom to the dentist's office. Humor provides physical relief through laughter, relaxes people emotionally, and takes them out of the characters they have been playing. Laughter is also a shared and common response from people who might not have much else in common, and it can provide insight and a change of perspective. In mediation the timing and focus of humor is critical. Mediators should leave their party routines at the door and use great sensitivity in the joke-telling department. If humor is used too early it may set a flippant tone and suggest that the mediator is not taking the matter seriously enough. It should preferably be aimed at mediators' own frailties ("Please speak up, I'm deaf in one ear and can't hear out of the other") or at the situation ("No one gets to relieve their bladder until we've settled") and

---

4. RUTH CHARLTON & MICHELINE DEWDNEY, THE MEDIATOR'S HANDBOOK 15 (2d ed. 1995).

should not be aimed at the parties. Jokes about mediators will no doubt emerge, but should be treated with great insouciance by serious practitioners.

9. MORE RITUAL FOR MEDIATION

Mediation in western societies has no established tradition of rituals. In communal societies, systems of conflict management have numerous rituals involving the exchange of gifts, eating, drinking and smoking, signs of respect, singing, and movement. Ritual lends a sanctity and mystique to the proceedings, suggesting that the business at hand has a social importance greater than the interests of the individuals. It also lends a sense of purpose and even-handedness to the proceedings. In the absence of equivalent rituals in western mediation, mediators need to consider spending time on preliminary courtesies among all present, on exchanging pleasantries, on initiating a formal round of introductions, on attending to how the parties should address one another, and on making some acknowledgment and affirmation of all parties present.

Mediators may also provide food, drink, and other refreshments that can be "ritually" served in a way that shows respect for all and the equality of all parties present. Consumption becomes a common activity, shared equally by all participants, which temporarily distracts attention from the negative features of the dispute during the settling-in phase. Imaginative mediators might develop additional rituals appropriate to the mediation process.

IV. Dealing with Intense Emotions

A. Overview

Intense and strongly expressed emotions can seriously affect the climate of a mediation. Strong emotions are often expressed in mediation, contrary to the naive view that because mediation is a "collaborative" and "non-adversarial" process all destructive and negative elements are miraculously avoided. This view confuses structure, on one hand, with style and behavior, on the other. Mediation is collaborative in structure, but this will not always prevent parties from being positional, adversarial, and mean-spirited in style and behavior. One of the difficulties with emotions is that they can be triggered more quickly than it takes the rational mind to assess a situation and decide how to react. While "positive" emotions, such as joy and contentment, are unproblematic, "negative" emotions, such as fear and anger, present a difficult challenge for most mediators.

Some mediators attempt to prohibit the expression of negative emotion because it is perceived to be dysfunctional in the mediation, though this prohibition might also be because these mediators feel uncomfortable with high emotion themselves or do not feel professionally equipped to deal with it. However, as the expression of emotion is an important form of communication, a blanket prohibition policy will restrict certain forms of communication and undermine many of the potential benefits of mediation. Legitimately expressed anger can have the advantage of indicating to others a depth of feeling, and even sincerity. However, anger can also change the parties' focus from the problem to the emotion, cloud their objectivity, and lead to angry retaliation.

There are various ways of dealing with strongly expressed emotions during the course of a mediation that can aid in maintaining a productive climate. There are differing views in the literature and among mediation practitioners about the most appropriate interventions. Here we provide opinions concerning the various approaches based upon the potential advantages and disadvantages of each. However, as in many of the interventions discussed, there is no hard and fast rule. As usual, these responses shade into one another and there may be elements of more than one in a single mediator intervention.

Five ways in which mediators might respond to intense feelings are set out below. Reference will be made to the following workplace fact scenario in assessing each approach.

Fact Scenario

Ian, the supervisor, has just demoted and changed the sales areas of Pat, a salesperson, for not meeting the specified performance criteria. Pat has lodged a complaint over the demotion and changed areas. In terms of company policy, the matter has come to an internal mediator. Pat has just had an intense outburst of anger and frustration over victimization, discrimination, and lack of training, allegedly arising from Ian's actions and inactions.

V. Discourage the Expression of Intense Emotion

As suggested above, discouraging the expression of intense emotion is often the practice of mediators who feel unable to deal with high emotion or regard it as irrelevant to the problem; they therefore attempt to prevent its expression as soon as it commences. Here is how a mediator pursuing this policy might handle the above fact scenario:

Mediator: *Look, Pat, it's not going to help here if you get angry and shout. Let's just talk about how you calculated your sales figures against the target figures for the last six months.*

This kind of response might be advantageous where resource limitations necessitate only a very short mediation and the parties need to be kept focused. It also might be useful in situations where a party simply cannot express the emotion without losing control and becoming threatening. However, this last situation might also raise the question of the appropriateness of mediation.

Discouraging the expression of intense emotion, on the other hand, has the potential disadvantage of causing further frustration and discontent for the emotive party and of jeopardizing the longer-term success of the mediation. It also reduces the amount of information a mediator will learn, some of it highly probative, about the party and the conflict. When and in what context intense emotions arise communicates valuable information. For example, if a party discussing the moment he or she learned that the other party wanted a divorce begins weeping uncontrollably, a mediator has learned something potentially valuable about the nature and degree of the loss that that party experiences. Accordingly, we believe that, as a general rule, discouraging intense emotion is not the best policy in most situations.

A. Ignore the Emotion and Proceed with the Mediation

Here the mediator does not intervene to suppress the expression of emotion, but ignores it and moves on. For example:

> Mediator: *Pat and Ian, I thought we were trying to provide some answers to the second question on the board, namely how can the sales areas be divided in a way which is fair to Pat and other salespersons. Now let's see how this can be done....*

In this example, the mediator uses the visuals on the whiteboard to focus the parties' attention on the problem and distract them from the interpersonal hostility. This has much the same advantages and disadvantages as the policy of discouraging the expression of emotions in the first place. A refinement of this strategy involves distinguishing between positive and negative emotions: mediators acknowledge and validate the former, for example, the optimism and hope present in the early stages of a joint initiative between the mediating parties, and ignore and disregard the latter, for example, intense anger over a party feeling betrayed.

B. Acknowledge the Emotion, and Then Continue

Here the mediator explicitly acknowledges the presence of the emotions and their intensity, whether they are expressed directly by the party or are merely evident from behavior, tone of voice, or body language.

> Mediator: *Pat, it sounds as though your treatment has made you extremely frustrated and angry and that your last four months at work have been exceptionally difficult. Is that correct?... Well, let's move on now and see how to divide up the sales areas....*

This approach is designed to give the emotive party the experience of being heard and understood by at least one professional. There is an expectation that this validation will encourage Pat to move forward from the emotional state to practical decision-making. This intervention also results in the other party having to listen to the emotion being identified and named by the mediator. Some mediators are nervous that such acknowledgment might provide a license for more extensive emotional outbursts and further complicate the dispute. However, acknowledgment does not equate with approval, and in our experience continued emotiveness is a rare occurrence where strongly felt emotions are expressed and then acknowledged. The mediator might wish to add an educational dimension to this approach by indicating that mediation in itself might not resolve the intense hurt or anger, as the case may be, and encourage the relevant party to seek other assistance. Accordingly, acknowledging the emotion makes a good default approach in most mediation situations. The mediator could then utilize less or more indulgent approaches as circumstances require.

C. Encourage Some Venting of the Emotion

Here the mediator explicitly invites an expression of emotion: in turn, the mediator might invite Ian to explain how he felt about making the demotion decision or how he feels now about Pat's condition. For example:

> Mediator: *Now Pat, tell Ian exactly what you felt about the demotion and what effect it had on you emotionally and physically....*

The advantage of this approach is that it allows the parties to get things off their chests, to release pent-up feelings, and, after an emotional catharsis, to move on to the problem at hand. Some judgment and control are required to ensure that neither party is injured by the other's emotional venting, and there also needs to be a limit on the duration of this exercise. This approach has the same potential benefits and disadvantages as the previous one. It might be particularly valuable where a party is inhibited or uncomfortable about expressing emotion without some encouragement from the mediator.

D. Identify and Deal with the Underlying Problem Therapeutically

In this approach, the mediator describes the response in therapeutic or psychological terms. This response is something that can only be undertaken by those professionally qualified to do so. For example:

> Mediator: *Pat, it sounds as though you have been traumatized by this ordeal, and that you have lost confidence and self-esteem. You may also be clinically depressed. Those issues need to be dealt with first....*

It has the advantage of dealing with underlying emotional or relationship difficulties which might prevent the parties from coming to a decision or which might jeopardize the long-term durability of any decision reached. It has the disadvantage of delaying the making of decisions on matters requiring immediate attention and of blurring the boundaries between mediation and counseling. Many mediators would adjourn the mediation and refer Pat to another professional if they decided that the problem needed therapeutic handling.

E. Selecting a Strategy

In selecting a strategy, the mediator needs to recognize the emotion distinct from the symptoms, diagnose it tentatively, and test out an intervention. If the diagnosis is that a party is deliberately using anger to force a compromise, the appropriate response may be to ignore it. If the mediator diagnoses a potential build-up in emotion, he or she may attempt to defuse it by humor. If the emotion is genuine but not too serious, the mediator might use behavioral techniques such as calling for an adjournment, bringing in the refreshments, conducting a round of separate meetings, getting the parties to write points on the whiteboard, and making other changes in the process to allow for a cooling-off. Mediators are providing a secure environment in which the dispute can be played out in a constructive manner. As with other skilled helpers, mediators also need to be attuned to their own responses to emotional outbursts and develop mechanisms to manage those without affecting the mediation.

F. Overcoming Clients' Fundamental Fears

It is clear from the previous sections in this chapter that mediators can have an important role in reducing the defensiveness of the negotiating parties. Many parties in mediation anticipate the worst possible outcome: that they will never see their children, that they will receive no compensation for their injuries. This common and understandable fear causes them to defend their positional claims at all costs. Of course, there may be some realism to this anxiety, but a party could also be negatively obsessed with an outcome that has not been decided and is not inevitable. In either event, this fear-induced defensiveness is not conducive to constructive problem solving.

Therefore, mediators should attempt to reduce the defensiveness of their clients. In the context of family mediations, the mediator might reduce the fear early in the intake by asking the parents, "What is the worst possible outcome of working with me?"[5] When each parent outlines this fear, it is usually an unrealistic concern, that is, one based not on fact but on emotion. The mediator then asks each parent if he or she can agree that the worst fear of the other parent will not materialize in the mediation. For example, if both parents state that the worst possible outcome would be "losing the children," the mediator asks each parent to affirm that the other will not lose their role in parenting the children in these negotiations. As this is understood and accepted by each parent, the need to defend against the possibility is

---

5. JOHN HAYNES & STEPHANIE CHARLESWORTH, THE FUNDAMENTALS OF FAMILY MEDIATION 162 (1995).

diminished, and each parent can spend their energy thinking about new solutions rather than defending against old fears. The same strategy can be adopted with respect to other kinds of meditations where the "fundamental fear" syndrome is evident or suspected.

VI. Exercises

1. Identify a dispute of some magnitude in which you have been involved as an employee, a consumer, a tenant, or a student. Write out a list of the things which the employer, retailer, landlord, or educational institution did or did not do between the emergence of the dispute and its "resolution" and describe the effect these factors had on your emotional state.

2. Assume you are the mediator between Sarah and Southern Gold Farms. What steps would you take to create a favorable climate for Sarah? What effect might these steps have on the representative of Southern Gold?

3. Discuss with a friend how each of you responds to intense sadness and anger. Together, develop some strategies you might use for dealing with these emotions if you were working as a professional mediator.

FOUR

Managing the Mediation Process

In all negotiations of difficulty, a man may not look to sow or reap at once, but must prepare [the] business and so ripen it by degrees.

—SIR FRANCIS BACON (WRITER AND PHILOSOPHER)

I. The Power of Process

Mediation is not encumbered by as many formal rules and procedures as litigation and arbitration, but it is not an unstructured, amorphous enterprise. Mediation follows a process, and it is from that process that it derives a significant source of its power to help parties make good decisions concerning their disputes. As we have said, mediation begins with the first moment of contact with the client during the intake process. However, there is a more formal stage of the mediation where the parties and the mediator meet as a group. In this chapter, "the process of mediation" refers to the stages mediation follows from the time the mediator and the parties first meet as a group until the mediation is concluded. Over the course of the mediation, the mediator assumes multiple roles: host, chairperson, guide, umpire, confessor, and police officer. These roles all concern the process of mediation, not its content. The mediator is responsible for conducting and managing the process of dispute resolution, while the parties are responsible for making decisions on its substantive content. The mediator therefore is a "process" expert in dispute resolution, and his or her success will be determined by the extent to which there is an effective process in place that is skillfully implemented.

Although the philosophy, purposes, and techniques of mediation can vary significantly, there is a common structure that most mediators follow regardless of style. This structure is designed to promote clear communication and thoughtful consideration of the problem. Not all mediation models are structured the same way. For instance, there are three-stage mediation models and twelve-stage models. The number of stages that a particular model contains, however, is usually a function of how broadly or narrowly one divides up the "traditional" mediation process and does not reflect a significant departure from the theoretical foundations of mediation. For our purposes, we will organize the mediation process into five stages: (A) *mediator's opening statement*, (B) *the parties' initial statements*, (C) *defining the problem*, (D) *problem solving and negotiation*, and (E) *final decision and closure*. See Table 4-1.

II. Stages in the Process

A. Mediator's Opening Statement

1. PURPOSE

The first stage of the mediation process is the mediator's opening statement. The mediator's opening statement occurs immediately after all the participants are assembled to work through the conflict for the first time. The opening statement serves several important purposes and should be given the utmost attention regardless of how much pre-mediation contact the mediator has had with the parties or how much experience the parties or their representatives have had with mediation. The most important purposes of the mediator's opening statement are as follows. First, the opening should explain the nature of mediation, paying particular attention to the roles that the parties and the mediator will play in the process. Second, the mediator's opening should explain the particular mediation process and rules that will be followed. As discussed above, the particulars of the mediation process vary among mediators, so the mediator should explain his or her particular style to help manage the parties' expectations and avoid misunderstandings during the mediation. Third, the mediator's opening statement should establish the mediator as the leader of the mediation session and provide him or her with the opportunity to establish credibility and gain the parties' trust.

Table 4-1: Five Stage Mediation Process

---

1. Mediator's Opening

- Explains the nature of mediation and the roles parties and mediator will play in the process
- Explains steps in the mediation process, mediator's particular style, and mediation guidelines
- Establishes the mediator as the leader of the session and provides him or her the opportunity to establish trust and credibility

---

2. The Parties' Initial Statements

- Provides parties the opportunity to participate directly in the process by explaining their problem
- Provides mediator with information about the problem
- Provides parties the opportunity to hear the other party's concerns from them directly in a controlled environment
- Helps parties to broaden their perspective of the problem

3. Defining the Problem

- Uncovers parties' concerns, needs, and desires (interests)
- Brings order and structure to ill-defined problems
- Provides mediator an opportunity to assist parties in developing an agenda, wherein parties can be assured that their concerns will be addressed

4. Problem Solving and Negotiation

- Assists parties in making good decisions concerning how to resolve the problem
- Assists parties in viewing the problem objectively
- Assists parties in avoiding common negotiation mistakes

5. Final Decision and Closure

- Assists parties to clarify terms of agreement
- Assists parties to finalize and, if appropriate, memorialize agreement in writing
- Brings closure to the matter
- Determines the extent to which the mediator needs to participate in post-mediation activities

2. PRINCIPLES

The opening statement is the mediator's opportunity to set the stage for the entire mediation. To the extent that it is delivered in an understandable, thorough, and professional manner, the mediation and the mediator will benefit immensely. A good mediator opening statement should be: (a) *clear*, (b) *concise*, (c) *conversational*, (d) *confident*, and (e) *constructive*.

a. *Clear*

A mediator should make his or her opening statement *clear* and understandable to the parties. It should be in plain English and should avoid legal or technical terms. While this may seem obvious, it is easy for professionals to unwittingly slip into professional "jargon." Plain language not only minimizes the chance for misunderstandings and confusion, but also lessens the intimidation factor that can start the parties off feeling inhibited and less willing to contribute to an open, honest discussion.

b. *Concise*

The opening statement should be *concise.* In most cases, a relatively short statement lasting no more than five minutes is sufficient. While more time may be necessary in highly complex matters or where parties have several questions, keeping the opening short will increase the likelihood that the parties will remember what you explained and remain engaged in the process.

c. *Conversational*

The opening should be polished, yet *conversational.* What we mean by conversational is that it should not be stilted and overly formal. If you have ever heard a professor reading without inflection from his or her class notes or an uninspired politician reading a speech, you know what we mean. Thus, we do not recommend that you read your opening statement to the parties verbatim. Rather, you should work from an outline of your opening, preferably memorized, so that you can put it into words extemporaneously. This will give the opening an orderly and thorough character, while still feeling fresh and unstilted.

d. *Confident*

The opening should be delivered in a confident manner. To the extent that the opening is given in a smooth and authoritative fashion, you establish yourself as credible and trustworthy. Rehearse beforehand if this is helpful to you. You want to avoid stumbling or stammering as this can be distracting to the listener, causing them to miss important information, and it generates very little confidence in your abilities.

e. *Constructive*

The opening statement should adopt a positive, *constructive* tone. While you cannot and should not promise a favorable outcome for the mediation, you can be hopeful about it. The parties are likely pursuing mediation because previous attempts at settlement have proved futile. They will often enter the mediation feeling frustrated, angry, anxious, or possibly feeling all of those emotions at once. Mood is contagious, and when the mediator projects a positive mood, it can contribute to creating a more productive atmosphere for discussing the problem.

3. ELEMENTS

The mediator's opening statement can be divided into five sections: (a) *preliminaries,* (b) *explaining the nature of mediation,* (c) *explaining the mediation process,* (d) *explaining the guidelines,* and (e) *commitment to begin the mediation.* While there is overlap between these sections and mediators may differ in how they present these elements, each is an essential part of a good opening statement. Although there is no magic about the order in which these elements are addressed, there are a couple of guidelines that are worth noting. First, they should be presented logically. Preliminaries such as the welcome and introductions must by necessity be explained first.

In addition, the nature of mediation and the mediator's role should be explained together because they are closely related. Second, a mediator should be mindful of the principle of primacy and recency. This principle says that when presenting information, listeners will be more likely to remember information presented at the beginning and end of the statement, and be more likely to forget the information in the middle. While all the information provided in the opening statement is important, a mediator should place information he or she particularly wishes to emphasize near the beginning or end, so long as it logically fits there.

a. *Preliminaries*

The preliminaries of an opening statement consist primarily of what might be considered "housekeeping" matters. While they may seem perfunctory, they are by no means trivial and a mediator should not underestimate their importance. They include introduction of the parties, introduction of the mediator, duration of the mediation, attendance by all necessary parties, and settlement authority.

Everyone should know who everyone else is before the mediation begins. Mediators should begin with a welcome and introductions where everyone in the mediation (even the observers) are introduced. Do not assume that everyone knows each other simply because they have been in conflict for years, especially in commercial disputes where companies may send representatives who were not involved in the disputed transaction, or where lawyers may have never met. Whether first names or last names are used is a matter of a mediator's personal style, the relationship of the parties, and the particular culture in which one is mediating. This said, many mediators prefer to use first names to emphasize the informality of the mediation process.

Next, you, the mediator, should introduce yourself. Some mediators also like to provide what is called a "credibility statement," which is a short explanation of the mediator's experience or training. This helps to generate confidence in the mediator's ability to successfully assist the parties. Whether and to what extent you provide a credibility statement will depend on how well the participants know you and how much interaction you have had with them in pre-mediation activities. Where some or all of the parties do not know you well, it is almost always good to provide a brief comment about your relevant experience or training. This is just one small way of building the trust and confidence that is so crucial for you to be effective in the mediation.

Other important preliminary matters to address are duration of the mediation, attendance by all necessary parties, and authority to settle. If the mediator has addressed these issues in pre-mediation, it is always advisable for him to at least remind the participants of what has been agreed upon. In other instances, especially in mediations conducted through a court or referral program, the mediator's opening statement will be the first opportunity to address these matters. As discussed above, we recommend that there be a time set to conclude the mediation, even if all the participants later agree to extend the duration. It is also advisable at the beginning of the mediation to make sure that all necessary parties are present and that those present have authority to settle. There is little that is more frustrating to the parties than toiling for hours to arrive at an agreement only to find that an essential party is absent or the party present lacks authority to finalize the agreement. This is not to say, however, that mediation cannot proceed if a party lacks ultimate settlement authority. In many circumstances productive mediations are conducted when one or both parties must obtain final approval of any agreement reached from a party or a group unable to be present in the mediation. Parties simply need to know the status of authority to settle at the start of the mediation so they are not negotiating under a false assumption that an agreement can be finalized that day.

b. *Explaining the Nature of Mediation*

The opening statement should explain the nature of mediation. This includes an explanation of mediation's voluntary nature, the mediator's impartiality, and the mediator's particular style. For mediation to be effective, the participants must understand the nature of the process in which they will be engaged and the roles and responsibilities of everyone involved. First, the mediator should explain that mediation is a "voluntary" procedure, to the extent that the parties decide whether they wish to resolve the matter or not. Even when a court compels parties to participate in mediation, it is entirely the parties' choice to reach a mutually acceptable agreement; the mediator has no authority to impose a solution on the parties in the way a judge or arbitrator would. Second, the mediator should explain that he or she is impartial and neutral concerning the parties and the dispute. This is sometimes referred to as the "impartiality and neutrality" statement, and it emphasizes that the mediator does not have a stake in the outcome of the matter. When addressing impartiality, it is also usually a good time for the mediator to briefly acknowledge and review any prior interactions with the parties. Finally, the mediator may want to address his or her particular mediation style and philosophy, to the extent that it is strategically appropriate to share this information with the parties. Concerning style and philosophy, a mediator might say the following in his or her opening statement:

> You should understand that different mediators have different styles of working. I view my role as primarily a facilitator of the discussion, making sure that all the things that you have to say are heard and considered. I also will try to help you see the problem objectively. You may be doing that already, but many very bright people in these situations sometimes lose sight of important facts or considerations because they have been dealing with the problem so closely for so long. So, to that end, I might discuss with you how you arrived at your thinking on some issues, and may even feel the need to bring up points to make sure that you have considered them. What I will not be doing is telling you what to do or giving my opinion on the strength of any particular argument. Some mediators do that, and I respect that, but that is not how I work.

c. *Explaining the Mediation Process*

The mediator's opening statement should also explain to the parties the particular process that will be followed. Providing this information helps to reduce anxiety participants may feel about how the mediation will be conducted by letting them know what to expect. Most parties have very little experience with mediation, and they care deeply about the issues being mediated. Providing a procedural roadmap eases trepidation about where the process will take them. Just as it is comforting for a patient to know that a physician has a systematic plan for treating his or her medical problem, it is comforting for a mediation participant to know that the mediator has a systematic plan for assisting him or her with the conflict. This informational step is an especially important one for mediators to take until such time as mediation becomes more commonplace in our culture and the public becomes more familiar with mediation processes.

Most mediators describe the mediation process at a fairly high level of generality during the opening statement. Participants, especially if mediation is new to them, can be easily overwhelmed with too much information. Thus, a healthy balance must be struck, providing enough detail to put a party at ease without encumbering them with more information than they need to know at this stage. For example, a mediator might explain the mediation process this way:

> The way we are going to work is that I will first give each of you a few minutes to explain your concerns that bring you here today. You will have an opportunity to go into greater detail later in the process. Then I am going to take a few minutes summarizing what I think those concerns are and make a list of the questions we need to discuss. Then we are going to work through those questions, and I am hopeful that we can come to a solution to this problem that will be acceptable to both of you.

Mediators should also indicate if and how they will use separate meetings during the mediation. A separate meeting, also known in mediation circles as a *caucus*, is a private meeting between the mediator and one party and/or the party's representative. Separate meetings are used for various reasons but most often are used to discuss matters privately that the party would be uncomfortable or unwilling to discuss in the joint session. Some mediators use separate meetings throughout the mediation (called "shuttle mediation"), some use them sporadically, and some almost never use them. By explaining the policy regarding separate meetings in the opening statement, the mediator establishes an expectation that such meetings are a normal part of the process. If the use of separate meetings is not explained at the beginning of the mediation, when one is called for the first time, parties might make some mistaken, unhelpful assumptions about why the meeting is being held. For example, a party might erroneously assume that something has gone wrong in the mediation or that the mediator favors the party with whom he or she has called the meeting. Once these assumptions are formed, they are difficult to dispel. The purpose and use of separate meetings is discussed in more detail later in this chapter.

d. *Explaining the Guidelines*

Although mediation is an informal process, there are a few practical guidelines or table manners that participants should be asked to follow to foster a productive environment. These are best explained in the opening statement in a proactive manner, rather than during the mediation in response to participants' behaviors. Presenting the guidelines this way gives them a spirit of empowering the parties, rather than carrying the tone of a reprimand. Different mediators may emphasize some guidelines over others, and sometimes the same mediator will modify the list of guidelines depending on the anticipated challenges of a particular matter being mediated. The following are common guidelines that mediators include as part of the opening statement.

e. *One Person Speaks at a Time*

Parties cannot communicate effectively if they are speaking over each other, which is a common and predictable occurrence during mediation. Mediators should instruct the parties not to interrupt one another while the other is speaking. However, this is easier said than done. The natural pattern of conversation, even amicable ones, is sometimes overlapping, with parties occasionally finishing each other's sentences. While a mediator can permit the natural flow of conversation, he should also ensure a balance of dialogue where each party has an opportunity to participate meaningfully. Such meaningful participation is threatened when parties attempt to take over the conversation by force of will. As we will see, this rule takes on a particular importance during the parties' initial statements where each separately explains their version of the problem to the mediator. During each of the parties' initial statements, uninterrupted time to explain their story is both psychologically important to the parties and important for the mediator to hear without distraction. The parties' initial statements are particularly vulnerable to interruptions because they may contain very different views of the factual events or the legal implications of the facts, often provoking an emotional response from the other party.

f. *No Personal Attacks*

Personal attacks, such as name-calling, sarcasm, and belittling, undermine the mediation process. These are common occurrences in highly acrimonious disputes and can be minimized if parties are asked to refrain from engaging in them before they enter into the heat of discussion. In situations where the mediator believes such personal attacks are likely, it is helpful for the mediator to acknowledge that such feelings are natural and understandable in such situations while emphasizing that they are particularly destructive to the mediation process.

g. *Anyone Can Take a Break at Any Time for Any Reason*

Although some mediators like to retain absolute control over breaks, we believe the better policy is to allow parties to take breaks as needed. Providing parties this type of control over the process usually has little negative impact on the mediation's effectiveness and provides parties with a valuable feeling of empowerment over the process.

i. No Binding Agreement Until Reduced to Writing and Signed by the Parties.

It is good policy that there is an understanding that no binding agreement can be reached unless it is put in writing. The mediation process works best when parties communicate ideas, opinions, and potential solutions freely and openly. Free and open discussion is muted, however, if the parties fear that off-handed suggestions might be unintentionally perceived as firm offers of settlement or where they believe a proposal needs to include every minute detail before being made. This rule also helps to prevent misunderstandings among the participants over the terms of the agreement. Oral agreements are often inexact and ambiguous in their language and thus can more easily lead to misinterpretation. Writing disciplines thought and thus is more likely to be clear. Accordingly, to promote open discussion and minimize the chance of disputes arising over the terms of the agreement, it should be explained to the parties at the beginning of the mediation that an agreement is not binding until reduced to writing and signed by the parties.

ii. Confidentiality Obligations.

It has long been deemed beneficial that mediation proceedings be confidential.[1] The underlying premise for confidentiality in mediation is that participants will be more willing to share information, interests, and concerns, and evaluate the relative merits of their positions more objectively if such information subsequently cannot be used against them if the matter is not resolved in mediation. Each jurisdiction governs its own law of confidentiality, and many jurisdictions provide for two distinct forms of confidentiality in mediation: *mediator confidentiality* and *party confidentiality*. Each plays a critical role in fostering the open and honest communication necessary for effective problem solving. Consequently, the mediator must be familiar with and explain the contours of confidentiality to the participants. Because of the importance of confidentiality and its complexity, we will explain it in detail below in Section 4—*Confidentiality in Mediation*, below.

---

1. Lawrence R. Freedman & Michael L. Prigoff, *Confidentiality in Mediation: The Need for Protection*, 2 Ohio St. J. Disp. Resol. 37 (1986).

iii. Commitment to Comply.

To increase the likelihood of compliance with mediation guidelines, the mediator should obtain an explicit commitment from the parties to follow them. Research has shown that people who publicly commit to abide by rules are more apt to follow them than those who are merely told the rules.[2] This is so because people wish to appear consistent with prior words and deeds. The effectiveness of this technique is illustrated by its use at a restaurant to address the problem of people who do not show up for table reservations. A restaurant owner told the receptionist to stop instructing patrons to, "Please call us if you change your plans." Instead, the owner told the receptionist to start asking patrons, "*Will* you please call us if you change your plans?" and wait for a response. By asking for a commitment from people to call if their plans changed, the reservation "no-show" rate dropped from 30 percent to 10 percent.[3] Moreover, even if the party does fail to follow a guideline during the mediation, a mediator has more influence over the party to bring them back into compliance because of the party's previous public commitment to comply.

h. *Commitment to Begin the Mediation*

Gaining a commitment from the parties to begin the mediation is the last step in the mediator's opening statement. It assists the parties in making the necessary transition from listener to active participants in the mediation process. Moreover, like commitment to the mediation guidelines, it provides general motivation to parties to live up to their promise of actively participating in the mediation. This is also a good time to ask if there are any questions about anything covered in the opening. Such questions should be answered clearly but succinctly. A delicate balance is required between the needs of the questioner on the one hand and avoiding over-elaborate answers and delay on the other.

4. CONFIDENTIALITY IN MEDIATION

Mediation is commonly described as a "confidential process" because it is usually conducted with a significant degree of privacy. The scope and degree of confidentiality required, however, varies considerably from jurisdiction to jurisdiction. The primary reason for mediation confidentiality is to promote candor in mediation discussions. Knowing the mediation communications are bound by confidentiality increases the likelihood that parties will be open and honest in their discussions, and the more that open and honest information is shared in a mediation, the more likely it is that the parties will resolve their problem.[4]

---

2. Robert B. Cialdini, Influence: Science and Practice 61 (2001).
3. *Id.* at 74 (the restaurant was Gordon's in Chicago).
4. Ellen Waldman, Mediation Ethics 227 (2011); Ellen Deason, *The Need for Trust as a Justification for Confidentiality in Mediation: A Cross-Disciplinary Approach*, 54 U. Kan. L. Rev 1387 (2006).

The purpose of this section is to introduce you to the nature of mediation confidentiality generally, so you can better navigate the often complex confidentiality rules in whichever jurisdictions you may serve as a mediator or participate in mediation, whether as an advocate or as a party. Understanding the rules of mediation confidentiality are particularly important for mediators because, as we will see, they have an obligation to explain confidentiality to mediation participants. This section will address seven aspects of mediation confidentiality with which a person participating in mediation, in any capacity, should be familiar: (i) a mediator's duty to not share what he or she has learned in the mediation process with anyone outside of the mediation, (ii) a mediator's duty to not share what he or she has learned from one mediation participant with another mediation participant without permission, (iii) a mediation participant's duty to not share information obtained in the mediation process with anyone outside of the mediation, (iv) exclusion of using mediation communications as evidence in subsequent legal proceedings, (v) exclusion of calling mediators as witnesses or of subpoenaing mediator notes in subsequent legal proceedings, (vi) exceptions to mediation confidentiality and evidentiary rules, and (vii) a mediator's duty to explain confidentiality rules to participants.

a. *Mediator's Duty to Keep Mediation Communications Confidential*

A mediator has a duty to keep information and observations acquired through the mediation process confidential. A mediator's duty of confidentiality goes to the very heart of the mediation process, and it has been correctly observed that "a mediator's duty to keep confidences is mediation's most compelling and straightforward ethical imperative."[5] The mediator's duty to keep confidences is usually embodied in a jurisdiction's rules, court procedures, or statutes that govern mediation. Yet a strong argument can be made that, as one of the helping professions, mediation creates reasonable expectations by clients that information they or their representatives share during mediation will not be disclosed by the mediator without permission, even absent explicit rules governing mediation privacy.[6]

Most U.S. jurisdictions have rules that govern mediation and mediator behavior. Many of these rules are based on the Model Standards of Conduct for Mediators, which state the following regarding a mediator's duty to keep party confidences: "A mediator shall maintain the confidentiality of all information obtained by the mediator in mediation, unless otherwise agreed to by the parties or required by applicable law."[7] The Model Standards further state: "A mediator should not communicate to any non-participant information about how the parties acted in the mediation. A mediator may report if required, whether parties appeared at a scheduled mediation

---

5. ELLEN WALDMAN, MEDIATION ETHICS 227 (2011).
6. OMER SHAPIRA, A THEORY OF MEDIATORS' ETHICS 271–72 (2016).
7. MODEL STANDARDS OF CONDUCT FOR MEDIATORS STD. V.

and whether or not the parties reached a resolution."[8] The high value that the Model Standards place on mediator confidentiality is followed in most jurisdictions.[9]

b. *Mediator's Duty to Keep Information Shared by One Party Confidential from Other Parties*

A mediator also has a duty to not reveal information to one party that he has learned in a separate session with another party without that party's permission. The Florida Rule is representative of similar rules throughout the country: "Information obtained during caucus [a separate meeting] may not be revealed by the mediator to any other mediation participant without the consent of the disclosing party."[10] A prohibition of sharing information learned from one party to another party, however, does not mean that a mediator cannot use that information to help the parties come to an agreement. If in a partnership dissolution dispute, for example, a mediator learns that one partner values certain partnership assets more than others, the mediator may employ this information without breaching his confidentiality duty by strategically shaping his questioning of the other partner to see if that partner has different interests and preferences about assets that may make a deal between the partners possible.

c. *Mediation Participants May Also Be Bound by Confidentiality*

Although less commonly codified than mediator confidentiality, some jurisdictions also impose confidentiality on mediation participants. For example, the Texas Civil Practice and Procedure Code provides the following: "[A] communication relating to the subject matter of any civil or criminal dispute *made by a participant* in an alternative dispute resolution procedure, whether before or after the institution of formal judicial proceedings, *is confidential*, [and] *is not subject to disclosure....*"[11] In contrast, California has no such provision. That said, it is common for mediation agreements to include a term similar to the Texas rule that imposes confidentiality on mediation participants. Indeed, in most instances, a jurisdiction's rules regarding mediation confidentiality are a default that the participants can contractually alter. However, there is an important exception to parties' ability to contractually impose confidentiality. Increasingly, jurisdictions are enacting legislation that prohibits settlement agreements from being confidential if the allegations involve sexual assault, sexual harassment, or discrimination.[12]

---

8. *Id.*

9. "A mediator shall maintain confidentiality of all information revealed during mediation except where disclosure is required or permitted by law or is agreed to by all parties." FLA. RULES FOR CERTIFIED AND COURT APPOINTED MEDIATORS.

10. FLA. RULES FOR CERTIFIED AND COURT APPOINTED MEDIATORS R. 10.360(b).

11. 2005 TEX. CIV. PRAC. & REM. CODE, Ch. 154. Alternative Dispute Resolution Procedures (emphasis supplied).

12. See, for example, California, which prohibits restricting disclosure of "factual information related to a claim filed in a civil action...or an administrative proceeding" that involves sexual assault, sexual harassment, or discrimination. CAL. CODE OF CIV. PROC. § 12964.5 (2021).

d. *Exclusion of Using Mediation Communications as Evidence in Subsequent Legal Proceedings*

By far the most common way that jurisdictions protect information obtained in a mediation is by establishing exclusions on the information that may be introduced as evidence in subsequent legal proceedings. These exclusions are usually styled as evidentiary rules that are distinct from the confidentiality rules imposed on the mediator and the parties, whether imposed by the jurisdiction or agreed to by contract. Examples of mediation communications that are usually the subject of exclusions in subsequent legal proceedings include settlement offers, admissions of responsibility for injury or liability, and concessions about the relative merits of legal arguments.

California has among the strictest mediation evidentiary rules in the United States. It states:

> No evidence of anything said or any admission made for the purpose of, in the course of, or pursuant to, a mediation or a mediation consultation is admissible or subject to discovery, and disclosure of the evidence shall not be compelled, in any arbitration, administrative adjudication, civil action, or other noncriminal proceeding in which, pursuant to law, testimony can be compelled to be given.

It is noteworthy to point out that the statute covers not only information obtained during the mediation but also during the "mediation consultation," which is not the case with many other jurisdictions. Further, the California Supreme Court has interpreted the statute to cover not only communications that occur in the mediation among the mediator and the participants but also communications between a party and his or her lawyer during the mediation but outside the presence of the mediator. In *Cassel v. Superior Court*, the California Supreme Court held that a private communication between a client and his attorney during the mediation, made outside the presence of the mediator or other participants, was covered by the evidentiary mediation communication statute and thus inadmissible in a malpractice action against the attorney for allegedly "badgering" his client to accept the settlement.[13]

However, it is important to appreciate that not all information communicated in a mediation can be excluded from evidence in subsequent legal proceedings. Generally, information communicated in a mediation will not be excluded from evidence when the information is known outside of the mediation or is available in discovery in litigated matters. For example, if a party in a personal injury litigation based on a

---

13. *Cassel v. Superior Court*, 51 Cal. 4th 113 (2011). *But see Alfieri v. Solomon*, 358 Or. 383 (2015), in which the Oregon Supreme Court interpreted a similar mediation communication evidentiary rule to allow a party suing their former attorney for malpractice to introduce evidence of communications that occurred in a meeting between them during a mediation, reasoning that the confidentiality rule only covered communications in which the mediator participated.

car accident explains what she saw and heard the day of the accident, she would not be excluded from sharing that same testimony at trial simply because she also previously shared it during the mediation. The California evidentiary statute is representative of many jurisdictions when it says that "[e]vidence otherwise admissible or subject to discovery outside of a mediation or a mediation consultation shall not be or become inadmissible or protected from disclosure solely by reason of its introduction or use in a mediation or a mediation consultation."[14]

e. *Exclusion of Calling Mediators as Witnesses or of Subpoenaing Mediator Notes*

Another way most jurisdictions protect mediation confidentiality is by excluding parties from calling their mediators as witnesses or subpoenaing their mediators' notes for use in subsequent legal proceedings. The Texas rule is typical of many jurisdictions: "Any record made at an alternative dispute resolution procedure is confidential, and the participants or the third party facilitating the procedure may not be required to testify in any proceedings relating to or arising out of the matter in dispute or be subject to process requiring disclosure of confidential information or data relating to or arising out of the matter in dispute."[15] There are, however, exceptions to mediator confidentiality and the exclusion of mediation communications from subsequent legal proceedings, as we will now explore.

f. *Exceptions to Mediation Confidentiality*

Mediation confidentiality is not absolute. Most jurisdictions compel, or at least permit, mediators to share mediation communications in circumstances where disclosure is necessary to protect important public interests.[16] Jurisdictions differ considerably in the degree and type of mediation confidentiality exceptions they permit. Thus, mediators and mediation participants must be familiar with those exceptions in the jurisdictions in which they practice. Below are the most common exceptions to mediation confidentiality:

- Threats of bodily injury or the commission of a violent crime.[17]

- Communications used to plan or commit a crime.[18]

- Evidence of abuse or neglect of children, the elderly, or the disabled.[19]

- Evidence of professional misconduct or malpractice by a party or representative of a party.[20]

---

14. CAL.. EVID. CODE § 1120.

15. TEX. CIV. PRAC. & REM. CODE ANN. § 154.053(b).

16. SHAPIRA, *supra* note 6, at 82.

17. UNIFORM MEDIATION ACT § 6(a)(3); N.C. Rules of Court, MODEL STANDARDS, STANDARD III (C)(2) (2010).

18. UNIFORM MEDIATION ACT § 6(a)(4); OR. REV. STAT. § 36220(6) (2010).

19. UNIFORM MEDIATION ACT § 6(a)(7).

20. *Id.* at § 6(a)(6). *But see Cassel v. Superior Court,* 51 Cal. 4th 113 (2011).

This is by no means a comprehensive list of exceptions to mediator confidentiality, but only the most common ones found throughout U.S. jurisdictions. For example, some jurisdictions create exceptions to mediator confidentiality specifically for fraud and threat of damage to real property.[21] Moreover, it is important to note that mediators must understand the contours and exceptions to mediation confidentiality not only so they can conduct a proper mediation and meet their reporting duties but also because they have an obligation to explain mediation confidentiality to participants.

g. *Mediator's Duty to Explain Confidentiality to Participants*

Mediators also have a duty to explain the mediation process to participants, and this often includes explaining mediation confidentiality. Indeed, many mediation codes specifically require a mediator to explain confidentiality to participants. For example, the Model Standards state that a "mediator shall promote understanding among the parties of the extent to which the parties will maintain confidentiality of information they obtain in a mediation."[22] California is a jurisdiction that explicitly prescribes a mediator's duty to explain the contours of confidentiality to mediation participants. The California Rules state that "[a]t or before the outset of the first mediation session, a mediator must provide the participants with a general explanation of the confidentiality of mediation proceedings."[23]

The potential complexity of mediation confidentiality presents a challenge for mediators in meeting their obligation to adequately explain confidentiality at the outset. This is particularly true because the mediator's opening statement should be relatively short while including a significant amount of other important information. Providing too much detail about confidentiality in the mediator's opening statement would render it too long and cumbersome, thereby diminishing its impact. Below are a few ways to make it easier for a mediator to fulfill his or her obligation to explain mediation confidentiality in a pre-mediation meeting or in a mediator's opening statement:

- Oral explanations should be relatively straightforward and short. But a mediator can supplement the oral explanation by providing more detail about confidentiality, especially about confidentiality exceptions, in the agreement to mediate.

- A mediator should tailor the confidentiality explanation to the matter at hand. If the matter involves a dispute about a property line between landowners, for example, a mediator need not include exceptions about evidence of child abuse in the oral explanation.

---

21. KAN. STAT. ANN § 5-512(b)(3) (2010) (exception for fraud); OR. REV. STAT. § 36.220(6) (2010) (exception for threat to real property).
22. MODEL STANDARDS OF CONDUCT FOR MEDIATORS STD. V.
23. CAL. RULES OF COURT R. 3.854.

- When parties are represented by counsel, a mediator can spend less time on the confidentiality explanation than when a party is unrepresented, because it can be assumed the party's counsel will answer any further questions a party may have about confidentiality.

Here is a sample mediation confidentiality explanation in a litigated case in which the parties are represented by counsel and in a jurisdiction that prevents parties from using mediation communications in subsequent legal proceedings but does not require party confidentiality:

> As your attorneys may have explained to you, mediation is a confidential process in several ways. First, I will not share anything we discuss today with anyone. Also, if one of you tells me something in a separate meeting, I will not share that with the other party unless you give me permission. By participating in mediation, you will not be able to use what we say here in a legal preceding if we do not resolve the matter today. For example, if one party makes an offer of settlement, the other party cannot introduce that offer into evidence at a trial for any reason. That said, information that is otherwise known outside the mediation or has been or can be uncovered during the discovery phase of the litigation will not be deemed confidential just because you bring it up in the mediation. For example, if one of you explains today what you saw and heard at the accident, you can also share that information at trial. You also have agreed not to call me as a witness or subpoena any of the notes that I make here today. The exceptions to my confidentiality are if I see credible evidence that requires me to prevent a crime, a fraud, or someone getting hurt. Any questions?

5. EXAMPLE OF A MEDIATOR'S OPENING STATEMENT

Every mediator's opening statement needs to be adapted to what is suitable to the parties, the dispute, the circumstances of the mediation, and other relevant factors. A "Mediator's Opening Statement Checklist" is included in Appendix 7. The following is an example of one such statement that contains implicit assumptions about all of the above matters. It would require significant amendments, including abbreviation, in many circumstances.

Welcome. My name is John Smith and I am the mediator today. You both know each other, but you may not know each other's attorneys. Jane, this is Patty Rushdie, who is assisting Peter. Peter, this is Alan Pope, who is Jane's attorney. Now please call me John... Are you also comfortable with first names...?	**(a) Preliminaries** Welcome and Introductions

Now before we get going, I would like to check with you on time. We originally agreed to meet today for up to four hours, can you all recommit to that…? Any parking limits or other time constraints…? I think we have everyone here that we need, and you both told me over the phone that you both have the authority to commit to an agreement today if it meets your needs. Is that correct…?

Checking time constraints, necessary parties present, and settlement authority

Now just by way of background, Jane, you approached me about having a mediation, and I spent some time talking to you on the phone and sent you out some written information, and Peter I did the same with you. And you both know that I have spoken to your attorneys by phone and have received the papers which you prepared for me. That is all the contact I have had about this matter, and I have had about the same access to both of you. Are there any questions about that…?

Disclosure of extent of prior contact with parties Checking for questions

Now you've made the decision to come to mediation yourselves and generally this is a better way of dealing with problems than going into battle. So that's a commendable start. Let me tell you briefly a few things about mediation, though I realize that you may have heard some of this before. Mediation is really a structured opportunity for those with a problem to make decisions about it themselves. My role as the mediator is not to make those decisions for you; nor is it to tell you what decisions to make or to advise you on the law or on technical matters. My role is essentially to assist you along the way in your own decision-making. Sometimes emotion or poor communication makes it difficult for people to deal with problems. The mediator's role is to guide them down the path of decision-making, so to speak, and help them to avoid the obstacles and pitfalls. In aiding your decision-making, I will make sure everyone has an opportunity to be heard and I may ask questions that might help to make sure that we fully understand the situation. Peter and Jane, you will be discussing the situation and making the decisions, and your advisers will assist you in that process. So the objective today is for you to make decisions on the issues you are facing, and my role is to assist you in that process. Any questions…?

(b) Nature of Mediation Explaining mediator style Checking for questions

Now I am a neutral and impartial party in the mediation and you do not have to try and persuade me about the merits of your case. If at any stage you feel a lack of impartiality, please let me know. As you know from the materials my office sent you, I practiced for ten years as a family law attorney, representing at different times both husbands and wives, and have been mediating divorce matters for the last five of those years. While every situation is unique, I have considerable experience in working through the kinds of problems we will be discussing today.

Neutrality and impartiality statement
Credibility statement

Now this is what will happen in the mediation process. Shortly, I will ask each of you in turn to explain to me what your main concerns are today. This need only be a brief overview as there will be time later to go into the details. After you have each made a statement I will summarize it back to you and then we will confirm the matters in respect of which there already is agreement and what matters still require decisions. I will then write these issues on the whiteboard and we can use it as an agenda for the discussion. We will then work through all the issues on the board, looking at options for dealing with them, and making as many decisions as we can.

(c) The mediation process

A normal part of the mediation process is for the mediator to meet separately with each of the parties. As you have advisers, I would meet with Jane and Alan together, and with Peter and Patty together. This gives me an opportunity to see how the mediation is going for each of you, it allows you to raise matters that have not come up when we were together, and it allows the other party to have a break and to think about settlement options. It is also an opportunity for refreshments and to make any calls if you so need. Normally I hold these sessions when we have already worked through most of the issues but you are free to ask for one earlier if you have the need. Are there any questions, Jane…? Peter…? Of course this is a flexible process and anyone can ask for an adjournment at any reasonable time.

Explaining the use of separate meetings

Now in my experience, mediation works best where we all observe some basic guidelines. It helps if we all speak one at a time, and even where emotions run high it is useful if no one denigrates the other. As you know this is a non-smoking building, and we should probably also make it a mobile-free zone while we are together. We could call these the table manners for the mediation. Can you commit to them, Peter...? Jane...?

(d) Explaining guidelines Obtaining commitment to guidelines

I just need to refer to one more matter before we begin. Mediation is conducted confidentially, which means that, in so far as the law allows, I will not disclose anything said here today. I will be taking some brief written notes, but these will be destroyed after the mediation and cannot be accessed by either of you. Mediation confidentiality also means that should the matter go to court, which we hope it will not, then neither of you can present evidence about what the other said at the mediation or produce documents that they made for the mediation. Do you understand the basic principles here...? The other important aspect of mediation confidentiality is that anything I learn in our separate meetings that you do not wish me to share with the other party, I will not share. Please check with your attorneys if you require more advice on these points.

Explaining confidentiality Checking for questions

As regards the outcome, the situation today is that any agreements will not be binding until they have been reduced to writing and signed by both of you. Is that understood?

Agreement not binding until put into writing

Now just before we begin, are there any questions that either of you have about mediation generally, or about what will happen here today? Jane...? Peter...?

Final check for questions

Good, are you both then prepared to continue along the lines I have discussed...? Thank you. Now Peter, since you approached me first about the mediation, I would like to start with you. Can you tell me what your concerns are here today...?

(e) Commitment to begin mediation Transition to party statements

6. OTHER MATTERS

a. *Omitting an Important Element of the Opening Statement*

What should be done if a mediator omits an important element of the opening statement? This depends, as with missing cooking ingredients, on when the discovery is made. Generally, a missing element can be added at any stage of the mediation, provided the mediator openly acknowledges the oversight and emphasizes its "normality" in mediation. For example, "I'm sorry that I forgot to tell you in the beginning that it is a normal feature of mediation that each party not interrupt the other during the initial statement." After a certain stage in the mediation, as with cooking, it will be too late to add the missing ingredient; in other words, adding an instruction in too late may result in it having little impact on the final product.

b. *Mediator's Opening Statement Where There Are Two or More Mediators*

There should be no sense of hierarchy between co-mediators, which entails that they should share the opening statement rather than leave all or most of it to one mediator. How they divide it up is a matter of logic, convenience, and training, subject only to the necessity of operating as a team. Because a division of tasks is more important during this stage of co-mediation than in later stages, co-mediators require a clear understanding of who will say what, and what their "cues" will be, in order to operate as a team.

B. The Parties' Initial Statements

The *parties' initial statements* stage of the mediation consists of two distinct but closely related tasks, the *parties' statements* and the *mediator's summary* of those statements. Each is addressed separately below.

1. THE PARTIES' STATEMENTS

a. *Purpose*

Immediately after the mediator's opening statement, the parties are invited to make their own initial statement. Here, parties begin to play the dominant role in the process for the first time, but in a controlled and structured way. A party's initial statement serves several important purposes. First, it allows each party to make their first contribution without interruption or confrontation. This satisfies their need to have their say and be heard. Second, it provides information to the mediator about the parties' concerns, which is especially important when the mediator has had no prior contact with the parties, as a basis for understanding the dispute and developing an agenda. Third, it provides an opportunity for each party to hear the other's presentation in the party's own words, which may promote a better understanding of each other's concerns. Fourth, it confronts each party with some aspects of the other's case in order to create doubt about their own position.

It is not within the purposes of the party statements to allow discussion, negotiation, or altercation between the parties at this stage, nor to allow the parties to propose and accept solutions. Mediators must be assertive in preventing these forms of interaction that experience and science suggest are premature and counterproductive. As in cooking, timing is important in mediation and the mediator controls the timer.

b. *Scope*

The parties' initial statements should deal with broad themes, not with matters of detail. This means that they need only be brief, often no more than five to ten minutes each. Of course, as the nature of the parties' situation increases in complexity, so too will the initial statement. Though this brief overview may appear at first blush to be inadequate, there will be opportunities later in the mediation process for the parties to elaborate. Requirements concerning time and level of detail should be explained to the parties, and where the statements become long-winded, repetitive, or excessively detailed, the mediator should refer back to these constraints. Loquacious parties might need to be reassured that matters of detail can be dealt with at later stages of the mediation.

This topic raises the question of the extent to which mediation clients should be able to "tell their stories." There are many advantages in encouraging storytelling by clients. It allows them to present things in their own words, it discloses relevant details, it allows the listener to identify client interests, and it provides satisfaction for the teller.[24] On the other hand, stories tend to focus on the past and reinforce blame and other negative judgments. Lawyers and courts tend not to allow free storytelling but rather encourage structured disclosures from clients. As we shall see below, mediation should provide more leeway than courts for storytelling. However, this need not occur entirely within the party statements. Keep the parties' initial statements short and direct; storytelling is to take place during the *problem solving and negotiation* stage. A benefit of proceeding in this way is that it encourages parties to focus on their most important issues and concerns in the initial statements. This can provide the mediator with helpful insights into the dispute that may become useful in later stages of the mediation.

c. *Focus*

One of the ways mediators help parties resolve disputes is by bringing order and focus to the seeming chaos of conflict. To do this, mediators can invite the parties to focus on specific information or factors in their statements. This increases the probability that the party will be succinct, although it certainly does not guarantee it. In

---

24. NADJA M. SPEGEL, BERNADETTE ROGERS & ROSS P. BUCKLEY, NEGOTIATION: THEORY AND TECHNIQUES 44–46 (1998).

other words, the wording the mediator uses to *invite* a party to provide an initial statement influences what the party will say.

What the mediator wishes the party to focus on in the initial statement will depend on the mediator's style of mediation. For example, a *facilitative* mediator may invite the parties to explain their "concerns," an evaluative mediator may invite the parties to explain their "arguments," and a transformative mediator may invite parties to explain issues concerning their "relationship" with the other party. The point is that the mediator must be intentional in the language he or she chooses to use in inviting the initial party statement as it is can bring a productive focus to the statement and to the discussion that follows. The following are different ways a mediator might attempt to focus the party statement through invitation:

- Fact-based: "*Tell me the history and facts in this case as you see them…*";
- Rights-based: "*Tell me what your arguments and evidence are…*";
- Positional: "*Tell me what you are here for, what would you like to achieve in the mediation…*";
- Legalistic: "*Tell me what the issues are between you today…*";
- Narrative: "*Tell me what happened and what effect it had on you…*";
- Interest-based: "*Tell me what your concerns are today…*";
- Problem solving: "*Tell me what decisions need to be made today…*"; and
- Procedure-based: "*Tell me first how you think we should go about resolving the problems that we are dealing with.…*"

Each approach has its advantages and disadvantages. The first four approaches are more typical of an *evaluative* mediation style, while the last four are more typical of a *facilitative* mediation style. Our preference is for using a more facilitative style, such as an interest-based or problem-solving approach, although the others do have their legitimate use. An interest-based or problem-solving focus will be counterintuitive for many mediation participants who want to be positional, legalistic, or rights-based, and will require some explanation and justification if the mediator wishes the parties to adopt one of them. For example, a mediator might say, "In my experience it helps if, instead of getting into a debate over who did or said what to whom, you each tell me briefly what your current concerns are that you would like dealt with in the mediation." In summary, the mediator should craft the invitation of the parties' initial statements to focus the discussion in a direction that is most productive for that particular problem.

d. *Who Makes the Party Statements?*

The parties themselves make the initial statements. However, when there are lawyers present, the practice varies. Some mediators insist that the parties make the statements and invite the lawyers or other advisers to supplement them if necessary. This is consistent with the philosophical assumptions of mediation and the need for the parties to feel that they have control over their own dispute. Other mediators request the lawyers to make the statements, and then invite the parties themselves to add their contributions. These arrangements give a dominant role to lawyers in the mediation process and reassure them that their clients will not prejudice their cases by admitting liability or making other detrimental statements. However, mediators should be careful about establishing a strong sense of hierarchy, lawyer domination, and exclusive focus on legal rights at the expense of client interests and party participation.

Our preferred practice is to allow the parties to decide among themselves who will speak first, and then ask the other participant if they have anything to add. For example, a mediator might say, "Ms. Jones (client) and Ms. Wang (lawyer), briefly tell me what your concerns are today." If Ms. Wang, the lawyer, starts, then the mediator might give Ms. Jones, the client, a chance to add to the statement. In this way, the parties retain some control over the process and feel a valuable sense of empowerment, even as the mediator retains the right to hear from everybody.

Where there are more than two people on a side, it may be advisable for the mediator to invite each side to nominate a single spokesperson to provide the initial statement and judiciously invite the others to add to it if necessary. If everybody is allowed to speak there is a legitimate fear that this stage of the mediation will become too protracted. The mediator can reassure the other participants that they will have opportunities to speak in later stages of the process.

e. *Party Speaking Order*

There is some significance, albeit limited, in who makes the first party statement. Research shows that the first speaker establishes a narrative framework that can predominate and be more influential on listening parties, such as the mediator, than subsequent statements. This is referred to as the "tenacity of the first voice."[25] In other words, mediators might be more inclined to believe the first speaker than the second or subsequent speakers where their versions differ from the first. Although mediators do not make binding decisions, their first impressions may affect the way in which they conduct the process. Another point of significance is that the second speaker is likely to be defensive and try to *deny, justify,* or *excuse* what has been said by the first, instead of providing his or her distinct concerns. This usually detracts from the objectives of the party statements. To address this problem, as discussed below, mediators often instruct later speakers that they are to give their own versions of events and not to respond to what they have heard.

Nevertheless, mediators would be wise to downplay the significance of speaking first. The mediator should remember that while they are responsible for conducting the process fairly, doing so depends on the overall conduct of the mediation and not on a single decision early in the process. Where parties express concerns over who

---

25. MARGOT COSTANZO, PROBLEM SOLVING 27 (1995).

speaks first, a mediator can explain that there is no major disadvantage in speaking second, and each party will have approximately equal speaking time. Also, there will be other occasions for parties to go first, for example, in the separate meetings, so that "going first" can be rotated.

f. *Deciding Who Speaks First*

Most mediators decide themselves who should give the first party statement. This is the preferred practice. It shows that the mediator is in charge of the process, and it prevents any conflict between the parties arising at an early stage. Moreover, there may be some strategic advantages or logical rationale in arranging for one party to speak before another. In supporting their decision concerning who should speak first, mediators need to have both a private rationale and a public explanation for it.

i. Private Rationales for Who Speaks First.

As in all other interventions, mediators require a hypothesis to support their decision on who should speak first. In cases in which a party is asserting a claim against another, such as in personal injury or contract disputes, the person making the claim usually speaks first. This is because it is logical to hear the nature of the claim before hearing why it is flawed, unreasonable, or invalid. It helps to set the parameters of the dispute. However, some disputes do not neatly create claimant and defender roles. Family conflicts and business disputes between partners, for example, often present joint problems over which the parties are simply divided. The following are some potential hypotheses for who speaks first:

- The perceived "weaker" party should speak first, to reassure them about the fairness of the process;
- The more anxious party should speak first, to settle them down;
- The less anxious party should speak first, so that the other can settle down;
- The party not legally represented should speak first, so that they do not feel disadvantaged; and
- The party claiming something from the other, such as a plaintiff in a civil action, should speak first, because they need to set the parameters of the negotiations.

This is not an exhaustive list. Nor is it possible to provide a general rule for what rationale works best in what circumstance. In deciding who should speak first, the mediator must use his or her best judgment based upon the type of matter and the personalities of the participants involved.

ii. Public Explanations for Who Speaks First.

In order to legitimize their decision and retain the parties' trust, mediators should give a brief explanation for their choice of first speaker. Clearly, mediators should not always express publicly an underlying rationale like those above for asking one party to speak first. However, they need to provide a plausible public reason, which may involve some mediator license, for example:

- "I would like John, the plaintiff, to begin because he is bringing the claim…";
- "I would like to hear from Marisol first because she approached the mediation center…"; and
- "I would like to hear from Al first because Marisol approached the mediation center…."

iii. Allowing the Parties to Choose Who Speaks First.

Some mediators avoid making a choice between the parties out of fear of losing the trust of the second speaker. They might ask the parties to decide themselves who should speak first. This may work well in some cases but create conflict in others. A mediator might resort to random choice, for example, by flipping a coin. This is quick and prevents any conflict but might be seen as a flippant way to commence an important negotiation. Our preference is for mediators to show leadership in selecting the first speaker and to use appropriate explanations to help the parties accept their decision, without making too big an issue of it. In practice, the mediator's choice is seldom challenged.

g. *Preventing a Defensive Response from the Second Speaker*

Mediators should not invite the second speaker to reply to the first party's statement. For example, a mediator *should not say*, "Now, Mr. McNair, how do you respond to what Ms. Hawke has said?" That approach will allow the first speaker's definition of the problem to predominate and the second speaker is likely to justify, deny, or make excuses in response. Rather, mediators should direct the second party to give his or her statement without reference to what they have just heard. They can also specifically instruct the second speaker not to respond to the first and instead to speak directly to the mediator. For example, a mediator should say, "Now, Mr. McNair, without responding to Ms. Hawke, please speak to me and tell me in your words what your concerns are today." In following this approach, the mediator has a much better chance of setting the parties up for a dialogue rather than a debate.

h. *The Party Statements Should Be Addressed to the Mediator*

As has already been suggested, the party statements should be addressed to the mediator directly and not to the other party. Additionally, it is important that no interruptions or interactions are allowed between the parties during their initial statements to ensure that there is an uninterrupted speaking opportunity. This is designed both to avoid an interaction between the parties that might derail an initial statement and to afford the mediator the opportunity to use good listening skills to ensure that the communication is accurately received and that the speaker feels heard. The mediator will dispense with this structured form of discourse later.

i. *The Mediator's Role During the Parties' Initial Statements*

The mediator's role during the parties' initial statements is to listen, keep the speaking party focused, and prevent interruptions. Listening requires mediators to exercise good attention and concentration skills and to display appropriate body language. The mediator may also have to ask questions, but these should mainly be open-ended questions. Open-ended questions are broad inquiries that require the party to provide explanations. For example, "Can you tell me more about your financial condition?" Some clarifying questions may also be necessary where a party is unclear or ambiguous, but this is not the time for seeking detailed information, asking probing questions, or otherwise embarking on a series of leading questions that will either detract from the party telling their own story or make them defensive. When a speaker stops talking, the mediator may invite more information by asking in an open-ended way, "Is there anything else?" or "Would you like to go on?"

As suggested above, mediator intervention will also be required where a party statement is excessively long or descends into unnecessary detail for this stage of the proceedings. In such a case, the mediator should both remind the parties that the purpose of the party statements is to provide a broad overview of the problem and to reassure the speaker that there will be a later opportunity to go into detail. Where there is repetition of a particular fact or theme, the mediator will need to acknowledge the point being made, and even write it down, to cure the "broken record" symptom.

As discussed above, the mediator should also pay particular attention to preventing interruptions from the other party. Although typically brief, the parties' initial statements have symbolic importance. It is usually the parties' first opportunity to share their concerns in a semi-formal, semi-public setting to an objective third party. Thus, parties should be encouraged to show one another respect and allow each other to provide a statement without interruption. Accordingly, just before inviting the first party to give their initial statement, the mediator should obtain an explicit commitment from both parties to not interrupt the other during the other's initial statement.

Finally, the mediator should respond immediately to any interruptions by reminding the party of his or her previous commitment and explaining that he or she will have the chance to speak. Most parties, most of the time, however, follow the guidelines set out. Once one party has given his or her initial statement without interruption, the mediator should thank the other party for following the guidelines. For example, in transitioning from one party's statement to the other, a mediator might say the following:

> Thank you, Thomas, for allowing Phillip to explain his concerns without interruption. I want to now give you the same opportunity. Thomas, I want to just ask if you could show Phillip the same courtesy he showed you while he

speaks. Can you do that, Phillip…? Now Thomas, briefly, what are the concerns you wish to discuss today?

After the second party has finished without interruption, the mediator should thank the first party for showing similar respect. Acknowledging the parties' cooperative behavior in this way accomplishes two tasks. It provides positive feedback for cooperation, which will increase the likelihood that the parties will continue to cooperate. It also emphasizes the cooperative and productive nature of communication between the parties, which in some conflicts is no small achievement.

j. *Note-Taking by the Mediator*

Many mediators find it useful to take notes during initial statements and the mediation generally. Most mediators take only brief notes, usually words or phrases to record key concerns, interests, common ground, offers, important figures, areas of potential agreements, and concessions. However, it is difficult to practice good listening skills and take comprehensive notes at the same time, though there can be a division of these tasks between two co-mediators. Thus, a mediator should take notes concerning only the most important information.

A common form of note-taking is as follows. The mediator divides a page with a vertical line and heads each column with the name of a different party. As the mediator records words or phrases under the appropriate column, he or she can connect concerns common to both parties with a line or numbered asterisk to assist with the later development of the agenda. For purposes of illustrating this mediator function, and others to follow, review the following fact scenario.

Case Illustration

There is a professional business partnership involving two partners, Fatima and Antonio. Fatima is the older partner in a firm established by her father many years ago. Antonio is the younger partner who was taken into the business when Fatima's son "defected" to another profession. The two have been in dispute over a number of issues for the past seven months and finally agree to sort things out at mediation

This is what the mediator's notes might look like at the end of the party statements:

Partner Fatima	Partner Antonio
Retain the partnership and name	Wants greater share of profits
Retain existing profit-sharing arrangement	More professional workplace needed
Golf and Rotary are important rain-making activities	Need client diversity

Wants to settle dispute here privately	Does not want this to get out of hand
Antonio has bad attitude	Fatima to spend less time on golf and Rotary business
Antonio's clients late in paying	Fatima to use support staff less for private activities
	Committed to retaining partnership

These notes allow the mediator to identify the parties' common interests in retaining the partnership and avoiding a court battle and to recognize that some of Fatima's concerns, such as the late payment of bills, are not shared by Antonio.

Mediators should be consistent with note-taking in that speakers will be conscious of sudden changes, such as the mediator's stopping or recommencing writing. Some mediators may use note-taking as a stream of consciousness or even as a strategic way of reducing the anger of a speaking party. For instance, a speaker may be encouraged to talk more slowly and less emotionally if the mediator insists he or she needs to take more detailed notes.

Finally, as a mediator you must be vigilant in keeping your notes private and confidential. An example will help illustrate the importance of this crucial practice. In a mediation simulation conducted by law school students, one of the student-participants returned to the mediation room following a separate session (caucus). Upon return to the mediation table, the student-participant found the mediator's notes, including a description of the other side's forthcoming offer, sitting openly and unattended; this illustrated not only a vivid breach of confidence by the mediator but also enabled the student-participant to strategically utilize the information if and how he pleased for his individual gain. Fortunately, in this example it was a student—and not a party in an actual mediation—who learned just how easy it can be to break the confidences of separate sessions through inadvertence. Keep your notes secure or with you at all times during the mediation.

k. *Requests for a "Right of Reply"*

The first speaker, or their adviser, might ask for a "right of reply" after listening to the second speaker. In most circumstances, this should be denied for the same reasons that the second speaker was asked not to respond to the statement of the first. Mediation is not a debate or a court-room combat, and a reply is likely to involve justification, denial, or excuse and lead to an adversarial confrontation too early in the process. A summary of the party statements is a more appropriate development at this stage, a topic to which we will now turn.

2. MEDIATOR SUMMARIES OF THE PARTIES' STATEMENTS

a. *Purpose*

Immediately after the parties provide their initial statements, most mediators briefly summarize those statements. The summaries of the parties' statements serve several purposes. For one, they reassure the parties that they have been heard correctly regarding the content of what they have said. Of equal importance, they provide acknowledgment and validation of the emotional side of the parties' statements. They also enable the mediator to check the accuracy of his or her understanding of what has been said and give the parties an opportunity to provide feedback to correct any misunderstandings or add to their statements. Finally, each party hears the other party's concerns from the mediator, which may incline them to listen more attentively.

b. *Process*

Some mediators summarize the parties' initial statements after both parties have made them, while others do so after each party has made their initial statement. To summarize the first statement directly after it has been made, some argue, would be to devote excessive attention to that party and to leave the other in the cold. However, the benefit of summarizing an initial statement immediately after it has been made is that the mediator may be able to summarize it more faithfully. We have no preferred practice in this area, each method having its own strengths and no significant disadvantages.

c. *Types of Summaries*

There are three types of summaries: *actual summaries*, *reframed summaries*, and *cross-summaries*:

i. Actual Summary.

Some of the parties' actual words and phrases are used so that they hear from the mediator's mouth the same terms they have used themselves. When using an actual summary, the mediator should be strategic in their word choices to make very clear they are explaining the parties' perspectives, and not their own. This distances the mediator from statements that are hostile to the other party. For example, in the Fatima and Antonio partnership dispute, an actual summary should begin as follows: "Antonio, *you* began by saying that this matter was quite simple, and that Fatima 'stresses you out' over her old-fashioned ways and needed to change to a more professional style." In contrast, the mediator should not say "Now by way of summary, Fatima stresses you out over her old-fashioned ways."

ii. Reframed Summary.

The mediator changes the perspective of the parties' statements so as to shift to interests, to remove the sting from harsh language, or to focus on the future. In this method, referred to as *reframing*, the mediator avoids the actual words of the parties and provides a sanitized summary. Thus, using the example of the actual summary above, a reframed summary might be phrased as follows: "Antonio, you began by suggesting that this matter should resolve easily and that you wished to discuss how the firm could adapt its practices for the future."

iii. Cross-Summaries.

The mediator asks each side to summarize what they have heard from the other in order for them to walk in each other's shoes: "Fatima, as I foreshadowed earlier, I would now like you to summarize what you heard Antonio say, and then I will ask Antonio to summarize your statement."

In most circumstances, the preferred practice is that of *actual* summaries, in particular because they give the parties the experience of being heard by the mediator. *Reframing* is a technique that should be used later in the mediation because it involves the mediator intentionally shifting the focus of the discussion. Parties are more receptive to this type of mediator control after the mediator establishes a degree of trust, which is usually not sufficiently established at this earlier stage of the mediation. The use of *cross-summaries* involves several risks for what we believe is marginal gain. The most significant of these risks is that the parties will do a poor job of summarizing, thus failing to accomplish many of the important purposes of the summaries and perhaps further exacerbating the conflict.

C. Defining the Problem

1. PURPOSE

A problem well-defined is a problem half-resolved. It is important to list and prioritize the issues comprehensively before moving on to their resolution. When parties spend inadequate time defining the conflict, the problem-solving process is more difficult and inefficient. Moreover, since parties often present the problem in simplistic and positional terms, their real concerns, needs, and desires are often obscured. Mediators can make a valuable contribution to the participants' negotiations by assisting them in defining the parameters of the conflict objectively and constructively, in all its complexity, taking special care to uncover the participants' true concerns, needs, and desires.

Defining the problem also brings structure to the mediation that provides several benefits to both mediator and participants. It first helps to harness the issues, which are often presented in chaotic and confusing terms. Once the issues are defined, the mediator can set an agenda for the rest of the mediation, prioritize issues, and subdivide the dispute into smaller parts to make it less formidable. Setting a clear agenda has several benefits. For one, the participants are reassured by a process where their concerns are noted at the outset, which in turn helps them gain confidence that their issues will be dealt with during the course of the mediation. In addition, where the participants have brought their own biased perceptions to the table, setting a clear agenda reframes the conflict in more objective and neutral terms. The agenda also confirms that the dispute is finite, shifting attention and focus to the matters on the list rather than all matters under the sun. Then, as the mediation progresses, both the mediator and the participants feel a sense of positive direction and accomplishment in checking off agenda items as they are discussed and resolved.

2. PROCESS

Mediators need to assume a significant leadership role in the problem-defining stage of mediation, as it is a sophisticated art. While setting the agenda is something that many parties to a mediation would find difficult to achieve on their own, it is also a complicated exercise for even the most experienced mediators. For this reason, some mediators lapse into ad hoc agenda-setting, allowing the parties to talk about issues randomly as they arise. At the other extreme is a very structured and elaborate approach involving considerable leadership and finesse from the mediator, in consultation with the participants. Dispute-resolution theory points to the benefits of the latter approach, which is what is described here. However, it is a challenging exercise that requires sound understanding and extensive practice to execute skillfully.

3. USING PRE-MEDIATION CONFERENCES

As you apply your skills to mediation, keep in mind that the pre-mediation process discussed previously is an alternate time at which to define the problem or to commence the pre-mediation conference process.[26] During the initial contacts with the parties and/or their representatives, the mediator can use many of the skills and techniques addressed in this section to bring focus to the problem. A particularly effective but underutilized method of defining the problem at the heart of the conflict is by conducting a pre-mediation conference. A pre-mediation conference is a separate meeting held with each party before the mediation. Holding a conference before the mediation will allow the mediator to spend a significant amount of uninterrupted time with the parties individually to learn about the parameters of the problem in an unrushed and more relaxed environment. This opportunity will not only afford the mediator more time to explore the problem but also to plan strategies for resolving it. In contrast, when the problem is first defined during the mediation, the mediator must develop strategies "on the spot," with no opportunity for reflection. The more mediators know about problems before the mediation, the better prepared they will be to deal with them. Regardless of the chosen approach, this section reviews essential skills and techniques for defining the problem either before or during the mediation.

---

26. *See* Chapter 2—*Establishing the Foundation: Introduction, Intake, Screening, and Preparation.*

4. UNCOVERING INTERESTS

a. *Positions and Interests*

A seminal element in defining the parameters of the conflict in mediation (or negotiation) is uncovering each party's interests. In other words, the contours of the problem are defined by where the parties' interests conflict and where they coincide.[27] *Positions* are the concrete demands or claims that parties in conflict make of the other side. The statement, "I don't want a halfway house for the mentally disabled in my neighborhood," is a position. Positions are particular solutions or preferred outcomes. Other terms for a position might be wish lists or wants. *Interests*, on the other hand, are the concerns or fears that underlie the parties' concrete demands or preferred solutions. They are the deeper needs actually motivating the parties in the negotiations. The following would be a more interest-based statement about the halfway house conflict: "I don't want a halfway house in my neighborhood *because I am concerned about increased crime and diminished property values.*" Increased crime and diminished property values are the party's underlying interests, and the party is trying to guard those interests through the particular solution of preventing the halfway house from being located in his neighborhood. In other words, positions are the parties' preferred solutions to the negotiating problem, while the parties' diverging interests actually define the negotiating problem to be solved.

b. *Types of Interests*

There are three types of interests in mediation: *substantive, procedural,* and *psychological.*[28] Substantive interests are those that relate to concrete factors, such as money, conditions of employment, or a specific kind of performance. Procedural interests are those relating to the way in which the dispute has been managed or mismanaged. Examples of procedural interests would be a lack of response to complaints, refusal to be flexible in dealing with exceptional circumstances, or inequality in the treatment of similar people. Finally, psychological interests refer to emotional needs, such as desire for vindication for past actions or acknowledgment of hurts and injuries suffered. A mediator must be attentive to all three types of interests.

c. *Uncovering Interests*

The parties' true interests are not always easy to uncover. One reason for this is that most people approach conflict positionally, making no distinction between their underlying concerns and the means by which those concerns may be satisfied. In other words, they conflate their positions and interests. People tend to focus more on how the problem should be solved rather than on understanding the problem itself. For example, the party challenging the planned location of the halfway house in his neighborhood likely sees no distinction between his position and his underlying

---

27. ROGER FISHER, WILLIAM URY & BRUCE PATTON, GETTING TO YES 40–41 (2d ed. 1991).
28. CHRISTOPHER W. MOORE, THE MEDIATION PROCESS 75 (3d ed. 2003).

needs; to him they are the same. Consequently, positional claims often disguise or conceal the party's real interests. This is common in all manner of problems. A custodial parent in a family mediation might make the positional claim that the children should have no overnight contact with the other parent, even though the custodial parent's real interest is in having one night to himself/herself every weekend. Likewise, a farmer in a farm-debt mediation might make the positional claim that she wants the loan restructured, when her real interest is to leave the farm with a sense of dignity after the next harvest. A mediator's job is to uncover those interests.

Positional claims also may be motivated by revenge, fear, ignorance, or professional advice, and they can disguise the parties' real interests even from themselves. For this reason, people often make agreements that they later regret because they failed to recognize what they truly needed to feel satisfied. Sometimes parties intentionally obscure their true interests because they believe revealing them will make them weaker in the negotiation. This is not an unreasonable fear because revealing their true interests can leave them vulnerable to exploitation by a less cooperative negotiator, something we will explore further in Chapter 7—*Facilitating the Negotiations*.

The best, most direct way of identifying interests is by having the parties focus on what it is they wish to accomplish in the mediation. Thus, the mediator should ask questions that focus on the party's "concerns," "needs," "desires," and "fears," as the case may be, because doing so is usually fruitful. A useful mantra for a mediator when trying to uncover interests is "ask, listen, and probe."[29] Ask the parties, usually in private sessions, direct questions about their interests. For example, a mediator might ask as follows: "What are the concerns that have brought you to mediation?" A helpful variation on this question is "What do you need?"[30] In whatever form you ask these interest-based questions, you must listen for the party's underlying interests that are animating the conflict. Sometimes the party will respond with actual interests. In the halfway house example above, for example, the party objecting to the location may respond to an interest-based question by saying, "I'm concerned with the safety of my children." This is an interest that provides valuable information that will be useful in crafting a settlement.

If, on the other hand, in reply to a question about his concerns, a party instead responds with a position, the mediator needs to continue to "probe" deeper for the party's interests. For example, the mediator should search beneath the position to uncover the corresponding interest by asking, "Why is that important to you?" This is not to suggest that mediators should regularly ask the "why" question, as it might elicit a defensive or protective response, but it demonstrates the relationship between positions and interests and can be useful in appropriate circumstances.

---

29. David Lax & James Sebinius, 3D Negotiation 77 (2006).
30. Alexandra Carter, Ask for More: 10 Questions to Negotiate Anything 142 (2020).

In the problem-defining stage of the mediation, there are two helpful techniques to encourage openness from a party whom the mediator suspects may be intentionally concealing his or her true interests. The first is to explain to the party the potential benefits to him or her of accurately identifying his or her interests. The most important of these benefits is to better equip the parties and the mediator to generate a solution that is highly responsive to the parties' concerns.[31] The second technique, as noted above, is for the mediator to attempt to uncover the party's true interests in the confidential environment of a separate meeting. The confidentiality of the separate meeting makes it more likely that the party will share his or her true interests because it reduces the risk of the other party exploiting the information. The mediator, however, knowing the party's true interests, can work to satisfy the party's underlying needs or concerns during the negotiation.

5. IDENTIFY AREAS OF AGREEMENT

Once a mediator has sufficiently uncovered the relevant information, issues, and interests, the next step in defining the problem is identifying those matters on which there is already agreement between the parties. Mutual antagonism and poor communication in conflict situations can often cause the parties to think that they disagree about everything. However, the mediator can perform an affirming role by pointing out areas where the parties are not in conflict either because they share common interests or because some of their independent interests are compatible. Highlighting areas of agreement places the mediation in a more positive light and provides a platform for further agreement and decision-making. These are sometimes called "easy agreements" or "cheap agreements," and they can generate a "climate of consent." They may involve: substantive issues, such as the amount of damages suffered; procedural issues, such as the acceptance of a particular appraiser's figures; or objective standards for decision-making, such as an agreement to adhere to current industry practices.

In the partnership mediation example referenced previously in this section, the mediator might indicate the common ground between the parties in the following way:

> Now you may not realize it, Antonio and Fatima, but there are many things on which you agree. You both agree that this is a profitable partnership that needs to remain competitive in the future. You agree that you have different professional strengths that you contribute to the firm, and you agree that there are different categories of clients being serviced, though there are some questions about their worth. And finally you both agree that you would like to sort things out today so that you can get on with the business. Is that correct?...OK, now let's look at the things we still have to work on....

---

31. For a detailed discussion of the benefits of identifying interests, see Chapter 7—*Facilitating the Negotiations*, section II C.

The mediator should describe the common ground in terms of the information provided in the party statements so that it does not appear contrived or imposed (or incorrect). The mediator's notes and summaries are instruments for achieving this goal. The mediator may present the areas of agreement visually on a board or butcher's paper and use them subsequently to emphasize progress and to maintain a sense of momentum.

Sometimes it may only be possible to identify agreements at a high level of generality, for example, that the interests of the children should prevail, that any outcome should uphold the principle of ecological sustainability, or that both parties would like an outcome that is fair and minimizes transaction costs. In these cases, the mediator must exercise a judgment about whether to leave out the stage of identifying areas of agreement on the grounds that, because of its high level of generality, it may appear trite, patronizing, or absurd. However, our own experience is that it is an important stage in the process and should be attempted in at least some form. Unfortunately, the evidence suggests that in practice many mediators omit this important intervention altogether.

6. DEVELOPING AN ISSUE AGENDA

a. *Crafting the Issues*

Mediators should assist the parties in crafting neutral issues that get to the heart of the conflict. Participants in a dispute are usually inclined to define the problem in a one-sided manner that implies that the other party is at fault and must rectify the problem. This creates a naturally defensive reaction from the other party, who in turn develops his or her own biased issue definition. Thus, it is the mediator's task to shift the focus of the participants away from their polarized viewpoints and toward more generalized and mutually acceptable definitions of the issues that distribute the burden of resolving the problem to both parties. For instance, in a dispute between a school board and a principal, a mediator might proceed as follows:

- *School board's definition of the problem*: The principal is not faithfully applying school policy set by the board and does not communicate adequately with the board. (Implication: the principal must change.)
- *School principal's definition of the problem*: The board is going beyond its policy-making role and continually interferes in matters of day-to-day school administration. (Implication: the board must back off.)
- *Mediator's definition of the problem*: What is an appropriate division of functions and responsibilities between the board and the principal, and how should future communication and cooperation take place between them? (Implication: both parties have to work on the problem.)

Note how the last definition implies no blame, provides a single common definition, is future-oriented, and presents the problem as an open-ended question that can be used to invite possible answers from the parties. By contrast, the other two definitions each have a biased approach to the problem that implies that the other side carries sole responsibility for finding a remedy.

The following are some general guidelines for mediators to follow to neutralize the parties' tendency to blame each other and to direct their attention toward their underlying interests:

- *Restate or reframe positional claims.* Phrase issues to reflect underlying interests and be precise in stating the parties' needs. For example, a claim for the family car may be motivated by a more general need for adequate transportation.[32]

- *Restate or reframe one-sided claims.* Phrase issues to reflect both sides of the problem when possible. By way of example, if parents each claim exclusive custody of the children, the mediator might suggest that they see the problem as one of reconciling each parent's need for appropriate involvement in the children's lives and having a good relationship with them.

- *Define the problem in a generalized or tentative manner.* A claim for 60 percent of the property might be depicted by the mediator as a need for a fair and equitable division of property that takes into account past contributions and future requirements. By ignoring the specific figure, the mediator opens up the negotiating process to more options.

- *Define the problem to include both sides' interests.* For example, in the school problem referenced above, the mediator might suggest that what is needed is the consideration of solutions that allow the school board to have overall supervision of policymaking in the school and allow the principal to have the final say on matters of administrative management.

- *Use neutral and non-provocative language.* The claim, "The tightwad managers must give us a raise or there will be hell to pay" could be redefined as, "So you want management to pay you an appropriate wage for the kind of work you do?"

- *Use open-ended problem-solving questions.* For example, "How can the loan be repaid in a way that satisfies both parties?" or "How can you each be assured of the reliability of future performances?"

- *"De-legalize" the problem.* Lawyers might define a problem as one of liability and compensatory damages, whereas a mediator should attempt to define it in non-legal terms when possible. Thus, in a traditional workers' compensation case, the mediator might redefine liability and compensatory damages by asking, "How can we deal with different versions of the accident?" or, "How have the various parties been affected by the accident?" or, "What actions are required to make good any losses suffered?"

---

32. For more on reframing, see Chapter 5—*Assisting the Communication Process*, section VIII.

- *"De-monetize" the problem.* In litigation, interests and issues are usually in-corporated into a monetary claim, whereas in mediation it might be better not to define the dispute in monetary terms so that other non-monetary factors are encouraged to emerge. Thus, an employee's claim for damages for wrongful dismissal might be redefined as, "What actions should the employer undertake to resolve the employee's grievances and claims?"[33]

b. *Different Levels of Defining the Issues*

There are different substantive levels on which a dispute may be defined, and mediators have some discretion and control in selecting the level at which to define the dispute. That discretion should be exercised in light of the mediator's evaluation of the circumstances of the dispute, the needs and desires of the parties, and the mediator's background and training. The three substantive levels are:

- *The legal level*: Has there been a breach of the employment agreement between the parties?

- *The commercial level*: What is an appropriate commercial arrangement to take account of past conduct and future business possibilities?

- *The personal level*: How can the employer's sense of betrayal and the employee's lack of acknowledgment be managed?

These levels are not mutually exclusive, and a combination of approaches may be appropriate. Mediators should try to avoid purely legal definitions because they do not promote negotiated decision-making, although they might be appropriate in some circumstances.

c. *Form for the List of Issues*

Some mediators use single words or phrases to define the parties' issues. The main advantage of this system is that it is easy to learn and quick to perform. Other mediators convert the issues into a series of problem-solving questions. The main advantage of this system is that questions beg answers and provide the mediator with a useful source of leverage for soliciting the parties' responses. For example, the mediator might say, "Now Fatima and Antonio, we are looking for possible ways of answering the third question, 'What is an appropriate client base for the firm?' What suggestions do either of you have?" Questions are also dynamic ways of presenting the issues because they contain action words, namely verbs (newspaper sub-editors know about this when writing headlines), that give the issue some "lift," a sense of purpose, something in which the parties can get involved. It is not easy to ignore a dynamically written question. For example, note how the following question promotes and focuses discussion: "How can we improve teachers' working conditions

---

33. The mediator skill most pertinent to the above interventions is that of *reframing*, which is referred to in Chapter 5—*Assisting the Communication Process*, section VIII.

so that schools and students will benefit?" A well-crafted issue is just as hard to ignore as a well-crafted, action-packed newspaper headline such as "Mediator Solves Bitter Teachers' Dispute in One Dramatic Night." The following table depicts the different approaches to issue identification in the same partnership dispute:

Single term	Phrase	Problem-solving question
Profits	Future profit shares	How should the partners share profits in the future?
Staff	Appropriate use of support staff	What is an appropriate use of support staff?
Billing	Faster billing	How can the billing system be made more efficient?
Retirement	Timing of Fatima's retirement	How should each partner's involvement with the firm be arranged over time?

d. *Avoid Framing the Problem as a Single Issue*

Mediators should try to avoid framing the negotiation as a single issue because single-issue negotiations end in deadlock more frequently than multi-issue negotiations.[34] Single-issue negotiations are less likely to succeed because when a negotiation focuses on one issue, such as money, parties are placed in a highly polarizing struggle over a finite resource. In an effort to claim as much of the finite resource as possible, parties tend to use competitive negotiation tactics that are more likely to escalate conflict, such as adopting rigid positions, making threats, and personalizing the conflict. This makes the conflict much more difficult to manage and resolve. Somewhat counterintuitively, the more issues a conflict contains, the easier it will be for the parties to resolve. Multi-issue conflicts provide parties the opportunity to trade concessions on different issues, which promotes cooperative behavior. It also gives the parties an opportunity to "create value" in the negotiation, a topic that will be covered in greater detail in Chapter.

Thus, mediators should, to the furthest extent possible, "unbundle" an issue or problem to uncover new relevant issues to add to the conflict. Although not always possible, unbundling issues and adding issues to a dispute can usually be accomplished by identifying hidden or unarticulated interests of the parties. To illustrate this, assume that a woman of Hispanic descent is fired from her job as a general manager and has filed a legal action alleging racial discrimination. The company argues that she was fired because of an unprofessional attitude and personality problems with other staff. If the mediator frames the dispute as, "How much money should the company pay to settle the lawsuit?" the negotiation is likely to be a highly confrontational power struggle over a monetary settlement amount. Alternatively, and preferably, the mediator could "unbundle" the issue by uncovering the parties'

---

34. Leigh L. Thompson, Mind and Heart if a Negotiation 80 (3d ed. 2005).

underlying needs, desires, and interests. The following are some examples of typical interests that parties to an employment discrimination dispute might have and how those concerns might be crafted into issues:

- How should the employee's future request for references be handled?
- How should the employee's need for medical insurance be addressed?
- How should allegations of discrimination be addressed at the company in the future?
- To what extent should any agreement reached be available to the general public?
- How should the employee be compensated for the time she is, and has been, unemployed?
- If money is paid to the employee as part of resolving the litigation, when should it be paid?

e. *Addressing "One-Party" Issues*

In some situations, one of the mediating parties may wish for a matter to be included in the list of issues, while the other insists that it is not appropriate for decision or even discussion. While there are risks to either including or excluding the issue, including the issue is preferable as doing so can be framed as benefitting both parties. For example, in the business dispute example above, a mediator accommodating Antonio's wish to discuss support staff might mitigate the impact of this accommodation on Fatima by saying something along the following lines:

> Look, Fatima, the use of support staff time is something that Antonio would like to talk about, and although you feel that it is not a matter requiring any decisions, I think we should let him refer to it. Likewise, you may wish to talk about some matters that Antonio does not think are necessary for today's decisions. Is that a reasonable arrangement for you both?

This choice of words gives due deference to the matter, although it slightly marginalizes its importance, and encourages mutual accommodation for issues raised by the other party. Thus, as mentioned, the essence of the rule is that both parties can benefit. Where time and resources allow, the mediator might take a more proactive approach by acknowledging to both parties before the problem-defining stage begins that differences of opinion on issue definition sometimes arise and by preemptively explaining how such potential issues will be managed. This approach has the advantage of the appearance of impartiality since the gain or loss of either party is not specifically at issue.

f. *Presenting the List of Issues Visually*

The list of issues is often presented visually on a whiteboard or butcher's paper. Although this is not required, it provides a point of common focus for the parties, a public checklist of matters to be dealt with, and a visible and visual point of reference for the mediator. Additionally, when the parties are interacting too intensely, the mediator could say, turning to the board, "I thought we were discussing item three. Fatima and Antonio, would either of you like to indicate some possible answers to that question?" There are a number of important techniques relating to this apparently simple function:

- Agenda matters should not be written up before they have been agreed to verbally between the mediator and the parties;

- Particular attention should be given to not including any judgmental or inflammatory terms in public view on the board;

- Caution should be exercised when erasing items from the list, as they might have symbolic significance to one party. Erasing a topic that has been covered to make room for new topics may give the impression that the matter has been "discarded." For this reason, if using butcher's paper, an ample supply is preferable where there is likely to be extensive writing;

- The mediator's handwriting needs to accommodate the visually-challenged;

- The board should be cleaned, or the paper disposed of, at the termination of the mediation so that it is not accessible to cleaners or the yoga class using the room subsequently; and

- The mediator should not spend the entire mediation at the board as this suggests an undesirable authoritarian position.

g. *Prioritizing the Issues*

Generally speaking, the issues at dispute are usually outlined—whether verbally or visually—in no particular order. The question of how to prioritize each issue now arises. Someone must take the lead in this process, either the mediator or the parties together. Either approach has its strengths and its shortcomings, but in either case the mediator should offer expert guidance on the prioritization of issues. Depending on the circumstances, this may require some finesse on the part of the mediator.

The first approach is where the mediator invites the parties to examine and jointly prioritize the issues. This approach acknowledges that the parties are in control of the dispute and that their subjective priorities are more important than the objective priorities of the mediator. Thus, the parties in a partnership dispute might want to talk first about urgent debts and insistent creditors before working through assets and valuations. The parties' priorities can be shown visually on a board against the list of issues. In practice there is usually little problem in the parties reaching agreement on priorities. However, where there are difficulties, the mediator is required to intervene, and it is advised to try and move through this stage quickly. The mediator might suggest alternating priorities, two "first" priorities with each dealt with for a limited time, or some random choice (flip a coin) on priorities.

The second approach, which we prefer, involves the mediator taking the initiative in prioritizing the issues. This avoids a situation where the parties do not agree on priorities. More importantly, it allows the mediator to use his or her expertise to guide the parties in the right direction. For example, good negotiating practice usually involves dealing with "easier" matters before moving on to those that are most difficult. This allows the parties to develop some early success and confidence and avoid becoming deadlocked too soon.

h. *Standard Issue Lists*

Experienced mediators can anticipate the predictable issues in their fields of expertise, even where they have no prior knowledge of the particular dispute. This is useful knowledge where the parties are hesitant about presenting the issues themselves. Through appropriate questioning, the mediator might be able to discern those issues that he or she knows, if only at a general level, are normal for the particular category of dispute. Of course, how mediators do this is important—they should not appear to be imposing their own agenda on the parties. Where there is time pressure, the mediator may even commence the mediation with the standard issues on the board, ask the parties whether they are relevant to their case, and invite them to add additional issues. The following is a standard list of issues in a dispute involving the dissolution of a professional partnership.

Standard Issues: Partnership Dissolution

- What are the assets and liabilities of the partnership?
- How should the assets be divided among the partners?
- What needs to be done in relation to the liabilities?
- How should the clients of the partnership be dealt with?
- What legal formalities are required for the dissolution?
- What else is required to finalize the matter?
- How should post-dissolution problems be dealt with?

i. *Using the List of Issues*

As has already been suggested, mediators can use the list of issues in various ways. They can direct the parties' attention to them when there is acrimony in the room, they can tick off completed issues to give a visual sense of progress, they can write up optional solutions next to each issue, and they can use the issues as a checklist to verify that the drafted agreement is comprehensive. They can add to the list if additional issues arise during the course of the mediation, and they can use the list in any other way that helps the mediation to progress.

D. Problem Solving and Negotiation

Once a prioritized list of issues is available, the mediation moves to the stage of discussing and refining the issues, considering options for resolving them, and negotiating specific outcomes. Generally, we might refer to this as the "problem-solving" stage of the mediation. The problem-solving stage can be approached in a variety of ways using a variety of skills and techniques. This section will outline in a general way the most common and useful problem-solving approaches. The specific skills and techniques for implementing these approaches are discussed in subsequent chapters.

1. PURPOSE

The purpose of the problem-solving stage is to help the parties make good decisions concerning how to resolve the conflict. Most often this means helping them arrive at some amicable agreement, but not necessarily. Sometimes the best course of action for a party is continued litigation and trial, taking the dispute to the "boss," or some other alternative, when the likely benefits of trial reasonably outweigh the benefits of a proposed settlement. Sometimes, the conflict is not ripe for resolution because the parties lack necessary information to make good decisions. Thus, we cannot emphasize enough that a mediator's role is to help the parties view the problem as objectively as possible and help them make reasoned, thoughtful decisions about it, not to "settle disputes." Mediators who view their primary function as settling conflicts run the risk of placing undue pressure on parties to settle, or of themselves becoming biased in their assessment of the conflict. These circumstances raise serious ethical concerns, expose the mediator to potential claims for professional negligence, and threaten the parties' self-determination. However, this is not to say that settling conflicts is not an important function of mediation; of course, it is—the very purpose of the mediation is to provide a venue for amicably resolving the problem. It is just important for mediators to help parties accomplish this by assessing the conflict objectively; by happenstance, mediators will facilitate the settling of the vast majority of the matters they mediate simply because in the vast majority of conflicts, amicable resolution is objectively the best course of action.

2. STYLE

There is significant variation in the processes, skills, and techniques used in the problem-solving stage of the mediation. The greatest influence on how the process will be conducted depends upon whether the mediator uses a *facilitative, transformative,* or *evaluative* mediation style. Facilitative and transformative mediation styles, while different in many respects, might be deemed the "directing traffic" mode. Using one of these styles, the mediator maintains order, provides structure, encourages discussion, and summarizes and reframes party statements. The advantages of such a style are that the mediator stays out of the fray, parties assume greater responsibility for solutions, and the mediator is more likely to maintain an open mind about the dispute. The disadvantages of these styles can include a lack of direction, the parties being unable to progress on their own, and the mediation becoming lengthy and unproductive.

A more evaluative approach might be deemed the "driving the bus" mode. Using this style, the mediator controls communications (sometimes by keeping the parties in separate rooms throughout the entire mediation, shuttling offers and information between them), uses leading questions, suggests options, encourages settlement, and may even give opinions on the merits of parties' arguments and claims. The potential disadvantages of this style are that the parties assume less responsibility for the solutions, the mediator might appear biased and lose the trust of the parties, and the parties may become resistant or later blame the mediator for the outcome.

It is also important to emphasize that facilitative, transformative, and evaluative mediation styles are not rigidly set roles. Many mediators do not fall neatly into one style or another. Moreover, a mediator may move between these styles in different mediations, or even in the same mediation, as the circumstances of the dispute and the personalities of the participants involved require.

3. STORYTELLING

a. *Benefits of Permitting Storytelling*

The problem-solving stage is the place in the mediation process where parties may elaborate on their stories in a way that is usually counterproductive in their initial statements. Although not all parties will have stories to tell, and not all mediations benefit from parties telling them, allowing a party to relate their version of events and how it has affected them is beneficial. Here are some potential benefits of allowing storytelling:

- Storytelling creates a powerful psychological benefit by giving the parties an opportunity for the cathartic experience of telling their story to an objective third party, often for the first and only time. This satisfies deeply rooted needs to be heard and acknowledged.

- Both sides can explain their motivations for past conduct and the significance of important events to them.

- Where emotions are high, there may be considerable venting of feelings as parties communicate with one another about the past.

- Storytelling helps to identify important interests. People telling stories will tend to emphasize those aspects that are most important to them. This can provide clues to the mediator about what issues and interests most need to be satisfied to resolve the problem.

- Storytelling includes more factual and emotional detail than if the person was asked to respond to a series of narrow questions.[35] People respond to

---

35. SPEGEL, *supra* note 24, at 42–44.

narrow questions using their neo-cortex, the critical analytical part of the brain.[36] As a result, they usually respond only to the narrow question asked. Thus, if the mediator fails to ask about an important aspect of the problem, this information may be missed. Conversely, people tell stories using their limbic system, a more emotionally centered part of the brain. When a person tells a story, whole sequences of events are recalled, along with the emotions associated with those events, such as anger, fear, or regret. Those emotions may further trigger other "chunks" or "sequences" of memory, providing even further information. Thus, storytelling increases the likelihood of a party providing a factually and emotionally richer account of the events surrounding the problem as compared to narrow questioning.

b. *Limitations of Storytelling*

Despite the benefits of allowing parties to tell their stories, mediators are advised to closely monitor and limit the time spent on discussing past events. Uncontrolled storytelling can become too protracted and complex. The very same qualities of storytelling that enable parties to provide rich factual and emotional detail also increase the likelihood that a party will ramble, take too much time, or become overly emotional. The other real danger in allowing parties too much time in storytelling is that parties may begin to see the process as a search for the "historical truth." However, mediation is not good at discovering the "historical truth," nor is that its purpose. The purposes of storytelling are to allow the parties to feel heard, provide the mediator with sufficient information to properly define the problem, and gather information that may be useful in developing a solution to the problem. Parties will often disagree on past events, and they do not need to agree to conduct a productive mediation.

Case Illustration: Factual Disagreement

An employment dispute was set for trial in which the pleadings identified a major dispute of fact and law: Had there, or had there not, been an oral variation of the service agreement? The case involved a substantial damages claim and was scheduled for three days of trial, during which each party would present a number of witnesses to support their case. At mediation there was about 30 minutes of discussion over the question of what the employer, the manager of a finance company, and the employee, an accountant, had said to each other three years earlier. While there was some clarification of the factual issues, there was no agreement on the essential facts of the dispute. This factor was acknowledged, and the parties moved on to find a commercial accommodation involving the finance company re-employing the accountant in one

---

36. *Id.* at 42.

of its subsidiaries. This was achieved without ever reconciling the different versions of the facts.

c. *Guidelines to Manage Storytelling*

The benefits of allowing storytelling outweigh the potential dangers it presents, especially when a mediator takes steps to minimize common pitfalls. The following are some useful guidelines that will enhance the quality and usefulness of storytelling in mediation. Not all of these guidelines will be applicable in every situation. Thus, mediators must utilize them judiciously depending on the circumstances, the parties' personalities, and the extent to which storytelling is part of the mediation process.

- *Emphasize the subjective nature of the storytelling.* Invite the parties to "tell your version" of the past, or "explain your understanding," or "explain how things seemed to you," as opposed to asking them to "explain what happened" or "state the facts."

- *Underscore the purpose.* Explain to the parties that the purpose in having them elaborate on the problem is not for the mediator to be in a position to make judgments about who is right or who is wrong but rather for all of them to better understand the issues that need to be addressed and to possibly uncover information that may provide solutions.

- *Focus the storytelling.* When inviting a party to tell their story, especially in a complex matter, it may be helpful to have the party focus on one aspect of the problem that the mediator thinks most productive to discuss instead of asking a more global question, such as, "What is your understanding of what happened?" For example, in a complex commercial lease dispute involving several issues, the mediator might ask a party to relate the circumstances of one issue at a time: "What's your understanding of what happened concerning the air conditioning?"

- *Obtain permission to interrupt.* When inviting a party to elaborate on a certain aspect of the problem, it may be helpful to also get the party's permission to interrupt them in order to refocus the story on a particular topic the mediator deems particularly relevant.

- *Discourage statements that assign blame.* Instead, encourage descriptions of events. In telling their stories, parties will often evaluate and judge the events that they are relating to. For example, in a case where an employee is alleging wrongful firing as a result of sexual discrimination, an employee might say, "My manager treated me differently and discriminated against me even before I was fired." In response to this, a mediator might ask the participant to specifically describe the employer's behavior. For example, the mediator might ask, "How, specifically, were you treated differently while you worked for the company?"

- *Discourage overstatements and generalizations.* Parties in conflict often become highly polarized and begin to demonize the other party. This leads to overstatements and generalizations about the other party that can be inflammatory. Common examples of this are statements such as "they never...", or "they always...". An effective technique for addressing this problem involves the mediator's reframing the statement to focus on the consequences of the behavior. So in response to a statement in a child visitation dispute between divorcing parents where a party says that "all the children do on their visits is watch T.V.," a mediator might respond by saying, "It would be helpful if you explained what about that upsets you."

- *Discourage interrupting by the other party.* Storytelling can trigger powerful emotional responses from the other party, especially if the story is peppered with blame statements and overgeneralizations. Thus, it is always advisable to obtain commitment from the other party to not interrupt before the story begins, or to remind the party of their commitment if they do interrupt.

- *Limit the use of documentary evidence.* Some parties, especially attorneys, will try to support their story by providing documents, such as letters, contracts, bank statements, expert reports, medical records, and legal pleadings. While some of these materials may be helpful, the introduction of too much documentation can bring mediation to a screeching halt. The best way to avoid this potential problem is for the mediator to have identified and reviewed these documents before the mediation. If this is not possible, then the mediator must exercise his or her judgment in declining to review certain documents, emphasizing the need to keep the mediation moving forward and the mediator's role as an objective facilitator, not as a judge or arbitrator who will render a decision in the matter.

- *Prevent one party's monopolization of the mediation.* A mediator should try to give each party relatively equal "airtime" in the mediation. Although this is not always possible because some parties are naturally more talkative or genuinely have more to say, it is an ideal to strive for. Unbalanced storytelling can create a perception that the mediator is biased in favor of the monopolizing storyteller. Moreover, limited opportunity to speak by one party can limit the amount of useful information revealed. Many of the techniques listed above will help to discourage parties from monopolizing the mediation. Mediators, however, must develop tactful ways of allowing parties equal opportunity to share information. Like in many mediation matters, managing party expectations goes a long way. A mediator who suspects that a party may try to monopolize the conversation might first obtain agreement that it is important that both parties have an opportunity to speak and that it would be appropriate for the mediator to interrupt if he or she thinks time necessitates such intervention.

4. PROCEDURE

a. *Packaging Issues*

The mediator need not only prioritize the issues but must also decide what issues are best addressed separately and what issues are best addressed together. This is sometimes referred to as "packaging issues."[37] There are two common pitfalls that parties fall into when discussing a multi-issue conflict unassisted. One pitfall is trying to discuss too many facets of the problem at the same time. Too many unrelated arguments, facts, and standards make productive communication extremely confusing and difficult. The other pitfall is discussing all issues sequentially, one at a time. Discussing all issues separately increases the risk of the parties missing opportunities for integrative solutions that can be achieved by strategically addressing *certain* issues at the same time, so that the parties can trade concessions on different issues. This is how value is created in negotiation.[38] Accordingly, negotiation is made more efficient by rationally packaging issues, separating issues that need to be separated, and connecting issues that need to be connected. Parties in conflict are often not very good at this type of coordination because they attempt to focus the discussion on either those issues most important to them or those on which they believe they have the best opportunity of prevailing.

Mediators bring great value to the parties' discussion by helping them navigate how and when each issue will be discussed. Unfortunately, there is no formula or comprehensive rule for identifying when an issue should be addressed separately and when issues should be addressed in concert. The good news is, however, that the logic of why issues might best be addressed separately or together is usually apparent to an objective person like a mediator who has no stake in the outcome of the dispute. For example, a couple in divorce mediation might have several important issues to resolve: custody of the children, visitation of the children, financial maintenance of the children, division of assets, and alimony. Each of these issues involves, to a lesser or greater degree, different facts, arguments, standards, and potential solutions. However, some are more closely related than others; for example, custody and visitation are closely related because it is foreseeable that one parent might be willing to give up sole custody if an acceptable visitation schedule can be reached. These issues are therefore closely linked and would benefit, at least in some cases, from being discussed together. Issues like child maintenance logically need to be discussed after the custody issue because in most states it is tied to income and assets of the non-custodial parent.

Sometimes issues that have been initially discussed separately can later be discussed together in the hope of uncovering the type of integrative opportunities that make agreements more effective and attractive. In the divorce situation above, if the

---

37. THOMPSON, *supra* note 34, at 160.
38. Detailed exploration regarding "creating value" in negotiations can be found in Chapter 7—*Facilitating the Negotiations*, section I D.

parties are having difficulty in reaching an agreement on alimony, revisiting the tentatively settled issue of division of property might prove helpful; a party that cares more about keeping their monthly expenses to a minimum might be willing to give away more property, whereas a person who wishes to maximize their monthly income might not care as much about his or her net worth. Therefore, we recommend that issues always be tentatively agreed to until all the issues are decided. This allows the parties to renegotiate "tentatively settled" issues to help resolve subsequent issues that prove difficult. This valuable technique is harder to use if previously discussed issues are viewed by the parties as "definitively" settled. Integrative agreements are also a way to satisfy the most pressing concerns of the parties, which are often different and complementary. This will be discussed in greater detail in Chapter 7.

b. *Problem-Solving Processes*

There are nearly as many different problem-solving processes as there are mediators. Most of these processes, however, fall into three broad categories. These categories of processes are *open discussion, interest-based negotiation,* and *positional negotiation.* These problem-solving techniques are not mutually exclusive and often all are used in the same mediation—sometimes on the same issue. Each has its appropriate uses, advantages, and disadvantages.

i. Open Discussion.

Open discussion is an unstructured, free-flowing dialogue among the parties and the mediator regarding a particular issue. The mediator might begin the discussion by saying something as general as "Let's talk about the division of assets." He or she would then wait for one of the participants to start speaking. Alternatively, he or she might begin the discussion with a narrower question, such as, "Baranjit, how do you think the assets should be divided?" This is not to say, however, that the open discussion is uncontrolled. The mediator will still enforce the general guidelines of mediation and employ several techniques that will help the parties to communicate effectively, such as allowing parties to finish their thoughts uninterrupted, paraphrasing, summarizing, and reframing.[39] The advantage of having an open discussion is that it gives the parties maximum control over the problem. In some mediations, once the issue is clearly defined, the parties need little assistance to resolve it other than the opportunity to discuss the problem civilly together. Notably, this process works best with highly cooperative parties and usually on less complex conflicts.

ii. Interest-Based Negotiation.

In this process, mediators encourage the parties to develop and explore a wide range of options that satisfy the parties' previously identified interests. The focus in this type of bargaining is on helping the parties distinguish between the means of

---

39. See Chapter 5—*Assisting the Communication Process,* explaining these techniques.

solving the problem (positions) and the problem itself (interests). One way of achieving an interest-based solution is through the device of *brainstorming*. Although brainstorming will be discussed in more detail in Chapter 7, it is useful to introduce its basic steps now.

Brainstorming consists of two steps: generating options and then evaluating the options generated. In the first step of the brainstorming process, all parties are invited to identify possible options for dealing with the dispute, regardless of how practical, reasonable, or viable they may be. The objective of the first step is to get the parties to think imaginatively about as many potential solutions as possible and to feed off each other's ideas, without the twin fears of being judged as stupid or being committed to their suggestions. A mediator may encourage brainstorming by asking hypothetical questions, such as "What could you think of in relation to...?" or "Can you think of ways in which other people have dealt with this kind of problem...?"

In the second step of the brainstorming process, the mediator encourages the parties to evaluate the options generated. Specifically, the mediator will encourage the parties to identify the options that encapsulate both the needs and interests of the parties as well as objective standards of fairness and reasonableness. The mediator should also invite the parties to consider the practical consequences of various options. Where no options satisfy both parties, the mediator may attempt to gain agreement based on principles. Below is an example of how this might work.

Case Illustration: Brainstorming

A mediation involved a local municipal authority and a property owner who had been affected by a major extension to the municipality's sewerage works that affected the property's future residential use. The municipality had offered to purchase the property, but no agreement could be reached on the purchase price. After other issues had been discussed, a brainstorm was held over options for the land. No fewer than 10 options were listed, including a joint commercial development between the municipality and owner, and the development of an environmental park named after the owner. The brainstorm ended with an evaluation of the options that resulted in mutual choice of the original option of a municipality purchase with the price to be decided by an agreed appraiser. While the exercise ended with the option they had first thought of, the process adopted gave the decision greater legitimacy and prompted the parties to fine-tune ways of achieving it.

Interest-based negotiations are the preferred process since they can often produce the most beneficial agreements for both parties by finding integrated solutions to the problem. This type of process works, however, only when there are multiple issues and interests at stake in the negotiation. It also takes considerable time, energy, and creativity.

iii. Positional Negotiation.

In this process, the parties focus primarily on trying to achieve a specific outcome or solution to the conflict and not on the underlying interests or concerns that those solutions are meant to address. Here, the mediator's primary role is to assist the parties in arriving at acceptable compromises by reasoning with them about the legitimacy and practicality of offers and counteroffers. For example, a mediation concerning how much an insurance company will pay a claimant in a personal injury matter generally will center around the single issue of money. The claimant may demand $100,000 and the insurance company may offer $10,000 in settlement of the matter. The mediator's role is to help the parties manage the concessions as the parties work their way to a mutually agreeable settlement amount. The mediator's role in the positional bargaining process is dealt with more extensively in Chapter 7.

E. Final Decision and Closure

1. PURPOSE

The primary purpose of the *final decision and closure* stage is to finalize any agreement made and to bring closure to the mediation process. What steps the mediator will need to take in ending the mediation will depend upon what the parties decide. Most mediations result in an agreement to resolve the dispute. In such circumstances, the mediator helps the parties solidify and clarify the terms of the agreement and may even aid in drafting a written agreement. In situations where the parties do not settle, it is often helpful for the mediator to review with the parties what issues have been identified in the mediation and review the progress that has been made. Whether the parties settle or not, however, the mediator should provide a concluding statement that brings a formal closure to the mediation process. Finally, it is also during this stage that the mediator and participants decide if, and to what extent, the mediator will be needed in any post-mediation activities. These activities range from making sure any tentative agreement reached in the mediation is subsequently formalized into a written agreement, to continuing working with the parties over the telephone and/or by e-mail to resolve issues that were not resolved during the regular mediation session.

2. THE AGREEMENT

a. *Level of Commitment*

Level of commitment refers to the manner in which the parties acknowledge their agreement to resolve the conflict, whether it be through an informal handshake or the filing of a 50-page settlement agreement with the court. Different types of conflicts require different types of commitments to promote compliance. It is the mediator's responsibility to work with the parties to determine what level of commitment is appropriate for the conflict. There are three different levels of commitments: *oral agreements*, *written non-binding agreements*, and *written binding agreements*.

i. Oral Agreements.

An oral agreement is where the parties verbally commit to the terms of settlement. Although these agreements can be legally binding in certain circumstances, we generally discourage the use of oral agreements in most mediations. State law application and interpretation is complex in this area, opening the door for legally insufficient agreements. Even where the oral agreement is legally binding, if a party fails to live up to the agreement, the aggrieved party would need to prove the existence and terms of the agreement, which can be difficult without written evidence of it. Oral agreements should only be used where legal enforcement is not desirable or possible if one of the parties fails to comply with the agreement.

For example, where a human resource manager has mediated a dispute between employees squabbling over the use of a shared administrative assistant, a written agreement might be appropriate because the terms of any agreement reached might be too vague to have enforceable meaning (*We agree to respect each other's work priorities*), but an oral agreement may be more suitable. For one, it is not the type of settlement that one would legally enforce by filing a lawsuit. Further, the parties likely will be motivated to comply with their oral agreement for other reasons, such as to avoid further contact with the human resources department or to prevent their conflict from reaching high levels of management.

ii. Non-Binding Written Agreements.

A non-binding written agreement is one where the parties reduce the terms of the settlement to writing but the writing has no legal effect. This type of agreement is sometimes referred to as a *memorandum of understanding* and has two common uses. The first common use is as the final agreement. For instance, a non-binding written agreement may be appropriate in employee disputes where there are concrete terms agreed to that might be practical to put in writing. For example, "The administrative assistant will give Jeff's work priority in the morning and Joan's work priority in the afternoon." The second common use for non-binding written agreements is in community disputes, such as those involving barking dogs or trespassing children. While such agreements have no binding legal effect, they do have a powerful moral effect. When people make commitments in writing, they usually live up to those commitments; even when a party initially fails to live up to their commitment, the writing may be used as a source of moral leverage by the other party to compel compliance.

The other common use for a memorandum of understanding is as a tentative agreement that will later be formalized into a binding agreement. Parties in mediation often are not prepared to commit to a legally binding agreement on the day of mediation. This may be the case for several reasons: sometimes they do not have final authority to bind the organization they represent; information needs to be verified before final commitment can be made; they wish to consult with trusted advisors; or simply because a party wishes to take more time with what are often important decisions. In such cases, reaching a tentative agreement by means of a memorandum of understanding is a way of giving the parties a sense of accomplishment and a taste of closure. In our experience, most memoranda of understanding are subsequently formalized without substantial alterations or difficulty.

iii. Binding Written Agreements.

A binding written agreement is where the parties reduce the terms of the agreement to a writing that is a legally enforceable contract, just like any other contract. If a party fails to comply with a valid mediated agreement, the other party can file a legal action, and the violating party can be compelled by a court to comply, pay damages, or both, depending on the nature of the agreement. Most mediations produce written binding agreements.

As stated before, we recommend that it be a term of the agreement to mediate that an agreement will only be binding once it has been reduced to writing and signed by the parties. This is an important precaution against disputes arising over whether an agreement has been reached and helps prevent misunderstandings over the terms of the agreement. In some situations, a binding agreement is drafted during the mediation and signed by the parties in rough form to be subsequently refined into a more formal document.

b. *Drafting the Agreement*

Where lawyers or other advisers are present, they usually draft the agreement, and the mediator has only a limited role of checking for completeness, accuracy, and clarity. The mediator generally can, however, assist the parties in drafting the agreement.[40] In most states, assisting parties in drafting a mediated agreement is not considered the practice of law and is therefore permissible by those mediators who are not licensed to practice law in that state. However, the law is not uniform on this issue, so mediators should be familiar with their state's law concerning the drafting of mediated agreements. Noting the wide range of views on this issue, the American Bar Association issued the following resolution. Although not binding, the statement has been highly influential on most states' thinking concerning the issue:

> **Drafting settlement agreements**. When an agreement is reached in a mediation, parties often request assistance from the mediator in memorializing their agreement. The preparation of a memorandum of understanding or settlement agreement by a mediator, incorporating the terms of settlement specified by the parties, does not constitute the practice of law. If the mediator drafts an agreement that goes beyond the terms specified by the parties, he or she may be engaged in the practice of law. However, in such a case, a mediator shall not be engaged in the practice of law if (a) all parties are represented by counsel and (b) the mediator discloses that any proposal that he or she makes with

---

40. Mediators are advised to check the law of the states in which they practice.

respect to the terms of settlement is informational as opposed to the practice of law, and that the parties should not view or rely upon such proposals as advice of counsel, but merely consider them in consultation with their own attorneys.[41]

In situations where the mediator assists in drafting the mediated agreement, the following principles should be considered:

- There should be close consultation with the parties over its precise wording;
- All drafting should be done in plain English and, where possible, the parties' own words and terms should be used;
- There should be a sense of balance in the agreement in that the parties' names are used alternatively and their rights and obligations are balanced against each other; and
- Each page and any alterations should be initialed, and the parties should sign the final page.

Samples of mediated agreements in commercial, family, and community disputes are included in Appendix 3.

c. *Content of the Agreement*

Inevitably, the content of the written document will reflect the terms of the parties' agreement. However, there are many different styles in which this can be recorded, ranging from a more flourishing style that deals with matters of principle in broad generality, to a focused legalistic style that records minute details with a view to legal enforceability, with many variations in between. The context and circumstances of the mediation will determine which of these styles should be used. Regarding the specific content of the agreement, however, the following are essential elements:

- Full names of parties;
- Effective date of the agreement;
- Reference to the transaction, incident, or conflict that is the subject of the agreement;
- Duties and responsibilities of the respective parties clearly explained in concrete terms;
- If payment is being made as part of the settlement, the agreement should include who is paying whom, the amount of payment, when it will be paid, and the form of payment (bank check, personal check, electronic transfer, etc.);

---

41. American Bar Association Section of Dispute Resolution, *Resolution on Mediation and the Unauthorized Practice of Law* (adopted Feb. 2, 2002).

- If the mediation involves a litigation matter that will be dismissed as a consequence of the mediated agreement, the agreement should include reference to that litigation by caption and docket number; and

- Signatures of the parties.

Terms that are sometimes included are the following:

- *Return to mediation*: "In the event the parties encounter any difficulties in the application of this agreement, they will use their best endeavors to settle the problems with the assistance of the mediator."

- *Supervision of any performance*: "The mediator will supervise the performance of any obligations or duties required in terms of this agreement."

- *Goodwill statement for the future*: "The parties agree that they will treat each other with courtesy and respect in the future and avoid any actions which might cause the conflict to recur."

3. CLOSING STATEMENT AND TERMINATION

Mediators should take some care in terminating the mediation, even if agreement has been reached on all matters requiring decisions. A sense of closure is an important part of honoring the parties' participation in the mediation. If properly done, a closing statement can increase the parties' commitment to honoring the agreement reached, or, in matters that did not reach agreement, inspire the parties to continue seeking an amicable resolution. It is also a way of signifying, in most cases, the end of the mediator's involvement in the conflict.

In situations where the parties have reached agreement, a short closing statement should possess the following elements and qualities:

- Conclude the proceedings on a positive note;

- Commend the parties for what they have achieved;

- Encourage compliance with the agreement;

- Normalize the "post-settlement blues" (that is, the prospect of the parties having subsequent misgivings over concessions they have made);

- Thank the lawyers or other advisers for their contributions;

- Reassure the parties as to the confidentiality of the mediation; and

- Invite the parties to return to mediation if that is necessary.

The closing statement should be tailored to the particular mediation, taking into account not only the subject matter but also the nature of the interactions that occurred during the mediation. The following is a sample of a more generic closing statement:

Now that the agreement has been signed, I just want to take the opportunity to thank you before you leave. These types of problems are almost never easy to resolve. But through your hard work and commitment to the mediation process you were able to reach an agreement that you both think will work for you. I commend both of you for the effort you put in to today. I want you to know that it is not uncommon for parties to second-guess themselves after reaching a resolution, but I hope you will not do that. I believe we have worked through the problem thoroughly, and you have had the advice of very fine legal representation that contributed greatly to the process. So, I think you should be comfortable in your decisions today. I also want to assure you that the matters discussed here will remain confidential and that the notes that I have taken throughout the day will be promptly destroyed. Thank you again for your cooperation, and please let me know if I can help with anything in the future.

In situations where the parties did not reach a full agreement, some additional principles apply in bringing closure to the mediation. The main guiding principles are that, no matter the level of party frustration or disappointment, the mediator should (1) terminate the mediation on as positive a note as possible, and (2) provide a basis for future settlement. To facilitate this, the mediator should attempt to generate a list of matters on which there is agreement and a list of issues on which agreement is still required. This will provide some sense of achievement. The mediator might also highlight other achievements, such as the sharing of information that has occurred in the mediation and has left the dispute in better shape than when the mediation started. It is also appropriate to normalize the inability to settle in order to reduce the parties' sense of failure. The mediator might advise the parties to take their time before deciding on their next course of action, particularly if they are in a state of agitation over the current impasse. Finally, the mediator might remind them of the option of returning to mediation should circumstances change at any time in the future. This is a possible mediator presentation for these situations:

> In some cases, mediations do not achieve settlement for a range of reasons, and this seems to be one of those cases in which we are not going to reach full settlement today. However, we have made progress and I have written up a list of issues on which there is agreement. Because of your hard work today, I think you have a better understanding of the dispute and of each other, and that in itself has value. Hopefully you will not have to re-open the issues you reached tentative agreement on today. It may also help that you now have a common list of those issues on which you have yet to reach agreement so that you can work in the future from the same list. Statistically it is unlikely that this matter will reach a court hearing and you should each feel free to approach me about resuming the mediation at any time. Let me reassure you about the confiden-

tiality of what has occurred here today, and I would like to wish you both well in dealing with this in the future.

4. EVALUATIONS

It is wise to provide the parties an opportunity to evaluate their mediation experience. A written evaluation is a way for a mediator to obtain constructive feedback and improve his or her skills. Participants are usually happy to oblige and it takes no longer than 10 minutes. A sample Participant Evaluation form is included in Appendix 6B.

5. POST-MEDIATION ACTIVITIES

Occasionally, the mediator's responsibilities do not end with the termination of the mediation meeting. Where the parties do not settle all of the issues, a mediator may continue working with the parties via telephone or e-mail to resolve those remaining. It will depend on the mediator's compensation policies whether he or she will charge for this additional service. In settlements that require continuing performance over a period of months or years, a mediator may be asked to monitor such performance and help resolve any disputes concerning it. Common examples of disputes that can require continuing performance are environmental cleanup matters, ongoing work relationships, child support payments, or any agreements that require payments or performance over time.

III. The Separate Meetings

A. Definition

Mediators often find it helpful to meet with the parties separately during the mediation. Here the term "separate meetings" is used to refer to the meetings between the mediator, on the one hand, and each party and their advisers, on the other. Other terms used for this part of the process are "private meetings," "separate sessions," and "caucuses." In some mediation models, the separate meeting is actually a stage in the regular mediation process. For example, in one mediation model, immediately after the parties' initial statements, the mediator will meet separately with each party (and their counsel, if present), usually to uncover any information that the party was uncomfortable sharing in the joint session in the presence of the other party. In our model, however, we use the separate meeting as a tool, rather than a fixed stage in the process. Separate meetings can occur at any stage of the mediation but are most commonly used during the problem-defining and the problem-solving stages.

There are many variations regarding these meetings, and the table below suggests distinguishing terms for different kinds of meetings:

Name	Those involved	Objective
Separate meetings	Mediator and each party with their own advisers	See discussion in text
Side meetings	Mediator and each party individually without advisers	To give parties opportunity to talk directly without adviser influence or pressure
Party meetings	Mediator and all parties without advisers	To avoid negative role of advisers, to get parties talking unadvised
Adviser meetings	Mediators with all advisers without parties	To explore realistic settlement options where both clients are "problematic"

The terms used above are by no means standard but are adopted here so as to distinguish among the different kinds of meetings that could be convened in the proceedings. In what follows, the emphasis is on *separate meetings*, as defined above, though many of the principles are equally applicable to other kinds of meetings.

B. Purpose

There should always be a reason for calling a separate meeting, and these reasons will vary according to the stage that the mediation has reached. Strictly speaking, a separate meeting should be called to serve the requirements of the parties and the negotiations, and not to serve the mediator's comfort needs or uncertainty about what to do next. Adjournments can be used to deal with the mediator's problems, ranging from confusion to thirst. There are many legitimate reasons for meeting separately with a party, far too many to provide a comprehensive list, as many are unique to the circumstances of the mediation. Nearly all of them, however, are attempts to propel the mediation forward or prevent or curtail destructive behavior. The following are some of the typical purposes for calling separate meetings:

- To provide relief from destructive emotions and high tension, allowing the relevant party to vent their feelings;
- To provide space and time for a weaker or disempowered party to recover;
- To establish whether there are any concerns that have not yet been raised but need to be addressed for the resolution of the dispute;
- To attempt to understand the motivations of the parties and their priorities;
- Where the mediator believes that there is additional information that he or she will not obtain in joint session;
- To deal with breaches of the mediation guidelines and threatened disruption of the process and to get the parties recommitted to the process;

- To attempt to break a deadlock by changing the dynamics of the negotiation process;
- To ascertain whether an apparently inflexible and intransigent party is open to further negotiation;
- To engage in "reality testing" with a positional or intransigent party or to encourage settlement in other ways;
- To coach the parties in constructive communication and productive negotiation strategies;
- Where the parties are unable to come up with settlement options in each other's presence, to provide a risk-free environment for considering such options;
- To privately check out the acceptability of an imminent agreement;
- To allow for last-minute consultation with the parties before the mediator terminates the mediation without agreement being reached; and
- To test the parties' perceptions of each other, for example, to ask Party A how they view Party B's interests and position.

C. Confidentiality in Separate Meetings

As has already been suggested, the conversations that occur in separate meetings are confidential. Mediators should emphasize confidentiality at the beginning of each separate meeting: "Xin, as I explained at the beginning of the mediation, everything we say in this meeting is confidential, and I will not share any information with the other party that you don't want me to." Emphasizing confidentiality at the beginning of the separate meeting encourages greater trust and openness from the party, making it easier for him or her to share information that might prove valuable in resolving the dispute.

Since mediators often discuss both confidential and non-confidential matters in the separate meetings, they should end the meeting by clarifying what, if anything, must be kept confidential. If the party has told the mediator throughout the meeting what information he or she wishes to keep confidential, the mediator should review that list before ending the meeting: "Maria, you told me that you do not wish me to tell the other party yet about your dire financial condition or that you recognize that your punitive damage claim is weak, is that correct?"

If the party has not identified any information as confidential, a mediator should still address confidentiality before the meeting ends. One technique for doing this is by framing the question so that the party must proactively identify confidential information: "Ben, is there anything we discussed that you wish me to keep between us for now?" Framing the question in this way performs two subtle but helpful tasks. First, it increases the chance that the party will permit the mediator to share more information because it requires him or her to identify it. Second, by ending the question with "for now," it foreshadows the possibility that the party might decide to share the information later in the mediation for strategic purposes.

D. When Separate Meetings Should Be Called

There are no hard-and-fast rules as to when separate meetings should be called. Where one of the above purposes can be pursued, it is an appropriate time to call separate meetings. Where the parties or their advisers request a separate meeting, it is appropriate to oblige, provided that it does not appear to be allowing the requesting party to manipulate the process. In some styles of mediation, as mentioned above, mediators call separate meetings directly after the parties' initial statements to establish whether there are any concerns that have not yet been raised or to gather information that has not been disclosed. Some mediations are conducted exclusively through separate meetings, but this involves a different concept known as "shuttle mediation."[42] As usual, all the variations have their strengths and shortcomings.

Our own preference is to convene separate meetings only after at least some, and often all, of the issues have been discussed in a joint session, at least provisionally. Our concerns with calling separate meetings immediately after the parties' initial statements include that it artificially prevents the conflict from occurring, it allows the parties to relapse into positional thinking, it introduces the confidentiality of the separate meetings too early in the process, it gives the mediator immense power, and it involves a default shuttle-mediation system without that option being expressly considered and chosen. However, in reality many attorney mediators, unpersuaded by this compelling logic, call separate meetings immediately after the party statements in commercial mediations, often never returning to a joint session.

Shuttle mediation is frequently used in the commercial context where there is a view that separate meetings are necessary when parties reach the stage of making offers and counteroffers to each other. While it might be necessary for parties to be able to confer alone and to consult with their advisers before making or responding to offers, it is not necessary that this be done exclusively through separate meetings. It is feasible to adjourn the mediation for such deliberations to take place and to resume the joint session thereafter.

The concern here is that the process should not move by default into shuttle mode, which should involve a conscious strategic decision of the mediator, after some consultation with the parties. It may be entirely appropriate to adopt shuttle mediation, but that should involve a deliberate and transparent decision. This is because the mediator's role in shuttle mediation is different from that in non-shuttle mediation. The mediator becomes the sole messenger for offers and counteroffers

---

42. For a detailed discussion of "shuttle mediation," see Chapter 10—*Variations in the Mediation Process*, section III.

and the sole conveyer of other information on the attitudes and behaviors of the parties. There are necessary limits on the confidentiality principle in this context, and the mediator acquires immense power. However, the practical reality is that many mediators lapse into shuttle mediation without any thoughtful selection of that option.

A comprehensive study of mediation strategies in same-day mediation in Maryland's District Court found significant negative impact as a consequence of excessive use of separate meetings.[43] One finding was that in "[t]he short-term analysis... the greater the percentage of time participants spend in caucus, the more likely the participants are to report that the ADR practitioner controlled the outcome, pressured them into solutions, and prevented issues from coming out."[44] The study further found that the "[g]reater percentage of time in caucus was also negatively associated with participants reporting that they were satisfied with the process and outcome, and that the issues were resolved with a fair and implementable outcome."[45] Finally, with regard to time spent in separate meetings (caucus), the study found that it was more likely that the parties would return to court within 12 months to enforce the mediation agreement because a party failed to follow through on the agreement.[46]

E. Separate Meetings and Physical Space

Normally the mediator remains in the joint venue with one party and directs the other to an alternative room. This is partly a practical arrangement, in that fewer persons have to move, but it also has symbolic significance in that the mediator is not relinquishing "control" of the principal mediation venue. Ideally, the excluded parties require a meeting room of their own, but in practice they are often dispatched to windy corridors or noisy foyers. In all events, mediators should ensure that the room in which the separate meeting is being conducted is soundproofed from those outside. Where the accommodation allows it, the parties can each be offered their own conference rooms and the mediator moves between them. This provides more exercise for the mediator, but gives him or her private space in the original venue. It also provides the best image of equality as between the parties.

---

43. Maryland Administrative Office of the Courts, *What Works in District Court Day of Trial Mediation: Effectiveness of Various Mediation Strategies on Short- and Long- Term Outcomes* (Jan. 2016), https://mdcourts.gov/sites/default/files/import/courtoperations/pdfs/districtcourtstrategiesfullreport.pdf.
44. *Id.* at 6.
45. *Id.*
46. *Id.*

F. How Dynamics Change in Separate Meetings

As compared with the joint sessions, there are two potential yet contradictory changes to the dynamics experienced in the separate meetings. These changes may be subtle or pronounced, depending on the style of the mediator and the requirements of the mediation. In a more relaxed setting, a separate meeting may facilitate a mediator in identifying with the relevant person and empathizing with their situation. This is sometimes referred to as "alliance formation," in that the mediator builds an alliance with the person so that he or she is perceived as their ally in relation to the problem they are facing. (In liturgical terms, the *guardian angel* function.) In the confidential setting of a separate meeting, the mediator can also be a harsher critic of the relevant person and be more forceful in assisting the party in seeing the downside of their position. This is referred to as "reality testing," in that the mediator uses a wide range of tactics to disenchant the person with their positional claims. (In liturgical terms, the *devil's advocate* function.) However, while many mediators regard the separate meetings as the critical stage of the mediation process, our experience is that in many cases they have only a limited bearing on the outcome. In some cases it is not even possible for the mediator to use disclosures made by the relevant party. This is illustrated in the following case study.

Case Illustration: The Separate Meeting and Confidential Information

In a mediation involving a division of matrimonial property, one party was being particularly intransigent and requested a separate meeting. In the meeting he informed the mediator that the reason for his attitude was that he had recently been diagnosed with glaucoma, and because he worked in the surveillance industry, he would lose his livelihood within the next 12 months. He did not want this disclosed to the other side (and had not even told his lawyer until then). The mediator empathized with the predicament and the desire not to disclose it. The mediator could not use the information in any other way, but the interest of the party in explaining and justifying his behavior to the mediator was satisfied, and the matter moved to quick resolution in the next joint session.

G. When to End Separate Meetings

1. DURATION OF SEPARATE MEETINGS

While there is no standard duration for separate meetings, in general, they should be kept relatively short. Keeping meetings short is motivated by two practical concerns. The first concern is that the longer the separate meetings last, the less time you, as the mediator, will have to use the information learned in the meeting to move the negotiation forward through problem solving or exchanging offers. For example, if you have a half-day to mediate a matter and spend 45 minutes in the first separate meeting and another 45 minutes in the second separate meeting, you have left little time to engage in the actual negotiations. Inadequate time to spend on problem solving and exchanging offers can decrease the likelihood of settlement. The second concern for keeping separate meetings short is that the longer you meet with a party, the more likely the other party is to speculate on what is happening in that meeting, sometimes in unhealthy ways. Accordingly, a separate meeting should be ended when the following occur: (1) it has served the purpose for which it was called, (2) the party involved has nothing further to say and the mediator nothing more to contribute, or (3) dramatic new information, threats, or final offers emerge, thereby returning responsibility to the parties.

2. CALLING AND MANAGING SEPARATE MEETINGS

The one qualification to the above guidelines for conducting and ending separate meetings is that a mediator should be sensitive to the parties' perceptions of inequity concerning how the separate meetings are called and managed. These considerations include the number of opportunities the parties have to meet separately with the mediator and in what order the mediator meets with the parties. Parties are often highly sensitive to and suspicious of unequal treatment in mediation, even if such behavior is for the common good. To lessen the likelihood of creating distrust, a mediator must be sensitive to the process of calling separate meetings. First, the mediator should meet separately an equal number of times with each party. If meeting separately with one party, the mediator should meet separately with the other even if there is no pressing need. This helps to maintain an appearance of neutrality. Somewhat less importantly, unless there is a good reason to do otherwise, the mediator should alternate which party is met with first when there is more than one round of separate meetings. For example, the mediator might say, "David, last time we broke for separate meetings, I met with you first, so I would like to meet with Lya first now."

3. BALANCING THE DURATION OF SEPARATE MEETINGS

Finally, and less within your control as the mediator, you should balance the amount of time you spend with each party in separate meetings. If you spend 30 minutes in a separate meeting with Party A and then only five minutes in a separate meeting with Party B, you run the risk of causing Party B to doubt your neutrality. However, there is often a good reason to spend significantly more time in separate meetings with one party than with another. One party may have more information about the conflict than the other, have a greater emotional need to tell his or her "story," or be more difficult to reason with. If there is a legitimate need to spend significantly more time with one party than the other, you should try to reduce the risk of appearing biased. One way to do this is to explain why you needed to spend more time with the other party. Honoring confidentiality, you might explain to the other party, "I appreciate your patience while I met with Clyde. He had a real need to explain to me how this conflict has affected his life. Although it took some time, I think it will have real benefits in helping us work through this process successfully." You should also help manage the parties' expectations about the separate meeting by stating how long you think it will take. "Mary, I am going to meet with Jim separately for about 20 minutes. If I think it will take longer than that, I'll come out and let you know how much longer I think it will be." Managing expectations about duration in this way reduces the risk of the mediation appearing biased.

H. The Separate Meeting Transitions

There are four significant transitions in relation to the separate meetings: (1) *breaking into separate meetings*, (2) *commencing a separate meeting*, (3) *ending a separate meeting*, and (4) *resuming the joint session*. As the transitions may invoke some anxiety and suspicion on the part of clients, the mediator requires a "patter" to explain and justify the change and to reassure the parties. Here is a model mediator patter for each transition, based on the scenario of Fatima and Antonio appearing earlier in this chapter.

1. BREAKING INTO SEPARATE MEETINGS TRANSITION

"As indicated earlier, it is normal practice for the mediator to meet with each of the parties separately, and to give the other some time out, and I should now like to do that with you. I will probably meet with you each for 10–15 minutes, and if I am going to be significantly longer than that with either of you, I will let the other person know. These are confidential meetings and I will keep anything confidential that you wish me to. Antonio, as I heard from you first when the mediation began, I will speak to Fatima first now. Would you like to go into the other room, have a coffee, and think about options for the billing system on your own? I will call you when I have finished with Fatima...."

2. COMMENCING A SEPARATE MEETING TRANSITION

"Well, Fatima, thanks for meeting with me separately. I want to first reassure you that what you say here and wish to be kept confidential will be kept confidential unless you ask me to convey some offer or message to Antonio.... Now, let's start by hearing how the mediation has been going for you so far.... Thanks, Fatima, now is there anything new you would like to raise with me that hasn't come up in the joint session...?"

3. ENDING A SEPARATE MEETING TRANSITION

"Now as I understand it, Fatima, when we resume the joint session, you would like to make an offer to Antonio along the lines that if he is willing to set up a more effective billing system for his clients, you are prepared to reduce the use of general staff on Rotary business and to spend only two afternoons a week on the golf course…. And you also said that while you were on your own you would consider ways of increasing Antonio's share of the profits on a phased-in basis. Is that correct…?"

4. RESUMING THE JOINT SESSION TRANSITION

"Well thank you, Fatima and Antonio, for meeting with me separately. That can sometimes be an important tool in a mediation, and it gave you time to consider settlement options and do some other homework. Now as a result of those meetings, is there anything which either of you would like to say to the other…?"

I. Potential Dangers with Separate Meetings and Ways of Handling Them

As with much of life, there is a series of risks relating to separate meetings; but in both, there are also ways of limiting and dealing with the risks. The following table deals with the separate meeting risks only.

Potential risk	Ways of dealing
Breach of confidential disclosure in separate meeting	Make written notes of confidences, limit length of meetings
Development of suspicion and distrust ("What is going on without me…?")	Educate parties, normalize this stage, keep to times, meet with both sides, give withdrawing party task to perform
Mediator miscommunicates an offer or information or dollar figure	Write down details and check with party before conveying them
Party becomes anxious over length of other side's separate meeting	Advise of likely duration, and tell waiting party if longer than expected
Party thinks mediator is on their side	Avoid sympathy, too much bonding and encouragement of their position
Creates too much power for mediator	Have co-mediator to keep honest, require mediator debriefing
No progress on resumption of joint sessions	Prepare parties at end of separate meetings for subsequent negotiations
Detachment of parties from each other and lack of "constructive confrontation"	Do not hold too early, resume joint sessions after served purpose

Due to these risks, and in particular, the potential loss of trust by one or both parties, some mediators never conduct separate meetings. In our experience, this precaution is unwarranted. However, the concern underlying this practice should be understood and dealt with through the expediencies of advance notice, explanation, confidentiality, and equality referred to in the above pages.

IV. Exercises

1. Find (or appoint) a volunteer and ask them to role play a party in a mediation who has no prior knowledge of the process. Make a mediator opening statement to them (use some poetic license to give the illusion that there are two persons present). Respond to any questions or concerns. After making the mediator's opening statement, ask the volunteer to give you feedback on what you did well and what you could have done differently. Evaluate your own performance against the standards found in this chapter.

2. With the same volunteer as before, practice the transition patter for the separate meetings. In light of this experience, modify the patter or your use.

3. Watch a video of a real or simulated mediation and identify differences in the structure of that process compared with that described here. Write out possible reasons for why the structures differ.

IV. Exercises

FIVE

Assisting the Communication Process

*The problem with communication... is the **illusion** that it has been accomplished.*

—GEORGE BERNARD SHAW (AUTHOR AND PLAYWRIGHT)

I. Introduction

One of the most important functions of mediators is to provide a context in which good communication can take place. Parties in conflict tend to communicate poorly, and disputes can be the result of bad communication. The goal of good communication is mutual understanding, that is, a meeting of the minds of those engaged in communicating with one another. This chapter deals with the mediator's roles in assisting the parties to communicate appropriately. The skills referred to here are clearly not peculiar to mediating. Many prospective mediators have good communication skills from past training and experience, which they need to adapt to the requirements of mediation. Many others do not have those skills and need to begin with the basics.

There are three broad responsibilities for mediators in relation to their communication roles. First, they must themselves be good communicators and model good communication practices, with words as their main, but not only, tool. Second, they must intervene in the parties' communications to make them more accurate, explicit, comprehensible, and appropriate. Third, they must "educate" the parties in good communication techniques.

Communication is an important ingredient in all forms of professional practice, and is also a major discipline in its own right. Thus, a book on mediation skills can only deal with some aspects of communication particularly relevant to that practice. Dedicated students of communication should consult the specialized literature on this subject for more theoretical and practical insights than can be provided here.

Communication assistance by the mediator is necessary during all stages of the mediation. Where communication is unclear, negative, or over-emotional, then his or her intervention is required. Where communications break down entirely, the mediator tries to keep them going, for example, by relying on the advisers or using informal channels. All dispute-resolution processes rely on good information, and where the mediator can enhance communication, it can serve the purpose of obtaining and making use of the best information. However, this is not a narrow instrumental role. Good communication is enhanced as much by context as it is by a good reframe or appropriate question. The other mediator skills required in building the foundations for mediation and conducting the process effectively are all significant in achieving good communication.

II. Communication and Culture

As referred to previously, this book does not attempt to deal in any significant way with the relevance of culture to many aspects of mediation. However, regarding communication, some reference, no matter how brief, needs to be made to the significance of cross-cultural realities.

Styles and methods of communication are affected by many factors, including class, gender, ethnicity, religion, education, and emotional state. Even the meaning of simple words or phrases can be different for people from middle-class or working-class backgrounds, or for members of the different genders. For example, "to negotiate," "matter of principle," "compromise," "agreement," and "commitment"' have different meanings in different cultures. Here reference is made only to the factor of culture and its significance for communication, but the general principles referred to have much wider applicability.

Culture is understood as the habits, behavior, attitudes, values, and unconscious knowledge of different social groups—in the present context, groups of identifiable ethnic or racial background. (One could also talk about different business cultures.) Culture shapes and affects approaches to many different facets of life, including the approach toward "negotiation" and "mediation." Different cultures also speak different languages, and while it is possible to translate the spoken word from one language to another, this will not necessarily convey the intended meaning across cultures. In her book, *Negotiating with the Chinese*, Bee Chen Goh points out that language may translate words but not meaning because, particularly across cultures, communication consists of more than words alone.[1] Where cultural factors are less visible, and even an unconscious part of behavior, they may lead to serious communication breakdowns as each side judges and evaluates the other in terms of their own cultural realities.

Goh develops this theme in relation to the different outlooks and perceptions of the Chinese and Western cultures. Chinese society has a collectivist (homocentric) conception in which the individual inhabits a web of relationships and conformity, which is highly regarded. Western society has an individualistic (egocentric) conception in which the individual self is of prime importance and self-actualization is admired. While harmony and interdependent relationships are a feature of collec-

---

1. BEE CHEN GOH, NEGOTIATING WITH THE CHINESE 20 (1996).

tivist societies, individualistic societies emphasize self-centered behaviors and competition.

Given the contrasts, communication can be expected to be highly different as between collectivist and individualistic societies. Collectivist cultures tend to have "high-context" communication, and individualistic cultures tend to have "low-context" communication.[2] In *low-context* communication, as we have in the United States, most information is conveyed in explicit verbal messages, with less focus on situational context. Communicators state opinions and desires directly and strive to persuade others to accept their viewpoint. Clear, direct, accurate speech and verbal fluency are admired. For example, when an American negotiator does not like an offer of settlement, he or she might say, "I think that offer is too low." This is a "low context" message because the message's meaning is clear without knowing much, if anything, about the situation (context) in which it was stated.

In *high-context* communication, on the other hand, important information is conveyed in contextual cues (time, relationship, situation), with less reliance on verbal messages. Communicators state opinions indirectly and abstain from saying "no" directly. Talking around the point, ambiguity, and silence are admired. For example, a negotiator from a "high-context" culture, like China, might respond to an offer of settlement he or she believes to be too low by remaining silent. The negotiator might also say, "I will need to think about that offer," the true meaning of which, in the context of the discussion, is that the offer is too low. Thus, there are increased opportunities for miscommunication and misunderstanding when people of different cultures are present in the mediation.

While there can be a tendency to stereotype cultural factors, and while not all individuals in a culture behave in identical fashion, the differences between high- and low-context communication styles are highly significant in mediation. This book is based on the low-context communication style that is part of the dominant American culture. In this context, mediators strive to get the parties to get to the point, say what they mean, and be explicit, direct, and unambiguous. This is appropriate for some cultural contexts but is inappropriate for others where indirectness, ambiguity, and situation are more relevant. In the latter context, mediators must adapt the suggestions in this chapter to take account of the subtleties of high-context communication.

Case Illustration: Multi-Cultural Miscommunication

In a commercial tenancy dispute, the shopping center was represented by its commercial manager, a traditional American, while the tenant, a new American from an Asian country, was representing himself. During the exchange

---

2. RONALD B. ADLER & GEORGE RODMAN, UNDERSTANDING HUMAN COMMUNICATION 102 (1994).

of information, the manager gave a lengthy account of why factors beyond the center's control had led to diminished revenue and how the center had no responsibility for the tenant's substantial drop in turnover during the past year. Throughout this presentation the new American listened attentively, nodded his head continuously, and made occasional affirmative noises. As soon as he began to speak it became apparent that he did not accept any of the landlord's explanation, and the manager was outraged. During the separate meeting the manager vented his anger to the mediator and asked how the other party could be so inconsistent. The mediator explained the cross-cultural misunderstanding to the traditional American, that for the new American his attending and nodding indicated that he was listening, but not that he was giving his assent.

III. Basic Issues in Communication

The beginner's guide to earthly communication would inform us that human communication involves at least two parties, a "sender" and a "receiver." The sender wishes to transmit a message to the receiver and sends it by way of verbal, vocal, and visual elements. The receiver takes delivery of the message, and the communication is complete. Unfortunately, it is not quite as simple as beginner's guides like to suggest.

A. Encoding and Decoding Messages

The passing of a message from one person to another is not as mechanical as the passing of a ball from one player to another. This is because both the sender and receiver are affected in the way they communicate by a range of factors: the context of the communication, the respective emotions of the parties, cultural expectations, past experiences, and assumptions and prejudices. These are all subjective and highly variable factors that can differ significantly from one person to the other, even when they are from the same cultural background. This means that the sender will "encode" his or her message—that is, the words used, the vocal effects, and the body language will be based on his or her perceptions of the world. Likewise, the receiver will "decode" the message in terms of his or her perceptions and frame of reference. Because of the subjective nature of both the encoding and decoding, there may be a substantial difference between what the sender thought they were communicating and what the receiver thought was being communicated. Hence the need for advanced guides to communication.

Of course, in reality, communication seldom consists of a single message from one person to another. In the mediation context, it involves a series of ongoing messages between three or more people. This makes things both easier and more complex at the same time. It is easier because the receiver of a message usually responds to it, and this response can help to clarify things. Receivers can give feedback to the sender through verbal, vocal, or visual means. Thus, the receiver may ask a question which gives the sender an opportunity to resend the message more clearly, more slowly, or more accurately than before. Moreover, the sender may detect from the body language of the receiver that the message has not been understood or has been misunderstood, and immediately clarify it.

Things are more complex in the mediation context because, as in any other conversation, all parties continually swap the roles of sender and receiver. During these exchanges many different facts, ideas, emotions, and attitudes are being exchanged. If the situation is tense and the communication fast and furious, the encoding of each party may be clumsy and the decoding may be faulty. Thus, where a receiver is intently focused on the words being used by the sender, he or she might pick up on the factual information of the message but fail to pick up on attitudes and feelings surrounding it. Likewise, where a sender uses aggressive body language, it may cause the receiver to overlook important objective information being conveyed verbally.

B. Professional Terminology

Professional frameworks also affect communication, whether lawyers, accountants, or psychologists are involved. For example, lawyers use accepted and well-understood terms to communicate in a kind of shorthand that is highly accurate and appropriate when they converse with one another. For example, lawyers in a personal injury mediation may happily swap terms such as "without prejudice," "compensatory damages," "special damages," and "future economic loss" with both ease and understanding. Unfortunately, these terms add another layer of complexity to the involvement of laypersons for whom legalese is unintelligible at best and alienating at worst. Mediators also have their in-house jargon such as "BATNA," "caucus," and "conditional linked bargaining" that should be used with caution, or not at all, in front of clients. hence the need for an outside party to assist with many facets of communication.

C. Experiences, Behavior, and Affect

In the classic work *The Skilled Helper*, Gerard Egan points out that clients of the helping professionals tend to talk about three things: *experiences, behavior,* and *affect*.[3] Experiences are "what happened" to them. For example, an employee says she has just been reprimanded and put on notice by her supervisor. Behavior is "what they do or refrain from doing." For example, the employee explains that the reprimand concerns her arriving at work late, making long personal phone calls, and missing deadlines. Affect is the feelings and emotions that arise from or are associated with experiences and behavior. For example, the employee expresses frustration about job advancement or anger over her treatment.

---

3. GERARD EGAN, THE SKILLED HELPER 81 (2005).

Most people are willing to talk about their *experiences* but are less willing to talk about their *behavior* and *feelings*. Experiences are easier to discuss because they usually involve something that has happened *to* the speaker and they entail no acceptance of responsibility. However, in mediation, communication is required on experiences, behavior, and affect in so far as this will promote resolution of the dispute.

In facilitating the parties' communication, the mediator should be attentive to the common tendency for people to talk about others' motives and to talk about the facts as though there is only one version of "what happened." The mediator might instruct the parties at an early stage of the mediation that they cannot claim to talk about "what happened" but only about "your memory of events." This builds in a qualification to whatever they might say. Likewise, the mediator might instruct them not to talk about what they perceive the other party's motives to be, but only about "your own motives and internal feelings" relating to past events.

IV. Communication Style and Terminology

Mediators need to develop an appropriate communication style and use of terminology. The style is an art, and the terminology is a science. In regard to style, much will depend on culture and context. However, there are no prizes for guessing that in most American contexts, mediators need to speak fluently in a quiet and confident manner and give complete and specific messages. They should use plain and intelligible words and avoid legal jargon and technical terms where these would not be understood by the parties they are helping. In other words, they should speak the parties' language (or languages).

In regard to terminology, some words and phrases are redolent of conflict, contestation, and struggle and are best avoided by mediators. Others could be seen as threatening or challenging to particular parties. There is much emphasis in mediation manuals on the need for "reframing" the inappropriate language of the parties to words and phrases that are positive instead of negative, constructive instead of destructive, and problem-solving rather than problem-reinforcing. However, instead of only being reactive through reframing, mediators should proactively use appropriate language as a model for that of their clients. This skill is called "framing." This can be illustrated in the following table.

Mediators should say	Instead of saying
Problem/situation	Dispute/conflict
Discussions	Negotiations
Current hopes	Claims/demands
Other party (Phyllis)	Opponent/defendant
Agree to	Concede

Give us your understanding	Tell us the facts
Make decisions	Reach agreement
So this is important for you	It's a matter of principle
Ways of compensating	Damages/award
Important issue for you	Fundamental to claim
I'm having trouble understanding you	I don't believe you

These and other positive terms are second nature to veteran mediators and are used from the earliest stages of mediation. The use of positive terms is designed to get parties to think about the dispute constructively. It attempts to restructure their perceptions. Where the parties adopt the positive term, it can open them up to a more constructive form of problem solving. Mediators also use a number of constructive "weasel" words such as "reasonable," "satisfactory," "appropriate," and "productive." These again lend a positive tone to the discussions. Where the parties use a negative term, the mediator reframes to the positive replacement term.

V. Non-Verbal Communication in Mediation

Conversing verbally is only one form of communication. Non-verbal communication is another. Non-verbal communication consists of those aspects of communication that can be seen by the other party (the visuals) and other forms of non-verbal communication which can be heard (namely, vocals).

A. Body Language and Visuals

Visuals refer to all aspects of communication that are observed, as opposed to heard, by the receiver and which convey messages to him or her. Body language is the most prominent form of visual communication. It involves all aspects of bodily appearance and movement that convey attitudes, feelings, emotions, and other important dimensions of communication. In practical terms, it could include the sender's clothing, posture, body and limb movements, hand gestures, facial expressions, eye motions, and physiological responses such as blushing and quickened breathing. The face and eyes are often portrayed as the most important conveyors of body language, but micro-signals in these areas are not always easy to read and interpret.

While parties can fake body language to some degree, for example, eye signals, tone of voice, blushing, or shortness of breath, doing so is not easy. Children in particular find it difficult to conceal body language, and the crossed legs or averted eyes can betray the apparent innocence of their spoken words. Unlike verbal communication, body language never stops, and when a person is verbally silent, it remains the only way in which they are communicating.

There are numerous specialized books on body language. A long-time favorite book is by Alan and Barbara Pease entitled *The Definitive Book of Body Language*. The authors make the following observations:[4]

- More than 65 percent of a message is conveyed non-verbally;
- Non-verbal communication has a significance in communication five times that of verbal communication;
- In general, non-verbal communication conveys interpersonal attitudes, while verbal communication is used to impart information; and
- Some non-verbal signals are learned and some are inborn.

A single gesture may have many meanings and should be interpreted in the context of associated verbal and non-verbal communication, the person's culture, and the environment in which it takes place. Some generalized features of body language in Western societies are:

- Open limb positions—receptivity toward what is being said;
- Crossed or folded limbs—defensiveness toward what is being said;
- Forward-leaning body posture—attentiveness to speaker;
- Backward stance—indifference to speaker;
- Open hands—plain dealing and honesty;
- Closed fists, pointed fingers—aggression, threatening attitude;
- Direct eye contact—sincerity, openness, honest dealing; and
- Averted gaze, avoidance of eye contact—deceit, guilt, embarrassment.

Body language can either confirm or contradict what is being said verbally, or it could simply confuse.[5] As mentioned below, when it comes to interpreting body language, it is dangerous to put too much weight on a single factor. As Egan suggests in *The Skilled Helper*, the trick is to spot the messages without making too much or too little of them.[6] Unfortunately for us, there are studies finding that people in the helping professions often misinterpret the non-verbal messages implicit in a series of photographs, while untrained people pick them correctly.[7] Lawyers have highly trained listening skills, but are not trained in observing behavior and are among the offenders.

---

4. ALAN PEASE & BARBARA PEASE, THE DEFINITIVE BOOK OF BODY LANGUAGE 8–11 (2004).

5. For a study of the relationship between facial expressions and emotions, see generally PAUL EKMAN, EMOTIONS REVEALED (2003).

6. *Id.* at 87–89.

7. JAY FOLBERG & ALISON TAYLOR, MEDIATION: A COMPREHENSIVE GUIDE TO RESOLVING CONFLICTS WITHOUT LITIGATION 117 (1984).

Visuals also refers to messages received from the broader environment, such as the size of an office, the shape of a table, the size and height of chairs, seating arrangements, spatial configurations, lighting, and the like. These factors can convey power, strength, status, influence, domination, equality, and other such messages more emphatically and unequivocally than words. Director Stanley Kubrick is reported to have spent five days arranging the lighting for a single scene in his final film, *Eyes Wide Shut*, but mediators seldom have such time, or flair. Nevertheless, without any language, body movement, or other overt communication, a whole mood and atmosphere can be conveyed by the environment and surroundings. The mediator is usually responsible for the mediation environment, and thus, should be attentive to the "message" the environment conveys.

B. Vocals

Vocal communication refers to the many oral messages that can be sent without using words and language. It is sometimes referred to as paralanguage. Some forms of this paralanguage are volume, pitch, pace, tone, inflection, emphasis, intonation, rhythm, resonance, inflection, and silence.[8] One may add laughter, sighs, gestures, and screams, although the last-mentioned is not encountered in the daily rounds of mediators. All of these disclose emotion, attitude, and other states of mind that are not conveyed through verbal communication.

Because all vocals are auditory signals, they are difficult to demonstrate through written words in a textbook. However, the following illustration shows the different meanings that the same five words can have depending on where the emphasis is placed by the speaker:

- *This* mediation book is brilliant (but not all the other mediation books).
- This *mediation* book is brilliant (but not their books on pottery and poetry).
- This mediation *book* is brilliant (but not their mediation videos).
- This mediation book *is* brilliant (I had my doubts, but now I've read it).
- This mediation book is *brilliant* (it's top class, of the highest quality).

As with body language, some forms of vocal communication are difficult to disguise. Where the vocal messages contradict the spoken words, listeners tend to be influenced more by the former. This can be demonstrated in relation to sarcasm, where emphasis and tone can give spoken words a meaning diametrically opposed to their literal meaning. Thus, if you say the above sentence (but preferably not too loudly) with the relevant emphasis and tone on both syllables of "brilliant," it can become a contemptuous rejection of the merits of the book. There are many more subtle deviations from literal meaning that mediators can detect from vocal communication.

---

8. Nadja Spegel, Bernadette Rogers & Ross P. Buckley, Negotiation: Theory and Techniques 151 (1998).

C. The Mediator's Role in Relation to Visuals and Vocals

One of the mediator's functions is to observe and interpret vocal messages and body language, though much micro-language in the face and eyes is not easy to read. From their observations, mediators need to make inferences, for example, that blushing or crossing of the limbs indicates anxiety or defensiveness, and plan their next intervention accordingly. This is part of the mediator's hypothesis development function.

However, observing behavior and inferring meaning are separate activities, and it is possible to accurately observe but assign a mistaken meaning to that behavior. Mediators therefore need to make tentative interpretations of behavior and check them out to see if they are correct. They should not read too much into a single cue. A sudden bodily movement by a young client, Jonathan, may be caused as much by discomfort, habit, or a medical condition as by anger or boredom. When an elderly client, Kerri, frowns at a document, she might be upset at what the paper says or be unable to see clearly without her glasses. Where behavioral signals occur in clusters, for example, dilation of the pupils, heavier breathing, and distressed hand movements, they are easier for mediators to diagnose tentatively than where they are single occurrences.

Non-verbal signals are most significant where they are incongruent with the verbal message. This is the situation, for example, where the words signify assent but the crossed legs or nervous eyes suggest resistance, or where the words suggest honesty but the voice's higher pitch suggests deceit. Mediators can use the separate meetings to raise and deal with incongruent factors such as these. They can check whether their understanding of a party's signals is correct and whether the other side might be aware of the message being sent.

D. The Mediator's Own Non-Verbal Communication

Mediators need to be attentive to their own body language and vocals, which could reveal bias, anger, impatience, or boredom. Some actions will be generally appropriate in mediation, for example, open body positions, direct eye contact, and congruent facial expressions. Others will usually be inappropriate, for example, frowning when a party is making their opening statement or folding the arms when a party is proclaiming the truth of their version of events. Yet others require the mediator to make judgments and adaptations for particular circumstances, such as choice of clothing, handshakes, touch, and facial expressions. Some long-held habits which could disconcert or mislead the parties may be unknown to mediators. Viewing videotapes of actual or simulated mediations can provide a useful learning tool and insight into reality. With that said, some long-held habits are notoriously difficult for even earnest mediators to change.

Because mediators' language and non-verbals can be just as significant as the parties', mediators must strive to achieve consistency in *their* verbal, vocal, and visual communication. Some "censorship" of body language might be required; for example, where the mediator feels annoyance or disbelief, he or she might have to control facial expressions so as not to display this inner reality. "Censorship" can develop into manipulation where mediators deliberately provide non-verbal signals that they think might be appropriate, such as a shake of the head to indicate disagreement with a client's proposal.

Mediators need to be attentive to their own physiological reactions, for example, tensing of the muscles or clenching of the fists. Likewise, the initial handshake can convey domination (crushed phalanxes), weakness (wet fish), or strength (firm grip). By being aware of these factors, the mediator can control his or her bodily reactions and prevent communicating anxiety, disapproval, or anger, as the case may be. Experienced mediators can also use body language as a form of constructive intervention, for example, to guide the conversation between the parties with simple hand directions to ensure that they are speaking to each other and not to the mediator.

Appearance is an important issue for mediators, though not entirely within their control. Appearance creates initial impressions that are difficult to change. Clothing can be changed but height cannot. Some male commercial mediators remove their suit jacket at the earliest opportunity to convey the message, without saying it, that this is an informal process. However, few would remove the tie as this might convey lack of commercial experience.

How mediators arrange the physical space is also significant. Reference was made previously to how people are seated in mediation.[9] Physical arrangements should always respect personal space. In a professional relationship there is usually more physical space between persons than in a personal relationship. Where the mediator knows a lawyer personally it might be appropriate to maintain a professional distance when the clients are present.

VI. Effective Listening

In a perfect world, mediation would not be necessary, as parties would listen to each other effectively. They would hear the messages that are "on the lines," usually factual content, as well as the messages that are "between the lines," usually emotions and feelings. Mediators would not be required to remind the parties to listen to each other to achieve proper understanding. However, in the real world, mediators are required for these purposes.

Most of a mediator's time should be spent listening to the parties. Effective listening skills are of major importance to mediators. They must listen effectively before they can get the parties to listen to each other. Effective listening involves more than

---

9. *See* Chapter 2—*Establishing the Foundation: Introductions, Intake, Screening and Preparation*, section VI F.

hearing spoken words. It involves properly understanding the meaning of messages, by grasping facts and information analytically as well as by picking up on their emotional content and the broad patterns and themes that they convey.

A. Causes of Ineffective Listening

Listening may prove to be ineffective for many reasons. Let us look at some common reasons for ineffective listening in relation to the *speaker*, the *listener*, and the *environment*:

1. *The speaker*: inaudibility, annoying mannerisms, physical appearance, tone of voice, speed of delivery, presentation, contentious content, and interruptions by others.

2. *The listener*: inattention, discomfort, fatigue, focus on responding to the speaker, ignorance of subject matter, psychological deafness, emotional involvement, lack of comprehension, inability to absorb, and judgmental attitude.

3. *Environmental factors*: external noise, bad lighting, poor acoustics, uncomfortable seating, outside interruptions.

B. Listening Effectively

There is a lot of hard work involved in listening effectively. It is not just a passive exercise, hence the use of the phrase "active listening." The listener must be physically attentive, must concentrate on and encourage the speaker, must display an attitude of interest and concern, be non-judgmental, not be preoccupied with responding to or questioning the speaker, and not be distracted by non-relevant matters. The effective listener is concentrating not only on words and sentences but also on patterns of thought, the organization of ideas, and the themes implicit in the speaker's communication. This requires considerable effort. "Pay attention while I speak" is not just a classroom cliché, but an important principle of effective listening. Active listening is important for mediators in relation to a number of other functions, such as summarizing, defining the issues, and making the best use of any valuable communications by the parties for negotiation.

VII. Elements of Active Listening

There are three elements to active listening: *attending skills*, *following skills*, and *reflective skills*. Each plays a part in making the person a "good listener." Let us explore each in more detail:

1. *Attending Skills:* This means being with the client physically and psychologically, making them feel important and trustful by use of physical atten-

tion, display of interest, appropriate body movements, encouraging noises ("I see…," "Uhuh…," "Yes…"). Gerard Egan, in *The Skilled Helper*, refers to listening skills in terms of the acronym SOLER:[10]

- *S*quarely face the client to show involvement;
- Adopt an *O*pen posture, literally and metaphorically;
- *L*ean towards the client at times;
- Maintain *E*ye contact most of the time;
- *R*elax, be natural in these behaviors.

2. *Following Skills:* This indicates that the listener is following the speaker by providing cues, not interrupting, asking clarifying questions, taking notes, summarizing, and refraining from giving advice.

3. *Reflecting Skills:* This involves giving feedback to the speaker about the listener's understanding of their meaning, with reference to feeling and content; identifying and acknowledging content and feeling; summarizing content and feeling; and asking empathic questions.

The speaker's frame of reference is always important in relation to listening. The listener needs to try to understand and comprehend this frame of reference and look for themes and patterns in the speaker's speech. The mediator also needs to be aware of his or her own frame of reference. In some situations, the mediator needs to modify the speaker's frame of reference through reframing.

Reading body language and vocal communication is an important element in active listening. As referred to above, the trick is to spot the messages in non-verbal behaviors without making too much or too little of them. These non-verbal messages can confirm the verbal message, contradict it, or confuse it. Much will depend on context.

A. Detracting from Effective Listening

Some of the natural impulses that detract from good listening by the mediator include the following behaviors:[11]

- Focusing on facts and information and ignoring the feeling and emotions: "So you just want $93,475.12 as compensation?"
- Asking too many questions, particularly closed, leading, or cross-examining questions: "But didn't you tell me earlier that you had not done specialist training?"

---

10. EGAN, *supra* note 3, at 75–76.

11. ROBERT BOLTON, PEOPLE SKILLS: HOW TO ASSERT YOURSELF, LISTEN TO OTHERS, AND RESOLVE CONFLICTS 15–16 (1986).

- Being judgmental and moralizing: "You did okay..."; "Everyone has to take the ups with the downs."

- Analyzing the reasons for parties' behavior: "You were obviously in denial when you refused help."

- Lapsing into clichés: "I hear what you're saying..."; "I know how you must have felt...."

- Becoming hooked into the other's emotions, values, or judgments: "So you felt you were entitled to some self-help against the bastard?"

- Engaging in self-exposure: "The same thing happened to me...."

- Finishing the parties' sentences.

VIII. Communication in Telephone Mediations

Despite the advent of quality video conferencing and its general availability, mediation via telephone or similar means that use solely audio communication still occur. Telephone mediation may be used because high-speed internet is unavailable to all participants. There are some instances where telephone mediation is used because some or all of the parties prefer it. That said, it is more difficult to communicate effectively over the telephone, which presents special challenges for the mediator. In telephone mediations, the mediator is entirely dependent on verbal and vocal communication and is unaware of the speaker's body language. As we have seen, body language accounts for a major part of the communicating message. The lack of visual-communication cues makes it more likely that parties will misunderstand each other, lose track of the conversation, and take offense to comments where no offense was intended. Thus, the mediator must make a special effort to ensure the parties are communicating clearly and minimize the chance of misunderstandings.[12] Here are some techniques that will make telephone mediations more productive:

1. *Summarize frequently.* Although summarizing is always important in mediation, it takes on a special importance in telephone mediations. Parties will often not know that they have misunderstood an offer or an argument, or they may be reluctant to admit that they have. Thus, summarizing at regular intervals helps to reorient participants who may have strayed from the discussion.

2. *Paraphrase frequently.* As with summarizing, paraphrasing ensures that the party's message has been understood correctly. It repeats the message a second time for those who might have missed it or misunderstood it the first time it was spoken.

---

12. James C. Freund, Smart Negotiating 218 (1993).

3. *Ask for clarification.* If you believe that a party's statement has a reasonable chance of being misinterpreted for any reason, ask the party to clarify it.

4. *Assist in balancing the amount of time each party speaks.* In telephone mediations, it is much easier for a participant to monopolize the discussion than in face-to-face mediations. In face-to-face meetings, mediators often rely on visual clues (facial expressions or body language) to determine when a party has something to add to the discussion. When a mediator sees that a participant wishes to speak but has been reluctant to interrupt the other party, the mediator can tactfully give the party an opportunity to speak. These important clues, however, are unavailable in telephone mediation, and, absent special efforts by the mediator, the party may become frustrated with their inability to contribute as they would like to the conversation. Additionally, participants will have different degrees of "tolerance" for silence in the telephone conversation. Consequently, one party after only a few seconds of silence will rush in to fill the "void" with an argument or opinion, often crowding out the contributions of less aggressive speakers. Mediators should therefore "check in" with less vocal participants more frequently to assure that their voices are heard.

5. *Explain telephone mediation pitfalls.* Explain to the participants at the beginning of the mediation some of the potential pitfalls of telephone mediation and what you intend to do to prevent them from falling prey to these. If the participants are aware of the potential for misunderstandings during telephone mediation, they are more likely to be more careful and clearer in their communications. Moreover, absent a rationale, a mediator's frequent summaries and paraphrasing may appear more disruptive than helpful.

Telephone mediations are sometimes necessary because time or cost make it impractical to meet in person. In circumstances where there is a high degree of animosity that would make an in-person discussion difficult or where there has been a history of violence, such as can be the case in domestic mediations, telephone mediation can provide a more appropriate mode of communication. However, in general, telephone mediations should be discouraged because face-to-face mediations are generally a more effective method of resolving differences. Parties who negotiate face to face are more likely to be cooperative than those interacting on the telephone.[13] Face-to-face negotiations enable participants to build rapport more easily and lessen the "psychological" distance that results between participants over the telephone. Finally, and perhaps most importantly, research has shown that negotiations conducted in person are more likely to reach agreement.[14] (Additional discussion of telephone mediation is found in Chapter 10—*Variations in the Mediation Process*, section V.)

---

13. LEIGH L. THOMPSON, THE MIND AND HEART OF THE NEGOTIATOR 305 (3d ed. 2005).
14. *Id.*

IX. Reframing

A. Reframing Defined

Reframing is closely related to active listening and is an important skill for mediators. It is the other side of the "framing" coin referred to earlier. Whereas framing is carried out proactively, *reframing* is a reactive mediator intervention. All parties communicate within a certain frame of reference based on how they see the world in terms of their culture, experiences, and sense of justice. The goal of reframing is to change this frame of reference in order to get the parties to think differently about things, or at least to get them to see things in a different light. It is based on the fact that the language we use affects how we perceive the world, that by changing language we can change perceptions, and that changed perceptions can lead to changed behavior. Reframing is a *translation exercise* through which the mediator changes the communication by moving it from one language to another, with the hope that in the second language the comment may be more palatable to the other side or more conducive to collaborative problem solving.[15] Acting as the "translator" is yet another role for the mediator.

Mediators accomplish reframing by using different words, concepts, terms, emphases, and intonations and by otherwise qualifying what the parties have themselves said to provide a different frame of reference. For example, suppose that in response to a proposed solution to the problem offered by the other party, a mediation participant says, "That is the craziest idea I ever heard!" A mediator might "reframe" the statement as follows: "John, what about Paul's suggestion do you think is impractical?" In this reframe, the mediator changed the words that the party used to sanitize the insult "crazy" and refocus the discussion on the more constructive topic of "practicality."

Reframing is used not only to change the words being used but also to change the context of a party's statement, for example, from positions to interests or from the past to the future. If a party in a mediation states, "I want $100,000 to settle this matter," the mediator can reframe that statement to "Betty, so you wish to be fairly compensated for your injury?" This attempts to shift the party's frame of reference from a position ($100,000) to an interest (fair compensation). When reframing is successful, it leads to a change in perspective or perception on the party's behalf. This altered attitude or view of the dispute can lead to changes in behavior. While the original frame of reference may have had a negative effect on the resolution of the dispute, the new frame of reference is conducive to constructive conflict management.

It must be emphasized that this is more than just a terminological exercise; it is about orienting the whole tone of the discussions. Where a party points out what is wrong, the mediator asks them to indicate what would be right for them. Where a

---

15. KARL A. SLAIKEU, WHEN PUSH COMES TO SHOVE 232 (1996).

party continually emphasizes what they do not want, the mediator gets them to talk about what they do want. Where a party goes on about what the other party wants, the mediator asks them to state what they themselves want.

1. A NOTE ON THE SIMILARITY BETWEEN REFRAMING AND THE DESIGN OF JOKES

A joke-teller encourages a certain point of view, but when the punchline is delivered, the listener is able to see the preceding story in a different light. On the face of it, the punchline is incongruous, but when the listener catches the joke by seeing the previous narrative in a different light, then the incongruous becomes congruous. For example:

> In the wee hours of the morning, a lawyer called the governor of his state to inform him that a noted judge had just died and the lawyer wanted to take the judge's place. The irritated governor assured him, "if it's okay with the funeral parlor, it's okay with me."[16]

Not such a great joke, but it makes the point. The humor is caused by the surprise, relief, or delight that occurs when the punchline is delivered and the listener has to change his or her erroneous expectation. In other words, a scene is first described from one viewpoint, and then rearranged, sometimes by a single word. Likewise, mediators, through reframing, have the capacity to restructure the parties' perceptions of a dispute situation. In joke telling the switch-over is temporary and gives rise to humor, whereas in mediation it can be permanent and give rise to insight. While the joke-teller reframes to achieve laughter, the mediator reframes to contribute to problem solving.

Case Illustration: The Custody Battle

In a lengthy family mediation, both parents began positionally by demanding "custody" of their two children and denying that the other was a suitable "residence parent." The mediator reframed this language to that of "discussing the most appropriate parenting arrangements for Mark and Matthew." Initially the parents resisted this definition of the problem and continued to assert their claim for custody or residence. The mediator persisted, and eventually one party, then the other, began using the new language. This shifted the focus from the parents to the children. It led to a constructive discussion of Mark and Matthew's needs and to eventual agreement on a parenting regime. In light of this arrangement, the legal concepts of residence and contact were dealt with in the final agreement.

---

16. LAWYERS, JOKES, QUOTES AND ANECDOTES 74, (Patrick Regan, ed. 2004).

B. Functions and Examples of Reframing

Reframing can serve a number of different functions. Clearly, no single reframe can perform each one of the functions at the same time, nor is reframing a constant form of mediator intervention. Instead, it is used selectively where it can perform one of the stated purposes. Here the various functions of reframing are illustrated in the context of a hypothetical dispute between a householder and the builder who was contracted to repair the chimney. The repairs were faulty, causing rain to leak into the lounge and on to expensive furnishings.

Function of Reframe	Statement by Party	Reframe by Mediator
It can detoxify language, by removing accusations, judgments, and other verbal stings and barbs.	"The builder is an idiot whose appalling workmanship has ruined my carpets."	"So this repair job has been a bad experience for both of you?"
It can focus on the positive, by removing references to negatives and other destructive elements in the language.	"The damage to the roof has caused me enormous losses…."	"So getting the roof fixed properly would be valuable for you?"
It can focus on interests, by removing references to positions and solutions and reframing to underlying needs and requirements.	"He must fix that roof tomorrow and give me $20,000 for the ruined carpets."	"So you need to stop the leaking as soon as possible and sort out your furnishings."
It can focus on the future, by removing references to the past and reframing to future needs and interests.	"He was always late, never returned my calls and left a mess all over the place."	"So you would like the future work to be done on a professional basis?"
It can mutualize problems, by avoiding one-sided definitions and reframing to dual-sided formulations.	"His stupid negligence has made me look a fool among friends and neighbors."	"So we also need to see how both your damaged reputations can be repaired."
It can soften and qualify demands, threats, and negotiation "bottom lines."	"If he does not pay me $20,000 dollars within 3 days I'll take him to court."	"So you're looking for a reasonable dollar settlement within a short time."

| It can turn an absolute demand or a position into one possible option. | "I demand the repair of the roof, $20,000, and a full apology." | "So your preferred option right now is an apology, money, and the repairs." |

Additional standard terms encountered in mediation, and ways in which mediators can reframe them, are contained in Appendix 4.

C. Potential Problems with Reframing

There are a number of potential problems with mediator reframing. The problems could arise because a suspicious or distrustful party finds it an alien experience, or it could be because the mediator does not carry out the reframing appropriately. In either event, the party's subjective assessment will be the same, namely, that the reframing intervention has not contributed positively to the mediation. More specifically, there are three common problems that can arise from reframing. First, reframing is a difficult art and if performed badly may be seen as mere parroting of the parties. ("Why does she keep repeating everything I say...?") Second, reframing could be seen as manipulating. ("That's not what I said, he keeps twisting my words....". Third, reframing could be perceived as the mediator favoring one party and losing his or her non-partisan role. ("She seems to be agreeing with the other party all the time....")

Nevertheless, appropriate reframing is a powerful mediator intervention and can be readily improved through practice. One of the golden rules for avoiding the potential problems is to retain neutrality in the reframing role and to use the intervention in relation to both parties' language. However, it takes some trial and error to achieve the correct balance, as illustrated in the following example.

Case Illustration: Finding the Balance in Reframing

The mediator's first reframe might be unsuccessful, in the sense that it is "rejected" by the party to whom it is directed. He or she could then try again. However, there are dangers in being too persistent. Assume in the following exchange that the mediator wants to soften, or at least qualify, Ned's positional claim in order to get some flexibility into his thinking:

Ned: *I want a million dollars.*

Mediator: *So you want to be reasonably compensated to settle this?*

Ned: *No, I told you I want a million dollars.*

Clearly the reframe has not worked as Ned has restated his positional claim, and he is also not happy with the mediator. The mediator could proceed with a softer reframe in the hope that Ned will accept it:

Ned: *No, I told you I want a million dollars.*

Mediator: *So at this point in time a million dollars would be reasonable compensation for you?*

Ned: *Yes ... I guess that is the case.*

The mediator now has two flexible concepts to work with, "this point in time" and "reasonable compensation." At a later stage she could make use of these concepts:

Mediator: *Ned, now that you have heard from the other side, what do you think a reasonable compensation would be?*

However, Ned might also reject the second reframe, with greater insistence than before. For example:

Mediator: *So at this point in time a million dollars would be reasonable compensation for you?*

Ned: *No, I've already told you twice, I will only ever settle for a million dollars, not a cent less.*

Here, Ned has entrenched himself in his positional claim and the mediator may decide not to make matters worse, acknowledge Ned, and move on. Alternatively, with some risk of losing Ned's trust, the mediator might try with the softest of reframes:

Mediator: *So, Ned, your preferred option is one million dollars, let's now look at Kelly's options and see where we can get.*

This has not contradicted Ned's positional claim, but it is calling it something else, namely, a "preferred option," which is opening the way for a consideration of other options.

Where should a mediator draw the line when reframing? It is impossible to define this in the abstract. There is inevitably some trial and error in this area. Our own preference is to be as persistent with reframing as the circumstance suggests is feasible.

X. Appropriate Questioning

A. Introduction

There are different views as to the nature and extent of the questioning mediators should engage in. In some models of mediation, the mediator conducts the process almost entirely through the use of questioning. In others, mediators ask very few questions of the parties but encourage them to explain certain facts or feelings directly to each other. The degree of questioning (and not the third degree) may also depend on the stage and phase of the mediation. Mediators may be reluctant to ask certain kinds of questions in joint session or early in the mediation but feel it is appropriate to ask them in separate session or toward the end of the mediation when greater trust and rapport have been established. The mediator also needs to control the questioning by professional advisers who may seek to interrogate or cross-examine the other party.

B. The Types of Questions

The following are some of the different categories of questions, an illustration of each, the objectives for which the category can be used, and the circumstances in which the particular category might be appropriate. They are based on a hypothetical mediation involving Kate, an employee, and Graham, the employer, over Kate's workers' compensation claim arising out of an injury sustained on the factory floor.

1. OPEN QUESTIONS

An open question invites the party to explain or elaborate on a particular topic, giving the parties wide latitude in answering: "Kate, would you like to describe in your own words how the accident at work has affected your life?" Opening questions are appropriate throughout the mediation and are an excellent way of encouraging the parties to share information. They are particularly useful in the commencement of joint and separate sessions. Because they are non-threatening and usually do not reflect bias, they are also useful in dealing with highly defensive parties.

2. FOCUSED QUESTIONS

A focused question seeks to uncover more detailed facts or information about a specific aspect of an event or incident: "Kate, can you tell me how the accident has affected your work performance in the last 12 months?" Focused questions are useful when there is time pressure or parties are rambling and the mediator needs to achieve direction.

3. CLOSED QUESTIONS

A closed question usually invites a "yes" or "no" response: "Graham, did your method of working contribute to the accident in any way?" Closed questions provide the mediator with more control over the conversation but are also more likely to trigger defensive responses from parties because they can appear suggestive of an answer or biased. Thus, they should be used sparingly and mostly in the later stages of the mediation or during separate meetings, where greater mediator control is better tolerated by parties.

4. CLARIFYING QUESTIONS

Clarifying questions help to elucidate the meaning of a participant's communication for the mediator: "Is it correct, Graham, that you were under the impression that the machine had been serviced shortly before the accident?" Clarifying questions should be asked where parties are not being sufficiently clear or specific on important matters.

5. REFLECTIVE QUESTIONS

A reflective question is one that asks a participant to think more about a particular aspect of the conflict that the mediator believes may be important to resolving the conflict. The mediator crafts a reflective question by isolating a particular word, phrase, or concept spoken by the participant and reframing it into a question: "So at the present time, Kate, you feel that you have little power?" Reflective questions are appropriate at all times during the mediation when a mediator believes that a party would benefit from deeper explanation of some aspect of the case, often an emotional one.

6. PROBING QUESTIONS

A probing question seeks further specificity or justification from a speaker concerning a narrow topic, or it attempts to learn more about a party's view of an option being considered: "Kate, if you are retrained, how will you deal with the new technology that was a problem in the past?" Probing questions are more appropriate in separate meetings to avoid defensive responses and toward the end of mediation to "road test" options.

7. LEADING QUESTIONS

A leading question is one designed to elicit information which the questioner already knows, to lead the speaker to a predetermined outcome. It suggests the answer: "Now, Graham, you were responsible for health and safety in the company when the accident happened, correct?" Although leading questions provide significant control over the discussion, they should be used sparingly in mediation because they are highly provocative. They should only be used when uncontroversial information needs to be elicited, but not otherwise.

8. CROSS-EXAMINING QUESTIONS

A cross-examining question is designed to test a party's accuracy, reliability, and general credibility. Its purpose is usually to expose contradictions and inconsistencies: "Graham, you are saying that there were adequate safety precautions, but did you not refer earlier to other accidents on this same machine?" Cross-examining should be saved for trial, and neither the mediator nor the lawyers representing clients in mediation should use them. They needlessly put parties in a defensive and sometimes embarrassing position. There are less aggressive ways of gathering the relevant information, such as through probing questions. If a mediator is compelled to use this type of question, it should only be asked in a separate meeting.

9. HYPOTHETICAL QUESTIONS

A hypothetical question gets parties to consider possible options without feeling committed to them: "Kate, if we could agree on the matter of compensation, what would you like to have done on the question of safety training?" Hypothetical questions are appropriate in the problem-solving stage of mediation. They are also particularly helpful when there are impasses or breakdowns in the negotiation process.

10. DISARMING/DISTRACTING QUESTIONS

A disarming or distracting question is intended to deflect attention from a destructive interchange between parties by redirecting them to a different topic: "How many employees were there in the company at the time?" This type of question is appropriate whenever there is a need to deflect from high emotions or destructive exchanges.

11. RHETORICAL QUESTIONS

A rhetorical question is intended to make a point dramatically or to produce an effect, not to solicit information: "Graham and Kate, which of you really wants to go through a tortuous trial?" A rhetorical question is appropriate when the parties need to be confronted with an obvious reality.

12. SUGGESTIVE QUESTIONS

A suggestive question is a method of suggesting possible or obvious options for settlement, to float options without parties feeling committed to them: "Graham, would it be possible for company resources to be used to assist in making alterations to Kate's house?" This is a fairly "interventionist" approach because the mediator intervenes in matters of content. Evaluative mediators frequently will use this type of questioning. Facilitative mediators use it rarely, as a last resort when parties are making no progress. Some facilitative mediators use it not at all.

C. Choosing the Appropriate Question

1. USE QUESTIONS JUDICIOUSLY

At a broad level, no type of question is unsuitable; it all depends on context and circumstances. However, some commentators suggest that questions for gaining information are the most overused tool in the novice mediator's toolbox: "If questions are used to the exclusion of other techniques, the conversation will cease to be an exchange and will become an unsatisfactory form of verbal ping-pong or interrogation.[17] We agree with this view. Thus, in the early stages of mediation, open questions are needed so that the parties can tell their stories without any suggestive

---

17. FOLBERG & TAYLOR, *supra* note 7, at 109.

leading questions. Only rarely will closed questions of the either/or variety, associated with selling techniques, be appropriate ("Shall I come on Wednesday or Thursday?" or "Would you like the green or blue one?"). The question "Do you want to settle at mediation or go to litigation?" has a powerful rhetorical effect but could be perceived as manipulative, and might even receive an unexpected answer.

2. THE HYPOTHETICAL QUESTION

The hypothetical question, sometimes known as the "what-if" or "if-what" question, is on the mediator's top 10 list of interventions. As illustrated above, it is used to get the parties to consider options hypothetically without feeling committed to them. The two forms of the hypothetical question are as follows:

Mediator: *Graham, what if Kate were to agree to accept the clerical position—would you then be able to make a commitment in relation to her retraining needs?*

A more elegant version looks like this:

Mediator: *Kate, if Graham would agree to pay for your retraining program, what would you be willing to accept in relation to the clerical position?*

In each case, the question allows the relevant party to make a settlement suggestion on one issue in the knowledge that it will not be binding unless the precondition on another issue is satisfied. If the condition is not satisfied, the party's concession can be withdrawn. This is related to the negotiation strategy of conditional linked bargaining.[18]

3. EMPATHIC VERSUS PROBING QUESTIONING

Stephen Covey in his bestselling book *The 7 Habits of Highly Effective People*, names empathic communication through actions, comments, and questions as one of the seven habits of effective people.[19] Empathy refers to the ability to put oneself in the shoes of another and to understand things from their perspective. Empathy does not signify agreement, nor does it amount to sympathy with or compassion for another. It involves convincing a person that the listener has entered their world of perceptions, even if only temporarily. Empathic questions show a sender that the receiver has understood what they said. They involve reflecting a feeling, or an act and a feeling, from the sender's statement. Examples of empathic questions are:

(a) "So, Kate, you felt unappreciated for a long period of time because you were not acknowledged in the reports?"

(b) "Is it correct, Kate, that you became more determined from then on?"

---

18. *See* Chapter 7—*Facilitating the Negotiations.*
19. STEPHEN COVEY, THE 7 HABITS OF HIGHLY EFFECTIVE PEOPLE 253 (1990).

(c) "It sounds, Graham, as if you were concerned about safety conditions after the accident?"

While empathic questions seek to check out the feeling or attitude behind a statement, probing or clarifying questions seek confirmation of facts and information. Probing questions seek more focus, concreteness, specificity, or accuracy. While they may be entirely appropriate in some circumstances, mediation is not the appropriate venue for an inquisition, whether by the parties, their advisers, or the mediator. It is likely to make the parties defensive and adversarial. Mediators do not need to know the full facts in order to fulfill their facilitation role. If there is a genuine need for additional facts, the mediator might discuss with the parties ways of engaging in a fact-finding exercise. Therefore, empathic questions are generally more important for mediators to understand and use than probing questions.

XI. Mediators' Tools to Promote Effective Communication

A. Reiterating

Mediators need to prevent anything of value from "falling off" the negotiation table. In the heat of the moment, it is possible for an apology, a concession, or a significant offer not to be heard by the non-speaking party because of their anger, psychological deafness, or emotional state. Here it is wise for mediators to ask the speaker to repeat the statement, when the timing is appropriate for this intervention:

> Mediator: *Now, Graham, I think you were making an offer about re-employment to Kate a few moments ago when we got side-tracked by the question of management attitudes to staff and I'd like you to repeat that offer now…*

Alternatively, mediators might themselves reiterate the statement of value when circumstances allow. For example,

> Mediator: *Now, a few minutes ago I heard Graham say that he would re-employ Kate in the sales department as part of a package of agreements involving other matters. Is that correct, Graham?*

Reiteration can be used to step up a weak signal from one party that is not being heard by the other. For example,

> Mediator: *Now Kate, Graham has indicated on a number of occasions that you have been a valuable and trustworthy employee, and that the conflict has arisen over broader pressures affecting the company, is that what you have heard?*

Reiteration is one of the tools in the mediator's toolbox that can be used in all situations in which the parties are talking past each other and not picking up on important messages.

B. Paraphrasing

Paraphrasing involves the mediator's controlling the dialogue between the parties and picking up on important issues. In particular, it involves capturing the emotional content of a message and ensuring that there is a response. Because it involves the mediator's intervening in the dialogue and reframing some of the language, it requires some delicacy and discretion in choice of language.

The following hypothetical dialogue is from a mediation involving a farmer and a bank representative, in which the representative of the bank, Mr. Nab, is negotiating with the farmer, Mr. Pigge, as a step prior to foreclosing on the family farm. It illustrates the paraphrasing method:

> Mediator: *Mr. Nab, Mr. Pigge is saying that although the bank was legally justified in its actions, the way it went about things caused him considerable stress and embarrassment in the community. Can you respond to him on that...?*
>
> Mr. Nab: *Yes, we do regret any embarrassment caused to you, Mr. Pigge. You were always a good customer and we acknowledge that the collapse of your farming operations was not altogether your fault. But at the end of the day a bank is a business not a charity and we need to get our money back....*
>
> Mediator: *Mr. Pigge, Mr. Nab has expressed his regret at the upset this has caused you and has emphasized that you were a good customer. Can you tell him how you feel now that you have heard that....*
>
> Mr. Pigge: *Well, it's the first time I've ever heard that kind of language from a bank, but I'd still like to keep the farm....*

Paraphrasing should be done in an even-handed way so that both parties' communications are paraphrased. It can be used to set up a pattern of direct communication between the parties. It can break what is called the "Oh but," "Yes but" pattern of communication:[20] "Oh but I didn't understand that's what you wanted." "Yes, but I had told you only two days before...." However, if this is the only way of keeping the parties communicating constructively, it will become strained and artificial.

C. Summarizing

Reference has already been made to the mediator's function of summarizing the parties' initial statements. In that context, the summary is intended to provide an accurate account of what each party has said in order to demonstrate that they have been heard and to allow the mediator to verify his or her understanding of what has been said. Summarizing can also be used in later stages of the mediation, and it will take on a different complexion in different contexts. Generally, summarizing involves the mediator's briefly restating or recapping important features of

---

20. RUTH CHARLTON & MICHELINE DEWDNEY, THE MEDIATOR'S HANDBOOK 158 (1995).

the preceding discussion and identifying the dominant feelings of the parties. Summarizing can be a powerful intervention that can achieve one or more of the following objectives:

- Provide a neutral and organized version of a course of discussion;
- Pick up on key issues which might otherwise have been overlooked;
- Simplify convoluted exchanges;
- Remind the parties that progress is being made;
- Provide acknowledgment to the parties that they have been understood;
- Establish a platform for the next round of discussion; and
- Assist the mediator to establish trust by using key words spoken by the parties.

Good summarizing requires a range of micro skills, such as retaining important information, recalling it, and condensing it. It is always a selective process, that is, the mediator picks up on the progress to date and presents this in a positive summarized statement. It is also selective in that the mediator picks up only on what is useful for mediation, as opposed to what would be useful for law or counseling. The reason why the mediator is selective in the summaries is that it provides a positive and encouraging basis for the parties to move forward with their negotiations. However, the summary also needs to be balanced in the sense that it deals fairly with what each party has said. The following is an example of a summary from the Pigge and Nab mediation:

> Mediator: *Now Mr. Pigge, you've told us that your financial difficulties were caused by wider economic factors, and that you felt the bank could have dealt with you more directly and sympathetically. You also acknowledged that you may not be able to trade out of your difficulties but that you would like to restructure finances for the short term so that you can consider your options for the future. And Mr. Nab, you said that things could have been handled differently with Mr. Pigge, particularly as he was a lifelong client of yours. You also said that banks have some discretion in these circumstances and that you would be prepared to look at some short-term financial arrangements, provided that these were appropriately monitored and reviewed. Is that correct…? Now Mr. Nab and Mr. Pigge, let's move forward and look at some options for the finances in the short term….*

There are two situations in which summarizing is particularly appropriate. It is useful after an adjournment or when a joint session resumes after separate sessions; here its function is to refocus the parties' attention on the state of the negotiations. It should also be used when the parties reach an impasse in their negotiations; here its function is to emphasize the positive progress to date and provide building blocks for the future. Although good summarizing can be one of the most effective interventions for mediators, it is probably one of the most under-utilized. It should now be added to your toolbox.

D. Note-Taking

Reference has been made to the mediator's role in note-taking during the parties' initial statements.[21] During the rest of the mediation, most mediators take only brief notes even though it is rare for proceedings to be recorded and a transcript to be produced. The following notes would ordinarily be required at the different stages of the process:

- *Preliminaries*: names of parties and advisers, time of commencement, special conditions for mediation, nature of queries by parties during this stage;

- *Mediator's opening statement*: important matters dealt with, such as confidentiality, separate meetings—can be checked off on a list;

- *Parties' initial statements*: main concerns, important facts, some record of feelings;

- *List of issues*: the mediator should keep a separate list in case the whiteboard is erased or changed;

- *Negotiation stages*: settlement options, concessions, acknowledgments, apologies, figures and amounts, sequence and timing of offers and counteroffers;

- *Separate meetings*: time of start and conclusion, exact offers if they are to be communicated by mediator, and record of matters to be kept confidential.

XII. Exercises

1. Develop a list of terms and words associated with conflict in your professional practice, work, educational institution, or home. Write out at least two positive replacement terms for the negative words or phrases and ask someone to assess their suitability. Try using the replacement terms in your particular situation.

2. Assume that an insurer's lawyer attempts to ask clarifying and probing questions of the plaintiff. You as the mediator are concerned that this might lead to a hostile interrogation. What procedures could you use to allow the lawyer to ask legitimate questions without the plaintiff's being cross-examined? (A clue for one procedure: the plaintiff also has a lawyer present.)

3. Form pairs and have one person begin talking about a subject of interest to them. The other person should mimic the speaker's body language (for example, fold their arms when the speaker folds their arms, smile when the speaker smiles). After a few minutes, swap roles. At the end of this exercise

---

21. *See* Chapter 4—*Managing the Mediation Process*, section II A 5(j).

both speaker and imitator should discuss what effect non-verbal communication can have on a conversation.

4. Think of a person you know who is a good listener. List the behaviors and qualities that make him or her a good listener. Think of a person you know who is a poor listener. List the behaviors and qualities that make him or her a poor listener.

Managing Conflict from Crisis to Opportunity

All polishing is achieved by friction.

—MARY PARKER FOLLET (MANAGEMENT CONSULTANT)

I. Benefits of Conflict

Society bombards us with messages that harmony is normal and that conflict is a deviation from the norm. When you see the word *conflict*, what is the first thing that comes to your mind? If you are like most people, you think of negative feelings and situations that most of us naturally want to avoid, including *war, fighting, frustration, stress*, and *anxiety*. Any form of disagreement or dissent, we are told, upsets the natural and desirable state of us all just "getting along." By contrast, harmony and agreement are viewed favorably and are often perceived as something to be achieved and maintained at all costs. Our society's negative attitude toward conflict is deeply rooted. In fact, the English word "conflict" is derived from the Latin word *conflictus*, which means "to *strike* together."[1]

Conflict, however, can be healthy and often benefits the parties involved. Improvements in relationships and the social condition are usually borne out of conflict, not harmony. Interpersonal conflict is a natural, essential, and permanent part of the human condition. Conflict is the active ingredient of interpersonal, social, and organizational creativity and growth. This is because when parties to a conflict find themselves having differing viewpoints and air those differences, there is an opportunity for acquiring a greater understanding of the other person, the situation, and themselves; to clarify goals and to shed prejudices; and to see the world in a new, less egocentric way.

Once we look for them, examples of the constructive power of conflict are easy to identify in all spheres of human interaction. In marriage, conflict between spouses can draw a couple closer together and fuel personal growth. For example, a conflict over child rearing responsibilities could potentially alter one spouse's long-held social prejudices concerning their child rearing role. In a business dispute, conflict

---

1. AMERICAN HERITAGE DICTIONARY (2d College ed. 1982).

can help clarify goals and issues, making communication more meaningful and coordinated action more likely. In the public arena, it is hard to think of any positive social change that did not arise as a result of conflict. Women's suffrage, civil rights, rights for the handicapped, and environmental conservation are all a direct consequence of conflict.

In addition to personal and social growth, conflict is essential to the effective functioning of small groups and organizations. Research shows that a leading cause of business failure is *too much* agreement among top managers.[2] Sometimes this agreement is created by a *false consensus*. False consensus is a situation where people agree with each other to avoid the unpleasantness or extra time involved with dissension, even when many of them may have strong opinions to the contrary.[3] Another pitfall is *groupthink*, a term coined by the eminent Yale psychiatrist Irving Janis.[4] Groupthink is where true consensus exists among the parties, but the convergence of thinking is more the result of the general homogeneous nature of the group and an organizational pressure for unity rather than objectivity.[5] The group dynamic promotes conformity and suppresses debate. In both false consensus and groupthink, the problem at hand is not addressed effectively because relevant information is not revealed. Thus, the problem is addressed from a narrow, often biased, perspective, and few alternative solutions are considered. This increases the likelihood that the participants will make bad decisions.

Commenting on the positive role productive conflict can play in the corporate environment, Michael Eisner, former CEO and Chairman of Disney, expressed it this way in discussing the Disney organizational culture, which at the time was considered among the most creative and productive in the industry:

> This whole business starts with ideas, and we're convinced that ideas come out of an environment of supportive conflict, which is synonymous with appropriate friction. We create a very loose environment where people are not afraid to speak their minds or be irreverent. They say what they think, and are urged to advocate strongly for ideas. That can be hard and somewhat uncomfortable at times as people say a lot of challenging, provocative things. However, this gets a lot of ideas out there so that we can look at them.[6]

Mr. Eisner's observation that the open and vigorous discussion of ideas can be "hard" and "uncomfortable" is supported by the research. While many organizations may claim to promote open and honest discourse where conflicts can be aired, the research suggests that most managers and executives avoid conflicts

---

2. DAVID A. WHETTEN & KIM S. CAMERON, DEVELOPING MANAGEMENT SKILLS 345 (6th ed. 2005).

3. HARVARD BUSINESS ESSENTIALS, CREATING TEAMS WITH AN EDGE 80–81 (2004).

4. *Id.*

5. *Id.*

6. Suzy Wetlaufer, *Common Sense and Conflict*, HARV. BUS. REV., Jan–Feb 2000, at 116.

whenever they can.[7] In avoiding conflict, however, they also diminish the creativity, innovation, and high performance that conflict can stimulate. The positive transformative power of conflict on performance and creativity is illustrated in the following classic experiment:

> Several groups of managers were formed to solve a complex problem. They were told their performance would be judged by a panel of experts in terms of the quantity and the quality of solutions generated. The groups were identical in size and composition, with the exception that half of them included a "confederate." Before the experiment began, the researcher instructed this person to play the role of the "devil's advocate." This person was to challenge the group's conclusions, forcing the others to examine critically their assumptions and the logic of their arguments. At the end of the problem-solving period, the recommendations made by both sets of groups were compared. The groups with the devil's advocates had performed significantly better on the task. They had generated more alternatives, and their proposals were judged superior. After a short break, the groups were reassembled and told that they would be performing a similar task during the next session. However, before they began discussing the next problem, they were given permission to eliminate one member. In every group containing a confederate, he or she was the one asked to leave.[8]

Every group in the experiment expelled the devil's advocate because that person created "conflict," even though the conflict is what provided the group with a competitive advantage in performance. If conflict can be both damaging and enlightening, the role of the mediator, whether assisting a couple with a divorce, litigants in a lawsuit, or an organization with a dysfunctional team, is to guide the participants in a dispute to interact productively. Like fire, conflict is neither inherently good nor bad but rather a force that can be managed productively or unproductively, and one of tremendous transformative potential.

Mediators, however, must overcome the cultural prejudice that conflict is simply a negative state to be avoided at all costs. They must adopt a richer, more comprehensive understanding of conflict, not just as a destructive force, which it can be, but also as a constructive force that can improve interpersonal relationships, business functioning, and society. The negative and positive aspects of conflict are aptly captured in the symbol that represents the Chinese word for *crisis*. The symbol consists of two characters. The top character of the symbol represents *danger*, and the bottom character of the symbol represents *opportunity*.

---

7. Whetten & Cameron, *supra* note 2, at 345–46.

8. David A. Whetton & Kim S. Cameron, Developmental Management Skills 346. ©1998, 1995, 1991, 1984. Reprinted by permission of Pearson Education, Inc., Upper Saddle River, N.J.

Conflict is a form of crisis, and the mediator must recognize and pursue the opportunities that such a crisis creates for positive change as well as manage its potential danger.

II. Productive vs. Unproductive Conflict

For mediators, productive and unproductive describes the *process* of conflict, not the result. When two or more people are in conflict, they "perceive that they have incompatible goals or interests and that the other is a source of interference in achieving their goals."[9] It is the *manner* in which two people attempt to reconcile their apparent differences that determines whether the conflict is productive or unproductive, not whether the conflict is settled.[10] Some conflicts that are accurately described as "unproductive" are resolved. For example, a couple who recently *resolved* a divorce through negotiation may have increased their animosity, may have spent tens of thousands of dollars over years of litigation, and may be unhappy with the resulting settlement. Likewise, productive conflicts may not be resolved in a way that maintains the parties' relationship. For example, two partners who have different views about the direction of their small company may not be able to reconcile those differences. One wants to grow it to maximize its value, while the other is satisfied with the modest profit it currently produces. Despite a productive conflict process, they might decide to dissolve the partnership. The difference between productive and unproductive conflict, for our purposes, is that productive conflict increases the likelihood of three things:

---

9. Joseph P. Folger, Marshall Scott & Randall K. Stutman, Working Through Conflict 5 (2001).

10. William A. Donohue & Robert Kolt, Managing Interpersonal Conflict 8–10 (1992).

1. That the conflict will get resolved;

2. That it will be resolved efficiently; and

3. That the relationship, to the extent possible, will not be impacted negatively, and may even be improved.

A. Identifying and Encouraging Productive Conflict

Three key features also distinguish *productive* from *unproductive* conflict. First, in productive conflict the parties remain focused on the relevant issue or problem.[11] Second, the parties are flexible in their negotiation style.[12] Third, the parties recognize that the other person has legitimate needs and that those needs must be satisfied if they are to reach an amicable agreement.[13] The mediator should encourage and support these behaviors.

Parties engaged in a productive conflict stay focused on the pressing substantive problems and issues surrounding the conflict. Going back to our definition of conflict above, the participants' perceptions are that their respective goals interfere with one another in some significant way. If the conflict process is to be productive, the dialogue must concentrate on the relevant substantive issues concerning the perceived obstacles to each party achieving their goals. While it may appear easy to maintain such a dialogue, as we will see below, there are forces in conflict situations that can lead parties astray from the real issues in the dispute. For example, parties often personalize the dispute. They begin to see the problem as one caused by the other person's personality flaws as opposed to a legitimate clashing of goals or perspectives.[14] This can often lead to one party demonizing the other, which is a destructive force in the process of resolving conflicts.

1. FLEXIBLE

Parties engaged in productive conflict are flexible in the *means* by which they achieve their goals while still being committed to the goals themselves. Parties' narrowly defining goals and rigidly holding on to those goals often characterize unproductive conflict.[15] For example, a party complaining about a neighbor's dog that barks incessantly during the early morning hours might care deeply about stopping the noise but may be flexible concerning how to remedy the problem—send the dog to obedience training, put it in the basement at night, etc. This would be a more productive approach than if the party took the inflexible position that the neighbor "must get rid of the dog." Parties engaged in productive negotiation usually strike a

---

11. *Id.* at 9.
12. WILLIAM W. WILMONT & JOYCE L. HOCKER, INTERPERSONAL CONFLICT 172 (7th ed. 2007).
13. ROXANE S. LULOFS & DUDLEY D. CAHN, CONFLICT FROM THEORY 16–17 (2000).
14. *Id.* at 126–27.
15. FOLGER, SCOTT & STUTMAN, *supra* note 9, at 9.

balance between competitive and cooperative behavior.[16] We address the relationship between productive conflict and conflict style in detail below in Section III, Conflict Style.

2. RECOGNITION OF OTHERS' NEEDS AND INTERESTS

In a productive conflict, the parties recognize that each sides' interests and needs must be at least minimally satisfied if an amicable agreement is to be reached.[17] Moreover, both parties demonstrate commitment in the negotiation to help the other party achieve their goals through collaborative or compromising negotiation behaviors. This does not mean that they are not competitive. Even in the most cooperative instances, negotiators often engage in competitive behavior in order to explain preferred solutions or express legitimate interests.[18] However, in productive negotiations, an appropriate level of cooperative behavior counterbalances this competitive behavior, whereas unproductive conflict usually lacks a cooperative counterbalance.

B. Identifying and Discouraging Unproductive Conflict

Unproductive conflict is characterized by personal verbal attacks, over-competitiveness, or focus on irrelevant issues in an attempt to gain power in the dispute.[19] Unproductive conflict is the type of conflict that harms relationships and is more likely to escalate, requiring increased commitment of energy, resources, and time without any increased likelihood of resolving the matter amicably. In one commentator's view, it "places heavy reliance on overt power and manipulative techniques."[20] Thus, mediators must learn to recognize and guard against unproductive conflict by using a variety of techniques that guide the participants toward more productive behavior.

1. PERSONAL ATTACKS

Personalized verbal or emotional attacks designed to hurt the other person are a common tactic in unproductive conflict. John Gottman, an authority on communication between couples, has identified four behaviors that are particularly destructive to interpersonal relationships. Gottman refers to these behaviors as the "four horsemen of the apocalypse" because when they "ride in" they "kill" relationships.[21] The destructive strength of these behaviors is so potent that Gottman is able to predict with greater than 90 percent accuracy whether a couple will divorce or remain married, within a period of years, by analyzing the first minute of a couple interacting in

16. LULOFS & CAHN, *supra* note 13, at 16.
17. *Id.*
18. FOLGER, SCOTT & STUTMAN, *supra* note 9, at 10.
19. DONOHUE & KOLT, *supra* note 10, at 10; LULOFS & CAHN, *supra* note 13, at 14–16.
20. LULOFS & CAHN, *supra* note 13, at 15.
21. WILMONT & HOCKER, *supra* note 12, at 16.

a conflict situation.[22] The relationship killing behaviors are as follows: *criticizing, defensiveness, stonewalling,* and *contempt*.[23] Let us now explore the nature of these behaviors and potential mediator interventions.

a. *Criticizing*

Criticizing takes the form of sweeping, negative generalizations about a person's character or worth. Negative comments that begin with the phrase "you always…" or "you never…" are particularly destructive.[24] These comments strike at the heart of an individual's sense of worth. The mediator can neutralize critical statements by encouraging the critiquing party to describe the offending behavior, its effect on them, and what behavioral change they would like to see, instead of making sweeping judgments and conclusions about it.[25] For example, let us look at a dispute between office mates where one party criticizes the other during the mediation, and how the mediator might intervene:

Jane: *He is lazy and never does his fair share.*

Mediator: *Jane, what behavior in particular concerns you?*

Jane: *Well, he doesn't help keep the office clean. Half the time, there is old rotting food lying around that stinks to high heaven, which makes it difficult for me to concentrate on my work. He always leaves the copier empty and leaves it to me to fill the paper, and he is constantly having private, or what should be private, telephone conversations with his girlfriend in the office, which I frankly don't wish to hear.*

Asking for more detail about the offending behavior shifts the conversation from the other party's personhood ("He's lazy"), to a productive discussion about his alleged specific behavior. From there, the mediator might summarize the party's concerns and then instigate a discussion regarding concrete solutions to these more specific concerns.

b. *Stonewalling*

Stonewalling is where the party appears to withdraw psychologically from the dispute.[26] The party makes little eye contact, his or her body language is closed and stiff, and he or she communicates little. It is both a defensive and aggressive tactic. It is a defensive tactic because it is often in response to attacks and criticism by the other party. It is an aggressive tactic in that the attacking party feels personally

---

22. *Id.* at 16. *See also* JOHN N. GOTTMAN & NAN SILVER, WHY MARRIAGES SUCCEED OR FAIL: WHAT CAN YOU LEARN FROM THE BREAKTHROUGH RESEARCH TO MAKE YOUR MARRIAGE LAST (1994).
23. WILMONT & HOCKER, *supra* note 12, at 16.
24. *Id.*
25. *Id.* at 17.
26. WILMONT & HOCKER, *supra* note 12, at 19.

affronted by the other's withdrawal from the discussion. In dealing with stonewalling, the mediator must assist the attacker in softening his or her tactics and draw out the stonewaller. The mediator can accomplish this, often in private meetings, by pointing out to the party the undesirable consequences that such tactics are having in creating animosity and stifling productive communication.

Let us look at the office mate conflict discussed above as an example. Assume that while listening to Jane's criticisms and complaints, her office mate, Bill, sits silently and stone-faced. When the mediator tries to encourage discussions about possible solutions, Bill remains detached and uncommunicative. The mediator might then call a private meeting with both parties. Here is an example of a portion of the mediator's private meeting with Bill, after the mediator has explained the general purpose of such meetings and discussed with him some possible solutions to the problem:

Mediator: *Bill, one of the things I would like to see happen when we meet with Jane in a few minutes is for you to share some of the ideas and concerns about potential solutions that you have just shared with me. Is that something you are willing to do?*

Bill: *She is just going to criticize anything I say, like she always does.*

Mediator: *If she does, I will step in and make sure your ideas are discussed fully. Bill, it is my experience that this process will work best if she hears your ideas and concerns from you. Once we get back together what I will do is ask that each of you provide some ideas to address the different concerns we have been discussing. I will ask that nobody comment on any of the possible solutions provided until we have come up with several for each concern. I'll ask Jane to make a specific commitment on that point. Once we have several possible solutions for each concern, we can then discuss what potential solutions would work best for both of you. How does that sound, Bill?*

Bill: *O.K., I guess.*

Mediator: *So, Bill, you agree to share your ideas for potential solutions when we get back together with Jane?*

Bill: *Yes.*

Here is an example of a portion of the mediator's private meeting with Jane, after the mediator has explained the general purpose of such meetings and discussed with her some possible solutions to the problem:

Mediator: *Jane, when we get back together in a few minutes with Bill, I want to spend a little time just listing the different potential solutions we have been discussing. Just get everything out on the table. Jane, how does that sound?*

Jane: *Good.*

Mediator: *It is my experience that getting a lot of ideas on the table and then picking out and discussing the most promising ones is the best way to proceed, but an important guideline of this process is that we first list these potential solutions, both yours and Bill's, without commenting on whether they are good or bad ideas.*

Jane: *But what is the point of listing a bad idea? How will that help the situation?*

Mediator: *Well, Jane, there are a couple of ways it can help. One way is that sometimes a bad idea can lead to a good idea. Bill might provide a solution that in the end might not be practical, but it triggers you to have an even better idea that might end up being a good solution. The other way it helps is that, if I throw out an idea and Bill criticizes it immediately, I'm going to be less likely to contribute other ideas or be less committed to the process. Maybe my next idea might have been a brilliant one, but you would never hear it, or maybe I would not have even thought of it, because I would have been afraid to have it criticized. So, the point of this two-step process is to get as many ideas as we can first and then, after we have a lot of them, some good and some not so good, evaluate them. Does that make sense, Jane?*

Jane: *I guess so.*

Mediator: *Jane, can you agree to allow Bill to list his ideas without commenting on them if Bill will show your ideas the same respect?*

Jane: *Yes.*

c. *Contempt*

This is a behavior where one person attempts to place himself or herself in a position of superiority over the other.[27] Often it involves sarcasm, mockery, and talking down to the other person. This is a particularly destructive tactic.[28] The mediator should not let contemptuous behavior go unchallenged—such is its destructiveness. The mediator should question verbal "put-downs" and label them as undesirable if the parties wish to achieve an amicable agreement. The following is an illustration of one way a mediator might address a display of contempt in a mediation.

Albert: *You are just being stupid!*

Mediator: *Albert, those kinds of comments are not going to help this process. Can you follow the guidelines we discussed?*

Albert: *Yes, but she makes me so mad.*

Mediator: *What specifically upsets you about Martha's idea?*

Here, the mediator immediately pointed out the unproductive behavior and referred to the mediation guidelines to which Albert previously agreed. As discussed, reminding the party of a previous commitment to follow the mediation guidelines is a significant source of mediator control, and it should be resorted to in

---

27. *Id.* at 19–20.
28. *Id.* at 18.

order to curb serious violations of protocol. After acknowledging the display of contempt, the mediator then explores the reasons for it, which may reveal information relevant to the problem.

d. *Defensiveness*

Defensive communication is a means of protecting oneself from perceived personal attacks.[29] This may take the form of blanket denials of responsibility, contrariness, or reciprocal personal attacks.[30] Defensiveness may be a legitimate response to contempt, criticism, or some other form of personal attack, or it may be a consequence of that person's sensitivity. In whatever case, defensiveness stymies communication and little real progress in working through the conflict can be made while it remains strong. A mediator often can minimize defensiveness through working separately with both parties. Like in the stonewalling tactic, the mediator needs to assist the perceived "attacker" by encouraging him or her to modify any overly threatening behavior, and assisting the defensive party to see the benefits of engaging in honest and open communication.

Let us look at one of the separate meetings in a mediation between the representative of an environmental group and a developer about the building of a residential community adjacent to protected wetlands. The mediator has called separate meetings because the representative of the environmental group, Steven, in a loud threatening voice, told the developer that the group would keep him in litigation "until he was a senile old man." The developer, still young and vigorous, shouted that the representative of the environmental group was a "crazy nut who cared more about tree-frogs than people." After some preliminaries, the mediator had the following exchange with Steven, the environmentalist:

Mediator: *Steven, I would like to get everyone back together to discuss the issues, but I will not do that unless I think we can discuss them with some civility.*

Steven: *He needs to hear it like it is. He needs to know we are prepared to go all the way with this. We have the money, and we have the will.*

Mediator: *I agree with you, Steven, one hundred percent that he needs to understand what the future is likely to be if we cannot work this problem out today. I promise you we will talk about that, but how do you think this conversation is affected when that important information is conveyed in a loud, threatening way?*

Steven: *I really don't care.*

Mediator: *Steven, I view part of my job as helping you to exchange important information in a way that is going to increase the likelihood of reaching a solution that works well for both of you, which I think is possible in this case. You know the developer. When you threaten, what is he likely to do...?*

---

29. *Id.*
30. *Id.*

Steven: *Make his own threats.*

Mediator: *Yes, or walk away from this discussion. Is that what you want to happen, Steven? Would you prefer to spend your group's financial resources litigating this matter for the next five years?*

Steven: *If that's what we have to do.*

Mediator: *I know you can do it, but is that your first choice?*

Steven: *No.*

Mediator: *If you are going to have a chance to resolve this matter, then loud threats are not going to help. I can appreciate that it might feel good, but it will not do any good. I know you are very committed to this problem, but we have to discuss it civilly. Can you do that?*

Steven: *O.K.*

Mediator: *Good, because if there are any more threats, I think that there is a good chance that he will walk out, maybe for good. And, at this point, I do not think that will be in your organization's best interest. Steven, does that make sense?*

Steven: *Yes, you're probably right.*

In this exchange, the mediator clearly explained to Steven the likely effect continued threats would have on the mediation. It is a mediator's responsibility to help parties appreciate the probable consequences of their behavior. The mediator might even suggest to Steven that an apology for his outburst would help repair some of the harm caused to the mediation process. Whether this would be an appropriate intervention at this juncture would depend on the degree to which the mediator has developed some rapport and trust with Steven and the degree to which Steven recognizes and acknowledges the harm caused. After the separate meeting with the environmentalist, the mediator would then meet with the developer.

2. OVER-COMPETITIVENESS

The over-competitive negotiator is one who typically takes inflexible positions and resists participating in meaningful problem solving or compromise. This kind of negotiation process is unproductive for several reasons. One, it often involves one or more participants trying to impose a solution on the other without consideration of the other's legitimate needs or concerns. This, of course, disenfranchises the other party from meaningful participation in the process or the outcome, which is anathematic to constructive conflict. Two, such behavior promotes positional bargaining and diminishes the chances for the parties to discover joint gains. Three, imposing one's will on another damages the relationship. No one likes to be controlled. Such attempts at control usually trigger unproductive defensive behavior. (See "face-threats" below).

Different reasons may be motivating over-competitive behavior, so, depending on the underlying motivation, different interventions will be necessary. If over-competitive behavior is a result of a negotiator's style preference, then private coaching in separate meetings can be helpful. In these private meetings, a mediator can reason with the participant about the consequences the behavior has on both the relationship and the quality of any resulting agreement. Another common reason for this type of over-competitive behavior in mediation is a mistaken belief that one is more powerful. The mediator can address this underlying motivation by helping the party objectively assess the nature of his or her power in the negotiation. The technique of assisting a party to evaluate objectively the strength of his or her position is often referred to as "reality testing," discussed in detail in Chapter 4. Thus, while competitive behavior is a natural and acceptable part of the mediation, too much competitiveness will damage the relationship, stymie communication, and increase the likelihood that the parties will not reach agreement.

3. ISSUE PROLIFERATION

Another important sign that conflict is heading down a destructive path is when parties attempt to expand the conflict to include additional issues, people, precedents, and principles that have little connection to the problem under discussion.[31] This is commonly referred to as *issue proliferation* and is a tactic used to gain power in the discussion, especially when one perceives that he or she is losing ground on a different, but usually more relevant, issue. For example, in a divorce mediation, when one spouse feels that they are losing the argument on the issue of visitation, they might bring up the other spouse's infidelity during the marriage. This is a way of embarrassing the other spouse or an attempt to gain moral superiority in the discussion. While it may have some relevance to the mediation, it is likely that it has little relevance to the issue of what is a fair visitation schedule. In such a situation, the mediator should refocus the discussion to the germane issue.

This is not to say, of course, that participants might not raise different, even more serious, issues during mediation that do warrant attention. Sometimes the initial issues the participants bring to the mediator are only symptoms of a much larger and more important issue lurking beneath. A contentious discussion over visitation with a divorcing couple may at its root be one spouse's legitimate concern over the other spouse's drinking problem, an issue relevant to the topic of visitation. Sometimes the mediator can effectively address these underlying issues that unexpectedly surface during the mediation, and sometimes it is more appropriate for the mediator to refer such issues to other professionals better trained to address them. In either circum-

---

31. LULOFS & CAHN, *supra* note 13, at 15. Issue proliferation should not be confused with "fractionating" or "unbundling" the problem. Fractionating and unbundling refer to breaking larger issues into smaller, more manageable ones, making the problem clearer, which is beneficial to the problem-solving process. Issue proliferation, on the other hand, is undesirable because it raises irrelevant issues.

stance, the mediator is in the best position during the mediation to identify those issues that are constructive to the discussion from those that are not.

III. Conflict Style

A. Introduction

Most people have a preferred style when dealing with conflict. Conflict style is an overarching strategy that a person has for dealing with the conflicts that life presents.[32] It consists of a collection of patterned responses, behaviors, and tactics that, for better or worse, a person uses most frequently when he or she has disagreements with his or her spouse over vacation plans, with co-workers over the best way to organize a particular project, or with a business partner over how to dissolve and divide the assets of a partnership. In other words, we do not reinvent ourselves anew each day.[33] We rely instead on well-worn behavioral patterns to navigate through our interpersonal relationships.

While most of us lead reasonably efficient lives, relying on our tried-and-true behavioral patterns, these patterns sometimes can prevent us from dealing effectively with conflict. Mediators, therefore, need to be aware of the different conflict styles, know how to recognize them, and work with them in mediation. There are five distinct conflict styles: *competing, avoiding, compromising, accommodating,* and *collaborating.*[34] Most of us make use of *all* of these conflict styles some of the time; but we also tend to favor *one* or *two* of these styles more than the others. Thus, most of us have a *predominant* conflict style.

The characteristics of *assertiveness* and *cooperativeness* are the building blocks of conflict style.[35] Each of the five styles represents the degree to which that style is assertive or cooperative. Assertiveness describes the "degree to which you try to satisfy your own concerns."[36] Cooperativeness, on the other hand, describes the "degree to which you try to satisfy the other person's concerns."[37] While conflict style encompasses more than these two dimensions, assertiveness and cooperativeness are the main characteristics that define it.[38]

Conflict style is a slice of one's personality and, like personality, it is acquired and influenced by many factors. Family upbringing, culture, genetics, and life experience

---

32. WILMONT & HOCKER, *supra* note 12, at 130.

33. FOLGER, SCOTT & STUTMAN, *supra* note 9, at 222.

34. These five conflict styles are based on KENNETH W. THOMAS & RALPH H. KILMANN, THOMAS-KILMANN CONFLICT MODE INSTRUMENT (1974).

35. KENNETH W. THOMAS, INTRODUCTION TO CONFLICT MANAGEMENT 3 (2002).

36. *Id.*

37. *Id.*

38. FOLGER, SCOTT & STUTMAN, *supra* note 9, at 220 (explaining that conflict styles also have other dimensions such as "disclosiveness, empowerment, activeness, and flexibility.").

are the major factors that influence a person's conflict style.[39] No particular conflict style is inherently better than any other style. Each style has its benefits, its costs, and its potential excesses. However, some conflict styles are more effective in dealing with some conflict situations than others, and people can learn to use different conflict styles. Thus, one of the goals in productively dealing with conflict is to apply the most appropriate conflict style to the conflict at hand. Some people do this instinctively and with great skill. Many other people are unaware that they even have a preferred conflict style, and even fewer purposely adapt their conflict style to the situation. Accordingly, many people unthinkingly approach a conflict with their preferred, or default, conflict style regardless of whether it is the most appropriate style for that particular conflict. Mismatching a conflict style with a dispute reduces a person's chances of resolving the conflict, and sometimes exacerbates it.

Mediators who understand the different conflict styles, the appropriate uses of them, and the potential benefits and costs of each style can help guide the participants in more productive ways of dealing with the dispute. Proper management of conflict style by the mediator leads to an increased chance of the parties communicating more effectively and making good decisions about the dispute. The role of the mediator in this respect, therefore, is to perform the following tasks: (1) assist the parties in avoiding unproductive tactics and excesses associated with their style; (2) encourage the beneficial aspects of their style; and (3) assist the person in shifting from their predominant style to one more appropriate, if their predominate style is an obstacle in managing the conflict.

B. The Styles

1. COMPETING — "MY WAY OR THE HIGHWAY."

Competing is an assertive and uncooperative conflict style.[40] A person using a competing style tries to satisfy his or her concerns at the expense of the other person's concerns. The competing person tries to force his will on the other. A person who has a predominantly competing style usually views negotiation as a battleground where there are clear winners and losers, and the goal is always to be the winner.

a. *Common Tactics*

The following are common tactics used by people who are employing a competing conflict style.[41]

---

39. WILMONT & HOCKER, *supra* note 12, at 130.
40. THOMAS, *supra* note 35, at 5.
41. *See* WILMONT & HOCKER, *supra* note 12, at 147 (general discussion of these competitive communication tactics); FOLGER, SCOTT & STUTMAN, *supra* note 9, at 241–53 (chart listing conflict tactics used by persons employing the respective conflict styles).

Inflexibility: Taking a hard line on positions, believing that there is only one way to satisfy his or her position. "I want the contract invalidated, and that's the only way this matter will be settled."

Personal Criticism: Remarks intended to demean the other person or injure them psychologically. "You're a liar; you never tell the truth."

Threats: An expression that the person will inflict some harm on the other if his or her request is not met. "If you don't pay me $100,000 to settle this matter, I will make this litigation very unpleasant."

Denial of Responsibility: Minimizing or completely rejecting any responsibility for the dispute. "If you had lived up to your end of the bargain, we would not be here."

Dismissal: Minimizing or completely rejecting the other party's arguments, factual information, or needs. "That's irrelevant…"; "That's ridiculous…"; or "That doesn't make any sense…."

Argument: Stating their position forcefully using reasoning, precedent, and supporting examples.

Not Sharing Information About Their True Underlying Needs and Concerns: While a person using a competing style might monopolize the conversation with arguments, those arguments will often try to mislead the other person and conceal their real needs and concerns. They do this because they believe that revealing their true needs and concerns will make them vulnerable to being exploited in the negotiation.

b. *Working with This Style*

The following are the appropriate uses, advantages, and challenges of a competing conflict style.

Appropriate Uses: An overly competitive style should usually be discouraged in mediation. As one can see from many of the tactics listed above, a competitive style can often be very destructive of the relationships in the mediation, further exacerbating animosity that stymies good communication. It also fuels unproductive personal conflicts and detracts from the more substantive issues to be resolved.[42] This is not to say, however, that a competitive style is inappropriate in all circumstances. Where there is a fixed resource or single issue at the center of the conflict, competitive tactics are often appropriate because integrative solutions are not possible. For example, in a personal injury dispute between an insurance company and the injured party, it is likely that the sole issue will be how much money the insurance company will pay to the injured party. In this situation, competitive tactics can be appropriate, especially because there will be no continuing relationship after the mediation is concluded.

---

42. THOMAS, *supra* note 35, at 21.

Advantages: Those using a competitive style also have qualities that benefit the mediation, and those natural tendencies should be encouraged. Those employing a competitive style are not typically reluctant to address issues head-on. They are often skilled at articulating their arguments clearly and forcefully.[43] They can also adequately defend themselves against other competitive negotiators, relieving the mediator from the awkward and often ethically tricky situation of balancing the power of the disputants.

Challenges: The goal of the mediator when confronted with a competitive conflict style is to make sure that the person does not become too inflexible, threatening, dismissive, or argumentative. Each of these aspects of the style can be counterproductive to resolving a dispute. A mediator, in some circumstances, can even encourage the party to adopt a conflict style more appropriate to the dispute. For example, where the mediator recognizes opportunities for integrative solutions, the mediator could explain the benefits of the party's use of a more collaborative style. Where neither a competitive nor a collaborative style is appropriate, the mediator could encourage compromising on certain issues. This can often be done through reframing (*see* Chapter 5), providing feedback, and coaching in private meetings or joint sessions.

2. AVOIDING — "I'LL THINK ABOUT IT TOMORROW."

"Avoiding" is an unassertive and uncooperative conflict style.[44] People who use avoidance as their predominant style abhor conflict and avoid it at all costs.

a. *Common Tactics*

The following are common tactics used by people who are employing an avoiding conflict style.[45]

Denial: Statements that explicitly or implicitly deny that a conflict even exists when it clearly does exist. "That's not really a problem."

Topic Shifting: Statements that move the discussion away from conflicted issues or terminate the discussion completely. For example, "Let's move on to something else," or, "I don't want to talk about this."

Psychological Withdrawal: Disengaging from the discussion, usually indicated by poor eye contact, closed body language, and remaining silent or inattentive. This can also be indicated by the person's making non-committal statements, such as "I am not sure how I feel about that offer."

---

43. WILMONT & HOCKER, *supra* note 12, at 145.
44. THOMAS, *supra* note 35, at 6.
45. WILMONT & HOCKER, *supra* note 12, at 143; FOLGER, SCOTT & STUTMAN, *supra* note 9, at 241–53 (chart listing conflict tactics used by persons employing the respective conflict styles).

b. *Working with This Style*

The following are the appropriate uses, advantages, and challenges of an avoiding conflict style.

Appropriate Uses: This style is most effectively applied to issues of little or no importance so that time and energy can be spent on concerns that are more important.[46] Similarly, minor personal verbal attacks and occasional sarcasm that sometimes occur during mediations are best ignored or minimized by the party on the receiving end of them. Focusing on these comments will increase their disruptiveness.

Advantages: A person who predominantly uses an avoiding style is less likely than most to get caught up in trivial or unimportant issues that can often use up precious time better spent on more central concerns to the problem. Another advantage is that such persons also more likely to ignore or forgive emotional outbursts and personal attacks that sometimes happen in mediation, helping to reduce tensions in the mediation and maintain focus on more relevant issues.

Challenges: The most common challenge that the avoiding style presents to a mediator is getting to the underlying needs and concerns of the party because of a tendency to minimize the problem. Thus, the mediator needs to work diligently, often in private meetings with the party, to ferret out his or her true concerns.

3. COMPROMISING — "HALF A LOAF IS BETTER THAN NONE."

A compromising conflict style is moderately assertive and cooperative.[47] It is a middling style in which the person believes that he or she will need to make some sacrifices to obtain a deal. The style's central values are practicality and expediency.[48] The compromising style is sometimes confused with collaborating, but the two styles are different. As will be discussed more below, the person using a collaborative style is more fiercely committed to all parties achieving their important goals and will spend considerable time, resources, and effort to accomplish this task, often engaging in creative problem solving that can generate value in the negotiation. The compromising style, by comparison, is less committed to goals and creating value. A person using this style is more concerned with dividing existing resources and arriving at an acceptable, if not optimal, outcome, with as little effort as possible.

a. *Common Tactics*

The following are common tactics used by people who are employing a compromising conflict style.[49]

---

46. THOMAS, *supra* note 35, at 17.
47. *Id.* at 6.
48. *Id.* at 32.
49. WILMONT & HOCKER, *supra* note 12, at 159; FOLGER, SCOTT & STUTMAN, *supra* note 9, at 241–53 (chart listing conflict tactics used by persons employing the respective conflict styles).

Appeals to Fairness: Persons employing a compromising style love using the word "fair," and will wield it extravagantly in mediation. "I just want a fair deal."

Trade-Offs: Willing to make concessions if he or she perceives that the other side is making relatively equal substantive sacrifices. "If you let me have the piano, I'll let you have the dining room set."

Seeks Quick Solutions: The compromising style is built for speed. Incomplete data or facts, or a little amount of time to mediate, is often no obstacle to obtaining an expedient solution.

b. *Working with This Style*

The following are the appropriate uses, advantages, and challenges of a compromising conflict style.

Appropriate Uses: Compromising is the most versatile of the conflict styles, being both mildly assertive and cooperative. It is most appropriate where the circumstances of the dispute do not lend themselves well to collaboration, such as when the parties need to divide a fixed resource.[50] It is also useful when time is short and the parties seek practical solutions.

Advantages: The person using the compromising style is usually very receptive to listening to the other party's arguments and suggestions and is flexible in constructing potential solutions to the dispute. In single-issue negotiations, such as where money is the central concern, they take a practical approach, recognizing that some sacrifice will be required to reach an agreement. They also do not get stuck on relatively unimportant issues on the grounds of "it's the principle of the matter," which can often undermine progress previously made on other issues.

Challenges: While one may think that mediators welcome the compromising style (and they often do), this style, like all conflict styles, has its dark side. First, those using this style are often too quick to make concessions, frequently making unnecessary ones. Repeated and unnecessary concessions by one party can lead the other party to mistakenly to believe that even more concessions can be made when, in fact, the supply of possible concessions has been exhausted prematurely. This can often lead to an impasse in the negotiation. Second, those using a compromising style tend to rush through the mediation process without taking the necessary time to seek out opportunities for joint gain. A person using a compromising style often spends too much time focused on how the negotiation pie will be divided and insufficient time on how he or she can enlarge the negotiation pie. This often leaves both parties feeling unsatisfied with the mediation process and outcome. There is a saying, in some mediation circles, *with which we strongly disagree*: "A successful mediation is one where both parties feel they have lost." A likely cause for this cynicism is too much compromising and not enough problem solving. Finally, as the mediation moves along quickly, a person using the compromising style will often ignore or minimize

---

50. THOMAS, *supra* note 35, at 33.

the importance of important facts or issues. Thus, mediators often need to slow down the mediation process so that a person using a compromising style does not become an unwitting victim of the style's challenges.

4. ACCOMMODATING — "I AM HAPPY TO OBLIGE."

The accommodating conflict style is non-assertive and cooperative.[51] The person employing this style tries to promote harmony and will often ignore or minimize their own needs and concerns in order to satisfy the needs and concerns of the other party.[52] He or she makes these sacrifices in order to maintain the relationship. Accommodation is different from avoiding. Unlike accommodation, the avoiding style is uncooperative, not caring greatly about the relationship or the other person's concerns or needs. The person using the accommodating style, conversely, cares deeply about the relationship and will do much to maintain it, even if it means making substantive concessions.

a. *Common Tactics*

The following are common tactics used by people who are employing an accommodating conflict style.[53]

Giving in: Placing a higher value on harmony than outcome, the accommodator will often volunteer substantive concessions or make concessions if there is the slightest sign of acrimony. "Why don't I just give you the house if you care so much about it."

Denial of Needs: Similar to the avoiding style, there is often a minimization or denial of their own needs or concerns, even when those needs and concerns might be very important to them. "I never liked the house anyway, and I can live with my mother."

Expressions of a Desire for Harmony: Persons employing an accommodating style will express a desire to work out the problem and emphasize the importance of the relationship to them. "I just want us to get along again."

b. *Working with This Style*

The following are the appropriate uses, advantages, and challenges of an accommodating conflict style.

Appropriate Uses: The accommodating style is useful where the issue is unimportant to one person but not to the other.[54] It is particularly appropriate where the value of keeping harmony in the relationship is more important than the outcome of a particular issue.

---

51. *Id.* at 6.
52. WILMONT & HOCKER, *supra* note 12, at 158.
53. *Id.* at 161 FOLGER, SCOTT & STUTMAN, *supra* note 9, at 241–53 (chart listing conflict tactics used by persons employing the respective conflict styles).
54. THOMAS, *supra* note 35, at 28–29.

Advantages: Persons using an accommodating style have a high degree of empathy and, therefore, have the ability to see the other party's point of view. This makes problem solving easier. The mediation can also proceed more smoothly because the accommodating style is very attentive to maintaining a harmonious relationship. People using this style are quick to give compliments and apologize for perceived offenses and less likely to make personal attacks on the other party. All of these characteristics promote a cycle of cooperation that can propel mediation along at a productive pace and in a promising direction.

Challenges: Accommodators can make very bad negotiating decisions in an attempt to make peace at any cost. Mediators have some responsibility for the quality of the agreements reached in the mediation in which they are participating.[55] A mediator's central role is to assist parties in making *good decisions* about the problem. How much responsibility a mediator has over the quality and fairness of the agreement is a subject of considerable debate in the field, a topic beyond the scope of this book.[56] At minimum, however, a mediator has the responsibility to help the parties realistically assess whether the agreement meets their minimum needs, as the mediator understands them, and whether the parties can practically implement any agreement reached. For example, neither party is well served if the mediator fails to question an agreed-upon payment plan in settlement of a contract dispute where he or she has reason to believe that the party promising to make the payments cannot do so; the parties will be back in court in a few weeks if the mediation is completed under these circumstances. What service is that to the parties? Thus, mediators need to be even more diligent with accommodators in helping them assess the viability and appropriateness of the agreements they reach. Moreover, like compromisers, accommodators will tend to rush through negotiations, which can result in not sharing information concerning their needs, or minimizing their needs, and ultimately missing opportunity for joint gain.

5. COLLABORATING — "TWO HEADS ARE BETTER THAN ONE."

The collaborating conflict style is both highly assertive and highly cooperative.[57] Persons employing this style are committed to satisfying their most pressing needs and concerns as well as helping the other party to satisfy their pressing needs and concerns. They view a dispute as a common problem to be solved by working together. They differ from people using a compromising style in that they will spend much more energy, time, and resources in working through the problem to maxi-

---

55. See Chapter 13—*Special Issues in Mediation*, section V.

56. *See* Lawrence Susskind, *Environmental Mediation and the Accountability Problem*, 6 Vt. L. Rev. 1 (1981); *but see* Joseph B. Stulberg, *The Theory and Practice of Mediation: A Reply to Professor Susskind*, 6 Vt. L. Rev. 85 (1981).

57. Thomas, *supra* note 35, at 5.

mize the results for both parties, whereas a compromising style seeks expedient solutions that at best will only partially satisfy the parties' needs and concerns.[58]

a. *Common Tactics*

The following are common tactics used by people who are employing a collaborating conflict style.[59]

Asking Questions: People using the collaborative style appreciate that information is the lifeblood of problem solving. Thus, they spend a significant amount of time asking questions to uncover the other party's needs, concerns, and perspective on the dispute. This is the opposite of the competitive style, where the party tries to monopolize the conversation but asks few questions.

Disclosing Information and Interests: Effective problem solving requires that information sharing be a two-way street. Collaborators share their underlying needs, concerns, and goals regarding the dispute.[60]

Flexible: Collaborators are strongly committed to satisfying their needs but are flexible as to how those needs are satisfied.

Supportive Remarks: Like the accommodating style, the collaborating style is highly cooperative, and the person using it will usually be attentive to maintaining a good relationship during the mediation. Collaborators build strong relationships by explicitly recognizing the merits of arguments made or the relevance of information presented by the other person. They are also quick to give compliments and make optimistic remarks concerning the likelihood of reaching an amicable resolution.

Acceptance of Responsibility: Parties employing a collaborative style accept responsibility for their role in the dispute and in resolving it. They are relatively open to criticism about past behavior.

b. *Working with This Style*

The following are the appropriate uses, advantages, and challenges of the collaborating style.

Appropriate Uses: A collaborative style works best when there are multiple issues and parties are committed to working together to arrive at integrative solutions.[61] This is also a particularly appropriate style when the parties are likely to continue a relationship after they complete the mediation, such as in disputes between divorcing spouses with minor children, disputes between parents and school administrations concerning special needs students, or disputes between business partners. The col-

---

58. WILMONT & HOCKER, *supra* note 12, at 162.

59. *Id.* at 165; FOLGER, SCOTT & STUTMAN, *supra* note 9, at 241–53 (chart listing conflict tactics used by persons employing the respective conflict styles).

60. WILMONT & HOCKER, *supra* note 12, at 165.

61. THOMAS, *supra* note 35, at 137.

laborative style does not work well in situations that revolve around a single issue, as in personal injury suits where money is the main concern.

Advantages: The collaborating style is a powerful problem-solving process that can produce highly satisfying solutions. The people employing this style are good listeners, share their needs and concerns openly, and are more likely to be respectful during the mediation.

Challenges: Those using a collaborative style can often spend too much time and energy on both trivial issues and important ones, exploring facts in such detail that the negotiation becomes smothered and stalled by the weight of all the information. Consequently, mediators need to guide people using this style to use their time and resources efficiently. A mediator may need to keep such parties aware of time constraints, keep them focused on the most salient issues, and encourage them to keep the discussion moving so that they can address all the important issues before time or patience is exhausted.

Mediators must also guard against a collaborative negotiator being taken advantage of by a more a competitive one. The collaborative style is open and honest about concerns and needs. Obviously, a competitive negotiator can exploit the collaborative negotiator by using their honest preferences against them in the negotiation process. For example, a spouse in a divorce mediation might be willing to share that his or her most important concern is to have ownership of the former family home to avoid spending the time, energy, and expense of finding a new one. A more competitive negotiator might feign interest in the family home simply to gain power in obtaining inequitable concessions in other areas of the divorce. In such cases, the mediator might encourage such transparency only in the private meetings with the mediator and not in the joint sessions in order to minimize the chance of exploitation.

IV. The Path of the Storm

A. Introduction

As chaotic as conflict can appear, there are discernible patterns. Just as meteorologists can often predict the path of a hurricane through comparison of historical weather patterns, so too might a mediator predict the likely course of a conflict through comparison of conflict patterns. As such, being aware of conflict patterns is enormously useful to a mediator. Knowing the next stage that a conflict is likely to pass through, and the attendant behaviors associated with that stage, provides the mediator with an opportunity to be better prepared for it, just like knowing the weather can help a person be better prepared by bringing an umbrella or dressing warmly. Unlike a meteorologist, however, knowing the path that conflict typically follows provides the mediator with more than just the ability to be prepared; it provides him or her with the ability to *influence* the path of the conflict.

Researchers have identified several different kinds of conflict cycles, but the one most useful for mediators to understand is the *escalation model*.[62] The escalation model is useful for mediators to know not only because it illustrates the most common conflict pattern, but it is also even more common in disputes that are likely to be mediated.

In his popular book *Story*, the screenwriting guru Robert McKee outlines the elements of dramatic structure in a way that can be adapted to the escalation model.[63] Indeed, as McKee's structure exemplifies, the crux of a good drama—whether in the form of a Hollywood movie, a Shakespearean play, or a Greek tragedy—is its believability; the believability of a good drama, in turn, stems from its accurate representation of our own experiences of conflict in the real world. The stages of a typical conflict escalation, like those in McKee's dramatic structure, are as follows: (1) *inciting incident*, (2) *progressive complications*, (3) *crisis*, (4) *climax*, and (5) *resolution*.

B. The Escalation Stages

1. INCITING INCIDENT

The escalation model, using McKee's terminology, starts with an "inciting incident." This is an event that "radically upsets the balance of forces in the protagonist's life."[64] Conflict researchers sometimes refer to this as the "triggering event."[65] An essential point for mediators to understand is that the inciting incident may be different for each party involved. For example, in a typical mediated conflict, it might be a refusal of a commercial tenant to continue to pay rent to the landlord. From the tenant's perspective, the inciting incident might be the landlord's failure to provide adequate air conditioning as provided for in the lease agreement. While it is important for a mediator to determine what the inciting incident was for each party, it is seldom important for the parties to agree on what the incident was that triggered the dispute. For if mediation has a theme, it is that it is a process for determining future behavior, not for assigning blame for past behaviors.

---

62. Two other common conflict cycles are the *conflict avoidance cycle* and the *chilling effect cycle*. LULOFS & CAHN, *supra* note 13, at 77. In the *conflict avoidance cycle*, the parties delay in dealing with a conflict because they are anxious about the confrontation with the other person or think that conflict is something negative, always to be avoided. The delay in addressing the conflict often complicates or exacerbates it. When the conflict becomes out of control and must be confronted, it is often handled poorly because the delay in addressing it has increased its intensity, thus confirming the person's negative view of conflict and reinforcing his or her future behavior in avoiding it. The *chilling effect cycle* is where there is increasingly diminishing communication between the parties because they believe that addressing the conflict is "not worth the time and energy." *Id.* at 79–80. As a consequence of decreased communication, there is a decrease in the commitment to the relationship, and the parties begin to view each other negatively and drift apart.

63. ROBERT MCKEE, STORY 181 (1997).

64. *Id.* at 189.

65. LULOFS & CAHN, *supra* note 13, at 91.

2. PROGRESSIVE COMPLICATION

If our mediated conflict were a movie, the next stage would be the "progressive complications" stage. Progressive complications are events that "generate more and more conflict as [the protagonist] faces greater and greater forces of antagonism."[66] In a movie, progressive complications are often caused by the circumstances in which the protagonist finds himself or herself, for instance, the protagonist has 24 hours to stop a terrorist cell from blowing up a famous bridge. Unfortunately, the protagonist's car will not start, the trains are not running, and the "bad guys" are trying to kill him or her. In a typical mediated conflict, on the other hand, the forces of antagonism come principally from the other party in the dispute. The distinguishing feature of this stage of a conflict is that the parties are often engaged in a cyclical pattern of increasingly aggressive behavior. One person's behavior triggers an aggressive response from the other and that, in turn, triggers an even more aggressive response, and so on.[67]

In the landlord-tenant dispute described above, the tenant might first call the landlord about the lack of adequate air conditioning. After receiving little assurance from the landlord that it will be fixed in a timely fashion, the tenant then might write a strongly worded letter demanding repair. The landlord might then send the tenant an even more strongly worded letter from the landlord's attorney explaining the landlord's legal rights under the lease. The tenant might then withhold rent, motivating the landlord to file legal action.[68] Obviously, there are endless variations on this theme, but the basic melody is the same—an alternating, ever-escalating use of aggressive tactics designed to achieve each side's respective goals in the dispute.

As in the best dramas, the progressive complication stage tends to be the longest and fullest stage of a real-world interpersonal conflict. Consequently, we will examine this stage and its mediation contours more in depth below, after outlining the remaining stages of a conflict.

3. CRISIS

Most dramatic movies have a crisis stage, and so do most real-life conflicts. A crisis, in the context of conflict, is where having "exhausted all actions to achieve a desire, save one, [the protagonist] now finds himself at the end of the line" with a crucial decision to make about his future.[69] At the end of the movie *Thelma & Louise*, two fugitive women become trapped between a cadre of police and the edge of the Grand Canyon. Their crisis decision is imprisonment or death.[70] They look at each

---

66. McKee, *supra* note 63, at 208.
67. Lulofs & Cahn, *supra* note 13, at 81.
68. This example mirrors a typical commercial dispute path from a "conciliatory" approach to conflict to an "adversarial" approach to conflict. Gerald R. Williams, Legal Negotiation and Settlement 86 (1983).
69. McKee, *supra* note 63, at 303.
70. *Id.* at 306.

other, silently decide, and proceed to drive their car into the gaping chasm. Mediated conflicts, thankfully, usually do not place the participants in such dire dilemmas. In mediated conflicts, the crisis decision usually arises because one or both of the participants have run out of faith in the effectiveness of their aggressive strategy or tactics, or have lost the ability to prosecute them. Therefore, they must choose a new strategy to address the conflict.

The crisis can come about for at least four distinct reasons. The first common reason is that one party has come to realize that his or her contentious tactics are just not working.[71] A second common reason is the exhaustion of resources.[72] Conflicts take time, energy, and often money to keep them going. As these resources diminish, so too does the ability to sustain the conflict. Third, people can become less committed to aggressively pursuing a conflict because of loss of social support.[73] People often rely on others psychologically and logistically to support them through conflict. Once this support wanes, the conflict becomes harder to maintain. Fourth, the participant perceives that the risks and costs associated with continuing the conflict outweigh any likely benefit.[74]

It is useful for a mediator to know the common reasons that motivate parties to abandon more aggressive tactics in favor of more cooperative ones. Knowing these common reasons, a mediator can move parties into the crisis stage sooner than they otherwise would on their own. Parties often employ aggressive tactics long after those tactics have become ineffective or, worse, counterproductive.[75] Mediators can help parties objectively evaluate the effectiveness of their tactics and assist them in choosing ones that are more fruitful. Mediators also can assist participants in evaluating the risks and costs of aggressively pursuing the conflict, something participants often minimize or ignore. It is critical for the mediator to appreciate that the crisis stage of a conflict is a *decision-making stage*. The party might choose to pursue a more cooperative strategy, or decide that their tactics have not been aggressive enough and redouble their efforts. The mediator's job is to help the parties make the best, most informed decision.

4. CLIMAX

The climax of an unfolding drama is that point in the plot where there has been "a major reversal."[76] In a conflict escalation cycle, the climax represents the decision by a party to "de-escalate."[77] De-escalation of the conflict occurs when one or both parties

---

71. DEAN G. PRUITT & SUNG HEE KIM, SOCIAL CONFLICT: ESCALATION, STALEMATE, AND SETTLEMENT 173 (2004).

72. *Id.*

73. *Id.*

74. *Id.* at 174.

75. *Id.* at 175.

76. MCKEE, *supra* note 63, at 309.

77. PRUITT & KIM, *supra* note 71, at 178.

behave more cooperatively.[78] Instead of making demands, they make compromises; instead of arguing, they problem solve; instead of accusing, they accommodate. The most critical feature of a party's decision to be more cooperative is that the party has undergone a fundamental conceptual shift in how he or she views the conflict. The party has shifted from believing that he or she can achieve his or her goals without any cooperation (by prevailing in a lawsuit, for example) to believing that he or she is dependent on the other party to achieve those goals. The party's view that he or she and the other party are *interdependent* is the vanguard of productive negotiation.

5. RESOLUTION

The final stage of all good drama is resolution.[79] In a movie, the viewer wants to know how things turn out. Does the hero foil the terrorist plot to blow up the famous bridge? Does the "regular guy" win the heart of the girl of his dreams? Most real-life conflicts are also resolved in some fashion, although not always as neatly as they are resolved in the movies. Some conflicts are resolved through agreement, as is often the case in mediation; some conflicts are resolved through parting ways with the other party; and some conflicts, unfortunately, are resolved through violence. In time, however, most disputes are resolved with or without the aid of a mediator. In fact, in the face of what may seem like overwhelming evidence to the contrary, humans tend to be adroit at resolving disputes. How many disputes do you have going on right now? Likely, few. How many lawsuits are you now personally a party to? Likely, none. Now, if we asked you how many disputes you have been involved with over the last year, the answer will likely be "too many to count!" The point being that conflict is a part of our daily existence, yet we seem to resolve most of them ourselves and move on with life. Disputes that are significant and intense enough to require a mediator are the exception, not the rule. Moreover, we believe that most parties, with few exceptions,[80] want to resolve their disputes and move on with their lives. Thus, in the vast majority of mediated disputes, the parties are the mediator's allies in trying to resolve it.

C. Complications that Occur During Conflict Escalation

As mentioned, the *progressive complication* stage is often the longest phase of the conflict cycle. It is during the progressive complication phase that the participants' animosity increases and the conflict intensifies. As the conflict intensifies, it can also transform in several ways that can further fuel escalation, making it more difficult to resolve the dispute amicably. The common types of transformation that occur during this stage of the conflict are as follows: (1) light tactics give way to heavy tac-

---

78. *Id.*

79. McKee, *supra* note 63, at 312.

80. Occasionally you will come across a "conflict junkie" who thrives on conflict, actively seeks it out, and attempts to unnecessarily sustain it. Fortunately, these people are the rare exception and not the rule.

tics; (2) issue proliferation; (3) sweeping generalizations; (4) increased commitment; and (5) proliferation of parties.[81] Not all of these complications occur in every conflict, but at least one or two occur in almost all conflicts. These complications undermine good decision-making, so the mediator must guard against, manage, and minimize them to the extent possible. When a mediator is engaged to assist the parties with the dispute, it is likely that some of these complications are already present. In this circumstance, the mediator's job, in part, is to work through these complications to minimize their impact. Just as often, however, these complications can arise during the mediation. In this circumstance, the mediator's job is to prevent them from interfering in the mediation's process.

Figure 6-1: The Path of the Storm

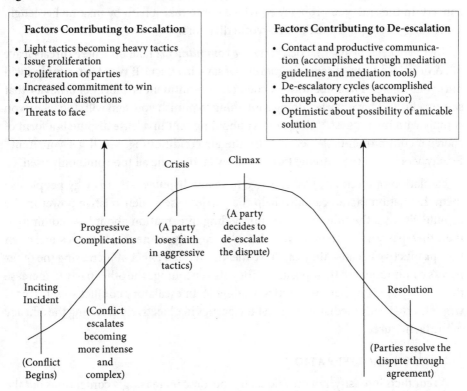

1. LIGHT TACTICS GIVE WAY TO HEAVY TACTICS

At the beginning of a conflict, most people begin by using "light" tactics to try to achieve their goals.[82] Light tactics might include ingratiation, promises to reward the other party for complying, or simply trying to persuade the other person to comply through reasoned argument.[83] If these tactics fail, most people up the ante; in other

---

81. Pruitt & Kim, *supra* note 71, at 89–90.
82. *Id.* at 89.
83. *Id.* at 65–66.

words, the light tactics give way to "heavy" tactics.[84] Heavy tactics include shaming and threats.[85] Let us take an example from home-life. You announce to your four-year-old daughter that it is bath time, but she flatly refuses to take a bath with a confident rigidity that only children and third-world dictators seem to be able to muster. Your first set of tactics might be to tell her what a good girl she has been all day and ask her politely again to take a bath (ingratiation). You might then promise an extra special nighttime snack (promises). You might even begin explaining the many health benefits of good personal hygiene (persuasion). When these tactics are met with the same defiant refusal, however, your tactics may become more severe. You might try *shaming* her by explaining how all her friends are taking a bath right now and she is the only one in noncompliance. You might then *threaten* to take away cherished privileges, like television or that planned trip to that special children's concert. In the end, you probably convince her to take a bath by making her laugh, something we might try with third-world dictators.

There are even heavier tactics. *Coercive commitments* take up where threats leave off. A threat is a form of *communication* that says, in effect, "If you don't comply, I will hurt your interests in some way." A coercive commitment is a form of *behavior* that says, in effect, "I have started doing something to punish you, and will stop when you comply with my request."[86] A tenant withholding rent in a lease dispute is a form of coercive commitment: "When you fix the air conditioning, you'll get your rent." Finally, violence is the extreme form of heavy tactics, one all too commonly used.

Escalation of tactics can be effective in many disputes—that is why people use them. Escalation tactics can also help the parties assess their relative power in the dispute *vis-à-vis* the other party and providing information about how committed the other party is to their goals. However, heavily contentious tactics are often non-productive because they can have the unintended effect of increasing the other party's commitment to their position. They also encourage the other party to increase the severity of his or her own tactics, leading to an escalatory conflict spiral. This is why it is crucial for mediators to assist the parties in objectively assessing the efficacy of the tactics used.

2. ISSUE PROLIFERATION

As conflicts intensify, not only do tactics become increasingly contentious but the number of issues tends to multiply.[87] An increase in the number of issues is neither inherently good nor bad. Often, new issues arise during the mediation that are germane and even vital to resolving the dispute. For instance, in an employer-employee dispute that was initially about interpretation of the employment contract, the

---

84. LULOFS & CAHN, *supra* note 13, at 81.
85. PRUITT & KIM, *supra* note 71, at 69–74.
86. *Id.* at 75.
87. *Id.* at 89.

employee might raise a valid issue of potential gender discrimination. The mediator will need to address both of these issues if the conflict is to be satisfactorily resolved. In such cases, the mediator's role is to manage how and when these issues are addressed. Where a conflict contains multiple issues, parties left to themselves will often try ineffective means of resolving them, such as attempts at addressing all issues at once, or attempts by one party to address one issue while the other party attempts to address a different issue.

As suggested earlier in our discussion of unproductive conflict, parties can also raise issues not relevant to the dispute. Sometimes these issues are raised as a ploy to gain power in the negotiation, whereas at other times, they are not appropriately addressed in mediation despite being valid. In either circumstance, the mediator should assist the parties in continuing to focus only on relevant issues. In short, a mediator assists the parties in coordinating when, how, and if an issue will be addressed.

3. SWEEPING GENERALIZATIONS

As conflicts intensify, people make generalizations about the issues over which they are conflicted and about each other.[88] An employee that fails to obtain a desired promotion because of perceived illegal discrimination, for example, may view the way the entire company is run as inept and most of the management as complicit in the discrimination. In other words, people mired in intense conflict tend to adopt broad general positions and negative attitudes. The longer and more intense the conflict, the more likely it will be that the parties will begin to see the other party in a negative light. As we will see below when discussing "attribution distortions," seeing the other party in a "negative light" distorts one's perceptions of the other party and the conflict, which can lead to further exacerbation of the conflict and poor decisions concerning its resolution.

4. INCREASED COMMITMENT

At the beginning of a conflict, the parties' primary objective is to achieve their goals.[89] They simply wish to do well, with no regard for how well the other party satisfies their goals. As the conflict escalates, however, parties become more competitive.[90] In becoming more competitive, parties commit increasing amounts of time, energy, and money to prosecute the conflict in order to "beat" the other side. In other words, the party shifts their perspective from merely doing *well* to doing *better* than the other party. If the conflict continues to escalate, each party can develop a desire to make the other party "hurt" as much as he or she has been hurt. This desire to financially or psychologically injure the other party can become so overwhelming that the party ignores or minimizes additional injuries he or she is inflicting on him-

---

88. *Id.*
89. *Id.* at 90.
90. *Id.* at 90 & 164.

self or herself.[91] A classic example of this phenomenon occurs in divorce litigation. A divorcing couple that has a total combined assets of $500,000 might spend a combined sum of $250,000 in attorney's fees to fund litigation! In negotiation terminology, this behavior is referred to as *irrational escalation of commitment*.[92] The mediator's responsibility when confronted with this type of destructive escalation is to point out the escalation cycle to the parties and then assist them in applying greater rational analysis to their negotiating strategy.

5. PROLIFERATION OF PARTIES

The number of participants often increases as the conflict escalates. To enhance their power and influence in the conflict, parties are motivated to seek practical and social support.[93] A common example is parties' commencing litigation and hiring legal representation as well as other experts. In non-litigation settings, this happens just as frequently. In an employment dispute, for example, as the conflict between a manager and an employee intensifies, the employee may seek the support of co-workers or other managers, while the manager might seek the support of human resources staff and executives. Increasing the number of participants is not inherently bad, but the mediator should appreciate that it changes the dynamics of the conflict and makes it more complex and time consuming to mediate. One reason it can render the mediation more time consuming is that there are simply more parties whose interests need to be addressed and satisfied. The additional time and complexity also increases the transaction costs of the dispute.

D. Other Factors Contributing to Conflict Escalation

1. ATTRIBUTION DISTORTIONS

Perception is how we organize and give meaning to the world around us. Because perception is an unconscious function, it appears a passive one.[94] Our brains create the illusion that the sights, sounds, tastes, smells, and tactile sensations we perceive come to us unmitigated, unfiltered, and untainted. Just the opposite is true. Our brains are non-stop "meaning-making machines" that mitigate, filter, and taint *every* perception.[95]

The way our brains organize and alter our perceptions of the world is a result of our unique experiences, attitudes, education, culture, gender, personality, and a myriad of other factors, which make perception highly subjective.[96] Three people witnessing the same event will not perceive it the same way: each will attend to dif-

---

91. *Id.* at 165–66.
92. MAX H. BAZERMAN & MARGARET A. NEALE, NEGOTIATING RATIONALLY 10–11 (1993).
93. PRUITT & KIM, *supra* note 71, at 89.
94. *See* DANIEL GILBERT, STUMBLING ON HAPPINESS 93 (2005).
95. WILMONT & HOCKER, *supra* note 12, at 49–50.
96. GILBERT, *supra* note 94, at 94.

ferent aspects of it; each will filter out different aspects of it; and each will assign different meaning to it. Perception is not something that happens to us, it is something that we do.[97] Although perception's proactive and subjective characteristics usually serve us well, they can contribute to the escalation of conflict.

In an unceasing effort to organize and make sense of the world, people in conflict make assumptions about the meaning of the behavior of the people with whom they are in conflict. We call these assumptions "attributions."[98] However, because people often have negative attitudes about the people with whom they are in conflict, these attributions are biased and frequently erroneous. In other words, people in conflict impute negative motives to the other person, even when such motives are absent.[99] Once a person forms a negative opinion of the other person as untrustworthy, malicious, or mean, all of that person's behaviors are filtered through that particular mental lens.[100]

In addition to perceiving those behaviors in a distorted light, people also "selectively process" information to confirm their negative opinion of the other person. In doing this, they over-emphasize the importance of words and deeds that support their negative opinion of the other person as untrustworthy and minimize or ignore words and deeds that undermine that opinion.[101] The result of selective perception is that

> there is nothing that the Other can do to dispel Party's negative expectations. If the Other behaves in a nasty way, this is taken as a true indicator of Other's hostile intentions, or belligerent disposition. If Other turns her cheek and displays friendly behavior, this is explained as a temporary fluke.[102]

Thus, "attribution distortions" create a constant stream of perceived aggressive action, some of which is likely imagined, feeding further escalation of the conflict.

Another aspect of attribution distortion is that people tend to judge their own contributions to the conflict in a much more forgiving light.[103] They see the other party's acts of aggression as evidence of bad character or unjust purpose, while they view their aggressive acts as necessary reactions to the situation. This, of course, makes it easier to blame others for the conflict situation and deny their contribution to it.[104]

The mediator's role in counteracting attribution distortions is to help the parties recognize that they may have based many of their conclusions about the conflict and

---

97. *See id.*
98. LULOFS & CAHN, *supra* note 13, at 126–27.
99. PRUITT & KIM, *supra* note 71, at 106, 159.
100. WILMONT & HOCKER, *supra* note 12, at 50.
101. PRUITT & KIM, *supra* note 71, at 156.
102. *Id.* at 159.
103. WILMONT & HOCKER, *supra* note 12, at 50.
104. *Id.*

the motives of the other party on erroneous assumptions. To accomplish this goal, the mediator can perform the following functions:

a. Explore the basis for the parties' beliefs and conclusions about the causes for the conflict and the other parties' motives;

b. Encourage the parties to question the other about the underlying interests and motivations for past and present behavior where it appears such behavior has proven an obstacle to progress in the conflict;

c. Encourage parties to explain their reasons for taking actions and positions in the mediation to prevent further misunderstandings and erroneous attributions.

d. Explain the natural tendency to negatively interpret the behaviors of the people with whom we are in conflict and stress the importance of using accurate assessments, not biased or distorted ones, to make decisions about how to address the conflict.[105]

2. FACE-SAVING

We all have a preferred image of ourselves and project that image to others in social situations.[106] One person may wish to emphasize his trustworthiness; another may wish to emphasize her intelligence. People have a deep psychological need for their image to be respected.[107] We call this self-image concept "face." In other words, "face is the communicator's claim to be seen as a certain kind of person."[108]

Being seen as a certain kind of person is a cooperative, not solitary, act.[109] It is an unstated social agreement. An example of this tacit agreement might be stated as follows: "I will let you believe that you are perceptive and witty, and you will let me believe that I am likable and trustworthy." In conflict situations, this common social contract is likely to be broken, especially where the parties are engaged in an intense conflict in which people often develop negative attitudes and perceptions about the other.

Threats to a person's self-image, or face, are of particular concern in conflict situations because they can intensify and complicate the conflict.[110] Face threats complicate conflict by introducing self-image issues to the dispute and complicate or detract from the substantive issues already under discussion. According to one researcher, "[i]n some instances, protecting against loss of face becomes so central

---

105. PRUITT & KIM, *supra* note 71, at 158 (The tendency to selectively process information is diminished "when people are strongly motivated to develop accurate impressions" (*citing* Neuberg 1989) and "are forewarned about the pitfalls of this phenomenon." (*citing* Swann 1987)).

106. FOLGER, SCOTT & STUTMAN, *supra* note 9, at 155.

107. LULOFS & CAHN, *supra* note 13, at 294.

108. FOLGER, SCOTT & STUTMAN, *supra* note 9, at 155.

109. LULOFS & CAHN, *supra* note 13, at 294.

110. FOLGER, SCOTT & STUTMAN, *supra* note 9, at 157.

an issue that it swamps the importance of the tangible issues at stake and generates intense conflicts that can impede progress toward agreement and increase substantially the cost of the conflict."[111] Increasing costs of conflict is a particular concern when face issues arise because a party's psychological need to "save face" can drive him or her to make self-destructive decisions.

A mediating party might feel they have lost face where they have made significant concessions from their original position. Their refusal to make further concessions, however commercially irrational, might be motivated by the need to maintain vestiges of face. Another common occurrence is for a party to be motivated by the fear of how they will appear to outside "ratifiers" if they make further concessions. In each case this subjective factor becomes the dominant interest of the party, as opposed to the objective factors over which they are negotiating. While the "face" phenomenon is probably common to all strands of humanity, it does have different significance in different cultures. In some cultures, any notion of compromise or concession on principle involves a loss of face, whereas in others the problem is less acute.

Accordingly, a mediator should employ "face-saving" tactics in the mediation. Face-saving tactics are attempts to "protect or repair relational images in response to threats, real or imagined, potential or actual."[112] Researchers have identified two distinct kinds of "face needs"—*positive face* needs and *negative face* needs.[113] Positive face needs concern a person's desire to be liked and respected. This is a need to be free from embarrassment or a need to be viewed as adequate and having integrity. Negative face needs concern a desire to be autonomous and independent. This is a desire to be seen as having power. There are several interventions a mediator can use to both prevent face issues from arising and repair them if they do.[114] We have discussed some of these interventions in other contexts in this book, but we list them again here because of their particular relevance in addressing face issues. These interventions are as follows:

a. Encourage the parties to treat each other with respect;

b. Encourage the parties to listen to the other party's positions, concerns, and interests;

c. Encourage the parties to see the dispute from the other party's perspective;

d. Encourage the parties to ask questions so that they may be able to better determine the other party's underlying motives and purposes for past behavior;

---

111. WILMONT & HOCKER, *supra* note 12, at 69.

112. FOLGER, SCOTT & STUTMAN, *supra* note 9, at 158.

113. LULOFS & CAHN, *supra* note 13, at 295.

114. *See generally* WILMONT, *supra* note 12, at 73–74; FOLGER, SCOTT & STUTMAN, *supra* note 9, at 175–82; LULOFTS & CAHN, *supra* note 13, at 296–312.

e. Encourage the parties to overlook or forgive momentary lapses in decorum in the mediation, such as interruptions or emotional outbursts;

f. Encourage parties who make significant "face" threats to the other party to apologize or explain their behavior;

g. Encourage parties to refrain from making ultimatums that threaten the other party's autonomy;[115]

h. Use "objective criteria" as a basis for getting a party's agreement rather than having them feel that they are conceding to the other side's proposal;

i. Use the technique of blaming a third party, such as the bank or the government (always a popular one), or an external factor, such as the economy or the weather, in order to remove blame and a sense of responsibility from the disputing parties;

j. Use the "scapegoat strategy," in which the mediation is engineered so that the parties can blame the mediator for a proposal or outcome, thereby allowing the parties to justify their own conduct;

k. Provide reasons for a change in negotiating position, for example, "in the light of the new information which we have heard for the first time today...," or "in light of the concessions you have heard them make...";

l. Use interim agreements. This is a classical negotiation strategy and is used to get deals accepted on a short-term basis ("say for the next two months...") without making any face-losing concessions on matters of principle which can still be negotiated in the future. In some cases "the temporary becomes the permanent," and the interim agreement is ratified without problem because it can be done without loss of face.

E. Factors Contributing to Conflict De-Escalation

In most conflicts, parties eventually lose faith in their escalatory tactics or dissipate the social or tangible resources that sustained the conflict. We have seen in the crisis stage of conflict how mediators can manage escalatory tactics. However, losing the will to escalate conflict is not the same as finding the will to de-escalate it.[116] Conflicts can languish for days, months, and even years betwixt and between escalation and de-escalation, the parties making little progress while continuing to expend considerable resources. Parties may find it difficult to de-escalate the conflict because they believe such a reversal of strategy would make them appear weak. Other times

---

115. For example, studies have shown that extremely rigid demands in business negotiations are one of the biggest obstacles in reaching an agreement because such demands create face-saving issues. LULOFTS & CAHN, *supra* note 13, at 299.

116. PRUITT & KIM, *supra* note 71, at 173.

it may be that the parties have become so alienated that almost all communication between them has ceased. It may also be that they do not know how to de-escalate a prolonged and intense conflict without "losing face."

Mediators can assist parties in overcoming many of these obstacles by creating the necessary environment and helping parties find the motivation to discover the path to de-escalation. Three tools are most useful in assisting in the de-escalation process: (1) *encouraging contact and communication*, (2) *initiating de-escalatory cycles*, and (3) *generating optimism*. While each in its own way is an effective tool for bringing about de-escalation, using these tools in concert has the greatest impact.

1. ENCOURAGING CONTACT AND COMMUNICATION

Parties engaged in intense conflict do not communicate effectively and often cease all communication, except through the aggressive tactics they employ to attain their goals. By simply getting the parties in the same place at the same time—having contact and communicating—the mediator can establish a necessary condition for making progress in the conflict.[117] During this contact, the mediator can use many different types of interventions, some which have been discussed above and others that will be discussed in later chapters, to de-escalate the conflict. For example, the mediator could encourage the parties to explain past behavior to overcome errone- ous attributions, or encourage the parties to share concerns and needs to allow for effective problem solving. These techniques, and others, can lead to greater empathy between the parties and counteract the inevitable dehumanization that occurs in conflict. Such productive transformations are only possible, however, through con- tact and communication.

Like all tools, encouraging contact and communication has its limits. For one thing, contact and communication work best shortly after the inciting incident of the conflict, before significant escalation has occurred, or later in the conflict when at least one of the parties has become dissatisfied with the escalatory nature of the conflict. In circumstances where both parties believe that escalatory tactics are working, contact and communication is at its least effective and can even further exacerbate the situation.[118] Sometimes parties need to escalate the conflict further before they are ready to de-escalate it. Indeed, there are mediators who argue that some parties will not be willing to participate in productive mediation until they have sufficiently "suffered." The authors are aware of one mediator who, when faced with parties in litigated matters who stubbornly continue unproductive, aggressive tactics and refuse even to explore the potential benefits of compromise or problem solving, approaches the situation by essentially saying the following:

> I think it is time to end the mediation, but before we do, let me share this with you. Ninety-five percent of these kinds of disputes settle before trial. In my

---

117. *Id.* at 181.
118. *Id.*

experience, this is not one of the five percent of cases that requires a trial or is likely to be tried. So, the question is not if it will settle but, rather, when it will settle. However, I don't think that either of you has suffered enough or spent enough money to fully appreciate that fact yet. So when you have suffered more and spent more, I will be happy to reconvene the mediation.

We do not share this statement necessarily to encourage such candidness with participants. Few mediators can be so direct without offending the participants. We share this statement because it captures the reasons why some parties may not be ready to mediate a dispute. Usually, a mediator will be able to determine the parties' willingness to de-escalate the conflict through pre-mediation interviews or separate meetings used during the mediation.

2. INITIATING DE-ESCALATORY CYCLES

Just as parties can become engaged in escalatory cycles, trading aggression for aggression, they can also become engaged in de-escalatory cycles where the parties' behavior becomes increasingly and alternately more cooperative.[119] De-escalatory cycles, like escalatory ones, are fueled by the rule of reciprocity. The rule of reciprocity states that the kind of behavior a person gives is the kind of behavior they are likely to get back.[120] Although the rule is not foolproof, it is a powerful principle of influence in human interactions. Parties are receptive to gratuitous conciliatory moves when their escalatory tactics appear ineffectual in the crisis stage of conflict. The act of a voluntary concession is called a *unilateral conciliatory initiative*.[121] To promote a de-escalatory cycle, a mediator can encourage a party to make such an initiative. Once one party makes the conciliatory initiative, the mediator is in the position to ensure the other party perceives this initiative as a sincere attempt to work through the conflict and not some trick or nefarious tactic (erroneous attribution). Moreover, the mediator can encourage the other party to make an appropriate reciprocal cooperative gesture. Whether the mediator conducts these discussions with all parties present or in separate meetings is within the mediator's judgment. Either way, this is one tactic a mediator can employ to energize a de-escalation cycle.

3. GENERATING OPTIMISM

Parties pursuing escalatory cycles do so because they believe aggression is the strategy that will most likely lead to achieving their respective goals. They are "optimistic" that a contentious strategy will work.[122] Conversely, to motivate parties to engage in de-escalation, the parties must become "optimistic" that cooperative behavior will help them achieve their goals.

---

119. *Id.* at 186.
120. ROBERT B. CIALDINI, INFLUENCE: SCIENCE AND PRACTICE 20–22 (4th ed. 2001).
121. PRUITT & KIM, *supra* note 71, at 184.
122. *Id.* at 179.

Mediators can generate optimism in three ways. One way mediators generate optimism is by being optimistic about the likelihood of success. Optimism, like laughter, is contagious. A second way is to share information with parties about the success of the mediation process in resolving similar disputes. Although a mediator should never promise a result, a mediator can be optimistic about reaching a favorable outcome. For example, a mediator might say, "Based on the excellent success rate in mediation and my experience with similar types of disputes, I feel we have a very good chance of resolving this matter in a way that will satisfy both parties." Finally, a mediator should reinforce the progress that the parties make during the mediation. Parties often lose track of progress made in mediation, focusing more on the time and energy expended and the issues that still divide them. Mediators need to emphasize the progress, however modest, and help the parties envision the benefits of an agreement.

4. DIAGNOSING THE DISPUTE

It is imperative for mediators to analyze and diagnose conflict situations in order to develop a theory on which to base an intervention strategy. Any diagnosis is always tentative. As we have seen, conflict is not a static phenomenon. It can escalate and de-escalate over time, necessitating a continual diagnostic assessment by mediators. Diagnosis can be done intuitively, as some mediator trainees would like to have it, or it can be done in a structured manner. As there is more to dealing with conflict than gut feeling, the structured approach is recommended here. It is also more appropriate for beginner mediators to learn through a structured approach rather than through the intestinal one. Structured diagnosis involves asking the following questions.

F. Who Are the Parties to the Conflict?

Mediators need to ensure that all relevant parties are playing an appropriate role in the mediation. In some cases, it is self-evident who they are and what their roles should be, for example, the person asking for something and the person being asked to provide it. In other cases, the situation is more complex and requires some investigation, analysis, and consultation with the parties directly involved to ascertain what other categories of parties should be included. Consequently, in mediation over a disputed development application, there might be a first category of parties (the developer, the objectors, and the local authority) and also a second category (comprised of residents, environmental groups, and business associations).

There may be a difference between the parties to the conflict and the appropriate parties for the mediation. For example, a doctor might not technically be a party to a medical negligence dispute between a patient and medical insurer, but his or her presence at the mediation might be an important ingredient for its success. Likewise, a party to the conflict might not be the appropriate person to attend the mediation. For example, a middle manager in a business dispute might have too much self-interest to be a useful participant in the mediation; a higher-ranking manager could attend instead.

A related question is who, apart from the parties to the dispute, should attend the mediation as observers or support persons, or in some other capacity. Where the parties have legal counsel, it is usually preferable for counsel to be present. This is particularly appropriate where the counsel has given the party a legal opinion about the merits and likely outcome of the dispute if the matter proceeds to a trial. However, practice varies significantly from state to state and from subject matter to subject matter. For example, in some states, attorneys frequently do not attend mediations with their clients in divorce matters, whereas in other states they do.

G. Why Are the Parties in Conflict?

Mediators need to develop a hypothesis concerning the probable causes of conflict because the mediation interventions and strategies will differ for each cause. Christopher Moore, in his classic book *The Mediation Process*, provides a helpful analytical structure for this purpose.[123] Moore identifies five major causes of conflict: (1) *relationship conflicts*; (2) *data conflicts*; (3) *interest conflicts*; (4) *structural conflicts*; and (5) *value conflicts*. For each of these types of conflict, he provides possible interventions. Some mediators find this level of analysis too technical and unnecessary—and sometimes it is. Often, the source of the conflict and the necessary interventions will be so clear that engaging in a significant analytical process is superfluous. However, many situations present greater challenges in identifying the cause of the conflict because the conflict is complex and/or there is more than one cause. In such cases, having an analytical tool kit to diagnose the sources of a conflict and select appropriate interventions can be invaluable. The following is an analytical structure based on Moore's "circle of conflict":[124]

1. RELATIONSHIP CONFLICTS

   a. *Causes*: Patterns of negative behavior, untreated emotions, the grieving process, stereotypes, psychological problems.

   b. *Example*: A supervisor in an organization is regarded by subordinates as biased, rigid, unreasonable, and unwilling to take risks.

   c. *Possible Interventions*: Acknowledge and validate emotions; avoid negativity through control of process through mediation guidelines and separate meetings; assist parties in clarifying purposes and testing assumptions; improve the quality of the communication through paraphrasing and reframing.

---

123. CHRISTOPHER W. MOORE, THE MEDIATION PROCESS 64–65 (3d ed. 2003).
124. *Id.* Adapted with permission by CDR Associates, Boulder, Colorado.

2. DATA CONFLICTS

a. *Causes*: Figures, data, or documents are incorrect, incomplete, lost or differently interpreted; different view of what is relevant; different view of assessment procedures.

b. *Example*: Valuers have different methods for assessing the value of goodwill in a business and produce widely different valuations.

c. *Possible Interventions*: Find, correct, and/or supplement data; develop objective criteria to evaluate information; use neutral expert to interpret data.

3. INTEREST CONFLICTS

a. *Causes*: Perceived or actual competition over goals, resources, or needs. These interests could be substantive, procedural, or physiological.

b. *Example*: The marketing department requires more products for new customers, while production wants fewer to ensure reliability of quality.

c. *Possible Interventions*: Emphasize interdependence; focus on interests, not positions; search for value, creating trade-off that satisfies parties with differing interests; stress implication of non-settlement.

4. STRUCTURAL CONFLICTS

a. *Causes*: Unequal access to authority, information, resources, professional advice, time, and other sources of power.

b. *Example*: Sales department's budget has increased 20 percent while the production department's budget remains unchanged.

c. *Possible Interventions*: Emphasize different sources of power; ensure fair decision-making power; focus on interests, not positions; define roles.

5. VALUE CONFLICTS

a. *Causes*: Competing ideologies, world views, religious and cultural values, basic assumptions about life and the universe.

b. *Example*: Employer and employee differ over whether touching on the shoulder constitutes collegial affection or harassment.

c. *Possible Interventions*: Clarify values and beliefs; search for an overarching common value or goal; focus on interests, not positions; educate on principle of "live and let live."

Interpersonal conflict is an ever-shifting landscape that requires the mediator to be continually on guard for new issues, interests, and information. Most conflicts that require mediation have more than one cause, some of which do not become apparent even to the litigants until well into the mediation. Mediators therefore must regularly update their hypothesis concerning the cause of the conflict and adjust their interventions accordingly. The interventions provided above are by no means a comprehensive list, nor should a mediator implement them in a mechanical way. Mediators must use their own judgment in what interventions are most appropriate to the circumstances of the conflict. However, having an intellectual framework for what typically causes conflicts and what interventions have proven effective in similar disputes is a useful platform from which a mediator can make strategic decisions about the most appropriate means to assist the parties.

V. Exercises

1. Identify the benefits you received resulting from a dispute in which you were personally involved.

2. Discuss with a trusted friend or co-worker your "predominant" conflict style in your workplace environment. Specifically identify attitudes toward conflict and the tactics you use most often.

3. Identify a significant dispute in which you have been personally involved and describe the course of the conflict according to the stages of the escalation model.

4. Identify a dispute in which you have been personally involved and analyze it in terms of the five sources of conflict referred to in this chapter. What other factors not referred to here might have caused the conflict to occur? What interventions worked or did not work in relation to resolving the dispute? How might a mediation have been designed to deal with the particular nature of this dispute?

5. Consult a newspaper for a news report on a dispute of some magnitude. What are the positional claims made by the parties to the dispute? What might be the interests and needs underlying these positions? As the dispute continues to be reported in the media, how do the parties' positions and interests change?

SEVEN

Facilitating the Negotiations

Never cut when you can untie.

—JOSEPH JOUBERT (MORALIST AND ESSAYIST)

I. The Mediator's Role in Negotiations

A. The Negotiation Expert

If there is a "golden rule" for contemporary mediators, it is that they need to become expert in the "art" and "science" of negotiation. Although mediators are not negotiators in the direct sense, mediation is a form of assisted negotiation, and mediators have a responsibility to improve the quality of the negotiations in which they participate. How mediators use their negotiation expertise is not, however, a straightforward matter. Assisting parties with their negotiation is a subtle and demanding skill that requires a balance between strong intervention and "benign neglect."[1] It also requires that mediators intervene for the common good of the parties or, at least, do not unduly advantage one party to the detriment of the other.

Mediators may assist parties with their negotiations at all stages of the mediation process: before the mediation, during joint sessions, during separate sessions, during the closing stage, and sometimes even after the mediation has ended. They also use a variety of methods in providing this assistance, such as advising, demonstrating, educating, and coaching. How a mediator goes about these tasks involves the use of discretion, judgment, and a sense of timing. For instance, there are practical restrictions on what interventions a mediator can use in joint sessions, while there is greater latitude for the kind of interventions available to the mediator in separate sessions. This chapter is organized into three topics: (1) the role mediators should play in the negotiation, (2) how mediators can prepare parties for the negotiation, and (3) what tools and techniques mediators can use to assist parties during the negotiation.

---

1. John M. Haynes & Gretchen L. Haynes, Mediating Divorce: Casebook of Strategies for Successful Family Negotiations 46 (1989).

B. Common Negotiating Mistakes

Mediators assist parties in negotiation by helping them avoid common and often costly negotiation mistakes often made by inexperienced or overly emotional negotiators. This assistance is very valuable. The following are common negotiation mistakes that we will pay particular attention to in this chapter:[2]

1. *Leaving Value on the Table:* This pitfall occurs when negotiators fail to recognize value-creating trade-offs in the negotiation. This is often a consequence of parties viewing the negotiation as a zero-sum game, a "your win is my loss" attitude.

2. *Settling for Too Little:* This pitfall occurs when negotiators make unneeded or inappropriately large concessions. As previously explained, we believe that mediators have some responsibility for assuring that agreements minimally meet parties' needs and concerns so that the terms of any agreement are likely to be implemented.

3. *Walking Away from the Table:* This pitfall occurs when a party rejects an offer from the other party that is *better* than any alternative that the party has or is likely to have. Assisting the parties in evaluating the adequacy of offers and terms is one of the central roles of a mediator. This pitfall is the result of unchecked emotionalism or failure to adequately assess alternatives. Mediators can provide considerable assistance in overcoming these obstacles.

4. *Settling for Terms that Are Worse than the Alternative:* This pitfall occurs when a party accepts terms less favorable than a readily available alternative; it is the inverse problem of *walking away from the table* pitfall. This pitfall is usually a consequence of a party's becoming overly committed to settlement or, as explained above, failing to thoughtfully evaluate alternatives to a negotiation.

C. Many People Are Ineffective Negotiators

Many mediation participants, including professional advisors, are ineffective negotiators. Sometimes this is because of "over-emotionalism" that can cloud good judgment, but just as often it is because most people have limited negotiation training and skills. People tend to rely on a few negotiating techniques and use them in all situations. Similar to mediation, negotiation is a skill that can be improved through the marriage of experiences, education, and constructive feedback. However, most people, even professionals who negotiate frequently, negotiate in isolation, receiving little feedback concerning their negotiation performance. Moreover, formal education in negotiation, even among lawyers and business professionals, is minimal and in many instances non-existent. Thus, most people approach negotia-

---

2. LEIGH L. THOMPSON, MIND AND HEART OF THE NEGOTIATOR 6 (3d ed. 2005).

tion in an instinctive, haphazard way with little planning or skill. These factors make them susceptible to the common pitfalls explained above and prone to other mistakes that we will address shortly.

Finally, because of a lack of training in negotiation, people often approach negotiation as a battle over a fixed resource that needs to be divided. This is known as the "fixed pie" syndrome, because the negotiator views the negotiation like a pie from which he or she wants the biggest slice. One study suggests about 80 percent of negotiators have this "fixed pie" mindset when they enter a negotiation.[3] This limited and often incorrect view of negotiation makes it more likely that parties will miss opportunities for joint gain and fail to engage in creative problem solving. It also increases the likelihood that negotiators will fail to reach an amicable resolution.

D. The Negotiator's Dilemma: Creating and Claiming Value

Assisting the parties in managing the *negotiator's dilemma* is an essential role of the mediator in the negotiation process. Negotiation presents an underlying tension between behaviors that *create* value and those that *claim* value. Creating value and claiming value are inextricably linked in all negotiations because they are countervailing forces. Thus, effectively managing the negotiator's dilemma involves applying and balancing methods of creating and/or claiming value to maximize the negotiation outcome for the participants.

Creating value in negotiation means to create *joint gains*. Joint gains are ones that simultaneously bring true intrinsic improvement to each side's position. A joint gain is not a beneficial compromise or "feeling good" about a particular contract term. Rather, it is an agreement that confers a tangible benefit on both parties.[4] For example, parties negotiating the settlement of a breach of contract dispute may discover that both sides benefit from delayed payment of the agreed upon monetary settlement for three months. Party A will benefit by the delay because it will not need to borrow money to pay the settlement, thereby saving interest on the loan; Party B will benefit because there will be significant tax benefits in receiving the settlement funds during the next fiscal year. This term represents a joint gain that *creates value* in the negotiation because it simultaneously confers value to both parties.

Claiming value in negotiation, on the other hand, means to obtain as much as possible from the fixed resource at stake in the negotiation. Claiming value often motivates stereotypical negotiation tactics, such as making high settlement demands, pretending to be more powerful than you are, or being inflexible concerning offers of settlement. In the breach of contract situation above, the amount of the settlement will be determined by *value-claiming* tactics. The more Party A pays to Party B, the

---

3. THOMPSON, *supra* note 2, at 6.
4. *Id.* at 70.

less Party A retains. So, it benefits Party A to use tactics that minimize the settlement amount, just as it benefits Party B to use tactics to maximize it.

The negotiator's dilemma arises because the negotiator must choose when to employ value-creating tactics and when to employ value-claiming tactics. It is called a "dilemma" because, as we will explore below, value-*claiming* tactics impede the creation of value, and value *creating*-tactics can leave a negotiator at risk of being exploited by value-claiming tactics used by the other party.[5] Certainly creating value is desirable because it enlarges the negotiation pie, but the parties' necessary transparency to accomplish this is risky. Claiming value is desirable because it maximizes one's share of the negotiating pie, but the overly competitive behavior dampens value creation so that there is less value to be divided. The trick in negotiation is to be aware of this tension and to properly manage it so as to optimize both value creating (so the negotiation pie is bigger) and value claiming (so you get your fair share of the bigger pie).

Let us examine how value-claiming tactics impede joint gains. Examples of value-claiming tactics include concealing information, minimizing the benefit of concessions received, exaggerating the value of concessions granted, setting high demands, and making threats. Coercive tactics such as these produce distrust between parties, making it less likely that they will share information. When parties conceal information, opportunities for joint gains that create value are significantly diminished. Value-claiming tactics also distort the parties' true needs and concerns, thereby further reducing the chances that the parties will discover joint gains. Thus, if the parties in the breach of contract example above hide that delayed payment is beneficial or mislead the other into thinking that it is unimportant, that joint gain would likely be unrealized, hurting both parties. The less information parties share, the less opportunity there will be to create value that could benefit both parties.

Creating value tactics, conversely, can place a party at risk of being taken advantage of by a more competitive negotiator. When one side truthfully reveals a preference, need, or concern, the other side may then use one of the value-claiming tactics discussed above to gain undue concessions in the negotiation, thus *claiming* a larger share of the negotiation pie. For example, if a spouse in a divorce matter is honest about a strong preference to retain custody of the minor child, the other spouse may feign a similar interest to gain leverage in forcing concessions on alimony—his true, more important concern.[6] The competitive spouse exaggerates the value of his concession on the issue of custody to claim more value regarding alimony.

Mediators are well positioned to manage the tension between cooperative and competitive impulses in negotiation. In some cases, the mere presence of the mediator in the joint session can influence parties to be more open and honest about their

---

5. David A. Lax & James K. Sebenius, The Manager as Negotiator 38 (1986).
6. *Id.* at 34–35.

concerns, thus making the discovery of joint gains more likely. An even more pow-erful tool that mediators possess in managing the negotiator's dilemma is the ability to meet with parties in separate private sessions. Parties that are reluctant to share true needs and concerns with the other party in joint sessions are often more willing to share those concerns with the mediator privately. Armed with this information, the mediator is in a position to search for opportunities for joint gains and the party's risk of exploitation is significantly reduced. A mediator's ability to simultaneously increase the opportunities for joint gain while also lowing the risk of exploitation is one of his or her most important contributions to the mediation process.

The other way for the mediators to manage the tension present in the negotiator's dilemma is to discourage overly competitive behavior or unchecked sharing of information. Mediators can educate parties about the unintended and unproductive consequences of overly competitive tactics in diminishing trust and causing resent-ment, which translates in diminished information sharing. They can also warn parties about sharing too much information that may leave the party vulnerable to exploitation. Assisting the parties in balancing these necessary but conflicting nego-tiating impulses increases the likelihood of achieving optimal agreements.

II. Assisting in Preparing for Negotiation

A. Nature and Importance of Preparation in Negotiation

Preparation is the most important part of any negotiation. Despite this unassail-able fact, many mediation participants do not prepare adequately for negotiation.[7] Lack of preparedness does not usually result because a mediation participant is lazy but rather because the participant does not know how to prepare for negotiation or believes that one cannot prepare for negotiation. Preparing for negotiating is not only possible, it is highly beneficial. Adequate preparation enhances the participants' ability to evaluate offers, manage concession-making, and create value.[8] These ben-efits also reduce the risk of parties succumbing to the common negotiating mistakes noted above.

A mediator can provide no greater service to the parties than assisting them in preparing for the negotiation when he or she has the opportunity. Mediators can arrange a pre-mediation conference to help parties prepare for mediation. (See Chapter 2, section VII B for a fuller discussion of pre-mediation.) Pre-mediation conferences are especially desirable in complex matters. Meeting before the media-tion enables the mediator to spend sufficient time with participants in working through the necessary aspects of negotiation preparation, time that often is unavail-

---

7. THOMPSON, *supra* note 2, at 13.

8. ROY J. LEWICKI, DAVID M. SAUNDERS, JOHN W. MINTON & BRUCE BARRY, NEGOTIA-TION: READINGS, EXERCISES, AND CASES 485 (5th ed. 2006).

able in the mediation. Pre-mediation conferences, however, are not always possible or practical. Thus, much of the assistance that a mediator provides parties in preparing for negotiation can and does occur during the mediation itself.

Three general principles should guide the mediator through the preparation stage: *simplicity, specificity*, and *flexibility*.[9] A simple plan can be more easily remembered and implemented. "Simple" is a relative term, depending on the nature of the dispute. Obviously, a negotiation preparation addressing the problem of a neighbor's incessantly barking dog will be far less complex than the negotiation preparation addressing an accounting dispute between two multinational companies. The mediator should use discretion to promote an approach that is tailored to the dispute and free from unnecessary complexity.

The preparation should also be specific. Specificity increases the likelihood that negotiators will achieve their goals. For example, as we shall discuss in greater detail below, specifically identifying a negotiator's alternatives to achieving his goals if no agreement can be reached makes evaluation of offers from the other party in the mediation more precise. Specifically identifying reasons that justify one's offers makes those offers more credible and persuasive.

Negotiation preparation should also be flexible. Invariably parties will base some of the preparation decisions on incomplete information or assumptions. As the parties acquire missing information and test their assumptions during the mediation, plans often need to be modified. To illustrate, let us look at a situation where a contractor has sued a homeowner for payment for installation of two bay windows. The homeowner says that the windows leak because they were improperly installed. In preparing for the negotiation, the contractor may have listed "I will repair any defect" as his preferred settlement option, only to find out during the mediation that the homeowner will not consider this option. Thus, the contractor will need to be flexible and focus on other potential solutions.

B. Setting the Stage—Gathering Information

Mediators must first assist the participants in preparing for mediation by gathering relevant information. There are four principal areas of focus in this effort: (1) *identifying the parties' interests*, (2) *evaluating alternatives*, (3) *identifying objective standards*, and (4) *generating potential solutions*. While there are certainly other matters that a mediator could address with the parties in preparing them for the mediation, these are the most essential. Once this basic information is known and evaluations have been made, the actual negotiations can occur.

The mediator's task is to explore these areas as efficiently and expediently as possible. Although preparation can be a lengthy process, it does not need to be. Any time spent on the preparation concepts listed above will pay dividends in the medi-

---

9. BILL SCOTT, THE SKILLS OF NEGOTIATING 77–87 (1981).

ation in both the quality of decisions made and the efficiency of the process. The earlier these areas are addressed in the mediation, the better. Using a pre-mediation conference for this purpose is best when possible. Keep in mind, however, that working through the preparation concepts is not always a linear process. Mediators may have to move back and forth between topics to sufficiently cover each area. Even when pre-mediation conferences have been held with the parties, the mediator will revisit these areas throughout the mediation as the parties reveal more information.

To help mediators with organization in overseeing this information gathering process, we have included in Appendix 8 the *Mediator Negotiation Preparation Worksheet* that can be a useful guide through the preparation process. Each party will need a separate worksheet. A mediation client and his or her representative(s) are considered "one party" for purposes of the worksheet. Mediators can use the worksheets to take notes, or the mediator and the party can work together to complete it.

C. The Parties' Interests

1. THE POWER OF UNCOVERING INTERESTS

Helping parties explore the relevant interests is central to helping them to uncover solutions to the conflict. As we have said before, interests define the dispute.[10] Interests are the parties' underlying concerns, needs, and fears that are motivating the conflict. *Interests* are to be contrasted with *positions*, which are the participants' preferred solutions to the problem. For example, an employer's wish to fire an employee for being habitually late for work is the solution (position) to his problem that the employee is disruptive to his business (interest). Thus, the first task of a mediator is to help parties uncover their interests. See Chapter 4, section II C (4), for a discussion of how to uncover the parties' interests.

Focusing on interests instead of positions has enormous potential benefits for participants. Most importantly, it helps participants discover solutions that are responsive to their true needs and concerns. For example, in the employment conflict above, the employer's true concern is running his business profitably without disruption. Quite possibly a better solution may be to work through the problem with the employee, who may bring value to the business despite her tardiness, by arriving at some agreement concerning her lateness. By finding a solution that enables the employer to keep an experienced and otherwise valuable employee, the employer saves the cost of rehiring and retraining a replacement.

Another benefit of focusing on interests rather than positions is that multiple potential solutions to the problem often become apparent. Focusing on interests encourages parties to resist the natural tendency to adopt the most obvious, self-serving solution without looking further. The more potential solutions that can be

---

10. ROGER FISHER, WILLIAM URY & BRUCE PATTON, GETTING TO YES 40 (2d ed. 1991).

identified, the more likely it is that one of those solutions will work for both parties, leading to an amicable agreement.

In some situations, as a result of focusing on interests rather than positions, the parties may discover that their interests are not completely in conflict with one another. This opens the door to potential solutions that were previously hidden from view when the negotiation was conducted on a more positional basis. An example of this is illustrated in the negotiation between Israel and Egypt at Camp David in 1978. The following is a recounting of the negotiation from the classic negotiation text *Getting to Yes*:

> Israel had occupied the Egyptian Sinai Peninsula since the Six Day War of 1967. When Egypt and Israel sat down together in 1978 to negotiate peace, their positions were incompatible. Israel insisted on keeping some of Sinai. Egypt, on the other hand, insisted that every inch of the Sinai be returned to Egyptian sovereignty. Time and time again, people drew maps showing possible boundary lines that would divide the Sinai between Egypt and Israel. Compromising in this way was wholly unacceptable to Egypt. To go back to the situation as it was in 1967 was equally unacceptable to Israel.
>
> Looking to their interests instead of their positions made it possible to develop a solution. Israel's interests lay in security; they did not want Egyptian tanks poised on their border ready to roll across at any time. Egypt's interest lay in sovereignty; the Sinai had been part of Egypt since the time of the Pharaohs. After centuries of domination by the Greeks, Romans, Turks, French, and British, Egypt had only recently regained full sovereignty and was not about to cede territory to another foreign conqueror.
>
> At Camp David, President Sadat of Egypt and Prime Minister Begin of Israel agreed to a plan that would return the Sinai to complete Egyptian sovereignty and, by demilitarizing large areas, would still assure Israeli security. The Egyptian flag would fly everywhere, but Egyptian tanks would be nowhere near Israel.[11]

When the Israeli and Egyptian negotiators focused on positions, the negotiation was deadlocked, even where compromise was attempted. It was only when negotiators focused on the parties' true concerns—their underlying interests—did a mutually acceptable solution emerge. The same process that brought peace to a small corner of the Middle East has the potential to bring peace to everyday conflicts, both big and small.

---

11. ROGER FISHER, WILLIAM URY & BRUCE PATTON, GETTING TO YES at 41–42 (2d ed. 1991). Copyright © 1981, 1991 by Roger Fisher and William Ury. Reprinted by permission of Houghton Mifflin Company. All rights reserved.

2. THE PROCESS OF UNDERSTANDING EACH OTHER'S INTERESTS

A mediator should not only help the parties to identify their own interests but also help them to appreciate the other party's interests as well. After exploring a party's interests, the mediator should explore what the party believes are the *other party's* concerns and needs concerning the dispute. This technique is intended to expand the parties' understanding of the problem and each other, laying the foundation for effective problem solving.

a. *Change the Parties' Point of View*

Skilled negotiators know the importance of considering the other parties' needs and concerns when preparing for a negotiation, and they spend up to four times the amount of time thinking about those concerns than average negotiators.[12] In fact, some research suggests that the ability to "see the other person's point of view" is the most important negotiation skill of all.[13] Henry Ford, the founder of the Ford Motor Company, said, "If there is any one secret of success, it lies in the ability to get the other person's point of view and see things from that person's angle as well as from your own." Henry Ford's secret of business success is also one of the secrets of negotiation success. Appreciating the other person's point of view is not an act of generosity; it is a self-serving and advantageous negotiation technique. This technique increases the likelihood that parties will be able to "create value" in the negotiation, which in turn increases the chances that any agreement reached will be more responsive to the needs of each party.

The mediator can provide valuable guidance in helping the parties see the other side's point of view. As we have discussed, many mediation participants are not skilled negotiators and are inclined to spend little or no time considering the concerns and needs of the other party. The mediator can assist the parties in understanding that negotiation is a "two-way street."[14] One way for the mediator to help each party understand the other side's point of view is to encourage each to walk down this "two-way street" in the other direction. This technique is called "role reversal."

b. *Role Reversal*

Role reversal is an effective technique for identifying the other side's interests. The party is asked by the mediator to imagine that he or she is in the position of the other party. This technique is usually performed in a separate session. While in the separate session, the mediator might ask, "What do you think your former employer cares

---

12. Neil Rackham & John Carlisle, *The Effect Negotiator—Part I: The Behavior of Effective Negotiators*, 2 J. OF EUROPEAN INDUSTRIAL TRAINING, no. 6, 1978, at 1; G. RICHARD SHELL, BARGAINING FOR ADVANTAGE 78 (2d ed. 2006); *see also* WILLIAM URY, GETTING PAST NO 19 (1993).

13. SHELL, *supra* note 12, at 80

14. *Id.* at 18.

most about in this negotiation?" or, "If you were in your wife's position, what would be your most pressing concerns?" Role reversal is challenging for some parties because it forces them to view the problem from the other side's perspective, perhaps for the first time. This can be quite an uncomfortable experience for a party, not just because it is perhaps a new experience but also because the party often realizes that engaging in such an exercise might result in them reevaluating their deeply held beliefs about the problem and the other person. Despite being an uncomfortable experience, however, most parties will engage in this activity with a little encouragement.

There will be times, however, when parties will resist role reversal. Common reasons parties give for resisting imagining the other person's perspective are that they do not know what the other party is concerned about, they feel "silly," or they believe it would be a waste of time. In such situations, a mediator should explain the potential benefits of role reversal and even provide some success stories. This is an area where mediators as "process experts" can and should apply some pressure to resistant parties. Helping parties see the problem objectively is often a critical step in resolving a dispute and one of the mediator's primary roles.

If educating the parties about the benefits of the technique fails, however, some mediators will offer up one or two of their own ideas about the other party's potential interests. This can be accomplished through leading questions. A mediator might ask, "Do you think that your wife is as concerned with your child's education as you are?" Then the mediator can coax the party to contribute: "What might one of her other important concerns be?" In this fashion, a mediator will likely be able to help the party identify many of the other side's interests. On rare occasions, parties have no idea what is motivating the conflict from the other side's perspective. In these circumstances, the mediator should try to have the other party share these concerns during the joint mediation sessions if appropriate.

3. SORTING AND PRIORITIZING INTERESTS

Once the interests have been identified, the mediator's task is to assist the parties in sorting and prioritizing these interests. This process involves identifying areas of common ground and areas where the parties' interests diverge. In addition, the mediator can also help the parties generally rank the issues in terms of priority.

a. *Identifying Common Ground*

By considering each other's interests, the parties are more likely to identify interests that they commonly share. As we have seen previously, when parties identify common ground, joint gains are created in the negotiation that can make proposals more attractive to each side. For example, a divorcing couple may have a shared interest in providing the best education possible for their minor child. Having identified this common ground, one spouse may be willing to pay more in child support and the other spouse may be willing to take less in alimony so that additional funds will be available to pay for a private school for their child.

Mediators bring tremendous value to the negotiations when they help identify common ground. Studies show that without assistance from a neutral third party, negotiators miss opportunities for joint gains about 50 percent of the time.[15] Finding common ground not only satisfies particular concerns of the parties, but it also builds momentum and good will that translate into a greater chance of success on more difficult negotiation issues where the parties' interests diverge.

b. *Identifying Divergent Interests*

Another important way value is created in negotiation is by identifying divergent interests. Divergent interests are those in which the parties place different values on their respective concerns or needs, or where the parties' interests are different. When parties value the same interest differently, they are said to have different interest preferences. Different interest preferences allow parties to create value and arrive at agreements that maximize the benefit for both of them. Inexperienced negotiators de-emphasize the differences they have with the other party, but in doing so they frequently miss opportunities for joint gain. A mediator can help the parties reach an agreement by identifying divergent interests and assisting parties in a mutually beneficial process of trading on those interests.

Let us take the simplest of examples: buying a television at your local electronic superstore. The reason why that transaction works is not because you and the superstore have common interests but because you value the same interests differently. While you and the superstore value both the television and money, the sale is completed because you value the television more than you value the $800 in your pocket; the superstore values the $800 in your pocket more than it values one of its televisions. The exchange makes you both better off because you each traded something of value for something you perceived to be of *greater value*. Accordingly, identifying preference differences help make deals happen.

Parties not only have different interest preferences; they often have different interests entirely. One party may care about what *form* the payment of settlement will take, and the other may not as long as the form of payment reflects an agreed-upon settlement value. Accordingly, in a negotiation between a company and a departing executive, the company might be willing to pay the executive $100,000 in severance as long as it is payable in stock options but only $90,000 if it is payable in cash. Assuming the stock options can be accurately valued and the executive has no preference concerning the form of payment, both sides can benefit from payment in stock options.

There are five categories of differences of which a mediator should be aware because they have the potential to create value in the negotiation. Being aware of these categories makes a mediator more efficient in identifying divergent interests

---

15. SHELL, *supra* note 12, at 79.

and, as a result, better at creating value in the mediation. The five categories of differences are as follows:[16]

i. Different Valuations.

This is where parties have different levels of preference for various issues. This technique is sometimes referred to as *logrolling*.[17] One party provides something of value to the other party in exchange for something that they value more highly. The Israeli-Egyptian negotiation mentioned previously in this chapter is an example of this. Although both countries might have valued the issues of security and sovereignty, they valued these issues *differently*. Thus, Israel was able to trade sovereignty for security, and Egypt security for sovereignty, each satisfying their most important interest.

ii. Different Expectations.

In this situation, parties differ in their predictions about some event. In a dispute between business partners over a buyout amount, for example, the crux of the disagreement may be different views about the future profitability of the company. The departing partner forecasts large profits and the remaining partner forecasts modest profits. In such a circumstance, a buyout agreement that is, in whole or in part, tied to actual future profits could resolve the dispute.

iii. Different Risk Attitudes.

Even where parties agree on what the future is likely to hold, they may differ in the degree of risk they are willing to take. For example, in a breach of contract situation where both parties predict that each has a 50 percent chance of winning at trial, if the claimant wins, the damage award will be $100,000. Thus, the expected value of the case is $50,000 (.5 x $100,000). However, the claimant may be "risk averse" and may be willing to accept only $35,000 to resolve the litigation, even though logically the litigation should settle closer to $50,000. Different attitudes toward risk can also make conflicts harder to resolve. For example, if the claimant in this case was more "risk seeking," he or she may not settle the matter for anything less than $60,000, even though the expected value is $50,000. Unless the other party is sufficiently risk averse, there will be challenges in resolving this matter. (See a more detailed discussion of how to calculate the "expected value" of litigated cases below in this chapter.)

iv. Different Time Preferences.

In this situation, parties place different values on when a particular event occurs. In a settlement of a personal injury claim, the injured party might place a higher

16. THOMPSON, *supra* note 2, at 84–85. These five categories are explained in a slightly different form in ROBERT H. MNOOKIN, SCOTT R. PEPPET & ANDREW S. TULUMELLO, BEYOND WINNING 14–15 (2000).

17. THOMPSON, *supra* note 2, at 84.

value on the settlement amount than on when the settlement is received. The insurance company responsible for paying the settlement, on the other hand, may place slightly more value on when the settlement is paid than on the total amount. Trading on these different preferences of timing, the injured party might be able to obtain a higher total settlement amount if he agrees to have it paid in installments over time.

v. Different Capabilities.

In this situation, parties differ in skills, aptitudes, and resources. One business partner may be skilled at "wining and dining" clients, while the other is skilled at financial matters. Each contributes their complementary skills to running a successful business. This kind of division of skills and resources can also be relevant in family conflicts.

D. Trading on Divergent Interests

Once the parties and the mediator have identified potential differences in valuation of interests, expectations, risks, time, and capabilities, the parties are well situated to begin trading on these differences. Not all of these categories of differences are present in every negotiation, but most negotiations possess at least one of these differences that can be exploited to create joint gain. The key to successfully *integrating* these differences is to help the parties identify "low-cost options" for them that address the other party's interests while advancing their own interests.[18] Low-cost options are those things a party has to offer the other side in exchange for things the other side can give of greater value. Discovering these types of mutually beneficial trades is more likely to occur if the parties prioritize their interests.

E. The Parties' Alternatives

1. BATNA—NEGOTIATING WITH THE LIGHTS ON

Parties negotiate to better their situation. Whether the conflicts with which the parties are involved concern spouses, employers, neighbors, business partners, or the government, they expend time, energy, and other limited resources on negotiating because they hope to achieve a better result than they could without negotiating. In other words, a party agrees to a resolution in mediation because he or she believes, all things considered, that his or her interests are better satisfied by making the agreement than not making it. To make such a determination with any degree of accuracy, however, the party must know what his alternatives are to making the agreement.

Alternatives should not be confused with *options*, as each has a different meaning for our purposes. An *alternative* is "outside the deal." It's a party's course of action if

---

18. SHELL, *supra* note 12, at 86.

they cannot reach a deal with the party with whom they are negotiating. For example, if you are negotiating to purchase a used Toyota Camry from a neighbor, possible alternatives would be to purchase a different car from someone else or a similar car from a car dealer, or keep driving the car you own. *Options*, on the other hand, are "inside the deal" and concern the particulars and terms of the agreement you might reach with a negotiating counterpart. Examples of options are as follows: Will you pay the entire purchase price now, or will it be paid in installments? Will she wash the car before she delivers it, or will you take it "as is?" Therefore, if a party is to make an informed decision whether to reject or accept a settlement offer, in the language of negotiation theory, he or she must know his Best Alternative To a Negotiated Agreement. This is commonly referred to as "BATNA."[19]

If a party does not know his or her BATNA, he or she is negotiating in the dark. Without knowing how or to what extent he or she can satisfy his or her needs and concerns in another way, it is impossible for him or her to know whether an offer of settlement is "good" or "bad." Without knowing his or her BATNA, he or she may fall into the trap of *accepting* an offer worse than one of his or her alternatives, or fall into the trap of *rejecting* an offer that is better than any alternative he or she has. Suppose, for example, a friend of yours recently paid $10,000 to purchase a 2005 Toyota Camry LX with 40,000 miles on it in very good condition. Our question to you is, did he make a wise purchase? We're waiting... did he? You cannot answer the question, of course, without more information, and the additional information you need is not the *Kelly Blue Book* value of the vehicle. The crucial missing information you need to properly evaluate whether the purchase was "wise" or "foolish" is your friend's BATNA at the time of the purchase. If your friend could have purchased the same car in similar condition with similar mileage for less just down the street, he made a foolish bargain, all else being equal. If he purchased the vehicle for less than any other reasonable alternative available to him, he made a wise bargain. Therefore, knowing one's alternative to a negotiation offer is essential to understanding the value of the offer.

2. MEDIATOR'S ROLE IN ASSESSING BATNA

Despite the importance of knowing one's BATNA, many parties enter mediation without having given it the least thought. Accordingly, mediators should ensure that parties have evaluated their alternatives to settlement or assist them to do so when they have not. In circumstances where parties have thought about their BATNA, the mediator should assure that the party has made an objective assessment of their BATNA. A BATNA is not what the party believes she deserves or something that she wishes for, *it is his or her most likely future* if no agreement can be reached.[20] In a conflict between two employees being facilitated by their supervisor over job duties,

---

19. FISHER ET AL., *supra* note 11, at 97–100.
20. *Id.*

what will the future hold for these employees if no amicable agreement can be reached promptly? Will the supervisor continue to suffer the work disruption? Will the supervisor request that the human resource department handle the dispute? Will one or both employees be terminated? Parties need to think about the consequences of not resolving the conflict because it affects choices that they will make negotiating the conflict. If, in this conflict, it is likely that the conflict will be taken to a higher level in the company and become a stain on their otherwise good reputation, the parties will likely be more "flexible" in trying to resolve the dispute.

3. RELATIONSHIP BETWEEN BATNA AND RESERVATION POINT

Reservation point, sometimes referred to as a bottom line, is a negotiating term that represents the most value a party is willing to give or the least value a party is willing to take, depending on one's perspective, to settle the matter.[21] Many parties enter mediations with a reservation point already determined. For example, a father in a divorce mediation might confidentially share with the mediator that he will not settle for anything less than having his minor child spend at least 50 percent of the nights with him at his home. Reservation points serve useful purposes. For instance, setting a reservation point can prevent a party from becoming committed to settling and accepting an unfair offer. There are, however, some downsides to reservation points of which mediators should be aware. Reservation points tend to be inflexible and a party can resist adjusting them even when new information learned during the negotiation reasonably justifies adjustment.[22] Moreover, because reservation points are by necessity crafted in concrete terms ("I will not accept anything less than having my child spend 50 percent of his nights with me at home…."), more creative solutions are sometimes missed. Most importantly, however, parties often set reservation points arbitrarily or base them on irrelevant information without consideration of their realistic alternatives.

Reservation points should be a reasonable "quantification of a negotiator's BATNA."[23] If the goal of negotiation is to put oneself in a better position than one's alternatives, then a reservation point should be slightly better than one's BATNA, but not too much better. As we discussed above, one should not accept an offer of settlement that is worse than one's BATNA. The more common problem, however, is for parties to set reservation points too high. When a party sets a reservation point significantly higher than her BATNA, that party runs the risk of rejecting an offer that is better than any alternative he or she has outside the deal. This, of course, is a bad negotiation decision that mediators should help parties avoid.

Let us return to the example of the father who wishes his minor son to spend "50 percent of his nights with him at home." Assume that the law of the state that applies

---

21. THOMPSON, *supra* note 2, at 16.
22. *Id.* at 98.
23. *Id.* at 17.

to the divorce proceedings requires a "custodial" or "primary" parent be appointed, so that in practice at least 60 percent of the child's nights must be spent in the custodial home. In this situation, the father's bottom line of having his son spend 50 percent of the nights with him is much better than his BATNA. Thus, if there is no settlement reached and a judge must render a decision concerning visitation, the best the father can hope for is having his son spend 40 percent of the nights with him at home, and he runs the risk of getting a less favorable visitation award. If the father's reservation point remains unchecked during the mediation, he might reject an offer of 40 percent of the nights with his son even though that is as much as he possibly could expect to get at trial, only he would need to spend many thousands of additional dollars and hundreds of additional hours of heartache to get it. Accordingly, mediators should assist parties in assuring that their reservation points are reasonably related to their BATNAs.

4. THE OTHER PARTY'S BATNA

Mediators should encourage parties to consider the other side's BATNA. Contemplating the other party's BATNA helps parties better assess their relative power in the negotiation and estimate realistic settlement ranges. Having a good BATNA gives one power in negotiation. The more attractive your alternatives outside the negotiation, the more value you can try to claim in the negotiation.[24] To put this another way, a party who has the ability to walk away from the deal has power. However, power in negotiation is a relative concept. Even if your BATNA is good, you may have less power in the negotiation if the other side's BATNA is better than yours. Conversely, even if you have a poor BATNA, you may be more powerful in a negotiation if the other side's BATNA is even worse than your BATNA.

Parties sometimes mistakenly assess their power in negotiation because they fail to consider the ability of the other side to walk away from the negotiation. The practical consequence of this miscalculation is that parties may be too aggressive or not aggressive enough in the negotiation. In other words, they may reject offers of settlement better than any alternative they have, or accept offers of settlement far worse than their alternative. These are both classic negotiation pitfalls that mediators can help parties to avoid. Mediators can and should help parties realistically assess their relative power so that parties can make good strategic decisions.

5. BATNA IN LITIGATED MATTERS

a. *The Decision to Go to Trial*

One of the most crucial strategic decisions a party makes when mediating litigated matters is whether to settle or go to trial. To determine whether it is in one's best interest to go to trial or to settle, a party must weigh the risks, costs, and poten-

---

24. THOMPSON, *supra* note 2, at 45; ROY J. LEWICKI, DAVID M. SAUNDERS & BRUCE BARRY, NEGOTIATION 230 (5th ed. 2005).

tial benefits of going to trial against any settlement offer. In other words, from the viewpoint of the plaintiff, one must determine whether accepting a particular settlement amount justifies abandoning the possibility of a more lucrative award at trial. From the viewpoint of the defendant, one must determine whether accepting a particular settlement amount justifies abandoning the possibility of having to pay far less, or nothing, at trial. Thus, in litigated matters and in those that will likely go to litigation if not resolved, both parties' BATNA is their evaluation of their probable outcome at trial. This analysis requires parties to determine the "expected value" of the case. In other words, the parties must decide whether the settlement amount offered is more valuable than the opportunity of trial, taking into consideration the "risks, costs, and potential benefits." This process is referred to as "valuing the case."

b. *Calculating Expected Value*

Mediators need to know how to determine the "expected value" of litigated cases. Understanding case valuation is an important mediator skill because in many mediations, especially where attorneys are involved, the discussion will focus on what is the fair settlement value of the case and how the respective parties arrived at that valuation. Mediators will need to be able to follow that discussion and ask appropriate questions to assure that evaluations are realistic because attorneys often inflate or deflate their case valuations in favor of their clients.

By assisting parties in valuing the case more objectively, mediators can help the parties close the settlement gap between them. In many situations, mediators not only help parties evaluate the case more objectively but actually walk parties through the case valuation process because attorneys do not know how to objectively determine settlement value. Included in Appendices 9A and B are *Expected Value Calculation Worksheets* to assist mediators and participants to value litigated matters more systematically. The Appendix 9A worksheet is for plaintiffs and the 9B worksheet is for defendants because the calculations of litigation costs are slightly different for each.

The idea that many attorneys do not know how to objectively determine the expected value of a case may come as a surprise. However, despite the obvious utility of the skill, it is one that most law schools do not require their students to learn.[25] Those attorneys that know how to value cases likely have learned it someplace other than law school or have figured it out on their own. Most attorneys do not apply any rigorous expected-value analysis to determine the settlement value of a case; they just "wing it" or "go from the gut."

---

25. Michael T. Colatrella Jr., *Learning "the True, the Good, and the Beautiful" in Law School: Educating the Twenty-First Century Litigator*, 33 Rᴇᴠ. Lɪᴛɪɢ. 741, 760–61 (2014).

Several research studies have demonstrated attorneys' significant decision errors when it comes to settlement, the most recent of which was reported in 2008.[26] In the 2008 Let's Not Make a Deal study, the researchers reviewed an impressive 2,054 contested litigation cases to determine if attorneys had chosen wisely in rejecting the last settlement offer before pursuing trial or arbitration.[27] In other words, the researchers studied the degree to which the litigants did better in the adjudicatory process after rejecting settlement. The study found that plaintiffs did worse at adjudication than the last settlement offer in 61.2 percent of the cases.[28] The average cost of this decision error for plaintiffs was $43,100. Defendants, by contrast, did worse at adjudication in only 24.3 percent of the cases.[29] Although defendants made fewer settlement decision errors, those errors were much more costly. On average, defendants' decision errors cost defendants $1,140,000.[30] This study, and similar studies that preceded it, demonstrate the importance of attorneys' understanding how to systematically and objectively as possible value cases.[31]

Arriving at an objective valuation of the case can be a simple or complex analysis depending on the nature of the case and the receptiveness of the parties to performing the calculations. In most situations, a simple analysis is sufficient to enable the parties to speak rationally about the value of the case and to increase the likelihood of the parties arriving at a mutually satisfactory solution. At a minimum, to properly value a case, *each* party needs be able to answer the following questions:

- What is the percentage chance that the plaintiff will win in court?
- If the plaintiff wins in court, what is the most probable damage award?
- What will it cost you to bring the matter to trial?

If the party or his or her attorney cannot answer all of these questions, he or she is not ready to settle the matter.[32] In fact, sometimes attorneys resist settlement because they are unprepared and have no idea what a "fair" settlement would be, and

---

26. Randall L. Kiser, Martin A. Asher, & Blakley B. McShane, *Let's Not Make a Deal: An Empirical Study of Decision Making in Unsuccessful Settlement Negotiations*, 5 J. EMPIRICAL LEGAL STUD. 551 (2008).

27. *Id.*

28. *Id.* at 567.

29. *Id.*

30. *Id.* The researchers surmised that defendants' average was so much higher than plaintiffs' because of "framing effects," where defendants are much more risk-seeking in their settlement decisions because they wish to avoid a certain payout. *See id.* For a robust exploration on decision making in settlement, see RANDALL KISER, BEYOND RIGHT AND WRONG: THE POWER OF EFFECTIVE DECISION MAKING FOR ATTORNEY AND CLIENTS (2010).

31. Although the research shows a substantial cause for concern regarding settlement decisions of litigated matters, a far-reaching study across eleven jurisdictions over a decade shows few complaints and malpractice lawsuits against attorneys for negotiated settlements. Michael Moffitt, *Settlement Malpractice*, 86 U. CHI. L. REV. 1825 (2019). Only 1.5 percent of complaints against attorneys and 1 percent of malpractice lawsuits were related to settlement. *Id.*

32. GERALD R. WILLIAMS, LEGAL NEGOTIATION AND SETTLEMENT 115–19 (1983).

instead of taking the risk of accepting a potentially unfair settlement, they refuse all offers, perhaps very reasonable ones. In most situations, however, even where an attorney has not thought about these questions, he or she knows enough about the case to answer them with reasonable certainty.

Once one has answered these three questions, one can determine roughly the fair value of the case. Let us start simply with just the first two factors: the percent chance that the plaintiff will win in court and the most probable damage award if he does win. Multiply these two factors together to arrive at the expected value of a case. For example, if the party believes that it has a 60 percent chance of winning at trial and, if it wins, it will likely be awarded $100,000, one would multiply these figures to arrive at an expected value of $60,000. In other words, "expected value" means that a 60 percent chance of winning $100,000 is worth $60,000. Thus, if the settlement offer is $60,000 or more, it would make sense to settle the matter. If the settlement offer is less than $60,000 it would not make sense to settle the matter. A decision tree is a useful way to represent this analysis. While it is not necessary to use a decision tree, it sometimes helps parties understand the concept or even helps the mediator to understand it more clearly. This example could be represented in a decision tree (*see* Figure 7-1).

Figure 7-1

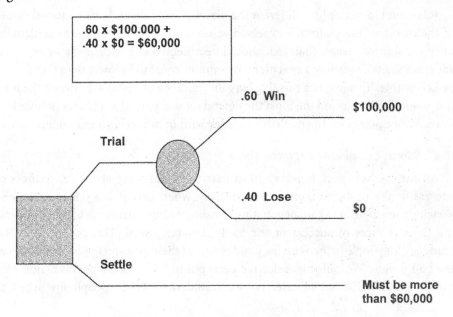

.60 x $100.000 +
.40 x $0 = $60,000

.60 Win — $100,000

Trial

.40 Lose — $0

Settle — **Must be more than $60,000**

The above example is the simplest form of the expected-value calculation. Despite its simplicity, it elevates the settlement discussion from phrases like "in my experience" and "I feel" to a discussion of probable degree of success at trial, which is a more productive conversation to have in a negotiation than one about "gut" feelings.

Any truly meaningful expected valuation, however, should include litigation costs. Litigation costs include attorney's fees and expenses. Commonly incurred major expenses in litigation are court costs, expert fees, and deposition transcription fees, although there are other less significant ones that can add up. It should go without saying that litigation is expensive, and many matters settle because the expense of litigating them through trial makes little economic sense, even when the chances of winning at trial are excellent. Thus, litigation costs must figure into the analysis if the parties are to arrive at a realistic value.

Let us assume the facts in the above example and add to it $25,000 in litigation costs, which is a rather conservative figure for anything but the most rudimentary of litigations. Costs are handled differently depending upon whether the party is the plaintiff or the defendant. If the party is the plaintiff, litigation costs serve to lower the expected value of the case. The reason for this is because the party will need to spend that money to get through trial. For example, in the case above, one would subtract $25,000 in litigation costs from $60,000 to arrive at an expected value of $35,000.[33] If the party is the defendant, on the other hand, litigation costs serve to raise the expected value of the case. This is because the party must spend that amount to defend the case through trial. For example, using the same figures above, the expected value for the defendant is $85,000, which represents $60,000 plus the $25,000 in court costs.

It is useful to notice how different the plaintiff's and defendant's expected values of the case are. The plaintiff's expected value is $35,000, meaning any settlement offer equal to or greater than that should be acceptable. The defendant's expected value is $85,000, meaning any settlement amount equal to or lower than that should be acceptable. This leaves a positive bargaining range of $50,000 between the least the plaintiff will take and the most the defendant will pay, which is a lot of "overlap" in resistance points for the mediator to work with in brokering a settlement.

c. Bias in Calculating Expected Value

As one might expect, however, most parties do not agree about the chances of success or the probable damage award. Even when parties are not intentionally skewing these figures to gain negotiating advantage, they usually are biased in assessing their chances of success or the likely damage award. This comes from the tendency for people to focus on the good points of their case and ignore or gloss over the bad points. We call this "selective perception."[34] The other phenomenon that causes biased valuation of cases is "overconfidence." When people are asked to

---

33. It should be noted that in situations where the plaintiff's attorney is hired on a contingency fee basis, such as in the case of most personal injury disputes, attorneys' fees are not deducted because the attorney is compensated by a percentage of the award or settlement. Litigation expenses such as expert fees should be deducted because they are paid for by the party.

34. Michael T. Colatrella Jr, *Learning "the True, the Good, and the Beautiful" in Law School: Educating the Twenty-First Century Litigator*, 33 REV. LITIG 741, 764 (2014).

"assess an uncertainty," like whether they will win at trial, they tend to be overly optimistic.[35] Thus, it is common in mediation that the parties' stated chances of success add up to more than 100 percent, for example, if both parties believe they have a 75 percent chance of winning (150 percent). Of course, somebody, or both, must be wrong.

Similarly, parties usually disagree on the likely damage award. The plaintiff might believe that a likely verdict will be $100,000, while defendant believes that a $50,000 verdict is more realistic. In one study performed with business and law students, those representing the plaintiff, using the same information given to defendants, on average estimated their chances of success 20 percent higher and their probable damage award 50 percent more than did defendants.[36]

Given the prevalence of biased assessments, mediators must help parties look at their case more objectively. In most instances, parties are willing to negotiate over both their chances of success and predicted damage award. Lawyers in particular realize that an analysis of expected value is only as reliable as the figures they use, and those figures are always, at best, educated guesses. Thus, most parties are flexible in adjusting their assessments so that the distance between the parties' respective values of the case gradually lessens. A party that originally stated that they had a 75 percent chance of winning might eventually concede, after the mediator has helped them work through the case more objectively, that their chance of winning might be as low as 60 percent. Using similar techniques with the other party, a mediator may be able to create a "positive bargaining range" where settlement makes economic sense for both sides. This is one way in which mediators bring about resolution.

d. *Other Factors that Affect Expected Value*

Another way that mediators can assist parties in realistically evaluating their BATNA in litigation is to raise issues affecting case value that parties often overlook. Although the following issues can be made part of a more complex expected-value analysis, it is usually sufficient to raise them and have the party assess some value for them, which will help to lower a plaintiff's settlement threshold and raise a defendant's settlement threshold.

i. Time Value of Money.

This issue is based on the principle that a dollar in one's pocket now is worth more than a dollar in one's pocket a year from now. Economists call this the "present value" of money. This is based on the concept that if you had a dollar now and put it in the bank for one year at simple 10 percent interest, at the end of that year you would have $1.10. Thus, to get an even more accurate expected value of a case, you could estimate when a trial might occur and further reduce the expected value

---

35. *Id.*
36. *Id.*

arrived at through the calculations above to present dollars. There are "present value" tables readily available that can help parties convert a potential future award into present dollars.[37]

ii. Other Costs.

Attorney's fees and litigation expenses are not the only costs of litigation. Litigation has emotional costs, time costs, business costs, and the potential for loss business.

- *Emotional Costs:* Months or years of worry and anxiety can take a physical toll on a person and their personal relationships. Moving on with one's life and eliminating the stress and the anxiety of litigation is worth something.

- *Time Costs:* Litigation not only takes up the lawyer's time for which the party is paying, it also takes up the party's time, which goes uncompensated. Parties often spend considerable time helping assemble relevant information and documents for trial. They also spend time discussing the matter with their lawyer (as well as glassy-eyed friends and relatives) and appearing at depositions and court dates. This is time that the parties might spend more fruitfully someplace else, such as with their spouse or children, or at their employment. What is this time worth?

- *Business Costs (Opportunity Costs):* When the client is a business, employees must support the litigation, providing documents and information, and appear at depositions and often court dates. It is common for a company to spend, in a moderately complex commercial or employment litigation, several hundred manpower hours in such activities. Some employees supporting the litigation would be low level, some would be high level, and many would be all levels in between. Assuming an average effective hourly rate of $50 per hour (remember this will include some highly paid managers and executives, so this is a conservative estimate) and a minimum of 200 litigation support hours, that would bring the value of the case up or down $10,000 depending on whether the party represents the defendant or plaintiff. This is a conservative example and business costs can run into the tens of thousands of dollars.

- *Loss of Business:* This refers to the effect that litigation can have on future business. Many parties and their counsel become so focused on "winning" the litigation that they often minimize or ignore significant collateral costs of battle. For example, many organizations, especially charitable ones, rely

---

37. Present value can also be calculated through a mathematical formula for more math-minded individuals, which is sometimes helpful in complex financial conflicts with sophisticated businesspeople. *See* Gerald Williams, Legal Negotiation and Settlement 121 (1983). Today, many sophisticated business calculators have the function pre-programmed. There are also websites that have calculating tools.

on their good name to generate income. If the litigation places that name in a bad light, how will that affect income? Sometimes the conflict is between two entities that formerly enjoyed a profitable relationship. Litigation usually destroys future business relationships, whereas mediation can repair them. If the litigation proceeds, what business profits will likely be lost?

iii. Benefits of Trial.

Although we have been focusing on reasons that make it economically more difficult to justify trial, a mediator's job is to help parties make good strategic decisions, not to push a party to settlement when it might not be in that party's best interests. Thus, mediators should help parties assess any benefits of trial above and beyond the specific amount awarded or saved as a result of obtaining a favorable verdict. Companies sometimes choose to spend $100,000 to litigate a matter that they could have settled for $10,000 because they expect similar suits in the future, and they wish to establish a favorable precedent or show that they will not just "roll over" and pay claims that they believe are unjust. In this way, they deter future litigation, which is likely to save them far more than the cost of defending a single matter through trial.

e. *Conclusion*

As you can see, the cumulative weight of all the factors listed above generally makes litigation hard to justify economically in most cases. This is why most litigated matters settle before trial. For example, a study of the federal district courts found that approximately 98 percent of civil cases filed are resolved without trial.[38] Thus, parties eventually suffer enough and pay enough in litigation expenses to recognize that the chance of winning does not justify the costs. One of the benefits that mediators bring to litigated matters is helping parties realize the economics of the situation sooner rather than later, which can save them significant time, energy, and money.

F. Identifying Objective Standards

Another area where mediators can contribute to thorough mediation preparation is assisting the participants in identifying *objective standards* applicable to the problem. Objective standards are those sources "independent" of a party's will or opinion that legitimize his or her offers, concessions, or solutions.[39] They come in many forms, but some common examples of objective sources are market valuations, precedents, scientific or professional opinions, costs, and traditions.[40] By including objective sources in their presentations, parties can greatly enhance their credibility. As with interests and BATNA, the mediator's task is to encourage the parties to iden-

---

38. Marc Galanter, *The Vanishing Trial*, DISP. RESOL. MAG., Summer 2004, at 4.
39. FISHER ET AL., *supra* note 10, at 85.
40. *Id.*

tify objective standards that justify their offers as well as those standards they anticipate the other party to rely upon in the negotiation.

There are several benefits imparted to the negotiation environment through the use of objective standards. First, objective standards increase the likelihood that parties will communicate more effectively. Second, they encourage the parties to trust each other more. Third, they increase the likelihood that any agreement reached will be "fair" and lasting. All of these advantages make it well worth the effort for mediators to explore applicable objective standards.

Identifying objective sources that justify a party's offer or potential solution helps parties communicate more effectively. When parties fail to justify offers of settlement with independent criteria, they may resort to a battle of wills. The battle of wills often takes the form of aggressive tactics, such as high demands, inflexibility, and threats. This "battle for dominance threatens the relationship."[41] In particular, it is a "face-threat" because it undermines a person's sense of power and autonomy.[42] This makes it more likely that a party will increase aggressive tactics to preserve "face." Justifying offers with objective standards, to the extent possible, makes negotiations more rational and less personal. Even where parties offer conflicting sources to justify their solutions, the conversation is more productive. In the medical negligence example, for instance, the insurer may make an offer of settlement of $50,000 based on previous settlements in similar cases and an expert opinion, while the patient may demand $100,000 based on costs, lost wages, and a different expert opinion. In this situation, the negotiation will focus on the appropriateness and the credibility of the various standards, which is a more relevant and less emotionally provocative discussion than a battle of wills, making more likely that the parties will reach an agreement.

Encouraging the parties to identify objective standards also increases the parties' trust levels. Parties in mediation often have a high level of distrust for each other, and high levels of distrust impede collaboration. Parties who distrust one another "will not accept information at face value but instead will look for hidden, deceptive meanings."[43] This is sometimes known as "reactive devaluation."[44] It is called reactive devaluation because parties "react" to the information by "devaluing" it because of its source. For example, when a car salesperson tells you that a particular car "is the best value on the lot," do you take him at his word? No, of course not, because he has an interest in selling the car. Thus, his comments are discredited to some degree.

Justifying offers by using objective standards, however, can diminish or even overcome reactive devaluation and other trust issues in negotiation. Parties who use credible sources to legitimize offers, concessions, or solutions are in effect saying,

---

41. *Id.*
42. Joseph P. Folger, Marshall Scott & Randall K. Stutman, Working Through Conflict 155–57 (2001).
43. Lewicki et al., *supra* note 24, at 138.
44. *Id.* at 161.

"Don't take my word for it; take this person's word for it that has no stake in this dispute." So the car salesperson who hands you a popular and credible consumer magazine article that says the car he is trying sell you is "the best value in its class," will be much more effective than one who says "take my word for it." The more relevant and credible the objective standard, the more effective it is in influencing the other party. Higher trust levels also lead to an increased sharing of information, an important component to uncovering a mutually acceptable resolution.

Finally, using objective standards increases the likelihood that any agreement reached will be fair and lasting. Although "fair" is a relative and often subjective term, using objective standards makes it less likely that negotiated outcomes will be based on some subjective and irrelevant rationale or solely on the relative skills or power of the negotiators. Agreements that are viewed as equitable by the parties, as opposed to those reached through acquiescing to overwhelming pressure, are more likely to be honored and implemented. This is usually in the long-term interests of both parties.

G. Generating Options

An important piece of the parties' negotiation preparation is generating options for resolving the dispute. Although the parties will have an opportunity to generate options during the mediation in joint sessions, significant benefits can be gained by encouraging the parties to explore potential solutions separately, either before the mediation in a pre-mediation meeting, as "homework," or during the mediation in separate meetings. Once the parties have considered their relevant interests, BATNAs, and objective standards, they are ready to begin generating solutions with an eye toward creating value in the negotiation. When inviting the parties to generate options, the mediator should emphasize that the options generated should attempt to address the other party's or parties' concerns as well as their own.

One benefit of generating solutions early in the process is that it promotes a more problem-solving approach to the mediation and emphasizes that amicable resolution is, at least in part, a cooperative effort. Having to consider the interests, parties can begin to develop "low-cost options" to satisfy the other's concern, thereby creating value in the negotiation. Generating options also suggests to parties that there is more than one way to satisfy their needs and concerns, increasing the likelihood that they will be flexible in considering potential solutions during the mediation. Finally, considering options as part of the negotiation preparation provides the mediator with a sense of the contours of a possible agreement. For example, in a medical negligence matter, by generating offers with both parties, a mediator can assess how far apart the monetary offers are and whether value can be created through differences in timing of payments, confidentiality concerns, or similar issues. Armed with this information, a mediator can bring a strategic focus to the negotiation.

III. Assisting the Negotiation Process

Once the mediator has assisted the parties in gathering the relevant information in preparation for the negotiation, attention will shift to the actual negotiation process where the parties will use that information to explore the issues and attempt to reach a resolution of the dispute. There are many different theories regarding the negotiation process, but the one most useful for our purposes is a model identified by Gerald Williams in his invaluable study of legal negotiations. Professor Williams recognizes that, similar to conflict, negotiation is a process that follows "reasonably predictable patterns."[45] Although his model was developed by observing legal negotiations, in our experience it is a useful tool in understanding most forms of negotiation. Under the model, negotiation is divided into four stages: (1) *orientation and positioning*, (2) *argumentation*, (3) *emergency and crisis*, and (4) *agreement or final breakdown*.[46] As with our study of the conflict escalation model in Chapter 6, understanding the pattern that human interaction typically follows in negotiation is a source of confidence and power for the mediator. It is a source of confidence because mediators who can reasonably anticipate negotiation behavior can be prepared for it and better able to respond to it. It is a source of power because each stage of the mediation presents, for the prepared and knowledgeable mediator, opportunities to positively influence the course of the negotiation.

To understand the relationship between the conflict escalation model and the negotiation model, the analogy to a "storm" or "hurricane" is again useful. The conflict escalation model is the path that the hurricane follows, and the negotiation model is the spinning of the hurricane along its course. Just as the intensity of a hurricane will affect its course, so too will the intensity of the negotiation affect the course of the conflict, making it longer or shorter, more or less "stormy." Although related, the escalation and negotiation models are different systems that influence the other. The following is a review of the stages in negotiation with particular emphasis on the techniques a mediator can use to assist the parties in negotiating productively.

A. Orientation and Positioning

1. ORIENTATION

In the *orientation* stage, parties adopt a negotiation style to address the dispute. The role of the mediator in this stage is to provide the parties with feedback concerning whether the type of negotiation style adopted by them and the behaviors and tactics associated with their styles are productive or counterproductive in the negotiation. As we discussed in Chapter 6, negotiation style is a combination of cooperative and competitive behavior, some styles being more cooperative, some more competitive, and some equally balanced between these two impulses. In the

45. WILLIAMS, *supra* note 32, at 70.
46. *Id.*

context of our discussion on conflict, we concluded that negotiation style directly affects the type of behavior and tactics a party will use in a negotiation. In most mediation cases, mediators will find that the participants have had some contact with each other before the mediation and have adopted, at least tentatively, a negotiation stance when they enter the mediation. To the extent the mediator is able to determine that a particular style is going to be counterproductive in the discussions, it is appropriate for the mediator to address this with the particular participant or representative at the earliest opportunity.

Mediators should be attuned to the different negotiation style "orientations" that the participants and their representatives bring to the negotiation. Some new mediators, especially non-attorney mediators, are surprised at the degree to which attorneys can become emotionally invested in the case that they are litigating. While attorney emotional investment in a case can have beneficial consequences, such as vigorous pursuit of a client's legal rights, it can also create obstacles to amicable settlement. It is sometimes the case, for example, that the clients are able to meet and discuss the problem civilly, while their attorneys are unable to sit in the same room together because of intense interpersonal conflict that has developed through the litigation or transaction process. Accordingly, mediators should be attentive to the negotiation style orientations of all individuals present and assist them in maintaining or shifting orientations as the needs of the dispute require.

2. POSITIONING

a. *Overview*

The next negotiation stage through which the mediator must guide the parties is *positioning*, which is closely related to, but different from, orientation. Positioning involves the parties and/or their representatives exchanging their opening offers of settlement.[47] If the parties have made no initial offers, the mediator's role is to help them to formulate and present their offers. In most instances, however, parties will make initial settlement offers very early in the conflict, prior to the involvement of a mediator, but will soon stall in their negotiation progress for months or even years. In some cases, stalling occurs because one party misinterprets or is offended by the other side's offer. Mediators are valuable here in helping the parties to better understand the other side's initial offer, enticing them back to the negotiation table. In other cases, the parties are not motivated to engage in serious negotiation until a trial date is set or the parties are induced by impatience or some other need to proceed to the argumentation stage where problem solving is conducted and concessions are made.[48] This common pattern often makes the orientation and positioning stage the longest stage in the negotiation process, especially in litigated matters. In such circumstances, the mediator's role is to motivate the parties to saddle up and enter the argumentation stage.

47. *Id.* at 78.
48. *Id.*

b. *Assisting the Parties in Formulating Opening Offers*

In formulating their initial offers, parties benefit from the experience of the mediator in helping them understand the different types of initial offers and the advantages and disadvantages of each. There are three ways in which parties can open negotiations: (1) *high/soft or low/soft offers*, (2) *reasonable/firm offers*, or (3) *integrative offers*. Once the parties understand what these are and how they apply in the context of their particular dispute, they can make an educated decision about which type of opening offer they want to use.

i. High/Soft or Low/Soft Offers.

In the case of the *high/soft* or *low/soft* opening offers, the party's opening offer is rather far from what they believe will likely be the negotiated outcome. In other words, the offer is much higher than what they really expect to get, or much lower than they really expect they will have to pay. We label this a "soft" offer because the party makes the initial offer fully intending to move away from it to a series of more reasonable positions during the course of the negotiation. There are several benefits of this type of offer. Because there is usually a time period in which the parties defend their opening offers, this delay gives the parties time to learn about the other side's positions and arguments and also gives the offer some time to have an "effect on the hopes and expectations of the other side."[49] In addition, it hides a party's true goal or bottom line, perhaps maximizing his or her share of the "negotiating pie" if matched with a less powerful or skilled negotiator.[50] It also is a way for a party to avoid underestimating his or her bargaining strength and making an offer that is so modest that it is readily accepted. For example, a common negotiating fear is that a party will make an initial offer of settlement, and the other party, with great alacrity, will say, "That's great, it's a deal!" This is sometimes called the "winner's curse."[51] Most importantly, high/soft and low/soft offers provide a party with room to make concessions during the negotiation. As we will see below, the ability to make concessions has an important role in resolving disputes. In arms-length negotiations, high/soft or low/soft opening offers should be one's default because research shows that on average, they create the most value for the negotiator and help to maintain good relationships with a negotiating counterpart.

On the other hand, the danger of this type of offer is falling within the other party's *insult zone*; offers in this zone are either so high or so low, as the case may be, that they offend the other party. This increases distrust in the negotiation. Mediators can caution the parties that opening offers that fall in the insult zone risk causing a "walk out" by the receiving party and may permanently harm the credibility of the offering party in negotiation discussions. This initial offer style is also highly positional and can encourage the type of aggressive tactics that are often counterproductive in

---

49. *Id.* at 77.
50. *Id.* at 74.
51. THOMPSON, *supra* note 2, at 48.

negotiation, especially negotiations where value-creating solutions are possible. Opening offers should be on the "far side of reasonable."[52] That rule has two parts: the offer should leave room for further concessions, but it also should be tethered to reality.

ii. Reasonable/Firm Offers.

With *reasonable/firm* opening offers, a party's opening offer is close to her preferred outcome. In other words, the party makes the offer with the belief that it is reasonable and that it is not in need of negotiation. It is "firm" in the sense that the party makes the offer without any intention of making meaningful concessions. This type of offer can reduce the likelihood of aggressive behavior in certain situations. It is particularly effective where there is a high degree of trust between the parties.[53] In most negotiation settings, however, there is not a high degree of trust, and so this type of offer tends to engender hostility from the other party. As a consequence of *reactive devaluation*, a concept we discussed earlier, the other party undervalues the offer. Moreover, making a first offer that is also a final offer is a *face threat*. Parties need to feel a sense of autonomy and independence in negotiation. Firm and final offers rob a party of this autonomy.[54] Parties expect concessions in negotiation.[55] There are other real benefits of reaching agreement through concessions that we will discuss below in this chapter.[56] Accordingly, reasonable/firm offers should be used only in negotiations where the parties trust each other, which in practice means that they should be used rarely.

iii. High/Low Firm Offers.

High or low firm offers occur when the negotiator makes an offer rather far from where an unequivocally fair offer would be but nevertheless refuses to make meaningful concessions. Such offers are typically made by inexperienced negotiators who have mis-valued the matter or have failed to understand the power of concession-making in negotiation. Experienced negotiators will sometimes make high or low firm offers where they assess that they have significant leverage in the negotiation. For example, leaving the relative merits of the matter aside, a litigant may not wish to take a dispute to trial because of a health issue that he or she fears a trial will exacerbate. If the opposing party perceives that the party's heath issue is a factor in the decision to go to trial, he or she may use that leverage to force a higher settlement than the merits of the issue would otherwise support. But high or low firm offers are risky and often rejected. They also may undermine the participants' relationship, thereby making future settlement more difficult.

---

52. *See* SHELL, *supra* note 12, at 160–61.

53. *Id.* at 77.

54. The tactic of first and final offer is known as "Boulwarism," after the former CEO of General Electric who used it in labor negotiations. It was later ruled an unfair labor practice by the National Labor Relations Board.

55. LEWICKI ET AL., *supra* note 24, at 93.

56. *Id.*

iv. Integrative Offers.

The third and final type of opening offer is an *integrative* or *interest-based* offer, where the offer is crafted to integrate the parties' needs and respond directly to the other parties' needs as well. As we have discussed, interest-based negotiation is grounded in a commitment by the party to look at the respective concerns and needs of the parties. Focusing on interests in this way, the negotiator is committed to satisfying those interests but is flexible as to how those interests are satisfied. Accordingly, integrative opening offers usually are made after the parties have discussed both the underlying interests and possible alternatives for satisfying those interests. Moreover, although an integrative opening may contain a monetary component, it is also likely to contain other non-monetary elements that trade on the parties' complementary interests. For example, an integrative offer in a dispute involving alleged sexual discriminatory termination might include a settlement amount along with terms such as confidentiality, installment payments to satisfy a party's tax consequences of settlement, and a provision addressing how future employment reference requests will be handled. As we expressed above, integrative solutions are best when possible because they "create value" for both parties in the negotiation. However, some disputes do not provide opportunities for this type of negotiation, either because they are single-issue driven or because one or both parties refuse to abandon overly aggressive negotiation styles.

c. *Understanding the Other Side's Initial Offer*

In addition to assisting the parties in formulating their opening offers, the mediator may also be useful in helping a party to receive, properly interpret, and understand the other side's offer. Mediators can educate the receiving party about the other party's potential motivations or habits, helping to increase the understanding of the offer's implications. For example, mediators can help to educate clients who are unfamiliar with the low/soft strategies of some large defendants, such as insurers and governments, by advising them not to allow this to exacerbate the conflict: "Yes, I can see you are aggrieved by their offer, but don't worry, the ABC Insurance Company always starts like that; if you hang in for a while, it is likely to improve its offer." In another example, a party who has made a high/soft offer needs to understand why the reasonable/firm approach of the other side leaves the impression that she is making all the concessions and feels as though she is negotiating against herself (see the case illustration below).

Case Illustration: Opening Offers

A matrimonial property mediation was conducted between the husband, Bob, and the wife, Rebecca. Bob began the positional bargaining with a high/soft claim of 55 percent of the value of the asset pool and made three incremental concessions in moving down to 45 percent. Rebecca commenced with a claim of 58 percent and had not moved from this position at all. During a separate session with the mediator, the husband complained about the lack of movement from the wife and about the fact that he had been "negotiating against myself." The mediator explained that the wife was operating under the "reasonable/firm" system and this made the situation at least understandable to the husband. They both made some further small concessions and settled.

To avoid this problem, at minimum, mediators can educate parties who are adopting the reasonable/firm approach to signal this fact, for example, by saying, "After careful consideration and in light of all the circumstances, I am asking for 58 percent of the asset pool...." Some lawyers hold themselves out as reasonable/firm negotiators who only ever make "one offer." For reasons discussed above, the "one-offer" tactic should be discouraged in most situations.

B. Argumentation

1. OVERVIEW

After the orientation and positioning stages, the mediator's role is to assist the parties through the argumentation stage of the negotiations. Here, the parties develop and implement appropriate negotiation strategies and tactics. They attempt to reconcile their conflicting interests that have been established by their opening positions. Further information is shared, arguments are made, and offers are discussed and exchanged. It is, in short, the stage where value is created and claimed in the negotiation. As discussed above, negotiators may use either positional bargaining methods or collaborative bargaining methods to resolve their differences. In most negotiations, however, the parties will use some combination of both forms of negotiation to attain their goals.

In performing this role, there are five areas in which research and experience have shown that mediators can provide the most beneficial service to parties: (1) *managing the rule of reciprocity*, (2) *managing the pattern of concessions*, (3) *assisting with the packaging and presenting of offers*, (4) *dealing with positional bargaining tactics*, and (5) *assisting with interest-based bargaining*. In examining these areas, we also address special negotiation techniques that can be helpful for the mediator to apply in certain factual situations to enhance productivity in the argumentation stage.

2. MANAGING THE RULE OF RECIPROCITY

The mediator's role in managing the rule of reciprocity is to help the parties appreciate the consequences of their negotiating behavior. The rule of reciprocity is one of the most dynamic and pervasive forces in negotiation. The rule states, "We should try to repay, in kind, what the other has provided us."[57] The rule is found in all human societies and has enormous influence on human interactions, especially in negotiations. At one level, the rule is important to negotiations because the gen-

---

57. ROBERT CIALDINI, INFLUENCE: SCIENCE AND PRACTICE 20 (4th ed. 2001).

eral attitude and behavior one party displays has a tendency to provoke similar attitude and behavior in the other party. Therefore, a party that uses a more aggressive and uncivil approach in negotiation is more likely to receive aggressive and uncivil behavior from the other party, even if the other party is naturally inclined toward cooperative and civil behavior. The reverse is also true. Cooperative behavior tends to beget more cooperative behavior from the other party. As we shall see, the rule of reciprocity is a deeply ingrained principle of human behavior, but one that participants in intense conflict overlook and find difficult to manage. Accordingly, mediators should assist the parties in recognizing the rule and help to manage it.

a. *Social Foundations of the Rule*

Understanding the reasons for the universal acceptance of the rule of reciprocity is important to understanding the reach of its influence in negotiation. As humans evolved, societies that operated under the rule of reciprocity gained enormous social and economic advantages. People who lived in societies that conformed to this rule felt free to share extra resources with others, such as time, food, or energy, because they were confident that in their time of need the resource would be repaid.[58] For example, if a person gave food to a hungry neighbor, that person now had someone upon whom to call if he became hungry. Instead of asking the neighbor to return the favor by repaying with a meal, however, he might ask them for help in digging a well. Thus, people in societies that operated under the rule of reciprocity did not actually give the resource away—they stored it as a "credit" to be redeemed when needed. Consequently, societies that operated under the rule of reciprocity were more efficient than those that did not. Reciprocity allows for division of labor, bartering, and the creation of close-knit societies.[59] All human societies came to practice the rule.[60]

Because the rule of reciprocity is so beneficial, societies take great pains to train their members to comply with it.[61] While there are certainly exceptions to the rule (and we probably all know one or two people), there is significant social stigma attached to people who regularly fail to comply with it. In our society, we call these people "moochers," "freeloaders," or "ingrates."[62] Cicero explained it this way more than 2000 years ago, "There is no duty more indispensable than that of returning a kindness. All men distrust one forgetful of a benefit." In maintaining an atmosphere of productive cooperation in the mediation, the rule of reciprocity plays a central role.

---

58. *See* MATT RIDLEY, THE ORIGINS OF VIRTUE 114–17 (1992).

59. CIALDINI, *supra* note 57, at 22.

60. Alvin Gouldner provided the first clear scientific articulation of the norm, even though norm has been with us since the dawn of our species. Alvin W. Gouldner, *The Norm of Reciprocity,* 25 AM. SOC. J. 161, 161 (1960).

61. *Id.*

62. *Id.*

b. *How the Rule Works*

Once a benefit is conferred on the other person, by whatever means, a reciprocal obligation is created. The obligation, while unstated, is powerful. To illustrate the power of the obligation let us examine a classic experiment, conducted in the late 1960s, related in Robert Cialdini's authoritative book on the subject, *Influence*.[63] A person was told that they were participating in an "art appreciation" experiment. In the experiment, the subject was asked to rate the quality of a set of paintings. This task was performed with another person. However, unknown to the subject, the other person was an "accomplice" working for the experimenter. The experiment was conducted under two different conditions. In the first condition, the accomplice performed a small act of kindness for the subject during a break, and in the second condition he did not. This was the favor: during a short break from rating paintings, the accomplice brought back a bottle of Coke for the subject, saying, "I asked him [the experimenter] if I could get myself a coke, and he said it was OK, so I brought one for you, too."[64] Except for the absence or presence of the favor, the accomplice acted the same in each trial of the experiment. After they were finished rating the paintings, in both versions of the experiment, the accomplice then asked the subject if he would buy raffle tickets to win a new car, explaining that he would win a $50 prize if he sold the most tickets. The accomplice added, "Any would help, the more the better."[65] The raffle tickets were 25 cents each (remember, this is in 1960s dollars).

After conducting many trials of this experiment, the experimenter then compared the average number of raffle tickets the accomplice sold under the condition where the accomplice performed the small favor of buying the subject a bottle of Coke with the average number of raffle tickets the accomplice sold under the condition where the accomplice performed no favor at all. Feeling the power of obligation, subjects bought *twice* as many raffle tickets from the accomplice in circumstances where he had performed a prior favor than in circumstances where he did not.[66] This in itself is an astounding result that demonstrates the power of the rule of reciprocity, but there are two additional insights into the rule that this experiment provides that are helpful for mediators to understand.

The first additional insight is that the rule of reciprocity works regardless of whether the parties like one another. In the "art appreciation" experiment above, after the subject was finished evaluating the paintings, the experimenter asked the subject to evaluate how much he liked his rating partner (the accomplice). Not surprisingly, subjects tended to buy more raffle tickets from the accomplice the more he or she liked him. The more surprising finding, however, and the one most relevant for mediators to appreciate, was that subjects who owed the accomplice a favor, even

---

63. *Id.*
64. *Id.*
65. *Id.*
66. *Id.*

if they indicated that they disliked him, bought as many raffle tickets as those who indicated they liked the accomplice. Thus, the strength of reciprocity "overwhelms" how the parties feel about one another.[67]

The second important insight from this study is that the rule of reciprocity can trigger "unequal exchanges."[68] At the time of the experiment, a bottle of Coke cost 10 cents. Subjects who owed the accomplice a favor bought, on average, two raffle tickets costing 25 cents each. Thus, the accomplice's favor netted him a 500 percent profit in return.[69] The impact of this rule in mediation is considerable. Behavior that is seen as kind and generous is likely to be returned in kind, and then some. This can initiate a constructive cycle of reciprocity. Conversely, aggressive behavior will likely be returned in kind, and then some. This can initiate an unproductive cycle of escalation: when you fight fire with fire, all you get is more fire.

c. *How Mediators Can Manage the Rule*

The seminal goal of mediators in applying their knowledge of the rule of reciprocity to mediation settings is to help parties appreciate the consequences of their negotiating behavior. When parties understand that a positive offering is likely to induce something positive for them in return, they may be more willing to soften a previously rigid position. Conversely, when parties realize how caustic negotiation moves are likely to incur a backlash against them, they may rethink that tactic. The challenge for negotiating parties, however, is that the destructive emotions of fear and anger that often accompany intense conflict blind them to the downstream effects of their actions. In other words, they neglect to apply the rule of reciprocity by themselves. Thus, the mediator provides a highly useful service by intercepting negative negotiation tactics and strategies and encouraging the parties to move in a less inflammatory direction. In the following actual case illustration, the mediator was able to use his knowledge of the rule of reciprocity to help a party avoid an unproductive tactic that would have likely made it more difficult, if not impossible, to resolve the dispute.

Case Illustration: Defusing the Bomb

A company filed a lawsuit against one of its former salespersons, Bill, alleging violation of an agreement not to compete. Non-compete agreements are common contracts that many salespeople sign at the beginning of employment in which they agree not to engage in similar sales in a specific geographic area for a set period of time after leaving the company's employ. Most jurisdictions enforce these types of agreements if they are valid and reasonable, striking a balance between the right of the salesperson to make a living and the right of

---

67. *Id.* at 23.
68. *Id.*
69. *Id.* at 33.

the company to protect contacts and propriety information the salesperson learned while working for the company. The company had obtained a temporary restraining order from the court that prevented the salesperson from selling in the area described in the agreement until the trial, which would be held in a few months. The court then ordered the parties to mediation.

Before the initial joint mediation session, the mediator met briefly with both sides. During the meeting with the company representatives, the company's lawyer informed the mediator that he had credible information that Bill had recently violated the temporary restraining order and they planned to file a motion the next day asking the court to fine and *imprison* the salesperson if a settlement was not reached that day. He then took out a 50-page motion with supporting documents and explained that he intended to give this to opposing counsel at the *beginning* of the mediation, making his plans to file the motion known.

The mediator first asked the company representatives what purpose letting the other side know their intent to file such a motion at the beginning of the mediation would serve. They explained that it would show Bill that they were serious about the issue, intended to pursue it vigorously, and thought it would give them a tactical advantage in the mediation. The mediator advised that it was not likely in their best interest to make such a threat at the beginning of the mediation if they had a desire to settle the matter amicably. The mediator explained that, in his view, Bill already knew that the company viewed the matter seriously and would pursue its legal rights vigorously based on the history of the litigation thus far. He also explained that the likely effect of the threat would be to anger Bill, making him more aggressive and defensive and render it less likely that the mediation would proceed in a constructive way. The other possibility, he explained, would be that Bill would refuse to negotiate under threat of imprisonment, and simply leave.[61] The mediator then advised that the motion not be mentioned but that the alleged violation of the agreement could be brought up and discussed. If a settlement were reached, the motion would be moot. If it appeared that a settlement was not likely to be reached, the company's plans to file the motion then could be revealed. The company followed the mediator's advice. The alleged breach was discussed amicably and the parties settled the dispute after a long and challenging day of discussion. The motion was never mentioned. Had this "bomb" been dropped at the beginning of the mediation, the animosity that would have been created between the parties likely would have prevented a settlement.[70]

---

70. The request for imprisonment, while technically available in cases of violation of a court order, would have been highly unlikely. This would have made the motion particularly offensive to the other party.

In addition to its role in managing negotiation behavior, the rule of reciprocity has an even more specific role concerning how concessions are made in negotiations.

3. MANAGING THE PATTERN OF CONCESSIONS

a. *Planning the Concessions*

The mediator at this stage of the negotiations may play a role in assisting the parties in planning a reasonable pattern for their concessions. Many negotiations involve dividing up a fixed resource. For example, a mediation involving the amount of compensation a defendant will pay in a personal injury matter resulting from a car accident will involve a monetary settlement. Here the plaintiff and the defendant are in competition over the fixed resource of money. Even where parties are able to "create value" through interest-based bargaining, there is usually a point in the negotiation where they have to "claim" their share of the value created. This apportioning of value is accomplished, in part, through concession making. Concession making is a series of incremental "giving up" of value from each side, sometimes referred to as the "negotiation dance." It involves each party making a number of concessions on their original position and on each subsequent position until they reach agreement. Many negotiations fail because parties fail to choreograph the timing or steps in the "negotiation dance" properly. Therefore, why, how, and when concessions are made are of particular importance to mediators.

In highly competitive settings, mediators can prevent the negotiation from becoming too confrontational, which can unproductively escalate the conflict. Some of the obstacles in reaching agreement through concession making are created because the process is by its very nature competitive. Parties are dividing a fixed resource—the more one party gets of it, the less the other party will get of it. This invariably creates competition. Where there has been significant cooperation on other issues in the negotiation, however, parties usually are able to manage concessions civilly and with little assistance from the mediator. On the other hand, where the negotiation is solely over a fixed resource, like money, or where aggressive negotiators are involved, parties will often resort to more competitive bargaining methods.

In attempting to influence the other side to back off their opening position and each succeeding position, the parties often resort to a range of tactics, including stonewalls, threats, anger, intimidation, ridicule, and tricks. Parties will use these tactics, where they have the aptitude, power, and incentive to do so, in order to "create doubt" in the mind of the other party. Where there is an inequality of bargaining power, these tactics may be highly successful. The weaker or more vulnerable party makes concessions as a result of the pressures and tactics applied by the other side, as they change their perceptions of their negotiation prospects and their own best interests.

An important technique for mediators to use in managing the pattern of concessions is to establish parameters for concessions in advance. When limited resources
are at issue, there are three fixed points that each party should set prior to making
any concessions in the negotiation: an *opening point*, a *reservation point* (sometimes
known as "bottom line"), and a *target point* (sometimes known as "goal"). These
fixed points should be known in advance so that a party is less likely to be induced
by high-pressure negotiation tactics to concede issues beyond the limits established
by these predetermined points. The easiest way to explain these concepts is by using
the limited resource of money as an example, although the dividing of any limited
resource would follow the same procedure.

i. Opening Point.

The opening point is a party's opening offer. At this stage of the negotiation, the
opening positions have already been established. Thus, the negotiation can be said
to be "bracketed," because the range of possible settlements has been set. For example, in a car accident mediation between an insurance company and a claimant
injured by one of the company's insureds, each would make opening offers. Let's
assume that the claimant demands $50,000 to settle the matter, and the insurance
company offers $5,000. This "brackets" the negotiation and leaves $45,000 to be
divided (*see* Figure7-2). The negotiation is deemed bracketed because if the matter
is resolved, it will be resolved within the range set by the opening positions, some-
where between $5,000 and $50,000.

Research has shown that once bracketed, negotiations tend to settle toward the
middle of the bracketed range. This is by no means a universal or rigid rule, and
there are other factors that influence the final settlement, such as the parties' relative
negotiation power and skill. However, there is a "gravity" that draws negotiators
toward the middle of the settled bargaining range. Thus, all things being equal, the
car accident negotiation has a high probability of settling near $27,500, the middle
of the parties' opening positions.

Figure 7-2

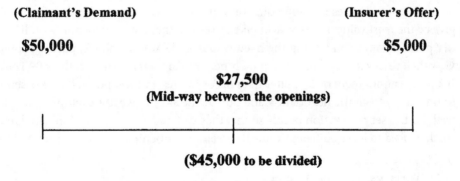

(Claimant's Demand)   **(Insurer's Offer)**

$50,000   **$5,000**

$27,500
(Mid-way between the openings)

($45,000 to be divided)

There is an advantage to making the opening offer in situations where a party is relatively certain of the value of the negotiation—the party making the opening offer can influence the midpoint of the bargaining range. A party wishing to favorably influence the bargaining range will usually make an extreme opening offer. This can have an "anchoring" effect on the perceptions of the other side and influence them to make a less extreme opening offer than originally intended. Research suggests that when negotiators have not adequately evaluated the value of the matter over which they are negotiating, they are highly susceptible to being influenced by the other party's initial offer.[71]

To illustrate this phenomenon, assume the above car accident example. Instead of making a $50,000 settlement demand, assume the plaintiff makes a $75,000 demand, which the plaintiff can reasonably justify. The other party may think, "I was going to make a $5,000 demand, but I may have undervalued the case, so I will offer $10,000." Two important things have happened here. First, by raising his opening demand from $50,000 to $75,000, the plaintiff has favorably shifted the mid-point of the bargaining range in plaintiff's direction. Second, the plaintiff's high settlement demand has influenced the other party to make a higher first offer, further shifting the mid-point in plaintiff's direction. Thus, in the first example above, the midpoint was 27,500, but now the mid-point is $37,500.

For opening offers to have the desired anchoring effect, however, they need to be in the "credible" zone. This means that there needs to be at least minimal objective reasoning justifying the offer, even if that reasoning is somewhat exaggerated. Offers that fall into the "insult" zone are usually counterproductive because they have no relation to the reality of the situation. Insulting offers are likely to produce deadlock in the negotiation, inspire the other negotiator to make an equally insulting counteroffer, or end the negotiation. Thus, a claimant may say to a party who makes an opening offer in the insult zone, "You have offered me so little that it is a joke; let me know when you are serious." The "credible" zone begins where the insult zone ends, though there is no precise point differentiating between the two.

ii. Reservation Point.

The second important concept for the parties in concession making is their reservation point. The reservation point, or bottom line, is the *most* value a person will give or the *least* value a person will take to resolve the matter, depending on his or her point of view, concerning the fixed resource. As we saw above, parties should view their reservation point as marginally better than their alternative, their BATNA. If a party cannot meet or do better than his or her reservation point, it makes sense to walk away from the negotiation and pursue the alternative, for example, going to trial. Parties set reservation points so that they can plan their concessions. In doing so, they need to leave sufficient value between their opening and reservation points

---

71. WILLIAMS, *supra* note 32, at 75.

to allow for meaningful concessions during the negotiation. These concessions are intended to "inspire" the other party to make concessions so that an acceptable compromise can be reached.

Parties almost never reveal their real reservation point, even to mediators. In the car accident mediation, for example, although the claimant demands $50,000 to settle the matter, they will secretly take as little as $25,000 to settle it. The insurer, on the other hand, secretly will pay as high as $30,000 to settle the matter. The parties' reservation points set a "bargaining range" in the negotiation. In this case, there is a *positive bargaining range* of $5,000. It is called a positive bargaining range because the parties' reservation points overlap: the plaintiff will accept as little as $25,000, and the defendant will pay as much as $30,000, permitting a $5,000 range of possible settlement (*see figure 7-3*).

Figure 7-3

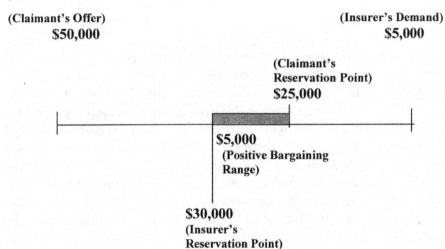

In some cases, there can be a negative bargaining range. This is where there is no overlap in the parties' reservation points. In the car accident case, for example, if the claimant would accept no less than $25,000 to resolve the matter, and the insurance company would pay no more than $20,000, there would be a $5,000 *negative bargaining range*. When there is a negative bargaining range, the only way the matter can be resolved is if at least one of the parties alters their reservation point to create a positive bargaining range or some interest-based solution is added to close the gap. For example, assume that the parties have reached the point where they are both at their reservation points, the claimant demanding $25,000 and the insurer offering only $20,000. If obtaining the settlement funds immediately rather than weeks later, as is typical, has some value to the claimant, a deal might be struck whereby the insurer overnights a settlement check to the claimant for the $20,000. Satisfying the claimant's underlying need for immediate payment closed the negative gap in the settlement range (*see* Figure 7-4).

Figure 7-4

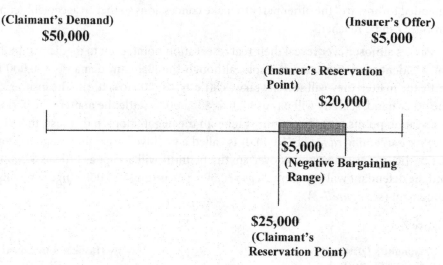

(Claimant's Demand)	(Insurer's Offer)
$50,000	$5,000

(Insurer's Reservation
Point)
$20,000

$5,000
(Negative Bargaining
Range)

$25,000
(Claimant's
Reservation Point)

One task for the mediator is to assess the validity of the parties' stated reservation points. Parties will usually attempt to keep their true reservation points secret. Even when parties say to the mediator in a separate meeting, "I will not pay more than $100,000 to settle this matter," they might be posturing. Thus, mediators should not take such pronouncements at face value. Because parties are less guarded with mediators, however, mediators are in a better position to estimate a party's true reservation point. Mediators should be attentive to subtle signals that parties send about their true reservation points. These signals sometimes take the form of parties never mentioning their reservation point again, or becoming less emphatic about it when the topic does arise. A party's willingness to at least listen to offers below/above their "stated" reservation point is another sign that the stated reservation point is just negotiation posturing. This is especially true at the beginning and middle parts of the negotiation. Toward the end of the mediation, a mediator should give more credence to stated reservations points because the parties will have a sense that the time for posturing is running out. The mediator will usually have a sense of what types of agreements are possible in the negotiation or whether an agreement is possible at all. This may take a little informed guesswork on the mediator's part.

Mediators should also appreciate that parties can change their reservation points during the course of the negotiation. Parties often enter the negotiation with a highly subjective view of the conflict and an incomplete understanding of the other party's positions, arguments, and interests. Thus, a party's view of the relative merits of their claims can be altered during the mediation as he or she gains a more complete picture of the situation. Gaining a more complete picture of the conflict can be a result of learning new information from the other party and through the mediator's efforts in assisting a party in objectively evaluating their true interests, alternatives, and relative merits of the arguments.

iii. Target Point.

The third concept that can affect a party's concession making is *target point*. A target point is the negotiator's goal. Target points are sometimes confused with reservation points, but the concepts are different. A reservation point is the minimum or maximum acceptable settlement point.[72] Anything that is not better than the reservation point is a deal not worth taking because, by definition, the alternative to the deal is better. Target point, on the other hand, is a negotiator's preferred outcome. Let us look at the target point from the claimant's perspective in the car accident example we've been discussing. We established that the claimant made an opening demand of $50,000 and has a reservation point of $25,000. In that situation, he might also have a $40,000 target point (*see* Figure 7-5).

Figure 7-5

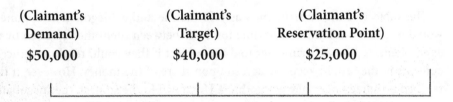

(Claimant's Demand)	(Claimant's Target)	(Claimant's Reservation Point)
$50,000	$40,000	$25,000

Experienced negotiators usually set target points because they know that this promotes success in the negotiation. In fact, research demonstrates that people who set *concrete and optimistic but justifiable* goals in negotiation out-perform those that do not, often by a significant amount.[73] Thus, mediators need to be aware that a party, especially an experienced negotiator, will often be making concessions to meet his target rather than his bottom line. This adds a new level of complexity for a mediator trying to estimate what that negotiator's true bottom line is.

b. *Reciprocity of Concessions*

Mediators should remind parties about the application of the rule of reciprocity in making concessions. Reciprocity is the engine that fuels concessions in negotiation. The rule says, in effect, that the recipient of a concession should respond in kind.[74] This does not necessarily mean that the concession will be of the same value or magnitude. As we will see, concessions can be larger than, equal to, or smaller than a previous concession, depending on a number of factors. It means that parties expect that they will take turns making concessions. Although most parties understand and follow this fundamental principle of negotiation, some do not.

---

72. SHELL, *supra* note 12, at 30.
73. *Id.*
74. CIALDINI, *supra* note 57, at 37.

Either because of ignorance, arrogance, or strategy, parties sometimes make a single offer with no intention of making concessions. For example, a party who believes he or she is more powerful may try to delay making concessions in an attempt to extract multiple concessions from the other party for every one concession of his or hers. In such cases, mediators should educate the party employing this strategy about the need to make reciprocal concessions. The reciprocity of concessions is a basic social contract that when broken angers the other party and makes settlement harder to achieve.

In addition to honoring an important social norm, negotiating through reciprocal concessions is usually in the best of interest of the parties. This is why we advise parties to set their opening position so as to leave room for concessions. Assuming the opening position is in the "credible zone," negotiating up or down from one's opening position, as the case may be, leads to better, more satisfying agreements. An experiment conducted by UCLA social psychologists demonstrates this point.[75]

The subject of the experiment was told that he and a "negotiation opponent" would be given a set amount of time to divide between them money given by the experimenters. The experimenter told the subject if they could reach an amicable agreement, they could keep the agreed upon share of the money. However, if they reached no agreement, they got nothing. Unknown to the subject, the "negotiating opponent" was a confederate working with the experimenter. The negotiation was conducted under three different conditions. With one group of subjects, the confederate "made an extreme first demand, assigning virtually all of the money to himself" and inflexibly persisted in the demand during the negotiations. With another group of subjects, the accomplice made a "demand that was moderately favorable to himself" and persisted in the demand during the negotiations. With another group of subjects, the accomplice "made an extreme demand and then gradually moved to a more moderate one" throughout the remainder of the negotiations.

The experimenter made three important findings.[76] The first finding was that starting with an extreme position and then gradually conceding to a more moderate one was the most profitable strategy of the three conditions. The second finding was that the subjects who were the *recipients* of the "conceding" strategy felt more responsible for the agreement. In other words, they felt that they had more control over the final outcome. When parties feel responsible for the outcome, they are more likely to implement the agreement. The third and perhaps most surprising finding was that parties who were the *recipients* in the conceding strategy were *more satisfied* with the agreement than those subjects in the other two conditions of the experiment. This was so even though, on average, they gave away more money than those in the other groups! This is why, as we recommended above, the high/low flexible concession pattern should be a default concession strategy.

---

75. *Id.* at 45.
76. *Id.*

c. *Concessions Are Communication*

Mediators should help parties appreciate the signals they are sending to the other party through their pattern of concessions. Both the magnitude and the timing of concessions signal to the other party a negotiator's intention and ability to make further concessions in the negotiation.[77] Although most parties appreciate the need to make reciprocal concessions, many parties fail to appreciate that concessions are a form of communication. Accordingly, parties frequently fail to plan their concessions in a strategic way, sometimes sending the other party a message that they did not intend. In this regard, mediators should encourage the parties to think about the *signal* they are sending with each concession and assist them in planning the concession to communicate the intended message.

i. Magnitude of Concessions.

The magnitude of the concessions communicates something about a party's ability to make future concessions. The larger the concession relative to the total resource being bargained over, the more likely it will be that the other negotiator will believe the party has more to give, even if they do not. Thus, a party that has a predominantly "accommodating" negotiation style might make large concessions in order to end the negotiation as quickly as possible to minimize the conflict. For example, in a dispute over a home remodeling fee overcharge of $5,000, a homeowner using an *accommodating* negotiation style might immediately agree to pay half, $2,500. This is a 50 percent initial concession. A more aggressive negotiator is likely to view this as a starting point not an ending point and believe that the homeowner will make further concessions. In the homeowner's mind, however, this may have been a fair offer to settle the matter (fair/firm offer), and he has no intent to concede much further. This unintended signaling creates a situation where the contractor expects more concessions, and when none or few are forthcoming, he is likely to become angry and distrustful of the other party. Increased anger and distrust make settlement less likely.

Conversely, concessions need to be large enough to "inspire" the other side to reciprocate with a meaningful concession of their own. For example, if in the remodeling mediation the contractor offered to accept $4,900, a concession of only $100 on a $5,000 claim, very little if any progress would be made in resolving the matter. As a general proposition, to indicate that one is getting close to the bottom line, concessions should begin to decrease in magnitude as the negotiation progresses. To our minds, there is no meaningful all-purpose rule for calculating the magnitude of concessions. Concessions are highly contextual acts. However, parties are well advised to leave room to make multiple meaningful concessions.

---

77. Thomas, *supra* note 2, at 51.

ii. Timing of Concessions.

The timing of concessions is another factor in communication. Timing of concessions refers to whether they are made immediately, gradually, or delayed.[78] There is a saying in negotiation that "the right offer at the wrong time is the wrong offer." Despite being rather simplistic, the maxim is useful to bear in mind. In most cases, as illustrated in the UCLA concession experiment above, a gradual pattern of concessions produces the best outcome.

The least productive pattern of concessions is when they are made immediately. Where a negotiating party receives a "favorable" offer too early in bargaining, there is a tendency to devalue what the other side has offered ("reactive devaluation") and to attempt to secure something additional from the negotiations. This might involve them backtracking and trying to recover even more than they initially sought. Thus, in a used car negotiation, if the purchaser were to offer the seller the ticket price of $1,800 immediately upon seeing the car, the seller might decide that he had asked for too little and should have asked for more: "I was going to accept $1,500 but the offer of $1,800 suggests the car is more valuable than I thought."

As we have seen, the same principle applies to the acceptance of offers. Where an offer is, in the perception of the offeror, accepted too eagerly by the offeree, the former may likewise have second thoughts about the wisdom of their offer and attempt to complicate the dispute in other ways ("the winner's curse"). Thus, in the used car example, if the purchaser offered $1,800 and this was immediately accepted by the seller, the former might become suspicious about the quality of the vehicle: "He seemed to jump at that offer rather quickly, perhaps I should take things a bit more cautiously here."

We have encountered commercial negotiators who, in conscious or unconscious application of the above maxim, deliberately idle away time before making or accepting offers. They are waiting for the timing to be "ripe." While this is hardly an exact science, mediators can discuss with the parties the possible implications of making offers or accepting them at particular times in the negotiations.

d. *Record of Concessions*

Mediators should always keep a written record of the parties' concessions, whether monetary or in other forms of value. They can be the honest keepers of accurate figures and value exchanged. This will assist them in assessing the extent to which the parties might be approaching their resistance points. It can also be used to show one party how much the other has conceded. It is a common feature of negotiations that each party feels that they have conceded more than the other, and objective facts and figures can be used to challenge this perception. Thus, in the divorce mediation scenario above, the mediator might say, "You may not realize it,

---

78. *Id.*

Rebecca, but your husband has moved down from a 55 percent claim at the beginning of the mediation to one of 45 percent now." This is an excellent technique to harness the power of reciprocity in obtaining further concessions from the parties.

4. RESPONDING TO AND PACKAGING OFFERS

Mediators can assist parties in framing the offers to enhance their attractiveness or minimize offensiveness.[79] Negotiations are complicated systems of actions, reactions, and interactions. Where a negotiating party is unhappy with a claim or offer, there is a risk that he or she will react in a retaliatory way and exacerbate the conflict. Thus, in the matrimonial mediation involving Chris and Rebecca, referred to above, Rebecca's claim for 58 percent of the asset pool could invoke a strongly negative reaction from Chris. The mediator can adopt strategies to avoid problems in situations such as these and can assist a party to make an offer or reject an offer in a constructive way. The following are some strategies for this purpose.

a. *Provide a Rationale for the Offer Before Making the Offer*

Any offer should be accompanied by a rationale and not consist of cold, hard figures or demands alone. The explanation serves to give some "rationality" to the offer and creates an opening for the offeree should they wish to respond constructively to it. The explanation for the offer or concession should be given *before* the offer or concession itself. This forces the party to listen to the explanation. When the party gives the offer before the rationale, it is much more likely that the other party will be distracted by thoughts about the acceptability of the offer and how to respond to it and pay little attention to the rationale for it. For instance, a party might say, "Before I respond to your offer, I want to give you my thinking about it. I don't accept the way you are valuing the business and my pension. Here is how I do the calculation.... Therefore, I believe 58 percent of the assets is my fair share." The reasons provide an indication of what the claimant needs to work on (in the last example, the valuations) in order to persuade the offeree to accept.

b. *Emphasize Areas of Agreement by Communicating Them First*

The offer should also be packaged in such a way that the most palatable parts are heard or seen first and those least attractive to the other side are presented last. This is sometimes referred to as "gift wrapping" the offer and is particularly feasible where the mediator is shuttling offers and counteroffers between the parties when they are in separate rooms. Thus, the mediator in shuttle might say, "Rebecca, when I take to Chris your claim for 58 percent of the asset pool, it would be helpful if I could first indicate what you agree with in relation to his arguments over his contributions, his valuations, and his claim to retain the business, before disclosing to him your actual figure." Or, if an offer is being rejected, a party might be coached to say, "Well, I can

---

79. For an excellent discussion of framing in negotiations, see Max H. Bazerman & Margaret A. Neale, Negotiating Rationally 31–41 (1992).

agree to your getting the family home, most of the furniture, and the Mercedes, but we need to do more work on the final percentages."

c. *Acknowledge Agreement at the Level of Principle*

If the general principle of the agreement is acceptable, but the details are not, it is best to acknowledge the common ground. Thus, the mediator may suggest that the response be made in a way that identifies the level of principle at which there is agreement, before rejecting the detail: "Well, obviously you are entitled to significantly more than I am, but I cannot agree to 58 percent at this stage."

5. DEALING WITH THE TACTICS OF POSITIONAL BARGAINING

a. *The Tactics*

Mediators need to be familiar with the predictable tactics associated with positional or competitive bargaining. These are sometimes referred to as "hardball" tactics. These tactics are designed to pressure the other party "to do things they otherwise would not do."[80] They are most effective on ill-prepared or inexperienced negotiators. Thus, to the extent the mediator has assisted the parties in adequately preparing for the negotiation, the negative impact of hardball tactics will be diminished. What follows is by no means a comprehensive list, but it does include the more common hardball tactics with which mediators are confronted.

i. Intimidation and Threats.

This general category of tactics is used by more powerful parties to force negotiators to make concessions based upon emotion rather than reason. "Well, Rebecca, if you don't become more reasonable, I'll call in the lawyers and take you through every court in the land."

ii. Stonewalling.

This tactic is characterized by refusing to make concessions. It is intended to pressure the other party to question their assessment of the value over which they are negotiating, and it is designed to force the other party to make a disproportionate amount of concessions in the negotiation. "Chris, my offer is eminently fair and reasonable and under no circumstances am I going to offer you another nickel."

iii. Phantom Trades.

This is when a negotiator pretends that an issue of actual little importance to them is of great value when conceded. This tactic is sometimes referred to as a "bogey." It is a method of gaining value on important issues for very little cost. "Well, I really wanted the pet gerbils, Chris, but I suppose I'll let you have them if you give me the dining room set."

---

80. Lewicki et al., *supra* note 24, at 103.

iv. Good Cop/Bad Cop.

This tactic is familiar from just about any police television show you have ever seen. One negotiator adopts an aggressive negotiating style, while his co-negotiator appears to adopt a more flexible, friendly negotiating style. This tactic is designed to enable the more agreeable co-negotiator to ingratiate himself with the other negotiator for the sole purpose of extracting concessions. For example, assume that the aggressive co-negotiator has left the room to make a telephone call. The more agreeable co-negotiator might say to the other party: "Bill, I am sorry about how my client is acting, but he is very emotional about this case, and I think he might force me to take it to trial, which I don't think is a good thing for either of us. What is the most you can offer?"

v. Claiming Lack of Authority.

A party using this tactic claims a lack of authority in order to impose pressure or gain an adjournment. This tactic has two purposes. The first is that a party who believes the other negotiator has to "convince" someone else that the proposed agreement is a good one will tend to make greater concessions.[81] The second is that it gives the party using it the opportunity to reject a tentatively accepted offer to extract one more meaningful concession. This is a particularly effective ploy because a party who has tentatively agreed to a deal and is anxious to resolve the matter is often inclined to provide the last request. "Well, that looks fine in principle, Rebecca, but I first need to consult my new spiritual adviser, Ramon."

b. *Possible Interventions*

As with their other functions in the mediation process, mediators have a range of tools in their toolboxes for dealing with these tactics. It will be a question of judgment as to which is appropriate, and there can never be certainty that a specific intervention will work. Mediators need to use the strengths of the mediation process and their understanding of negotiation to attempt to counteract the use of these tactics. By way of example, they might:

i. Educate.

Point out the downsides of a particular strategy, particularly in the separate sessions: "You know, Chris, in my experience those kinds of threats normally make the other side even more resistant."

ii. Anticipate.

Anticipate some of the tactics and attempt to pre-empt them by alerting the parties generally to their possibility. In a separate session, you might say, "Now, Rebecca, it is best that whatever opening offer you make, you leave yourself some room to make concessions. People usually don't expect the first offer to be the final offer."

---

81. Roger Dawson, Secrets of Power Negotiating 48 (2001).

iii. Identify.

Identify the tactic ("name the game") and question its wisdom as a way of shaming the relevant party: "Rebecca, that deal over the gerbils and the dining room set sounds to me like you're pretending to care about something that you really don't. Do you think it's wise to persist with it?"

iv. Enforce.

Enforce the mediation guidelines and intervene strongly when they are breached: "I have mentioned before that mediation works best when you speak one at a time and avoid personal attacks. Now can you both recommit to those principles?"

6. MEDIATOR'S ROLE IN PROMOTING INTEREST-BASED BARGAINING

Much mediator training and mediation literature focuses on the roles and functions of mediators in shifting the parties' negotiations away from positional and toward interest-based bargaining. Interest-based negotiation is encountered in all forms of conflicts but is particularly useful in ones in which the parties have an ongoing relationship, such as those involving partnership conflicts, business disputes, organizational conflict, planning disputes, and parenting disputes. We have already explored the benefits of interest-based negotiation and have encouraged its use when possible. The following are some of the tools and techniques mediators can use to assist parties in adopting an interest-based negotiation approach and to manage the process effectively when they do.

The following scenario will be used to illustrate points made in this section.

Case Illustration: Promoting Interest-Based Bargaining

A large corporation, Resources International, supplies raw materials to a medium-sized manufacturer, Home Supplies Ltd, which exports most of its products abroad. Before expiration of the supply contract, Home Supplies indicates that it will make use of an alternative supplier in the future. Resources International immediately stops delivery of raw materials and Home Supplies sues for damages arising from the breach of contract. Both sides agree to come to mediation, where Resources International is represented by Ms. Greene and Home Supplies by Mr. White.

a. *Shifting Focus from Positions to Interests*

The distinction between the terms "positions" and "interests" has been explained already. It was shown that positional claims can lead to impasses and obscure what people really want. Mediation provides a process in which the focus can be changed to the underlying interests, that is, the motivating needs, desires, concerns, and fears of the parties. When the focus shifts to interests, the problem becomes better defined and better understood by all concerned. The disclosure of interests can also reveal what is really motivating the parties and what is preventing a resolution of the dispute. As people are motivated mainly by self-interest, this approach opens the way to dealing with the dispute creatively in terms of the parties' own priorities.

The main stratagem of interest-based bargaining is to put more "negotiating chips" on the table. Thus, where the parties make positional claims over money, this approach seeks to disclose the interests underlying that claim and make them objects of negotiation. In the above scenario between Resources International and Home Supplies, the "chips" could include:

- Preservation of a tough image by Resources International;
- Ability of Home Supplies to deal with its pressing creditors;
- A quick and confidential settlement for both parties;
- Reducing opportunity costs for Home Supplies and transaction costs for Resources International;
- Keeping open Home Supplies' prospect of future business dealings with Resources International;
- Maintaining face for Home Supplies with overseas customers.

These multiple interests, dealing with the present and the future, provide a more constructive basis for fashioning a negotiated settlement than the single-issue obsession with financial damages.

The role of the mediator is to encourage the parties to negotiate in terms of their own and each other's interests. One way in which the mediator can focus the parties on their interests is to ask them why a position is important to them. He or she can also help the parties to try to persuade each other on the mutual benefits of requests, rather than trying to convince the mediator of the justice of their cause. In some cases, the mediator might be able to point out why certain settlement options could in fact be in both the parties' interests.

b. *Considering Creative Settlement Options*

Mediators can encourage the parties to be creative in fashioning their settlement outcomes. In order to be creative, there needs to be a broad consideration of possible settlement options. This involves three facets: (1) *developing options based upon the parties' interests*, (2) *evaluating options*, and (3) *selecting options*. This rarely happens in an orderly textbook fashion, but there is an important underlying principle: good negotiation requires expansionary thinking before contractionist thinking takes place. Mediators can educate the parties about this principle and its possible applications. Thus, in the distribution of property in a matrimonial or partnership mediation, a positional approach might lead to a crude 50:50 division, whereas a creative-interests approach could allocate specific possessions, assets, or other forms of property to the side which places the most value on them.

There are several strategies for assisting the parties to be creative in developing options. Mediators might use a direct strategy in asking the parties in the above scenario, "Ms. Greene and Mr. White, can you think about and suggest possible options?" They may do it analogously by asking, "Mr. White and Ms. Greene, can you think of ways in which other people have dealt with the problem in question?" Or they may proffer a contribution themselves by saying, "I can share some creative ideas with you about what others in similar situations have considered....."[82] There are several factors that might make it difficult for the parties on their own to develop options creatively. One is the assumption that there is only a single answer to the problem, a second is the perception that there is a "fixed pie" to negotiate over, and a third is the tendency for a party in dispute to judge negatively options mentioned by the other party.

c. *Brainstorming*

Brainstorming is one technique designed to overcome these obstacles and to assist the parties to think creatively and constructively about settlement. The objective of brainstorming is for the parties to develop and consider a wide range of alternatives for resolving the problem at hand. In brainstorming, parties are invited to think creatively and laterally and to propose settlement options, however unrealistic they might be, without having to justify or defend their suggestions. Other parties are not allowed to comment on, evaluate, or criticize the option so as to reduce defensiveness and inhibitions and to provide for risk-free ideas without any party being committed to specific proposals. The technique is designed to get the parties to feed off each other's insights and to illustrate the wide number of conceivable ways of dealing with the problem.[83]

The guidelines for the *first stage* of brainstorming are as follows:

- All ideas, without exception, are allowed;
- Parties are encouraged to feed off one another's ideas;
- No interruption or criticism of others is permitted;
- No evaluation or ranking of options is allowed.

During the *second stage* of brainstorming, the parties:

- Categorize the options into relevant groups;
- Develop some interest-based criteria for evaluating them;
- Discard the worst options, in terms of those criteria;
- Undertake a cost-benefit analysis of the best options.

---

82. John M. Haynes & Stephanie Charlesworth, The Fundamentals of Family Mediation 41 (1996).
83. Fisher et al., *supra* note 10, at 58–67.

In the context of mediation, the mediator can suggest brainstorming as a way of moving forward when the negotiations have bogged down. When the first stage of brainstorming is complete, the options can be evaluated and selected in terms of their desirability, practicality, and cost. Even where this brings the parties back to the unpalatable option first thought of, this option is shown to be the only realistic one in the circumstances and it therefore acquires more credibility. In the dispute between the supplier and manufacturer referenced previously, brainstorming could lead to a range of creative options. For example, it could be agreed that, while the manufacturer, Home Supplies, would abide by its decision to use the alternative supplier, it would purchase another product from Resources International at a discount that would "compensate" it for losses suffered, and that both parties would enter a joint research and development project for new export products.

d. *Eliciting Participants' Solutions*

In many instances, simply eliciting participants' solutions to the problem is an effective mediation strategy. Once the issues have been identified, the mediator asks a participant for a potential solution to the problem. He then summarizes the solution and checks in with the other party to inquire of the solution works for him or her. If the other party rejects the solution, the mediator probes why the solution is unworkable for them. This inquiry will often lead to a counter proposal. This process is less formalistic than brainstorming and typically involves an informal shaping of solutions through dialogue. Eliciting participants' solutions is also associated with positive perceptions of the mediation process. A study of the effectiveness of mediator strategies conducted in Maryland same-day mediations found that this strategy was "positively associated with participants reporting that they listened and understood each other in the ADR and jointly controlled the outcome."[84] Participants who reached agreement by presenting their own solutions were less likely to return to court to enforce the mediated agreement because of failure of one of the parties to follow through on the agreement.[85]

7. SPECIAL TECHNIQUES IN NEGOTIATION

The following is a discussion of several different negotiation techniques about which a mediator should be knowledgeable so that they may be used in appropriate circumstances.

---

84. Maryland Administrative Office of the Courts, *What Works in District Court Day of Trial Mediation: Effectiveness of Various Mediation Strategies on Short- and Long- Term Outcomes* 7 (Jan. 2016), https://mdcourts.gov/sites/default/files/import/courtoperations/pdfs/districtcourtstrategiesfullreport.pdf.

85. *Id.*

a. *Reframing to Enhance Negotiability*

Reframing has particular application in the fiery crucible of negotiation. Here it has the objective of reorienting the parties' perceptions toward a more "negotiable" view of the problem. There are many possibilities, of which the following are just examples:

- *Where a negotiator makes blanket demands*: Mary says, "I need more training and assistance to be able to cope with the new demands of the job." The mediator can focus her on the underlying needs that would be served by the training and resources: "Tell us what the new demands of the job are over a weekly period and how training would assist you in coping with them."

- *Where a party is continuously complaining about what they do not want from the negotiations, the mediator can reframe to focus them on what they do want from the process*: "Mary, don't tell Jo what you don't want her to do when you bring problems to her, tell us what you do want her to do."

- *Where a party talks only in broad generalities*: Mary says, "The supervisor always gives the good projects to other employees." The mediator can focus her on the specifics: "What do you mean by always, and what in your mind constitutes a good project?"

- *Where a party is focused on the past, the mediator can refocus them on the future*: "Jo, you've told us about the difficulties in supervising Mary in the past, now tell us what a good working relationship between you and her would look like in the future."

b. *Shifting Between Principle and Detail*

Where the parties are stuck on matters of detail, the mediator can attempt to move the discussion to a more abstract level in order to achieve agreement "in principle." For example, in a dispute between apartment neighbors Andrew and Bernard over children's noise, the mediator might attempt to get the parties to agree in principle on the need for all children in the units to have "reasonable time to play and express themselves." With the "in principle" framework in place, the parties can then work on the details of times, kinds of activities, and decibel levels.

Conversely, where the parties cannot agree on matters of principle, because doing so is seen as too abstract or too compromising, the mediator can attempt to move the discussion to a more concrete level and try to reach agreement on some of the details. Thus, in the above example, neither party might want to agree to the "in principle" arrangement, and the mediator can then focus on the specific details of activities, times, and noise levels. In dealing with the details, the parties might creep up to the level of "in principle" agreement. The mediator's ability to move the discussions between principle and details is a significant way of keeping them moving productively.

c. *Making More than One Offer Simultaneously*

Mediators often find it useful to encourage the parties, usually the defendant or respondent, to make more than one offer at an appropriate time. This gives the other side, usually a plaintiff or claimant, a sense of power and control through the choice, albeit limited, that is being provided. Thus, in a matrimonial property mediation, a party might be encouraged to say, "I offer either 60 percent of the asset pool based on my valuations, or 54 percent based on your valuations." In a mediation involving the payment of damages, the defendant might be encouraged to say, "I offer a $20,000 lump sum within 14 days and 24 monthly installments of $3000, or a $50,000 lump sum within 14 days and 36 monthly installments of $1000."

Apart from the choice element that these offers provide, there can also be real value for a claimant who is not receiving what they really want from the defendant in dollar terms. They can at least opt for the scheme that is otherwise best suited to their needs, for example, in relation to taxation or cash flow or what they will tell their children.

d. *Linked Bargaining*

Linked bargaining involves the conditional coupling of one negotiation issue with another. As discussed above, this is a technique for creating value in the negotiation: a party gives on issues he cares less about to gain on issues he cares more about. It is sometimes called "conditional linked bargaining," which highlights its two closely related elements. The first is the *linking* of one negotiation issue to another so that there is a package of two issues; the second is the *conditional* way in which the linked issues are presented. It is best illustrated by way of example.

Case Illustration: Linked Bargaining

Suppose that there is a mediation in a residential tenancy dispute involving the agent, Alex, and the tenant, Catherine. The agent is seeking compensation for early termination of the tenancy agreement by the tenant and for damage to the carpets beyond normal wear and tear. The tenant is claiming that the lessor was in breach of the contract and is also claiming for damage allegedly caused to the tenant's furniture by the lessor. The following dialogue indicates how linked bargaining could be pursued in respect of two of these issues.

Mediator: *Catherine, if you were to get a satisfactory outcome on Alex's claim for compensation, what would you be prepared to offer Alex in relation to the carpets?*

Catherine: *Well, I suppose if I could be really satisfied on the compensation issue, I would be prepared to get the carpets cleaned at my expense.*

Mediator: *Now Alex, you've heard what Catherine said. If she is prepared to pay for the carpet cleaning, what could you do about the contract issue?*

Alex: *Well, it all depends. But I suppose if she undertakes to have the cleaning done immediately at her expense, and if I approve of the quality, then I might be able to write off most of the compensation claim. Not all of it, but certainly most.*

Its objective is to free up some space in which either Catherine or Alex might feel free to make an offer on one issue in the knowledge that it is contingent on their being satisfied on another. It is designed to open up the process without either side feeling that they are at risk. If Catherine makes a constructive suggestion on the question of the carpets, it will not constitute a unilateral concession to the agent, and the mediator can then focus attention on the conditional factor, namely the compensation. Likewise, if Alex concedes conditionally on the compensation issue, the mediator can focus on the carpets as the way of ensuring that the concession can be attained. If the conditions are not met on either side, the relevant party can withdraw their offer without being inconsistent or losing face.

This approach forces the parties to focus on a specific issue without sliding off into other issues, as frequently happens in negotiations. For example, Catherine might ordinarily say, "I'm not prepared to talk about the carpets while he wants damages in lieu of rent." The mediator's intervention makes her concentrate on one issue by reassuring her on the other. It also involves a key reframe by the mediator, using words such as "reasonable," "fair," and "appropriate" in the conditional term. This avoids an expectation in Catherine's mind that she will get what she wants on the compensation issue; it reduces the expectation to a "satisfactory outcome." This method of bargaining involves some level of sophistication but, if the mediator initiates it, can become a pattern for the deal-making phase of the negotiations.

e. *Accommodating Future Contingencies*

A recurring problem in negotiations is that decisions often have to be made in the face of uncertain future contingencies. The contingencies could relate to many kinds of external factors involving other parties, the establishment of facts, or developments in the economy or the marketplace. There are many examples: a grandparent has to be asked to transport children at the beginning and the conclusion of contact; property has to be sold and distributed while the sale price, and even the likelihood of a sale, are unknown factors; a bank has to be asked to release a debtor from personal guarantees in a partnership dissolution. Where this problem arises in a mediation, there are various ways in which mediators might guide the parties on dealing with the future unknowns. As with other difficulties in mediation, they should first normalize the situation: in many negotiations, and other life situations, the relevant people, and often their professional helpers as well, have to make decisions in circumstances of uncertainty. In addition, mediators could use different methods to guide the parties:

- *Wait-and-See Method*: Reach agreement on matters that can be settled, adjourn the mediation, then resume it when the formerly uncertain events have become clear;

- *Default Method*: Make an assumption as to what will occur, and base the settlement on this assumption, with a covenant that if the assumption proves to be incorrect, the parties will revisit the agreement on which it was based;

- *Formula Approach*: Develop a formula, involving percentages, proportions, or ratios, which can be applied to facts or figures when they eventuate;

- *Process Method*: Develop a process for resolving the uncertainty involving the parties, fact-finding, external experts, and the like; and

- *Rough-as-Guts Approach*: Have the parties base their agreement on an average or a median price or other relevant factor, using their own figures or the estimates of their advisers or experts.

C. Emergence and Crisis

The next stage of negotiations requiring management by the mediator is the *emergence-and-crisis* stage, where the parties have nearly exhausted their patience or resources for making further concessions or trades.[86] Often there is still some "gap" separating the parties from resolving the matter and neither side wishes to be the one to make concessions to close that gap for fear of being exploited. It has been observed that in this stage in many negotiation situations one party will make a "take it or leave it" offer. This is always a precarious moment in negotiations because it is framed as an ultimatum. To less imaginative parties, the ultimatum appears as "take it" or we end negotiations and pursue our alternatives, like going to trial, for instance. However, these types of offers implicitly leave room for coming up "with something else."[87] As negotiations progress, parties often become more positional and narrow their potential solutions. Mediators must help parties resist this tendency and appreciate that creative solutions may still be possible even at this late stage of the negotiation. Mediators should also appreciate that "final offers" are sometimes not as "final" as they first appear, either because they are tactics or because parties eventually recognize that further concessions are in their best interests. Mediators confront two common obstacles in this negotiation stage: *crossing the final gap* and *impasses*.

1. CROSSING THE LAST GAP

The last gap is a special type of deadlock that can be encountered in negotiation. It occurs where the parties have made decisions on all issues except one and have reached a deadlock on that one. It often involves an amount of money—the last ten

---

86. Williams, *supra* note 32, at 81.
87. *Id.*

dollars or the last one million dollars, as the case may be. The last gap is difficult to cross because both parties feel that they have conceded too much and they would lose face or compromise an important personal principle if they made the final concession. Even where it makes commercial sense to compromise on the last gap, these non-commercial factors make it difficult to do so. There are clearly no guaranteed strategies for dealing with the last gap. Mediations do sometimes fail to reach settlement. Mediators can, however, be mindful of the following possible approaches for dealing with crossing that last gap that have proven successful in many instances.

- *Split the Difference.* This is the classical compromise arrangement in which the parties meet each other halfway.

- *Random Chance.* This is where the parties flip a coin, draw straws, or write out a series of figures between the last two offers (for example, $2,000, $3,000, $4,000—up to $10,000) and have one selected randomly with the agreement that it will constitute the settlement figure.

- *Third-Party Gift.* This is where the parties agree to give the benefit or value being argued over to a third party, for example, to charity or to the children, or to purchase a lottery ticket.

- *Develop Sub-Issues.* This is where the parties focus on their interests to develop sub-issues to add value to the deal. This is a form of "unbundling" the problem discussed above. Examples of this technique are timing of payment, method of payment, confidentiality agreements, etc.

- *"You Cut, I Choose" Routine.* This is where one party divides up the chattels or other objects of value and the other party has first pick of the "piles."

- *Confidential Last Offers.* This is where each party gives the mediator their last and best offer in private, and if the gap between these last offers is less than a predetermined amount, the mediation proceeds, otherwise it is discontinued.

- *Mediator Proposal.* This is where the mediator proposes a settlement, often a final settlement number. This is a more evaluative technique, although it does not necessarily mean that the mediator is truly valuing the dispute. It often means the mediator is proposing a settlement that she thinks can resolve the dispute by a fair closing of the "last gap." If a mediator intends to use this technique, she should first ask the parties for permission. Then, after making the proposal, each party tells the mediator separately and confidentiality if they accept the proposal. If both accept the proposal, the mediator reports that there is a deal. If either party rejects the proposal, then the mediator reports there is no deal. In this way, if the parties do not reach a deal, they remain in their former negotiating positions with the other party knowing whether or not they made a further concession.

- *Deciding on Appropriate Procedural Options.*
  - Refer the liability or damages question to an expert and continue the mediation in light of their opinion.
  - Change the process, for example, to "med-arb."
  - Refer the issue to a "higher authority," such as an arbitrator or court.
  - Defer treatment of the last gap to a fixed time and implement the remainder of the agreement in the interim.
- *Adjournment Options.*
  - Adjourn and have both parties exchange "final offers" directly with each other or through the mediator, within a specific period.
  - Adjourn and have one party accept or reject the "final offer" of the other party at a specified date and time.
- *Involve Attorneys.* The mediator can ask the attorneys to put the same question to their clients, namely, whether, if the other party moves up/down to a specified figure, will their client move down/up.
- *Mediator Makes Up the Difference.* This is where the mediator offers to pay the amount of the discrepancy himself or herself, in the hope that the parties will be embarrassed and do it themselves. (It is a risky strategy as the parties might accept the offer.)

Ultimately, of course, it is best to anticipate and avoid the last-gap phenomenon. Mediators should consider warning the parties early in the mediation about the potential problem and discuss ways of avoiding it, for example, by keeping more than one issue to negotiate over.

A Note on Splitting the Difference

Splitting the difference is the classical form of compromise and might be the appropriate strategy in some cases, even though compromise is sometimes looked on as a simplistic "cop out" in the mediation movement. Some mediators say that the problem with splitting the difference is that it rewards the bigger liar, in that the point of compromise will favor the party who made the more extreme opening demand. Nevertheless, in the right circumstances it might be highly appropriate. It can be introduced by the mediator as an honorable option, "You need to give a little to get a little," or with a small homily, "In my view a little give and take by each of you will settle this matter."

Mediators should be alert to the problem of only one party offering to come halfway to cross the last gap; the danger is that the other party will then split the remaining difference, and so on. For example, if there is a last gap of

$10,000 and one party offers to move $5,000 the other might respond with an offer of only $2,500. Therefore, in joint session the mediator might say, "Are you both prepared to meet halfway...?" Or in separate session, "Are you prepared to concede half the disputed amount on condition that the other side also does so...?" Care should also be taken with language on this issue, as the term "compromise" might not be appropriate in some cultural contexts where it might suggest the sacrifice of principle.

2. DEALING WITH IMPASSES

Impasses are situations in which one or both negotiating parties refuse to make further concessions on a particular issue and the negotiations are threatened with termination.[88] The differences between impasse and the final gap are that impasses do not involve the very last issue or concession. They can occur anywhere in the negotiation, but usually occur in the final stage of the negotiation where substantial concessions have already been made. Many negotiation and mediation texts provide long lists of "things to do" in the face of impasses, such as "move on to another issue," "take an adjournment," and "have a beer." There is some value in these suggestions, but they all require concrete circumstances to indicate their appropriateness. Here the list system is also used, without the beer, with an attempt to provide a more systematic approach to the problem.

As with other problems in mediation, the mediator needs to diagnose the situation and develop a hypothesis about the reason for the impasse before selecting an intervention. There can be three broad types of impasses. They can arise over *substantive* issues, where parties will not shift from their positional demands because their monetary or other substantive interests are not being met. They can arise over *procedural* issues, where the parties' interests in a fair and appropriate procedure are not being satisfied. And they can arise over *emotional* issues, where a party's emotional interests are not being met. (And of course, they can arise for mixed reasons.) In each situation, the affected party will engage in grand-standing, table-thumping, threatened walk-outs, and other dramatic displays of negotiation impasses.

Based on their tentative hypothesis, mediators decide on an appropriate intervention. What follows are some possible mediator interventions in lists that recap on many of the tactics discussed in this book. At the end of each subsection, an illustration is provided from the residential tenancy mediation involving Alex and Catherine.

---

88. Different expressions are used for the situation in which the mediating parties *get stuck*. Some mediators avoid the word *deadlock* as it implies a complete breakdown in negotiations and is too negative; the same applies to *stalemate*, which suggests that there can be no resolution. The term *logjam* suggests that with some bumping and jostling it might be possible to find a solution, although the metaphor might not be universally understood. The term *impasse* is rather abstract but does not have any of the negative connotations of the others. It is the term used (mainly) here but might not be appropriate for some clients.

a. *Possible Interventions for Substantive Impasses*

- Refocus the parties' attention on interests and away from their positions;

- Investigate the possibility of a further exchange of information and data;

- Shift from the substantive issues to alternative processes for dealing with the problem;

- Conduct brainstorming or another creative option exercise;

- Clarify communication and the understanding of the parties;

- Develop sub-issues;

- Link negotiation issues in a packaged system;

- Emphasize costs and other downsides of not settling; and

- Have one key witness give "evidence" after which the parties discuss its significance.

Case Illustration: Substantive Impasses

If Alex and Catherine are in dispute over questions of fact relating to what happened during the tenancy, the mediator might suggest that they invite the resident manager of the units, a relatively independent party in the eyes of both agent and tenant, to provide some information at the mediation and to be asked questions of clarification, after which Alex and Catherine could resume their discussions.

b. *Potential Interventions for Procedural Impasses*

- Summarize in a positive way and invite the parties to continue;

- Reassess the effect of the venue, seating, visual aids, and the like;

- Use separate meetings to ascertain why and how the process is not satisfying the parties;

- Explain and make transparent aspects of the mediation and negotiation processes;

- Use visuals to depict the situation more graphically;

- Investigate the possibility of changing the mediator (last resort); and

- Ensure stronger enforcement of the mediation guidelines.

Case Illustration: Procedural Impasses

If Alex and Catherine have reached an impasse because Alex is dominating the process, talking over Catherine, and otherwise ignoring the mediation guidelines, the mediator might identify the problem, restate the guidelines, get the parties to recommit to them, and resume the process with a more forceful application of the rules than before.

c. *Potential Interventions for Emotional Impasses*

- Consider changing the principal negotiators, or support persons;
- Allow some controlled venting of feelings;
- Acknowledge deeply experienced emotions of the parties;
- Deal with destructive tactics being used by one or both parties;
- Consider appropriateness of language, terminology, and non-verbals;
- Consider the relevance of mutual apologies;
- Attempt to quantify value disputes; and
- Identify an exception or other basis to bend the rules.

Case Illustration: Emotional Impasses

If Alex and Catherine have reached an impasse because Alex cannot afford to lose face in the eyes of other tenants, the mediator might discuss with him in separate session a basis for distinguishing Catherine's situation from those of other tenants so that he can have a reason for bending the rules, for example, that she has a less attractive unit or has been in the building for considerably longer than other tenants.

D. Agreement or Final Breakdown

The last stage of the negotiation for the mediator to work through with the parties is bringing closure to the discussions, either through agreement or final breakdown of the negotiations. In situations where the parties have reached an agreement, the mediator should assist the parties in finalizing the agreement to assure that all issues have been addressed. The mediator might even assist in drafting the agreement. In situations where the parties have not reached an agreement, the mediator should help the parties through the final breakdown stage, in which the parties agree to end the discussions and pursue other avenues for meeting their goals. This stage coincides with the *final-decision-and-closure* stage of mediation, and the same mediator responsibilities and duties apply.[89] The mediator should provide a sense of closure to the proceeding by making a concluding statement. A mediator's closing statement can help review the agreement, summarize the progress that has been made, or identify those matters that are still in dispute. This can form a basis for further negotiations after the mediation.

A common problem specific to the final stage of the negotiation is *dealing with the last-minute add-on.* The last-minute add-on is an additional claim where settlement has been tentatively reached on all declared issues. For example, in a real-life employment mediation where it was alleged that a former employee violated a

---

89. *See* Chapter 4—*Managing the Mediation Process*, section II E.

non-compete agreement, after the agreement had been reached on all issues that had been raised in the mediation, the employer raised the question of putting in a penalty clause if the mediated agreement was breached. This is sometimes known as a "liquidated damage" clause. The employee became so upset at this last-minute add-on that he declared that the entire agreement "was off." It took another two hours to finalize the agreement that included a nominal penalty clause.

Thus, the mediator's first responsibility is to attempt to diagnose the significance of the add-on and to base an intervention on that provisional diagnosis. If it appears to be an oversight, then some explanation and face-saving is required. If it is a tactical ploy, then several interventions can be considered: asking the other party if they also have any additional items, re-opening earlier issues to discuss together with the additional one, resorting to separate meetings, confronting the party who raised it, or using some of the techniques discussed in relation to the last gap.

Where a mediator suspects in advance that the add-on problem might occur, he or she can inform the parties about the problem in a generalized way, thereby lessening the chances of it being used as a tactical ploy. The mediator could even ask the parties to agree at that point on how to deal with the problem should it arise. Another way of pre-empting the problem is by asking the parties periodically whether all relevant issues have been disclosed, in an attempt to make it less easy to sabotage the process at the end.

IV. Exercises

1. Identify an upcoming negotiation situation in which you will be involved and prepare for the negotiation using the four principles discussed in this chapter: (1) identify the parties' interests, (2) evaluate alternatives, (3) identify objective standards, and (4) generate potential solutions.

2. Discuss with a friend or colleague how the rule of reciprocity has evidenced itself in past social interactions and negotiations.

3. Reflect on the last time that you negotiated something of significance, such as purchasing a car or negotiating job compensation. What one specific insight from this chapter would cause you to negotiate differently if you were to take part in that same transaction again? What principle of negotiation did you learn in that encounter that is not referred to in this chapter?

4. Role play with a partner a negotiation between a consumer and a retailer over the former's attempt to return a vacuum cleaner on the grounds that it is defective. Each of you must use a range of relevant tactics, including lies, bluffs, and threats, to "create doubt" in the mind of the other. Use great poetic license. Debrief each other on the effects of these tactics on each of you. How might a mediator have dealt with the doubt-creating tactics and their effects that you experienced?

5. You have been appointed to mediate a dispute between two factions in a voluntary organization. They have the time and resources to allow you to have preliminary meetings with each faction, during which you plan to educate them about and train them in negotiation skills. Write out a list of the *three* negotiation principles which you think are the most important and upon which you will enlighten them in the preliminary meetings.

EIGHT

Encouraging Settlement

The only way on earth to influence the other fellow is to talk about what he wants and show him how to get it.

— DALE CARNEGIE (WRITER)

I. Introduction

Most mediation training is based on the distinction between process and content. This distinction implies that the mediator should conduct the mediation process and allow the parties, consistent with the principle of self-determination, to come to their own decisions on matters of content. Some people assume that in conducting the process the mediator does not "influence" the parties' decisions concerning settlement. This assumption is incorrect. Although mediators should not coerce parties to resolve their dispute, the methods mediators use to assist the parties to better view the problem do influence their decisions and encourage settlement. This should come as no surprise because mediation is a process to bring about amicable resolution of the conflicts. Therefore, mediators do wield power over the direction of the conflict and influence the outcome. This chapter explores several of the most important methods mediators use to influence the parties' perspectives on the problem that help them arrive at amicable solutions.

II. Sources of Mediator Power and Influence

Mediators have considerable potential power even though they do not possess the authority to impose binding decisions on parties. Power is understood here as the ability to affect the perceptions, attitudes, and behavior of others. Some of the sources of mediators' power are as follows:

- *Associational Status:* the power they derive from their membership of a mediation service or professional association that "accredits" mediators, or from a court or government agency that appoints them to mediate.

- *Individual Status:* the power they derive from their credentials, experience, personality, and reputation.

- *Presence:* the power that they have to affect the parties' behavior to act more civilly merely because they are being observed by a neutral third party to whom they wish to appear reasonable.

- *Expertise:* the power that derives from their knowledge and understanding of conflict, of the mediation process, of negotiation behavior and of other aspects of dispute resolution, and, in some situations, their substantive knowledge about the matters in dispute.

- *Control of the Process:* the power deriving from their role as chair and manager of the mediation process, including the ability to make decisions on procedural matters, such as who speaks first, when to move from the discussion of one issue to another, or when to adjourn.

- *Personal Attributes and Skills:* the power deriving from their personality, interpersonal skills, intellectual capacity, linguistic abilities, and the like.

- *Access to Restricted Information:* the power that derives from knowing the parties' interests, their priorities, the factors that are motivating them, and other information they may disclose to the mediator on a confidential basis.

- *Ability to Transmit Messages:* mediators derive considerable power from their position as the sole source of communication between the parties where they are in separate sessions or the mediation is being conducted on a shuttle basis.

- *Ability to Evaluate and Sanction:* some mediators have structural sources of power, for example, where they are required to evaluate mediation behavior and make recommendations (which could lead to sanctions for one or both parties) to outside bodies.

- *Moral Pressure:* mediators have power where, by virtue of their neutrality and independent status, they can invoke ethical standards or moral judgments that might affect and influence the parties.

At least some of these sources of power exist in all mediations. The next question for discussion is how mediator power can be used to encourage settlement and the making of other relevant decisions.

III. Categories of Encouragement to Settle

There are many ways in which mediators use their power to encourage settlement. Here reference is made to five categories of interventions that encourage settlement: (1) *providing information,* (2) *expressing an opinion,* (3) *advising,* (4) *being judgmental,* and (5) *acting as the agent of reality.* However, a semantic problem crops up here. It is clearly not always easy, for example, to be precise about the distinction between the provision of "information" and the furnishing of an "opinion," or between expressing an "opinion" and giving "advice." Thus, most of the following categories have some potential overlap with one another.

A. Providing Information

The first way in which mediators can encourage settlement is by providing *information* to the parties. Here "information" is understood as referring to statements asserting the objective truth about matters, as opposed to providing an evaluation or expression of opinion. Mediators can provide information in this sense in relation to the following matters:

1. *The Mediation Process.* The mediation process is one of the mediator's most powerful tools for encouraging settlement. Mediators should explain and be transparent about how each step in the process works and what it is intended to accomplish: "In mediation we first define the problem before considering options for its settlement. This makes it more likely that the options we generate will meet your needs."

2. *Negotiation Behavior.* A mediator is the parties' negotiation advisor and coach, helping them to avoid negotiation mistakes: "Negotiations work best where there are no last-minute add-ons as this can prejudice the progress made."

3. *Legal Rules or Principles.* Providing information about the law is a controversial but common practice. In many jurisdictions it constitutes the practice of law, and thus only should be performed by mediators who are also lawyers.[1] Even where the mediator is also a lawyer, explaining legal rules increases the mediator's liability exposure:[2] "Pensions in this jurisdiction are not treated as an asset in the distribution of matrimonial property."

4. *The Legal System.* Providing information about how the legal system works is not legal advice and can be performed by informed non-lawyers. Assisting parties to think about what their future litigation experience will look like if the matter is not resolved is part of a mediator's responsibilities: "Realistically, you would likely not get a trial date in this jurisdiction for two years."

5. *Aspects of Conflict Behavior.* Mediators should become experts in interpersonal conflict dynamics and provide expert information to parties that help them behave productively: "If you threaten John, he is likely to threaten back."

6. *Realities of the Situation.* Another source of mediator influence is his her objectivity. Parties in conflict can become blind to the practical realities of the dispute: "Don't forget that while you are arguing over the sizes of the slices, the 'cake' is getter smaller because of legal fees and other expenses."

---

1. The definition of the practice of law is controlled by state law, and mediators should be familiar with the definition in the states in which they practice.

2. *See* Michael Moffit, *Ten Ways to Get Sued: A Guide for Mediators*, 8 HARV. NEGOT. L. REV. 81 (2003).

7. ***About the Situation.*** Mediators can be conduits for passing information that is relevant to resolving the dispute that one party is reluctant to share directly with the other party: "Paul has given me permission to tell you that if your claim is successful that he will need to file for bankruptcy, and he is prepared to show you the financial data to prove it."

Clearly some kinds of information will be more "objective" than others. The statement, "In this state you cannot get damages that are too speculative," will, if correct, be more objective than the statement, "It's normal for depression to lift once the anxiety of a court hearing is removed." Similarly some kinds of information when furnished by the mediator will have a greater effect in encouraging settlement than others.

B. Expressing an Opinion

The second way in which mediators can encourage settlement is by expressing an opinion to the parties on a particular matter. Here, an "opinion" refers to a considered view on some matter or a personal evaluation about a state of affairs, but without any firm advice or recommendation on which course of action to pursue. Opinions can be expressed on the same matters as those on which information can be provided.

The expression of an opinion would normally be a more "interventionist" contribution by a mediator than the provision of information, and therefore more likely to be viewed as encouraging settlement. Some mediators distinguish between a *professional* opinion (for example, "As an engineer, my view is that there was probably insufficient ballast for the size of the ship....") and a personal opinion (for example, "If I were you, I'd probably forget about trying to get them to apologize if they agree to more than $120,000 in damages..."). Some mediators feel that their professional opinions are more appropriate in mediation than their personal opinions. However, the subtleties of this distinction may not be appreciated by mediation clients for whom any expression of opinion by an authoritative mediator might influence them into making decisions in accordance with the opinion. See Chapter 12 for a full discussion on evaluative mediation.

C. Advising

The third way in which mediators can encourage settlement is by advising one or both parties on a particular issue or course of action. Here, the term "advise" refers to the mediator's making a suggestion or recommendation based on his or her professional assessment of the situation or on personal experience. Advice denotes more than just an expression of opinion—it has attitude as well. In mediation, advice can relate to one or more things:

1. ***Substantive Advice.*** Mediators with an evaluative philosophy often provide substantive advice concerning the adequacy of offers: "Well, $120,000 does not sound like adequate compensation for your injuries when your medical problems could continue for many years to come."

2. ***Legal Advice.*** Legal "advice" differs from legal "information" in that the mediator is applying a legal principle to a party's particular situation and not just telling them what the law is. This constitutes practicing law in all jurisdictions and should only be performed by a lawyer: "Well, you might find that you have a problem in court with statute of frauds, which states that contracts for land need to be in writing and signed by the parties."

3. ***Advice on Conflict.*** Utilizing their theoretical knowledge of interpersonal conflict, mediators can tell parties what actions likely will yield the best results in resolving the matter: "This dispute was the result of a breakdown in your working relationship caused by poor communication, and now that you have demonized each other you should look at your relationship before discussing the money."

4. ***Negotiation Advice.*** Similar to providing advice concerning interpersonal conflict, mediators can recommend to parties strategies and tactics that will increase their chances of settling the matter: "In this type of negotiation it would be best for you to keep something up your sleeve and not to make your best offer at this stage."

5. ***Advice on Court Behavior.*** Mediators sometimes recommend that a party take a course of action based on the mediator's knowledge of the court system. Like providing legal advice, this is an evaluative and risky intervention: "Judges here are not very sympathetic to those kinds of arguments nowadays, and you would be advised to drop the idea that you can pursue them there."

6. ***Advice on the Facts and Arguments.*** Mediators can assist parties in organizing their facts and arguments so that they are clear and concise: "Your facts about the accident are disorganized and inconsistent and will have to be presented in a comprehensive and systematic way if you are to persuade anyone on the liability question."

One of the most discernible trends in certain areas of contemporary mediation practice, particularly in mediations connected to the court systems, is that of the mediator "advising" the parties in some or other way. The question of whether mediators should ever, or sometimes, give advice in one of these forms is a major one in mediation circles. As with the other categories of encouraging settlement, it is dealt with further below.

D. Being Critical or Judgmental

The fourth way in which mediators can encourage settlement is by being "critical" or "judgmental" of one or both parties on a particular issue or proposed course of action. This category is closely connected to that of the mediator advising but implies a more severe evaluation of the parties' statements or behavior. There are many ways in which mediators can encourage settlement by being critical or judgmental of the parties. Apart from direct judgmental or critical statements, one of the most likely ways is by asking certain categories of questions. When asked in the relevant context and with the appropriate tone, questions that are critical, suggestive, or judgmental could be a significant factor in encouraging settlement by the parties. Questions are addressed in detail in Chapter 5—*Assisting the Communication Process* but are also introduced here because of their relevance to encouraging settlement. The following are examples of such questions.

1. *Rhetorical Questions:* These are intended to make a point, not to solicit an answer: "Well, do you want to settle on those terms now, or do you want to spend more time and money and settle in a year's time on the court steps?"

2. *Closed Questions:* These ask for a "yes" or "no" response: "Now, do you want to take either the reduced amount in cash, or do you want the larger sum of money in installments over three years?"

3. *Suggestive Questions:* Such questions provide a suggestion regarding a solution to the problem or course of action: "Would it be possible for you to agree on the amount of damages and get an expert to give you an opinion on the liability question?"

4. *Cross-Examining Questions:* These questions test accuracy and reliability: "But didn't you say previously that you did not want to pursue that point any further?"

5. *Probing Questions:* These questions explore a topic more thoroughly: "You've said that you are strong on the liability question, but could you tell me what case law supports the defense you are raising?"

Criticizing and judging should be used sparingly and only in separate sessions. As previously discussed, some mediators view it as an inappropriate and ineffective mediator behavior.[3] There is always a chance when criticizing or judging an aspect of the dispute or the parties' actions that a mediator will appear biased, but that chance is somewhat lessened if it is done outside the presence of the other party.

3. Robert Benjamin, *What Is Mediation Anyway? Ethical Issues, Policy Issues, and the Future of the Profession*, NIRD NEWS, Jul./Aug. 1996; Kimberley Kovach & Lela Love, *Evaluative Mediation Is an Oxymoron*, 14 ALTERNATIVES TO THE HIGH COST OF LITIG. 31 (1996).

E. Acting as the Agent of Reality

The fifth way in which mediators can encourage settlement is by acting as "agents of reality," a method known as "reality testing." The term "agent of reality" is used frequently in relation to the role of mediators. The phrase suggests that they can encourage parties to face the realities of their situations where they are being unrealistic, uninformed, or just intransigent. The purpose of reality testing is to make the relevant party reflect on a position, behavior, or attitude, to think of future consequences that they have not considered before, and to change their behavior. In short, the purpose of reality testing is to ensure that "parties are making sound and informed decisions."[4] The phrase is part of the jargon of mediation and is usually used in a way that denotes a sacred legitimacy to the function. (It has an almost biblical ring—angel of reality.) In negotiation terms, it is the mediator's way of "creating doubt"; he or she is the "devil's advocate." Heaven and hell create interesting metaphors here.

In fact the "agent of reality" terminology is a loose and rather unhelpful description for many of the interventions referred to in this section as well as for many of the interventions discussed in the conflict and negotiation chapters that help parties see the problem more objectively. Thus, the mediator can perform the agent-of-reality function by providing information, by advising one or both parties, by expressing an opinion on the matters in dispute, by asking critical or judgmental questions, or by assisting parties in assessing their alternatives. Essentially the mediator is inviting the party to see the weaknesses as well as the strengths of their case, the downsides as well as the upsides.

In helping a party to see the merits of his or her case more objectively, a mediator increases the probability that the party will make better decisions concerning settlement. Helping a party to see a case more objectively is most often about making sure that they have not forgotten, ignored, or minimized important information. We believe that the most effective way to perform reality testing is through appropriate questioning of the participants. In other words, instead of first *telling* participants that a certain fact affects the strength of their position, first *ask* the party what facts they considered in analyzing the merits of his or her case. If important information or facts are left out, a mediator might ask whether those facts have an impact on the case, and if not, why. Question that do not imply judgment are less interventionist—more facilitative—and show greater respect to the policy of party "self-determination" that is so important to the mediation process.

Although there are many areas in which reality testing is useful, there are two categories of special importance: *weaknesses* and the *quality of the agreement*.

---

4. Michaela Keet, *Informed Decision-Making in Judicial Mediation and the Assessment of Litigated Risk*, 33 Ohio St. J. on Disp. Resol. 65, 73 (2018).

1. WEAKNESSES

Parties tend to minimize or ignore facts that weaken their position. Thus, mediators serve clients well when they ask questions that are designed to force parties to confront the weaknesses of their own cases. For example, a mediator might ask in a private meeting, "What aspects of the case do you think weigh in the other side's favor?" When attorneys are involved, mediator Gary Friedman frames this question another way, "Assume you have gone to court and you've lost. Explain to your client all the reasons why that could have happened."[5] This forces the client to hear from his or her attorney's lips, perhaps for the first time, the reasons why he or she may lose the case if it goes to court.

A good place to start with reality testing is to simply ask the party to explain how they arrived at a position or an argument. Being forced to articulate a position or argument often reveals obvious flaws in the party's thought process that can serve to inspire the party to make adjustments in the position or argument that will get the parties closer to a settlement. For example, in litigated matters, a mediator could ask the plaintiff to break down their damage request. More times than one might suppose, the damage breakdown doesn't support the actual request. Or the damage breakdown reveals significant exaggerations or unsupported damages. This gives the mediator an opportunity to close the gap between settlement offers by simply pointing out the discrepancies or probing the unsupported damages more closely.

Further, in litigated matters, mediators can ask the parties more pointed questions about the risks involved in a claim or defense. For example, a mediator could ask the following question: "In proving this claim...what is your greatest risk at trial...?"[6] Once the party has articulated the risk, the mediator can then ask the party the likelihood that the risk will be realized. Taking the parties through "their proofs" is a mild form of reality testing that can be extremely effective.

If more mild forms of reality testing prove ineffective, a mediator can escalate to more directive forms of reality testing, depending on his or her comfort level with a more evaluative mediation style. For example, after hearing what seems like a highly subjective argument, a mediator might imply critical judgment by explaining his or her doubt about the argument. For example, he or she might pose questions like this: "I'm having trouble understanding your take on the second paragraph in the *Smith* case...Can we go over it again, to be sure that I understand well enough to convey your interpretation to the room?"[7] Of course, as we will see below, a mediator can be even more directive in his or her reality testing. But it is important to keep in mind

---

5. SAVING THE LAST DANCE: MEDIATION THROUGH UNDERSTANDING (Video, Program on Negotiation & Center for Mediation in Law 1996, with Gary Friedman, Jack Himmelstein and Robert H. Mnookin).

6. Keet, *supra* note 4, at 88.

7. Dwight Golan & Marjorie Corman Aaron, *Beyond Abstinence: Safe and Impartial Evaluation Can Be Effective in Mediation*, 25 DISP. RESOL. MAG., Issue 4, Summer 2019, at 22, 25.

that nearly all reality testing involves an evaluation by the mediator as to the merits of the dispute and of the relative objectivity of the participants. A mediator usually doesn't usually become an agent of reality unless she thinks a participant's reality is askew.[8]

2. QUALITY OF AGREEMENT

As we have expressed previously, helping parties enter into impractical agreements is not good mediation practice. Thus, mediators should help parties assess the quality of their proposed agreement. One way to do this, as we explored in the previous chapter, is to assist parties in comparing the proposed agreement to their best alternative to the deal, sometimes known as their Best Alternative to a Negotiated Agreement, or BATNA.[9] This is also known as a risk assessment because it weighs the risks of not settling.

There are, however, other areas that can be explored to ensure a proposed agreement is workable. Checking in to see if any important issues have been forgotten is one area. For example, in a divorce case where alimony has been agreed to, a mediator might ask, "Are there any expenses that you left out or may have forgotten?" Ensuring that the agreement is workable in the future is another area. For example, in the divorce matter where alimony was agreed to, the mediator might ask, "Do you anticipate any changes in your financial need over the next year?" Finally, it is often helpful to consider how the agreement might affect non-parties. For example, in a family matter where there is a proposal for child visitation, a mediator might ask, "How will the child's grandparents feel about the arrangement?"

It must be emphasized that reality testing is a relatively interventionist technique even when done through artful questioning. Parties can sometimes perceive questions about their assessment of the case as a form of criticism even if the mediator did not intend to criticize. Accordingly, reality testing should generally be performed in a separate meeting so parties are not made to feel vulnerable in front of the other party.

IV. Methods of Encouraging Settlement

A. Modes of Encouraging Settlement

As with most other mediator functions, there are many styles of encouraging settlement. The following are the modes by which mediators encourage settlement.

---

8. *Id.*
9. *See* Chapter 7—*Facilitating the Negotiations,* section II D.

1. VERBAL

There are numerous ways in which mediators can encourage settlement through verbal interventions. These include questioning, reframing, summarizing, and rewording of the list of issues. As words are the main tool of the mediator, most encouragement to settle is likely to be provided in verbal form.

2. NON-VERBAL

The various verbal and non-verbal forms of communication relevant to mediation have been referred to above. They too can potentially be used to encourage settlement, for example, through a mediator's sarcastic or disbelieving tone of voice, or through his or her shrugging of the shoulders or raising of an eyebrow, with or without verbal accompaniment. Another non-verbal form of pressure is the use of silence. Mediators can use silence strategically to induce a party to make an offer or proposal that might not otherwise have been forthcoming. The circumstances will determine whether this is an appropriate method of furthering the negotiations. It could be a manipulative strategy if one party is uncomfortable or embarrassed by silence and, in order to "fill the vacuum," volunteers information which might otherwise have remained confidential or makes an offer, concession, or compromise that he or she might not otherwise have made.

3. PROCEDURAL AND STRUCTURAL

Again, there is a wide variety of procedural interventions that mediators might use to encourage settlement. Some of these interventions include hurrying the parties quickly through the list of issues, keeping them at the negotiation table for lengthy periods, imposing deadlines on them, or resorting to shuttle mediation so that the mediator can use his or her mediator power more forcefully. Employing these interventions implicitly acknowledges that even the standard procedural tasks of mediators are not always neutral and passive functions but can be experienced by the parties as influencing, pressuring, or even coercing them into making decisions.

4. ENVIRONMENTAL

Design and manipulation of the environment can also be factors in encouraging the parties to settle. This includes the choice of venue, use of space, seating arrangements, and the like. However, even where time is limited, mediators are not advised to provide the parties with uncomfortable seats so that they are pressured by discomfort to agree and get out of there.

5. VISUAL

Mediators can use visual effects to make a point about a proposed settlement. In a parenting dispute, they could visually represent the days and weeks on a sheet of butcher's paper to depict graphically the overall effect, and its fairness or unfairness, of a proposed plan. Likewise, in a commercial mediation, mediators can write up lists of offers and counteroffers to show how much each party has conceded since the negotiations commenced, or they can perform mathematical calculations that can be more easily assimilated by the parties.

B. Styles of Encouraging Settlement

Each of the different methods of encouraging settlement can vary in style and intensity. An intervention could be tentative, assertive, and so on, along a continuum of high to low intensity. The point at which it is located on this continuum will depend on the nature of the intervention, the intention of the mediator, and the perception of the party or parties concerned. Here are some points on this continuum, based on a fictitious family mediation involving a parenting dispute. They range from the strictly non-interventionist to the forcefully interventionist style. These styles overlap to some extent with the five categories of encouraging settlement referred to above, but they are provided to illustrate degrees of intensity and not the different categories as such.

1. *Non-Interventionist:* "No, I cannot advise you in any way on what you should do about moving out of state, nor on your legal rights. If you need that kind of advice we will have to adjourn and you can approach someone who can assist with that."

2. *Minimal Interventionist:* "Well, I cannot give you any advice, but in my experience with these disputes there are three basic ways of dealing with the Christmas issue. Shall I tell you what they are, and you can decide if you will opt for one of them?"

3. *Mildly Interventionist:* "Of course it's not for me to say what you should do, but as an outsider I might be inclined to drop the request for make-up contact if you can get unsupervised contact sooner."

4. *Moderately Interventionist:* "You know, it's up to you to decide, but in my experience people in these situations normally have a phase-in period of supervised contact until the child is comfortable with the parent it has not seen for a long time. This is also the likely approach of a court."

5. *Reluctantly Interventionist:* "Well, I won't be recommending anything now about the custody issue, but sometimes if both parties ask me late in the day I will make a suggestion, but it would clearly not be binding on you."

6. *Strongly Interventionist:* "Look, the Family Court will certainly listen to the argument for unsupervised contact, but frankly you have more chance of winning the lottery than of getting it straight away."

7. *Forcefully Interventionist:* "You're crazy to think about it, no court would keep a child away from its father just because he belongs to a different religious denomination than the child."

Again, the extent to which the different styles of encouraging settlement are appropriate or inappropriate will be covered below.

C. Using Power to Encourage Settlement: Some Illustrations

Following are some further illustrations of ways in which mediators could encourage settlement through influence, pressure, or other uses of mediator power. They involve the application of principles referred to in this chapter. The illustrations are based on a workplace dispute over the introduction of new information technology systems into the production and management system of a small publishing company. Those involved in the mediation are Bernadette, representing the chief executive officer, Ray; the human resources manager, Leigh, representing the workers; and John, a union official. As usual, some poetic license is required in relation to some of the illustrations. It should be emphasized that *some of these examples might be highly inappropriate in some circumstances.* Mediators *need to be selective in choosing* among them.

1. *Congratulations, Flattery:* "Well done to you all on coming to mediation, smart people tend to do that, whereas the ignorant and stubborn tend to fight it out in court...."

2. *Setting High Expectations:* "Most disputes settle and very few ever go to formal adjudication. In mediation up to 90 percent of cases can be settled, and nothing I have heard from any of you suggests that you are in the other 10 percent..."

3. *Shaming:* "Well Ray, Bernadette, John, and Leigh, you've been arguing for seven hours now with plenty of acrimony but very little progress. Do you think that sort of behavior is of any benefit to the business or to the workers employed in it?"

4. *Using Time Limits:* "Now unfortunately there are only 15 minutes of mediation time left, after which there will be no further opportunity to mediate, so why don't you use the time productively to make some breakthroughs..."

5. *Referring to BATNA:* "Look, if you don't reach an agreement here today, this matter will go to adjudication and a judge will make decisions about the business and working conditions about which he or she will know very little. Would either of you want that alternative?"

6. *Depict a Limited Range of Options:* "Look, you all want the business to remain profitable and competitive. So there are only two options, either we introduce the new technologies or we look for other ways of cutting expenses and being more productive. Now which of those options should we work on?"

7. *Becoming Evaluative:* "Well, it seems to me that you're all going to have to be more flexible. Bernadette and Ray, you'll have to consider conceding on the employees' demand for more training within working hours, and Leigh and John, you're going to have to consider conceding on the introduction of electronic forms of production as has happened throughout the industry."

8. *"Gift-Wrapping" Offers or Counteroffers (During Shuttle Mediation):* "Now, Ray and Bernadette, we're making good progress; Leigh and John are still committed to coming to an agreement, they're now prepared for the company to introduce some new technology, and they're committed in principle to seeking worker support for what is agreed among us today. However, at this point in time they can't quite agree on the nature and timing of the new systems you propose, and we'll also have to do some further work on the training issue."

9. *Educating and Coaching in Separate Meetings:* "Now, John and Leigh, in negotiations it is usual for one side to make a concession in response to the first concession of the other side. This keeps the negotiations moving, is a sign of good faith, and can establish a pattern for the rest of the negotiations. Now John and Leigh, would you like me to assist you in making a counteroffer to Bernadette and Ray in a way which is most favorable to you?"

10. *Trivializing Differences:* "Well, now we're arguing over whether the new system will be introduced on the 23rd of October or the 30th of October. How important do you think that difference is in light of the bigger picture that we've been dealing with and have largely agreed on?"

11. *Emphasizing Common Objective Standards:* "Look, you're all committed to the continuing viability of the company. Now all the experts indicate that new technology requires adequate training in order for it to be used to the optimum extent. And the suppliers have standard training packages that can be purchased by users. Let's focus on the details of those packages for a while."

12. *Creating Doubt Over Professional Advice:* "You both have good legal advisers, but it is logically not possible for both lawyers to be right. At least one is wrong, and it may be that both are wrong. However, it is logically impossible for both to be right."

13. *Creating Dissonance:* "John and Leigh, what would you need from Bernadette and Ray in order to get you to agree to their proposal on when the new systems should come into effect?" or, "John and Leigh, what could you offer Bernadette and Ray to get them to agree to your proposal on the new remuneration package?" or, "Bernadette and Ray, if I were an adjudicator here and I were to say that there was going to be the kind of training and support being requested by Leigh and John but that you could define the timing and extent of that training, then what would you suggest should be those terms and conditions?"

14. *Threatening to Quit:* "Well, you've been arguing on that point for several hours, and not only are you making no progress, but you seem to be slipping backwards. It seems that there is no real negotiability between you, and my only option is to terminate the mediation...unless of course either of you has an offer to make."

As already indicated, there are possible dangers in the use of these forms of encouraging settlement and these are referred to in the following section.

V. Dangers in Encouraging Settlement

There are dangers in any situation in which a mediator uses his or her power to influence or pressure the parties to enter an agreement that they might not otherwise have entered. Some of the dangers relate to the parties and their agreement, others relate to the mediator, and yet others relate to the reputation of mediation as a whole.

A. Dangers Relating to the Parties and Their Agreement

Dangers of encouraging settlement related to the party and the agreement are as follows:

- The mediator's own interests in achieving a mediated settlement, such as his or her success rate and reputation, could take precedence over the interests of the parties.
- The mediator's own perceptions, values, and preferences about what is appropriate might come to the fore and affect the outcome more than the parties' views affect it.
- There is a possibility of greater pressure being applied to or experienced by the weaker party because he or she is more likely to be affected by mediator power and more likely to make concessions.
- The mediator's pressure could be based on objective, normative standards (legal rules, company policies, and so on) and not on the subjective interests and needs of the parties.
- One or both parties might not abide by the mediated agreement because they feel that they were pressured and forced to compromise in the mediation.
- The legal validity of the mediated agreement might be challenged on grounds of duress or undue influence.

Case Illustration: Too Much Encouragement

In a mediation involving a bank's attempt to foreclose on the family property, all parties were legally represented. The mediator was determined to maintain the momentum when the parties were making progress and continued the mediation without significant breaks into the late hours of the night. Eventually settlement was reached, and all parties signed the mediated agreement. Sometime later, the owner of the property brought legal proceedings in an attempt to have the mediated agreement set aside as not being valid in law. The court was asked to review the contract in the light of the undue influence and duress that was allegedly affecting the owner when the agreement was signed. The court found that the party had established these factors and refused to uphold the agreement. The action was brought against the party's own lawyer and not against the mediator, but the argument was that the circumstances of the mediation created an oppressive climate for this party.

B. Dangers Relating to the Mediator

Dangers of encouraging settlement related to the mediator are as follows:

- The mediator might lose his or her status of independence and neutrality in the eyes of a party who felt pressured into reaching settlement.

- Disciplinary action might be brought against the mediator for breach of relevant standards or ethical guidelines.

- The mediator might be sued in negligence or for breach of the Agreement to Mediate.

- The pressure experienced by the parties might affect the reputation of the mediator among potential users of his or her services.

C. Dangers Relating to the System of Mediation

Dangers of encouraging settlement related to the system of mediation are as follows:

- Bad experiences or the inappropriate use of mediator power might adversely affect the reputation of mediation in the marketplace.

- Significant inconsistencies could arise in the practice of mediation among different mediators and in different contexts.

- Users and potential users of mediation might become confused about the nature of mediation and the mediator's role.

VI. Creating the Balance

As indicated in the introduction to this chapter, the most difficult issue relating to the mediator's role in encouraging settlement is how interventionist or non-interventionist mediators should be. On the one hand, parties in mediation usually require a settlement to their problems, and that might only be forthcoming with some encouragement from the mediator (see the case illustration below). On the other hand, too much encouragement could create problems for the parties, the mediator, or the mediation profession.

Case Illustration: Too Little Encouragement

An experienced attorney, Viktor, recommended the choice of a particular mediator, Tony, because he was an expert in the subject matter of the dispute, had held a high position in the relevant law society, and was regarded as a wise eminence in the profession. Because his client was resistant to his own recommendations on a commercial settlement, Viktor thought that the right signs from a neutral mediator with Tony's status would have the desired effect. Tony had recently completed a mediation training course and was committed to conducting the process without using his power to encourage settlement. The mediation did not produce a settlement. In a subsequent interview, Viktor indicated that his client had been on the brink of coming to a commercial settlement and required just a little more encouragement from the mediator. When this was not forthcoming, his resistance resurfaced and he was able to justify to himself his decision to walk away without reaching agreement.

It is not easy to talk in abstract terms about the proper balance between the parties' right to self-determination and the mediator's function of encouraging them to make decisions. Much will depend on context and culture. In relation to context, *timing* is an important factor. Thus, in terms of its likely receptiveness and effectiveness in influencing a party, encouragement of settlement should not occur before trust has been established; it should come later rather than sooner in the mediation process.

Another dimension of context is the relevant *stage* of the mediation process, which is distinct from, though related to, the timing question. Thus, there will normally be more latitude for mediators to encourage settlement in the separate sessions than there will be in joint session.

The *attitude and circumstances* of the parties will also be an important contextual factor. If the parties jointly ask the mediator for an opinion, it is likely to be experienced as less coercive than if they have not done so. Likewise, if a party has professional advisers or lay supporters present, he or she is less likely to experience pressure or coercion (at least from the mediator) than a party without such support.

Finally, as pointed out in the introduction to this chapter, whether a mediator intervention is one of influence, pressure, or coercion will also depend on the *personal disposition* of a party, their educational status and emotional stability, and how as individuals they react to the various forms of encouraging settlement referred to in this chapter.

There is little doubt that in practice some mediators are chosen because they have a reputation for being "assertive" in their interventions. Likewise, a particular model of mediation might have been chosen because it allows the mediator to make a greater contribution on matters of content as opposed to matters of process. Where a mediator does not encourage settlement sufficiently in these circumstances, he or she might not be doing what is required by the circumstances.

At the same time, some of the methods of encouraging settlement referred to in this chapter would be regarded by many as illegitimate exercises of mediator power in many circumstances. This all suggests the need for a delicate balance between assertion and oppression, between persistence and pressure, and between patience and endurance. In some ways this is easier to understand in the context of mediation simulations, case studies, observation studies, and other concrete mediation situations. For beginner mediators (which includes all within their first five years of practice), it is recommended to err on the side of encouraging settlement as little and as mildly as possible.

VII. Exercises

1. All professionals have different sources of power in the practice of their particular professions. (A doctor's power is different in nature than a teacher's.) What is inherent in the nature and process of mediation that gives particular powers to mediators? What are some of the dangers created by these powers?

2. Refer to the practical illustrations of ways in which mediators can encourage settlement referred to above. Which of these interventions do you think are generally legitimate, which are illegitimate, and which would have to be assessed in light of the particular mediation circumstances in which they were used?

3. Observe a video of a simulated or real mediation and make notes of the different ways in which the mediator encourages settlement as described in this chapter. Are there any ways in which he or she encourages settlement that are different from those referred to here?

NINE

Managing Power in Mediation

Justice and power must be brought together, so that whatever is just may be powerful, and whatever is powerful may be just.

—BLAISE PASCAL (FRENCH PHILOSOPHER)

I. Introduction

At the heart of all mediations is a negotiation—one in which a third party, the mediator, assists the parties in the negotiation process. By participating in the mediation, the parties implicitly and explicitly acknowledge the mediator's role to intervene in the negotiation in ways that will aid in "their decision making about the dispute."[1] Robust party participation conducive to effective decision making is sometimes stymied where parties come to the mediation with a significant asymmetry of negotiation power. In fact, the more pronounced the power imbalance, the more difficult the mediation is likely to be.[2] Thus, one powerful category of intervention techniques a mediator can use involves the managing of negotiation power between the parties. In this chapter, we will explore the mediator's duty to manage negotiation power, the nature of negotiation power, and mediator interventions that may help to lessen the power gap among parties so that the mediator can conduct a procedurally fair mediation.

Managing negotiation power refers to an array of potential interventions that are designed to assure that parties can participate as completely and as fully as possible in a procedurally fair mediation, or, in other words, to exercise their right of self-determination. Indeed, a mediator's duty to manage power arises primarily out of the common mediation principles of party self-determination and procedural fairness. Party self-determination, as defined by the Model Standards, is "the act of coming to a voluntary, uncoerced decision in which each party makes free and informed choices as to process and outcome."[3] Procedural fairness is reflected in the following instruction taken from the Florida Rules for Certified and Court Appointed Mediators, which is representative of many jurisdictions' mediation codes:

---

1. *See* Chapter 1—*Introduction to Learning Mediation Skills and Techniques*, section I A.
2. ELLEN WALDMAN, MEDIATION ETHICS 87 (2011).
3. MODEL STANDARDS OF CONDUCT FOR MEDIATORS STD. I(A) (2005).

A mediator shall conduct mediation sessions in an even-handed, balanced manner. A mediator shall promote mutual respect among the mediation participants throughout the mediation process and encourage the participants to conduct themselves in a collaborative, non-coercive, and nonadversarial manner.[4]

Thus, once parties enter mediation, many of the tactics and strategies that they might have used with impunity in a negotiation to gain an advantage, like intimidation, threats, or monopolizing the conversation, are behaviors that a mediator is obligated to mitigate or eliminate to promote party self-determination and procedural fairness. The ethical challenge for mediators is to manage disruptive power imbalances in ways that maintains mediator impartiality and does not cross over into advocacy for any one party.[5] John Paul Lederach, the noted conflict-resolution scholar, instructs that "advocacy chooses to stand by one side for justice's sake. Mediation chooses to stand in connection to all sides for justice's sake."[6] Before exploring specific tactics and strategies to promote justice in mediation, we will discuss what we mean by "negotiation power."

II. What Is Negotiation Power and Why Does It Matter?

A. Negotiation Power Defined

A party's power in mediation or negotiation is not necessarily the same thing as being powerful in society in general. One may be wealthy and have an influential job or elevated status in the wider community but be relatively powerless in a particular negotiation scenario. This is because, as we will explore below, negotiation power is multifaceted and is measured relative to another's power in a specific circumstance. Negotiation power is "the probability that a person can carry out his or her own will despite resistance."[7] Put slightly differently, power in negotiation can be defined as "the ability to convince the opposing party to give her what she wants even when doing so is incompatible with the opponent's interests."[8] Consequently, the degree of negotiating power will affect the negotiator's performance and outcome.

---

4. FL. ST. MED. R. 10.410.

5. For a fuller exploration of the ethical limits of balancing power, see Michael T. Colatrella Jr., *Informed Consent in Mediation: Promoting Pro Se Parties' Informed Settlement Choice While Honoring the Mediator's Ethical Duties*, 15 CARDOZO J. CONFLICT RESOL. 705 (2014).

6. JOHN PAUL LEDERACH, PREPARING FOR PEACE: CONFLICT TRANSFORMATION ACROSS CULTURES 14 (1995).

7. Peter H. Kim, Robin L. Pinkley & Alison R. Fragale, *Power Dynamics in Negotiation*, 30 THE ACAD. OF MGMT. REV. 799, 800 (2005).

8. RUSSELL KOROBKIN, NEGOTIATION THEORY AND STRATEGY 151 (2002).

The primary characteristic of negotiating power that a mediator should under-stand is that it is situational. A party's power is relative to those with whom he or she is negotiating. Although having substantial financial resources and social status may contribute to negotiation power, other factors may render these more traditional indicia of power relatively inconsequential. One example of the relative nature of negotiation power is related in G. Richard Shell's excellent book on negotiation, *Bargaining for Advantage: Negotiation Strategies for Reasonable People*.[9]

As Mr. Shell explains, in the 1970s, real estate developers were buying property in Atlantic City, New Jersey, with the prospect that the city would soon legalize gam-bling, making the real estate more valuable and sought after. Vera Coking, an elderly widow of modest means, owned a boarding house in a coveted Atlantic City loca-tion. In hopes of building a casino on Ms. Coking's land, Bob Guccione, the wealthy publisher of *Penthouse* magazine, purportedly offered Ms. Coking $1 million for her home—many times the fair market value. But Ms. Coking refused. Mr. Guccione gave up trying to persuade Ms. Coking to sell her boarding house after he failed to secure a preemptive gaming license for the premises.

Then primarily a real estate developer, Donald Trump entered the picture. Like Mr. Guccione, Mr. Trump was interested in purchasing Ms. Coking's property; how-ever, he was not willing to offer an exorbitant sum. Instead, Mr. Trump initiated a series of lawsuits and brought his considerable influence to bear on city officials to obtain the property, including convincing the Atlantic City Casino Authority to try to have the property condemned as an "eyesore."[10] All of Mr. Trump's machinations ultimately failed. Despite Mr. Guccione's and Mr. Trump's wealth, social status, and influence, Ms. Coking had the dominant negotiating power in this situation because she had considerable substantive negotiation power—she owned the property and could not be forced to sell it.

B. Why Does Being Attentive to Negotiating Power Matter?

Experienced mediators know that the more "symmetrical" the parties perceive their negotiation power to be, that is, the more they view their negotiation power as being relatively equal, the more likely it is that the parties will "favor cooperation, function more effectively, and behave in a less exploitative or manipulative man-ner...."[11] Conversely, parties who feel overly empowered are more likely to be inflexible, making a mutually agreeable settlement more difficult to attain and often damaging their own interest in the process. For instance, parties who feel particularly empowered are less likely to be collaborative and are more likely to use coercive negotiation tactics, like intimidation or monopolizing the conversation.[12] Simply put,

---

9. G. RICHARD SHELL, BARGAINING FOR ADVANTAGE 108–09 (2d ed. 2006).
10. *Id.*
11. CHRISTOPHER W. MOORE, THE MEDIATION PROCESS 389 (3d ed. 2003).
12. *Id.* at 390.

overly empowered parties are more likely to engage in behavior that undermines "the ability of the parties to work together cooperatively."[13] Parties who fail to work together cooperatively frequently miss opportunities for joint gains that can benefit all participants. By being attentive to negotiating power, a mediator will be better able to intervene as needed to alleviate potential issues caused by power asymmetry.

Although symmetrical power is the ideal in mediation, few parties enter mediation in such equipoise.[14] Also, as we will see, not all power imbalances are disruptive or unfair. Often, because of the law, or facts, or both, a party will have power because the relative substantive merits of the dispute tend to favor his or her version of events, as in the case of Ms. Coking in the Atlantic City real estate example above. Yet there are circumstances where power imbalances may require mediator intervention. One such scenario is where one party is represented by legal counsel and another is not. This is an all too common occurrence in modern litigation. In some family courts, for example, as much as 80 percent of cases have at least one unrepresented party.[15] Even in federal civil matters, 28 percent of cases have at least one unrepresented party.[16] When only one party to a mediation has legal representation, there is increased risk for significant power imbalances that could severely undermine procedural fairness if the mediator fails to intervene to mitigate the power asymmetry.

C. Types of Negotiation Power

Negotiation power is multifaceted, deriving strength from many different sources. We can, however, characterize these power sources into three general categories: (1) *substantive power*, (2) *personal power*, and (3) *relationship power*.[17] We explore each in turn below.

1. SUBSTANTIVE POWER

Substantive power derives strength from actual facts, circumstances, and merits of the dispute. For example, a landlord who has filed a legal action to evict a tenant for failure to pay rent may have the facts and law on his side. He may have a valid lease and fulfilled all his obligations under it. The tenant, however, has not paid the

---

13. *Id.*

14. Waldman, *supra* note 2, at 76.

15. Nat'l Center for State Courts, Family Justice Initiative, *The Landscape of Domestic Relations Cases in State Courts*, at 2 (2018) (A study of domestic relations cases conducted across 11 large urban courts in the U.S. between 2016 and 2017 found "[i]n some courts, upwards of 70 to 80 percent of cases reportedly involve at least one self-represented litigant.").

16. Mark D. Gough & Emily S. Taylor Poppe, *(Un)Changing Rates of Pro Se Litigation in Federal Courts*, 45 Law & Soc. Inquiry 567 (2020) (In an investigation of federal civil filings between 1999 and 2019, "28 percent of all cases filed [] involved at least one pro se party").

17. *See* Roy J. Lewicki, Bruce Barry & David M. Saunders, Essentials of Negotiation 185 (6th ed. 2016); *see also* Leigh L. Thompson, The Mind and Heart of the Negotiator, 159–74 (4th ed. 2009). A full exploration of the sources of negotiation power are beyond the scope of this chapter.

agreed upon rent in a timely manner without a colorable defense. In such a scenario, the tenant will have no reasonable chance of succeeding in court. Thus, in mediation, any settlement will reflect the merits of the dispute that are highly skewed in favor of the landlord. There are five common categories of substantive power, also known as "leverage," with which mediators need to be familiar. These are (a) *positive leverage*, (b) *normative leverage*, (c) *negative leverage*, (d) *best alternatives to making a deal*, and (e) *asymmetry of information*.

a. *Positive Leverage*

This form of power is having something that the other side needs. In the Atlantic City boarding house negotiation described above, Ms. Coking had an enormous amount of positive leverage because she owned land in a "prime" location; something both Mr. Trump and Mr. Guccione thought they needed, considering the enormous resources they spent in trying to obtain it.

b. *Normative Leverage*

Normative leverage is the "skillful use of standards [and] norms to gain advantage or protect a position."[18] Standards and norms are a form of objective sources and are most powerful where your negotiating counterpart views them as "legitimate and relevant" to the negotiation.[19] Normative leverage is premised upon two common human tendencies. First, people often tend to wish to appear consistent and reasonable, so they are inclined to act consistently with past behavior and opinions.[20] Second, they tend to be influenced by objective data and arguments. Normative leverage, thus, aligns with a person's wish to seem reasonable and to act consistently.

Normative leverage typically stems from a purely objective third-party source. For instance, utilizing the *Kelly Blue Book* value is a common form of normative leverage in purchasing a car, just as obtaining expert opinions is for litigation. Normative leverage can also be based on a party's past behavior. For instance, an employer who has paid computer programmers $100,000 per year will likely be convinced to pay a new qualified programmer similarly, even though there may be many other eager and qualified applicants who would gladly accept far less compensation.[21]

c. *Negative Leverage*

Negative leverage describes the power to take something away from a party that he already has. Sometimes this is called "threat-based" leverage.[22] This is a particularly potent form of leverage because people will often go to great lengths to protect

---

18. SHELL, *supra* note 9, at 44.
19. *Id.*
20. LEWICKI, BARRY & SAUNDERS, *supra* note 17, at 104.
21. See Chapter 7—*Facilitating the Negotiations*, section II E, discussing gaining normative leverage by using objective sources.
22. SHELL, *supra* note 9, at 103.

what they have and value. A common example of this type of leverage is between employee and employer. Whatever the subject matter of the negotiation is between employee and employer, the employer has the power to fire the employee—to "take away" something he values, his job. Even if it remains unspoken, as it most often does, the employer has a powerful source of negative leverage.

An objectively powerless party in mediation can also possess negative leverage. For example, a party making a particularly offensive discrimination claim against a large company may have the ability, simply by publicly and persistently asserting the claim, to diminish a company's otherwise valued reputation as a "good" corporate citizen. This may force a company to agree to a large settlement, even if it believes the discrimination would likely not be proven.

d. *Best Alternative to a Negotiated Agreement (BATNA)*

The best alternative to a negotiated agreement, commonly known as BATNA, is the best course of action that a negotiator can take if he or she cannot reach an agreement in the mediation. In other words, if the mediation fails, what is the next-best path for the parties to take to resolve their problem? Note that the "best alternative" may be more beneficial to one party than another. For example, in litigated matters, the parties' BATNA is the likely result at adjudication, where it is likely one party will fare better than the other as opposed to coming to a mutually beneficial agreement in a negotiation.

The authors of the classic negotiation book *Getting to Yes* illuminate this concept by explaining that "the reason you negotiate is to produce something better than the results you can obtain without negotiating.... What is that alternative?"[23] In the landlord-tenant scenario earlier, the landlord's BATNA is almost certainly obtaining an eviction if the matter proceeds to a court hearing, and the tenant's BATNA is almost certainly being evicted. Considering probable future outcomes if the parties do not resolve the dispute in mediation provides important information on what settlement might be fair. In fact, a party's BATNA is the best measurement for a party to determine whether to make a deal or not.[24] A party should only accept an offer in a mediation if she deems it more favorable than her BATNA. For a fuller discussion of BATNA, see Chapter 7, section II D.

e. *Asymmetry of Information*

Information also can be a source of substantive power. Parties often come to mediation with an "asymmetry of information."[25] Information imbalances often arise because parties in conflict stop communicating and because, in litigated matters, mediation often occurs before discovery is complete. In a personal injury mediation resulting from a car accident, for example, the plaintiff may have superior

---

23. ROGER FISHER, WILLIAM URY & BRUCE PATTON, GETTING TO YES 102 (3d ed. 2011).
24. *Id.*
25. MOORE, *supra* note 11, at 391.

information about her medical condition, treatment, and prognosis than the defendant has. Similarly, a defendant in an employment discrimination lawsuit may have access to relevant witnesses and documents that provide crucial information about the relative merits of the allegations not yet available to the plaintiff, depending on the status of discovery in the litigation. Information asymmetry is a common source of power imbalance in many types of mediation.

2. PERSONAL POWER

Personal attributes are also a source of negotiation power. These attributes can be associated with one's skills, such as having a facility with negotiation or "a head for numbers." They can also be personal traits like persistence and likeability, both of which can contribute to a negotiator's formidability. Personal attributes can also include financial resources and social status. Certainly, Bob Guccione's and Donald Trump's wealth and social status made them more powerful than less affluent and socially connected people might have been in the negotiation with Ms. Coking over her Atlantic City boarding house. People with substantial wealth can often afford to fight longer, harder, and better, exhausting their negotiating counterpart's resources and energy. Additionally, a negotiator can use one's elevated social status as a means of subtle, or not so subtle, intimidation of their counterpart to obtain concessions that the counterpart may not have necessarily made with others of lessor status.

3. RELATIONSHIP POWER

Finally, relationship dynamics can create power imbalances of which a mediator should be aware. In business disputes, for example, there are often organizational hierarchies, such as manager and employee. Business partners and domestic partners also will bring to the mediation a relationship history where one party may be substantially more dominant than the other to such a degree that it could threaten party self-determination. Without some form of mediator intervention, a party in a demonstrably inequitable relationship may not feel free to share important concerns, information, and preferences that could be vital to creating fair and lasting agreements.

III. Mediator Interventions to Manage Power

A. Introduction

It is important that we emphasize, as stated above, that when parties participate in mediation they implicitly and explicitly consent to the mediator's intervening in their negotiation. The very purpose of the mediator is to guide the participants through a productive dispute-resolution process, which may be very different from the one that the parties may have been following on their own or would follow if left to their own devices.

At its best, the mediation process is one that is informed by science-based nego-tiation and conflict-management practices. Our view is that in applying a productive negotiation process to the dispute, the mediator's interventions are potentially appli-cable and helpful to all parties. In practice, the mediator should use a variety of interventions, adjusting his or her tactics as needed across parties and as negotia-tions unfurl. Such an approach "recognizes that mediation parties might have different intelligence, skills, knowledge, economic resources, social status, and so forth."[26] In other words, because participants come to mediation with different resources and abilities, mediators may need to help each in different ways. As an example, for a mediator to conduct a productive and fair process, he or she may need to help one party more fully appreciate its concerns and needs, and help another party itemize and objectify damages so that they are more comprehensible and cred-ible. Accordingly, a mediator should inject good negotiation and communication practices wherever and whenever needed.

Relatedly, mediator interventions are not always "equal" because one party may need more assistance than another party. Such practice does not offend common understandings of impartiality.[27] Indeed, many mediation codes require such inter-ventions. For example, the Model Standards provide that "[i]f a party appears to have difficulty comprehending the process, issues, or settlement options, or diffi-culty participating in a mediation, the mediator should explore the circumstances and potential accommodations, modifications or adjustments that would make possible the party's capacity to comprehend, participate, and exercise self-determi-nation."[28] It is with this understanding that we explain several common mediator interventions for managing power.

B. General Interventions

There are three mediator activities in which mediators engage as part of the gen-eral mediation process but which also have a meaningful power-balancing effect. These are (1) *mediator presence*, (2) *educating the parties about mediation*, and (3) *modeling appropriate communication and behavior*.

1. MEDIATOR PRESENCE

As a general proposition, the mediator's presence in the mediation usually has the effect of placing participants on their best behavior. Parties, generally, wish to appear reasonable in the presence of a third party, here the mediator. Moreover, even where the mediator is operating under a facilitative mediation model, participants often

---

26. Omer Shaperia, *Conceptions and Perceptions of Fairness in Mediation*, 54 S. Tex. Law Rev. 281, 305 (2012); *see* Janet Rifkin, Jonathan Millen & Sara Cobb, *Toward a New Discourse for Me-diation: A Critique of Neutrality*, 9 Mediation Q. 151 (1991); *see also* Sara Cobb & Janet Rifkin, *Practice and Paradox: Deconstructing Neutrality in Mediation*, 16 Law & Soc. Inquiry 35 (1991).
27. Omer Shaperia, A Theory of Mediators' Ethics 212 (2016).
28. Model Standards of Conduct for Mediators Std. VI (A).

will try to convince the mediator that their arguments are more valid, their version of events truthful, or that they are simply more worthy of the mediator's sympathies. Consequently, the very presence of the mediator is sometimes sufficient to inspire the parties to treat each other respectfully and to behave cooperatively.

2. EDUCATING THE PARTIES ABOUT MEDIATION

Parties will often come to mediation with differing levels of experience with the process. This is especially true where one or more parties are unrepresented by counsel and other parties are represented. Mediators can minimize the power imbalances that may emanate from this disparity in experience by educating them about the mediation process. For instance, although all mediators will explain the process as part of the mediator's opening, a mediator may choose to take more time and provide more detail about the process and the parties' role in it when she knows that some parties are new to the experience. This places inexperienced parties more at ease because they have a better appreciation for what to expect in the mediation and greater guidance regarding how to participate most productively. This scenario is also an example of an intervention in which the mediator may help one of the parties disproportionately while still behaving impartially.

3. MODELING APPROPRIATE COMMUNICATION AND BEHAVIOR

It is standard practice for a mediator to model good communication and behavior, but such practice also aids in managing power. As the leader of the mediation, parties will look to the mediator to set expectations about the kind of communication and behavior that is appropriate in the process. To the extent that the mediator treats participants with respect and kindness, for example, he or she is more likely to inspire participants to act similarly. If she listens attentively, doesn't interrupt other speakers, and frequently summarizes to check for understanding, participants will be more likely to imitate these good communication practices, benefiting all parties. Thus, with such practices, participants are less likely to attempt to dominate the process or use undue intimidation practices that could undermine the power balance between the participants.

C. Balancing Substantive Power

As explained above, substantive power derives from actual facts, circumstances, and merits of the dispute. The mediator may employ some of the interventions listed below to mitigate disruptive power balances among the parties, although these interventions may also be used for other reasons as well.

1. ENCOURAGE PARTIES TO SHARE INFORMATION

As mentioned earlier, it is common for parties to enter mediations with an asymmetry of relevant information about the problem. Yet the more symmetrical the parties' knowledge about the relevant information, the more fully and productively they can collaborate to craft a resolution. Thus, to help facilitate party self-determination and an effective mediation, mediators should encourage the sharing of information.

Mediators can promote the sharing of information among participants by first creating opportunities for the parties to do so, most notably in the parties' initial statements. Often the mediator will need to suggest to parties that they should share information not known to the other party or parties. For example, a tenant in a rent dispute with a landlord may tell the mediator in a separate meeting that they had repaired various items in the apartment because the landlord had not responded to their requests. In such a situation, the mediator should then encourage the tenant to share with the landlord an itemized list of these repairs because it may be relevant to the back-rent discussion. The sharing of this information between the landlord and the tenant here will thus likely promote their coming to an agreement efficiently and effectively, as is common when the sharing of information is encouraged in a mediation.

2. HELP PARTIES OBJECTIVELY EXPLORE THEIR BATNA

Mediators can manage power imbalances by helping parties objectively explore their BATNA. As explained above, BATNA is a crucial negotiating concept for negotiating participants to understand as objectively and with as much detail as possible because it is a potent source of negotiation power. A party who has a good alternative to making a deal in a mediation has greater leverage in the negotiation.[29] Because a party has a good alternative to an agreement, there is no reason for making a bad deal in the mediation. Conversely, a party who has a poor alternative to reaching an agreement has less leverage in the negotiation and thus may be more incentivized to make the mediation work. To the extent a party understands his or her BATNA and seeks to understand the other party's BATNA, he will have a more accurate picture of the parties' relative negotiating power. This will help the parties make more informed settlement decisions.

For example, in litigated matters where the parties' BATNA is likely their continuing to adjudication, there are various matters that may impact the BATNA. Is it possible the case can be dismissed on a dispositive motion? If the matter goes to trial, what are the chances of the plaintiff winning, and if he wins, what is the most likely trial award? As importantly, what will the cost be to litigate the matter through trial? Parties, minimally, must assess the answers to these questions to arrive at the expected value of the case and determine their BATNA. See Chapter 7 for a detailed discussion of BATNA and expected value in litigated matters.

---

29. SHELL, *supra* note 9, at 101.

3. ASSIST PARTIES IN UNDERSTANDING THEIR INTERESTS AND THE INTERESTS OF OTHER PARTIES

Mediators can manage power imbalances by assisting parties in understanding their interests and the interests of other parties in the mediation. Interest-based negotiation lies at the very heart of facilitative mediation. As discussed in Chapter 7, negotiations are fueled by the parties' underlying interests. For instance, parties negotiate to alleviate a concern, meet a desire, satisfy a need, or quell a fear. Yet many parties enter a negotiation with only a superficial appreciation of their interests and the interests of their negotiating counterpart.

Instead, many parties to mediation focus on positions. Positions are what the parties want; they are solutions to underlying interests. For example, "I want $100,000 to settle this litigation" is a position. Positional bargaining can result in sub-optimal negotiation outcomes and are more likely to result in failed mediations because the parties can be too focused on a narrow end-result than on having their more meaningful interests met.

When mediators help parties to probe interests and help them to prioritize those interests, the parties become empowered because they are in a better position to craft a solution that is best tailored to the underlying problem. In a mediation where one party has less knowledge of the interests involved, the mediator may need to spend a disproportionate amount of time with that party to ensure that they understand their interests. Again, it is not in any way inappropriate or impartial for a mediator to work harder and longer with one party to help that party fully appreciate the extent of their interests at issue in the negotiation. Doing so helps ensure a better-balanced mediation; it is not done to help one party gain an advantage over the other. For a fuller discussion of the importance of understanding the parties' interests in negotiation, see Chapter 7—*Facilitating the Negotiations*, section II C.

4. RECOMMEND THE USE OF EXPERTS, LIKE LAWYERS, ACCOUNTANTS, FINANCIAL ADVISORS, OR OTHER EXPERT SOURCES OF INFORMATION

When a mediator recognizes that a party needs expert information or advice to make informed settlement decisions, the mediator should recommend that the party consult with such experts. This scenario is common when a party is self-represented. Such mediator interventions are ethical and encouraged by most mediation codes. The California mediation code is representative of many mediation codes, and it states, "A mediator may recommend the use of other services in connection with a mediation and may recommend particular providers of other services."[30] This advice is often hollow, however, because parties are usually self-represented because they do not have the financial resources to hire counsel or other experts. That said, many courts have free self-help resources that can aid participants in a mediation.

---

30. Cal. Rules of Ct. R. 3.857(e).

These free resources often provide litigants with information about their legal rights in a variety of commonly litigated matters, such as domestic disputes and land-lord-tenant disputes. Mediators should be fully apprised of these resources in their jurisdiction so they can direct parties to them as needed.

5. PROVIDE LEGAL INFORMATION TO PARTIES

As explained above, mediation participants will come with varying degrees of knowledge about the legal system and their legal rights. Mediators can manage power by providing legal information that can help parties make better settlement choices. Like most mediation codes, the Model Standards explain that "[a] mediator may provide information that the mediator is qualified by training or experience to provide, only if the mediator can do so consistent with these standards."[31] "[C]onsistent with these standards" means that a mediator can provide information that would not otherwise cross the line of impartiality, transforming him or her from mediator to advocate. While that line is not clear-cut, most mediator codes, for example, would prevent a facilitative mediator from explaining to a party that he had claims or defenses that he did not raise. The California Rule states this more clearly: "Subject to the principles of impartiality and self-determination, a mediator may provide information or opinions that he or she is qualified by training or experience to provide."[32]

Providing legal information comes in many different forms. A mediator might provide formal information about the legal system, such that a party has the right to try to dismiss the case through motion in court or that one party could try to compel the other to produce certain information in discovery if the matter proceeds to trial. Or the mediator could provide more informal legal information, for example, "It will take two years to get a real trial date in this county." Such information could be highly relevant to a party's decision to settle and for what amount. Yet it falls short of providing an evaluation or advice, as prescribed by the Model Standards and most other mediation codes.

Another type of legal information a mediator may provide to the parties is the applicable legal standard controlling the case. For example, Section 1983 civil rights claims filed by prisoners are a common feature of the federal civil dockets, and allegations of inappropriate medical care represent significant percentages of these lawsuits. Notably, as most prisoners are self-represented, they often come to the mediation lacking legal expertise. Consequently, many prisoners enter the mediation mistakenly assuming that the prison physicians owe them a duty of "reasonable care," as would be the case for non-prisoners. However, the federal legal standard to prove inappropriate medical care for incarcerated individuals is more rigorous and difficult to meet. Indeed, prison physicians must be found to be "deliberately indifferent" to the prisoner's care to be found liable, which is to say that they were

---

31. MODEL STANDARDS OF CONDUCT FOR MED. STD. VI(A)(5).
32. CAL. RULES OF CT. R. 3.857(d).

"conscious" or had "reckless disregard" of the consequences of their "acts or omissions."[33] In such a case, a mediator could intervene to apprise the prisoner of the proper legal standard. Although this type of information inches closer to a more evaluative approach to mediation, the mediator can inform the prisoner without giving an opinion regarding whether he can meet the standard. Armed with more accurate legal information, the prisoner is better empowered to make better settlement choices.

6. PROVIDE AN EVALUATION

Providing evaluations in mediation is controversial, a topic we explore at length in Chapter 12—*Use of Evaluation in Mediation*. Many mediators view evaluations as undermining party self-determination and as being inconsistent with a collaborative problem-solving process.[34] Yet, other mediators and mediation participants view evaluative mediation as a useful tool in assisting parties with a dispute.[35] Assuming a mediator follows the best practices for providing an evaluation, evaluations can be effective in managing substantive power.[36] In an employment discrimination matter, for example, a mediator might provide an evaluation of a reasonable range of possible damages that could help to bring the parties closer to settlement. Or a mediator in a divorce mediation may recommend a division of marital assets because it is consistent with the state's marital property law.

Evaluations can be particularly helpful in mediations where one or more parties are unrepresented. In such circumstances, a common mediator concern is that the unrepresented party will make poor settlement decisions because he or she does not fully take into account all of his or her legal rights, rendering his or her settlement decisions uninformed.[37] Here, a mediator who is an expert in the legal matter at issue can level the playing field by providing an evaluation that enables the unrepresented party to take into account the laws or standards that would control if the matter was adjudicated. This, to a significant degree, mitigates the concern that a party would resolve the matter without sufficient knowledge of his or her legal rights. Yet, as we explore in Chapter 12, mediator evaluations present other potential risks that the mediator should weigh before using this highly directive strategy.[38]

---

33. *See Farmer v. Brennan*, 511 U.S. 825 (1994).

34. *See* Lela P. Love, *The Top Ten Reasons Why Mediators Should Not Evaluate*, 24 FLA. ST. U. L. REV. 937 (1997).

35. *See* Dwight Golann & Marjorie Corman Aaron, *Using Evaluations in Mediation*, 52 DISP. RES. J. 26 (1997).

36. See Chapter 12—*Use of Evaluation in Mediation*, section IV B, discussing best practices for providing an evaluation in mediation.

37. *See* Jacqueline M. Nolan-Haley, *Informed Consent in Mediation: A Guiding Principle for Truly Educated Decisionmaking*, 74 NOTRE DAME L. REV. 775 (1998).

38. See Chapter 12—*Use of Evaluation in Mediation*, section III, discussing risks of evaluative mediation.

D. Managing Personal Power

People bring to mediation personal traits that can affect their mediation performance. Some are good negotiators, some are not. Some are verbally nimble, and some are verbally inhibited. Some are more assertive, and others more passive. Some are affable, and some are irascible. To promote full, meaningful party participation, below are interventions to help mediators manage power imbalances that result from personal power. These interventions are as follows: (1) *ensure that each party has their say*, (2) *paraphrase and summarize frequently*, and (3) *encourage persistence and patience*.

1. ENSURE THAT EACH PARTY HAS THEIR SAY

Regardless of their negotiating or verbal ability, mediators should ensure that parties have the opportunity to express their views, interests, preferences, and arguments. It is easy for more assertive mediation participants to monopolize the mediation. In these circumstances, mediators need to create space in the mediation for less assertive participants to express themselves. This can be done by creating guidelines that discourage interruptions when another participant is speaking. It also could mean allocating a period for each party to speak. Or it could mean calling more frequent separate meetings so that a party can communicate important information to the mediator without pressure or intimidation from a more assertive participant.

2. PARAPHRASE AND SUMMARIZE FREQUENTLY

Mediators can manage personal power by paraphrasing and summarizing frequently. Many participants who are new to negotiation easily lose track of important facts, offers, counteroffers, and the progress of negotiation. Frequently paraphrasing and summarizing mitigates this imbalance, keeping all parties engaged and better-informed about the negotiation status.[39]

3. ENCOURAGE PERSISTENCE AND PATIENCE

Mediators should assume that parties unfamiliar with formal negotiation processes will give up more easily than those who have significant experience with negotiations. This is particularly true of unrepresented litigants. As experts in negotiation, mediators know that impasses and slow progress, especially at the beginning of the negotiation where parties often test each other's resolve, are common features of negotiation. Thus, mediators should "normalize" common negotiation obstacles like these. Mediators also should encourage parties to persist in the negotiation to the extent that the mediator, in his or her experience, believes that persistence and patience have a reasonable chance of paying dividends.

---

39. See Chapter 5—*Assisting the Communication Process,* section X, discussing assisting in the communication process through paraphrasing and summarizing.

E. Managing Relationship Power

Related to personal power, relationship power refers to the interpersonal dynamic the parties developed before the mediation. Power imbalances can occur where one party has acquired dominance over the other to such a degree that full and meaningful participation in the mediation for the dominated party is threatened. Put another way, relationship power imbalances pose a risk that the dominant party will unduly control and suppress the other party's ability to exercise self-determination, thereby undermining the mediation process. Relationship power dynamics frequently arise in domestic disputes where partners have spent years or even decades cultivating communication and dominance patterns. But relationship power imbalances also result from business partnerships and employee-employer relationships, as well as from racial, gender, social, or cultural differences that arise from explicit discrimination or implicit bias. The following are interventions that can help to mitigate relationship power imbalances: (1) *assure party safety*, (2) *tailor mediation and communication guidelines to manage undue power imbalances*, and (3) *use separate meetings and breaks liberally.*

1. ASSURE PARTY SAFETY

When a mediator suspects a relationship power imbalance, he or she should assure that the parties *feel* safe and *are* safe. Safety concerns are a common feature of domestic mediations in particular because of the high rate of domestic violence, both physical and mental.[40] But safety issues are not restricted to domestic partners. They can arise in almost any mediation. For example, safety concerns are also prevalent in employee-employer relationships and business partner relationships because of opportunity to foment intense interpersonal conflict over a long period of interaction. If there is credible evidence of potential violence, mediators should assess whether mediation is even appropriate for the dispute. Mediation would be inappropriate for a dispute where the mediator believed that sufficient steps could not be taken to assure the physical and psychological safety of a participant.[41]

---

40. Amy Holtzworth-Munroe, Connie J.A. Beck & Amy G. Applegate, *The Mediator's Assessment of Safety Issues and Concerns (MASIC): A Screening Interview for Intimate Partner Violence and Abuse Available in the Public Domain*, 48 FAM. CT. REV. 646 (2010); *see* Amy Holtzworth-Munroe et al., *Intimate Partner Violence and Family Dispute Resolution: 1-Year Follow-Up Findings from a Randomized Controlled Trial Comparing Shuttle Mediation, Videoconferencing Mediation, and Litigation*, 27 PSYCHOL. PUB. POL'Y & L. 581, 582 (2021) (At least 10 percent of children are exposed to domestic violence every year, and, as of 2014, "24.3% of women and 13.8% of men report having have experienced severe physical intimate partner violence."); *see also* Anne Fuchs, *Considering the Needs of Domestic Violence Victims: The Exceptions to Minnesota's Alternative Dispute Resolution Rule 114*, BATTERED WOMEN'S JUSTICE PROJECT (2011) (explaining that careful screening procedures and safeguards for domestic violence should be put in place to protect victims, promote self-determination of both parties, and increase mediation effectiveness).

41. *See* Sarah Krieger, *The Dangers of Mediation in Domestic Violence Cases*, 8 CARDOZO WOMEN'S L.J. 235, 247 (2002) (explaining that a victim may be at most risk of violence during the

If the mediator deems a mediation appropriate even amidst safety concerns, he or she should take steps to ensure the safety of all participants throughout the proceedings. Common safety steps for face-to-face mediations are to arrange for participants to arrive and leave the mediation at separate times and for the mediator to never leave the parties unsupervised when in joint sessions or even on breaks. As an alternative, the mediator could conduct the entire process in separate sessions. Virtual mediations, using videoconferencing software, is also now an attractive option where safety issues are present (*see* Chapter 11—*Virtual Mediation*). However, videoconferencing will not mitigate safety concerns if the participants are in the same home or office when conducting it, as was sometimes the case during the COVID-19 pandemic in domestic mediations.

2. TAILOR MEDIATION AND COMMUNICATION GUIDELINES TO MANAGE UNDUE POWER IMBALANCES

As with potential personal power imbalances, relationship power imbalances can be managed by crafting mediation guidelines to mitigate dominating behavior. For example, if a mediator suspects there is a strong likelihood that a party will become overly aggressive in the mediation, he or she could add the following guideline in the mediator's opening: "It is important that everyone has a chance to express themselves in the mediation. Thus, can we agree that there will be no interruptions or personal verbal attacks like name calling? And if there are, you understand that I will jump in to remind everyone of this guideline. Can we agree to that?" This is not a guideline that we would typically include in a mediation unless we felt aggression a potential problem. Also note, as we explain in Chapter 4, that we ask for participants to affirmatively agree to the guidelines by saying "yes" or "I agree," or by giving a nod of the head. This public agreement, as opposed to only a mediator instruction, renders infractions less likely to occur and makes controlling infractions much easier later in the mediation.[42]

3. USE SEPARATE MEETINGS AND BREAKS LIBERALLY

Separate meetings are an effective tool to mitigate against aggressive or dominating participant behavior. When a mediator suspects that there is potential for aggressive or dominating behavior, the mediator should emphasize during opening that each party has a right to call for a separate meeting or break at any time for any reason. The mediator should also call separate meetings and breaks frequently to check in with parties about concerns or information that they may have felt uncomfortable sharing in the joint session because of party dominance.

---

period between separation and divorce, and that placing victims in non-adversarial situations like mediation "with their abusers puts them in greater danger of being beaten, harassed, or stalked"); *see also* Fuchs, *supra* note 40, at 9, explaining the importance of pre-screening and rescreening mediation participants for abusive behaviors to determine if mediation is appropriate.

42. ROBERT B. CIALDINI, INFLUENCE 294 (rev'd ed. 2021).

Of course, the mediator has the option of conducting the entire mediation in separate meetings if he or she feels this is warranted. But mediators should not be too quick to resort to this type of shuttle diplomacy because self-determination is most fully realized when parties work directly together. Having parties work together in joint session as much as practical is particularly important when they will have an ongoing relationship after the mediation, such as in domestic disputes where the parties will co-parent minor children, in employee-employer matters, in landlord-tenant matters, and in many more.

F. Dangers in Managing Power Imbalances

Interventions for reducing the power of stronger parties involve some potential deviation from the mediator's neutrality and impartiality. These interventions may involve the mediator's creating doubt in the mind of the stronger party over the facts, the law, the evidence, and the party's likelihood of being successful in litigation. Intervening in this way can engender risk that the mediator becomes too involved in increasing the power of the weaker party and decreasing that of the stronger, leading to the mediator's becoming the advocate for and protector of the weaker party.

Indeed, when managing power imbalances, a mediator can be at risk of losing his or her impartiality, or being seen as having lost his or her impartiality, in "taking sides" with the perceived weaker party and against the perceived more powerful party. A mediator who has lost his or her impartiality may be inclined to impose his or her own standards and values over those of the parties, which goes against the fundamental mediation principles of facilitating party self-determination and procedural fairness. Consequently, it is important for mediators who find themselves in situations where they must manage negotiation power among participants to be mindful to avoid falling into these traps.

IV. Exercises

1. Observe a mediation, real or simulated, and assess which party has the most negotiation power based on the negotiation power principles explained above.

2. Observe a mediation, real or simulated, and note the interventions the mediator uses or might have used to appropriately manage the negotiation power between the parties.

TEN

Variations in the Mediation Process

We shape our buildings: thereafter they shape us.

—WINSTON CHURCHILL
(ENGLISH PRIME MINISTER AND STATESMAN)

I. Introduction

There are many possible variations that can be made to the "standard" mediation process described in Chapter 4, as mediation is adapted and modified to suit the circumstances in which it is being used. The variations could be required or dictated by a wide variety of circumstances: the needs of the parties, the nature of the dispute, the resources on hand, the amount of time available, the strategic judgments of the mediator, and so on. Generally, it will be the mediator who makes a discretionary decision in relation to most of these variations. However, a variation may also be requested by the parties and their advisers or be demanded by the objective circumstances of the mediation. This chapter deals with a few of the many variations that can be made to the so-called standard mediation process.

II. Multiple Meetings

Mediations can be held over two or more separate sessions conducted on different days, different months, and different centuries. Mediators can, in their discretion, call adjournments after consultation with the parties. They can also call them in response to reasonable requests from the parties or their advisers for breaks and postponements in the process.

There are many reasons for the calling of adjournments. Some relate to the subjective requirements of one or both parties, such as their need for some respite from intense emotions or the need for external assistance and advice. Others relate to the objective requirements of the process, such as the need for further information, further planning and deliberation, or a fresh mandate from constituents.

In some mediation contexts, there is a policy of having multiple meetings as standard practice. An example of this would be parenting disputes in which the mediation is provided by social services. The parties are given a break of up to four weeks to enable them to consider the progress they have made, reflect on provisional agreements, and acquire information or make arrangements for the subsequent mediation meeting. The adjournments also serve to prevent either parent from feeling pressured into making hasty decisions. In other contexts, adjournments are held with some reluctance, for fear that the momentum of the negotiations may be lost and the parties might move further apart during the period of interruption. This is the case in commercial mediation.

Where multiple meetings are held, it is advisable to commence each new session with a review of developments since the last meeting. This allows both parties to indicate where they currently stand on important issues, what changes have occurred since the last meeting, and what new information has been obtained. It also provides the opportunity to reconsider provisional agreements; however, it is sometimes discovered that the "temporary has become the permanent." Indeed, one of the advantages of multiple meetings is that parties can use the factor of time to secure agreements that would otherwise be problematic to achieve. See the following case illustration.

Case Illustration: The Temporary Becomes Permanent

In a mediation that was scheduled to run over several sessions, the parties agreed to an interim arrangement for the four-week period between the first two meetings. This agreement was acceded to with some reluctance by both parties, and only because it did not involve a permanent commitment by them. When the second mediation session was held, the interim arrangement was reviewed, and both parties agreed to commit to it permanently. At that point, they moved on to discuss other issues. The parties had felt safe in committing to it in its temporary form and then, having satisfactorily "road-tested" the arrangement, were able to commit to its continuation on a permanent basis.

Unfortunately, the converse can also occur, where after an adjournment there is some "slippage." This is where one or both parties resiles from previous agreements or raises unexpected new issues in the negotiations. While this is not easy to avoid, some mediators attempt to prevent it by having personal contact with each party during the adjournment and discussing with them the possible consequences of any slippage for which they might be responsible.

III. Shuttle Mediation

A. Shuttle Mediation Defined

Reference was made in Chapter 4 to the concept of "shuttle mediation." This involves the parties being based in different physical locations, whether rooms or countries, and the mediator moving continuously between them, shuttling messages back and forth and becoming their sole avenue of communication. The system is named after the "shuttle diplomacy" that sometimes occurs in international disputes involving nation states and political groupings. It was pointed out previously that shuttle mediation should be distinguished from a mediation in which there is a series of separate meetings, as there are practical and qualitative differences between the two.

B. Differences in Shuttle Mediation

Shuttle mediation differs from a series of separate meetings in mediation in several ways. In shuttle mediation, the parties are kept in separate rooms or venues from the start of the mediation or immediately after making opening statements, and it is understood that the full mediation will be conducted in this way unless the parties make a conscious decision to come together. In separate meetings, on the other hand, it is understood that the parties will return to a joint session after the purpose of the separate meeting is achieved. Additionally, in shuttle mediation, all communications are conveyed through the mediator, which gives him or her enhanced control and power. Finally, the usual confidentiality principle is modified to allow the mediator to convey messages between the parties.

Because of these differences, it is important that mediators should not transform a conventional mediation into shuttle mediation by default, that is, by lapsing into a prolonged series of separate sessions. There should always be a specific reason for shuttle mediation, and where the mediation does not begin in this mode, the parties should be made aware of any change into shuttle and of its implications for their communications and the confidentiality principle.

C. When to Use Shuttle Mediation

Shuttle mediation can be an effective tool for resolving disputes under the appropriate conditions. Mediators might consider the use of shuttle mediation in the following circumstances:

1. There are legal or safety reasons why the parties cannot be together, for example, the existence of restraining orders or domestic violence.

2. One of the parties feels intimidated or afraid, or there are other high emotions that would be exacerbated by meeting in each other's presence.

3. There is a gross imbalance of bargaining power because of differences in verbal ability, size of the groups, number of advisers, and the like.

4. There would be very poor communication in joint sessions because of linguistic or cultural factors.

5. The parties cannot afford for their constituents or followers to see them together, for example, in international disputes or high-profile domestic disputes involving political parties or ethnic groups.

In these circumstances it could be the case that there will either be shuttle mediation or no mediation at all. Some commentators, however, argue that shuttle is not true mediation in that the parties do not work collaboratively on the problem. They also do not learn how to negotiate with one another, and do not have the opportunity to improve their relationship for the future. We do not share this view, however, and believe shuttle mediation is an effective and necessary tool in some conflicts.

However, shuttle mediation is often used unnecessarily and to the parties' detriment, especially by those mediators who take a solely evaluative approach to mediation. This type of mediation philosophy has been dubbed the "trashing" method.[1] The trashing method is where the mediator's primary tool is to "tear apart" each side's arguments to encourage them to make more realistic settlement offers.[2] This direct form of "reality testing" can only be performed in separate meetings, thus leading to shuttle mediation. While there is nothing inherently wrong with direct reality testing by those competent to do it, the indiscriminate use of it is problematic. Shuttle mediation should be used as rarely as possible. There are significant potential downsides to the parties' perception of the mediation with such an approach, as with the parties' follow-through with the agreement. See Chapter 4, section III D for a more detailed explanation of these dangers.

D. Practical Considerations

Mediators need to attend to a number of practical matters in relation to shuttle mediation. Here is a list of practical considerations for shuttle mediators, with examples of the kind of language they might use in dealing with them:

1. Explain to the parties the ground-rules and the practicalities of the process: "Because this is shuttle mediation, I will be transmitting all messages between you and the others. Please be patient when I am not with you as this kind of mediation can take some time. However, when I leave you to see the others, I will suggest matters on which you can do some homework while I am away. You will also have plenty of time for your coffee fix...."

2. Establish a clear basis for what can be disclosed and what is to remain confidential: "Please indicate clearly what you would like me to say to the others and what should remain confidential. This includes not only facts and figures, but also reasons and explanations both for your proposals and for your response to their proposals. Only if I know what is confidential can I avoid unwanted disclosures."

3. Be alert to the parties' sensitivities over the amount of time spent with the other side: "I will now convey your proposals to the other side and I expect

---

1. James J. Alfini, *Trashing, Bashing, and Hashing it Out: Is this the End of "Good Mediation"?*, 19 FLA ST. U. L. REV. 47, 67 (1991).
2. *Id.*

to spend about 15 minutes with them. However, in shuttle mediation it is difficult to predict exactly how much time I will spend with either of you. If I am going to be longer than expected, I will come back and let you know."

4. Avoid losing impartiality by becoming the advocate of one or both parties: "Now I can tell them why you are not accepting their offer, convey your counter-proposal to them, and provide the explanation and reasoning which you have just given me. However, I cannot become your advocate and persuade them to accept your proposal, just as I cannot do that to you with any of their proposals."

5. Take precautions against making mistakes in conveying the parties' messages to each another: "Now your offer is quite a complex one, so I would like to write down the various dollar amounts and times of payment that you are proposing and then go over with you the justification for your proposal that you would like me to present to them."

E. Some Potential Drawbacks and Dangers in Shuttle Mediation

There are a number of potential drawbacks and dangers in shuttle mediation. The process itself has some transaction costs not found in non-shuttle mediation. It could take considerably more time, and it is susceptible to mistakes and misunderstandings. Communication is liable to be distorted and to focus more on substantive content and less on emotional content. From the point of view of the parties, shuttle mediation can create dynamics not usual in non-shuttle mediation. Because they are each located in their own "locker rooms," there is a danger that the parties will engage in bravado, fighting talk, and team "war cries," and even that they will backtrack without shame in the absence of the other side. This is because it can be easier to engage in positional bargaining, threats, bluster, and other negotiation tricks when not facing the other mediating party. Shuttle mediation can also result in attempts by the parties to persuade the mediator instead of each other, or in unconsciously using the mediator as their agent to advocate their case to the other side.

Shuttle mediation also creates the potential danger of an abuse of mediator power deriving from his or her position as the sole conduit of information between the parties. This point can be illustrated by reference to the range of options a shuttle mediator has when asked to convey an offer from one party to the other.

Case Illustration: Shuttle Mediation

Assume there is a shuttle mediation in a dispute relating to a deceased father-husband's will. The parties involved are the executor of the estate, the deceased's widow, and the deceased's two sons. There is agreement between the relatives that reasonable provision should be made for all of them and the executor has agreed to go along with any satisfactory proposal to which they can commit. The widow wishes to make a monetary offer to her two sons through the shuttle mediator. Here the mediator has several options. He or she can convey:

1. The cold factual offer without anything else: "Your mother is offering you each $50,000 and one-quarter of the proceeds of the family farm when it is sold in ten years' time."

2. The monetary offer with other information, which could be general or highly selective, explaining and justifying the offer: "Your mother is offering you each $50,000 because that will allow you to finish your education abroad. In addition, you will receive one-quarter of the proceeds of the family farm in ten years' time because she would like to retain it and bring to fruition your father's vision of a 20,000-tree olive orchard producing oil for export."

3. The monetary offer together with the emotional dimensions surrounding it: "Your mother is offering you each $50,000 and one-quarter of the proceeds of the family farm when it is sold in 10 years' time. She feels very upset at the strain that this dispute has put on the family, she is sad about the fact that some of your father's often-stated wishes might not be carried out, and she is concerned that the value of the estate is diminishing while you quarrel over it. Your mother feels that her proposal will put all this behind you and improve family relations."

4. The monetary offer enclosed in "gift wrap" to make it more palatable to the others: "Now, your mother is committed to coming to an agreement today; she wants it to be fair and reasonable to both of you as well as to her, and she would like to talk about family reconciliation once this is settled. She would also like you to be consulted on the development of the olive project. Now her offer at the moment is...."

5. The offer, plus the mediator's intimation as to whether there might be a further offer: "Well, at this point in time your mother would like to make an offer. This is based on the various discussions we have had thus far. It might be that with further information and negotiation her position will change. However, at the moment her offer is...."

Each of these approaches has advantages and disadvantages, and mediators will have to make tactical judgments as to which is appropriate at different stages of the mediation proceedings. Note, however, the degree of control the mediator has in the way the offer is "packaged." The mediator's control over what information is conveyed and how it is conveyed imbues him or her with significant power over the parties.

The mediator also has considerable power over the timing of offers, "coaching" the parties about negotiation, getting them to anticipate possible responses to their offers, and other features of the negotiation process referred to in this book. It is conceivable, for example, that a mediator might be tempted to refuse to convey certain offers and accompanying sentiments because, in his or her judgment, it would be unwise to do so. He or she might even "misrepresent" an offer, for example, indicate to one side that they will get $x when the mediator knows that the other side is in fact offering the greater amount of $x + y, so that the "excess" of $y can be disclosed later when, in the mediator's discretion, the timing is "ripe" to do so.

These possibilities are referred to here without any approval but in order to highlight the extensive power that mediators derive from shuttle mediation. In fact, the above strategies have considerable potential dangers if the mediator is caught or the strategy backfires and the parties lose both trust in the mediator and faith in the process. This kind of control also increases the likelihood of disciplinary or legal action being taken against the mediator.

F. Ways of Improving Shuttle Mediation

Despite the drawbacks and dangers, shuttle mediation is a fact of life in many situations where mediation would not take place in any other form. Here mediators should be transparent with the parties about some of the potential problems and about ways in which they might be kept in check. They should also attend to practical matters, like keeping written notes of offers and counteroffers, or getting the parties to write these out for transmission to each other. Where shuttle mediation is an option but is not obligatory, mediators could explain to the parties the advantages of not using it unless necessary. In relation to the power of mediators and the temptations it brings, there is sometimes the option of having co-mediators conduct the shuttle process so that they keep each other honest—a variation that is discussed in greater detail below.

IV. Using More than One Mediator

In co-mediation, there are two or more mediators. The co-mediation process is essentially the same as that in solo mediation—the mediators' functions are similar, and the same skills and techniques are required. However, there are some slight differences that are important to note. For one, there are some additional techniques, skills, and behaviors that are required of the co-mediators. Additionally, skillful preparation is even more important to an effective mediation process when multiple mediators are involved. Below, we will discuss each of these considerations in more depth.

A. When to Adopt Co-Mediation

Co-mediation is only a feasible prospect where circumstances and resources allow for both the additional expense of an extra mediator and the prospect of the mediation taking a longer time. The following are situations in which it might be appropriate to have more than one mediator:

1. Where additional mediator resources are needed—the "two heads are better than one" principle—for example, in a lengthy mediation over policies in a large organization which would require considerable mediator energy, patience, and persistence.

2. Where balance and matching are needed in respect to the gender, race, age, or other attributes of the parties and the mediators; some individuals might feel uncomfortable where the mediator, other party, and all the advisers are of the gender other than their own. (Of course, others may feel very comfortable with it.) For example, some divorce mediation practitioners work in female and male teams.

3. Where a specific professional background or experience is needed for a particular dispute, for example, an engineer in a construction dispute or a social worker in a parenting dispute, with one mediator being a mediation specialist and the other a specialist in the relevant field.

4. Where there is need to stabilize the dynamics because there might be attempts at manipulation or "triangulation," four people being a more stable number than three.

5. Where there is a need to provide experience and continuing training for new mediators and additional work for the mediation profession.

6. Where, as referred to in the previous section, there is a need to provide greater accountability, with co-mediators able to keep each other honest in their confidential and sometimes powerful role.

7. Where there is a desire to bring greater diversity of thought and to counter implicit bias among mediators or parties.[3]

B. Creating a Favorable Environment in Co-Mediation

1. PLANNING AND ORGANIZATION

As mentioned, preparation for the mediation is of particular importance when co-mediators are involved. For instance, the presence of an additional person in co-mediation requires attention to seating arrangements. Usually, the co-mediators will sit next to each other and apart from the parties to symbolize their "partnership" in a mediator team. Seating arrangements should not suggest that one co-mediator is the advocate or champion of a particular party. With a round table or circular seating arrangement all persons at the mediation can be seated equidistant from one

---

3. Implicit bias is defined as "attitudes or stereotypes that affect our understanding, actions, and decisions in an unconscious manner." Audrey J. Lee, *Implicit Bias in Mediation: Strategies for Mediators to Engage Constructively with "Incoming" Implicit Bias*, 25 HARV. NEGOT. L. REV 167, 169 (2020). *See generally* Sharon Press & Ellen E. Deason, *Mediation: Embedded Assumptions of Whiteness?*, 22 CARDOZO J. CONFLICT RESOL. 453 (2021).

another without detracting from the co-mediators' leadership position and their status as partners in the mediator team.

In the mediation planning stages, consideration can also be given to "creating balance" in co-mediation teams along the lines of professional qualifications, gender, age, or ethnicity; note that these factors are subject to the qualifications mentioned in the previous section. In addition, the co-mediators should give consideration to all the pre-mediation preparation responsibilities referred to in previous chapters; in particular, co-mediators should strategize how they will conduct the process together.

2. CONDUCT OF THE PROCESS

The process and stages of co-mediation are the same as those for solo mediation. However, co-mediation requires common understandings as to the different roles and functions of the co-mediators and as to the division of labor between them. This is usually more important during the early stages of the mediation when there can be a clear division of roles in the mediators' opening statement, in note taking, in attending and following during the party statements, in developing the list of issues, and in using the whiteboard. Later in the mediation there tends to be no clear division of labor between the mediators.

Teamwork and common understandings are important ingredients of successful co-mediation, and these are greatly assisted by the mediators' having attended the same training program where ways of dividing and sharing the tasks can be discussed and role-played. Here is one system for dividing the mediation tasks:

- *Meeting, Greeting, Seating:* Shared by mediators on an informal basis;
- *Mediator's Opening:* Clearly divided between mediators, each presenting different parts of the statement in alternating roles;
- *Party Presentations:* One mediator (M1) attends and follows and the second mediator (M2) takes notes;
- *Summaries:* Given by the mediator who took notes (M2);
- *Identification of Common Ground and Listing of Issues:* Lead taken by other mediator (M1), but with open collaboration between mediators and with parties;
- *Writing up of issues and prioritization:* Managed by second mediator (M2), with assistance from the first (M1);
- *Problem Solving and Negotiation:* Managed by both mediators equally;
- *Separate Meetings:* Mediators stay together when meeting with each party;
- *Drafting of Agreement:* One co-mediator can be principally responsible for drafting the agreement, while the other is responsible for checking the agreement against the agenda and ensuring matters of detail are accurately recorded; and

- *Closure:* Like the mediators' opening statement, the closing statement should be clearly divided between both mediators, each presenting different parts.

3. USING EACH MEDIATOR'S EXPERTISE

Where co-mediators have been chosen for their complementary expertise, each may be more active than the other at different stages of the mediation. An engineer co-mediator in a construction dispute would be expected to have a more active involvement in the discussion of technical matters, while a co-mediator skilled in the mediation process would be expected to be more active in the early stages. There is no objection to these shifts in the relative ascendancy of each.

The "non-active" mediator can still be performing a useful function in observing the parties' reactions, taking notes, considering options, and otherwise observing and analyzing the negotiations. These activities can provide the basis for an appropriate contribution at a later stage in the process. In the separate meetings, there might also be unequal contributions because of the mediators' respective strengths, experiences, or personal attributes. For instance, it might be appropriate for a male co-mediator in a family mediation to speak more in the separate meeting with the husband. Co-mediators can still model respect and equality even though they are contributing in differing ways and to different degrees. However, they should not model to the parties, whose collaborative endeavors they are attempting to facilitate, a hierarchical relationship between themselves.

4. AVOIDING BIAS AND PARTIALITY

Where the co-mediators are selected to reflect the age, gender, class, or ethnic attributes of the different parties, they should be conscious of the possibility that a particular party might perceive them as their representative or champion. Where they suspect that this is happening, they should be attentive to their own body language, be observant of the other party's reactions to the proceedings, re-emphasize at appropriate points their neutral role in the mediation procedure, and confer with one another on this issue when there is an opportunity to do so.

5. STAYING TOGETHER

Co-mediation is a team effort in which the co-mediators should at all times perform their functions together and not separately. They should meet and greet the parties together, be present together throughout the joint sessions, and remain together during the separate sessions (each should not meet with a different party). Co-mediators may call an adjournment so they can meet on their own to discuss joint progress in the mediation, to review differences in their approaches, or just to deal with their individual problems, such as emotional fatigue. There is no reason not to be transparent to the parties about the reasons for calling such an adjournment wherever this is possible.

6. IMPROVING THE COMMUNICATIONS IN CO-MEDIATION

Both co-mediators are responsible for improving the communication of the parties.[4] In furtherance of this, the co-mediators need to model good communication between themselves. This includes not interrupting one another, listening actively to what each other is saying, asking clarifying questions of each other where appropriate, and reframing each other's statements. By modeling such constructive communication techniques, the co-mediators illustrate to the parties crucial tools for problem solving. Appropriate body language also provides a subtle way in which co-mediators can communicate with each other, but it is also permissible to be quite transparent to the parties about communication differences between themselves. Moreover, the communication techniques referred to in this book are instructive not only for facilitating communications between mediators and parties but also for facilitating communications between co-mediators.

7. FACILITATING THE NEGOTIATIONS IN CO-MEDIATION

Both co-mediators are responsible for facilitating the negotiations of the parties.[5] As with communication, the co-mediators need to model good negotiation skills between themselves for the benefit of the participants. This is particularly relevant where the co-mediators differ in their opinions about the mediation process or about the nature of their interventions. Here, interest-based negotiation is the appropriate behavior that the parties need to see demonstrated by their skilled helpers. Needless to say, the co-mediators may have to use adjournments to discuss ways of overcoming negotiation difficulties between them and avoiding such difficulties in the following sessions. However, it will often be necessary for the co-mediators to negotiate between themselves without any interruption of the process. Thus, it is crucial for the co-mediators to be able to do so in a way that models good negotiation skills for the parties.

The following dialogue illustrates how co-mediators might negotiate in an interest-based way over an assumed difference between them. The co-mediators are Michael and Priyam, and the parties are Gerrard and Sally.

Case Illustration: Co-Mediation

Michael: *Now Gerrard has asked for a separate meeting with us. Shall we consider that request now?*

Priyam: *Yes, as I understand it, Gerrard would like some time out to consult his lawyer and to get some advice on Sally's offer.*

---

4. *See* Chapter 5—*Assisting the Communication Process.*
5. *See* Chapter 7—*Facilitating the Negotiation Process.*

Michael: *Yes, and it appears that Sally is interested in getting to a more advanced stage in the discussions so that these consultations will not have to be repeated. She is also concerned about the overall time question.*

Priyam: *Well, we do have some time limitations. We also agreed at the beginning that Sally and Gerrard could obtain outside advice when that was necessary for them. What if we continue for about 15 minutes to keep up the momentum and then adjourn for a short period so that both Gerrard and Sally can obtain professional advice?*

Michael: *Yes, that might meet the various interests. Gerrard and Sally, how would that arrangement suit your needs?*

C. Avoiding Traps in Co-Mediation

Traps are preventable problems caused by mediators themselves or by the predictable difficulties inherent in the negotiation process. Some of the general traps for mediators are referred to in Chapter 14-*Avoiding Mediator Traps*. There are some other traps which derive from the situation of having more than one mediator at the head of the table.

1. GOOD COP-BAD COP ROUTINE

This involves the "bad cop" co-mediator using his or her power forcefully and coercively while the "good cop" co-mediator acts more empathically in an attempt to draw out a reticent party who perceives this mediator as having a sympathetic ear. The problem is caused by mediators watching too much bad television. Co-mediators should avoid any impression of playing this routine as it could jeopardize their appearance of neutrality and cause them to be seen as manipulative and coercive (which the routine undoubtedly is).

2. MODELING INEQUALITY OR LACK OF TEAMWORK

As already indicated above, co-mediators should not model any sense of hierarchy or inequality between them. This requires particular attention where they have different levels of experience or expertise, and where societal inequalities based on class, gender, or race are reflected in the mediator team. They should also not model any lack of teamwork when their objective is to move the parties toward collaborative problem solving themselves.

3. APPOINTING INCOMPATIBLE PERSONALITIES

Co-mediators should not be appointed where there are serious incompatibilities in their personalities. Mediation provides the opportunity for the mediators to model constructive problem solving. It would be unnecessarily inviting trouble to create incompatible teams of co-mediators. While this does not have to involve personality testing for co-mediators, it does require some selectivity and honesty in their appointments.

D. Preparation for Co-Mediation

The following questions can be regarded as important for mediators to consider in their joint preparation for a co-mediation:

1. How can we ensure appropriate "balance" in the mediation team?

2. Where it is not possible to match gender, age, and other attributes, how can we reassure and encourage the mediating party who is not "matched" (for example, a teenage party where both mediators are middle-aged)?

3. How should we divide our functions during the early part of the mediation?

4. How should we deal with differences of opinion or strategy between ourselves during the mediation?

5. How can we model equality, good communication, and constructive problem solving between ourselves for the benefit of the parties?

6. How should we alert each other to problems that we think the other is causing?

7. How should we signal to each other, for example, where one of us wishes to pursue a particular topic or line of discussion?

8. How can we use each other constructively in the post-mediation debriefing?

E. Debriefing by Co-Mediators

It is recommended that all co-mediators take time to debrief one another after each co-mediation. There are two major objectives or rationales that support debriefing between co-mediators. The first is to provide a venue for co-mediators to deal with any emotional trauma they may be experiencing as a result of the mediation session. The second is to provide a venue for co-mediators to reflect upon their performance, particularly on the skills and techniques each mediator demonstrated or failed to demonstrate.

A co-mediation debriefing, as compared to solo mediation, is an especially beneficial platform for co-mediators to reflect upon their performance. For example, co-mediation allows for immediate debriefing between the mediators; it can be undertaken directly after the mediation has finished, making it more accurate and undistorted than if undertaken later with outside mentors, as is required in a solo mediation. Additionally, debriefing following a co-mediation allows for an objective evaluation of each mediator's performance by someone who has observed it personally—it does not rely only on self-assessment, though this can be a part of the debriefing process. Unfortunately, despite the great potential, co-mediators are not always, in our experience, candid and open about each other's performance. They may require an honest broker to facilitate the debriefing process.

V. Telephone Mediation

Virtual mediation and telephone mediation are alternative venues for holding a mediation. We use the term "virtual" mediation to represent mediations conducted primarily via teleconferencing software.[6] For a full exploration of virtual mediation, see Chapter 11. Even though high-quality video conferencing software is widely available, parties my opt to mediate by telephone for any number of reasons. The most common reason is that parties may not have access to high-speed internet or a computer or smart phone. A party may also feel more comfortable mediating by telephone precisely because of the less personal aspects of the technology. Like virtual mediation, mediation might be conducted by telephone conference in the following circumstances: (1) where the parties are geographically distant from each other, (2) where there is great urgency to resolve a matter, (3) where resources do not allow for the parties to come together in the same location, (4) where there is concern over the safety and well-being of one party, or (5) where there is a protection order in place which prevents them from being in each other's company. In the latter cases it might still be preferable to arrange shuttle mediation.

Where there is a choice between having a face-to-face mediation, a virtual mediation, or telephone mediation, it should be kept in mind that the last option has several potential disadvantages:

- It is more difficult for mediators to establish rapport and trust with the parties through telephone conversations only;
- Mediators cannot observe and react to some of the non-verbal communications of the participants, such as their body language;
- Separate meetings lose their immediacy and personal touch;
- The parties may be less committed to the process because there is less time and fewer expenses invested in convening the mediation;
- Visual aids cannot be used to focus the parties' attention on an agenda, diagrams, facts and figures, and so on;
- There is less scope for parties to learn conflict management skills; and
- Technology often follows Murphy's law and goes wrong when it is most needed (see the Case Illustration below).

Where telephone mediation is necessary or is chosen, it would normally operate as follows. Pre-mediation activities are the same as for face-to-face mediations, save

---

6. There are certainly more expansive definitions of virtual mediation, ones that include only written exchanges or some combination of face-to-face and online components. N. Ebner & D. Rainey, *ODR and Mediation*, *in* ONLINE DISPUTE RESOLUTION: THEORY AND PRACTICE 410 (Mohamed S. Abel Wahbe, Ethan Katsh & Daniel Rainey, eds. 2d ed. 2021).

that there is unlikely to be a preliminary conference. A date, venues for the participants, and contact numbers are arranged for the mediation meeting. A conference
call is set up with a local telephone conference call service where each participant is
given a conference call telephone number and identification code so they need only
call into the conference at the prearranged time. It is advisable that speaker phones
are used so that hands are free for taking notes or retrieving documents; this is a
necessary arrangement where there are several persons at the same venue, for example, a client, an adviser, and a witness.

The mediator follows the standard stages of mediation. Parties should be asked to
identify themselves each time they speak as there can be damaging confusion over
who says what—for example, Party A may think that a "suggestion" from the mediator is an offer or concession from Party B.

Confidentiality requires particular diligence in telephone mediation. If there are
to be separate meetings, the safest arrangement is to call on a different line (cell
phones work well for this function) or disconnect the conference line and to make
individual contact with each party in turn, before returning to the conference call. It
is dangerous to speak with one party confidentially while the others have left their
room for a consultation as it may not be apparent when the latter have returned.
When it comes to finalizing the agreement, it is advisable to use e-mail or facsimile
to circulate drafts while all parties are still present and not to "leave the finalization
until later."

Here are some additional guidelines for telephone mediation based on the harsh
lessons of experience:

- The mediator should recommend that the discussions not be recorded by
  the parties, or at least develop a policy on this issue with the parties;

- The mediator should ask each party to disclose who is physically present
  with them during the mediation so that this does not complicate the situation later. Needless to say, there is no guarantee that others will not also be
  present and overhear the conversation;

- Because of the possibility of misunderstanding and confusion, the mediator needs to listen harder, ask clarifying questions, and summarize more
  frequently. (For additional advice on how to promote effective communication in telephone mediations, see Chapter 5–*Assisting the Communication
  Process*, section VII);

- The mediator should be particularly diligent about noting and recording
  the concessions and agreements of the parties so that there is no misunderstanding on these between them; and

- When in the same building as one of the parties, the mediator should allow
  the party to leave the premises first so that there is no post-mediation contact with that client alone.

Case Illustration: Murphy's Law Comes to Telephone Mediation

In a mediation concerning an estate dispute conducted by telephone conference, the following applications of Murphy's law provided some "lessons learned":

1. There were four separate lines, one for the two co-mediators and one for each of the three parties and their advisers. During the exploration stage, one party and their adviser seemed to be silent for an extended period. Upon investigation, it transpired that they had been accidentally disconnected and had missed at least six minutes of the discussions.

2. At one point, a co-mediator made a settlement "suggestion" without any prior identification of who was speaking. One of the parties seized on this proposal, thinking it had been made by one of the other parties. It took some time to convince them that this was not so.

3. Late in the mediation, it became obvious that there were frantic discussions taking place at the venue of one of the parties, and significant slowing down of the process. It transpired that the party had invited four other family members into the room to confer on the impending settlement, and this incident almost caused one of the other parties to abort the mediation.

4. As the co-mediators left their room after the mediation, they were accosted by one of the parties who had been in the same building. The party requested that they witness their faxed copy of the agreement to "give it more weight."

VI. Med-Arb

Med-arb is a dispute resolution process that combines mediation and arbitration. When using med-arb, a selected neutral ("the neutral") first serves as a mediator. If mediation fails to produce an agreement, the neutral then assumes the role of a binding arbitrator. Med-arb is popular in labor, commercial, and family disputes. The advantages touted by admirers of med-arb are its efficiency and finality. Med-arb can be more efficient than a separate mediation followed by a separate arbitration because it minimizes transaction costs. If the mediation fails, a separate arbitrator does not need to be retained, and a separate proceeding does not need to be arranged. Moreover, the neutral will not need to be "re-educated" about the dispute as would a new arbitrator, saving time and expense. Unlike mediation, med-arb provides the parties assured finality because the matter will proceed to binding arbitration if they cannot reach a mediated agreement.

Critics of med-arb argue that the process's efficiency and finality do not outweigh its disadvantages. Parties who know that the mediator may also decide the dispute are likely to be less candid about their true concerns and needs, making integrated agreements less likely. Parties that do share their true concerns and needs during the mediation phase of the process may unwittingly bias the neutral's decision if they assume the role of an arbitrator. For example, a claimant who admits in a private meeting with the "mediator" that he or she would settle a $60,000 claim for $30,000 because he or she is in desperate financial circumstances might provide the "mediator" who subsequently assumes the role of "arbitrator" a rationale to make a less favorable arbitration award, even if the merits of the dispute justify a higher one.

There are variations to med-arb. One variation is to the make the arbitration phase of the process advisory instead of binding. This variation, some argue, makes it more likely that parties will share true concerns and needs because the neutral has no binding authority. Because any arbitration award is non-binding, it also diminishes the cost of bias as a result of information learned in the mediation phase of the proceeding. Another variation is for the neutral to first assume the role of arbitrator and then mediator. This variation is called "arb-med." Although arb-med addresses the possible disadvantage of tainting the arbitration process with a party's interests and willingness to compromise, it also may unnecessarily prolong the process by starting with an adjudicatory process when a more informal and less time-consuming process like mediation might have resolved the dispute.

VII. Other Variations in the Mediation Process

A. Alternating Venues

Occasionally the mediator in consultation with the parties might select different venues for different sessions of a mediation. There are three reasons for doing this. The first is to demonstrate fairness and even-handedness to both parties, for example, by using the premises of each party, or their lawyers, in turn. The second is because a particular need can be served by changing the venue, for example, in an industrial dispute it might assist all concerned to have part of the mediation on the factory floor where the safety-related disputes actually arise, or in a commercial lease dispute it might clarify matters if options are considered at the shopping center where the retailer is a tenant. The third is because it can be more convenient for all concerned to change the venues. An example of an appropriate use of alternating venues is in a major land use mediation which takes place over a long period of time and involves multiple parties and advisers.

B. Variations in Separate Meetings

There are several common variations of the separate meetings mediators may hold during the course of a mediation. In each case, the mediator makes a discretionary judgment as to who should be in attendance, with some degree of consultation with the parties. Two common variations include the *side meeting* and the *party meeting*. Legal advisers normally will be present at separate meetings held with their clients, but on occasion the mediator may meet separately with each party alone without their adviser (side meetings) or with both parties together without their lawyers (party meetings). Where the mediator meets with the parties alone, the parties should be reassured that they will be able to consult their advisers before agreeing to any settlement. If advisors are present, the mediator should obtain the permission of advisors for such a separate meeting.

Another variation includes the mediator meeting with the lawyers without the parties (*adviser meetings*).[7] Sometimes, for example, it is necessary to meet with the advisers to educate them about their appropriate role in mediation or to challenge their obstruction of the mediator. This also provides the lawyers an opportunity to communicate outside of the presence of their client information that the client may need to hear from the mediator to help the client see the issue in a broader, more productive light. The mediator also may meet separately with the experts from both sides. Importantly, mediators should be sensitive about meetings between professionals alone being regarded with suspicion by the parties. Thus, for all separate meetings, the mediator's judgments should always be explained and the parties reassured.

C. Involving Support Persons

The flexibility of the mediation process allows for the involvement and participation of a wide range of "support persons" in mediation. The disputing parties can bring friends, family members, work colleagues, and other relevant individuals to assist them in the process by providing advice and reassurance or to merely make up numbers for negotiation. In some cases, it may be necessary for supporters to remain outside the mediation room because there is insufficient space or because not all parties agree to their presence. In these situations, there might have to be agreed-upon protocols for keeping them informed of developments. In other cases, they may be in the meeting room for all or part of the mediation. Here they might be allowed to participate in all stages of the mediation, have a limited participation, or be silent observers. Mediators are required to exercise some discretionary judgments in relation to these options and to consult with the parties as appropriate. They will want to allow for constructive contributions from "outsiders" but avoid the "cheer squad" syndrome. All support persons should be required to sign a confidentiality agreement before being admitted to the mediation room.

---

7. See Chapter 4—*Managing the Mediation Process*, section III, for more detailed discussion of variations concerning separate meetings.

D. Consultation with Outside Parties
Before Ratifying Agreement

In some cases, parties may need to confer with outside managers, boards, or committees to obtain the formal approval required to make a provisional agreement final. As this approval is an issue for both parties, it can be discussed openly with them in the mediation meeting. With the approval of the parties, the mediator should offer his or her services to contact the ratifying body and convey to them some of the dynamics of the mediation not apparent from the drafted agreement.

VIII. Exercises

1. You are about to represent a client in a mediation that will be conducted on a shuttle basis. Write up a list of precautions you feel should be taken to ensure the following:

   a. The parties do not lose trust in the mediation process when the mediator is absent from them;

   b. The mediator is accurate in conveying messages back and forth; and

   i. The mediator does not abuse the vast power which he or she will derive from being the sole source of communication between the parties.

2. In a co-mediation it is useful if the co-mediators can avoid any personality conflicts between themselves. Write out some of your personality traits and then generate two lists of personality traits, one listing those factors which would tend to make a co-mediator compatible with you, and one which would tend to make them incompatible.

3. You wish to develop a business that conducts mediations over the internet. Investigate and describe ways in which information and communications technology could be used to maximize the advantages of this kind of mediation and to minimize any drawbacks.

ELEVEN

Virtual Mediation

> *However revolutionary it may be, the Internet still hasn't altered the basic law of the human condition: Being nice to your interlocutors is a good way to start any negotiations, particularly, when being hostile is an open invitation for a cyber-fight.*

—EVGENY MOROZOV (WRITER)

I. Introduction to Online Dispute Resolution

Online dispute resolution, commonly referred to as ODR, generally refers to the use of online platforms as a channel of communication and/or the use of technology to assist parties to resolve disputes.[1] ODR grew out of the rise of the internet in the 1990s. It began as a means to efficiently resolve a voluminous number of relatively low-value disputes that stemmed from internet commerce, where parties were in different states or even in different countries. Today, ODR has evolved to include a broad range of processes, from those as simple as using an email exchange to negotiate a contract, to those as sophisticated as using a computer program to aid in the resolution of a dispute.[2] If you have ever resolved a dispute as a buyer or a seller on eBay or similar ecommerce platform, then you have participated in ODR.[3]

---

1. Noam Ebner & Daniel Rainey, *ODR and Mediation, in* ONLINE DISPUTE RESOLUTION: THEORY AND PRACTICE 410 (Daniel Rainey, Ethan Katsh & Mohamed S. Abdel Wahab, eds. 2d ed. 2021).

2. For a comprehensive review of the history and types of ODR, see ONLINE DISPUTE RESOLUTION: THEORY AND PRACTICE (Daniel Rainey, Ethan Katsh & Mohamed S. Abdel Wahab, eds. 2d ed. 2021).

3. For an excellent review of ODR and eCommerce, see AMY J. SCHMITZ & COLIN RULE, THE NEW HANDSHAKE: ONLINE DISPUTE RESOLUTION AND THE FUTURE OF CONSUMER PROTECTION (2017).

II. Virtual Mediation

This chapter will focus on one specific type of ODR: virtual mediation. For our purposes, virtual mediation is a mediation conducted in a videoconferencing environment from beginning to end.[4] This chapter first will explore the advantages and disadvantages of virtual mediation and will then provide best practices in conducting a virtual mediation. Although the use of virtual mediation has a long history, it was used sporadically and in limited circumstances up until the onset of the COVID-19 pandemic in March of 2020. For two years thereafter, virtual mediations were used almost exclusively in many states and countries. Because of the necessity of using virtual mediations during the COVID-19 pandemic and the relatively recent availability, affordability, and quality of videoconferencing, virtual mediations have become prevalent in a post-pandemic world, and all indications are that they will remain a popular forum for mediation. As we will see, virtual mediations offer many advantages over face-to-face mediation but also present disadvantages and challenges that a mediator should consider when deciding which mediation forum to use.

III. The Advantages of Using Virtual Mediation

Virtual mediation offers several advantages over traditional face-to-face mediation. We will discuss the most common advantages, which include the following: (a) *decreased demands on time and money*, (b) *ease of attendance and enhanced participation*, (c) *heightened ability to manage negotiation power among parties*, and (d) *high efficacy*.

A. Decreased Demands on Time and Money

Participants save time, money, and energy by not needing to travel to the mediation location. If attorneys are involved, clients also save money if the attorney charges for her travel time, which most do. In complex, multi-state disputes, for instance, travel and time costs may be significant, as air travel, hotels, ground transportation, and much else may be required. While virtual mediation necessitates access to the internet which, to an extent, involves time and money, these demands are generally far exceeded in face-to-face mediations.

---

4. There are certainly more expansive definitions of virtual mediation, ones that include only written exchanges or some combination of face-to-face and online components. *See generally* EBNER & RAINEY, *supra* note 1, for broader definitions of virtual mediation.

B. Ease of Attendance and Enhanced Participation

One of the greatest benefits of virtual mediation is that the logistics of attending are simplified. The improved ease of attendance has numerous potential benefits, most predominantly that it leads to enhanced participation in the mediation. For example, parties to a virtual mediation are more likely to be open to multiple mediation sessions because of the logistical convenience of participating, and multiple mediation sessions can be particularly fruitful to an effective resolution for more complex mediation matters.

The improved logistics also make it easier for various participants to attend the mediation. For instance, mediators using virtual mediations during the COVID-19 pandemic found that it was far easier to get high-level decision makers, like company executives, to attend a virtual mediation because of the convenience of videoconferencing. This can be particularly important to the outcome of a mediation because absent the participation of ultimate decision makers, mediation participants can only make tentative agreements, which can evaporate once the parties leave the mediation "room." Participation by expert witnesses in mediation are also made easier and less costly because of the ease of participation. Additionally, people who are unable to travel or participate in in-person interactions, such as those who have certain health risks, can attend the mediation without physical exposure to other people.

The increased ease of attending virtual mediations may lead to enhanced participation for several other reasons as well. First, some people simply feel more comfortable and safe discussing difficult issues in the familiar environment of their homes or offices. Second, there is anecdotal evidence that parties are "more active" in the more informal environment of virtual mediations.[5] Lastly, virtual mediations better allow clients to select mediators outside of their geographic area, which, in traditional face-to-face interactions, was only an option for clients of significant financial means. Increasing the pool of available mediators allows parties greater control over cost of and accessibility to mediation.

C. Heightened Ability to Manage Negotiation Power Among Parties

Mediators have an obligation to manage power among the participants so that all parties can participate meaningfully in the mediation process, and virtual mediation can aid in the task.[6] Specifically, the nature of virtual mediation may help diminish

---

5. Dwight Golann, *"I Sometimes Catch Myself Looking Angry or Tired…": The Impact of Mediating by Zoom*, 39 ALTERNATIVES TO THE HIGH COST OF LITIG. 79, 80 (2021) (Professor Golann interviewed 20 mediators from the United States and Britain who collectively mediated over 1,000 disputes during the pandemic about their views on virtual mediation.).

6. *See* Chapter 9—*Managing Power in Mediation*.

some kinds of procedural power imbalances that undermine procedural fairness and party self-determination. For example, just as the lack of physical presence in the same room at the same time makes trust and rapport more difficult to establish, it also makes intimidation more difficult to achieve. The lack of physical presence and the diminished non-verbal cues in virtual mediation mitigate intimidating words and behavior; parties are secure in their homes or offices, and there is no possibility of physical violence in the virtual mediation.

Physical safety is one of our foundational needs, and loud, strident words and aggressive body language can, consciously or unconsciously, create a threat to one's physical safety, which can result in diminished participation by the threatened party. The threat to physical safety and resulting threat to party participation is severely lessened in virtual mediation. This does not mean that if parties become aggressive or overbearing in the virtual mediation that the mediator should not use common interventions that he or she might also use in face-to-face mediations, such as reframing, redirecting, controlling who is speaking, or entering a separate meeting. It simply means that the force of unduly disruptive behavior is less impactful in a virtual setting and thus is easier for a mediator to address.

Because of the mitigating effect of virtual mediation on intimidation and the increased physical safety it provides to participants, virtual mediations may be an option where the parties have a history of violence and face-to-face mediation is unwise. This certainly would apply in family disputes where there is a history or credible evidence of domestic violence. In face-to-face mediations where domestic violence is a factor, mediators need to do safety planning for the mediation.[7] For instance, parties are often scheduled to arrive and leave at separate times to avoid unsupervised contact. In some cases, there are no joint sessions conducted where all parties are present. But the lack of direct, contemporaneous communication between the parties can undermine the effectiveness of the mediations, especially in family disputes where child custody and co-parenting terms and schedules must be negotiated. Thus, virtual mediation provides an option where joint sessions can be conducted safely and with greater mediator control over communication and power dynamics among the participants.

D. High Efficacy

Thrust abruptly to the forefront of the industry by the COVID-19 pandemic, virtual mediation's widespread use is such a relatively new phenomenon that there are as yet no major studies to determine its efficacy in resolving disputes as com-

---

7. Anne Fuchs, *Considering the Needs of Domestic Violence Victims: The Exceptions to Minnesota's Alternative Dispute Resolution Rule 114*, BATTERED WOMEN'S JUSTICE PROJECT (2011) (explaining that careful screening procedures and safeguards for domestic violence should be put in place to protect victims, promote self-determination of both parties, and increase mediation effectiveness).

pared to face-to-face mediations. However, the early anecdotal evidence suggests that virtual mediations are as effective as face-to-face mediations in most circumstances. Eric Galton, a noted mediator with offices in Austin, Texas, reports that in 18-months during the COVID-19 pandemic, his mediation firm performed over 1,000 virtual mediations with settlements that were "the same or slightly higher than in-person mediations."[8] A survey conducted in May 2021 of 500 prominent mediators across the Americas, Europe, Central Asia, Asia Pacific, and Africa also suggests that virtual mediations had no meaningful change in settlement rates.[9] Finally, an EEOC study of its ODR mediation program was "effective across all EEOC charge bases (race, gender, age, etc.)."[10] The study also reported no significant difference in settlement rates.[11]

Given the success that many mediators experienced in conducting virtual mediations during the COVID-19 pandemic, all indications are that many mediators will continue to use virtual mediations on a regular basis even as in-person mediations have become once again practical. This greater use of virtual mediations will undoubtedly produce welcome research into virtual mediation's efficacy. It will be especially important to better understand which types of disputes are more effectively settled via virtual mediation, and which are better settled via traditional face-to-face mediation. Perhaps the research will reveal that in most instances, there is no practical difference in the efficacy between virtual mediations and face-to-face mediations.

IV. The Disadvantages of Using Virtual Mediation

Even with these advantages to virtual mediation, mediators must be aware of its attendant disadvantages so that they are equipped to choose the best path forward. We will discuss the most common disadvantages, which include the following: (a) *diminished non-verbal communication*, (b) *increased difficulty in building trust and rapport*, (c) *risk of technical and practical problems*, (d) *videoconferencing fatigue*, (e) *confidentiality and privacy concerns*, and (f) *perceptions of diminished procedural justice*.

---

8. Eric Galton, *The Remarkable (and Often Very Surprising) Benefits of Virtual Mediation*, MEDIATE.COM (June 25, 2021), https://www.mediate.com/the-remarkable-and-often-very-surprising-benefits-of-virtual-mediation/.

9. James Claxton, *Mediators Like Online Mediation and Other Verifiable Facts*, MEDIATE.COM (June 4, 2021), https://www.mediate.com/mediators-like-online-mediation-and-other-verifiable-facts/ (71 percent of the surveyed mediators reported no change in virtual mediation settlement rates, 10 percent reported settling more cases online, and 10 percent reported settling fewer cases online).

10. Patrick McDermott & Ruth Obar, *Equal Employment Opportunity Commission, Mediators' Perception of Remote Mediation and Comparison to In-Person Mediation* (2022) (the study was based on 139 mediator survey responses.).

11. *Id.*

A. Diminished Non-Verbal Communication

Even with the availability of high-quality videoconferencing, interpersonal communication in virtual mediations is diminished as compared to face-to-face mediations. In any situation, the relative robustness of communication is affected by the number of "channels" of communication available. Channels of communication refer to the modes by which we communicate messages.[12] In face-to-face communication, we use multiple channels to communicate. We use words, tone, inflection, eye contact, proximity, facial expressions, hand gestures, body posture, body movement, and touch. Whether we are conscious of it or not, smell and taste are also potential communication channels.[13] In his now classic study, Albert Mehrabian determined that 93 percent of all communication in face-to-face interactions is non-verbal.[14] Moreover, communication is deemed "rich" where there is an unfettered array of channels available and considered "lean" where some communication channels are unavailable or significantly diminished.[15]

Videoconferencing uses many of the same channels as face-to-face communication, so it can be deemed a relatively rich form of interpersonal communication. Participants can hear the words, the tone of voice, and the vocal inflection of the communication. They can also see facial expressions and, in some cases, see the position of a person's upper torso and hand gestures. But videoconferencing also impairs or completely obscures some important communication channels; there is no real eye contact, the ability to determine body posture is diminished, and there is no ability to touch or to obtain a sense of physical proximity. This diminished non-verbal communication is meaningful in videoconferencing as it can make accurate and comprehensive communication more difficult.

B. Increased Difficulty in Building Trust and Rapport

Trust is crucial to a successful mediation. With the participants' trust, mediators are better positioned to manage the mediation process and assist the parties through various mediator strategies and interventions. For example, a mediator's guidance to promote more productive participant behavior or suggestion to share information will likely be heeded more readily when the participants trust the mediator. With a high degree of trust, mediators can also help parties more effectively see the dispute in a more objective light through reality-testing questions, as parties will likely be more open when they trust the mediator. Parties also benefit from building trust with one another during a mediation; the more the parties trust one another, the more information they will share, and the more flexible they will be.[16] With trust, deals get done.

---

12. JOSEPH A. DeVITO, THE INTERPERSONAL COMMUNICATION BOOK 35 (14th ed. 2015).

13. *Id. See also* Jean R. Sternlight & Jennifer K. Robbennolt, *In-Person or via Technology: Drawing on Psychology to Choose and Design Dispute Resolution Processes*, 71 DePAUL L. REV. 701, 707 (2022).

14. ALBERT MEHRABIAN, NON-VERBAL COMMUNICATION (1972).

15. *Id.*

16. *See* CHRISTOPHER W. MOORE, THE MEDIATION PROCESS 280 (3d ed. 2003).

Rapport is a crucial component of trust. Rapport can be defined as the "mutual positivity and interest that arises through the convergence of non-verbal behavior and interaction,"[17] and it is built primarily through non-verbal communication channels. Unfortunately, as we have seen, several important channels of non-verbal communication are absent or severely compromised in virtual mediation. For example, open and forward-leaning body postures are difficult, if not impossible, to assess in videoconferencing. The diminished non-verbal communication in virtual mediation makes it more difficult to establish rapport both between the mediator and the participants, and among the participants. This makes engendering trust more difficult, thereby decreasing the likely effectiveness of the mediation. Thus, it is important for mediators to consider the ways in which virtual mediation can impact rapport, trust, and ultimately the effectiveness of communications when determining whether to proceed with virtual mediation.

C. Risk of Technical and Practical Problems

Virtual mediations are not without potential logistical problems. Parties must have a reliable internet connection and know how to use the videoconferencing software. Even though videoconferencing is now extremely common, people dropping off the conference, screens freezing, and audio issues are still common occurrences which disrupt the mediation. Participants are also more prone to distractions that are not in the mediator's control, such as barking dogs and children underfoot.[18] Additionally, many people only have internet access through their smartphones. In our experience, mediation participants are typically much less engaged when they are participating from their phones. One reason for this may be because they cannot see all the participants at one time as would be the case on a computer or a tablet and thus often do not know who is speaking. These potential concerns notwithstanding, the logistical benefits of virtual mediations, as discussed above, are considerable and make this mode of communication highly desirable to many mediators and clients alike.

D. Videoconferencing Fatigue

Both scientific and anecdotal evidence suggest that participants fatigue more quickly in virtual mediations than in face-to-face mediations—a phenomenon sometimes referred to as "Zoom fatigue," in reference to the popular videoconferencing software.[19] One theory for fatiguing more quickly in virtual mediations is that

---

17. AIMEE L. DROLET & MICHAEL W. MORRIS, *Rapport in Conflict Resolution: Accounting for How Face-to-Face Contact Fosters Mutual Cooperation in Mixed-Motive Conflicts*, 36 J. EXP. SOC. PSYCHOL. 26, 27 (2000).

18. *See* Golann, *supra* note 5, at 79, where mediators report that being introduced to pets and children may make for a welcome distraction and can build a human connection.

19. Julia Sklar, *"Zoom Fatigue" Is Taxing the Brain. Here's Why that Happens*, NAT'L GEOGRAPHIC (Apr. 24, 2020), https://www.nationalgeographic.com/science/article/coronavirus-zoom-fatigue-is-taxing-the-brain-here-is-why-that-happens.

videoconferencing cuts off or diminishes non-verbal communication channels to such an extent that participants need to put forth more intellectual effort to process the spoken word.[20] Another possible source of fatigue is the added effort that participants need to expend in deciding where to focus their attention on the screen.[21] In videoconferencing, it is often difficult to discern who is talking to whom, which impedes the natural eye-wandering that usually occurs seamlessly in face-to-face mediations. There is also the added distraction of seeing oneself on the screen! Both participant and mediator fatigue are important to monitor in mediations because, when fatigued, people are less patient, make less objective decisions, and are more emotional—all of which could undermine the mediation.

E. Confidentiality and Privacy Concerns

Virtual mediations present confidentiality and privacy concerns that are not present in face-to-face mediations. Of course, the mediator must assure that the videoconferencing software is private and secure. However, even beyond those assurances, it is relatively easy for one or more of the parties to secretly record the mediation. Additionally, because video cameras have a limited view, there may be people—whose presence other participants are unaware of—who are attending the mediation or coaching one of the parties. Thus, mediators will need to take additional precautions to assure the confidentiality of the mediation, precautions we will provide later in this chapter.

F. Perceptions of Diminished Procedural Justice

Procedural justice refers to the parties' sense that they are being heard in a fair process.[22] Procedural justice is just as important in mediation as it is in a court adjudication. There is some empirical evidence, however, that videoconferencing can diminish a participant's feeling of being fully part of the proceeding. For example, one study found that prisoners in court proceedings via videoconferencing felt "disempowered" and "disconnected."[23] Not being physically in the courtroom led to some prisoners disassociating from the process. However, it is important to note that a robust study by the Equal Employment Opportunity Commission of its Online Dispute Resolution (ODR) Mediation Program found that participants were overwhelmingly satisfied with the procedural fairness. In a survey conducted of both charging parties and employers in employment discrimination matters, 92 percent of charging parties and 98 percent of employers "view the overall ODR process as fair."[24] Therefore, it may be important for a mediator to place extra emphasis on

---

20. *Id.*

21. Sternlight & Robbennolt, *supra* note 12, at 718.

22. *Id.* at 39.

23. *Id.* at 40.

24. Patrick McDermott & Ruth Obar, Equal Employment Opportunity Commission, *Mediation Participants' Experience in Online Mediation and Comparison to In-Person Mediation* (2022) (the study was based on 1,234 participant survey responses).

ensuring that parties to a virtual mediation feel empowered and are connected to the process, as this will help to increase their self-determination and the overall procedural fairness of the mediation.

Table 11-1: Major Pros and Cons of Virtual Mediation

Below is a table discussing the above-mentioned pros and cons of virtual mediation along with several other related or more minor considerations not fully discussed above.

Pros	Cons
Participants often find it more comfortable participating from their home or office.	Loss of richness from communication because of diminished capacity to observe non-verbal communication, like body posture.
Loss in formality: Anecdotal evidence suggest that clients are more active because of the less intimidating environment.	Loss in formality: Anecdotal evidence suggests that clients take the proceedings less seriously because of the more causal environment.
Savings of time, energy, and cost from no traveling.	Inability to make direct eye contact.
Ability to have the simultaneous presence of many parties without the hindrance of needing personal attendance at a specific place and time.	Concerns that other participants are recording the mediation or being coached by someone unknown to the other participants.
Ease of moving between separate sessions among parties.	People that are unsure about technology may have additional stress.
Initial concerns about confidentiality have been reduced as neutrals and participants have learned to put safeguards in place that ameliorate or eliminate many potential issues.	Evidence suggest that mediation participants fatigue more quickly in videoconferencing ("Zoom fatigue").
Participants may be more amenable to schedule additional mediation sessions, when appropriate, because of the ease of videoconferencing.	The diminishment of non-verbal communication and lack of physical proximity may make it difficult to build trust.

Continued

Continued

Encourages more participants, especially high-ranking executives in business mediations and expert witnesses in complex mediations.	Needing to have backup forms of communication if the internet goes out. Potentially having to cancel if the internet is not working.
The internet is also a neutral platform for negotiation because, unlike an attorney's office or other settings, neither party controls it, which reduces the potential for power imbalances.	The issue of confidentiality and data protection must be considered when selecting the software for online mediation.
The borderless nature of the internet resolves issues raised by international parties.	Many mediators cite the severely restricted transmission or the complete lack of non-verbal signals as the greatest challenge.
The intervention of the mediator will also be perceived as less in online mediation than in face-to-face mediation.	Losing connection or waiting for parties to join or re-join the "room" can lead to a loss of momentum during the negotiation process.
Disruptions from pets and children may help to humanize the participants and build connection.	Participants may be more easily distracted by interruptions, as from pets and children.

V. Best Practices in Conducting Virtual Mediation

Below are suggestions for arranging and performing virtual mediations. While some of these suggestions are just good videoconferencing protocol, most are designed specifically for virtual mediation and thus should be incorporated into your mediation agreement.

A. General Considerations

In addition to researching best practices in videoconferencing, such as how to best frame your image, obtain good lighting, and arrange an appropriate background, below are several other important general considerations for virtual mediation:

1. Ensure all participants have reliable access to the internet.

2. Know the technology well and how to troubleshoot common issues.

3. Agree in advance on what process will be used if a participant unexpectedly drops off the conference. For example, the participants will agree to immediately contact the mediator by text to apprise him of the issue. The mediator will agree to do the same if experiencing technical issues.

4. Agree in advance about what will happen if the technical issues cannot be resolved. For instance, the parties will determine whether to continue through another medium, like telephone, or will instead reschedule the mediation.

5. Have parties share relevant documents in advance of the mediation so there is no unnecessary delay in the discussion while documents are shared and reviewed.

6. Take breaks more frequently than you would in a face-to-face mediation to manage fatigue.

7. Encourage parties to use headphones if they have access to them because it cuts down on ambient noise.

8. Encourage parties to participate from their own computer instead of having multiple parties using the same computer because this necessitates placing the camera further away, which makes the illusion of "eye-contact" more difficult.

9. Discourage participants from using more than one computer in the same room for the mediation because it can cause sound problems.

10. Instruct parties to keep an eye on their computers when you are in a separate meeting with another party, so they know when it's their turn for a separate session or when the joint session is resuming.

B. Use of Videoconferencing Platform Features

It is important before the virtual mediation begins that the mediator establishes what videoconferencing features may be used and how to use them. The mediator can create these guidelines based on her experience, or the mediator and parties can decide on these conventions as a group. Either way, it is best practice to agree on these guidelines as soon as practicable. In doing so, the following should be considered:

1. Whether or not to use the chat function and who can use it. A chat function allows parties to write messages to the whole group or to individual participants privately. Many mediators turn off the chat function because they

find it distracting. Some limit the chat function so that the participants can only communicate with the mediator. Some mediators find the ability to message attorneys privately to be a helpful communication channel when the mediator wishes to communicate with the lawyer without the client knowing.

2. Decide if and when the video feed can be turned off. Sometimes participants will need to turn off their live video feed because of connectivity issues or to attend to some issue on their end. However, it can be distractive if participants turn off a video feed to disengage from the process.

3. Decide how a participant indicates that they wish to speak. For example, participants can indicate that they wish to speak by electronically raising their hand through an icon, by raising their real hand, or by just speaking up.

4. Decide whether participants should be muted when not speaking.

5. Decide if pop-up icons or electronic reactions can be used.

6. Decide who will have the ability to share their screen or documents.

C. Protect Confidentiality

As discussed elsewhere in this book,[25] confidentiality is a crucial component of an ethical, lawful, and effective mediation. Thus, protecting confidentiality is an important consideration for all aspects of mediation. However, virtual mediation provides for unique confidentiality hurdles, as discussed earlier in this chapter, such as the risk of unknown outside parties attending the mediation or covert recording of the mediation. Therefore, mediators should consider the following practices to help protect confidentiality in virtual mediations:

1. Have parties agree in advance that they will participate in the mediation from a private location.

2. Have parties agree that they will not record the mediation.

3. Have parties agree that all participants can be seen on the video, or at least are known to the other participants if they are off screen.

4. Have parties agree on no virtual backgrounds. This bolsters assurance that participants are participating in the mediation from a private location.

---

25. *See* Chapter 4—*Managing the Mediation Process*, section II A 3 (d)(v).

VI. Exercises

1. Interview three mediators who mediate via videoconferencing to learn about the virtual mediation rules they usually establish and how they conduct their mediations.

2. Try at least three videoconferencing platforms to see which work best for you.

3. Conduct a simulated mediation using a videoconferencing platform and obtain feedback about the experience from participants.

TWELVE

Use of Evaluation in Mediation

How little do they see what really is, who frame their hasty judgment upon that which seems.

—DANIEL WEBSTER (LAWYER AND U.S. SENATOR)

I. Introduction

Although our book primarily promotes and explores a facilitative mediation model, we believe it is important to address evaluative mediation in greater depth because of its widespread use and potential utility. A mediator utilizing a facilitative approach "assist[s] disputing parties in making their own decisions and evaluating their own situations."[1] Conversely, a mediator using an evaluative approach "guides and advises the parties on the basis of his or her expertise with a view to reaching a settlement that accords with their legal rights and obligations, industry norms, or other objective standards."[2] In other words, without providing his or her own substantive input on the matter, a facilitative mediator strategically *supports* the mediation in a way that helps empower parties to make decisions on their own. In contrast, an evaluative mediator also employs his or her substantive expertise and knowledge to provide the parties with an *evaluation* of the issues and possible adjudicatory outcomes, which can help the parties make more informed and objective decisions. Evaluative mediation is controversial among mediators because its directive nature can undermine party self-determination in important ways.[3] However, evaluative mediation is permitted in nearly all U.S. jurisdictions and can be an effective tool if used judiciously, appropriately, and wisely.

Evaluative mediation is widely used, especially in mediations conducted by lawyers. Indeed, one study found that legal representatives overwhelmingly preferred evaluative mediation when mediating litigated matters.[4] One lawyer's comment

---

1. Lela Love, *Top Ten Reasons Why Mediators Should Not Evaluate*, 24 FLA. ST. U. L. REV. 937, 939 (1997).

2. Chapter 1—*Introduction to Learning Mediation Skills and Techniques*, section V A 3.

3. *See* Murray S. Levin, *The Propriety of Evaluative Mediation: Concerns About the Nature and Quality of an Evaluative Opinion*, 16 OHIO ST J. ON DISP. RESOL. 267 (2001); *see also* Kimberlee K. Kovach & Lela P. Love, *"Evaluative" Mediation Is an Oxymoron*, 14 ALTERNATIVES TO THE HIGH COST OF LITIG. 31 (1996).

4. TAMARA RELIS, PERCEPTIONS IN LITIGATION AND MEDIATION 207–10 (2009).

from the study is representative of many lawyers: "I much prefer an evaluative approach.... Each side can make their pitch and have some feedback from somebody with expertise and skill in the area...and [who] can facilitate the thinking through the positions and the risks...."[5] Although some mediators use an exclusively facilitative approach and some use an exclusively evaluative approach, many mediators use aspects of both approaches, even when they may not have been fully conscious of using more evaluative tactics.[6] The goal of this chapter is to explain the potential benefits and dangers of evaluative mediation and to provide guidance on the best practices as to when and how to use it effectively.

II. Benefits of Evaluative Mediation

On January 20, 1977, his first day in office, President Jimmy Carter surprised many when he announced that peace in the Middle East was his top priority. This was surprising because most of the people who had experience with Middle East peace negotiations, including Henry Kissinger, Presidents Nixon's and Ford's Secretary of State, had advised Carter against getting involved because of the likelihood it would result in failure and political harm to his presidency. President Carter's focus on Middle East peace was also surprising because his previous post as Governor of Georgia had ill-prepared him for international negotiation on such a grand scale. Naysayers notwithstanding, President Carter invited Egyptian President, Anwar Sadat, and Israeli Prime Minister, Menachem Begin, to Camp David to try to bring peace to the Middle East. Beginning on September 17, 1978, the meeting, entitled "Framework for Peace in the Middle East," was centered on bringing an end to the hostilities between Egypt and Israel, who shared a disputed border and had fought three wars in the preceding thirty years.

Over the first three days of the summit, President Carter took on a facilitative approach with the parties.[7] However, by day four it was clear that this approach was yielding no meaningful progress. Accordingly, on day five President Carter shifted to a more evaluative approach by creating an American proposal for peace between the two warring countries. The President's proposition focused the parties' negotiations over the next eight days at Camp David, and it ultimately formed the basis of a peace treaty between Israel and Egypt that has lasted over 50 years. Although this is one of the most famous uses of evaluative mediation, it is a mediation model whose benefits help to resolve thousands of disputes each day and offers several benefits to mediating parties.

---

5. *Id.* at 209.
6. *Id.* at 198.
7. For an excellent account of the Camp David negotiations between Israel and Egypt, see LAWRENCE WRIGHT, THIRTEEN DAYS IN SEPTEMBER: CARTER, BEGIN, AND SADAT AT CAMP DAVID (2014).

Beyond helping to resolve major international disputes, evaluative mediation can provide several benefits for more commonplace conflicts. Below are the primary benefits of providing evaluations that a mediator can keep in mind when strategizing a mediation.

A. Provides Parties With a Better Understanding of the Issue(s)

One of the chief benefits of evaluative mediation, as mentioned above, is that the mediator engages his expertise to conduct an evaluation of the substantive issues involved in the mediation. Through his evaluation, the mediator might also provide a prediction of how a court may view a dispute, which may provide helpful information and insight to the parties of which they may not have otherwise been aware. With this input from the mediator, parties may be more equipped to make an informed decision regarding whether and how to resolve the issues in mediation.

B. Provides Objective Insight

While a represented party may be able to obtain an evaluation of the substantive issues of the mediation without the help of the mediator, their evaluation is at risk of being overly subjective. Indeed, because parties and their advocates are concerned with the perceived "success" of their side, they often fall into common cognitive traps that can make objective assessment of the dispute difficult. For example, parties will often place too great of an emphasis on law or facts that bolster their version of the dispute, while unduly deemphasizing or ignoring law or facts that undermine it. Such subjectivity imposes a significant bias in their evaluation of the relative merits of the problem that may create a formidable obstacle to resolution.

The primary quality that a mediator brings to an evaluative mediation, therefore, is his or her objectivity. While no mediator is truly and completely objective, mediators are arguably *more* objective than the parties. This objectivity permits a mediator to analyze and reflect upon the matter at issue more clearly. This clarity positions the mediator to more accurately predict how a judge or jury may assess the dispute or some important aspect of the dispute. An evaluative mediator, therefore, may be able to provide the parties with a more objective and thus realistic understanding of the matter and its probable adjudicatory outcome, which can be helpful in eroding unrealistic party views that can hinder negotiations.

C. Especially Beneficial for Unrepresented Parties

A mediator's evaluation is most beneficial for educational purposes when one or all parties are self-represented and may know very little about their legal rights or the legal system. The mediator's evaluation, by necessity, parses out the respective rights and obligations of the parties under the law or other relevant norms. This makes it less likely that self-represented litigants will be taken advantage of in the mediation. For example, in a tenant eviction matter, a knowledgeable evaluative mediator would assess the legality of the eviction, considering both appropriate notice and process as well as any colorable substantive defenses the tenant might possess. Absent such an evaluation, many self-represented tenants would be unaware of potential defenses to their eviction. Considering its educational value, evaluative mediation can thus also be a helpful tool in managing negotiating power between represented and unrepresented parties.

D. May Provide a More Cathartic Experience

The evaluative mediation model emphasizes past behaviors of the parties and how those behaviors should be assessed under the law or some other norm. The backward-looking focus of an evaluative mediation enables parties to spend more time explaining their "stories" or version of events, unlike an interest-based facilitative mediation where the mediator steers parties away from unnecessary discussions of past events and assignment of blame to instead focus on future agreements. Evaluative mediations thus may allow parties an important and needed opportunity to release emotions and thoughts, providing them a cathartic and symbolic "day in court." However, it is important for a mediator to keep in mind that what may be a cathartic experience for one party may be frustrating or upsetting to the other. Thus, an evaluative mediator must remain attentive and mindful because a party's emphasis on blame and past behavior over interests and their future can mire the mediation in the past and undermine negotiations.

III. Dangers of Evaluative Mediation

As we embark on an exploration of the potential dangers of using evaluations in mediation, it is first useful to distinguish between mediator impartiality and mediator neutrality. Although there are no definitive definitions of these terms, and although they are often used interchangeably, it is useful for our purposes in this chapter to assign different meanings for them. Most mediation codes state that a mediator must be "impartial." Impartiality is usually defined as being free from bias. For example, the Model Standards define impartiality as being free from "favoritism, bias, [and] prejudice."[8] Mediator neutrality, on the other hand, is often described as a mediator not providing an opinion on matters at issue in the mediation.[9] Thus, an evaluative mediator might be impartial in that he or she is unbiased, but the mediator would not be neutral once he or she provides an opinion in the dispute that

---

8. MODEL STANDARDS OF CONDUCT FOR MEDIATORS STD. II (2005).

9. *See* Joseph B. Stulberg, *Must a Mediator Be Neutral? You'd Better Believe It!*, 95 MARQ. L. REV. 829 (2012).

favors one party over another. With these definitions in mind, we will now investi-gate dangers that evaluative mediation may pose to the success of a mediation.

A. Risk of the Mediator Being Perceived as Having Lost Neutrality

Because the nature of evaluative mediation involves the mediator's offering insight into the strengths, weaknesses, and, in some instances, the likely adjudica-tory outcome of the substantive issues of the mediation, there is a danger that a party may perceive the mediator as having lost neutrality. For instance, once Party A perceives the mediator as favoring Party B's view on an issue important to the mediation, there is a significant risk of the mediator losing Party A's trust. It is often rightly stated that the "coin of the realm" for mediators is trust. Once trust is under-mined or lost, a mediator's efficacy is greatly diminished. The mediator's ability to influence participant behaviors, have parties follow a productive problem-solving process, share information, and much else may be stymied because he or she is no longer seen as neutral and, consequently, is viewed as untrustworthy. Hence, an evaluative mediator must not only *be* impartial as is required by most mediation codes but must also be cognizant of the potential loss of neutrality so as not to lose the participants' trust.

B. May Discourage Interest-Based Problem Solving

Offering an evaluation may also discourage interest-based problem solving by the parties. Once a mediator offers an opinion about rights or obligations in the media-tion, one of the parties may feel vindicated and refuse to discuss any other settlement options that do not incorporate the mediator's opinion, even where the party might once have been receptive to more creative, interest-based solutions. For example, in an employment discrimination matter where the plaintiff's employment was allegedly illegally terminated, the plaintiff might have initially been receptive to dis-cussing the possibility of the defendant re-hiring the plaintiff as part of a settlement. But a mediator's prediction of a potentially large monetary award may completely shut this line of discussion down. It can also have the effect of making the parties less flexible in their negotiations because the "objective" mediator has provided a predic-tion supporting their demand.

C. Threatens Party Self-Determination

Among the most concerning potential dangers of evaluative mediation, however, is that it threatens party self-determination, especially when one or more parties are self-represented. Mediators are often seen by parties as authority figures in the medi-ation process. This is, in part, what gives mediators their influence and power. Because of this authority, mediator opinions can have undue influence on parties so that their goals and needs are ignored in favor of a mediator's view of the matter. In some cases, mediator opinions might be expressed so forcefully that they cross the line from influence into coercion, which, of course, is unethical. The Model Standards explain that "party self-determination is at the heart of the mediation process. A mediator shall conduct a mediation based on the principle of party self-determination. Self-determination is the act of coming to a voluntary, uncoerced decision in which each party makes free and informed choices as to process and outcome."[10] Parties that come up with their own solutions to problems tend to be more satisfied with the agreement and the mediation process. For example, in a study of mediation strategies conducted of same day mediations in Maryland District Court, it was found that a mediator offering "opinions and solutions" was "*negatively* associated with participants' report[ing] that the outcome was working, [that] they were satisfied with the outcome, [that] they would recommend ADR...."[11]

D. Evaluations Can Be Flawed

Last, but not least, is the significant danger that mediators may be wrong or unconsciously biased in their evaluations. As discussed above, it is usually the case that mediators will be more "objective" in their evaluation of an important issue in the matter than the parties or even their lawyers. This can have value where the assessment of the relative merits of the matter has been the primary obstacle to settlement. Nevertheless, experts, even when presented with identical information, can vary widely in their opinions. This makes expert opinions of limited value. An excellent demonstration of the limited value and subjective nature of expert evaluation can be found in the Douglas Rosenthal study of the expert assessment of personal injury cases.[12]

Rosenthal chose sixty-one personal injury matters that had been settled and then asked four experienced personal injury lawyers and one experienced insurance claims adjuster to review the actual case files and assess the cases' settlement value. Thus, the study produced six values per case: the actual settlement amount and five assessments of the value by experts. The degree of variability among the expert assessors was dramatic. In one case, which was typical of the degree of variability, the five assessors valued the case as follows: $11,600, $7,500, $12,500, $20,000, $15,000, and $3,000, respectively. The case settled for $5,000. Given this outcome, it would not be outrageous to suggest that had the expert who valued the case at $20,000 been a mediator in this dispute, a proposed settlement of $5,000 would be deemed self-evidently "unfair." Yet, to the other expert who valued the case at $3,000, the $5,000 settlement looks like a good deal. In another case the experts varied considerably in

10. MODEL STANDARDS OF CONDUCT FOR MEDIATORS STD. I (2005).

11. Maryland Administrative Office of the Courts, *What Works in District Court Day of Trial Mediation: Effectiveness of Various Mediation Strategies on Short- and Long- Term Outcomes*, 7 (Jan. 2016) https://mdcourts.gov/sites/default/files/import/courtoperations/pdfs/districtcourt-strategiesfullreport.pdf.

12. DOUGLAS ROSENTHAL, LAWYER AND CLIENT: WHO'S IN CHARGE? 204–05 (1974).

their valuation, with values spanning from \$2,000 to \$30,000, where the actual settlement was \$5,250. This case had a coefficient of variability of 0.8950, which means that there was nearly a 90 percent variation from the mean.[13] The Rosenthal study demonstrates, as do similar studies, the significant subjectivity inherent in evaluative mediation and why propping up mediators as arbiters of substantive fairness of mediated agreements is potentially problematic.

Table 12-1: The Benefits and Potential Dangers of Evaluative Mediation

Below is a table discussing the above-mentioned pros and cons of evaluative mediation.

Pros	Cons
Evaluative mediators can apply their knowledge and expertise to provide the parties with a better understanding of the substantive issues of the mediation.	There is risk that a mediator's evaluation may be flawed, which may lead parties to rely and act upon inaccurate information.
Evaluative mediators can supply more objective insight, which may provide parties with a more realistic understanding of the pros, cons, and likely adjudicatory outcome of the matter.	Evaluative mediation may discourage interest-based problem solving because the needs and interests of parties may be put aside or disregarded in response to the mediator's evaluation.
Evaluative mediation is especially beneficial for unrepresented parties who may have less knowledge or understanding of the substantive issues of the mediation and the likely adjudicatory outcomes.	Parties may rely too heavily on the mediator's evaluation, which increases risk to party self-determination.
Evaluative mediation can be used as a tool to manage the negotiating power between represented and unrepresented parties.	Due to the nature of providing opinions, even if objective, there is a substantial risk that the mediator may be perceived as having lost his or her neutrality if he or she indicates favor for one party's side or view over the other, and this may lead to distrust and less effective negotiations.

Continued

13. *Id.*

Continued

Evaluative mediation may provide a more cathartic experience by allowing parties to express their point of view and feelings about past events, making them feel as if they got their "day in court."

Allowing parties to relive the past carries the risk of frustrating or upsetting the parties and stagnating cooperation. Over-emphasizing blame and past behavior over interests and the parties' future may mire the mediation in the past and undermining negotiations.

IV. Recommendations for Using Evaluative Mediation

Although the use of evaluative mediation remains controversial in some mediation circles, we believe that the larger issues are that it is commonly performed unnecessarily and poorly. In many evaluative mediations that occur every day around the United States, evaluative mediators begin evaluating, analyzing, and suggesting solutions shortly after the parties' initial statements, and they persist in making evaluations throughout the mediation. In this section, we are going to explore best practices in evaluative mediation that are designed to mitigate the potential dangers of using such a directive strategy.

A. Familiarize Yourself with Jurisdictional Variations

A threshold question that a mediator contemplating using an evaluative mediation strategy must answer is whether the type of evaluation he or she wishes to employ is permitted in the jurisdiction. For example, in California, evaluative mediation is expressly permitted. Under California law, "a mediator may provide information or opinions that he or she is qualified by training or experience to provide," as long as the mediator can do so impartially and without undermining party self-determination.[14] Maryland, on the other hand, prohibits evaluative mediation. Here is the relevant Maryland rule:

> Mediation means a process in which the parties work with one or more impartial mediators who, without providing legal advice, assist the parties in reaching their own voluntary agreement for the resolution of all or part of a dispute…[15] While acting as a mediator, the mediator does not engage in any other ADR process and does not recommend the terms of an agreement.[16]

---

14. CAL. RULES OF CT. R. 3.857(d).
15. MD. RULES R. 17-102(g).
16. MD. RULE R. 17-103.

Florida is another jurisdiction that limits the type of evaluation a mediator may offer. While a mediator may discuss possible court outcomes and the relative merits of the arguments on each side, he or she cannot offer a prediction of how a court would likely rule on the matter. Here is the relevant Florida provision:

> A mediator shall not offer a personal or professional opinion intended to coerce the parties, unduly influence the parties, decide the dispute, or direct a resolution of any issue. Consistent with standards of impartiality and preserving party self-determination, however, a mediator may point out possible outcomes of the case and discuss the merits of a claim or defense. *A mediator shall not offer a personal or professional opinion as to how the court in which the case has been filed will resolve the dispute.*[17]

Most U.S. jurisdictions either expressly or impliedly permit evaluations of all kinds in mediation. That said, mediation rules are dynamic, and mediators must keep apprised of the laws and rules that govern mediation in the jurisdiction in which they are operating.

B. Use Best Practices in Evaluative Mediation

Despite the ubiquity of evaluative mediation, there is relatively little scholarly writing or science-based knowledge on how to perform it well. This stands in stark contrast to the vast array of scholarly material on the tools, strategies, and best practices in the use of facilitative mediation. Thus, we are fortunate that Professors Dwight Golann and Marjorie Corman Aaron have focused their considerable talents to better understand how evaluative mediation can be used in ways that take advantage of its potential benefits and minimize its potential dangers. Below are best practices in evaluative mediation that are, in substantial part, based on their work.[18] The best practices are as follows: (1) *choose to evaluate judiciously*, (2) *have relevant expertise*, (3) *ask permission to evaluate*, (4) *emphasize that it is only your opinion*, (5) *evaluate as narrowly as practicable*, (6) *delay an evaluation as long as possible*, and (7) *provide evaluations to parties privately*.

1. CHOOSE TO EVALUATE JUDICIOUSLY

Once you have determined that your jurisdiction permits evaluations in mediation, the next step is to determine if you should use it. Even when using these recommended best practices, evaluative mediation is still an inherently risky strategy because of the potential dangers reviewed above. Thus, a mediator should be judicious in his or her use of evaluative mediation; if you believe that it is likely the parties can make good decisions about the matter without an evaluation, you should

---

17. FLA. RULES OF MED. R. 10.370(c) (emphasis supplied).
18. *See* Dwight Golann & Marjorie Corman Aaron, *Using Evaluations in Mediation*, 52 DISP. RESOL. J. 26 (1997).

not use it. Professor Golann analogizes evaluative mediation to surgery. "Most people," Golann explains, "would not choose a doctor whose first response to every illness was to bring out a scalpel. At the same time, few would feel comfortable with a physician who refused to perform surgery regardless of the need."[19]

To determine if an evaluation is necessary, a mediator should begin by reviewing the nature of the conflict at issue. Before providing an evaluation, a mediator should assess what obstacles are in the way of resolving the problem(s) between the parties. For instance, differing views between the parties on the interpretation of law or other relevant data are common mediation obstacles that suggest an evaluation may be helpful to resolving the dispute. Conversely, if resolution has been stymied because of miscommunication or an asymmetry of relevant information that could be remedied through the sharing of information among the parties, an evaluation is likely not called for.[20] Accordingly, treat evaluation as a potentially helpful strategy only when less directive strategies have failed or are deemed likely to be ineffective because of the nature of the conflict.

2. HAVE RELEVANT EXPERTISE

You must have relevant expertise to evaluate. Like California, many jurisdictions expressly require that the mediator be a subject matter expert in the topic at issue as a prerequisite to offering an evaluation. Thus, you should know what you are talking about before you render any kind of evaluation. It is insufficient that you have a general knowledge of the area; you should have specific expertise in the matter at issue. For example, if you are mediating a litigated case over an alleged patent infringement, you should have intimate, current knowledge of patent infringement law. It would not be enough if you were a lawyer who took a Patent Law course in law school five years ago. If you were a psychologist inclined to offer an opinion in a child custody matter, you should have a specialty in child psychology and not general psychology. Your evaluations, whether followed or not, will have significant impact on the mediation, so you should make them responsibly by knowing the subject matter well.

3. ASK PERMISSION TO EVALUATE

Even where the jurisdiction permits evaluations and you deem an evaluation beneficial to assist in resolving the conflict, you should ask permission to perform the evaluation. In asking this permission, you should also explain any significant risks in undermining the mediation process that performing the evaluation might involve, just like a physician would explain risks when advising about an invasive medical procedure. Like a physician, you need not explain every possible risk, but you should explain those risks that are most likely to materialize. For example, in a divorce

---

19. Dwight Golann, Mediating Legal Disputes 145–46 (2009).

20. For an excellent analysis of the causes of conflict, see the "Circle of Conflict" chart in Christopher W. Moore's classic mediation text The Mediation Process 60–61 (2d ed. 1996).

mediation you might say, "I think it would be helpful if I provided a prediction whether a court in this jurisdiction would rule that this asset would be included in marital property because it seems to be a significant obstacle to resolving this matter. However, before I proceed to give you my opinion—and it is just an opinion—I want you to be aware that evaluations like this sometimes can make the parties less flexible in the negotiation process moving forward, which might make it less likely that we will resolve this matter. That said, I think an evaluation will help and is worth that risk. Can I proceed in providing my opinion?" This kind of request for permission and explanation of risks assures that the parties can provide informed consent when mediators are inclined to use this riskier mediation strategy.

4. EMPHASIZE THAT IT IS ONLY YOUR OPINION

As suggested in the requesting permission example above, mediators should emphasize that the evaluation is only an opinion. Too often, mediators present evaluations as fact or unimpeachable truth. This type of emphatic evaluation can be at worst tantamount to coercion or at best undermine party self-determination. Sophisticated mediators appreciate that resolving conflicts, legal or otherwise, is a human endeavor and therefore imperfect and unpredictable. All one needs to do is to review the data from the Rosenthal experiments detailed above to appreciate that predictions are no more than educated guesses that will vary considerably depending on the person making the prediction.

Even though a court adjudication is unpredictable, evaluations can still be helpful and valued. Indeed, there is empirical evidence to support that lawyers and clients alike value mediator opinions. In an extensive study on the perceptions of mediation participants, Dr. Tamara Relis found that "most legal actors preferred evaluative, rights-based mediators to facilitative, interest-based mediators."[21] This preference, in part, is because mediators are more objective than the parties or their representatives because they do not have a stake in the outcome. Therefore, mediators are less likely to fall prey to common decision errors in the evaluation of the case, such as minimizing the impact of facts or law that undermine the merits or arguments of one party over the other. One defense lawyer-participant in Dr. Relis's study stated, "In these actions...it is key to have some evaluation from someone considered authoritative...for plaintiffs and/or their lawyers...to hear from someone other than me...[that] they're on the wrong track [or have]...misconstrued evidence."[22]

5. EVALUATE AS NARROWLY AS PRACTICABLE

A way to minimize the chance of undermining party self-determination is for mediators to evaluate as narrowly as practicable. Too often evaluative mediators make predictions regarding how a court, tribunal, or other ultimate authority would

---

21. RELIS, *supra* note 4, at 207.
22. *Id.* at 209.

decide the dispute. This kind of global assessment increases the chance of realizing many of the dangers associated with evaluative mediation explored above. Instead, if possible, a mediator should focus his evaluation on a more discrete issue in the mediation that appears to be a key obstacle in the dispute.

In a divorce mediation, for example, a key obstacle could be division of a specific asset; in a personal injury mediation, it could be a particularly contentious aspect of damages; or, in an employment discrimination matter, it could be the likely amount the court would award in future compensation. By providing evaluation on these more discrete but important issues, the mediator may help to bring the parties closer to agreement; indeed, by narrowing the scope on the issues, the mediator can use more facilitative tools and tactics to resolve a dispute. If narrowly evaluating fails to break negotiation impasse, the mediator can then become progressively more expansive in his evaluation if he or she thinks it appropriate.

6. DELAY AN EVALUATION AS LONG AS POSSIBLE

Offering an evaluation, even one focused on a narrow issue, should be delayed as long as practical in the mediation. As explained in the danger section above, an earlier evaluation is likely to make parties less flexible and undermine interest-based problem solving. In contrast, delaying the evaluation promotes a robust exchange of information, exploration of party interests, and a fuller understanding of the parties' arguments. This provides time for more facilitative—and less risky—mediator tools and strategies to work their magic. Later evaluations tend also to be more informed because the parties have exchanged more information.

7. PROVIDE EVALUATIONS TO PARTIES PRIVATELY

Generally, evaluations should be offered privately in separate meetings to minimize the chance of the mediator being seen as biased. Inevitably, parties will perceive evaluations as favoring one party over another. When evaluations are offered when all parties are present, there is a greater likelihood that one party will believe that the mediator is taking sides, no matter how objectively the mediator explains the evaluation. Once the mediator has lost the trust of a party, he or she will have a more difficult time managing the mediation in a productive direction. The same evaluation, if given privately to each party, is much more likely to be perceived as objective rather than biased.

V. Conclusion

Its widespread use notwithstanding, especially among lawyer-mediators, evaluative mediation remains a controversial mediation strategy among many mediators. Yet, as we saw in President Carter's Camp David mediation between Israel and Egypt, some disputes appear resilient to more facilitative mediation tools and tactics. Thus, there are mediation scholars who believe that evaluative mediation "is a legitimate weapon in the mediator's arsenal."[23] If you deem evaluative mediation a valid strategy, be mindful that it can be "either effective or explosive depending on how and when it is used."[24] Thus, when using evaluations in mediation, we encourage mediators to follow the best practices explored in this chapter.

VI. Exercises

1. Conduct a simulated mediation first using an evaluative mediation style, and then, using different parties, conduct it using a facilitative style. Compare the two experiences.

2. Observe real mediations with a mediator using an evaluative mediation style, and then observe a mediation where the mediator uses a facilitative style.

3. Interview parties to a mediation who have participated in an evaluative mediation and parties who have participated in a facilitative mediation and inquire of them what they liked and did not like about their respective mediations.

---

23. Golann & Corman Aaron, *supra* note 18, at 27.
24. *Id.*

THIRTEEN

Special Issues in Mediation

Our circumstances answer to our expectations and the demand of our natures.

—HENRY DAVID THOREAU (PHILOSOPHER)

I. Introduction

This chapter deals with some of the special issues that can arise in mediation. Each of the issues can have important implications not only for the success of individual mediations, but also for the reputation of the mediator and mediation, and for broader societal interests as well. While there are no unifying themes among this array of single instances, a number of them do touch on the question of power in mediation. What makes an issue "special" is not entirely obvious. The term "special" denotes something out of the ordinary that will be encountered in only exceptional circumstances in mediation and not as part of the routine. The term "special" does not imply that these issues are more important than others already dealt with in this book.

There are many special issues that can arise, and those dealt with here are based on relevant literature, stories about actual mediations, and the authors' experiences and reflections. They are not raised for the purpose of providing any specific solutions but rather so that you may consider the skills and techniques mediators might use in dealing with them.

II. Dealing with Violence

A special form of the power problem arises where there has been a history of personal violence between the parties or there is ongoing violence between them. This is most pertinent in relation to domestic violence between spouses or partners, but is also relevant in other situations, for example, personal violence in the workplace or within schools. The same skills and techniques relating to power imbalances have applicability here, but there are some additional policy and practical considerations.

A. Policy Issues

The literature and policy guidelines deal extensively with the issue of when mediation should be regarded as entirely inappropriate because of the violence factor. It is argued that the fear, apprehension, and intimidation experienced by the abused party may render him or her incapable of negotiating and making decisions in mediation, and that such problems should be dealt with elsewhere. Whatever precautions are taken in the mediation, the argument goes, mediation will still be a fundamentally unfair process for the victim, and possibly even a dangerous one.

Notwithstanding these policy arguments, practicing mediators (including the authors) are often involved in cases where violence, such as domestic violence, has occurred between the parties, including where protection orders are actively in place. Domestic violence mediations, in particular, usually take place in the context of legal aid schemes and others involving services from agencies where there are scarce resources, limited dispute-resolution options, and some measure of pressure on the parties to participate in mediation. In these settings, mediators are seldom privy to the true realities of the violence, and rarely receive any follow-up regarding the mediated agreements. Regretfully, while mediation is hardly an ideal option in such circumstances, it might be the only one.

Thus, while it is never ideal to mediate where there is a history of violence, it may be the only realistic option for some parties, such as those with scarce resources or those who need to make practical arrangements over children and property. The focus is therefore on ways in which this reality can be best dealt with by thoughtfully modifying and adapting the mediation process.[1]

B. Screening for Violence

As has been noted, pre-mediation screening for evidence of violence is one of the most important precautions in this context. Screening is designed both to provide hard information on matters of violence and to create opportunities for clients to disclose their feelings and concerns about the problem. It allows the person conducting the screening to assess the victim's capacity to participate effectively in mediation and to assess the perpetrator's capacity to function appropriately. Pre-mediation screening can have two significant outcomes. First, it allows for the identification of situations that are unsuitable for mediation, which can then be referred to another form of skilled help. A sample of some helpful questions intended to identify domestic violence are as follows:[2]

---

1. Rene L. Rimelspach, *Mediating Family Disputes in a World with Domestic Violence: How to Devise a Safe, Effective Court-Connected Mediation Program*, 17 OHIO ST. J. ON DISP. RESOL. 95 (2001).

2. These questions are part of Rene L. Rimelspach's informative article on the topic. For a more complete list, see *id.* at 112 (Appendix A).

- Do you have concerns about the mediation?
- Is there anything you feel you can't say in front of your partner?
- Have there ever been any instances of abuse in your relationship?
- Has your partner ever intimidated or threatened you?
- Have the police ever been called out to your home to settle a dispute?

These are by no means a comprehensive list of questions required to appropriately screen for domestic violence. Moreover, mediators and staff who are to be tasked with conducting the screening and interpreting the responses should obtain advanced training.

The second outcome of pre-mediation screening is that it allows for adequate preparation by the mediator where mediation is to go ahead despite a history of violence. In some settings, mediators are directly involved in the screening function, and in others it is performed by designated staff with specialized training in this area. In both contexts, mediators can plan strategies and interventions for dealing with the violence factor. However, as screening is not infallible and might only be available in a rudimentary form, mediators need to be generally prepared in all cases where there might have been a history of personal violence.

C. Mediator Interventions in Relation to Violence Issues

Before planning their interventions, mediators need to be able to understand and read the indicators of violence. To achieve this, all mediators involved in family mediations would benefit from training on the nature of domestic violence and its consequences for both victim and perpetrator. One of the many advantages of training is that it can assist mediators to recognize indicators of domestic violence. On the part of the victim, this might include continually waiting for the other to speak, glancing timidly at the perpetrator, or always trying to smooth over points of conflict; on the part of the perpetrator, it might include dominating the conversation, aggressive body language, impatience, or threatening tone of voice. Of course, these are only indicators, and the mediator might need more information in order to understand the situation fully.

In light of this understanding, the mediator is able to adapt and modify the mediation process to suit the circumstances. For instance, practical steps a mediator might take include:

- Investigating the possibility of the victim taking out a protection order before the mediation;
- Organizing separate arrival times and supervised waiting rooms for the parties;
- Having more than one session, and keeping them relatively short, to provide the victim party with additional time to seek counsel and support;

- Always, as a matter of inflexible policy, conducting separate sessions, and holding these more than once where circumstances require it;

- Making strict arrangements for the victim party's safety during the mediation session;

- Making use of written details of tasks that the parties are required to perform between sessions. For example, in a divorce mediation, parties need to list personal items that they wish to be included in their property distribution;

- Considering the safety aspects of contact visits and other post-mediation meetings between the parties (with reference to neutral public venues, supervision, and so on);

- Assessing the victim's comfort level throughout the process;

- Undertaking any termination of the mediation in such a way that it does not antagonize the offender toward the victim;

- Ensuring that the victim is able to leave the mediation first and has sufficient time to leave the premises before the perpetrator departs; and

- Discussing with the victim party beforehand ways of dealing with their problems in the mediation (see the case illustration below).

Case Illustration: Dealing with Violence Symptoms in Mediation

In the preparatory stages of a voluntary mediation, the mediator, who was aware of a history of personal violence between the parties, conducted personal interviews with both parties. The victim, who was legally represented, was willing to take part in the mediation process jointly with the perpetrator provided her lawyer was present but was concerned that she would become intimidated and quiet if the perpetrator raised his voice and became threatening. She would also feel nervous about asking for a separate meeting with the mediator or an adjournment to speak with her lawyer.

The mediator discussed with her options for dealing with this predicament. They agreed that as soon as she felt intimidated, she would give the mediator a secret hand signal, and this would cause him to suggest an adjournment a few minutes later. This occurred twice in the mediation, after which the victim had developed enough confidence in the process and in her abilities to be able to continue through to agreement, despite continuing threats from the perpetrator.

Mediators have some important responsibilities on the violence issue, but they alone cannot guarantee the safety of the victim. In relation to the responsibilities which they do have, there is comprehensive advice available from many mediation service providers and agencies operating in this area.

III. Using Interpreters in Mediation

The need for and use of interpreters in mediation is another aspect of the power dynamic, this time created by linguistic disadvantage. Normally it is clear as to whether an interpreter should be used in mediation, namely, if one or more participants is unable to understand the language in which it is conducted. However, mediators should not be too gullible regarding the issue. It is not uncommon for parties to ask for an interpreter despite their being fluent in the language of the mediation. The use of the interpreter then becomes a device for the relevant party to have time to think, and it provides the presence of a "professional friend" in the mediation process.

Where an interpreter is necessary for the successful conduct of the mediation, the following guidelines are appropriate for mediators:

- It is clearly preferable to use professionals as interpreters (as opposed to using friends, the mediator, or one of the parties involved);

- A clear role definition is important for the interpreter as well as for the party for whose benefit the interpreter is present. Where an interpreter is being used for the first time, even if he or she is professionally qualified, the interpreter should be fully briefed on the nature of the mediation process and on his or her role in it;

- The mediator should explicitly direct the interpreter to avoid adopting a quasi-mediator role or engaging in giving advice or evaluation;

- The mediator should get the interpreter to sign a confidentiality agreement before the mediation commences;

- The mode of interpretation should be specified and understood: either one that is consecutive (where the interpreter translates the party's statement after the statement is complete), or simultaneous (where the interpreter translates the party' statement as the statement is spoken);

- The interpreter should be seated next to the mediator to symbolize neutrality of the interpreter. This also serves to maintain focus on the mediator, as opposed to another professional present at the foot of the table;

- The mediator should communicate via direct speech with the party. Mediators should avoid indirect speech, for example, "Interpreter, please tell the party that I am going to summarize now...." The mediator should simply state to the party, "I'm going to summarize now." The interpreter will then translate the statement.

- The mediator should intervene if the interpreter and the party engage in conversation outside the scope of mediation.

- Mediators should avoid slang, excessive side commentary, and colloquialisms during mediation because these forms of expression are difficult to translate.

- Mediators should be more vigilant than usual in their efforts to minimize the parties cutting each other off mid-sentence when an interpreter is being used, for it is unrealistic to expect an interpreter to effectively translate cut-off sentences and interruptions.

Where interpreters are used, mediators are advised to prepare for a lengthier mediation to accommodate the additional person, longer speaking time, and inevitable difficulties. In regard to the quality of the interpreter's work, this is very difficult for a mediator to monitor. This requires the mediator to be particularly observant in relation to the reactions of the parties to see if one or both seem concerned at what is being said. However, even active listening and body language can be problematic, given the cultural differences that operate in these situations.

IV. Dealing with Proposed Settlements "Outside the Range"

Mediator trainees often ask what they should do when the parties are about to settle on something that is "outside the range" of usual settlements for a particular kind of dispute. The range could involve the formal, conventional, or usual ways in which such disputes "normally come out." The range could be derived from court decisions, on industry norms, on community standards, or on simple common sense ("One party should not be getting everything and the other nothing…."). It is, however, seldom a matter of scientific measurement, hence the use of the term "range." Here are some examples of "outside the range" situations:

- A self-represented plaintiff in a personal injury mediation is about to settle for less than he might otherwise obtain because he has entirely overlooked claiming damages for pain and suffering;

- A sexual harassment complainant is about to settle only for an apology, in circumstances where she would usually be awarded monetary compensation; and

- A husband is entering a matrimonial property settlement in which no account is taken of his wife's pension entitlements.

The "outside the range" problem extends to other situations in which one party is at a disadvantage, whether because of ignorance, emotional stress, lack of advice, or other considerations. The question arises as to what techniques a mediator can use in the face of these imminent settlements "outside the range."

It is useful to start from first principles. The mediator's role is primarily to assist the parties to come to their own decisions and not to protect the interests of the weaker party. Moreover, mediators should be aware of the non-pecuniary interests, both procedural and emotional, which parties might have in settling for less than might otherwise be obtained. They may not want to come within the "range." Thus, plaintiffs and claimants might settle for less money than they are entitled to in order to achieve finality in the dispute, to avoid the uncertainty and stress of litigation, to get a lesser amount now rather than a greater amount sometime in the future, or in order to turn a corner and get on with their lives. Defendants and respondents might also agree to a commercial settlement to avoid bad publicity or to save further legal costs, despite virtually no prospect of their being found liable in a legal forum. It is consistent with the mediation principle of party autonomy to allow parties to give their informed consent to a settlement even if it is outside the range.

These principles suggest that one possible response is for the mediator to do nothing and to allow the parties to settle on their intended terms—the *sign them up* approach. This is an extreme non-interventionist approach that might be suitable for some clients in some situations. In other circumstances, however, the *sign them up* approach could have serious long-term consequences for one party, in particular where their "consent" is not informed. It could also damage the reputation of mediation as a dispute resolution process.

Therefore, another possible response is for the mediator to adopt a strong interventionist approach of assisting such a party by advising him or her directly about a matter that has been overlooked or forgone. This is the *let me tell you* approach. However, using this approach could result in the non-assisted party's losing trust in the mediation process, and it could also lead to confusion in the marketplace about the nature of mediation.

Between the two extremes of the *sign them up* and *let me tell you* approaches are a number of intermediate responses, each having some advantages and some shortcomings. Here, reference will be made to the personal injury scenario referred to above, where the unrepresented plaintiff is Lindsay, and Isaiah is representing the defendant. The mediator could:

1. Work systematically through the proposed agreement, checking it against the list of issues, to verify that the parties are consenting to each detail: "Lindsay and Isaiah, now that we have agreement on principle on these matters let me take you through them one by one to make sure that you are entirely clear on each of them."

2. Ask the parties in joint session whether there are additional matters they would like to have dealt with in the mediation: "Lindsay and Isaiah, now that we have agreement in principle on these matters, let me check with you whether there are any additional matters or issues you would like dealt with today."

3. Question the parties in joint session as to whether they would like to obtain advice before making final decisions: "Isaiah and Lindsay, before we go any further, would either of you like an adjournment to consult other people about the settlement we are about to reach today?"

4. Adjourn the mediation on the pretext that this is "normal practice" in such matters, in the expectation that the disadvantaged party will have the opportunity to reconsider the settlement or seek advice: "Well, we have nearly reached settlement, and it is my normal practice to have an adjournment at this stage, for about an hour, so that both of you can reconsider what you have agreed to and obtain advice on any matter on which you are uncertain or unclear."

5. In a separate meeting with the weaker party, Lindsay, the mediator could act as the agent of reality in relation to the extent to which the proposed agreement is in their best interests: "Lindsay, you are entitled to make your own decisions here, but this needs to be in your long-term interests. Once you agree to this settlement, you will have no further opportunity to claim damages. I should also point out that this is a technical area of the law and many people in your position seek advice on what is best for them."

6. In a separate meeting with the stronger party, Isaiah, the mediator could point out the potential legal, ethical, and reputational consequences of their agreeing to a settlement that disadvantages the weaker party: "Now Isaiah, you are about to sign-off on a settlement which you know is considerably less than Lindsay would obtain in court. What if Lindsay finds out later and seeks to review it? How will that affect your company, and for that matter, your professional reputation?"

7. Raise the prospect of including a "cooling-off" clause in the mediated agreement: "Isaiah and Lindsay, in cases like this where one party is in the position of a consumer and the other is a big organization, it is often fair to have a three-day cooling-off period to allow either of you to get out of the agreement. Is that something which might be used here?"

8. Withdraw from the mediation, after explaining that the mediator is not willing to continue mediating where parties propose to settle "outside the range": "I'm in a difficult position here, Lindsay and Isaiah. While my role is not that of judge or jury, I have to be able to live with the outcome you agree on. If you insist on going ahead with an agreement which is, in my judgment, not within the bounds of reasonableness, I shall have no choice other than to terminate the mediation."

These options become increasingly more "interventionist" as far as the mediator is concerned. Which of them is appropriate will be a matter of judgment for the mediator in the particular circumstances of the mediation.

V. Dealing with Absent Parties

Reference has already been made to the question of how mediators might deal with the need for formal ratification of mediated agreements by company boards, chief executives, government ministers, and other outside ratifying parties.[3] In many mediations there are also significant *absent parties*, that is, individuals who are not present at the mediation but who, without being required formally to ratify the mediated agreement, may have considerable influence over one or the other party. In some cases, the existence of an absent party may be obvious to the mediator from the facts and circumstances of the case or from an admission to this effect by a party. In other cases, the mediator might suspect the influence of an absent party from the reticence of one party or the intransigence of another.

The following are some illustrations of *absent parties* a mediator might encounter:

- New partners of former spouses in matrimonial property mediations, who are strong influences on the mediating parties and who will themselves be affected by the outcome in the mediation;

- Grandparents of children in parenting mediations, who have their own interests in seeing the children and who might also be used for supervised contact or as go-betweens for the parents;

- External advisers and support persons, whether religious, spiritual, or emotional, who hold a powerful sway over the parties and their view of what is right or wrong;

- Members of social networks, clubs, and associations to whom a mediating party will "report back," and who may criticize, ridicule, or otherwise undermine their commitment to the mediated outcome; and

- Outsiders who are directly funding one of the parties, such as the concerned parent who is paying the costs of the mediation on behalf of their child and who has high expectations of the process.

Where the mediator suspects the existence of a significant absent party or is informed about this person in a confidential separate session, he or she should work in private with the relevant party on options for dealing with the problem. Here, the mediatory method is used to identify interests, priorities, options, and choices for that party. Assume, for example, that there is a mediation between Mark and Philippa, both employees of a church school, involving sexual harassment. It becomes evident that Philippa, the complainant, is concerned about how her fellow employees will react to any compromise she reaches. The mediator might say in separate session: "Philippa, you have raised this fear about your colleagues' reactions. How important is that to you, and what ways do we have for dealing with it?"

---

3. *See* Chapter 10—*Variations in the Mediation Process*, section VIII D.

If, however, the absent party is known about by both parties, the mediator can deal with the problem in joint session, where he or she can explain that dealing with this outside person is a common problem for them both. In mediation terms, another issue goes up on the board. In the above example it might be, "How can the church community's anticipated criticism of a settlement be dealt with?" or, "How can we prevent the church community from sabotaging the mediated agreement?" The mediator can then ask Philippa and Mark for ideas on dealing with the joint problem.

In dealing with the "external ratifier" discussed in Chapter 4, reference was made to the need for the mediator to make contact with that person and present to him or her an authentic "blood, sweat, and tears" version of the mediation. This will not be possible where the "absent party" is not known to one mediating party and may still not be easy where he or she is. However, the same principles apply, and the parties might agree to the mediator having a major role in this regard. In practice, some elaboration in the drafting of the mediated agreement, to include reasons and explanations, makes the relevant party more confident of dealing with their "absent party."

VI. Involving Children in Mediation

Reference has been made to the importance of involving in mediation those who, while not direct parties to the dispute themselves, are sufficiently important to warrant some inclusion in the mediation. Examples of such people are senior executives in commercial mediations where middle managers were responsible for the original problem, or vehicle drivers and employers in personal injury mediations although insurers are the parties currently involved in dispute resolution. Children in family mediations constitute a different category of those who might be involved, in that it is their interests that are directly and intimately affected by decisions taken. While there will sometimes be a court-appointed separate legal representative to uphold the children's rights in mediation, the focus here is on the direct involvement of the children themselves.

There are four logical approaches to the involvement of children in mediations dealing with disputes between their parents over custody and contact:

1. No involvement at all for the children, with the parents responsible for any communications to them about the process and its outcome;

2. Involvement of the children after the mediation has concluded, by setting up a meeting with the mediator, with or without assistance from the parents, where the mediator informs the children about the outcome and its practical implications for them;

3. Partial involvement of the children, in joint or separate sessions, for the purpose of listening to their views about parenting arrangements but without their having any role in the final decision-making; or

4. Full involvement of the children in all stages and aspects of the mediation.

The fourth option is rare in practice and could only operate with older children of significant maturity, with the full consent of all parties and with the approval of the mediator. The first is common in mediation practice. It is justifiable with children of tender years or where there is likely to be major confrontation between their parents. It is also supported on policy grounds by those who claim that children should not be involved in the drama of family mediations or feel the burden of choice and decision-making. However, this approach is often adopted with little consideration given to the feasibility of the second and third options in light of the children's maturity, understanding, and ability to cope.

It might be entirely appropriate for the mediator to inform and educate the children about the parenting agreement and its practical implications, for example, how it might be amended in the future to take account of their changing needs. This is likely to be a more independent and objective version of the settlement and its practical consequences. Likewise, where children are at the age where they might be consulted about their preferences, they could be involved in relevant parts of the mediation, subject to safeguards and protections. Because adolescents can cause the breakdown of a carefully crafted parenting regime even before it has commenced operation, there might be good practical reasons to involve them in some way in making the arrangements. However, there is always a cautionary aspect to any involvement: children should never have adult responsibilities imposed on them and they should not feel that they are choosing between their parents.

Ultimately, as with other special issues, there are many ways in which mediators can adapt the mediation process to deal with children's needs and interests. One such option is using the children as an "advisory panel" to reality test a proposed parenting arrangement.[4] Here the mediator or parents would seek the children's reactions before the parents sign a final agreement. It maintains the parents' obligation to make decisions while allowing the children a sense of involvement in reviewing and commenting on the outcome. This part of the process can take place informally without the children coming to the mediation meeting itself. However, it is advisable that both parents be involved in a collaborative way so that together they can clarify any ambiguities in the agreement and questions from the children. Where there is too much antagonism between the parents, the mediator should be involved, but preferably with the parents present. As with all forms of child involvement in mediation, it is possible for other trusted adults to accompany them into the mediation room and to be with them before and afterwards.

---

4. JAY FOLBERG & ALISON TAYLOR, MEDIATION: A COMPREHENSIVE GUIDE TO RESOLVING CONFLICTS WITHOUT LITIGATION 182 (1998).

VII. Dealing with Experts in Mediation

A common feature of litigation is the involvement of competing experts present-ing evidence. A frequent problem in the system is that because they often differ fundamentally from one another, dual experts become dueling experts, with non-ex-perts such as the judge or jury having to decide between them. The dueling-experts phenomenon is a product of the adversarial nature of the litigation process. Adver-sarialism provides that the parties themselves are responsible for conducting the investigation, preparation, and presentation of their respective cases. The judge's or jury's traditional role is limited to that of adjudicating on the merits of the two pre-sentations, and it does not conventionally extend to establishing the truth through investigation, fact-finding, and the calling of independent expert witnesses. In many cases, the available remedies require the judge or jury to give an either/or verdict based on the evidence and arguments presented by the parties.

The adversarial system encourages each side to make the best possible case it can, to be as extreme in its presentation as is possible, and to use a range of tactics and arguments to weaken the case of the other side. Each side engages its own expert who presents reports and evidence in favor of that side's case and in contradiction to the other's. There are three possible reasons as to why experts give contrasting evi-dence:

1. There may be genuine differences in their observations, evaluations, and opinions, as is the case in many technical areas, from the causes of indus-trial accidents to the long-term effects of physical injuries;

2. The experts' views may be based on different versions of the facts or on partisan perceptions of events. For example, accountants may have different valuations of a business because they have been given access to different books of accounts and figures; or

3. The individuals may have been retained because they have established rep-utations in their areas of expertise and can be expected to behave more as advocates than as experts, for example, "plaintiff" and "defendant" doctors in personal injury disputes.

There are different ways in which dispute-resolution processes can avoid the syn-drome of dueling experts. Some processes are themselves "expert"-based. For example, in case appraisal, the expert gives an indicative opinion based on limited presentations of the case by each side and its experts. In this model, the case appraiser acts as a third independent expert who renders his or her opinion in the knowledge of the views of the parties' experts. Although this opinion is "non-binding," it can be very helpful to parties because it provides them with a glimpse as to how they may fare at a subsequent trial, thereby helping them prevent possible cost penalties that may come as a result.

In mediation, it is the flexibility of the process that can be deployed to avoid the dueling-experts syndrome. The mediator needs to diagnose the reason for the differences between the experts, in light of the three possibilities referred to above, and then adapt the process with this diagnosis (which is always tentative). This is illustrated through two case studies in which different approaches are taken to the problem.

Case Illustration: The Case of an Outside Engineer

There had been a number of disputes between a developer and a local authority over the years. The developer had become accustomed to lax enforcement of development regulations over a long period of time. He had adopted an aggressive, combative style and tended to get his way with all his applications. The current problems began when the local authority appointed a new manager of the development department who was young, enthusiastic, and wanted to do things "by the book." A poor relationship developed between the two and there were a number of court hearings on various development applications and related matters. Eventually, one of the long-standing matters was brought to mediation. Progress was made on a number of issues, but there was an impasse over a seemingly minor issue, namely the appropriate depth for sewerage pipes. Each side had an expert's opinion on this matter. After discussion, the parties agreed to engage an independent engineer to give an opinion that they would both accept. There was no consensus on the identity of the expert, but they invited the president of the local chapter of the American Arbitration Association to nominate a suitable engineer. They further agreed on what information to provide to the expert engineer, and on what access she would have to the parties. Once the technical issue had been resolved, the mediation continued on other matters.

Case Illustration: The Case of the Collaborative Accountants

Legal proceedings were afoot between a father and daughter over the validity of his late wife's and her late mother's will, respectively. The usual legal challenges were being brought against the validity of the will and the case was set for a court hearing. The stakes were high in that the estate had a net value of approximately $9 million, including family businesses and farms. At the mediation, there were some preliminary skirmishes over the validity of the will, but the focus soon shifted to the underlying issue, the deterioration of the father-daughter relationship over the years. This was discussed for a while with some progress being made, after which they reverted to the distribution of assets. Now that a breakthrough of sorts had been made in the relationship, the parties allowed their accountants to work together on their respective valuations and other aspects of the businesses and properties. The accountants spent several hours together outside the mediation room and returned with virtual unanimity on all issues. Some simple trade-offs were possible on the outstanding valuation issues, and the parties were able to agree on all financial matters. While the accountants were collaborating, the parties and the mediator continued to look at relationship issues. The lawyers also played a collaborative role in their joint drafting of a complicated tentative agreement.

Here are other possible ways in which the problem of competing experts can be dealt with in the mediation process:

- By requesting them to identify the common ground between them and to provide specific reasons for their differences, particularly where valuations are in dispute.

- By conducting a "mini moot" in which the experts act as "witnesses" for a short period of time so that each side, and their advisers, can hear the best case of the other. Here, protocols are required to allow some questioning of the experts without it deteriorating into cross-examination or interrogation.

- In so far as the experts' views relate to the question of liability, by circumventing the liability question altogether, by making a commercial decision on damages and other aspects of the dispute.

- By allowing the mediator to give a decision on a point of expertise, thus converting the process into mediation-arbitration, with all the advantages and shortcomings of that system.

VIII. Dealing with Lawyers and Other Professional Advisers

A. Issues for Professional Advisers

Some references have been made earlier in the book to the roles of lawyers in relation to the preliminary conference, the party statements, the separate meetings, and the drafting of the agreement. Here the subject of professional advisers is looked at from the mediator's side of the fence, and not from the side of the lawyer or accountant assisting a client in mediation. Generally speaking, clients and their advisers are responsible for their own participation and behavior in mediation. However, mediators can have both proactive and reactive roles in this regard. They can, for example, educate all participants beforehand about their appropriate roles in mediation, and they can intervene reactively where advisers transgress the mediation guidelines and play inappropriate roles.

Having advisers present at mediation increases the transaction costs of the process. This is because an agent's interests are never identical with those of the principal and there are more needs to accommodate. More specifically, professionals have a strong interest in maintaining satisfied clients, in being seen to perform their role in front of other professionals (including the mediator), in maintaining their desired reputation, and in not being sued by their own clients. There are also the many factors deriving from the complexities of the human condition which affect advisers as much as their clients: personal fears and anxieties, past (and future) relationships with other advisers, the nature of the relationship with their client, demands from colleagues and supervisors, and time pressures. This makes for a complex mediation situation.

This is not, however, to suggest that mediation involving professional advisers is impossible. On the contrary, many mediations would not have succeeded without the appropriate professional involvement of lawyers and other advisers. The real questions are: *what* can mediators do to guide the participation of professional advisers, and *how* should they go about doing it?

To take the *how* question first, the preliminary conference provides an early opportunity for the mediator to inform and explain to advisers what is expected of them in mediation. This can be reinforced with written guidelines or protocols for advisers that can be distributed at the preliminary conference or sent out in advance of the mediation. Some mediators request advisers to sign these codes as a way of reinforcing their commitment to them. More formal still are the occasional attempts to incorporate into the Agreement to Mediate some protocols on the behavior of advisers and to have the advisers, as well as their clients, sign this agreement. However, in this department there is much to be said for the less formal approach, namely, that of educating, explaining, and guiding the advisers.

Regarding the *what* question, mediators need to educate, explain, and guide advisers on the philosophy and objectives of mediation, the central participatory role of their clients, the survey findings that clients appreciate mediation because it allows them to speak and to be heard, the importance of focusing on interests as opposed to legal rights, and other principles and values of the mediation process. In regard to their role, it should be emphasized that advisers function best when they work informally, as supporters and not advocates, and with less emphasis on legal rights and more on needs, interests, and the future. The assumption is that advisers who understand the nature of mediation will be less defensive about their own roles, and the less defensive they are, the more likely they will be to allow the mediator to conduct the process appropriately. However, this is also a somewhat optimistic approach, and the ego, personality, and tactics of advisers have been known to disrupt the process, notwithstanding their full understanding of mediation. Inexperienced or youthful mediators can also anticipate attempts by older and more worldly professional advisers to dominate them and subvert the process.

Case Illustration: The Case of the Controlling Lawyer

A senior attorney was representing a daughter who was suing her father over her late mother's will (see above *Case Illustration*). The attorney flew into town for the mediation and in pre-mediation discussions indicated that her client could not bear to be in the same room as her father and that the mediation should be conducted on a shuttle basis. The client "confirmed" this, in the presence of her attorney, and the mediation commenced with the parties in separate rooms. After two futile hours of ferrying messages, the mediator confronted the attorney and insisted on a face-to-face meeting. The attorney eventually relented and the client "acquiesced." After father and daughter had been in the same room for ten minutes, the daughter moved to the whiteboard and drew a map of the family properties being discussed. This led to an extended personal discussion between the clients about the decedent, family relations, and the future of the family businesses and properties. This led, albeit eight hours later, to full agreement on the distribution of assets and on the future of the business. The formerly controlling attorney played a more passive, but still significant, role in the traditional mediation process.

B. Degrees of Involvement by Advisers

There are variations in relation to the degree of mediation involvement by professional advisers. Assume, for the purposes of the discussion in the following sections, that Dr. Baker is appearing in a mediation relating to allegations of professional misconduct and he consults Ms. Yang, an attorney. Ms. Yang could advise Dr. Baker on how to represent himself in mediation and have no further involvement herself; she could attend a preliminary conference and leave her client to participate in the mediation meeting on his own; she could be present during the mediation and participate fully throughout the process; she could be present at the mediation but have only a restricted participation (for example, observe for the first two hours and participate directly thereafter); she could be physically absent from the mediation but be accessible to Dr. Baker for involvement by phone or through fax; or she could join the mediation only after her client and his patient have reached agreement in order to advise the doctor legally and to undertake the drafting of the settlement agreement. All of these variations are encountered in American mediation practice. Good lawyers are comfortable about considering such options, together with their clients and the mediator, so as to suit the needs, circumstances, and resources of the relevant dispute.

Within the mediation process there is also sufficient flexibility to allow for a number of other modifications involving professional advisers. The mediator might:

- Meet with the advisers together without the clients (adviser meetings);
- Meet with the clients together without the lawyers (party meetings);

- Ask to meet with an individual client without his or her lawyer (side meeting); and/or
- Ask the lawyers to meet together on their own, with a specific aim of assisting in the settlement process.

C. Seating of Advisers

Reference has been made before to the Great Seating Debate in mediation.[5] One of the reasons why mediators need to control the physical environment (and arrive early) is so that they can take charge of the seating arrangements. Many professional advisers, such as Ms. Yang, like to be seated near the mediator in a hierarchical arrangement where they are the experts "representing" their lay clients. It is preferable for mediators to make the strategic decisions about seating. It is clearly more in the spirit of the mediation process and client self-determination for Dr. Baker and the other party to be seated in the places of precedence near the mediator, with the professionals seated further away in their supportive role. However, as in all other aspects of the process, the mediator needs to develop a hypothesis on this matter before the mediation and might have good reasons for indicating other seating arrangements.

D. Documentation

Lawyers have expertise in developing and systematizing relevant documentation for dispute-resolution processes. Mediators can attempt to manage the lawyers' documentation functions in relation to the specific needs of the mediation. In some court-referred mediations, mediators have delegated authority to order the production of documents and other materials. In these situations, it is not unusual for lawyers to have much of the documentation necessary for litigation available at the mediation. How essential or relevant this is depends on the circumstances. One mediator makes a great show of having a file in front of him containing the court documents, correspondence, reports, and other papers sent to him by the lawyers. He picks up the file, deposits it on the floor and announces to the meeting, "Ladies and gentlemen, we may get back to this, but let's see if we can solve the problem first without it." This is a dramatic, if unusual, way of emphasizing that in mediation the clients' personal and commercial interests are of more importance than their legal rights. This might entail that the craftsmanship of their lawyers in providing documentary support for their legal rights has only limited significance in mediation.

---

5. *See* Chapter 2—*Establishing the Foundations: Introductions, Intake, Screening and Preparation*, section VI F.

E. Parties' Initial Statements

Reference has already been made to the desirability of the parties themselves making the party statements and for the professional advisers then to expand on these where necessary. Again, this principle might need modification, but the mediator, and not the professional advisers, should be the one to assume control over this aspect of the process. This may require some quiet mediator assertion, but diplomacy and tact are not incompatible with such control. Again, it is useful for the mediator to be educative and to normalize. He or she might say, "Ms. Yang, in my experience mediation works best where the client makes the opening statement and the adviser is then given an opportunity to expand on it. This would allow Dr. Baker to indicate what his personal concerns are here today. This is also how I normally conduct mediations. So, Dr. Baker, would you like to begin?"

F. Accommodating the Need to Be Involved

One of the needs of professional advisers is for them to be seen as involved. There is a danger in having advisers present when they do not feel fully engaged in the mediation. It can lead to problems, ranging from an overt hijack of the mediation process to subtle forms of sabotage. To avoid these consequences, mediators should ensure that there is scope for the appropriate involvement of all advisers. Thus, a mediator might invite lawyers to exchange views on legal issues and even to ask clarifying questions of the "opposing" party, as long as this does not lead to a form of cross-examination. Legal advisers also have a significant role at the settlement-agreement drafting stage, and the mediator from the earliest stages can foreshadow this involvement. Thus, the mediator might say, "Although mediation is essentially an opportunity for you, the clients, to sort things out yourselves, you can always call on your lawyers for advice and support. I would also anticipate the lawyers drafting the settlement agreement, and perhaps that is something they could have in mind as we move along." Some lawyers have refused to participate in drafting because they did not feel sufficiently involved in the previous stages of the mediation. Mediators can prevent resentment from forming by keeping professional advisors engaged in the mediation process.

G. Taking Instructions

Lawyers in mediation often say to the mediator, "I'd just like to take instructions from my client on this matter." If the mediation is in joint session, this would entail a short adjournment; if the mediation is in separate session, the mediator would leave the lawyer alone with the client. When a lawyer uses this time-honored phrase in mediation, however, it could mean one or more of the following:

- "I need to ask my client what they think about an offer, counteroffer, and so on, and about what they would like me to do"—the expression means what it says;

- "I need to advise my client on the current offer and where the negotiations might be heading"—the lawyer needs to take control;

- "I am not sure what to do next and need some time to reflect and consider options"—the lawyer is in trouble and needs a time out;

- "I need to ask my client about important new information which has come up for the first time"—the lawyer is surprised by developments and needs to reconsider strategies; or

- "I need a break and a cup of coffee"—the lawyer needs the amenities and a caffeine fix.

In most of these scenarios, either the lawyer is taking instructions with the objective of advising he or she client or there will be an opportunity to provide advice. The mediator should therefore inquire of a lawyer who has expressed the need to take instructions what he or she will be advising their client: "Now, Ms. Yang, you have said that you wish to take instructions from Dr. Baker, but it is my experience that in complex situations like this, clients want advice from their lawyer. Perhaps you can indicate to me just what you will be recommending to Dr. Baker about the offer...." This clearly cannot be done in open session, and even if asked in the corridor the lawyer may not be forthcoming in response. However, it accords with the realities of many client-adviser relationships, namely, that under the guise of "giving instructions," clients often ask the professional what they should do. Where the mediator takes this proactive step, it gives him or her an opportunity to act as reality agent if the adviser is about to give extremely unrealistic or unhelpful advice.

H. Assisting Advisers in Modifying Their Advice

Sometimes a professional adviser has given a clear statement of advice to their client, often incorporating a monetary figure, and this has been reinforced publicly in front of the other party and their adviser. For example, Ms. Yang may have said before the mediation and again in the joint sessions, "There is no basis in law for holding Dr. Baker liable, and the most the claimant could recover is the cost of the medical consultations." This public statement creates difficulties where the lawyer is required to back off this advice because it is hard to do so without losing face.

Mediators can make the situation easier for the adviser by providing a pretext for them to change their advice. For example, the mediator might say, "Ms. Yang, now that you have heard the other side's version of the incident, which you were not aware of before, how do you see Dr. Baker's position?" or, "Ms. Yang, now that you have seen the documentation on medical expenses, how would you suggest that we deal with the damages question?" By giving this opening to the adviser, the mediator is attempting to allow them to change their prior recommendations without losing face.

I. Using the Advisers as Quasi-Mediators

In the final result, mediation-friendly advisers can be an extremely valuable resource in mediation. They can serve as quasi-mediators in many ways: in managing their clients' expectations, in keeping the lines of communication open, in acting as constructive negotiators, and in serving as reality agents when they know their client is being unrealistic. It is wise mediation practice to use this potential resource to the greatest extent possible. Professionals can be either dealmakers or deal-breakers, and mediators have the responsibility to aim for the former.

Sometimes the question is asked, "Is it appropriate to have lawyers in the mediation?" This closed question is unhelpful, as the roles and contributions of advisers can vary considerably. Some mediations would not have been successful had it not been for the advisers, while others failed because of them. The better question is, "What kinds of legal representation are appropriate, and what kinds are inappropriate in different kinds of mediation?" In any case, lawyers will be involved in many mediations, particularly where mediation is the result of court referral. In general terms, advisers should support all aspects of the mediation process, but there could be a whole chapter on the specific roles and interventions that are appropriate.[6]

IX. Dealing with Complex Multi-Party Disputes

Some mediations are complicated by the wide range of issues involved, the diversity of subject matters, and the large numbers of participants. There are many examples: environmental disputes, corporate mergers, and long-standing conflicts within community organizations. Sometimes these mediations also involve broad issues of public policy, for example, in relation to town planning matters; provision of infrastructure, such as mobile telephone towers; and location of controversial facilities, such as prisons. These mediations are characterized by a high degree of intensity; the need for significant resources such as time, information, and money; the complexity of decision-making; and potential problems in the performance and enforcement of settlement agreements.

This is another topic that warrants considerably more treatment than is possible here.[7] It is important to bear in mind that in complex disputes, the core principles of mediation are still relevant—they just need to be applied in a modified framework. Some matters requiring particular attention include:

---

6. Harold I. Abramson, Mediation Representation: Advocating in a Creative Problem-Solving Process (2004).

7. Some relevant issues have been raised in the discussion of team negotiations in Chapter 2—*Establishing the Foundations: Introductions, Intake, Screening and Preparation*. However, complex multi-party disputes require special procedures to mediate effectively. Two excellent resources on the topic are Suzanne Ghais, Extreme Facilitation (2005), and Maggie Herzig & Laura Chasin, Fostering Dialogue Across Divides (2006).

- The identification of key stakeholders before the mediation meeting;
- The appropriate qualifications of the mediator, or mediators, with relevant personal attributes or professional background;
- Extensive pre-mediation preparation with all so as to manage expectations, secure commitment, and agree on decision-making protocols;
- Consideration of important procedural matters, such as mediation guidelines, speaking time, use of separate meetings, and use of "shuttle diplomacy";
- Ways of preventing and dealing with anticipated difficulties over resources, mandates, timing, and ratification and finalization of formal agreements;
- The need to draft a customized Agreement to Mediate;
- Consideration of who not to involve in the round table discussions, such as those with long-term bitterness, and ways of preventing sabotage attempts by those excluded;
- The creation of a "process control group," with representatives from each set of stakeholders, to advise the mediator on progress in the conduct of the mediation;
- Development of a broad-based report-back system to keep external groups informed, involving the mediators where necessary;
- Extent of privacy and confidentiality, on one hand, and publicity and media statements, on the other; and
- Ongoing monitoring of complicated agreements with continuing obligations for the parties.

Case Illustration: Complex Multi-Party Mediation

A mediation was required for a large number of residents of a housing development who had been in a state of hostility for many months. Because of the numbers involved, three mediators were appointed, and they spent considerable preparation time together to design the mediation process, define their respective roles, and discuss how to deal with problems arising among the mediators. A lack of resources precluded lengthy pre-mediation contact with the individual parties. The mediators' opening was comprehensive and dealt with a wide range of questions and concerns from the participants. Each participant was allowed to make a brief opening statement and at least one concern from each was listed on a white board. A system of voting was used to prioritize the issues for discussion. Strict rules were imposed on speaking times to prevent domination by the angry and verbose participants. One mediator acted mainly as scribe and noted all concessions, agreements in principle, and other matters of value mentioned by any party. Another mediator acted mainly as "process observer" and noted which participants were "stabilizers" and useful catalysts for achieving settlement. No separate meetings were held as there were no identifiable factions among the participants. Agreement was reached in principle on a number of issues, and the mediators drafted this up for signature by those present. A representative group was appointed to investigate implementation of these agreements, with the option of returning to mediation if necessary.

X. Dealing with the Walk-Out

Occasionally, a party moves beyond idle threats and starts to walk out of the mediation. The mediator needs to think and act quickly. The mediator may try to dissuade the party before he or she reaches the door and encourage him or her to stay or suggest a separate meeting. Where the party has already left, the mediator might make contact once the party has cooled down. Ultimately, the party's right to terminate should be respected, but some mediator persistence is compatible with this principle. There is always the prospect that a walk-out is a power play designed to force concessions from the other side. These possibilities are illustrated by the two types of walk-outs illustrated by real situations.

The genuine walk-out: An unrepresented party had been giving some warning signals and suddenly walked out of the joint session of the mediation with the parting shot that he would see the other side in court. Four hours later, there was a telephone call to the mediator from a lawyer. The client had immediately sought legal advice, and it was recommended that he accept the latest proposal on offer. The matter was settled on this basis.

The strategic walk-out: A couple, who were business partners and represented by counsel, walked out of a mediation while the mediator was with the other party. Their lawyer suggested that the mediation continue and that if there were significant progress, she would be able to contact the couple on their mobile phone. The other side, also represented by counsel, immediately made a major concession. After further negotiations, the couple was contacted and returned to sign the settlement agreement.

XI. Exercises

1. Interview an experienced mediator about "special issue" situations he or she has encountered. Draw up a list of such issues, ways in which they were dealt with by the mediator, and other options you think may have worked.

2. Assume that you are a mediator in a case where an employee who has been unlawfully dismissed is about to settle for a fraction of the monetary compensation to which he or she would be legally entitled. With reference to

the ways referred to in this chapter for dealing with these situations, write out a list of ways that you consider most appropriate for dealing with this scenario.

FOURTEEN

Avoiding Mediator Traps

Man is the only kind of varmint sets his own trap, baits it, then steps in it.

—JOHN STEINBECK (NOVELIST)

I. Introduction

Dispute resolution is a complex phenomenon, and there are many potential traps into which a mediator may be snared in the mediation process. The parties set some of these traps, and there is little that even a well-prepared mediator can do to avoid them, for example, a sudden walk-out, a physical attack, or a client dismissing their lawyer. Others are created by external circumstances, for example, representatives of the media bursting into the mediation room or the lights failing. In these abnormal situations, presence of mind is more important for the mediator than preparation or planning.

There are also potential traps in mediation that are, at least to some degree, created by mediators, in the sense that they are the result of practices or interventions, or the lack of practices or interventions, which are attributable to the mediator and not to the parties or to external factors. These traps are easier to avoid through planning and preparation, though presence of mind is also useful when the mediator stumbles upon them.

What follows is a description of some of the traps that could be created by mediators themselves, together with potential strategies for avoiding them. As is usual, there is no single strategy that will guarantee that a trap does not eventuate and frustrate the mediation and all participating in it. There are only options and choices.

Some mediator manuals provide lists of "do's and don'ts" for mediators. This approach has some value, though there can be resistance to learning through negatives. In a sense, this chapter provides the "don'ts" of mediation, but they are presented in a constructive fashion (so mediational). Because this chapter contains some repetition from previous chapters, albeit from a different perspective, there is not extensive cross-referencing.

Unless otherwise indicated, the following fact scenario will be used to illustrate some of the issues raised in this chapter.

Case Illustration: Golf Course Mediation

The Parties

Party A: John and Helen Cavanagh

Lawyer: Not present at mediation

Party B: Nicki Coots

Lawyer: Josh Viser

The Dispute

The Cavanaghs live in a property adjoining the Paradise Eden Golf Club of which Nicki Coots is the manager. They undertake a major landscaping and pool construction project on their land for which they require access through the golf course grounds for an extended period of time. The club grants access upon payment of a $6,000 bond which is to be returned with interest once the grounds are restored to their original condition.

After completion of the work, the Cavanaghs request repayment of the bond. The manager, Ms. Coots, returns $1,200 and retains the balance for tree planting and drainage works required "to restore the grounds to their original condition." The Cavanaghs write to the club board, which confirms the manager's decision. The Cavanaghs retain a lawyer who writes a letter of demand to the club, which in response retains its own lawyer. The Cavanaghs begin badmouthing the club publicly and seek support from neighbors who have had their own problems with the golf course in the past.

The Mediation

The Cavanaghs contact the local community mediation service that obtains the agreement of the club to participate in mediation, on the provision that its lawyer may be present. Co-mediators are appointed. The Cavanaghs elect not to have a legal adviser present at the mediation.

II. Unrealistic Expectations

A. The Trap

One of the themes of this book is that the mediator is a manager of client expectations (the *M* and *E* in *Me*diation, remember?). The trap occurs where the mediator fails to manage client expectations from the very beginning of the mediation process, or where the mediator inadvertently increases the unrealistic expectations of the parties through word, action, or omission. The mediator is not responsible for all unrealistic expectations that often are found in mediation, but there are some that he or she should manage, or at least not exacerbate. An unrealistic expectation can relate to the process of mediation (for example, the Cavanaghs think that "the mediator will listen to our case and find in our favor.")

and can relate to anticipated outcomes of the process ("We'll get back our $4,800 plus interest immediately.").

B. Avoidance Strategies

Informing and educating the parties is the best way to deal with unrealistic expectations. This can be done in relation to both the mediation process ("John and Helen, mediation is not a miracle pill, but it can assist to deal with this problem in a constructive way if you are both committed to seriously considering an amicable resolution...") and to the problem itself ("In my experience, John and Helen, claimants who have difficulty with their facts and evidence usually have to compromise to some extent in cases such as this..."). It will always be a matter of judgment as to when and how the informing and educating should take place. The sooner it occurs in relation to the process and nature of mediation, the better. In relation to the outcome of the dispute, this will depend on when the expectation first comes to the mediator's attention, how unrealistic it is, and the influence of professional advisers in creating it. This is illustrated below.

Case Illustration: The Trap of Unrealistic Expectations

In a personal injury mediation, a young plaintiff injured in a motor vehicle accident had an expectation of receiving $800,000 in damages. The "normal" range for this kind of injury was $200,000–$300,000 only. The unrealistic expectation had been generated by her lawyer, who was present in the mediation and persisted with the unfounded stance on damages.

In the negotiations, the lawyer operated in aggregate terms of damages on the basis of his "extensive experience" and refused to justify and quantify specific kinds of damages. During the separate sessions, the mediator attempted to influence the lawyer and there was some success, but the client whose expectations had been raised seemed inhibited by the lawyer's approach, on which she was heavily reliant. There was no settlement despite the fact that the insurer was offering $275,000. In hindsight it would have been helpful for the mediator to have anticipated this problem, to have had prior contact with the lawyer, and to have acted as agent of reality on the issue of damages. This would not necessarily have solved the problem, but it was the appropriate route to take in attempting to change the client's expectations.

III. Losing Impartiality

A. The Trap

There are many ways in which mediators can forfeit their impartiality, or the appearance of impartiality. It is important to recognize that partiality is as much a matter of party perception as it is of objective behavior, a factor that makes it more difficult for the mediator to manage and control. Irrespective of the reason for it, the loss of impartiality can lead to the collapse of one or both parties' trust and the failure of the mediation process. Some of the ways in which the perception of partiality can arise are through the mediator's

- Not being even-handed in conducting the process (for example, consistently giving more attention to Nicki Coots and her lawyer than to the Cavanaghs);

- Arguing with one of the parties and appearing to oppose their viewpoints;

- Acting as advocate for one of the parties and representing their arguments to the other, which can happen unwittingly with unrepresented parties like the Cavanaghs;

- Interrogating and cross-examining one of the parties (for example, Nicki Coots over the nature of the remedial work required);

- Inappropriately disclosing his or her evaluation of and opinion on what a party is saying or his or her assessment of the merits of the case;

- Not being conscious of his or her own biases that might be detected by one or both of the parties; and

- Responding to triangulation. Triangulation is an attempt by a negotiator to put the mediator in a position of supporting him or her. Every triangulation strategy is dangerous to the mediator. If the mediator responds in the terms the negotiator is looking for, the mediator will alienate the other negotiator. If the mediator tries to check the triangulator, the mediator is likely to alienate him or her.

Note on Implicit Bias

Research over the last several decades demonstrates that we all possess implicit bias.[1] Implicit bias is unconscious "attitudes or stereotypes that affect our understanding, actions, and decisions...."[2] For example, a mediator may give more or less weight to one party's statements or suggestions because of their "race, ethnicity, age, or appearance."[3] Because these biases reside "deep in the subconscious" they have the ability to negatively affect the mediator's decisions and interactions with participants, undermining the fairness of mediated outcomes.[4] Thus, mediators should seek to identify their implicit biases

1. Audrey Lee, *Implicit Bias in Mediation: Strategies for Mediators to Engage Constructively with "Incoming" Implicit Bias*, Harv. Negot. L. Rev 167, 168 (2020); Carol Izumni, *Implicit Bias and the Illusion of Mediator Neutrality*, Wash. U. J.L. & Pol'y, 71, 87 (2010).

2. Lee, *supra* note 1, at 169.

3. Shadeequa M. Smith, *Implicit Bias and the Case for Testing and Redress Prior to Mediation*, 35 Ohio St. J. on Disp. Resol. 169, 173 (2019).

4. *Id.* at 172.

and engage in activities and training to mitigate them. Although there are several implicit-bias self-inventories available, the best known is the Implicit Association Test ("IAT"), developed in 1998.[5] But learning about one's implicit biases is only the first step in mitigating them. Armed with information about one's implicit biases, a mediator should seek professional training to erode and manage these biases productively. Implicit-bias training is now readily available, often at no cost, especially if one is associated with a university as student, staff, or faculty member.

B. Avoidance Strategies

Avoidance strategies that can aid a mediator falling into the *losing impartiality* trap are as follows:

1. The mediator should be "eternally vigilant" on the impartiality issue, particularly where he or she is an expert in the subject matter of the dispute, for example, an attorney in personal injury mediations;

2. The mediator should be aware of his or her own biases where there are important value issues at stake, for example, allegations of environmental degradation or victimization in the workplace, on which it is likely that they would have personal views;

3. The mediator needs to treat the parties comparably, for example, in summarizing both the Cavanaghs' and Nicki Coots's opening statements and not only that of one party, or in devoting approximately the same time to each party in separate sessions;

4. The mediator could invite the parties to comment on any perceived deviation from his or her impartiality, in either joint or separate sessions—"Now Nicki, John, and Helen, as indicated earlier I will be impartial here today but if any of you think that this is not the case, then please let me know";

5. Where there are co-mediators, as in the golf club mediation, they could provide feedback on the impartiality concern to each other.

6. The mediator could take an implicit bias inventory. The IAT, one of the most well-regarded, is available online at no cost.[6]

7. The mediator could seek-out professional implicit-bias training.

---

5. Lee, *supra* note 1, at 170.
6. Project Implicit, *Take a Test*, HARVARD UNIV., https://implicit.harvard.edu/implicit/takeatest.html.

IV. Dominating the Process

A. The Trap

Many survey studies have shown that one of the aspects of mediation evaluated favorably by clients is the direct participation it allows them in the process of resolving their dispute and the control they experience in respect to the outcome of that process. These benefits are derived from a faithful adherence to the different stages and elements of the mediation process, to the extent that this is possible. Mediators can fall into the trap of undermining these potential benefits by engaging in the following behaviors:

1. Talking too often and for too long, and generally dominating the airwaves;

2. Interrupting the parties too much, particularly in the early stages of the process;

3. Cross-examining the parties and pointing out inconsistencies in what they have said;

4. Not allowing the parties to tell their own story in their own time and manner and thereby preventing important information from being disclosed;

5. Using closed, leading, and interrogatory questions to constrict the parties' contributions; and

6. Assuming a narrow notion of what is relevant in the mediation, for example, by restricting discussion to matters covered by the legal pleadings.

B. Avoidance Strategies

Here are some actions that mediators might consider to avoid dominating the process:

1. Using open and clarifying questions, particularly in the early stages of the process: "Nicki, how did you understand the original agreement and the responsibilities of each side?";

2. Practicing active listening as a major ingredient in successful mediation: "So Helen, it sounds as though you were angered and stressed by the club's attitude?";

3. Inviting the parties to indicate to the mediator if they feel they are unable to speak their mind and are not being heard: "Now, do you all feel you have had your say and been heard on the drainage question?";

4. Checking with the parties in separate sessions about how they are experiencing the process: "Helen and John, how do you feel the negotiations are going for you?"; and

5. Using language and terminology that allows the parties to understand and "own" the mediation process and avoiding the technical and arcane (see the *Case Illustration* below).

C. Avoiding Technical Language

An indirect way of dominating the process is for the mediator to use technical language or jargon which is not understood by one or more parties. This is tempting in cases where technical issues are in question, such as in medical negligence or building or computing disputes (e.g., "intermittent claudication" and "paroxysmal nocturnal dyspnoea," or, "RSJs" and "cost-plus contract," or "gigabytes" and "ISPs"—simple and self-evident to insiders, gibberish to outsiders). Likewise, professional jargon ("taking it on spec" or "Front-Pay") or trade usage ("an ambit claim" or "a conjunctional sale") is problematic when parties external to the relevant occupation or trade are present.

Mediation has its own jargon, first instilled in initiates during their training courses. It is best left to seminars and learned papers unless it can be easily explained for the uninitiated. Thus, terms such as "caucus" (for separate meeting), "conditional linked bargaining," and "reframing to interests" should best be avoided—unless you are mediating between two mediators.

Mediator domination through the use of this kind of terminology could lead to loss of face for a party where he or she makes inquiries and to a loss of understanding for a party when he or she does not. Rather than allowing this problem to manifest, it is incumbent on mediators to resolve it when it arises through the technique of "mediator vulnerability." Thus, in the golf club mediation, when Josh Viser or Nicki Coots uses a legal or technical term that is not understood by the Cavanaghs, the mediator should ask for clarification on behalf of himself or herself so that John and Helen can benefit from it without having to appear ignorant themselves.

V. Losing Control of the Process

A. The Trap

This is the converse of the dominating-the-process trap. Mediators must provide a reasonable measure of structure and control for the mediating parties. While they may share some of their control with their clients, for example, over whether there should be an adjournment or whether advisers can be present, they should also retain ultimate control over the process, particularly on the important procedural issues. Control is lost where mediators allow the following to occur:

1. The parties break the ground rules consistently without the mediator's attempting to intervene in any way, for example, Nicki talks over John whenever he speaks;

2. Professional advisers subvert the process and revert to their accustomed "comfort zone" of operation;

3. A party manipulates the process, for example, by imposing unilateral time limits or causing disruptions, having multiple adjournments, and the like, for example, Helen insists on taking mobile phone calls during the mediation; and

4. Unrepresentative outsiders are present and become involved in the mediation in a fashion that is not constructive for the progress of the negotiations, for example, John invites a large group of neighbors to come into the mediation room to support his case.

B. Avoidance Strategies

As with many of the avoidance strategies, sound common sense suggests that mediators should be attentive to the control factor from the earliest stages. This involves a balancing act between appropriate control, on the one hand, and inappropriate authoritarianism, on the other. Thus, each of the following strategies requires some basic judgment and diplomacy in their execution:

1. Prior education of the parties about the importance of structure in effective dispute resolution: "Now Nicki, John, and Helen, it is important to deal with these issues in an orderly way, and I can help you to have that structure during the mediation."

2. Early assertion of the mediator's authoritative role on questions of process: "Now you've all asked me to act as mediator for you, so I would suggest that you follow the guidelines as regards speaking in order."

3. Positive reinforcement of compliance with the mediator's requests and directions: "Thank you for being patient and not interrupting, Nicki, now that the Cavanaghs are done speaking, would you like to give me your opening statement?"

4. Appropriate enforcement by the mediator of the mediation guidelines: "Now, we did agree at the beginning that there should be no denigration of one another, which there has been, and I would like to suggest that you all recommit to that agreement."

5. Using the separate meetings to reassert control and warn about the consequences of continued lack of orderliness: "Helen and John, you have had

difficulty in listening to Nicki's case and have interrupted her continually. If this continues there is a possibility that she and Josh will walk out. Can we reduce the likelihood of a walk-out that will be in no one's interests?"

6. Securing renewed commitment to the guidelines where they have been consistently breached: "Now you have all had difficulty in keeping to the speaking guidelines, so I am going to restate them now and ask you to give your commitment to them for the next phase of the mediation."

C. The Trap of Allowing Professional Advisers to Dominate the Process

Professional advisers play an indispensable role in the success of some mediations, but in others their involvement is highly problematic and leads to failure. Generally speaking, advisers are a problem where their own interests diverge from those of their clients and where the advisor's interests are allowed to surface and dominate in the mediation. Some of those interests are listed here:

1. The professional interest of being seen to act as the zealous promoter of their client's cause and not being called into question by the client;

2. The reputational interest of being known as a tough negotiator;

3. The competitive interest of needing to win and not showing weakness toward or making concessions to the other professionals present; and

4. The accountability interest of being able to render a flattering report to outside partners, supervisors, and colleagues.

Dealing with professionals involves a delicate balance for mediators: they cannot allow advisers and their interests to dominate, but if they deal with the problem undiplomatically, the advisers may become defensive and even more problematic. Thus, the timing of interventions and who is present when they are made are important matters to consider. The following actions can help avoid the trap:

1. Prior education of professional advisers about their appropriate role in mediation;

2. Making advisers signatories to a protocol of conduct for the mediation (*see* Appendix 5—*Guidelines for Lawyers Representing Clients in Mediation*);

3. Using adviser meetings to speak to advisers about the nature and consequences of their dominating behavior; and

4. Making mild intimations about unprofessional conduct or professional misconduct.

VI. Ignoring Emotions

A. The Trap

There is a danger in mediators' ignoring the emotional factors which arise in mediation. It has been shown that most forms of mediation do not involve a therapeutic relationship between the mediator and the parties. Nevertheless, the process allows for the expression, acknowledgment, and validation of deeply felt emotions more than some other forms of dispute resolution. Where mediators attempt to force the parties into a "cool, rational, and objective" discussion of their problems, there is a danger that they will not be ready or willing to move toward a settlement, or that a settlement will come undone at a later stage. The complete disregard of emotions could also result in the parties' finding the process alienating and unsatisfying.

Conversely, mediators should avoid the trap of identifying with one side emotionally, for example, with the weaker party or with one whom the justice of the situation seems to favor. Particularly where there are significant imbalances of power, mediators need to maintain an objective stance to avoid falling into this version of the trap.

B. Avoidance Strategies

The standard mediation process is designed to prevent intense emotional feelings from being disregarded and to deal with them in appropriate ways. More specifically, the mediator is able to do the following:

1. Facilitate wide-ranging communication by the parties on matters of concern to them, whether or not they are within "the pleadings": "Helen, tell us how the incident has affected you personally over the past six months."

2. Encourage some ventilation of emotion in joint or separate sessions: "John, it sounds as though your treatment by the club made you frustrated and angry. Would you like to tell us about that?"

3. Acknowledge the parties' deeply held feelings: "So Nicki, it sounds as though this has been a very stressful and damaging episode for you and the board."

4. Validate some implicit feelings: "It's not unusual for parties in mediation to feel apprehensive about conceding too much to the other side."

Mediators can anticipate the kinds of emotions that are likely to be present in an approaching mediation and plan ways of dealing with them. They should also be conscious of their own reactions to emotion and deal with these appropriately.

VII. Moving to Solutions Too Quickly

A. The Trap

This book has emphasized the importance in dispute resolution of first defining the dispute comprehensively in terms of underlying needs and interests before moving into possible solutions. This is because where mediators allow parties to move too quickly into solutions, it increases the likelihood of several dangers occurring: (1) that the parties will focus only on monetary or material factors and ignore matters of procedural or emotional significance; (2) that the parties will move too quickly into incremental positional bargaining and fail to close the final gap; (3) that the parties will reach a settlement that does not exploit all the potential value at the negotiation table; and (4) that the parties will be discouraged from revealing information that might be influential in reaching a settlement.

B. Avoidance Strategies

Here are some of the factors that mediators might consider in order to avoid falling into the trap of allowing the parties to move too quickly into solutions:

1. Being transparent with the parties about the advantages of discussing the general circumstances of the dispute before dealing with the money or other "hard" solutions: "In my experience it would help to talk a little about how this incident arose and what effects it had on each of you in order to get a fuller perspective on the problem, before we discuss the question of money."

2. Asking each party to explain how they approach the question of monetary figures before they actually make a dollar offer or counteroffer: "John, you've acknowledged that you should not receive the full bond back. Before you mention the figure you do want, explain to Nicki and Josh how you have gone about quantifying this amount."

3. Seeking agreement on matters of principle before moving into the financial details: "Let's see if there is agreement on the following matters before discussing the money: You'd all like to settle the matter today. Helen and John, you agree that you can't recover the full amount you deposited with the club, and Nicki and Josh, you agree that you need to itemize the expenses which you have incurred in restoring the grounds. Are we all agreed in principle on those matters?"

4. Coaching the parties in separate sessions on how to package deals so that the money is not the only point of focus: "John and Helen, you are about to ask for some money, but perhaps you could first tell Nicki, as you've told me, that you are prepared to stop badmouthing the club, to stop any further agitation by the neighbors, and to consider this dispute settled once and for all. This may make them more receptive to your figure."

Case Illustration: Delaying the Money Moves

In a mediation involving losses incurred in first mortgage lending, the lender sued the valuer for alleged negligence in drawing up his valuation. The valuer denied liability but was prepared to offer a small monetary amount in order to reach a financial settlement. The plaintiff had some legal and evidential difficulties on the liability question and had financial pressures that demanded a commercial settlement. In order to keep the parties from moving too quickly into the figures, the mediator requested the valuer's lawyer to explain how they were approaching the monetary settlement, which he did in terms of risk assessment and costs recovery. The plaintiff was asked to respond along the same lines, and although this highlighted substantial differences in approach between the two sides, it did provide a theoretical point of reference when they bargained on the money. The monetary negotiations were successful, despite the plaintiff's having to accept only 15 percent of what he had lost. Had there not been the "philosophical initiation," the deal on the money may have been difficult to attain.

VIII. Pushing the Parties

A. The Trap

This trap involves the mediator's expressing judgments and personal views on what is important for resolving the dispute or on how it should be resolved, or otherwise pursuing his or her own agenda in the mediation. It includes the situation in which the parties have provided their own list of issues and the mediator insists that the mediation should also deal with other matters that they themselves have not raised (e.g., "You cannot finalize these neighbor disputes without discussing how to deal with such problems in the future"). Likewise, the mediator might insist that a particular issue, for example, the question of interest to be paid or the drafting of a confidentiality agreement, be dealt with in accordance with his or her preferred approach to the matter.

There are several reasons why there is a trap in pushing the parties to the mediator's preferred approach or outcome:

1. The mediator can only view the dispute from an objective "rights-based" perspective and not from the subjective "interests-based" perspectives of the parties;

2. The mediator may only have a restricted knowledge of the facts, the law, and other relevant factors and may push toward an "incorrect" outcome;

3. At least one party may become more intransigent where the mediator's view appears to favor them;

4. At least one party may lose trust in the mediator if they would not stand to benefit from the expressed view;

5. The mediator may base his or her view, in part, on information disclosed during the confidential separate sessions;

6. It may confuse clients who did not expect such interventions from a mediator, and it may result in confusion in the marketplace over the nature of mediation;

7. The mediator may breach a code of conduct or ethical standard and be sued for negligence; and

8. The mediator may no longer be "mediating" and may thereby lose any applicable statutory immunity.

This trap is particularly problematic where both parties request the mediator to provide an opinion or make a recommendation. While this expressed consent will obviate some of the problems referred to above, it might create difficulties of its own. Thus, one party, or conceivably both parties, may, in asking for the mediator to express a view, be influenced by what they perceived to be the mediator's support for them in a separate session. If this is the case, they will be at least surprised and possibly disappointed about the actual opinion expressed or recommendation made by the mediator.

B. Avoidance Strategies

It is more difficult for some categories of mediators to avoid the "pushing the parties" trap than it is for others. Mediators with high levels of expertise in the subject matter of the dispute will be more likely to push to their preferred position than those selected because of their skills in the process of mediation. Regardless of these variables, the following strategies will minimize the worst dangers of this trap:

1. Defining from the earliest stages of the mediation the nature of the mediator's role and reinforcing this definition in the minds of the parties wherever necessary: "I am not here to make any decisions for you, or to advise you on the law, or to recommend outcomes for you. I am here to assist you in other ways…";

2. Deflecting requests for advice or opinions in terms of the stated mediator's role: "You've asked my advice on what are reasonable deductions from the bond, but, as I've indicated, that is not my role. What ideas do you have on that issue?";

3. Identifying the concern or interests underlying any request for this kind of mediator intervention and attempting to address those motivating factors: "Now Helen and John, based on what you've just asked, you seem to be uncertain over your legal rights. Does this mean you'd like to consider ways of dealing with that uncertainty?"; and

4. Avoiding the seductive nature of the power conferred by shuttle mediation (see below).

C. Distorting the Parties' Views During Shuttle Mediation

It has been indicated already in this book that mediators acquire immense poten-tial power during shuttle mediation by virtue of their control over the communications between the parties. This power can be used to push unsuspecting parties to the mediator's preferred outcome. As the holding and conduct of shuttle mediation is largely within the mediator's control, the abuse of this power is a trap that mediators can avoid by

1. Delaying the holding of separate meetings until discussions are advanced, and avoiding lapsing into shuttle through default rather than by design;

2. Checking with the parties as to what is and what is not to be conveyed back and forth between them;

3. Reducing the parties' offers to writing before conveying them to the other side;

4. Bringing the parties back together if the reasons for adopting shuttle no longer exist; and

5. Continually reflecting on how they are performing their shuttle role, and where possible, conferring with their co-mediator on this point.

IX. Assuming a Differing Professional Role

A. The Trap

All occupations and professional practices have boundary problems involving what someone can legitimately do and what is in the province of others. A difficult boundary problem in mediation arises where the mediator feels required to play the role of adviser, advocate, counselor, or lawyer. This is a particular problem where only one party has professional advice or other skilled assistance in the mediation, although the trap could still be present where both parties are professionally advised. As usual, there are semantic issues in relation to the differences between the legiti-mate functions of mediators and those of lawyers, counselors, or other professionals. It is nevertheless possible to envisage some functions that would not be regarded as part of a mediator's role. Thus, some mediators might be inclined to advise John and Helen legally about their situation, while in other situations they might attempt to counsel a grieving party. The mediator is more likely to be drawn into playing the role of the absent professional in the separate sessions.

There are many problems associated with the transgression of professional boundaries. Essentially, these problems revolve around what parties expect or can legitimately expect when they come to a mediation. Despite all the debate over the exact contours of the mediator's role, there are clear transgressions that should not occur. Thus, in the golf club mediation, the co-mediators should not counsel the claimants over their loss and grief, advise them on their legal position, or calculate the legitimate deductions that could be made by the club. Such interventions could create confusion among clients, loss of trust in mediation, and subsequent problems for mediators.

B. Avoidance Strategies

The following are some strategies that might be successful in avoiding the trap of adopting an inappropriate professional role:

1. Providing as clear a definition as possible of the mediator's role before the mediation, in the Agreement to Mediate, and during the mediator's opening statement: "Our role today is not to give you legal advice, to act as therapists or counselors, or to assess and quantify the alleged damages."

2. Discussing in separate meetings the implications of not having professional advisers present: "Now John and Helen, you have decided not to have advisers here, and I cannot give you legal advice. How is that affecting your participation in the mediation?"

3. Exploring options for obtaining professional advice when the parties are not represented: "Now it seems clear that you need to be advised on the liability question. How can we modify the mediation process to make that possible for you?"

4. Pointing out the difficulties and possible negative consequences for the parties of the mediator's transgressing professional boundaries: "The problem with my giving you a view on the reasonable deductions which could be made from the bond are that I do not have all the facts at my disposal, I might get it wrong, and it might affect the long-term viability of the agreement you make."

X. Being Unprepared

A. The Trap

Implicit in many of the above traps is a lack of preparation by the mediator. Being unprepared is also a trap of its own. Mediators need to be prepared on the specific features of the case in which they are involved, including the nature of the dispute, the possible causes of conflict, potential mediator interventions, and ways of dealing with predictable problems. They also need to be prepared in a more generalized way in relation to theories of conflict, negotiation dynamics, communication requirements, dealing with impasses and emotions, and on the other skills and techniques required in mediation. In many cases there will be no occasion for specific preparation as the mediator receives no prior knowledge of the case, making only generalized preparation is possible. Being unprepared in either sense is one of the most prevent-able of the mediator-generated problems.

B. Avoidance Strategies

The main avoidance strategy for unpreparedness is an obvious truism: prepare. Throughout this book there are indications of how mediators should prepare for their task and of the factors on which they should be prepared. Where circumstances and resources allow, specific preparation can be done before a mediation commences, for example, by obtaining necessary information and having appropriate contact with the parties. Where circumstances and resources do not allow for systematic prior prepa-ration, a snatched conversation in the corridor with parties and advisers will have to suffice for the impending mediation. In all situations, mediators can improve their generalized preparation, for example, by revising their understanding of basic frame-works of conflict and negotiation, with particular reference to the predictable problems which can occur. This should be an ongoing process: systematic reflection on yester-day's mediation constitutes a form of preparation for tomorrow's.

XI. Allowing the Agreement to Be Left Undocumented

A. The Trap

It is now common practice for Agreements to Mediate to stipulate that no deci-sion made in mediation will be final and binding until reduced to writing. Whether this condition applies or not, the problem of leaving the agreement hanging in the air can still arise where the parties feel drained and exhausted and they would rather go home than write up their terms of settlement. The trap results in the parties either forgetting what they have agreed upon or returning to adversarial combat the next day despite having reached agreement. In either case, the efforts of the mediating parties could be rendered futile.

B. Avoidance Strategies

Mediators can avoid the trap of leaving agreements undocumented by doing the following:

1. Reinforcing throughout the mediation the requirement that agreements be reduced to writing in order to make them binding: "Nicki, John, and Helen, we have agreed on what additional work is required on the course grounds, and that will be binding once we have reduced it to writing.";

2. Maintaining lists of matters agreed on by the parties to assist the parties in the drafting process;

3. Recommending abbreviated memoranda of understanding or statements of agreement for later redrafting into a detailed agreement;

4. Working off standard form agreements or using modern technology, such as laptop computers, to shorten the required drafting time; and

5. Allowing clients time out from the mediation while professional advisers, or the mediator, undertake the drafting exercise.

XII. Ignoring External Parties

A. The Trap

Reference has been made to the problems of the "external ratifier," whose formal approval is required for any mediation agreement, and the "absent party," who is not directly involved in the mediation but who could destabilize any agreement after the event. While it may be opportune in terms of reaching agreement to ignore these persons in the short term, failure to take account of them can result in jeopardizing long-term viability of the mediated agreement. This is one of the predictable potential problems in any mediation that mediators can take steps to prevent.

B. Avoidance Strategies

The following avoidance strategies may be successful:

1. Before commencement of the mediation, checking with the parties about the existence of stakeholders whose approval is, formally or informally, a required factor for success: "Nicki, what sort of formal and informal ratification will you require for any mediated agreement?";

2. Keeping a note of any reference by the parties to significant external individuals or bodies and referring to them at appropriate times: "John, you have referred several times to the neighboring Simpsons. What will their interests be in the mediated outcome?";

3. Checking with the parties in separate meetings as to whether there are any ratifiers or absent parties who have not yet been identified: "Helen, are there any other people who will be insistent on knowing from you how this matter settled, and will that cause you any problems?";

4. Emphasizing to the parties that the existence of a ratifier or absent party is a problem that both of them needs to address: "John and Helen, you have heard Nicki say that she requires board approval for this agreement, and I think it would be helpful if we all discussed that requirement.";

5. Developing options with the parties for dealing with the ratification issue, with consideration of the mediator's involvement: "Now, what are the op-

tions for persuading the board to endorse this agreement, and would my services be useful in this regard?"

XIII. Exercises

1. Select an area with which you have some familiarity or expertise, for example, studying law, working in a take-away food outlet, playing a particular sport, or practicing as a professional. Draw up a list of some of the traps which, through experience, you have learned to avoid in this area of activity. What do you think might be some of the counterpart traps for mediators?

2. Write up a guide for professional advisers who will participate in mediations you conduct that defines their role, the preferred approach to their tasks, their rights and responsibilities, and the attitude and demeanor expected of them. Ask a lawyer you know to comment on the guide.

3. Prepare a set of lists, tables, or mind maps which set out important features and principles of conflict and negotiation and make these into manageable and accessible cards for use on trains, planes, and cranes as memory aids for your mediation practice.

FIFTEEN

Becoming a Mediator, Careers in Mediation, and Establishing a Private Mediation Practice

The best augury of a man's success in his profession is that he thinks it the finest in the world.

—GEORGE ELIOT (NOVELIST)

I. Introduction

The rapid growth of mediation in both the public and private sectors is a welcome development for the career mediator. For decades, federal and state court systems in the United States have recognized the tremendous value of mediation programs to litigants, including greater control and participation in resolving their legal disputes, more opportunities for creative, interest-based solutions not attainable through litigation, and less case congestion in the courts. Mediation has also found wide acceptance in many governmental agencies. More recently, increasing numbers of private organizations across all industries have begun to value mediation and conflict-management programs as a means to avoid costly and time-consuming traditional litigation. Not surprisingly, the increased demand for mediation has fueled the expansion of educational choices for those who wish to become trained as mediators or dispute-resolution professionals and has created significant employment opportunities for mediators.

The sections that follow provide an overview of some of the education options and career opportunities available to those in the field of mediation. We also address some of the fundamentals of marketing and starting a private mediation practice. This chapter is designed to provide a general introduction to a mediation career.

II. Developing Mediator Credentials

A. Training and Qualifications

Before the 1980s, mediation scarcely existed in the United States as a distinct profession. When people wished to mediate their disputes, they sought the assistance of clergy, respected merchants, or other professionals, such as psychologists, lawyers, or judges. Mediation then was not yet a recognized profession but rather a service that other professionals provided. As a consequence, most who practiced mediation did so on a limited basis and relied on their personal observations, experience, analytical instincts, and abilities to become more effective mediators.

As the practice of mediation increased, however, there was a growing awareness of the benefit of having mediators who were formally trained in three areas: *knowledge* about mediation, development of *skills and techniques* in mediation, and *attitudes* toward standards and ethical requirements. Today, an array of formal training options is available to provide this basic foundation for mediators. The options include a variety of training sources as well as a choice of substantive training programs.

1. WHERE TRAINING IS AVAILABLE

Formal mediation training is available through four sources: (1) *community mediation centers*, (2) *professional mediation and dispute-resolution organizations*, (3) *private mediators*, and (4) *colleges and universities*. The first three share the benefit of offering relatively low-cost and conveniently located mediation training. Certificates and degrees from academic institutions are usually more costly, but the cost is often justified by the quality and scope of the educational experience.

a. *Community Mediation Centers*

Community mediation centers are found in many communities throughout the United States. They are non-profit organizations that are funded, all or in part, by municipal, state, or federal government. These centers provide free or low-cost mediations to the community. As part of their mission, they also offer mediation courses taught by local mediators. The courses offered are limited to a basic mediation class, and sometimes one or two more specialized or advanced mediation courses. The benefits of this type of training are its low cost, convenience, and the opportunity it gives students to observe and participate in actual mediations through the center as part of their training.

b. *Professional Mediation and Dispute-Resolution Organizations*

Professional mediation and dispute-resolution organizations also offer workshops and seminars in mediation. These are non-profit organizations comprised of local mediators who have organized to promote the mediation profession as well as their own professional development. Similar to community centers, the training is limited in scope, relatively low in cost, convenient, and provided by local mediators or sometimes more well-known mediators. On the other hand, such organizations do not offer mediation services, so the student does not receive exposure to the process of mediation in the context of actual disputes.

c. *Private Mediators*

Private mediators sometimes teach mediation as a way to earn income and promote their own mediation practice. The student earns a mediation certificate for completing the private course. This form of training is not standardized and the quality varies considerably from mediator to mediator, depending upon the mediator's experience, education, ability as mediator, and skill as a teacher. The courses are low cost and convenient but are limited in scope and lack the opportunity for the student to participate in actual mediations.

d. *Colleges and Universities*

Many *colleges and universities* offer degrees, certificates, and seminars in mediation and dispute resolution, and many new programs are being added as the field expands. Although these programs are often more expensive than those offered through other venues, they offer several distinct advantages. The faculty members who teach in these programs typically will have had significant formal training in mediation as well as a scholarly interest in mediation. Graduation from these training programs is considered more prestigious in the field than the other options just discussed, particularly if it leads to an academic degree or certificate, which is often beyond most states' requirements to serve as a mediator in a "court-connected" dispute. These programs usually offer a practicum or clinic experience that enables students to observe and participate in actual mediations in the local community. Academic institutions offer a much wider range of dispute-resolution courses that can broaden and deepen the student's understanding of mediation well beyond that which one might receive in the other training venues. Other advantages of the academic setting might include access to the most recent scholarship in the field, study-abroad programs, career guidance, and placement services.

Certainly, each training program must be evaluated on its merits, and quality training can be found in any of the above venues. The serious student of mediation would be well advised to research the individual programs for issues of quality and practicality prior to making a selection.

2. BASIC MEDIATION TRAINING

All the training providers discussed above offer the basic mediation training course. The basic mediation training course is what most states require an individual to complete before he or she can serve as a mediator in a state-sponsored mediation program in that state.[1] After successful completion of the course, the participant

---

1. Requirements and procedures for becoming a mediator in government-connected conflicts vary considerably from state to state. We encourage mediators to research the requirements for states in which they intend to practice.

typically is able to mediate community and civil disputes, although some states require separate training for mediating civil disputes.

The length of this course varies from state to state, but the most common length is forty training hours. The typical mediation curriculum explains the process of mediation and introduces some of the seminal techniques mediators use to improve communication between the parties and aid them in making better decisions about the dispute. It also introduces the applicable ethical guidelines for mediation practice and provides the student with the opportunity to practice his or her skills and techniques through exercises and role plays where simulated disputes are mediated and discussed.

Additional training beyond the basic mediation course is almost universally required in the United States if a mediator wishes to mediate family or divorce disputes. Most often an additional twenty-four hours of training is required. Family mediations, especially those that involve custody and child support issues, present unique challenges for the mediator. Mediations involving family matters can be highly emotional conflicts that have been developing for years or decades. The disputants are often highly polarized. These types of disputes can also involve issues that raise public concerns, such as spousal, elder, or child abuse. Accordingly, some knowledge of family social dynamics, crisis intervention, and the applicable state family law is needed to mediate them effectively.

Other substantive areas involve unique issues, dynamics, and challenges where additional training is beneficial although typically not required by the state. For example, additional training is available and advisable if you intend to mediate disputes involving employment, environmental, securities, or public policy.

3. ADVANCED TRAINING

Mediation is a complex skill that usually requires hundreds of hours of study and practice to develop a reasonable level of competency. The forty hours for basic mediation training that most states require is an arbitrarily chosen duration that has little correlation to the time and experience it takes to become a skilled mediator. Thus, individuals who are serious about becoming mediators should pursue advanced study. Advanced study in mediation and dispute resolution is now available in the form of graduate academic certificate programs and both undergraduate and graduate degree programs at many colleges and universities across the United States, which is a sign of the growing acceptance and integration of dispute resolution in our society.

A graduate academic certificate program consists of several courses in dispute resolution that can be taken for credit or non-credit and requires in the range of 15–21 credit hours. Taking a combination of required and elective courses fulfills these credits. The required courses are a selection of introductory courses that survey the fields of dispute resolution, mediation, and negotiation. The advantage of a graduate academic certificate over a basic mediation training course is that it provides a broader and deeper understanding of dispute resolution in general, and mediation in particular, as well as a greater opportunity to develop the necessary skills to become a good mediator. For example, since mediation is often defined as "assisted negotiation," a prospective mediator would benefit from courses in negotiation and communication. Yet these topics cannot be covered in depth in a basic mediation training course.

Master's degrees in dispute resolution are also now available. These programs may be styled as Master of Arts, Master of Science, or LL.M programs (for lawyers). They range from 32 to over 60 credit hours. Like the certificate programs, the curriculum for a master's program consists of a combination of required and elective courses, often including a clinical experience component. There are at least two distinct advantages that a master's degree in dispute resolution has over a graduate academic certificate. The first advantage is that the additional credit hours allow a student to specialize in a particular aspect of dispute resolution. For instance, a person interested in family mediation may take additional courses in divorce mediation, family dynamics, family law, and counseling and interviewing. The second advantage of earning a master's degree is that it carries increased value in the job market. Most mediators in the United States have only taken the basic course in mediation. As mediation and dispute-resolution procedures become more widely used, competition for jobs in the field will also increase. A master's degree is a distinguishing credential that enhances the attractiveness of the mediator.

4. MAKING THE DECISION

Where and what type of formal mediation education one chooses to pursue is a personal decision that must take into account many factors, not the least of which is time and expense. But there are three considerations in particular that you should take into account: First, how do you plan on using your mediation skills? If you intend to use your knowledge of mediation to enhance an already existing career, then a basic course in mediation may serve your purposes. For example, if you are a manager of a manufacturing plant who regularly must address disputes among employees, taking the basic mediation course would help you build a core set of skills to help you perform that aspect of your job better. If you are planning on having a significant part-time or full-time career as a mediator or dispute-resolution professional, however, the greater time and financial investments involved in earning an academic certificate or master's degree would certainly be justified.

Second, it's also important to evaluate the quality of the program you are interested in. Presently, there is little governmental supervision of mediation education programs. While most states have some criteria for accrediting a person or organization to teach mediation and/or dispute-resolution courses, the oversight is minimal. Thus, there is a considerable range of quality among mediation training programs. To better protect your investment of time and money, it is best to review the institution and proposed curriculum carefully and compare it to competing institutions and courses. Speaking to the instructor or director is another good way to get an idea of whether he or she can communicate the topic effectively. Asking for references from previous attendees is invaluable. One of the best ways to assess the quality of a mediation course or program is to sit in on a small portion of a course before taking it. Most quality programs have no hesitation in granting this request.

Third, and finally, you should consider the program's reputation in the community in which you plan to practice mediation. Reputation is an especially important consideration, for those who intend to present themselves as career mediators in the marketplace. As is the case with any business or profession, the reputation of the mediator's school program is relevant to the individual's marketability, especially at the beginning of a career. Sometimes more reputable institutions are more expensive or less convenient than other sources of mediation training, but your marketability upon graduation may be worth the additional investment.

B. Licensure, Certification, and Accreditation

Presently, there is no formal process for review and approval of a mediator's qualifications prior to his or her practicing mediation at either the national or state level. Anyone can hold themselves out as a "mediator" regardless of training, education, or experience. If one wishes to mediate in connection with a court- or state-sponsored mediation program, however, most jurisdictions require minimum mediation training.[2] For example, to be listed on a roster of mediators in a specific state or federal court or as a mediator in special needs education matters, a jurisdiction will have training and education requirements that must be met. Yet, the length of such trainings varies widely.[3] Forty hours of mediation training is one of the minimum requirements for many court-connected mediation programs across the country, but there is no standard curriculum.[4]

Various initiatives around the country to impose some professional licensure, certification, or accreditation standards on mediators have thus far been unsuccessful.[5] The reasons for a jurisdiction's adopting some form of regulation over the mediators are the same as they are for any service profession that works to solve problems in the community, like lawyers or doctors. One significant reason for regulation is to protect the public from "bad actors, incompetent practitioners, and unqualified providers."[6] Such regulations, along with meaningful education and training requirements, would also enhance mediator skill level and bolster the credibility of the mediation as a profession.[7]

---

2. Art Hinshaw, *Regulating Mediators*, 21 HARV. NEGOT. L. REV. 163, 172–73 (2016).
3. *Id.* at 172.
4. *Id.* at 173–74.
5. *Id.* at 208.
6. *Id.* at 199.
7. *Id.* at 201.

Absent government regulation, the practice of mediation has been guided by private associations and organizations through a disparate and often conflicting assortment of codes and ethical guidelines that often conflict from state to state, as well as within the same state. These organizations have no real power, however, to enforce the rules and codes they adopt, except for disqualifying a mediator's membership. That said, these national, state, and local dispute-resolution organizations have provided a degree of credibility for mediators and the profession by promoting mediation, holding valuable professional conferences, promoting public awareness of mediation, and offering professional education.[8]

At present, the most comprehensive effort to bring national coherence to the field of mediation in the United States is the Uniform Mediation Act (UMA). The UMA was approved in 2001 by the National Conference of Commissioners on Uniform State Laws (NCCUSL), a non-profit, state-sponsored organization that provides model legislation to bring clarity and uniformity to various areas of the law. The UMA has no force of law in and of itself. Rather, it is prototype legislation for states to adopt, in whole or in part, to govern legal and policy issues regarding mediation. The NCCUSL is a highly regarded institution that has been responsible for a large number of now well established and respected laws such as the Uniform Commercial Code, to name one of its better known efforts. The UMA was created through a joint effort between the NCCUSL drafting committee and a drafting committee from the American Bar Association's Section of Dispute Resolution. Those committees also received considerable academic support and drafting suggestions from many other institutions and organizations with a particular expertise in mediation.[9]

A significant motivation in creating the UMA arose from the proliferation of conflicting state statutes addressing mediation.[10] The most common areas in which these statutes differed were in the definition of mediation, the scope of confidentiality, and the exceptions to confidentiality.[11] Accordingly, the UMA attempts to create a comprehensive and uniform policy on the most important aspects of the mediation process. In particular, the UMA aims to

---

8. Some of the more prominent of these national organizations are the American Arbitration Association, the American Bar Association Section on Dispute Resolution, Association of Conflict Resolution, Academy of Professional Family Mediators, International Academy of Mediators, U.S. Ombudsman Association, and the National Academy of Distinguished Neutrals.

9. Notable academic support was provided by Harvard University Law School, Missouri-Columbia School of Law, Ohio State University College of Law, and Bowdoin College. Drafting advice was contributed by numerous dispute-resolution organizations, such as the Association for Conflict Resolution, National Council of Dispute Resolution Organizations, American Arbitration Association, Federal Mediation, and Conciliation Service.

10. The drafters also found statutory conflicts within state laws, as there were more than 2500 different laws nationally addressing some aspect of mediation.

11. UNIFORM MEDIATION ACT (2005) (Prefatory Note).

- "promote candor of parties through confidentiality of the mediation process, subject only to the need for disclosure to accommodate specific and compelling societal interests…";
- "encourage the policy of fostering prompt, economical, and amicable resolution of disputes in accordance with principles of integrity of the mediation process, active party involvement, and informed self-determination by the parties…"; and
- "advance the policy that the decision-making authority in the mediation process rests with the parties."[12]

Uniformity in the rules regulating mediation promotes predictability and confidence in mediation. For example, when laws concerning mediation confidentiality differ from state to state, a statement made by a party in mediation in one state might nevertheless be admissible in evidence in another state. Moreover, mediations are increasingly being conducted simultaneously in multiple jurisdictions via telephone, the internet, and other technologies. In such situations, conflicting mediation laws can raise uncertainties about what rules govern the mediation process and may lead to additional disputes. These ambiguities and inconsistencies, as well as others, undermine public confidence in mediation and make mediation more complex to administer.

In addition to these benefits, there is enormous value in the fact that experts in their respective fields are responsible for drafting uniform laws. These laws are not a product of a state legislature that often has far less time and fewer expert resources to craft highly specialized legislation. The UMA represents years of work by dozens of the most respected authorities in mediation, with contributions from hundreds of other mediation experts. Thus, while not everyone will agree with all the drafters' policy choices, the UMA nevertheless is a manifestation of the best thinking of some of the best minds on the topic. It is thus afforded considerable respect and authority.[13]

The mediator should familiarize himself or herself with the individual state's statutes, court rules, and regulations that typically prescribe some ethical guidelines. Mediators should also be familiar with the training a mediator must have to mediate a dispute, in situations where the dispute is in some manner connected to a government system, like litigation or an agency proceeding. This governmental oversight is not a license or a certification.

---

12. *Id.*

13. As of this writing, the following states and territories have enacted the UMA: District of Columbia, Georgia, Hawaii, Idaho, Illinois, Iowa, Nebraska, New Jersey, Ohio, South Dakota, Utah, Vermont, and Washington. *See* Uniform Law Commission, *Mediation Act*, https://www.uniformlaws.org/committees/community-home?CommunityKey=45565a5f-0c57-4bba-bbab-fc-7de9a59110#LegBillTrackingAnchor.

C. Gaining Experience as a Mediator

Mediation is a skill, like playing the piano, playing golf, or painting landscapes. Like all skills, you must practice it to master it. Gaining experience as a mediator, therefore, is critical to a mediator's education. Experience also plays a critical role in marketing oneself as a mediator. While the experience gained in the formal mediation education process through exercises, observations, and role plays builds skills, a mediator's education is incomplete without having had the opportunity to confront real conflicts involving real people. This invaluable mediating experience can be acquired through both formal and informal means.

1. FORMAL AVENUES FOR DEVELOPING EXPERIENCE

Volunteering one's mediation services is an excellent way to gain valuable experience. Community mediation centers, churches, legal aid organizations, governmental agencies, and courts frequently seek out volunteer mediators to assist in resolving disputes. These organizations, unlike paying clients, often place little emphasis on past practical experience. They typically require only that the volunteer have the necessary formal training required by the state. The stakes are also frequently low. This is an excellent opportunity, particularly for the beginner mediator, to hone one's mediation skills while also providing a valuable community service.

2. EXPERIENCE THROUGH CO-MEDIATION

Another way of developing experience is through a co-mediator relationship with an experienced mediator. This apprenticeship or mentoring arrangement is most often available through community mediation centers and the academic programs. However, some private mediators are also willing to establish mentoring relationships. Developing a mentor-mentee relationship with an experienced mediator provides the dual benefit of honing one's mediation skills and obtaining invaluable advice from someone more experienced. This is a great way to accelerate your learning.

3. REFLECTIVE PRACTICE

Where beginner mediators are able to gain practical experience, they are advised to follow the principles of reflective practice in order to develop their skills and expertise. This involves learning from experience through self-debriefing, mutual debriefing with a co-mediator, or supervisory debriefing with an experienced external mediator. Another way to develop the benefits of reflective practice is by conducting follow-up surveys of those who have attended the mediation, including clients and professional advisers. These "audit" activities provide both an "objective" appraisal of what mediators are doing well and what they could be doing differently as well as subjective evaluations of effectiveness from clients and their advisers. In all cases it is advisable to focus on qualitative as well as quantitative indicators of effectiveness. (Appendix 6 contains debriefing forms for mediators, and for the parties and their lawyers.)

4. INFORMAL METHODS FOR DEVELOPING MEDIATION EXPERIENCE

Where there are limited options for gaining experience in formal mediation, it is still possible to do so informally. In many situations outside formal mediations there will be opportunities to apply some of the process and many of the skills and techniques. Here are some of the many areas in which this is possible:

- In *chairing* meetings of businesses and voluntary associations;
- In holding *planning meetings* for partners and associates;
- In conducting hearings in *disciplinary tribunals*;
- In teaching in small *group seminars*;
- In *managing grievances* in employment situations and complaints from customers;
- In dealing with *aggrieved shareholders* or other passionate and committed people; and
- In dealing with crowds in *emergency or crisis* situations.

III. Employment Opportunities

Mediation skills are a valuable and marketable asset for any businessperson in almost any job that involves interaction with people. This is especially true in supervisory, managerial, and executive positions. In addition, there are significant employment opportunities available in both the private and public sectors that require mediation or dispute resolution as their central skill set, and these opportunities are growing. The following are some of the more commonly advertised positions.[14]

A. Opportunities for Salaried Positions

1. COURT-CONNECTED PROGRAMS

The federal and state trial and appellate court systems offer opportunities for mediators to find employment either as the director or coordinator of the court's mediation program or as a mediator of selected cases on the court's docket. Every federal trial and appellate court in the United States and nearly every state court system offers a mediation program to help litigants resolve their disputes. A full-time ADR coordinator typically administers these programs. This position is actually mandated for the federal district courts by the federal ADR Act of 1998.[15] Similar

---

14. *See generally* PETER LOVENHEIM & EMILY DOSKOW, BECOMING A MEDIATOR: YOUR GUIDE TO CAREER OPPORTUNITIES (2004).
15. 28 U.S.C. 651 (2000).

ADR coordinator positions are available in the state courts at both the trial and appellate levels. With regard to the actual mediations, most mediations in court-connected programs are performed by mediators in private practice, either on a volunteer or fee basis. However, several trial courts are also hiring full-time mediators in an effort to emulate the success of the federal appellate court mediation programs. In the federal appellate court mediation programs, all but one of the thirteen circuit courts employs full-time mediators. Federal appellate programs have been very successful in resolving cases and easing the crowded appellate dockets. Several commentators have attributed the success of federal appellate mediation programs to the use of full-time mediators.

2. STATE AND FEDERAL AGENCIES

State and federal administrative agencies have come to recognize that the use of ADR processes, especially mediation, in resolving disputes can save time and money and improve their services. Thus, many agencies hire individuals with mediation skills. In the federal system, all agencies are required by the Administrative Dispute Resolution Act to incorporate ADR procedures into their dispute-resolution processes.[16] While there is significant diversity in how and to what extent the different federal agencies use mediation, many agencies rely heavily on mediation in their daily activities. These federal agencies include the Equal Employment Opportunity Commission, the Internal Revenue Service, the Environmental Protection Agency, and Medicare, to name just a few. Another important source of potential employment for mediators is the Federal Mediation and Conciliation Service.[17] This agency has been mediating disputes between employers and unions since its founding in 1918 and has regional offices throughout the United States.

3. COMMUNITY MEDIATION CENTERS

Community mediation centers are private, non-profit, or governmentally funded organizations that offer low cost mediations to the communities that they serve. These centers handle civil disputes, neighborhood disagreements, and minor criminal complaints. Like court-connected programs, these centers employ coordinators who need to be trained mediators. The center's coordinator is often both an administrator as well as one of the center's mediators. Mediation centers, depending on their size and funding, often employ full-time mediators as well, although most mediations are performed by volunteers.

4. COLLEGES AND UNIVERSITIES

Colleges and universities are among the fastest growing source of employment for people trained as mediators to handle internal disputes. These highly diverse and

---

16. 5 U.S.C. 571–84 (2000).

17. Information about the Federal Mediation and Conciliation Service can be found by visiting www.fmcs.gov.

usually non-profit organizations often face significant administrative challenges and have strict budgets. As a result, they benefit tremendously from establishing designated positions for addressing conflicts promptly and efficiently as they arise in specific operational areas. For example, disputes between students can be efficiently handled by the manager of the Student Dispute Resolution Office. Employment disputes might be managed by a designated ombudsman who is trained in the handling of employment issues. When these matters are handled promptly in house, the organization realizes general administrative cost savings including those arising from litigation avoidance.

5. CORPORATE

In 2003 the American Arbitration Association, a national, non-profit dispute-resolution organization, published a study that found "companies that embrace a 'dispute-wise' approach to managing business and workplace conflicts enjoy lower operating costs and are more successful at preserving business relationships than those who favor litigation." Among other things, "dispute-wise" companies relied upon arbitration and mediation to resolve disputes.[18] The study involved 100 Fortune 1000 companies and explains why many companies throughout the United States are hiring people who have expertise in dispute resolution, mediation in particular. Such companies are hiring managers and supervisors with formal education in dispute resolution and human resources specialists who are trained in dispute resolution. Many companies are even creating dispute-resolution offices that need staffing, using ombudsmen to help address disputes before they escalate, implementing in-house dispute resolution systems and policies, and conducting employee training in mediating conflicts.

6. PRIVATE DISPUTE-RESOLUTION COMPANIES

A dispute-resolution practice company is a group of two or more mediators or other dispute-resolution professionals who form a group for the purpose of providing ADR services. They are similar to law firms or medical group practices. Depending on its business structure and the nature of the position being offered, a mediator might obtain a flat salary or some combination of salary and profit sharing. These groups usually offer a host of ADR services. In addition to mediation, an ADR practice group might offer other services like arbitration, dispute resolution system design, or training in mediation or negotiation.

---

18. American Arbitration Association, *Dispute-Wise Business Management* (2006), www.adr .org.

B. Private Practice

Mediators who desire to be their own boss and have the flexibility of owning their own business might consider starting a private mediation practice. The private mediator might choose to handle a wide range of matters involving any substantive area, or he or she might choose to specialize in one or more areas, such as family conflicts, labor and employment matters, or international conflicts. Private mediators can work full-time, part-time, or even on a volunteer basis for personal satisfaction. Because well trained mediators are still a rarity in the field, high-quality mediators who commit themselves to excellence and build a solid reputation in the community have the opportunity to cultivate a successful and lucrative mediation practice.

Establishing a private mediation practice carries with it some challenges as well. For example, while mediation is becoming increasingly popular, many organizations and people remain uneducated about its availability and benefits. Therefore, mediation is not considered in many disputes that would benefit from it. It is also a challenge to distinguish oneself in the field as the requirements for becoming an "approved mediator" are still rather minimal. Effective marketing strategies will be discussed in detail below.

C. Mediation-Related Employment

1. TEACHING

As the popularity of mediation grows in the United States, the number of mediation education programs is expanding, creating more opportunities for mediation faculty, instructors, and program administrators. These opportunities exist in both undergraduate and graduate academic institutions, as well as with private mediation organizations. Most teaching positions in the mediation field are part-time, but there are increasing numbers of full-time positions available at colleges, universities, and other organizations for those with advanced degrees. A well-educated and experienced mediator who has teaching ability usually has opportunities to do so in his or her community.

2. ASSOCIATIONS AND ORGANIZATIONS

Across the United States, there are hundreds of dispute-resolution associations and organizations that offer administrative employment to individuals with a mediation background. These organizations, whose membership is mostly comprised of mediators and other dispute-resolution professionals, provide information and special events for their members. They often employ full-time staff to assist with organizing conferences, editing newsletters, making presentations to the community or other dispute resolution professionals, tracking legislation, and even writing books, papers, or briefs in connection with policy initiatives important to the dispute-resolution community.

3. CONSULTING

Mediation professionals can also provide consulting services to private organizations or public entities regarding a wide variety of issues involving conflict management and dispute-resolution policy and process. As companies seek to incorporate dispute-resolution principles and practices into their operations to create better business relationships and more efficient functions, they may prefer to hire the services of a consultant rather than invest in a full-time professional. The services required may vary significantly in duration and substance from client to client. For example, a mediator could provide guidance in setting up an in-house dispute resolution process to assist the organization in managing workplace disputes. A mediator could also provide educational lectures and workshops for the organization's managers or employees on conflict management, dispute resolution and mediation, or negotiation in the workplace.

D. Developing Frontiers

1. VICTIM-OFFENDER MEDIATION

Victim-offender mediation is a process that provides crime victims and their offenders an opportunity in a "safe and structured" environment to discuss the crime and negotiate the best manner to bring justice to the situation.[19] Victim-offender mediation is a form of "restorative justice," the focus of which is to repair the physical and psychological damage done by the crime. The nature of the crimes most frequently mediated involve property damage and minor assaults, although some programs have reported benefits in mediating more violent crimes such as rape and murder.[20]

Unlike our traditional criminal legal system, the goal of restorative justice is not punishment, but healing. The specific goals of most victim-offender programs are to increase victim involvement and healing, to get the offender to take responsibility for his or her actions and learn from the experience, and to provide restitution to the victim for the harm caused. Restitution can take many forms depending upon the nature of the offense and the damage inflicted. Restitution might be made in dollars, community service, work performed for the victim, and/or an agreement by the offender to attend a treatment program. Restitution is often of secondary importance to the victim. Many participants report that the opportunity to talk with the offender about the effect the crime had on them is its most satisfying aspect.[21]

---

19. Mark S. Umbreit, Robert B. Coates & Betty Vos, *Victim-Offender Mediation: Evidence-Based Practice Over Three Decades, in* THE HANDBOOK OF DISPUTE RESOLUTION 445, 456 (Michael L. Moffit & Robert C. Bordone eds., 2005).

20. Marty Price, *Personalizing Crime: Mediating Produces Restorative Justice for Victims and Offenders,* 7 DISP. RESOL. MAG. 8, 11 (Fall 2000).

21. Umbreit, Coates & Vos, *supra* note 19, at 445, 456.

There are currently over 300 victim-offender programs in the United States and Canada, and each year the number of programs increases as the parties report satisfaction with the process and the benefits of such programs are more thoroughly explored and understood. One of the additional benefits of victim-offender programs, especially among youth offenders, is a decrease in recidivism. For example, the Northwest's Victim Offender Mediation Program in Multnomah County, Oregon, reported a 22 percent drop in recidivism during a one-year follow-up between youths that participated in the victim-offender program as compared to those youths who did not.[22]

2. PRIVATE INTERNATIONAL MEDIATION

Private international mediation refers to mediation between private citizens or organizations from different countries.[23] In recent years, as a greater number of people have come to embrace mediation to solve their domestic business disputes, they have also sought mediation to help solve their private and business international disputes. Historically, private companies have used arbitration for international disputes.[24] Although arbitration can overcome many of the challenges of resolving disputes between people and/or organizations with different legal traditions and processes, arbitration is still an adversarial, time-consuming, and expensive endeavor. Consequently, many organizations are using mediation in their international disputes for the very reasons that they are using mediation in their domestic disputes: mediation is, on average, less costly, less time-consuming, and provides participants greater control over the outcome than either arbitration or litigation. Perhaps most importantly, mediation is a less adversarial process that offers the increased possibility of parties continuing a profitable relationship after the dispute is resolved. This feature of mediation is especially attractive to those businesses and people with long-term business relationships. As globalization of the world economies continues, parties will increasingly seek international mediation as an attractive dispute-resolution option.

3. ONLINE MEDIATION

Coinciding with the commercialization of the internet in the mid-1990s, online mediation emerged as a significant and distinct form in the alternative dispute resolution landscape.[25] Online mediation combines the principles of mediation with the power and convenience of the internet. What started out as a means for techni-

---

22. *Id.* at 463.

23. Andrea Kupfer Schneider, *Public and Private International Dispute Resolution, in* THE HANDBOOK OF DISPUTE RESOLUTION 438, 443.

24. Jeswald Salacuse, *Mediation in International Business, in* JACOB BERCOVITCH, STUDIES IN INTERNATIONAL MEDIATION 213 (2003).

25. For a comprehensive review of the history and types of ODR, see ONLINE DISPUTE RESOLUTION: THEORY AND PRACTICE (Mohamed S. Abel Wahbe, Ethan Katsh & Daniel Rainey, eds. 2d ed. 2021). For an excellent review of ODR and eCommerce, see AMY J. SCHMITZ & COLIN

cally inclined people to resolve specialized disputes has burgeoned into a multi-million dollar a year mediation industry that services a wide range of people with all manner of disputes. One of the most common forms of disputes addressed by online is commercial internet transactions, but other types of disputes such as real estate and family disputes are becoming more common. Most importantly, online mediation provides an inexpensive and convenient forum for resolving conflicts for people and organizations when geography or legal systems divides them.

Online mediation is more than dispute resolution by e-mail. Like "off-line" mediation, it assists parties in clarifying issues, uncovering interests, and thinking objectively about the problem so that they can make good decisions on how to address it. Although a mediator is often involved, some of the analytical functions of the mediator are enhanced (or replaced) by computer programs that take participants through a series of issue-clarifying questions or which help parties identify and rate the importance of needs and concerns in resolving their dispute. There are even programs that will generate potential solutions.[26]

Private businesses, non-profit organizations, and governmental entities have embraced online mediation, and it is among dispute resolution's fastest growing fields. Despite this, the field is still young and provides the interested mediator with boundless opportunity for innovation and growth. (For a detailed discussion of virtual mediation, which we define as mediation via videoconferencing, see Chapter 11 — *Virtual Mediation*.)

IV. Marketing Your Private Mediation Practice

A. Introduction

Like any business professional, a private-practice mediator or mediation group will need to engage in marketing efforts to develop an established business. It is not enough to be good at what you do. Even excellent mediators need to market themselves beyond placing an advertisement in the local phonebook to generate significant business. You must get the word out that you are good and that you are available to provide services. There are many ways to effectively market your practice, depending on a variety of factors, such as location, field of practice, and your skills and personality.

In addition to marketing yourself, however, you might also want to give some thought to how you can help promote the mediation profession as another way of

---

RULE, THE NEW HANDSHAKE: ONLINE DISPUTE RESOLUTION AND THE FUTURE OF CONSUMER PROTECTION(2018).

26. SmartSettle is one company that utilizes software to improve parties' decision making in negotiation. Using patented algorithms, it advertises that it will assist parties in achieving fair and efficient solutions. *See* www.SmartSettle.com.

increasing your professional business opportunities. Because the mediation profession is still relatively young, there is a lack of education in society about the existence and benefits of mediation. Sometimes the people who would benefit most from your mediation services and who serve as the gatekeepers of disputes, such as lawyers, business professionals, court personnel, and governmental employees, are either unaware of how mediation can improve their business functions or they have a bias against mediation because of their lack of experience with quality mediators. The United States legal system has a long and venerable history. Despite widespread lamenting about clogged courts, a costly litigation process, and dissatisfaction with traditional litigation results, our society still feels a gravitational pull to the almighty courtroom to solve disputes. As Jerold Auerbach observes in his insightful book *Justice Without Law*, in America "law is our national religion; lawyers constitute our priesthood; the courtroom is our cathedral, where contemporary passion plays are enacted."[27]

Mediators who combat misinformation and misconceptions about the mediation profession help to elevate the status of all mediators everywhere. In doing so, their individual mediation practices will undoubtedly reap the benefits of their efforts as well—"a rising tide raises all ships." There is already some generic marketing of mediation by governments, courts, and agencies that portrays it to the public as a legitimate and attractive form of dispute resolution. This generic publicity provides a solid foundation for the marketing of specific mediation services.

Successful marketing is a continual, steady process. It should not be viewed as a single event or even a series of unrelated events. It must be part of a coherent plan of getting known, staying known, and being seen as a valuable resource to the people who are your potential clients.

In the context of private mediation practice, the prevailing approach to marketing is focusing on elements of client satisfaction. In the *satisfaction* story,[28] satisfaction is measured in terms of cost, time, effectiveness, privacy, and other attractive features of the process. For example, private mediation may be competing with a free or subsidized dispute-resolution service provided by courts or government agencies, in which case the mediator might sell his services by emphasizing the privacy or quality of the process. In other situations, prospective clients might be more attracted to mediation's potential for preserving existing business relationships where there are no alternative commercial options available to them. Finding ways to appeal to client satisfaction is the prevailing concept in the current promotion of mediation and in this book.

---

27. JEROLD S. AUERBACH, JUSTICE WITHOUT LAW? 9 (1984).
28. ROBERT A. BARUCH BUSH & JOSEPH P. FOLGER, THE PROMISE OF MEDIATION: RESPONDING TO CONFLICT THROUGH EMPOWERMENT AND RECOGNITION 20 (1994).

B. Mediation Is a Service Industry

Mediation is a personal service, and so when you market your mediation services you are marketing yourself.[29] Unlike the sale of tangible goods, where the qualities and attributes of the item are most important to the buyer, when you are selling a personal service, *your* qualities and *your* attributes are what are most important. To some extent, all salespeople are in the business of selling themselves and engendering trust and respect in the prospective buyer, even when they are selling a tangible good, like televisions. But in a private mediation practice, you are both the salesperson and the commodity.

1. CHARACTERISTICS OF SUCCESSFUL MEDIATORS

Successful mediators run the gamut of personalities and mediation styles, but the fundamental qualities that will likely earn you respect and a healthy client base fall into the following four categories: (1) *people*, (2) *passion*, (3) *excellence*, and (4) *authenticity*.[30]

a. *People*

Mediation is a "people" business. Thus, your ability to make personal connections with people and inspire them to trust and respect you are essential to building a successful and profitable mediation practice. Your ability to achieve this does not depend so much on your personality as it depends on your willingness to take an interest in your clients as people and to show respect for them at all times. Maintain a sense of calm and grace, especially when the participants' emotions are running high. Be professional in your appearance and manner. Be punctual. Be honest and truthful. Your clients will notice and remember.

b. *Passion*

Demonstrating passion for your work is a wonderful way to inspire people to hire you. Most successful mediators view their mediation practices as a "calling," not just a job. If you are entering a mediation career simply to make money, you should rethink your decision. There are easier and more lucrative ways to make a living. Successful mediators love to mediate and gain great satisfaction from the process of helping people resolve their problems. Although the work often can be difficult and exhausting, successful mediators are energized by the challenges and thrive in the intense, sometimes chaotic melee of problems and people. They are fully committed to and have faith in the process. Participants and potential clients see that commitment, faith, and passion and are motivated to work harder at the process of mediation themselves.

---

29. *See generally* FORREST S. MOSTEN, MEDIATION CAREER GUIDE 170–83 (2001).
30. *See generally* JEFFREY KRIVIS & NAOMI LUCKS, HOW TO MAKE MONEY AS A MEDIATOR 9–31 (2006).

c. *Excellence*

Striving to maintain a standard of excellence in your mediation practice is a good way to distinguish yourself in a relatively young profession with many seat-of-the-pants mediators. Make an effort to regularly evaluate your skills and ask yourself after each mediation, "How could I improve my performance next time?" even if the case settled. Regularly attend advanced training seminars and stay abreast of new developments in the field to sharpen and deepen your skills and knowledge. In short, immerse yourself in the profession and it will show in the quality of your work.

d. *Authenticity*

Authenticity is another hallmark of most successful mediators.[31] Being "authentic" in this context means not trying to be something you are not. Do not try to be funny if you do not have a comedic personality. Success does not require the stereotypical gregarious and witty "sales" personality. Some mediators may use humor to create personal affinity, others may be thoughtful and sensitive, and still others may be serious and intense. Do not attempt false subtlety when your natural manner is more direct. A genuine nature will inspire trust and respect from the disputants. Most people are good at detecting insincerity, and when they encounter it, trust is undermined. Mediators who act authentically get selected more often and conduct higher quality mediations.

2. IMPORTANCE OF REPUTATION

Unlike a car, clients cannot take you for a test drive, so it is your reputation as a mediator that counts most in your marketing efforts. Much of your business will come from repeat business and referrals, so establishing and maintaining a good reputation are your top priorities. The principal factors that define your reputation as a mediator are how effective you are at assisting the clients in resolving their disputes, particularly the difficult ones, and whether the clients feel good about the process.

Most mediators keep track of their settlement rates, and many advertise them as part of their marketing strategy. For better or worse, it is one way a potential client can judge quality. A potential client's thought process might be that a mediator who settles 80 percent of the cases he or she mediates must be better than one who settles only 50 percent of the cases he or she mediates. While this is not necessarily true, as settlement rates are affected by many factors including the types of cases a mediator handles, the number of mediations done, and sheer luck, certainly mediation skill is also a factor.

One way to increase your settlement rate is to adopt a policy of remaining assigned to a dispute until the end. For example, if you calculate your settlement

31. *Id.* at 38–41.

rate by simply calculating what percent of cases are settled, in whole or in part, on the day of the mediation, you might have a 75 percent settlement rate. However, if you make it your policy to follow the dispute even after the parties leave your office and, with their permission, continue mediating the dispute by telephone and e-mail or even in an in-person follow up session, your settlement rate is going to increase, perhaps by ten percent or more. This is both a function of your ongoing mediation efforts as well as the reality that time settles most matters. For example, a study of U.S. federal civil cases found that approximately 98 percent of cases are resolved before trial.[32] So the longer you stay with a litigated dispute, the more likely your clients will become part of that statistic. Thus, continuing with disputes until the end not only enhances your reputation for commitment to client service but also improves your settlement rate.

Your ability to make participants feel comfortable and satisfied during the mediation process is another key factor in developing a positive reputation in the community. The more you can make participants feel positive about themselves and their situation in the mediation, the more they will feel good about you. The reason for this is twofold. First, it is self-evident that a mediator who interacts in a positive manner with clients and is well received by them will develop a good reputation in the community, regardless of the outcome of the mediation. However, an additional benefit to positive interactions with clients is that they will be more likely to trust you, become an active participant in the process, and listen to reasonable suggestions from you regarding the process and settlement options. Developing this rapport with clients involves demonstrating the specific "characteristics of successful mediators" discussed in the previous section.

C. Determine Your Desired Level of Practice

Success means different things to different people. You must determine what being a successful mediator means to you. While your definition of success will likely change over time, when embarking on a mediation practice, it is best "to begin with the end in mind."[33] There are at least four levels of mediation practice to which you might aspire: (i) *volunteer practice*, (ii) *part-time practice*, (iii) *full-time practice*, and (iv) *premier practice*.

1. VOLUNTEER PRACTICE

Many people enter the field of mediation never intending to make any money doing it. They are drawn to mediation as a form of community service and self-fulfillment. This level of practice involves volunteering as a mediator in community mediation centers, court mediation programs, or industry-specific mediation pro-

---

32. Marc Galanter, *The Vanishing Trial*, DISPUTE RESOL. MAG., Summer 2004, at 4.
33. STEPHEN R. COVEY, THE 7 HABITS OF HIGHLY EFFECTIVE PEOPLE 97–98 (1989).

grams that are now found throughout nearly every community in the United States. For thousands of individuals, helping people resolve their disputes as a form of community service constitutes a successful mediation practice.

2. PART-TIME PRACTICE

For others, a successful mediation practice means profiting financially for their labors, often as a means of supplementing their main source of income. Many professionals, such as lawyers, accountants, psychologists, and businesspeople, have part-time mediation practices where they might do a few mediations a month or only a few a year. Frequently, these mediation practices are related to the mediator's primary profession. For example, a patent lawyer might also market herself as a mediator in patent cases, or a psychologist specializing in family therapy might also market himself as a mediator in family disputes. The income for a part-time mediator can be substantial, even approaching what others might consider a full-time salary. This is especially true where the mediator is experienced and well regarded and can therefore command a significant hourly or daily rate. For instance, an average daily rate for an experienced mediator in a typical metropolitan area at the time of this writing is about $2,000 a day for a two-party mediation. A mediator who is able to perform, on average, two mediations a month could earn $48,000 a year in supplemental income. A part-time mediation practice can be a very attractive path for helping professionals to expand their services and income or as a way to gradually transition into a full-time mediation practice.

3. FULL-TIME PRACTICE

A full-time mediation practice is one where the mediator spends most of his or her time working as a mediator or providing other dispute-resolution services, such as training or designing dispute-resolution systems for organizations. A typical full-time mediator will have a relatively steady source of business, charge close to the average local market rate for his or her services, and earn a respectable living from the business. Nonetheless, full-time mediator earnings vary greatly. As with many other self-employed professionals, there is little data available revealing what the "average" full-time mediator earns. It is also difficult to identify the average mediator income because it is difficult to define what an average mediator is. Mediators' salaries vary depending on experience, skill level, nature of mediations conducted, geographic location, and business acumen. For instance, a successful New York mediator who handles business and commercial disputes will likely earn more than a similarly situated Dallas mediator. The successful Dallas mediator who handles mass tort mediations will likely earn more than the similarly situated Dallas mediator who handles business and commercial disputes. There are, however, in every substantial city in the country, full-time mediators earning professional salaries, many extending into the six-figure incomes.

4. PREMIER PRACTICE

Income is the defining factor that distinguishes a premier mediation practice from a full-time practice. The premier mediator is one who has reached the highest level in the profession, in his or her geographic and/or practice area.[34] Premier mediators can charge as much as $10,000 a day or more. Their yearly incomes are often in the mid- to high-six figures, some well into the seven figures. These mediators often have national or international reputations and can be very selective about the disputes they take on. Often their mediation schedules are booked months in advance.

D. Developing a Marketing Plan

Once you have determined what level of mediation practice best suits your particular situation, you need to develop a strategic marketing plan to help you create a successful practice. A strategic marketing plan assesses how your goals and capabilities can satisfy present or future market needs. At minimum, it should do the following: (1) define the category of clients to which you intend to market, (2) include measurable business goals, and (3) identify appropriate strategies for reaching your business goals, such as how you plan to reach your target client base.[35] The more significant the mediation practice you wish to create, the more time and energy that must be invested into a comprehensive strategic marketing plan.

1. IDENTIFYING THE TARGET MARKET

a. *Market Segmentation*

It is best to narrow your marketing efforts in some way, such as by limiting your target market to substantive disputes in which you have a particular interest or background or to disputes arising within a particular geographic area. A common misstep made by many mediators starting a new practice is to try to be all things to all people. One-size-fits-all marketing is ineffective for the private mediator and leads to little business.

Focusing on a particular category of disputes in a particular geographic area is known as "market segmentation."[36] The purpose of market segmentation is to identify parts of the market in which the mediator might have a competitive edge and then to focus marketing efforts on those areas.[37] This has the benefit of directing limited resources to where they will have the most impact. It also enables the mediator to be in a better position to spot market opportunities because he or she has a better understanding of the clients' particular and often changing needs.

---

34. L. Randolph Lowry, Get Busy, Get Paid: Strategies to Develop a Financially Successful Mediation Practice (2003) (video and notes).

35. *See* Philip Kolter, Thomas Hayes & Paul N. Bloom, Marketing Professional Services 23–34 (2002).

36. *Id.* at 175.

37. *See generally* Mosten, *supra* note 29, at 100–07.

In defining your market segment, therefore, you should rely heavily upon your previous training and experience. Since conflict is ubiquitous, it does not matter in what area you have substantive knowledge. A civil litigator who practices in Essex County, New Jersey, would market to other civil litigators and civil judges in that county. Even if the litigator is just embarking on a mediation practice, the litigator's previous experience and reputation provides some level of credibility when marketing their mediation practice.

b. *Market Niche*

The next step in defining your target market is to identify one or two "market niches." A market niche is a "more narrowly defined group" within your market segment. Mediation lends itself to considerable specialization. For example, there are mediators who specialize in disputes within religious congregations and who accept mediatable disputes from members of all faiths. Other mediators specialize in racial discrimination cases. Emerging technologies in the information technology field will inevitably attract specialist mediators.

Again, it is most effective to build on what you know. Clients are attracted to mediators who are experts in the topic of the dispute. Having substantive knowledge of the topic being discussed in a dispute increases your credibility with the prospective client and gives you greater authority in the mediation. Identifying one or two niche markets also makes marketing more effective because there are fewer people to market to, your qualifications are better aligned with clients' needs, and there is often less competition. For instance, if you have had a previous career as an insurance adjuster who handled a significant number of medical negligence disputes, medical negligence disputes would be an attractive market niche for you to explore. In such a dispute, all other qualifications being equal, a mediator with more generalized insurance dispute experience would be less attractive to prospective clients than you. Effective niche marketing leverages previous experience, knowledge, or training, and is by its nature limited to one or two narrowly defined topics.

2. INCLUDE MEASURABLE BUSINESS GOALS

As part of a larger business plan it is essential to set specific, measurable performance goals for your mediation practice. The goals should be realistic, but also optimistic.[38] Goals should be optimistic because the best, most effective goals are the ones that challenge us. However, they should also be realistic, grounded in an honest evaluation of your situation, training, and experience and logically achievable. If you are a recent law school or business school graduate, setting a goal to establish a premier mediation practice within one year is likely not realistic and thus unhelpful. There are several scientific studies providing compelling evidence that setting appropriate goals in any area of life triggers physiological "striving" mechanisms that focus

---

38. *See* G. RICHARD SHELL, BARGAINING FOR ADVANTAGE 28–30 (2d ed. 2006).

our energies in productive ways and enable the goal-setter to outperform those who do not set goals.[39] A mediation practice should not be initiated with the attitude of "let's see what happens" or "I am going to do the best I can." It should begin with a specific and optimistic set of goals. For example, a person who wishes to have a part-time mediation practice might set the following goal: "Within two years, I want to be conducting an average of one mediation per week, at the market rate." Setting specific performance goals provides direction to your mediation practice and will help you make better strategic decisions concerning it. Simply put, setting goals increases the likelihood that you will be successful.

3. STRATEGIES FOR REACHING THE TARGET MARKET

Before you begin your mediation practice, you should identify how you intend to market yourself. Mediators approach this important aspect of the profession differently, depending upon their resources, background, personality, and skills. The following section will survey some of the more common ways mediators "get known" and "stay known."

a. *Professional Networks*

Building professional networks is the most important form of marketing a mediator can engage in because professional networks provide the main source of client referrals that are the lifeblood of a mediation practice.[40] Professional networks fall within two broad categories, *internal networks* and *external networks*. Internal networks are those relationships you build with other mediation or dispute-resolution professionals, either informally or formally, usually through involvement in dispute-resolution organizations. External networks are those you build with people and organizations within your market segment or niche. Internal and external networks are both important components of building a successful mediation practice, and while each helps to generate referrals, each does so in different yet complementary ways.

i. Internal Networks.

Establishing relationships through internal networking primarily helps you to establish respect and credibility within your profession, which indirectly enhances your reputation in your external networks. Internal networking means getting to know and socializing with other mediators and dispute-resolution professionals. The most convenient way to meet other mediators is to be active in local and national mediation or dispute-resolution organizations. There are hundreds of these organizations spread throughout the country. Some are local organizations and others are national organizations with local chapters. The mission of most of these organiza-

---

39. *See, e.g.,* J.P. Meyer, *The Effect of Goal Difficulty on Physiological Arousal, Cognition, and Task Performance,* 77 J. OF APPLIED PSYCHOL., no. 2, 1992, at 694–704.

40. *See* KRIVIS & LUCKS, *supra* note 30, at 53–75.

tions is to promote and support the practice of mediation and/or dispute resolution, usually through educational programs for members and the general public, as well as to perform charitable work. Many of the most successful mediators are active in these organizations and hold, or have held, leadership positions in them. Aside from the satisfaction of serving your profession, leadership positions in such organizations are a positive addition to your resume and help to distinguish you from the other mediators in the eyes of prospective clients. Stated plainly, they help make you more marketable to your external network.

A secondary but still important function of an internal network is as a source of client referrals. Internal networks are typically not an abundant source of referrals because your peers are not the gatekeepers of disputes but rather are people looking for work just like you. If you establish a good reputation among your peers, however, some referrals are likely to come your way. Mediators refer work to other mediators they know and respect for a variety of reasons. Some common reasons are ethical conflicts, scheduling conflicts, or situations in which the matter may be outside their expertise. It is not an uncommon arrangement, in fact, for a mediator who specializes in a certain type of dispute, civil litigation for instance, to have a reciprocal referral arrangement with a mediator who specializes in, for example, family mediation. Although internal networks can produce referrals, they primarily assist the mediator in establishing a reputation within the profession and should not be considered a substitute for building external networks.

ii. External Networks.

External networks supply the main source of business for most mediation practices. This network is composed of the gatekeepers for the type of disputes in which you specialize. If you are a family mediator, your external network includes family judges, family lawyers, and psychologists. This network would be different if you were a mediator that primarily handles commercial and business disputes, or one that handles public policy disputes. The gatekeepers are the people who recommend mediation to the disputants and who are in the best position to influence their choice of a mediator. These are the generalists in dispute resolution, and they all need to be educated about the appropriateness of mediation as a "specialist" referral option. They are the groups to which mediators should direct some of their marketing. But whatever the level of understanding, referrals in this area are likely to be no different from referrals in other services that are based on personal knowledge of the practitioner, previous experience, or a quality reputation.

There is an ancient tradition among professionals to refer their failures or hopeless cases to other professionals or to other disciplines. Mediation is at times a target for this dumping phenomenon. A danger signal is when a referring lawyer says to the mediator, "Do I have an interesting case for you!" While mediators can have their own screening mechanisms to assess suitability for mediation, it also makes sense to secure some preliminary screening from referrers. Such referrers may require some education and training so that they can conduct this screening themselves. For mediators this may be a worthwhile long-term investment in avoiding the dumping phenomenon.

Self-referral occurs when the disputants bring their dispute directly to a mediator. At present, there is little "self-referral" in mediation. Although self-referral business is increasing as a consequence of a greater public awareness of mediation and its benefits, there is still a long way to go before the general public considers mediation a mainstream process for dealing with conflict. Thus, little business will come directly off the street. Potential mediation clients will usually make primary contact with counselors, lawyers, medical professionals, accountants, government agencies, and other institutions that in turn refer them to mediators they know and esteem.

Mediation panels are formal lists of mediators maintained and managed by either a private or public entity that acts as a clearinghouse or broker for disputes. When the organization gets a dispute, the client either picks a mediator from the panel or is assigned a mediator by the organization. The panels are often organized by area of specialty. In the case of private mediation panels, the organization usually takes a percentage of the mediator's fee for the referral. For this fee percentage, the organization often takes care of the business end of the mediation, such as coordinating the mediation and billing. Sometimes, panels will even provide conference facilities as part of the arrangement. Public panels, on the other hand, are those that are run by court systems or state or federal agencies. These panels typically do not take a percentage of the mediator's fee and usually permit the mediator to charge his or her regular market rate. But some public panels set a fixed rate for panel members and impose other obligations, such as requiring a panel member to perform a certain number of pro bono mediations during a set time period. Panels are a mixed bag providing some mediators with significant income but others none at all. You should make inquiries into the mediation panels in your area and assess their value to your business. Very often, joining a panel is a matter of spending thirty minutes filling out paperwork. Even if you receive only a single mediation per year from the panel, the small effort in joining is worth it.

b. *Speaking Engagements*

If you have good presentation skills, professional speaking engagements are an effective way to increase your visibility and credibility within your professional networks. Public speaking, either in-person or via videoconferencing, gives people an opportunity to get to know you personally and to assess your intelligence, both of which are important factors in selecting a mediator. Your professional speaking engagements should be before both your internal and external networks, but remember it is your external networks that will produce the most business. It is typically easier to find opportunities to speak about mediation and dispute resolution at meetings and conferences that are directed toward other dispute-resolution professionals. Therefore, many mediators do most of their speaking before these groups. But if generating business is your goal, spending too much time speaking before your internal network is a misuse of your precious marketing time and energy. If you are a business and commercial mediator you should be seeking out speaking engagements at your local chambers of commerce, at rotary clubs, and at professional conferences and/or bar meetings in substantive areas that coincide with your mediation practice.

When speaking before your external markets, seek to provide some tangible value to your audience. This value might be educating them about the potential benefits of mediation and other methods of managing disputes differently from traditional litigation. Alternatively, it could be explaining practical methods of managing disputes more productively in both private and professional matters. The more the audience believes that they have received something of value from the presentation, the greater your credibility, and thus, the more likely it will be that they will call you the next time they need a mediator.

c. *Training and Teaching*

Many practicing mediators conduct mediation training workshops or teach dispute resolution part-time at a college or university. In addition to maintaining and developing their theoretical understanding in the field, it provides opportunities for networking and marketing of their services in the same way that public speaking does. It also has the added advantage of supplementing their income. Mediation training is best conducted by a practitioner in the field. Thus, the mediation discipline requires both scholar-practitioners and practitioner-scholars.

d. *Publishing*

Similar to public speaking, writing is a way to build credibility and visibility within your professional networks. Like speaking, writing should be directed at both your internal and external networks in equal measure. The dispute-resolution field offers countless opportunities to publish. There are scholarly journals, dispute-resolution organization magazines and newsletters, and online publications, all looking for quality articles and commentary. Publication of a book on mediation or conflict management adds considerably to one's reputation in the field.

There is also ample opportunity to write about mediation, conflict management, or dispute resolution in non-dispute-resolution arenas, depending upon the market segment you are trying to reach. For example, a mediator who desires to build or grow an employment mediation practice should try to publish articles in human resources publications, business trade journals, and state bar journals. Those in the best position to refer to work will read these articles. Publishing bestows the mediator with credibility because so few people have the time, inclination, or background to write extensively. We have already discussed the benefit of finding ways to distinguish yourself in a field that is flooded with people of rather minimal qualifications who share the title of "mediator" with those who are dedicated to the profession. Writing is an effective way to distinguish yourself and your practice.

e. *Website and Social Media*

An important component of successful marketing practice is having quality marketing materials that educate people about you and your mediation practice and that make it easy for them to contact you. Having a website and being active on social media are essential. Websites enable prospective clients to quickly and conveniently learn about your education, professional experience and qualifications. Because of the creative options available in the way of website design, it also provides an avenue for expressing to prospective clients aspects of your personality that you wish to emphasize, like being trustworthy, innovative, or service-oriented. Having a website also lends professionalism and credibility to your practice at a relatively low cost. Similarly, having a social media presence and providing information about mediation and conflict-resolution matters and news is a great way to establish yourself as a knowledgeable professional.

V. Practical Business Considerations

A. Meeting Facilities

A mediator should have appropriate facilities in which to conduct the mediation. Although some clients will have conference rooms available to meet in, many do not. Moreover, when mediations are held at a client's place of business, the mediator has less control over the appropriateness and comfort of the facilities. Some mediators also have a concern that other participants may view holding the mediation at one of the participants' facilities as a sign of bias or something that provides some advantage to the hosting participant in the mediation. For these reasons, it is best for the mediator to provide a neutral place for the mediation.

There are a few requirements that an appropriate mediation facility should meet.[41] It should have a main meeting room large enough to comfortably accommodate all the participants as well as at least one separate room in which to hold separate meetings. Additional meeting rooms will be needed if you perform mediations with more than two parties. Facilities should have access to a telephone, fax machine, photocopier, whiteboard or butcher paper, and to refreshments and restrooms. While not absolutely required, it is ideal for the facility to have internet access as well as a computer with a printer so that settlement documents can be drafted, signed, and distributed.

The good news is that appropriate mediation facilities are relatively easy to find if you do not already have your own office with sufficient space for conducting mediations. A popular solution for many part-time and even full-time mediators is using "executive suites." Executive suites are facilities that rent out conference space by the hour or day, and they are found in every metropolitan area. These suites are profes-

---

41. *See* MOSTEN, *supra* note 29, at 125.

sional in appearance, centrally located, and provide all of the office support systems listed above. They vary in price level and quality, so you should visit the facility and choose one that meets your needs and budget. A similar, equally acceptable solution is to establish a relationship with one or more other professionals with permanent office space, such as lawyers or accountants, and rent their conference space on an as-needed basis.

Another acceptable alternative, albeit less attractive, is renting space at colleges or universities, churches, and other local charitable organizations. These institutions often have meeting space available at a relatively low cost. The downside to these facilities is that they may appear less professional and may lack access to all of the business amenities listed above that are often needed during the mediation.

Finally, in a post-pandemic world, it is possible to set up an entirely virtual mediation practice. This is how many meditators functioned for nearly two years during the COVD-19 pandemic. Most reported no meaningful decline in settlement rates and effectiveness, and many preferred this mode of mediation. See Chapter 11—*Virtual Mediation* for a fuller discussion of the advantages and disadvantages of virtual mediation.

B. Getting Paid

Fee arrangements for mediators vary. In general, the amount of the fee is a product of several factors: reputation, experience, skill, geographic area, and other well-known market forces.[42] In setting fees, you should canvass mediators in your geographic area to determine the average fee in similar practice areas. In most instances, mediators' fees are easily viewed on their websites. Once you know what the average fee is, you should set your own fees appropriately, depending on your experience level and training.

The two most common ways to bill for mediation services is by the day or by the hour. Billing by the day, or half day, has much to recommend it. If you bill by the day, you can collect your mediation fee in advance of the mediation, which saves administrative time billing clients and handling billing issues, like overdue or unpaid invoices. Whether the mediation settles in an hour or takes a half-day or whole day, the mediator collects the entire fee. Yet other mediators prefer to bill clients after the mediation on an hours-incurred basis. Billing by the hour means more administrative time but may appear more equitable to the client. However, it is always difficult to give clients cost estimates when billing is calculated on a time basis. Although most mediations finish within eight hours or less, situations involving complex legal, financial, technical, emotional or relationship issues, or multiple parties and advisers, may prolong the process and require additional time.

---

42. KRIVIS & LUCKS, *supra* note 30, at 137–55.

Many mediators use a hybrid approach to billing, where they combine full-day and half-day rates with hourly rates. If a half-day is booked and the mediation runs over that time, the participants are then charged on an hourly basis for the additional time. Some mediators even allow the client to choose whether they wish to be billed by the day or by the hour. Each method of calculating the mediation fee has its advantages and disadvantages. In the end, however, it is a highly individualized choice that should be informed by the prevailing practices in the market in which you practice.

C. Business Entity

Many mediators practice through the same business entity that provides other professional services, such as a law partnership or accountancy firm. They could also practice through the use of sole proprietorships or through partnerships with other mediators. With the trend toward multi-disciplinary partnerships, mediators could also combine with lawyers, accountants, or social workers, where professional regulations allow. In order to limit their individual legal liability, mediators could also, singly or collectively, incorporate as a private company.

D. Professional Indemnity Insurance

Professional indemnity insurance is advisable for mediators who neither work for a government agency nor enjoy broad statutory immunity from liability. Some professionals, such as lawyers, may be covered by their existing professional indemnity insurance policy, provided their mediation work is part of their normal course of business. Professional liability insurance for mediators is relatively inexpensive, usually only a few hundred dollars a year, and is available through those insurers who offer professional liability insurance to other professionals. Several mediation organizations, however, offer group rate insurance as a membership benefit.

E. Client Satisfaction Surveys

These have been referred to earlier as an aspect of reflective practice. Individual surveys provide feedback on specific cases, and collectively surveys can provide statistically significant indicators of various aspects of client attitudes and mediator performance. Longitudinal surveys can trace subsequent attitudes of clients as well as the longer-term viability of mediated agreements. For a sample of a client survey form, see Appendix 6B.

F. Conclusion

As with any other venture, the larger and wiser the investment in mediation, the greater the likelihood of return. The investment comprises the costs of training, materials, association memberships, conference attendances and marketing, and the opportunity costs which all of these entail. As with other investments, there are no guaranteed returns and some risk assessment is required. The increased use of alternative dispute resolution in our government and private organizations has created hundreds of new career opportunities for those with mediation skills, and these career opportunities will continue to expand and grow as dispute resolution establishes itself as part of the mainstream American consciousness.

VI. Exercises

1. Peruse a few daily newspapers and use news articles, editorials, job advertisements, and other sources to develop a list of potential areas in which mediation might be applied. What modifications would be needed to make mediation suitable in each situation, and how might it be marketed and to whom?

2. Write a proposal to an educational institution, voluntary association, or other organization in which you point out the advantages of developing a mediation system for relevant disputes facing the organization and suggest ways in which you might be able to contribute to the system. Ask a knowledgeable person to comment on your proposal.

3. Examine current advertising and marketing campaigns for mediation and other dispute-resolution services in the press, in the Yellow Pages, on television, on websites, and in other relevant places. Which *models* and *brands* of dispute resolution are being marketed, and what messages are being provided about the nature of these processes?

4. Visit mediator and dispute-resolution websites to assess the type of services they provide. What qualities of the websites do you like? What about the websites do you not like? Make a special effort to find out market rates for mediation services in your area.

Standard Forms for Mediation Practice

A. Cover Letter

[Letterhead should contain mediator contact information: address, office phone, facsimile, e-mail and Internet address]

Ms. Jane Gerrard
49 Baltimore Drive
Plano, Texas 75024

Dear Jane:

Re: Information about mediation

Thank you for your recent telephone inquiries about mediation and the services which I provide.

As promised, I am sending you some information on the mediation process in the form of commonly asked questions and answers. The same information is being sent to the other parties who might be involved in this matter.

Please take time to consider this information and to discuss it with your advisers, if any. You or your adviser are welcome to contact me at any time should you have any further queries.

If you wish to go ahead with the mediation, please let me know. As soon as all parties have agreed to participate in the mediation, I shall send you my usual Agreement to Mediate, Guidelines on Preparing for Mediation, and Fee Agreement.

If I do not hear from you before, I will contact you in about two weeks to find out whether or not you would like to go ahead with the mediation.

Yours sincerely,
John Smith, Jr.

B. Information about Mediation

1. What is mediation?

Mediation is a process in which an outside person assists two or more people or organizations in dispute to communicate, to negotiate and to make mutually satisfactory decisions on the disputes between them. It is a form of "assisted decision-making."

2. What are the events leading up to mediation?

Every mediation process is different, but normally a mediation involves the following initial steps:

- The mediator is approached by one person or organization with a request for information or mediation assistance.
- The mediator contacts the other persons or organizations involved and asks if they are willing to consider mediation.
- The mediator sends to each person or group information about mediation and about the mediator, and a mediation contract for the parties to complete. Sometimes the mediator requests written background information on the dispute.
- The mediator makes contact with each individual or organization to explain the process and to assess the suitability of the dispute for mediation. This may involve telephone contact or personal meetings in which the mediator prepares each side for the mediation.
- A time and place, suitable for all persons, is arranged for the mediation meeting.

3. What happens in the mediation meeting?

The mediator welcomes each person and explains the mediation process. He or she first asks each person to talk in turn about their principal concerns.

The mediator clarifies the parties' concerns and translates them into issues for discussion. The issues are written up and listed in order of priority. The mediator then defines the areas where the parties are in agreement or disagreement, and provides a structure for the discussions. Each party is asked to give their views and explain their perceptions to the other on each issue, and together the parties explore options for resolving the points of difference. Thereby an agreement is pieced together, like a jigsaw.

4. Who can be present and how confidential is it?

Advisers, supporters, witnesses, and other persons can be present at the mediation if the parties both agree, and if those attending sign a confidentiality undertaking.

The parties can agree on what will be said publicly about the mediation. Neither party can introduce evidence in court about what was said in the mediation, nor produce in court documents prepared for the mediation.

5. What is the legal status of agreements reached at mediation?

This depends on the wishes of the parties. The parties and their advisers, with assistance from the mediator, will record the outcome in a draft agreement document which contains both matters that have been agreed and the issues, if any, which are still to be settled. The parties can redraft the agreement into a legally binding document after receiving advice from their lawyers or other professional advisers.

6. What if I feel uncomfortable in the mediation?

It is a normal part of the mediation process for the mediator to meet separately with each party on a confidential basis. You can also ask to speak to the mediator alone or you can ask for the mediation session to be adjourned if you have the need. You can always express any concerns openly in the mediation and the mediator will try to deal with them there and then.

Some of the mediator's tasks are to create a favorable environment for dispute resolution, to assist each side to negotiate, and to minimize intimidation or other causes of anxiety in the parties.

7. What does it cost?

Mediators charge at an agreed daily or hourly rate for preparation, for actual meeting time, and for other expenses, if any, such as travel. Many mediations are complete after 4-10 hours of work.

8. What happens afterwards?

One aim of mediation is to model a method of working through disputes so that the parties can solve their own disputes in the future. Mediated agreements often contain a dispute resolution clause in terms of which the parties commit themselves, in the event of a breach of the agreement, to come back to mediation before initiation of court proceedings.

C. Professional Biography

[*The following is a sample professional biography in a short format. It could be used as part of the initial materials sent to clients, on a website, or as part of a brochure. Mediators should also have a comprehensive résumé. Topics that should be in a professional biography are Mediation Training and Experience, Dispute Resolution Association Memberships, Education, and Contact Information. Other areas that might also be included are Employment History, Publications, Speaking Appearances, Dispute Resolution Teaching, Bar Memberships, Community Service, and Honors.*]

Marie Portland, J.D.

200 Main St., Plano, Texas 75024-3547
Phone: 972-555-1111
Fax 972-555-2221
Marie@PortlandMediation.com
www.Portlandmediation.com

Mediation Experience and Qualifications

Practice Areas and Experience: Practice in the areas of community, employment, personal injury and commercial mediation. Conducted over 200 mediations since 2003.

Training: Graduate Certificate in Dispute Resolution and Conflict Management from the Center for Dispute Resolution and Conflict Management at Southern Methodist University in Plano, Texas. (The certificate consists of 21 credit-hours, which is over 300 hours of classroom and practical study.)

Dispute Resolution Association Memberships

Association of Conflict Resolution

Texas Association of Mediators

Texas Bar Association, Alternative Dispute Resolution Section (member of the Liaison Committee, National Issues Project 2005-2006)

American Bar Association Section of Dispute Resolution

Employment

Adams and Hay LLP, Dallas, Texas, 2001 to present:

> *Litigation Associate*, handling all aspects of sophisticated litigation matters involving commercial law, employment discrimination, contract disputes, consumer finance and product liability.

Education

Southern Methodist University, Graduate Certificate in Dispute Resolution, May 2004

University of Texas School of Law, Juris Doctorate, May 2000

Stanford University, BA in Psychology, June 1996

Bar Memberships

Texas (2001) and California (2001)

APPENDIX TWO

Forms Related to the Agreement to Mediate

A. Agreement to Mediate

The undersigned party agrees to enter into mediation with John Smith, Jr. as mediator (hereinafter "mediator") with the intention of reaching a consensual settlement of their disputes concerning the matter of

[Insert name of matter, and court docket number if applicable]

The undersigned further agrees and understands that mediation will take place on the following terms:

The Nature of Mediation and Role of the Mediator

1. The mediator is a facilitator who will assist the parties to reach their own settlement. The mediator will not make decisions about "right" or "wrong," tell the parties what to do, or impose a decision on them. Any comments, opinions, suggestions, statements, or recommendations made by the mediator are not binding on any party.

2. The mediator will not offer legal advice nor provide legal counsel. Where applicable, each party is advised to retain his or her own lawyer or other adviser in order to be properly counseled about his or her legal interests, rights, and obligations.

3. Once the mediator has acted as a mediator, he cannot subsequently act for either party as a lawyer in relation to the same or related disputes between the parties, nor can he act as an arbitrator in the same dispute. [*This clause should be removed for non-attorney mediators*]

Confidentiality

4. It is understood that in order for mediation to work, open and honest communications are essential. Accordingly, all written and oral communications, negotiations and statements made in the course of mediation will be treated as privileged settlement discussions and are absolutely confidential. Therefore:

   i. The mediator will not reveal anything discussed in mediation unless compelled by law. It is understood that the mediator is *not* required to maintain confidentiality if he has reason to believe that a child is in need of protection or if either party is in danger of bodily harm or there is imminent danger to property.

ii. The parties agree that they will not at any time, before, during or after mediation, call the mediator or anyone associated with the mediation as witnesses in any legal or administrative proceedings concerning this dispute.

iii. The parties agree not to subpoena or demand the production of any records, notes, discs, or the like of the mediator in any legal or administrative proceedings concerning this dispute.

iv. The exceptions to the above is that this *Agreement to Mediate* and any *settlement agreement* resulting from the mediation may be produced in any subsequent court proceedings.

Cooperation During Mediation

5. Each party will enter into this mediation with the intention of achieving a settlement of the dispute. To this end the parties will:

   i. undertake to negotiate with commitment and in good faith;

   ii. cooperate with the mediator in the conduct of the mediation;

   iii. do their best to comply with reasonable requests made by the mediator to promote the efficient resolution of the dispute;

   iv. meet with the mediator at mutually agreed premises and dates.

Full Disclosure

6. It is understood that full disclosure of all relevant and pertinent information is essential to the mediation process. Accordingly, there will be a complete and honest disclosure by each of the parties to the other and to the mediator of all relevant information and documents. This includes providing each other and the mediator with all information and documentation that would usually be available through the discovery process in legal proceedings.

Mediation is Voluntary

7. While both parties intend to use the mediation process with a view to reaching an agreement, it is understood that any party may withdraw from mediation at any time. It is agreed that if one or all of the parties decide to withdraw from mediation, best efforts will be made to discuss this decision in the presence of all the parties and the mediator.

8. If the mediator determines that it is not possible to resolve the issues through mediation, the process can be terminated once this decision has been conveyed to the parties.

Settlement

9. If the parties reach a settlement at the mediation, the terms of this settlement will be written down and signed by the parties. No agreements reached at mediation will be binding until reduced to writing and signed by the parties.

Mediation Fees

10. The parties agree to share the costs of mediation equally. Each party is responsible for paying its own costs and expenses of the mediation according to the attached *Mediation Fee Schedule*.

By:_____

On behalf of:_____, Date:_____

And

By:_____

On behalf of: John Smith, Jr., LLC, Date:_____

B. Mediation Fee Schedule

Mediation Fee Schedule
John Smith, Jr. LLC

1. Full day mediation fees are $1000 per party. A mediation day is from approximately 9:30 a.m. to 6:30 p.m.

2. Half-day mediation fees are $650 per party. A half-day mediation is from approximately 9:30 a.m. to 1:30 p.m.

3. Mediations that go beyond the scheduled hours are billed at $350 per hour, divided equally among the parties. Additional fees will be invoiced to the parties and due 30 days after receipt of bill.

4. Mediations include preparation time and pre-mediation conferences, when appropriate.

5. All people or organizations represented by one lawyer or law firm are considered "one party" for purposes of billing. A Pro Se party is deemed a separate party for billing purposes.

6. Complex matters requiring extensive preparation may require additional fees. Such fees will be discussed with the parties in advance of mediation.

7. Mediator's fees and expenses shall be paid to the mediator along with the signing of the *Agreement to Mediate* before the mediation begins. Checks are to be made out to John Smith, Jr., LLC.

(*Print name of party*)

(*Print name and title of representative, if different from above*)

C. Pro Se Waiver Form

Pro Se Litigant Waiver and Consent Form For Mediation

Initial the following:

As a Pro Se litigant I am fully aware that I am mediating without the representation of an attorney.

As a Pro Se litigant I am also fully aware that the mediator cannot and will not give me legal advice or guidance.

As a Pro Se litigant I am fully aware that I am expected to follow all the rules of the court and the mediation procedure as an attorney would.

As a Pro Se litigant I am fully aware that if I violate any of the court or mediation guidelines there may be sanctions granted against me by the court.

As a Pro Se litigant, I understand and agree to the above.

SIGNATURE/DATE

D. Prior Contact with Participant Waiver Form

I, the undersigned, acknowledge that John Smith, Jr., the mediator in the matter of [insert name of matter, has informed me that [describe prior contact with mediation participant].

Mr. Smith further explained that his prior contact with [insert name of participant(s)] would in no way affect his ability to impartially facilitate the mediation.

Having been informed of the above, I, the undersigned, voluntarily consent to proceed with the mediation with Mr. Smith as mediator.

(Print name of party)

(Print name and title of representative, if different from above)

(Signature of representative)

Date:

(Print name of party)

(Print name and title of representative, if different from above)

(Signature of representative)

Date:

Mediated Agreements

A. Family Dispute (no children)

NO.

IN THE MATTER OF	
THE MARRIAGE OF	IN THE DISTRICT COURT
PETITIONER	JUDICIAL DISTRICT
AND	DALLAS COUNTY, TEXAS
RESPONDENT	

MEDIATION SETTLEMENT AGREEMENT

A. Introduction

1. The parties to this action are: PETITIONER (hereinafter sometimes referred to as "Wife") and RESPONDENT (hereinafter sometimes referred to as "Husband"). The parties have reached the following agreement in mediation.

2. The parties agree that either party shall be entitled to a final divorce decree that shall reflect the terms of this agreement. In the event that either party obstructs the entry of a final judgment consistent with this agreement, the prevailing party on a motion for summary judgment, motion for entry or other similar action, shall be entitled to reimbursement of that party's reasonable attorney fees and costs associated with such action.

3. Prior to filing any motions with the court, the parties further agree that they shall attempt to resolve any disputes regarding the interpretation or performance of this agreement, including the necessity and form of closing documents, through a conference call with the mediator.

B. Spousal Support

1. Husband shall pay spousal maintenance to wife in the amount of $1,000 per month for twelve consecutive months with the first payment being due on January 15, 2xxx, and a like payment due on the same day of each month thereafter until December 15, 2xxx.

2. Spousal maintenance shall terminate upon the first to occur of the following events: 1) death of husband; 2) death of wife; 3) remarriage of wife; or payment of $12,000.

C. Property

Husband is awarded all right, title and interest in the following property:

H-1. All clothing, jewelry, and other personal effects in Husband's possession shall be the property of the Husband, unless express provision is made herein to the contrary.

H-2. All household furniture, furnishings, fixtures, goods, appliances, and equipment in Husband's possession shall be the property of the Husband, unless express provision is made herein to the contrary.

H-3. The following items of personal property in the possession or control of Wife shall be made available to Husband by Wife to pick up on January 15 between the hours of 6:00 to 8:00 p.m.:

> DVD Player
>
> Widescreen television

H-4. Any and all sums, together with all future increases, related to any profit-sharing plan, retirement plan, pension plan, or like benefit program, such as social security, existing by reason of Husband's past, present, or future employment, shall be the property of the Husband.

H-5. Any and all sums of cash in Husband's possession or subject to his sole control, including money on account in banks, savings institutions, or other financial institutions, which accounts stand in his sole name or from which he has the sole right to withdraw funds, or which are subject to his sole control, shall be the property of the Husband.

H-6. The Husband shall have sole title to the 2006 Ford F-150 Truck, together with all applicable warranties and insurance, keys, and title documents. The Wife shall cooperate with Husband in transferring title.

H-7. All frequent flyer miles in Husband's name shall be the property of Husband.

H-8. The Husband shall possess an undivided ½ interest in and to the real property located at 2121 Wall Rd, Dallas Texas, subject to the terms and conditions for sale of the real property set forth below.

Wife is awarded all right, title and interest in the following property:

W-1. All clothing, jewelry, and other personal effects in Wife's possession shall be the property of the Wife, unless express provision is made herein to the contrary.

W-2. All household furniture, furnishings, fixtures, goods, appliances, and equipment in Wife's possession shall be the property of the Wife, unless express provision is made herein to the contrary.

W-3. Any and all sums, together with all future increases, related to any profit-sharing plan, retirement plan, pension plan, or like benefit program, such as social security, existing by reason of Wife's past, present, or future employment, shall be the property of the Wife.

W-4. Any and all sums of cash in Wife's possession or subject to her sole control, including money on account in banks, savings institutions, or other financial institutions, which accounts stand in her sole name or from which she has the sole right to withdraw funds or which are subject to her sole control, shall be the property of the Wife.

W-5. The Wife shall have sole title to the 1999 Ford Taurus, together with all applicable warranties and insurance, keys and title documents. The Husband shall cooperate with Wife in transferring title.

W-6. Cash amount of $5,000 is payable to Wife by Husband on or before January 15, 2xxx by cashier's check.

W-7. All frequent flyer miles in Wife's name shall be the property of Wife.

W-8. The Wife shall possess an undivided ½ interest in and to the real property located at 2121 Wall Rd, Dallas Texas, subject to the terms and conditions for sale of the real property set forth below.

D. Sale of Real Property

1. The parties agree that the real property and all its improvements commonly referred to as 2121 Wall Rd, Dallas, Texas will be sold.

2. The real property is to be sold under following terms and conditions:

   a. The parties shall list the property with a duly licensed real estate broker having sales experience in the area where the property is located, provided further that such real estate broker shall be an active member in the Multiple Listing Service with the Texas Board of Realtors.

   b. The property shall be sold for a price that is mutually agreeable to Husband and Wife. Should Husband and Wife be unable to agree on a sales price, upon the application of either party to this suit, the property shall be sold under such terms and conditions as determined by a court-appointed receiver.

   c. The Husband shall continue to make all payments of principal, interest, taxes, and insurance on the property UNTIL the sale, and the Wife shall have the exclusive right to enjoy the use and possession of the premises until closing. The Wife shall cooperate with real estate broker in making the real property available for showing to prospective buyers. All maintenance and repairs necessary to keep the property in its present condition shall be paid by Wife.

   d. Upon the sale, the proceeds remaining after payment of all mortgage indebtedness, commissions, fees, taxes, liens, and other related expenses shall be shared equally between husband and Wife.

E. Debts

1. The Husband shall be responsible for all debts incurred by either party before October 1, 2xxx that remain outstanding.

3

2. As part of the division of the estate of the parties, Husband shall pay and indemnify and hold Wife harmless from all debts incurred by Husband from and after the date of the parties' separation on October 1, 2xxx.

3. As part of the division of the estate of the parties, Wife shall pay and indemnify and hold Husband harmless from all debts incurred by Wife from and after the date of the parties' separation on October 1, 2xxx.

F. Attorney's Fees

Each party shall be responsible for their own attorney's fees and costs.

G. Federal Income Taxes

The parties shall be liable for federal incomes taxes as follows:

   a. Both are Jointly Liable for all taxes due from the date of marriage through date of divorce.

   b. Husband shall be responsible for and shall pay and hold wife harmless from all taxes due for the period after the date of divorce for income earned or received by him.

   c. Wife shall be responsible for and shall pay and hold Husband harmless from all taxes due for the period after the date of divorce for income earned or received by her.

H. Execution of Agreement

The parties agree to execute all instruments necessary to effect this mediation settlement including but not limited to the following documents:

Final Decree of Divorce Deed

Special Warranty Deed

Deed of Trust to Secure Assumption

I. Mediation

1. The parties agree to mediation with Jane Smith for conflict resolution prior to instituting any enforcement proceedings.

2. This agreement is made and performable in the county of suit, and shall be construed in accordance with the laws of the State of Texas and commenced upon the date of signing herein.

3. Each signatory to this settlement agreement has entered into same freely and voluntarily and without duress after having consulted with legal or other professionals, or, after having been given an opportunity to consult with legal or other professionals elected not to do so.

AGREED TO

THIS_____   DAY OF_____

Husband_____

Wife_____

Attorney for Husband_____

Attorney for Wife_____

WITNESSED:_____

_____

JANE SMITH, Mediator

B. Commercial Dispute

NO.

IN THE MATTER OF	
THE MARRIAGE OF	IN THE DISTRICT COURT
PETITIONER	JUDICIAL DISTRICT
AND	COLLIN COUNTY, TEXAS
RESPONDENT	

TERMS OF SETTLEMENT

WHEREAS:

A. The plaintiff alleges that without authorization, the defendant failed to advertise the plaintiff's business in its 2006 publications.

B. On or about 16 June 2006 the plaintiff commenced proceedings against the defendant in the District Court of Colin County, Texas in relation to the advertisements.

C. The plaintiff has claimed damages in the amount of $125,000 in respect of an alleged breach of agreement ("plaintiff's claim").

D. The defendant has denied the plaintiff's claim.

E. The plaintiff and the defendant are desirous of settling and resolving this proceeding.

NOW THESE TERMS OF SETTLEMENT WITNESS AND IT IS HEREBY AGREED THAT:

1. The parties hereby agree to an order that the legal action shall be dismissed with no order as to costs.

2. The defendant shall pay to the plaintiff, and the plaintiff shall accept from the defendant, the sum of $29,000 (which includes $4000 for legal expenses) in full and final satisfaction of the plaintiff's claim, inclusive of interest ("settlement sum").

3. The defendant shall pay the settlement sum to the plaintiff's lawyers within twenty-one (21) days of receipt by the defendant of an executed copy of these terms, failing which the plaintiff will be entitled to enter judgment against the defendant for the amount of $29,000. Payment shall be made in the form of a certified bank check.

4. The plaintiff and the defendant hereby agree to release each other and their officers, employees, contractors and agents from any and all claims, demands, actions, and suits whatsoever arising out of the subject matter of the proceeding.

5. The plaintiff further agrees, in consideration of the terms of this settlement, to indemnify and keep indemnified the defendant and all its officers, employees, contractors and agents from and against all and any proceedings, claims or demands made at any time by the plaintiff or another person in relation to, arising out of, or in connection with the plaintiff's claim.

6. All information exchanged between the parties under these terms of settlement or during the course of negotiations leading to the completion of these terms of settlement and the contents of these terms of settlement are confidential between the parties and their advisers and may not be disclosed to any person except as required by law or otherwise agreed to by the parties in writing.

7. Each party to these terms shall take all steps, execute all documents and do all things as may reasonably be required by the other party to give effect to these terms.

EXECUTED as an agreement of 1 August 2xxx.

SIGNED by

_____   in the presence of_____

as authorized representative for

S M Allbusiness   _____

                                                  Signature of witness

                                         _____

                                                  Name of witness (block letters)

_____   in the presence of_____

as authorized representative for

B Igbusiness   _____

                                                  Signature of witness

                                         _____

                                                  Name of witness (block letters)

C. Community Dispute

TERMS OF AGREEMENT

Because Bill and Syd had difficulties as neighbors they made use of mediation to deal with their problems and reached the following agreements:

1. Syd and Bill agree that they wish to resolve all matters discussed by them at the mediation.

2. Bill agrees not to use his power tools before 7:00 am Monday-Saturday, and only between the hours of 3:00 pm and 6:00 pm on Sundays.

3. Syd undertakes to complete the unfinished fence between the two properties within two months of this agreement, using treated pine of 5 feet in height.

4. Within seven days of Syd providing him with the invoice, Bill will pay Syd 40% of the cost of the fence timber and the other costs of the fencing will be borne by Syd.

5. Both parties agree to discuss future problems directly with each other before involving neighbors and other outside persons.

6. Syd and Bill agree to treat each other with mutual respect in the future.

Signed *Bill Smith*   Signed *Syd Brown*

                                                 July 1, 2xxx

Reframing

Table of Examples

Client's negative term	Mediator's replacement term
He's telling lies.	So you see the facts differently?
It's all her fault.	So you had different expectations?
I have my rights.	So you wish to exercise your options?
I want residence of the children.	So we need to discuss parenting arrangements?
I have a serious grievance against them.	So this is a situation you're not comfortable with?
He abused me verbally.	So you felt his language was inappropriate?
His repair work was shoddy.	So he did not work according to specifications?
I can't stand it when…	You feel uncomfortable with…
She totally ignored me.	There was inadequate consultation?
We had no room to move.	So you felt that you had limited options?
I think he was stealing.	So some funds could not be accounted for?
I'll destroy you in court.	So litigation is a possible option?

Guidelines for Lawyers Representing Clients in Mediation

A. Nature of Mediation

Mediation is an informal and flexible process in which the relevant parties can make decisions about disputes in which they are involved. The parties themselves have a direct and continuing participation in this form of dispute resolution. Professional advisers can be important ingredients in the success of mediation, provided they play a supportive and encouraging role to the parties. The main functions of lawyers in respect of the mediation process are outlined below.

B. Lawyer's Functions

Before the mediation meeting

- To educate their clients about the nature of mediation and its procedures.
- To prepare their clients for participating in the mediation process.
- To prepare necessary documents, reports and other materials necessary for successful mediation.
- To give clients realistic and clear estimates about the expenses and likely cost recoveries of other dispute resolution processes, including litigation, and to refer to both best- and worst-case outcomes.
- To advise their clients on relevant legal issues, including the Agreement to Mediate (Appendix 2).

During the mediation meeting

- To allow the mediator to conduct the process and to provide support to the mediator where appropriate.
- To permit and encourage their clients to participate fully and directly in the process.
- To assist clients to focus on their real personal and commercial interests as opposed to their legal rights.
- To assist clients to communicate accurately and comprehensively and to negotiate constructively and productively.

- To provide to their clients legal information and advice, where appropriate, on their rights and duties.
- To give ongoing realistic predictions about likely outcomes in court or other non-mediation processes and their relative advantages or disadvantages.
- To assisting in the drafting of agreements and the formalization of the mediation in appropriate ways.

After the mediation meeting

- To undertake any activities required for the formalization or ratification of the mediated agreement and to liaise with other lawyers where necessary.
- To reassure clients who have second thoughts and to inform them about the options of dealing with problems in the implementation of the agreement, including through return to mediation.
- To maintain the confidentiality of the mediation meeting.

For exercise in forums other than mediation

- Acting as the adversarial advocate of their clients' legal rights.
- Raising technical procedural points or insisting on formality.
- Engaging in other adversarial or combative strategies.

APPENDIX SIX

Evaluation

A. Mediator Self-Assessment Form

1. Names of clients:

_____

_____

2. Date and venue of mediation:

_____

_____

3. Referral source:

_____

_____

4. Nature and sources of conflict:

_____

_____

5. Escalation/de-escalation factors:

_____

_____

6. Pre-mediation conference:

_____

_____

7. Participants at mediation and their roles:

_____

_____

8. Major issues, agenda items, hidden agendas:

_____

_____

9. The following went well:

_____

_____

10. With hindsight the following could have been done better:

_____

_____

11. How clients/advisers assessed the process:

_____

_____

12. One lesson learned for future:

_____

_____

B. Evaluation Form For Party or Adviser

In order to assess and improve our mediation services, we would like to receive your comments about the performance of your Mediator.

1. Mediation date:

_____

2. Mediator's name:

_____

3. Your name/name of lawyer:

_____

4. Was the mediation: (please check)

Ordered by court   ☐

Agreed by the parties   ☐

Recommended by legal advisers   ☐

Other (please specify)   ☐

5. Type of Dispute: (please check)

Banking/finance ☐

Building/construction ☐

Partnership/joint venture ☐

Planning/local government ☐

Insurance ☐

Estates/wills ☐

Professional malpractice/negligence ☐

Intellectual property/IT ☐

Contractual ☐

Corporate ☐

Industrial Relations/workplace ☐

Other (please specify) ☐

6. To what extent did the dispute settle at Mediation?

Fully ☐   Partially ☐   Not at all ☐

7. The performance of your Mediator (please circle your response)

	Poorly/extremely well	Other comments
Explained nature of mediation and answered your queries	1 2 3 4 5	
Helped me prepare for mediation	1 2 3 4 5	
Explained the mediation process	1 2 3 4 5	
Identified relevant issues	1 2 3 4 5	
Understood your side of the dispute	1 2 3 4 5	
Helped the parties generate options	1 2 3 4 5	
Made communication easier	1 2 3 4 5	
Kept the process on track	1 2 3 4 5	
Helped reach a good result	1 2 3 4 5	

8. Please name one thing the Mediator did particularly well:

_____

_____

9. What would you have preferred the Mediator to do differently?

_____

_____

10. Would you recommend to others?

(Please give reasons)

Mediation   Yes   No

_____

_____

The Venue   Yes   No

_____

_____

Your Mediator   Yes   No

_____

_____

Other comments or evaluations:

_____

_____

_____

_____

Mediator's Opening Statement Checklist

I. Preliminaries

a. Welcome

b. Introductions

c. Check that all interested parties are present

d. Time limitations

e. Collect relevant forms and payment (Agreement to Mediate, waivers, etc.)

f. Explain policy concerning breaks and location of bathroom facilities

II. Explaining the Nature of Mediation

a. Agreement is Voluntary

b. Parties create the solution

c. Mediator impartiality and neutrality statement

d. Not an adjudication

III. Explanation of the Mediation Process

a. Mediation process and mediator style (party opening statements, issue identification, problem-solving, etc.)

b. Use of separate meetings procedure

c. Mediator note-taking procedures

IV. Guidelines

a. Speak one at a time

b. No personal attacks

c. No agreement until reduced to writing and signed

d. Confidentiality

e. Obtain commitment from parties to the ground rules

V. Commitment to Begin Mediation and Questions

a. Check for questions

b. Obtain commitment from parties to begin

Pre-Mediation Conference Preparation Form

Party	Interests	Alternatives	Objective Sources	Options

Instructions: Each party will require a separate form. The mediator should first explore the interests of the *party being interviewed* and then ask the party to imagine what *the other party's* interests are. Then proceed to *alternatives*, first exploring the alternatives of the party being interviewed and then asking them to consider the other party's alternatives. Then proceed to explore the *objective sources* that the party being interviewed will use in the negotiation that supports their view of the problem, and then ask them to imagine what objective sources the other party will use. Finally, ask the party being interviewed to list possible *options* that would resolve the matter, reminding them that these options should take into account the interests of the other party. The mediator can use the worksheet as a guide, or can work together with the party to complete it.

Expected Value Calculation
Form—Plaintiff

Legal Costs (*Transactional costs*) Discovery, motions, court costs, trial	Business Costs (*Opportunity Costs*) Lost work time, disruption of business, reputation	Personal Costs Affect on relationships, stress, health, leisure	Benefits of Trial Obtaining legal precedent, deterrence, vindication	Calculating the Expected Value
				Multiply probable damage award by plaintiff's chance of success at trial: $ _____ -(subtract) Benefits of trial: $ _____ +(add) Combined legal, business & personal costs: $ _____ = (equals) Expected Value: $ _____

Expected Value Calculation Form—Defendant

Legal Costs (*Transactional costs*) Discovery, motions, court costs, trial	Business Costs (*Opportunity Costs*) Lost work time, disruption of business, reputation	Personal Costs Affect on relationships, stress, health, leisure	Benefits of Trial Obtaining legal precedent, deterrence, vindication	Calculating the Expected Value
				Multiply probable damage award by plaintiff's chance of success at trial: $ _____ + (add) Benefits of trial: $ _____ −(subtract) Combined legal, business & personal costs: $ _____ = (equals) Expected Value: $ _____

Ethical Standards

Model Standards of Conduct for Mediators

AMERICAN ARBITRATION ASSOCIATION

(ADOPTED SEPTEMBER 8, 2005)

AMERICAN BAR ASSOCIATION

(ADOPTED AUGUST 9, 2005)

ASSOCIATION FOR CONFLICT RESOLUTION

(ADOPTED AUGUST 22, 2005)

SEPTEMBER 2005

The Model Standards of Conduct for Mediators 2005

The Model Standards of Conduct for Mediators was prepared in 1994 by the American Arbitration Association, the American Bar Association's Section of Dispute Resolution, and the Association for Conflict Resolution.[1] A joint committee consisting of representatives from the same successor organizations revised the Model Standards in 2005.[2]

Both the original 1994 version and the 2005 revision have been approved by each participating organization.[3]

Preamble

Mediation is used to resolve a broad range of conflicts within a variety of settings. These Standards are designed to serve as fundamental ethical guidelines for persons mediating in all practice contexts. They serve three primary goals: to guide the conduct of mediators; to inform the mediating parties; and to promote public confidence in mediation as a process for resolving disputes.

---

1. The Association for Conflict Resolution is a merged organization of the Academy of Family Mediators, the Conflict Resolution Education Network and the Society of Professionals in Dispute Resolution (SPIDR). SPIDR was the third participating organization in the development of the 1994 Standards.

2. Reporter's Notes, which are not part of these Standards and therefore have not been specifically approved by any of the organizations, provide commentary regarding these revisions.

3. The 2005 version to the Model Standards were approved by the American Bar Association's House of Delegates on August 9, 2005, the Board of the Association of Conflict Resolution on August 22, 2005 and the Executive Committee of the American Arbitration Association on September 8, 2005.

Mediation is a process in which an impartial third party facilitates communication and negotiation and promotes voluntary decision making by the parties to the dispute.

Mediation serves various purposes, including providing the opportunity for parties to define and clarify issues, understand different perspectives, identify interests, explore and assess possible solutions, and reach mutually satisfactory agreements, when desired.

Note on Construction

These Standards are to be read and construed in their entirety. There is no priority significance attached to the sequence in which the Standards appear.

The use of the term "shall" in a Standard indicates that the mediator must follow the practice described. The use of the term "should" indicates that the practice described in the standard is highly desirable, but not required, and is to be departed from only for very strong reasons and requires careful use of judgment and discretion.

The use of the term "mediator" is understood to be inclusive so that it applies to co-mediator models.

These Standards do not include specific temporal parameters when referencing mediation, and therefore, do not define the exact beginning or ending of mediation.

Various aspects of mediation, including some matters covered by these Standards, may also be affected by applicable law, court rules, regulations, other applicable professional rules, mediation rules to which the parties have agreed and other agreements of the parties. These sources may create conflicts with, and may take precedence over, these Standards. However, a mediator should make every effort to comply with the spirit and intent of these Standards in resolving such conflicts.

This effort should include honoring all remaining Standards not in conflict with these other sources.

These Standards, unless and until adopted by a court or other regulatory authority do not have the force of law. Nonetheless, the fact that these Standards have been adopted by the respective sponsoring entities, should alert mediators to the fact that the Standards might be viewed as establishing a standard of care for mediators.

STANDARD I. SELF-DETERMINATION

A. A mediator shall conduct a mediation based on the principle of party self determination: Self-determination is the act of coming to a voluntary, uncoerced decision in which each party makes free and informed choices as to process and outcome. Parties may exercise self-determination at any stage of mediation, including mediator selection, process design, participation in or withdrawal from the process, and outcomes.

1. Although party self-determination for process design is a fundamental principle of mediation practice, a mediator may need to balance such party self-determination with a mediator's duty to conduct a quality process in accordance with these Standards.

2. A mediator cannot personally ensure that each party has made free and informed choices to reach particular decisions, but, where appropriate, a mediator should make the parties aware of the importance of consulting other professionals to help them make informed choices.

B. A mediator shall not undermine party self-determination by any party for reasons such as higher settlement rates, egos, increased fees, or outside pressures from court personnel, program administrators, provider organizations, the media or others.

STANDARD II. IMPARTIALITY

A. A mediator shall decline mediation if the mediator cannot conduct it in an impartial manner. Impartiality means freedom from favoritism, bias or prejudice.

B. A mediator shall conduct mediation in an impartial manner and avoid conduct that gives the appearance of partiality.

1. A mediator should not act with partiality or prejudice based on any participant's personal characteristics, background, values and beliefs, or performance at a mediation, or any other reason.

2. A mediator should neither give nor accept a gift, favor, loan or other item of value that raises a question as to the mediator's actual or perceived impartiality.

3. A mediator may accept or give de minims gifts or incidental items or services that are provided to facilitate mediation or respect cultural norms so long as such practices do not raise questions as to a mediator's actual or perceived impartiality.

C. If at any time a mediator is unable to conduct mediation in an impartial manner, the mediator shall withdraw.

STANDARD III. CONFLICTS OF INTEREST

A. A mediator shall avoid a conflict of interest or the appearance of a conflict of interest during and after mediation. A conflict of interest can arise from involvement by a mediator with the subject matter of the dispute or from any relationship between a mediator and any mediation participant, whether past or present, personal or professional, that reasonably raises a question of a mediator's impartiality.

B. A mediator shall make a reasonable inquiry to determine whether there are any facts that a reasonable individual would consider likely to create a potential or actual conflict of interest for a mediator. A mediator's actions necessary to accomplish a reasonable inquiry into potential conflicts of interest may vary based on practice context.

C. A mediator shall disclose, as soon as practicable, all actual and potential conflicts of interest reasonably known to the mediator and could reasonably be seen as raising a question about the mediator's impartiality. After disclosure, if all parties agree, the mediator may proceed with the mediation.

D. If a mediator learns any fact after accepting a mediation that raises a question with respect to that mediator's service creating a potential or actual conflict of interest, the mediator shall disclose it as quickly as practicable. After disclosure, if all parties agree, the mediator may proceed with the mediation.

E. If a mediator's conflict of interest might reasonably be viewed as undermining the integrity of the mediation, a mediator shall withdraw from or decline to proceed with the mediation regardless of the expressed desire or agreement of the parties to the contrary.

F. Subsequent to mediation, a mediator shall not establish another relationship with any of the participants in any matter that would raise questions about the integrity of the mediation. When a mediator develops personal or professional relationships with parties, other individuals or organizations following a mediation in which they were involved, the mediator should consider factors such as time elapsed following the mediation, the nature of the relationships established, and services offered when determining whether the relationships might create a perceived or actual conflict of interest.

STANDARD IV. COMPETENCE

A. A mediator shall mediate only when the mediator has the necessary competence to satisfy the reasonable expectations of the parties.

1. Any person may be selected as a mediator, provided that the parties are satisfied with the mediator's competence and qualifications. Training, experience in mediation, skills, cultural understandings and other qualities are often necessary for mediator competence. A person who offers to serve as a mediator creates the expectation that the person is competent to mediate effectively.

2. A mediator should attend educational programs and related activities to maintain and enhance the mediator's knowledge and skills related to mediation.

3. A mediator should have available for the parties' information relevant to the mediator's training, education, experience and approach to conducting mediation.

B. If a mediator, during the course of a mediation determines that the mediator cannot conduct the mediation competently, the mediator shall discuss that determination with the parties as soon as is practicable and take appropriate steps to address the situation, including, but not limited to, withdrawing or requesting appropriate assistance.

C. If a mediator's ability to conduct mediation is impaired by drugs, alcohol, medication, or otherwise, the mediator shall not conduct the mediation.

STANDARD V. CONFIDENTIALITY

A. A mediator shall maintain the confidentiality of all information obtained by the mediator in mediation, unless otherwise agreed to by the parties or required by applicable law.

1. If the parties to mediation agree that the mediator may disclose information obtained during the mediation, the mediator may do so.

2. A mediator should not communicate to any non-participant information about how the parties acted in the mediation. A mediator may report, if required, whether parties appeared at a scheduled mediation and whether or not the parties reached a resolution.

3. If a mediator participates in teaching, research or evaluation of mediation, the mediator should protect the anonymity of the parties and abide by their reasonable expectations regarding confidentiality.

B. A mediator who meets with any persons in private session during mediation shall not convey directly or indirectly to any other person, any information that was obtained during that private session without the consent of the disclosing person.

C. A mediator shall promote understanding among the parties of the extent to which the parties will maintain confidentiality of information they obtain in mediation.

D. Depending on the circumstance of mediation, the parties may have varying expectations regarding confidentiality that a mediator should address. The parties may make their own rules with respect to confidentiality, or the accepted practice of an individual mediator or institution may dictate a particular set of expectations.

STANDARD VI. QUALITY OF THE PROCESS

A. A mediator shall conduct mediation in accordance with these Standards and in a manner that promotes diligence, timeliness, and the safe presence of the appropriate participants, party participation, procedural fairness, party competency and mutual respect among all participants.

1. A mediator should agree to mediate only when the mediator is prepared to commit the attention essential to an effective mediation.

2. A mediator should only accept cases when the mediator can satisfy the reasonable expectation of the parties concerning the timing of mediation.

3. The presence or absence of persons at mediation depends on the agreement of the parties and the mediator. The parties and mediator may agree that others may be excluded from particular sessions or from all sessions.

4. A mediator should promote honesty and candor between and among all participants, and a mediator shall not knowingly misrepresent any material fact or circumstance in the course of mediation.

5. The role of a mediator differs substantially from other professional roles. Mixing the role of a mediator and the role of another profession is problematic and thus, a mediator should distinguish between the roles. A mediator may provide information that the mediator is qualified by training or experience to provide, only if the mediator can do so consistent with these Standards.

6. A mediator shall not conduct a dispute resolution procedure other than mediation but label it mediation in an effort to gain the protection of rules, statutes, or other governing authorities pertaining to mediation.

7. A mediator may recommend, when appropriate, that parties consider resolving their dispute through arbitration, counseling, neutral evaluation or other processes.

8. A mediator shall not undertake an additional dispute resolution role in the same matter without the consent of the parties. Before providing such service, a mediator shall inform the parties of the implications of the change in process and obtain their consent to the change. A mediator who undertakes such role assumes different duties and responsibilities that may be governed by other standards.

9. If mediation is being used to further criminal conduct, a mediator should take appropriate steps including, if necessary, postponing, and/or withdrawing from or terminating the mediation.

10. If a party appears to have difficulty comprehending the process, issues, or settlement options, or difficulty participating in mediation, the mediator should explore the circumstances and potential accommodations, modifications or adjustments that would make possible the party's capacity to comprehend, participate and exercise self-determination.

B. If a mediator is made aware of domestic abuse or violence among the parties, the mediator shall take appropriate steps including, if necessary, postponing, withdrawing from or terminating the mediation.

C. If a mediator believes that participant conduct, including that of the mediator, jeopardizes conducting mediation consistent with these Standards, a mediator shall take appropriate steps including, if necessary, postponing, and/or withdrawing from or terminating the mediation.

STANDARD VII. ADVERTISING AND SOLICITATION

A. A mediator shall be truthful and not misleading when advertising, soliciting or otherwise communicating the mediator's qualifications, experience, services and fees.

1. A mediator should not include any promises as to outcome in communications, including business cards, stationery, or computer-based communications.

2. A mediator should only claim to meet the mediator qualifications of a governmental entity or private organization if that entity or organization has a recognized procedure for qualifying mediators and it grants such status to the mediator.

B. A mediator shall not solicit in a manner that gives an appearance of partiality for or against a party or otherwise undermines the integrity of the process.

C. A mediator shall not communicate to others, in promotional materials or through other forms of communication, the names of persons served without their permission.

STANDARD VIII. FEES AND OTHER CHARGES

A. A mediator shall provide each party or each party's representative true and complete information about mediation fees, expenses and any other actual or potential charges that may be incurred in connection with mediation.

1. If a mediator charges fees, the mediator should develop them in light of all relevant factors, including the type and complexity of the matter, the qualifications of the mediator, the time required and the rates customary for such mediation services.

2. A mediator's fee arrangement should be in writing unless the parties request otherwise.

B. A mediator shall not charge fees in a manner that impairs a mediator's impartiality.

1. A mediator should not enter into a fee agreement which is contingent upon the result of the mediation or amount of the settlement.

2. While a mediator may accept unequal fee payments from the parties, a mediator should not allow such a fee arrangement to adversely impact the mediator's ability to conduct mediation in an impartial manner.

STANDARD IX. ADVANCEMENT OF MEDIATION PRACTICE

A. A mediator should act in a manner that advances the practice of mediation. A mediator promotes this Standard by engaging in some or all of the following:

1. Fostering diversity within the field of mediation.

2. Striving to make mediation accessible to those who elect to use it, including providing services at a reduced rate or on a pro bono basis as appropriate.

3. Participating in research when given the opportunity, including obtaining participant feedback when appropriate.

4. Participating in outreach and education efforts to assist the public in developing an improved understanding of, and appreciation for, mediation.

5. Assisting newer mediators through training, mentoring and networking.

B. A mediator should demonstrate respect for differing points of view within the field, seek to learn from other mediators and work together with other mediators to improve the profession and better serve people in conflict.

Index

A

Aaron, Marjorie Corman, 47
Active listening. See Listening
Agenda, 52, 73, 90, 100–01, 105, 110
Agreement, mediated, 120–23
    Content, 123–24
    Drafting the agreement, 122–23
    Levels of commitment, 120–22
        Binding written agreements, 122
        Form, App. 3
        Non-binding written agreements, 120–21
        Oral agreements, 121
Agreement or final breakdown, 232, 266
Agreement to mediate, 46, App. 2
Anchoring effect in negotiation, 244
Apology, 16, 164, 200, 266
Appropriate questioning. See Questioning
    Appropriateness for mediation, 39
Asymmetrical (Asymmetry), See Power.
Assisting in the communication process, 21, 137–65
Authority to settle, 41–42
    Claiming lack of, 253
    Limited, 42
    Necessary parties, 75–76
Avoiding mediator traps, 377–94

B

Bargaining
    Collective, 9
    Interest-Based, 254–57
    Linked, 141, 160, 259
    Positional, 120, 177, 252–54, 297
    Power, See Power
    Range, 243–45
BATNA
    Defined, 219–20
    Litigated matters, 222–29
    Mediator's Role, 220–21
    Relationship between BATNA and reservation point, 221–22

Becoming a mediator, 47, 395, 397, 404
Bias,
    Calculating expected value, 226
    Implicit, 301
    Of mediator, 113, 314
    Of participants, 101, 105–06, 112, 197, 226–27
Binding agreement, 79, 89, 121, 122
Brainstorming, 22, 119, 256, 257, 265
Breaks, 79, 302, 305, 335
Business considerations
    Facilities, 21,47, 49, 50, 420, 422, 423
    Getting paid, 423
    Insurance, 424
    Surveys, 424. App. 6

C

Careers in mediation, 395–425
Caucuses, See Separate meetings
Certification, 400, 402
Children, 11, 15, 61, 124
Cialdini, Robert, 239
Civil Cases, 10
Clients, Satisfaction of, 44, 411
Climate, creating a favorable, 55–70
    Reasons for poor climate, 56–59
    Strategies for Improving climate, 59–65
        Acknowledging concerns, 63
        Generating trust, 60
        Getting out of the past, 63
        Humor, 64, 413
        Mutualizing unhappiness, 64
        Normalizing, 60, 63
        Optimism, 62, 67, 202
Closing statement and termination, 124–26, 266
Coaching, 207
Co-mediation, 311–17
    Appropriate situations, 311
    Communication, 315
    Debriefing, 317

Environment 314–15
Facilitating negotiations, 314
Preparation, 317
Traps, 314
Communication, mediator assisting in, 137–64
Channels, 137, 330–332
Culture, 138–140
Encoding and decoding messages, 140–41
Generally, 21, 113, 137, 140–42
High and low context, 139
Listening, 146–50
Non-verbals, 143–45
Body language, 143–45
Mediator's non-verbals, 146–47
Visuals, 143, 145, 146, 265
Vocals, 145
Paraphrasing, 150, 162, 300
Professional terminology, 141
Questioning, See Questioning
Reframing, 99, 100–01, 106, 116, 142–43, 149, 152–156, 260, 447
Reiterating, 22, 161
Style and terminology, 142–43
Community disputes, 9, 10, 50, 121, 123
Community mediation centers, 10, 396, 405, 414
Confidentiality, 80–86, App.6
Duty to explain, 85–86
Exceptions, 84–85
Generally, 80–84
Conflict
Attribution distortions, 195–98
Benefits of, 166–70
Complications
Heavy tactics, 192–194
Increased commitment, 172, 193, 195
Issue proliferation, 178, 193, 194
Light tactics, 192–194
Proliferation of parties, 193, 196
Sweeping generalizations, 173, 193, 195
De-escalation factors contributing to, 196, 200–03
Discouraging unproductive conflict, 172–79
Encouraging contact and communication, 201
Encouraging productive conflict, 171–72

Escalation stages (model), 188–200
Face-saving, 24, 198–200, 267
Interest-based conflicts, 118
Optimism, 62, 67, 201–203
Productive conflict, 170–72
Relationship conflicts, 204
Structural conflicts, 204, 205
Unproductive conflict, 170, 172–75
Contempt, 175
Criticizing, 173
Defensiveness, 176
Issue-proliferation, 178–79
Over-competitiveness, 176–77
Personal attacks, 176, 183
Stonewalling, 173–74
Value conflicts, 204–05
Conflict style, 179–88
Accommodating, 185–186
Avoiding, 182–83
Collaboration, 186–88
Competing, 179–181
Compromising, 183–185
Conflict waiver form, 436–37
Confucianism, 24
Covey, Stephen, 160
Creative solutions, 7, 18, 221, 261, 343, 395
Culture Communication, 22–23,138–40, 142, 144

D

Debriefing, by
Co-mediators, 317,
Reflective practice, 403
Defining the problem, 100–11
Agenda, 105–07
Areas of agreement, 104–05
Crafting issues, 105
Interests, 102–04
Levels of defining, 107
"One-party" issues, 109
Positions, 102–03, 108
Pre-mediation conferences, 101
Presenting issues visually, 109–10
Prioritizing issues, 110–11
Process, 101
Purpose, 100–01
Single issue, 108
Standard issue lists, 111
Types of interests, 102
Using separate meetings, 101

Deskilling, 18

Developing mediator credentials, 396–404
    Licensure, certification and
        accreditation, 400
    Professional organizations, 396
    Training and qualifications, 396
        Advanced training, 398–404
        Availability, 396
        Basic mediation training, 397–99
        Gaining experience, 403–04

Diagnosing dispute, 203

Dispute Entering Complex multi-party,
    372–73

Distributive bargaining, See Positional
    Bargaining

Diversity, 312, 469

Documentation, 369

Drafting of mediated agreement, 122

Dueling experts, 364

E

Educating the parties about mediation,
    42–47, 295

Effective listening, 147–149

Eisner, Michael, 168

Emery, Robert, 58

Emotion, dealing with, 21, 56, 58, 65–70,
    113, 208, 266, 342

Employment opportunities related
    mediation, 404–09

Encouraging settlement, 269–85
    Advising, 272–275
    Being critical, 274
    Creating a balance, 283
    Dangers, 282–83,
    Providing information, 271
    Reality testing, 275

Entering the dispute, 30–32
    Introductions and communications, 30
    Joint introductions, 30
    One-party approach, 32
    Preliminary conferences, 31, 32, 53

Environment, 30, 45, 49, 62, 69, 278

Ethics
    Appropriateness for mediation, 39
    Attitude toward, 167
    Confidentiality. See Confidentiality
    Competence, 39
    Conflict of interests, 38
    Disciplinary action, 283, 311
    Impartiality, See Impartiality
    Model Standards of Conduct for
        Mediators, 38–39, 47, 81, 85, 287,
        294, 298, 463
    Negligence, 283, 389
    Neutrality, See Neutrality
    Self-determination, See Self-
        determination

Evaluating effectiveness, as a mediator 24

Evaluation, Mediator's use of, 339–51
    Benefits, 340–43
    Dangers, 342–45
    Recommendations, 346–51

Expected value, 223–29
    Calculation form (Plaintiff), App. 9A
    Calculation form (Defendant), App. 9B

Experience, Gaining Experience, 16, 403,
    404

Experts, dealing with, 364–366

Expressing an opinion, See Evaluation

F

Face
    Cultural differences, 24, 301, 358
    Face-saving, 199–200
    Loss of, 198–200, 230, 235, 267

Facilitative mediation, 15, 18–20, 92,
    112–13, 159, 275, 297–98, 339–40,
    350

Facilities, 49- 50, 429

False consensus, 168

Fears (clients'), 69–70

Fees, mediator's, 46–47, 423–24

Final decision and closure, 120–26
    Agreement, 120–23
    Closing statement and termination,
        124–26
    Evaluations, 126
    Post-mediation activities, 126
    Purpose, 120

Framing, 142–43

Functions of a mediator, generally, 20

G

Generating options, 119, 128, 159, 219, 231,
    255–57, 262–63

Goh, Bee Chen, 23, 138

Golann, Dwight, 347–38

Groupthink, 168

Guidelines (mediation), 78–79

H
Humor, 64, 69, 153, 413

I
Impartiality, 76, 288, 294, 298, 303, 379–381, 465
Impasses, 163, 184, 261, 264–66, 300
Implicit bias, 301
Insurance, liability as a mediator, 424
Intake and screening, 29–38
    Educating the parties, 42–43
    Entering the dispute, 30–31
    Gathering information, 33–34
    Identifying issues, 35
    Identifying participants, 34
    Preliminary conferences, 31–32
Integrative negotiation, See Problem Solving
Interests, 102–20, 213–14
    Common ground, 216–17
    Identifying divergent, 217–19
        Different capabilities, 219
        Different expectations, 218
        Different risk attitudes, 218
        Different time preferences, 218
        Different valuations, 218
    Sorting and prioritizing, 216
    Trading on divergent interests, 219
    Uncovering, 102, 213–14
Interpersonal conflict, 167–68, 206
Interpreters, 357–58
Interventions by mediator
    Conflict, 204–06
    General, 20
    Impasses, 364–66
    Managing power, 293–303
    Positional Bargaining, 352–65
    Violence, 255
Issues
    Defining the problem, 100–01
    Developing list, 313
    Forms of, 107–08
    Guidelines for crafting, 105–06
    Identifying, 35
    Levels of defining, 107
    Multiple interests, 108–09
    Prioritizing, 110–11
    Purposes, 100
    Using list, 111

J
Janis, Irving, 168
Joint introductions, 30
Judgmental, 274
Jurisdictional variations in mediation, 346
Justice, 288, 332–33, 408

L
Labor disputes, 9
Lawyers, mediators dealing with, 366–74
Learning mediation skills (reflective learning), 16, 403
Leverage, See Power
Licensure, 400
Listening, 147–50
    Active, 147–48
    Detracting from, 149–50
    Effective, 147–50

M
Managing conflict, see Conflict
Managing power, 287–303
    Dangers, 303
    Mediator interventions, 293–303
    Power defined, 288–89
    Types of power, 290–94
        Personal power, 293
        Relationship power, 293
        Substantive power, 290–93
Marketing mediation practice, 410–22
Mckee, Robert, 189
Med-Arb, 263, 320, 321
Mediated agreement, 13, 439
Mediation
    Benefits of, 5
    Defined, 3
    Stages, 72–126
        Defining the problem, 90–111
        Final decision and closure, 120–26
        Opening, 72–90
        Party initial statements, 90–100
        Problem solving and negotiation, 112–120
    Uses of, 9
    Variations in, 305–23
    Virtual Mediation, 325–38
Mediator
    Credentials, 396
    Functions and roles, 20–23

Assisting in communication, 21
Creating favorable conditions, 21
Cultural awareness, 22
Encouraging settlement, 22
Facilitating Negotiation, 21–22
Styles, 44
Model Standards of Conduct for Mediators, 38–39, 47, 81, 85, 287, 294, 298, App. 10

N
Needs, See Interests
Negotiation
Agreement or final breakdown, 266–67
Alternatives, see BATNA
Argumentation, 232, 233, 237
BATNA
Defined, 219–20
Litigated matters, 222–29
Mediator's Role, 220–21
Relationship between BATNA and reservation Point, 221–22
Brainstorming, 22, 119, 256–57
Claiming value, 209–10
Common mistakes, 208
Leaving value on the table, 208
Settling for terms worse than the alternative, 208
Settling for too little, 208
Walking away from the table, 208
Concessions, managing, 242–50
Creating value, 209, 210, 218, 231, 259
Common ground, 216
Different capabilities, 219
Different expectations, 218
Different time preferences, 218
Different valuations, 218
Distinction between "positions" and "interests," 254–55
Emergence and crisis, 261–66
Crossing the last gap, 261
Dealing with impasses, 264, 391
Expected value, 457, 459, 461, 218, 223, 225–227, 296
Mediator's role in, 220–21
Other party's BATNA, 221–22
Relationship with reservation point, 222
Facilitating, 21, 207–68
Generating Options, 21, 231

Impasses, See Impasses
Ineffective negotiators, 208
Interest-based, 92, 102–03, 118–19, 254
Brainstorming, 22, 119, 256, 257, 265
Creative settlement options, 255
Mediator's role in, 53, 254
Interests, See Interests
Issues, See Issues
Last gap, 245, 261–264, 267
Last-minute add-on, 266, 267
Licensure, certification and accreditation as a mediator, 400–02
Linked bargaining, 141, 160, 259, 383
Negotiator's dilemma, 209–211
Objective standards, 19, 104, 119, 212, 229–231, 267, 281, 282, 339
Opening offers, 234–36
High soft / low soft, 234
Integrative, 236
Optimism, 62, 67, 201–03
Reasonable firm, 235
Understanding the other side's, 236
Packaging offers, 251
Pattern of concessions, 242–50
Communication, 249
Magnitude of, 249
Opening point, 243–44
Planning, 242–43
Reciprocity, 247–48
Recording of, 250–51
Reservation point, 244–46
Target point, 247
Timing of, 250
Positional bargaining
Defined, 120
Interventions, 252–54
Tactics, 252–54
Preparation,
For co-mediation, 317
For mediation by mediator, 47–53
For negotiation by parties, 211–31
Pre-mediation conference preparation form, App. 8
Problem Solving, 112–20
Procedure, 118–20
Interest-based, 118–20
Open discussion, 118
Positional, 120

Purpose, 112
Storytelling, 113–16
Style, 112–13
Reciprocity, rule of, 202, 237–40
Concessions, 247–51
Defined, 202
How it works, 239–40
How mediators can use, 240–42
Managing, 241–51
Social foundations for, 238
Negotiator's dilemma, 209
Neutrality, 5, 32, 38, 155, 283, 303, 342, 388
Evaluative mediation, 343
Impartiality, difference from, 342–43
Notetaking, by mediator, 97, 164

O
Objective standards (criteria), 200, 205, 229–31
Offers
More than one simultaneously, 259
Opening offers (point), 252
Packaging, 251–52
Responding to, 251–52
Opening statement (mediator's), 72–90
Checklist, App.7
Co-mediation, 90
Elements, 74–80
Explaining guidelines, 78–80
Explaining the mediation process,77–78
Explaining nature of mediation, 76
Preliminaries, 75–76
Omitting important element, 90
Principles, 73–74
Purpose, 72
Opening statements by parties, See Initial statements by parties
On-line mediation, See Virtual mediation

P
Packaging offers, 251–52
Paraphrasing, 150, 162, 300
Parties' initial statements, 90–100
Deciding who speaks first, 94–95
Focus, 91–92
Mediator's role, 96–100
Note-taking, 96
Purpose, 90–91

Scope, 91
Speaking order, 93–94
Summarizing, 99–100
Who makes it, 92–93
Pattern of concessions, 242–50
Communication, 249
Magnitude of, 249
Opening point, 243–44
Planning, 242–43
Reciprocity, 247–48
Recording of, 250–51
Reservation point, 244–46
Target point, 247
Timing of, 250
Physical space, 21, 130
Positions, See Positional bargaining under Negotiation
Post mediation activities, 126
Power (leverage)
Alternatives (BATNA), 219–30
Asymmetrical (Asymmetry) of information, 292–93
Encouraging settlement, 280–83
Imbalances among parties, See Managing power
Negative leverage, 291–92
Negotiation power defined, 288–89
Normative leverage, 291
Managing Power, 287–303
Mediator's power, 269–70,
Positive leverage, 291
Process power, 71
Sources of mediator power and influence, 269
Types of, 290–93
Working with, See Managing power
Preliminary conferences, 31–32
Pre-mediation conferences, 53, 100–01, App 8
Private international mediation, 409
Problem solving, See under Negotiation
Procedural justice, 332
Process (of Mediation)
Stages, 72–134
Defining the problem, 100–11
Final decision and closure, 120–26
Mediator opening, 72–90
Parties' initial statements, 90–100
Problem solving and negotiation, 112–20

Separate meetings, 126–35
Variations, 305–23
  Alternating venues, 321
  Co-mediation, 311–17
  Consultations with outside parties, 323
  Internet mediation, See Virtual mediation
  Involving support persons, 322
  Med-Arb, 320–21
  Multiple meetings, 305–06
  On-line mediation, See Virtual mediation
  Shuttle mediation, 306–11
  Telephone mediation, 318–320
Professional advisors, 208, 370
Professional biography, 43, App. 1
Pro se party, See Self-represented party
Pro se waiver form, App. 2
Public policy disputes, 9, 12

Q

Questioning, 156–61
  Choosing, 159–61
  Emphatic and probing, 160
  Types of, 157–59
    Clarifying, 157–58
    Closed, 157
    Cross-examining, 158
    Disarming / distracting, 159
    Empathic, 160
    Focused, 157
    Hypothetical, 159
    Leading, 158
    Open, 157
    Probing, 158
    Reflective, 158
    Rhetorical, 159
    Suggestive, 159
    "What if"?, "if what"?, 160

R

Rapport, with mediator, 29, 31, 60, 318, 330–31
Reactive devaluation, 230, 235, 250
Reality testing, 19, 42, 128, 131, 178, 275–277, 308
Reciprocity, rule of, 202, 237–40
  Concessions, 247–51
  Defined, 202

How it works, 239–40
How mediators can use, 240–42
Managing, 241–51
Social foundations for, 238
Referrals, 30, 43, 413, 418–20
  Mediation panels, 420
  Networks, 418
  Self-referrals, 420
Reframing, 152–55, App. 4 (examples)
  Dangers, 155
  Defined, 152
  Functions,154
Reiterating, 161
Restorative justice, 9, 408
Right to reply, dealing with, 98
Ritual, 50, 65

S

Safety, 45, 49, 301–02, 318–22, 328
Screening, See Intake and screening
Seating, 50–51,
Self-determination, 6, 287–88, 293–94, 296, 298–99, 301, 303, 328, 333, 339, 343–45, 347, 349
Self-represented parties, 297–98, 341–42
Separate meetings, 27, 53, 77–78, 82, 100, 104, 113, 126–35, 178, 202, 211, 209, 216, 237, 281
  Calling, 132
  Coaching, 281
  Confidentiality in, 128–29
  Controlling aggressive or dominant behavior, 302–03
  Dangers, 134–35
  Definition, 126
  Duration of, 132–33
  Dynamics, 131
  Negotiator's dilemma, 209
  Purpose, 128–29
  Shuttle mediation, See Shuttle mediation
  Transitions, 133–35
    Breaking into, 133
    Commencing, 133
    Ending, 133–34
    Resuming, 134
  Variations, 321–22
  When they should be called, 129–30
  When to end, 131–32
Shell, G. Richard, 289

Shuttle mediation
    Defined, 77, 129
    Distorting views, 390
    Drawbacks and dangers,
    Dynamics, how changed, 131
    Gift wrapping offer, 281
    Practical considerations, 130
    When to use, 129–30
Slaikeu, Karl, 37
Stages of mediation, See under Mediation
Storytelling, 113–16
    Benefits of, 113–14
    Guidelines, 115–16
    Limitations of, 114–15
Summarizing, 99–100, 162–63
    Assisting in communication, 162–63,
    Parties' initial statements, 99–100
        Actual, 99
        Cross summaries, 100
        Process, 99
        Purpose, 99
        Reframed, 99–100
Surveys, client satisfaction, 424, App.6B

T
Team negotiations, 52–53
Telephone mediation, 150–51, 318–20
    Communication in, 150–51
    Disadvantages, 318
    Guidelines, 319
    When appropriate, 318
Training, as a mediator, 396–99
Transformative mediation, 19, 92, 112–13
Traps, for mediator, 377–94
    Allowing professional advisors to
        dominate, 385
    Assuming differing professional role,
        390–91
    Being unprepared, 391–92
    Dominating process, 382–83
    External parties, ignoring, 392–93
    Ignoring emotions, 386
    Losing control of process, 383–85
    Losing impartiality, 379–81
    Moving to solutions too quickly, 387–88
    Pushing the parties, 388–90
    Undocumented agreement, 392–93
    Unrealistic expectations, 378–79
    Using technical language, 383

Trust, 59–61
    Importance of, 59–60
    In mediation process, 60
    In mediator, 60
    With parties' own negotiating abilities,
        61

U
Uniform Mediation Act, 4, 401
Unrepresented parties, See Self-
    Represented
Uses of mediation, 9–14
    Business, 11
    Civil Cases, 10
    Community disputes, 10
    Family matters, 10
    International commercial, 12–13
    Labor disputes, 9–10
    Limitations of, 14
    Public policy disputes, 12
    Special education, 11

V
Variations, in process, See Process
Venting, 68, 113, 266
Victim-offender mediation, 408
Videoconferencing, See Virtual mediation
Violence, 40–41, 353–57
    Assuring safety, 301
    Factors unsuitable for mediation, 40–41
    Mediator interventions, 355–57
    Policy issues, 354
    Screening, 29–31, 354–55
Virtual mediation, 325–37
    Advantages, 326–29
    Best practices, 334–36
    Disadvantages, 329
    Pros & Cons list, 333–34
    Videoconferencing,
        Diminished non-verbal
            communication, 330
        Fatigue 331,
        Platforms, 335
Visual aids, 52

W
Walk-out, 264, 274
Website (mediator's), 31
Williams, Gerald, 232